I0806434

THE MARKET FOR SKILL

The Princeton Economic History of the Western World

Joel Mokyr, Series Editor

A list of titles in this series appears in the back of the book.

The Market for Skill

Apprenticeship and Economic Growth in Early Modern England

Patrick Wallis

PRINCETON UNIVERSITY PRESS
PRINCETON AND OXFORD

Published by Princeton University Press
41 William Street, Princeton, New Jersey 08540
99 Banbury Road, Oxford OX2 6JX

press.princeton.edu

Library of Congress Cataloging-in-Publication Data

Names: Wallis, Patrick
Title: The market for skill : apprenticeship and economic growth in early modern England / Patrick Wallis.
Description: Princeton : Princeton University Press, [2025] | Series: The Princeton economic history of the Western world | Includes bibliographical references and index.
Identifiers: LCCN 2024023715 (print) | LCCN 2024023716 (ebook) | ISBN 9780691265315 hardback | ISBN 9780691265896 ebook
Subjects: LCSH: England—Economic conditions | Apprenticeship programs—England—History | Occupational training—England—History | Apprentices—England—History | BISAC: POLITICAL SCIENCE / Political Economy | BUSINESS & ECONOMICS / Economic History
Classification: LCC HD4885.G7 W35 2025 (print) | LCC HD4885.G7 (ebook) | DDC 331.25/9220942—dc23/eng/20240910
LC record available at https://lccn.loc.gov/2024023715
LC ebook record available at https://lccn.loc.gov/2024023716

British Library Cataloging-in-Publication Data is available

Editorial: Hannah Paul, Josh Drake
Production Editorial: Elizabeth Byrd
Jacket: Haley Chung
Production: Erin Suydam
Publicity: William Pagdatoon (US), Charlotte Coyne (UK)
Copyeditor: Anne Davidson

Jacket Credit: Private Collection / Bridgeman Images

Printed in the United States of America

10 9 8 7 6 5 4 3 2 1

MIX
Paper
FSC
FSC® C183721

CONTENTS

LIST OF FIGURES AND TABLES

Figures

Tables

ACKNOWLEDGEMENTS

This book started with an argument in a pub more than twenty years ago. Much of my professional life since then has flowed from that encounter with the late Larry Epstein. I only wish he was here to see where it has led me. Larry brought me to economic history, both intellectually, through the rigour and stimulus of his ideas, and practically, when he recruited me to the London School of Economics. He and I never agreed about apprenticeship. And that was entirely the point.

While Larry provoked me to think seriously about apprenticeship as system of training, doing this in a satisfying way has involved the work of many hands. This book is built on a wealth of evidence that has been transformed from an impassable mountain range of manuscripts into a digital treasurehouse by the indefatigable work of some extraordinary scholars. Cliff Webb has played a transformative role in this, through his gargantuan enterprise of transcribing and indexing apprenticeship records, and his own thinking on the topic. Without him, this book could not have been written. More recently, Michael Scott has been a wonderfully generous partner, sharing his ever-expanding research on London freely and opening new parts of the archive.

Working out how to use these riches brought its own challenge, and many of the approaches in this book were developed in partnership with my colleague Chris Minns in a sequence of papers in which we explored patterns of persistence, migration, and guilds. Chris's influence and ideas run through many parts of the book, and my debt to him is enormous. In addition to Chris, an array of wonderful co-authors have worked with me on these themes, each of whom has made fundamental contributions to the findings I discuss here: Clare Crowston, Bert De Munck, Marcel Hoogenboom, Chris Kissane, Mark Klemp, Claire Lemercier, Tim Leunig, Maarten Prak, Ruben Schalk, Cliff Webb, and Jacob Weisdorf. This has been a long process, and earlier versions of the ideas and evidence presented here have been published in the *Economic History Review*, the *Journal of Economic*

History, the *Journal of British Studies*, the *Journal of Interdisciplinary History, Explorations in Economic History*, the *European Review of Economic History, Social History*, and *Continuity and Change*. I am grateful for their permission to reuse this material.

Maarten Prak was also in that pub, and since then, he and I have been having a conversation about apprenticeship—and other things—that has enriched my thinking enormously. Margaret Pelling's deep knowledge and endlessly generous mentoring constructed most of the foundations on which I stand as a historian; Mark Jenner built the rest. Maggie and Maarten both kindly read earlier versions of the book. Jane Humphries's own work on apprenticeship has influenced me profoundly, and she commented on versions of this book and earlier work. Karine van der Beek, too, has generously shared evidence and ideas over many years. STICERD and the British Academy kindly funded early work on this topic. From 2013, I had the good fortune to be part of a project on European citizenship, bEUcitizen, supported by the European Union, with Raoul De Kerf, Bert De Munck, Marcel Hoogenboom, Chris Kissane, Claire Lemercier, Philippe Minard, Maarten Prak, and Ruben Schalk. That project led to other work with Claire Crowston and Claire Lemercier and a comparative book on European apprenticeship involving Joel Mokyr, José Antolín Nieto Sánchez, Victoria López Barahona, Beatrice Zucca Micheletto, Giovanni Colavizza, Riccardo Cella, Anna Bellavitis, Georg Stöger, Reinhold Reith, Merja Uotila, Ruben Schalk, and Annelies De Bie. This group have taught me a great deal, and I am deeply grateful for their friendship and help. Two vitally important books on this topic appeared too late for me to incorporate them here. Steve Kaplan's magisterial history of French apprenticeship, *Transmettre, soumettre, socialiser*, and Anna Bellavitis and Valentina Sapienza's *Apprenticeship, Work and Society in Early Modern Venice*. We await the next from Joel Mokyr, who has been both a brilliant contributor to this discussion and an insightful and generous editor for this book.

I owe a great deal to conversations with many colleagues and friends, including—but far from limited to—Ian Archer, Jonathan Barry, Helen Berry, Dan Bogart, Jeremy Boulton, Bruno Blondé, Justin Colson, Nick Crafts, Matthew Davies, Sandra de Pleijt, Amy Erickson, Ian Gadd, Laura Gowing, Paul Griffiths, Julian Hoppit, Stephanie Hovland, Mark Jenner, Steve Kaplan, Deborah Simonton, David Mitch, David Mitchell, Joel Mokyr, Craig Muldrew, Gilles Postel-Vinay, Raphaelle Schwarzberg, Richard Smith, Judy Stephenson, Jan Luiten van Zanden, and Phil Withington. Referee 2 has also been a vital critical voice. She knows who she is. My fellow Institute of

Historical Research seminar convenors keep the fire lit. My colleagues and students in the Department of Economic History have taught me a great deal and it remains an enormous privilege to work and teach in such a wonderful community.

I have benefited from the generosity of Ancestry.com, the Centre for Metropolitan History, the Lincoln Family History Society, Bristol & Avon Family History Society, Durham University Library, Michael Power, the Pewter Society, the Society of Genealogists, Shropshire County Archive, Bristol City Archive, the London Metropolitan Archive and Guildhall Library. Jill Barlow, Aske Brock, Philip Clarkson, Alyssa Levene, Mark Merry, and Melanie Winterbottom each made important contributions by sharing their research, skills, or resources. Several London livery companies have been particularly supportive, including the Apothecaries, the Goldsmiths, the Leathersellers, the Pewterers, and the Stationers. Parts of this project were developed while I was a visiting professor at Tsinghua University, kindly hosted by Long Denggao, and a visitor at the Guanghua School of Management at Peking University, hosted by Se Yan. Over the years, I was helped by the assistance of Michael Aldous, Claire Benson, Carlos Brando, Jens Christiansen, Eilish Gregory, Santosh at Hitech Infoserv, Joe Lane, Katrina Maydom, and Michaela Summerer. I am also a grateful beneficiary of the research, techniques, and tools developed at the Cambridge Group for the History of Population and Social Structure, especially by Gill Newton and Leigh Shaw-Taylor.

Projects like this are personal as well as professional. My friends have kept me mostly sane, particularly Jeremy, Mark, Dave, Dan, Miriana, Rich, and Paul. It would have been written more quickly without the Beijing journos footy game, but I'd have enjoyed it less. My parents, Richard and Maureen, have watched with love and bemusement as this (and other projects) have absorbed years of my life; they have been a source of immense support and practical help. While this all started with my disagreement with Larry, the spur to write the first draft of my response was the chance to come to London to join my partner, now wife, Rosie. She has suffered through years of my work on this topic, and read and commented on many early versions. She and our amazing children, Eva and Joseph, surely the two best to ever be born, have taught me a great deal more about love and learning than any archive could. This book is dedicated to them.

ABBREVIATIONS

BRO Bristol Record Office

CLRO City of London Record Office (now in LMA)

GL Guildhall Library

LMA London Metropolitan Archive

ODNB *Oxford Dictionary of National Biography*

SRO Shropshire Record Office

TNA The National Archives, UK

THE MARKET FOR SKILL

1

Introduction

On 1 July 1805, at not quite thirteen years of age, John Carter started his apprenticeship as a tailor. It marked a turning point in his life. He had worried that his parents 'were too poor to be able to apprentice me to any suitable trade', while he was 'too feeble to be put to any very labourious occupation . . . there seemed to be no good prospect in regard to my future'. As he later recalled, after several decades working as a tailor, 'my going into this situation I regard as having been by far the most important incident of my early years, inasmuch as all my subsequent experiences took its general complexion therefrom'.[1]

Globally, apprenticeship is one of the most durable and widespread economic institutions. Understood broadly as an agreement to exchange labour for training in a trade over a specific period, apprenticeship is almost a human universal, found everywhere from the shop floors of advanced engineering companies to the tracks trod by Kalahari hunters, from classical Rome to modern Japan.[2] Yet, in few periods or places has it equalled the prominence that it possessed in early modern Europe. There, a specific form of apprenticeship defined by a formalised contractual agreement enforceable at law became a near ubiquitous experience for youths with any aspiration beyond a life of farming, service, or unskilled labour. Carter's view of the transformational impact of apprenticeship was shared by many of his peers in England between the fifteenth and early nineteenth centuries. In England, when the share of youths training through apprenticeship reached its peak, up to one-third of teenage males would be indentured to serve a master and learn one of a myriad of crafts or trades. Until 1800, the amount of time and money directly invested in human capital formation through apprenticeship outstripped that spent on primary, secondary, or tertiary schooling.

The impression of premodern apprenticeship given by much popular and academic writing is of an archaic, inflexible, overly long period of training rooted in exclusive guilds that monopolised trades. Children had little choice about their futures. Apprenticeship was highly traditional. It had little, if any, connection to innovation. And, in England at least, it had 'failed' by the nineteenth century, or 'declined' even earlier.[3] In parallel, but now less prominent, is another, more romantic version in which every artisan had an apprentice, and 'skills were recognised, valued and freed'.[4] Both are misleading.

This book presents a new account of apprenticeship and the market for skill.[5] It examines how apprenticeship operated in England from the early sixteenth to the start of the nineteenth century and the consequences this had for economic and social development in this transformative period. This was the era of the Statute of Artificers (1563), the Elizabethan law that made service as an apprentice a legal requirement for those working in many occupations outside farming. Its abolition in 1814 is the event that provides the endpoint for this study. It was also a time of remarkable urbanisation, structural change, and economic development—changes that flew in the face of the intentions of those who wrote the statute, and that I argue were made possible, in part, by the way apprenticeship mobilised labour and diffused knowledge in the English economy.

Premodern societies are sometimes mischaracterised as possessing little human capital.[6] There is truth in this if we focus on the number of years of education or levels of literacy, both of which are common measures of human capital today.[7] But the problems with this idea are obvious if we think of the amount of physical skill and tacit knowledge and understanding possessed by craftsmen, traders, and farmers as they wrestled with the everyday challenges of economic life, their depth of understanding about the materials and markets they worked within, and the body of slowly acquired techniques and 'recipes' they possessed, the prescriptive knowledge that was integral to production and exchange. It is more accurate to see premodern societies as endowed with high levels of tacit and prescriptive knowledge.[8]

One reason for this mistaken assumption about the level of premodern human capital is what came next. Industrialisation and modern economic growth have involved a parallel and mutually supportive expansion in education and technology, even a 'race' between them in Goldin and Katz's powerful interpretation.[9] This has been tied to a general shift in the scale and contribution of science and research to the economy, which increased the pace with which technology advanced and prosperity grew.

Accompanying this has been an equally important change in the structure of production that has led to greater differentiation in skills between roles and workers. The increasing division of labour, standardisation, and new tools and machines all served to lower the degree of embodied manual skill required of many roles. As the great economist Alfred Marshall noticed in 1890, with industrialisation the 'kinds of manual work [that] require long-continued practice in one set of operations . . . are becoming rarer: for machinery is constantly taking over work that requires manual skill of this kind'.[10] In this context, general academic skills and knowledge—literacy, numeracy, science—become more important than technique, and their distribution may become more unequal in sectors or occupations where the workforce becomes divided between a small elite of 'thinkers' and a larger body of 'labourers'. As a result, one kind of deskilling, a loss perhaps in the degree of manual dexterity or craft technique that Marshall noted, can coexist with an increase in skill or human capital in another dimension, produced through general and higher education.[11]

Apprenticeship had two critical roles in the premodern economy. Craftsmen and traders' skills, their techniques and knowledge of how to make and sell, were fundamental to production and commerce. Reproducing these essential skills between generations of workers was a lengthy and challenging process, one that relied on observation and extended practice through immersion in the work itself because much of the knowledge was 'tacit' in the sense of being hard, even impossible, to articulate and communicate by description. This continuous replenishment of human capital was largely achieved through apprenticeship.

However, apprenticeship did not just maintain the aggregate stock of economically useful knowledge that skilled workers possessed. It also enabled its expansion and diffusion. The combination of different types of skills, particularly the complementarity between prescriptive and propositional knowledge, made the techniques inculcated through apprenticeship crucial to the realisation of innovations, to turning ideas into machines, materials, and products. Apprenticeship was also a key mechanism for the next step in this process: the spread of new skills, techniques, and technologies. Apprenticeship was one of the factors setting the pace at which innovation occurred and diffused.

To talk about the premodern economy in this way may seem surprising. Was this not a time of Malthusian stagnation? Maybe so—although that debate continues.[12] However, Malthus's insight was that technology would not improve living standards in the longer run if fertility was unrestrained, not that technology and productivity would not change. There is a more valid tension with the characterisation of the premodern economy contained in unified growth theory. In that model, premodern parents invest little in their (many) children's human capital. It is only with the transition to modern growth that parents begin to invest heavily in their children and move from 'quantity to quality', breaking the Malthusian pincer grip on living standards.[13] One implication of the scale of apprenticeship that is described here is that unified growth theory under-estimates the importance of human capital formation in the premodern period by neglecting occupational or vocational skills. Fortunately, this can be reconciled because this investment in human capital was deferred until adolescence and largely paid for by the child's labour, not their parents' (although many parents did pay as well).[14]

Who can gain skills matters, too. Indeed, this is critical for social mobility, openness, and equity, as is obvious today from the inclusion of education in indices of human development to the politics of university access. Access to training mattered in premodern societies for much the same reason: human capital lifts human capability and, with that, people's living standards and their aspirations for the future. In anthropological and historical accounts, apprenticeship appears as a vital way to acquire knowledge from individuals outside the family group.[15] Restrictions on who can gain access to apprenticeship are, therefore, a particularly pervasive and consequential form of injustice, limiting the opportunities of those excluded, as well as imposing deadweight costs on society as a whole.[16]

In medieval and early modern Europe, access to apprenticeship was linked to central and local laws and to the decisions of courts and guilds, as well as to cultural and social norms about work, particularly the gendering of occupations. Because apprenticeship often brought with it the right to work in an occupation—privileges akin to occupational licensing as a lawyer or nurse nowadays—or provided a claim to local urban citizenship, the issue of who was able to gain access to apprenticeship, and who completed their training, mattered greatly for cities and guilds. As a result, apprenticeship was integrated tightly into the hierarchies that structured early modern societies.

How these influential bodies shaped apprenticeship, whether they nudged it towards greater inclusivity or exclusivity, was therefore a major determinant of the openness of their societies. That this mattered normatively should be self-evident. That it also mattered economically has been the thrust of much recent work exploring how institutions and political economy shaped growth. North, Wallis, and Weingast see 'open access orders' as the defining feature of modern developed societies, and they list 'entry into economic, political, religious and educational activities without restraint' as one of their five features.[17] In a similar vein, Acemoglu and Robinson similarly emphasise that prosperity relies on 'broad-based economic opportunities'.[18] Early modern England features frequently in these studies. Most of the attention has been given to political and financial markets, however. Here, I show that a large part of the labour market can also be characterised as relatively open—far freer of frictions, barriers, and exclusions than the superstructure of guilds and privilege might seem to imply.

The relationship between the system of apprenticeship and these two themes of economic development and opportunity are the focus of this book. Like any of humanity's most widespread institutions—marriage, the state, the firm—there is no single type of apprenticeship. Rather, each society has a specific variant that forms part of a wider constellation of institutions. The argument I present in this book is that early modern England's variant of apprenticeship worked positively to support economic development and helped rather than hindered spatial and occupational mobility.

In terms of development, apprenticeship in England was effective at moving people and ideas. It integrated markets in labour and knowledge. It concentrated training in centres of best practice, allowing skills to diffuse outwards. This occurred through several complementary channels. Apprenticeship enabled individuals to match their aptitudes to a wide range of opportunities found in places and occupations that were distant to their families. It allowed choices to be revised as a youth's ability was revealed in the workplace. It led to training being focused in the workshops and counting houses of the most able artisans and traders. As a result, each new generation on average acquired better knowledge than the last and took this forward, lifting productivity as ideas and techniques were diffused and adopted.

For opportunity, English apprenticeship was, in practice, largely open, with few meaningful barriers to entry beyond nationality and the powerful force of the patriarchal imagination that constrained young women's participation—and even that was frayed to some degree. Apprenticeship gave a measure of security that encouraged intergenerational leaps of faith, emboldening youths to cross long distances and wide gaps in experience into occupations where they had no connections. It did not produce a rapid reshuffling between rich and poor, however; the opportunities open to the young reflected the wealth their families possessed.

Underlying this was a specific form of apprenticeship that was rooted in a particular institutional context: a simple contract that lowered transaction costs, and a set of local tribunals that acted to support apprentices' freedom to exit from situations that were serving them poorly. This was a flexible form of apprenticeship, one that could be adjusted or ended early. The effect was to encourage families from the full breadth of society to place their children into apprenticeship in their thousands and to speed urbanisation and structural change.

Apprenticeship: The Debate

The apprenticeship contract was the formalised expression of an intent to exchange training for labour. How that exchange operated in practice and what it meant for the English economy and society has been debated for well over a century. We can set much of the detail aside for the present. However, it is useful to highlight three clusters of ideas that will appear repeatedly.

The first position dates to the earliest writings in political economy and is fully expressed in Adam Smith's view that apprenticeship was primarily designed to 'restrain the competition to a much smaller number than might otherwise be disposed to enter into the trade. The limitation of the number of apprentices restrains it directly. A long term of apprenticeship restrains it more indirectly, but as effectually, by increasing the expense of education'.[19]

The result was higher earnings for masters and journeymen—and higher prices for consumers. Although Smith's analysis might stand on the restrictions set by corporations on the scale, length, and location of apprenticeship, he extends it to challenge the value of apprenticeship as a whole, in a famous passage that argues that 'long apprenticeships are altogether unnecessary'.[20] Smith's concerns share similarities with modern analyses of education that critique it as credentialling or screening.[21] The content of training is not the point, these suggest; the qualification is what matters, and, in many analyses, the system that produces it exists primarily to generate rents for educators (masters) and those who possess the credential.

Smith's argument, and later versions of it, draw our attention to the effect of institutional constraints on the supply and demand for training, the necessity of apprenticeship for learning, and the link between apprenticeship and growth. Was this system driven by the appeal of rents from licensing, and did growth depend on its erosion, for example?

The second position is more recent, rooted in modern economists' work on human capital and incomplete contracts which asks how training could be supplied despite the potential for opportunism by master and apprentice. The core model of 'human capital' used in this approach was set out by the American economists Gary Becker and Jacob Mincer in the 1950s and 1960s, in studies inspired largely by observations of US industry.[22] The value of training was not in doubt here. Instead, the question was, who pays for it? The distinction Becker drew between specific and general human capital, with the former of use solely within a firm and the latter portable to other employers, offered a way to explain when firms do and do not invest in training, when and why workers will accept lower wages while they are training, and a host of related labour market phenomenon; all depended on whether or not workers' productivity was increased in one firm or many, and so whether they could leave and capture the returns elsewhere. To the extent that apprenticeship provided general skills that could be taken to many other firms, 'the cost as well as the return from general training would be borne by trainees, not by firms.'[23] Apprentices' lower wages were the way they repaid their employer's investment in their training.

Becker's answer to the question of who would pay for training was conceptually powerful, but it generated a plethora of empirical challenges. If the apprentice captured the returns and paid for their training, why would a firm offer training in the first place? How could a firm be confident that an apprentice would hang around to repay their investment if they could earn more elsewhere? How could an apprentice be sure they were getting the training they were paying for, not being exploited as semiskilled labour, when they were acquiring tacit knowledge?

That apprentices and masters entered a contract with each other to work and teach, respectively, was not in itself a solution. As Joel Mokyr points out, 'The full details could not be specified ex ante, nor could they be observed with much accuracy ex post, due to the tacit nature of the service provided'.[24] Apprenticeship contracts are inherently incomplete, beset with the risk of opportunism on both sides, asymmetric information, and agency problems. How could masters and apprentices solve this?

A rich body of theory and analysis exists to answer these questions. Many economic explanations of apprenticeship centre on the link between training and subsequent employment, but the situations they analyse are so different to those present before 1800 as to be misleading.[25] A distinct literature in political science and sociology emphasises the way cooperation between employers, unions, and the state can create a situation in which sustained investment in apprenticeship by firms coexists with highly portable, certified skills that are recognised and rewarded in the labour market. This generates the abundance of highly skilled workers seen in countries such as Germany and Denmark.[26] However, the answers on how apprenticeship succeeds which are contained in this literature still depend on the incentives faced by modern firms operating in more or less imperfect labour markets.

In part because these explanations do not map well onto earlier periods, economic historians have suggested that the institutions that shaped the early modern economy might explain how apprenticeship contracts could be enforced, or made self-enforcing. Guilds feature prominently in this literature, largely because of S. R. Epstein's hypothesis that they provided the monitoring and enforcement that allowed apprenticeship to work.[27]

Epstein's revisionism inverts Smith's condemnation of the guilds, and it has been challenged in part on that basis.[28] To evaluate it, we need to look at the activities of the guilds and other institutions, as we will do directly. We must also consider whether the problem of enforcement was solved at all, or if apprenticeship operated in another, perhaps less efficient, mode.

Finally, apprenticeship has acquired a new prominence in attempts to explain the sources of modern economic growth in the characteristics of Britain's premodern economy. The older literature generally echoed Adam Smith's views in seeing apprenticeship as part of a heavy blanket of legal and customary regulation that bore down on the economy, stifling the market until the decline of the guilds and the eventual removal of the Statute of Artificers freed the English economy to flourish.

Now, Joel Mokyr and other authors offer a quite different story: they highlight the role of highly skilled artisans in England who provided much of the technical knowledge that was employed by innovators as they advanced the frontier of knowledge.[29] Apprenticeship becomes an ingredient in industrialisation, not a brake on it. The availability of skilled workers and the pace with which skills and techniques spread all depend, in part, on the way apprenticeship operated to reproduce human capital. This novel analysis suggests a quite different trajectory for apprenticeship in the eighteenth century, one that we will consider in some detail.

Apprenticeship: The Contract

Before launching into the book, we need to introduce the document that created every apprenticeship: the indentures. This type of contract was named after the jagged cut that separated and identified the two identical copies held respectively by master and apprentice. What did it say about the relationship between them?

The content of the apprenticeship contract used in London had become fixed for the most part by the fifteenth century and was conventionally used across England in the same format. The contract defined what each party would do. The master promised to instruct his apprentice in his craft or trade and to provide him with subsistence—food, clothing, and housing. The apprentice promised to work under his master's direction, to keep his secrets, and to accept his orders. The master was entitled to all the benefits of his apprentice's work, whether in his own workshop or if dispatched to assist another.[30]

This agreement was not reduceable to training and work, however. Like a marriage contract, the apprenticeship contract defined expectations about behaviour. The apprentice was forbidden from marrying, gaming, haunting taverns, and taking wages. He promised good conduct and civility. This was backed up by a public oath taken by apprentices in many cities. Apprentices were, in theory, settled in modest subordination within a well-ordered household. Their master's role was, as Jeremy Bentham put it, 'compounded of that of master and that of guardian'; it encompassed a degree of responsibility beyond that of an employer.[31] Like most such relationships in early modern households, the weight of social discipline was asymmetric, and the expectations placed on masters were a less tightly defined, 'paternalistic' role.

The very fact that training was agreed through a legal contract is, in itself, one of the most distinctive features of apprenticeship in premodern Europe. Apprenticeship in other regions of the world (including some areas of Europe) was and is often made through an oral or customary agreement. In Europe, indentures formed an identifiable and reasonably coherent genre from the earliest evidence of apprenticeship in the twelfth century until they gradually lost their distinctive form over the nineteenth and twentieth centuries.[32]

Thinking about the form of the indentures helps make clear three important characteristics of premodern apprenticeship. First, indentures are clearly very different to the modern contract of employment that might be entered into by an apprentice today: they agree an exchange of a fee (always the youth's labour and sometimes a sum of money) for a service (training), not a position in a career trajectory. They were also markedly different to the agreements underpinning most employment in this period: although apprentices were still subordinates, the indentures gave them greater rights than servants or hired workers, both in their right to instruction and subsistence and in their claim to a right to work in their trade, the property in skill they gained on completion.[33]

Second, the standard design of the English contract left only one major aspect of the apprenticeship agreement that could be varied: the price. This balanced the relative costs and benefits of the arrangement, most often by supplementing the value of the apprentices' work. The best-known example of how this was achieved was the 'premium', the fee that families often paid to the master; an alternative was a longer duration for the contract. At other times, when masters struggled to recruit youths, apprentices might be promised a payment or gift, such as tools or clothes, at the end of their term.[34] In addition, apprentices' families sometimes underwrote the honesty of their child, entering a bond for 'truth' that insured the master against embezzlement or loss.[35] These side-contracts were never regulated by guilds or the state, though, and were often not recorded on the main contract.[36] The other core elements of the contract—the minimum seven-year term, the expectation of training, the lack of wages for labour—were all set by statute, custom, or case law.[37] The contract was so standardised that most were printed forms by the middle of the seventeenth century.[38]

Third, and critically, because apprenticeship was organised through a legal contract, contract resolution was a matter for legal recourse. The courts were intimately involved in apprenticeship in early modern England, and this mattered greatly for the way the system functioned. Legal disputes are not a good guide to everyday behaviour, but they are one of the main ways in which the boundaries of behaviour are defined, and behaviour under contract exists in the shadow of the law. Apprenticeship contracts are sufficiently vague that their impact can be transformed by the way they are enforced. The use of 'apprenticeship' in the nineteenth century to control former slaves after abolition is the most egregious example of this, but magistrates' strict readings of youths' obligations—and lenient views of their employers' responsibilities—would limit workers' wages and freedom in nineteenth-century Britain.[39] As we will see, the treatment of apprentices in early modern English tribunals was very different—that is, more equitable and more lenient than these later examples. While the wording of the apprenticeship contract gave no method for early exit, the courts often provided one.

The standardisation of apprenticeship contracts mattered for the scale and openness of training. They were reliable, transparent, and predictable, with questions of law mostly settled and the meaning of terms fixed. This strong standardisation—what Kahan and Klausner describe as 'learning externalities'—removed drafting costs and uncertainty over terms, lowering the transaction costs incurred in accessing training.[40] These gains were particularly important for people who had no experience of the contract, which was true for many parents in this period. Full standardisation avoided the need to involve expert advice and the danger of agreeing to ill-conceived terms. This was not inevitable: bespoke contracting was the norm in France, where notarial archives reveal a variety of specialised—and so, more costly—contracts that depended on the involvement of legal specialists.[41] It also created its own costs. Term lengths, for example, were carefully adjusted to account for uncertainty and expected productivity in eighteenth-century Montreal, as Hamilton has shown. That the initial terms of English contracts were so constrained helps explain the need for post hoc revision, through the institutional mechanisms I describe in the second part of the book.[42]

The Basis and Structure of the Book

This is not the first book on apprenticeship in premodern England. It is more than a century since Dunlop wrote the foundational study.[43] Others have taken up the topic since then.[44] However, this is a somewhat different type of book, because we now have the opportunity to look at apprenticeship at a higher level of resolution. Where earlier researchers largely relied on traces left in court or guild records and snapshots of apprentice listings, I have been the fortunate beneficiary of a deluge of digital datasets that allow me to examine apprenticeship in many of the guilds of London, the dominant centre of training, and a broad swathe of other centres, including expanding port cities such as Bristol, England's second city, and smaller, less rapidly changing places such as Gloucester, Lincoln, Liverpool, Leicester, Shrewsbury, and Boston. In addition, for the eighteenth century we can now observe apprenticeships for which fees were paid from across the whole of England.[45]

For some decades, we know the names, backgrounds, and masters of one in ten English teenagers as they chose an occupation. Information on this scale—and the combined count of individual English apprentices in this study exceeds 1 million—allows us to think about old questions in new ways and ask new questions that would have been impossible to pose previously, just as similar troves of data are changing research on other parts of Europe.[46] (It is worth mentioning that to make it digestible, some of the technical details have been banished to appendices, to which the enthusiastic reader is directed.) To understand and find meaning in this evidence, we have to marry quantitative analysis with qualitative sources, from the rich trove of city and court records, guild minutes, and memoirs and diaries that survive.

There are some boundaries to the project. I begin with the early sixteenth century, when England was a relatively poor and largely undistinguished agrarian economy whose external trade largely centred on wool and cloth exports to Northern Europe. At this point, the amount of information in surviving civic and guild records begins to increase in scale.[47] This allows us to observe aspects of apprenticeship for several decades before the Statute of Artificers was passed. I end at the start of the nineteenth century, as the statute's limitations are removed, and the main archival sources cease—and as industrialisation is transforming parts of Britain. I have restricted my scope to England, in order to avoid dealing with more than one legal framework, and because similar urban records for Wales are not easily available. And perhaps most importantly, I focus on private apprenticeship, not pauper apprenticeship. The role of parishes in placing poor children into apprenticeships, and compelling households to accept them, was important to human capital and welfare. However, it largely operated under different rules and expectations and sat outside the market for training that is explored here.

The book is divided into three sections. The first section examines the relationship between apprenticeship and economic development in England between 1500 and 1800. I begin in chapter 2 by providing a new accounting of the scale and geography of human capital formation through apprenticeship over this period. The chapter shows the singular importance of apprenticeship to investments in human capital. Apprenticeship was critical to the period of growth and structural change that centred on London's booming economy in the sixteenth and seventeenth centuries. However, the relationship between apprenticeship and growth changed—and weakened—with industrialisation. The accounting also shows how much apprenticeship occurred successfully outside the guilds.

In chapter 3, I focus on how apprenticeship affected the reproduction and pace of diffusion of knowledge. What was the quality of skill that was being shared? The chapter presents evidence that apprentices were concentrated in the hands of the most skillful and successful masters. Reconstructing the 'training careers' of large samples of citizens and freemen from London, Bristol, Gloucester, and Boston, I show that most apprentices were trained by the minority of leading masters who trained multiple youths. The effect was to disseminate new ideas and practices rapidly as parents sought to give their children the best possible start.

Chapter 4 looks at the way apprenticeship integrated the English labour market. It explores the movement of young people from different places and occupational backgrounds into apprenticeships, showing the way that labour mobility was facilitated by this system of training. The scale and extent of apprenticeship make a strong case for the openness of apprenticeship and its importance in reallocating labour. The chapter also shows the way the market for training set boundaries on the social mobility it permitted, as the price of training meant that aspiration was constrained by affordability.

Part 2 of the book provides a new description of the system of premodern apprenticeship that produced these effects. It begins by considering what training in apprenticeship involved, in chapter 5, contrasting the reliance on learning by immersion and observation evident in premodern apprenticeship with alternative forms of teaching that were important in later systems of apprenticeship and occupational training. This form of training was pedagogically suited to acquiring embodied, tacit skills and knowledge.

It was also well suited to a setting in which employers could not be sure they would recover the value of any investment in training, and chapter 6 shows that premodern English masters faced a high chance that apprentices would not serve their entire term with them. Apprenticeship was in practice flexible: the frequency and timing of apprentices' absences and exits from their masters' workshops show substantial mobility and high rates of early departure. Pedagogically, this may have been virtuous, allowing apprentices to gain experience with several different masters. Economically, low levels of persistence challenge the viability of any model of training that relies on contracts being enforced for their entire duration.

That so many apprentices were absent raises a question about what the institutions that enforced their contracts were doing. In chapter 7 I look directly at the work of the guilds and urban courts in England. I show that guilds did very little to monitor or enforce apprenticeship. Local urban law courts were far more important. Their effect was to legitimise flexibility, by providing apprentices with a way to exit contracts legally and recover part of any premium. This was most developed in London, where a right for the apprentice to exit at will was designed into many contracts, but it was also present elsewhere in England. Avoiding lock-in, I suggest, encouraged families to invest in human capital in an environment with high levels of asymmetric information and uncertainty.

The outcomes of apprenticeship are the subject of chapter 8. Premodern apprentices' employment with their masters almost always ended at the point when they completed their contracted term of service; few would remain as employees with the same master. Having completed their apprenticeships gave them an entitlement to enter guilds, become a citizens, and set up independently, if they were in a corporate town. While the barrier to taking this next step was modest, only a minority would become freemen. 'Insiders' were more likely to do so, as were the better off, but they did not make up the majority of new masters. The rest were not necessarily failing; a significant number of migrant apprentices took their skills back home, spreading connections and knowledge.

The third and final section of the book focuses directly on the openness of this system, addressing the impact of three enemies of opportunity that could have limited and biased its effects. Chapters 9 and 10 survey the set of formal rules that were created in England by guilds, cities, and the nation-state and then evaluate their impact. Some rules did matter, particularly the link between a seven-year apprenticeship and the ability to work, set by the Statute of Artificers. This encouraged apprenticeship, as did Poor Law provision, but few of the formal boundaries to accessing training seriously affected recruitment.

Informal cultural barriers to training could potentially be more pernicious than formal rules in limiting opportunity. Chapter 11 examines the impact of social norms in two areas where we might expect recruitment to be limited: the gender and birth order of apprentices. Gender, especially, strongly affected the likelihood a child would be apprenticed. Young women were much less likely to serve apprenticeships than young men. Some did, however, and this included children from well-off families. Birth order, too, mattered, but largely when linked to the probability of inheriting land. Norms were most damaging for women.

A third potential enemy of opportunity is the effect of social networks. Apprenticeships involved matching a master with a child. If matches can only be made between people who already know and trust each other—those they share strong ties with—then young people's opportunities will be seriously constrained. By looking at the evidence for different types of family, occupational, or geographical connections between apprentices and masters, I show in chapter 12 that these were present for only a minority of apprentices. Most apprenticeships forged new links. Social ties were used to discover opportunities, rather than provide them. This allowed skills to spread and diffuse; it also helps explain the importance of flexibility in the contract.

The aim of the book is to give a balanced account of how apprenticeship worked and what this meant for economic and social life in premodern England. To be clear, I do not claim here that apprenticeship was the magic ingredient in England's economic success or that this variant was limited to England per se. As an institution, apprenticeship helps explains the path of development in England, but it did not determine it. There is good reason to believe that many of its features were shared with apprenticeship found elsewhere across Europe. We should also not be blind to the failings and costs involved in apprenticeship. The system was not optimal, in some efficiency-maximising sense, and training could have been faster and better. It created and benefited from economic rents that were born by the population. It did exclude some young people. It may, however, have been better than some of the alternative forms of training that existed in other regions of the premodern world that were less open, less flexible, and less effective at moving labour and knowledge.

That apprenticeship had these impacts also did not mean that it was without problems. Workshops possessed hierarchies that could be brutally enforced. Some youths were beaten and abused, exploited, and neglected; we will meet some later in the book. For that matter, so were some masters, though surely much less often. An excellent body of social history of childhood and work means that there is no need to cover that terrain here in detail.[48] For poor children, this was even more true: apprenticeship under the Poor Law could amount to little more than child slavery, hard labour, hard knocks, and no end in sight for more than a decade, though it is also clear that it need not always have been so.

The effects of English apprenticeship were not the result of farsighted design by progressive actors. Nor were they inevitable. In several areas, rules and practices pull in opposite directions, and the contradictions between regulation and reality have generated much of the debate around apprenticeship. Long terms of service fixed by guilds and later by statute were burdens that had to be quietly evaded with the compliance of masters, guild officials, and civic bodies to reduce the burden they imposed. In short, this is not a hymn to premodern institutional design or English exceptionalism, but an attempt to better understand one of the fundamental institutions of the premodern economy.

PART I

Apprenticeship and Development

2

The Rise and (Partial) Fall of Apprenticeship

Two stories that have global consequences are often told about England's economic development in the three centuries since the early sixteenth century. The first is about the nation's rise from a peripheral and relatively undistinguished place in Europe's economy to become the commercial and manufacturing powerhouse of Europe in the mid-eighteenth century, equalled only by the Netherlands. This period of expansion was inseparable from the rise of London, from a mid-sized city of 40,000 to Europe's largest urban centre and biggest port with a population of 740,000 in 1750. It saw the nation's rapid urbanisation from a relatively low level well below Europe's leaders to one of its most urbanised. It involved one of the earliest and most dramatic periods of structural change, with the share of the male workforce in agriculture declining from around 1600 to fall below 50 per cent by 1700, as manufacturing and services boomed. And it saw the expansion of England's influence across the globe, with the foundation of colonies and the expansion of overseas trade, including the Atlantic slave trade and the establishment of the East India Company's initial position in India, developments coordinated by English merchants and spurring further changes in manufacturing.

The second story was even more momentous: it is the story of the Industrial Revolution, which took hold initially in England's northern counties from the middle of the eighteenth century. The Industrial Revolution introduced a new mode of production tied to mechanisation, large firms, factory production, and inorganic energy, and a new pace of innovation and progress based on an alliance of science and industry.

These well-known stories have deep and complex roots that economic historians have traced and debated at length. This chapter and the two that follow address the part that apprenticeship played in them. They consider three ways in which apprenticeship contributed to these two connected periods in England's extraordinary and precocious economic development: first, the role apprenticeship played in the supply of human capital; second, the connection between the concentration of apprenticeship and the diffusion of knowledge and innovations across the economy; and third, the level of geographical and occupational mobility in the labour market that apprenticeship supported.

Rise and Fall?

The rise and partial fall of apprenticeship in early modern England is expressed most simply in figure 2.1, which shows estimates of the share of English male workers employed outside of agriculture who had started apprenticeships.[1] In effect, it measures the importance of apprenticeship to the supply of skilled labour in manufacturing and services in England.

Figure 2.1 contains three different estimates of apprentice totals. Two are for 'guild' apprentices: those registered by members of a guild in London; and the national total of guild apprentices, combining those in London with estimates of those enrolled by other incorporated urban centres and guilds. Guild apprentices are countable—because they were registered. They also qualified for guild membership or urban citizenship because they were registered to a guild member or citizen.[2] The third, the shortest line, is for 'all apprentices' across the eighteenth century, derived from apprenticeships with premiums for which stamp tax was paid. This includes youths trained in guilds and outside of them, but only if their master received money to train them.[3] There is some measure of uncertainty about both the numbers of apprentices and the sectoral shares, but probably not enough to change the basic trajectory suggested by this rough accounting of the supply of human capital.[4] There are also still some blank spaces, the most important of which are pauper apprenticeships provided by parishes, and training outside guild towns before 1700.

Let us begin with that shortest line, which is based on the first set of national totals for apprenticeship in England. It indicates that half of all

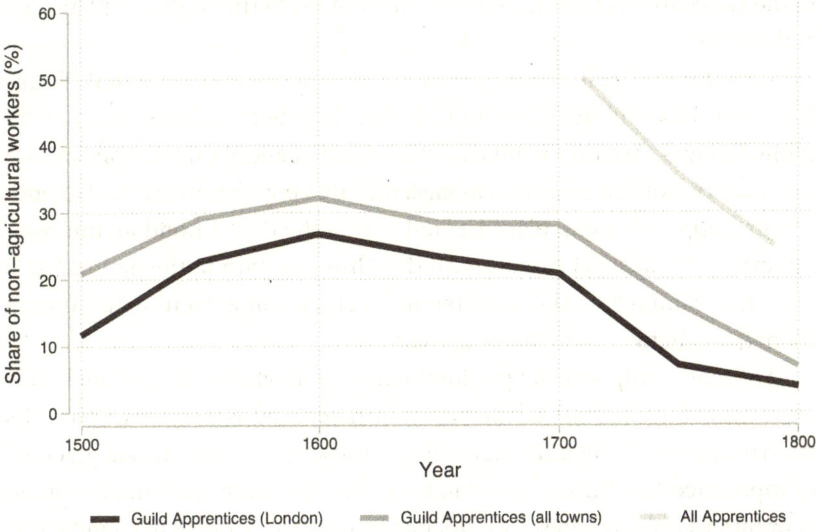

FIGURE 2.1. Apprenticeship and the English male workforce outside agriculture. The figure reports the share of male workers active in non-agricultural occupations who started an apprenticeship: (i) in a London guild; (ii) in an incorporated 'guild' city or town with a population over 5,000 (inc. London); (iii) in any location, assuming that the total of premium apprentices is 50% of the number of private apprentices once those not paying premiums or receiving charitable assistance are accounted for. See appendices 2 and 3.

male workers outside of agriculture started apprenticeships at the start of the early eighteenth century (assuming the estimate that 50% paid no premium is correct). Given that no adjustments have been made for unskilled jobs in these sectors—labourers, porters, messengers, soldiers, and so on—apprenticeship (within and outside guilds) must have been the most common mode of training outside agriculture, exceeding the share who trained solely within their family.

About half of these apprenticeships were registered within guilds. If we look at the two longer lines showing the share trained in guilds from 1500 to 1800, we see that the contribution of London's guilds to the nation's stock of human capital was increasing rapidly until c. 1600. The distance between the two lines is so narrow because guild apprenticeship was exceptionally concentrated within London in the sixteenth and seventeenth centuries, and as a result, other towns and cities had comparatively small numbers of guild apprentices. London's guild members trained one in ten men employed outside agriculture in 1500, and around one in four by 1600. London's role in training was always larger, and its growth outpaced that of other centres in the sixteenth century. London's contribution to training then plateaued and slid back

This flood of youths into London brought creative potential, financial resources, and the capacity to learn. Even before these youths were trained, it was a transfer of human capital and financial capital from around the country, not just a way to replenish the city's population. In the sixteenth century, apprenticeship played a vital part in the rise of London, the commercial and industrial powerhouse that drove growth in the nation.[5] This started to diminish in the seventeenth century, but even in 1700 London trained one in five men outside agriculture.

Apprenticeship was the predominant way in which occupational skills were gained at the start of the eighteenth century. Ninety years later, its contribution had fallen dramatically. In these terms, we can see 'decline' in apprenticeship. This is visible in both the 'all apprentices' and the 'guild apprenticeship' estimates. By 1790, just 30 per cent of males in manufacturing and services started apprenticeships.

This decline was almost all relative. The absolute number of apprentices grew in the eighteenth century, and the share of teenagers entering apprenticeship was largely stable until the 1790s. Apprenticeship remained the largest single focus for investment of time and money in human capital formation. However, apprenticeship had been outpaced by continued structural change, as employment in industry and services had grown from around 48 to 64 per cent of male workers. Manufacturing boomed in regions that had previously been farming areas.[6] Proto-industry expanded to meet the demand for consumer goods from the English middling sort and overseas markets. New ways of organising work and new forms of training accompanied these developments. Whereas apprenticeship had fuelled growth in the sixteenth and seventeenth centuries, it had a more muted role outside of a few occupations in the eighteenth and nineteenth centuries. The early modern apprenticeship boom fizzled out.

Figure 2.1 also holds a powerful message about the role of guilds in apprenticeship in England. The connection between guilds and apprenticeship eroded rapidly from the later seventeenth century. Apprenticeship experienced—and survived—this major change in its institutional context. If we consider guild apprenticeship in all of England's towns and cities, the share of training by guild members recorded in their records peaked at around a third of teenagers employed off the farm in 1600. In short, *guild* apprenticeships were never the source of training for the majority of English manufacturing and service workers. Some among the plurality of youths without guild apprenticeships would have been relatively unskilled, but apprenticeships *outside* guilds and informal training within families must have always accounted for most skill transmission in early modern England.[7]

The trends in figure 2.1 set the stage for this chapter. The first part looks further into training in London and other corporate towns during this process of urbanisation, commercialisation, and structural change. The second part turns to the eighteenth century and the changes in training that occurred as industrialisation took hold.

Apprenticeship in London and the Nation, 1500–1800

The epicentre of early modern guild apprenticeship in England was London. This single city rose to dominate guild apprenticeship during the sixteenth and seventeenth centuries to an unprecedented degree. This was not due to growth in the number or reach of its guilds: although some were established through the division of old groupings or for new occupations, such as distillers and spectacle-makers, most of the city's economy was governed by guilds by the fourteenth century. Rather, it was the sheer number of apprentices that changed. By the late sixteenth century, the great majority of England's urban apprentices were in London—almost 80 per cent, or 3,500 out of roughly 4,500 youths who were starting guild apprenticeships each year.

London's guild members recruited three to four times the number of apprentices training in all of England's other large towns combined in 1600. A century before, only around half had been indentured there. London played a large but not outsized role in training during the late medieval period. It then swelled into a leviathan. Never before or since would human capital formation in England be as concentrated into one location as it was in the early 1600s.

The scale of London's contribution to human capital formation can be seen clearly in figure 2.2, which presents estimates of the number of guild apprentices training in four categories of town and city: the first category consists just of London; the second is England's major towns and cities, taken as those with over 10,000 inhabitants; the third is the array of smaller towns with populations of more than 5,000; the fourth is a constellation of smaller boroughs that possessed some form of self-governance, but in this period, few residents. The latter three series are extrapolated from estimates of apprentice numbers per inhabitant, drawn from a sample of surviving records and then extrapolated across the towns known to exist in each category; the process is detailed in appendix 2, and there are substantial margins for error, especially in 1500 and 1800. The estimates of guild apprenticeship in London are increasingly precise as record survival improves, but the

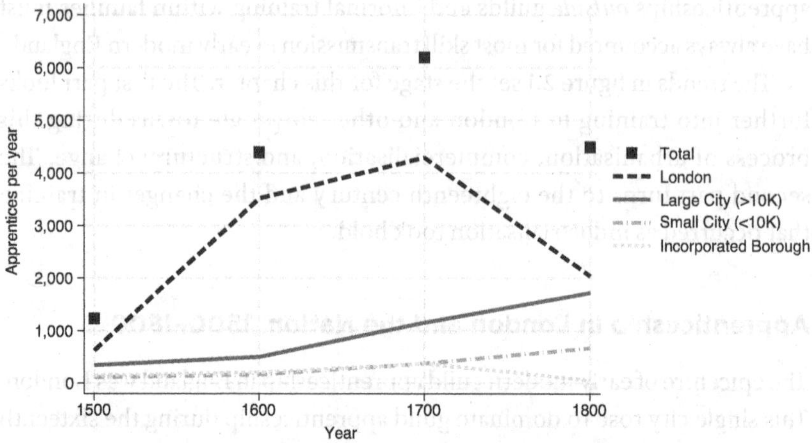

FIGURE 2.2. English guild apprenticeship, 1500–1800. The figure reports estimates of the number of new apprentices indentured per annum at each benchmark year. See appendix 3.

estimates of training elsewhere are rougher and reflect changes in urbanisation. Nonetheless, the dominance of London means that it is unlikely that any revision to the underlying numbers could change the basic pattern.

As well as the centrality of London, the rise and fall of guild apprenticeship more generally is clear here: the number of youths—mostly young men—starting apprenticeships with a guild master rose steeply from 1500 to 1700. The dramatic expansion in guild apprenticeship far outstripped the growth in England's population, even if it did not keep up fully with the pace of structural change in the seventeenth century. Apprenticeship quadrupled in the 1500s while the nation's population doubled from around 2.2 million to 4.1 million. In the 1600s, guild apprenticeship continued to outstrip population growth, but less dramatically. Apprenticeships increased by 44 per cent over the seventeenth century while the population grew by 26 per cent, reaching 5.2 million in 1700.[8] From then, however, guild apprenticeship entered a secular decline, falling to fewer than 5,000 new apprentices per year by 1800, while the nation's population grew quickly, to 8.6 million in 1800.

To put this in context, in 1500, about 7 per cent of English teenage males started a guild apprenticeship. By 1600 this had increased to 11 per cent, and by 1700 it was 16 per cent. One hundred years later, the share had fallen back to 8 per cent despite the continued growth of services and manufacturing. Even this figure may be generous, because in established guild towns apprenticeship was often occurring outside the corporate framework by

1800, and the total is increasingly reliant on the estimate of training in small boroughs which were now growing in population, but for which the least information survives.

London's rise in providing training for the nation overshadowed England's other towns. England's second and third tiers of cities played a much smaller part in guild apprenticeship in the sixteenth and seventeenth centuries. Where London attracted a flood, these cities received a trickle. In Lincoln—population c. 4,000 in 1700—just fourteen new apprentices a year were indentured in the mid-seventeenth century. New Woodstock, a borough that was little more than a village, averaged two a year in the early seventeenth century.[9] In Gloucester, a county town with around 5,000 residents, some forty to fifty apprentices were indentured each year in the seventeenth century. Even Bristol, the country's third-largest city, received only 180 apprentices annually around 1600 and about 250 around 1700, when its population reached about 24,000 people. It was only in the eighteenth century that these centres started to supply a more proportionate share of training.

The difference in the scale of guild apprenticeship between these towns and cities and London is hard to grasp. Every year, more apprenticeships were registered by some of London's larger guilds—the Merchant Taylors, Haberdashers, Weavers—than in the whole of the city of Bristol. And Bristol was relatively important in training: its density of apprentices came close to that of London, and like London, it was growing rapidly and seizing new overseas trading opportunities.[10] Almost 7 per cent of Bristol's population were apprentices in 1600, and around 4 per cent in 1700 (assuming 60% remained in their contracts to the end of their terms).

Even in their own hinterlands, England's provincial cities were secondary to the metropolis at its magnetic height. Almost twice as many youths from Gloucestershire were bound in London's guilds as in the city of Gloucester between 1590 and 1730. More than twice as many from Oxfordshire trained in London as in Oxford in the seventeenth century.[11] The figures look similar for Lincoln and Shrewsbury. These comparisons understate the metropolitan advantage, as not all London records survive, while those cities' registers are fairly complete for these periods. It was only those youths who had been born and raised in provincial cities who preferred their local options to the opportunities available in London; for everyone else, the fact that an apprenticeship gave a worker the right to remain and work only in the guild or city where they trained created a strong incentive to crowd into the largest and most lucrative labour markets at the outset.[12] Once London started to grow, success generated its own momentum.

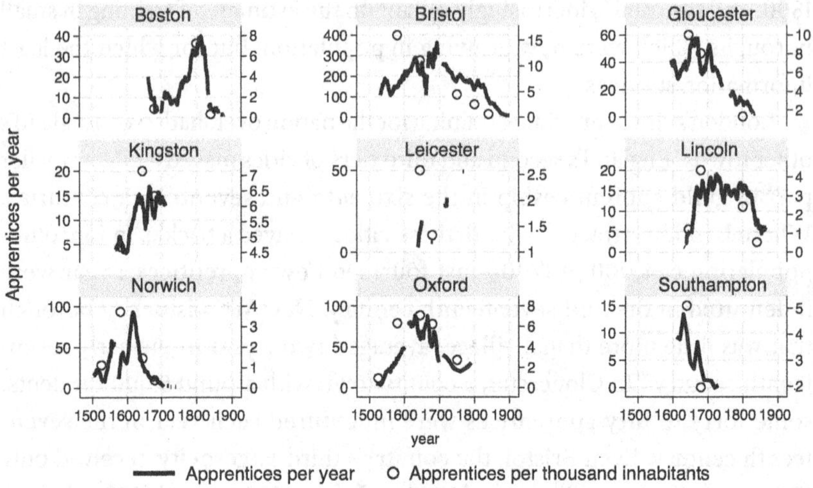

FIGURE 2.3. Annual entries to provincial urban and guild apprenticeships, 1500–1900. Apprentices per year are reported on the left-hand axis; apprentices per thousand inhabitants on the right-hand axis. For most series, the figure reports the number of apprenticeships registered each year in city registers of indentures; for Oxford post-1700 and Southampton, these are averages per decade. Population estimates are drawn from de Vries 1984; Langton 2000; Clark and Hosking 1993.
Source: See appendix 1.

To give a better sense of the scale and trajectory of 'guild' apprenticeship outside London, figure 2.3 presents individual series of annual totals of new apprentices registered in the city records of apprentices kept by a range of provincial towns and cities of differing sizes, alongside estimates of apprentices per thousand inhabitants. These towns represent a range of institutional settings; all of them linked the completion of registered apprenticeships to gaining exclusive local economic and political rights, but not all involved urban citizens being organised into guilds as such.

The diversity of numbers and trends in apprenticeship between different cities is the overwhelming impression given by figure 2.3. The evidence for a Tudor and Elizabethan growth spurt seems compelling. A clear upward shift in numbers of apprentices recorded over the sixteenth century is apparent in the figures for Oxford and Bristol, the two centres with substantial records from the period. Kingston upon Thames, where records commence in the 1560s, shows a similar upsurge. This rise in corporate apprenticeship aligns with a broader strengthening and regularisation of incorporated towns and cities over this period.[13] Peaks in guild apprenticeship occurred at wildly different times, however: in the 1640s and 1650s in Southampton, Gloucester, and Oxford; in the 1660s in Kingston upon Thames; around 1700 in Bristol; and in the late eighteenth century in Leicester and Boston. Lincoln appears to lack any distinctive peak.

Guild apprenticeship in England's guilds and corporate cities was a wave that crested at different times, and its ebb was equally unsynchronised. To suggest, as some have, that guild apprenticeship reached a nationwide high point at any specific moment before declining would seem too strong a generalisation.[14] We can observe an outer marker, in the mid-nineteenth century, when the last remaining series of registrations end. This coincided with the reform of urban government that occurred in this period, doing away with the ancient corporations and the apparatus of guilds that they maintained.[15] In Lincoln and Bristol, series stop, rather than falter, as a result of these reforms. Yet, several provincial cities had already ceased registering apprentices some decades before. In much of continental Europe, politics, and Napoleonic reforms especially, put paid to many guilds.[16] In England, the state quashed guild apprenticeship in some parts of urban England, but in others central government actions were only one small part of the explanation. The variety of trends suggests that local economic and political factors mattered more in most towns and cities.

If we turn back to London, what this boom and bust in guild apprenticeship meant for the place of apprentices and apprenticeship in the metropolis becomes apparent if we look not just at counts of new apprentices, but at the share of the city's population they formed. Table 2.1 presents estimates of annual number of new apprentices, and the stock of former apprentices who had completed training that they imply, to show the number of new apprentices each year per inhabitant, and the proportion of the city's population and its working-age males (those aged fifteen to fifty-nine) who were currently apprentices or had once trained as an apprentice. As many youths left contracts early, these estimates assume that three-quarters completed their terms of service.[17]

Between the late sixteenth and late eighteenth centuries, these estimates show that London experienced a fundamental shift in the degree to which it was a corporate city in which male working lives were structured by a regulated and predictable series of institutional and economic stages.

At the start of the sixteenth century, apprenticeship was pervasive, as it had been for a century or more. These estimates begin in 1500, but the limited evidence that exists suggests the number of apprentices recruited per capita was similar in the fifteenth century.[18] In the mid-sixteenth century, there was a surplus of apprentices compared to the number of working-age

TABLE 2.1. The importance of guild apprentices to London's workforce, 1500–1820

	1500	1550	1600	1650	1700	1730	1760	1790	1820
Apprentices p.a. (N)	627	1,729	3,512	4,359	4,285	2,731	2,239	1,803	1,873
Per 1,000 inhabitants	15.7	23.1	17.6	10.9	7.5	4.0	3.0	2.0	1.5
Former apprentices (N)	11,497	39,318	93,445	135,826	152,446	129,017	84,511	69,545	61,964
CURRENT APPRENTICES									
Share of London's population (%)	10	14	11	7	5	2	2	1	1
Share of London's working males (%)	28	42	30	19	13	7	5	4	3
FORMER APPRENTICES									
Share of London's population (%)	22	39	35	25	20	14	9	6	4
Share of London's working males (%)	63	117	98	71	57	39	25	17	11
BASELINE TOTALS									
London, population (N)	40,000	75,000	200,000	400,000	575,000	675,000	740,000	900,000	1,247,000
London, males, 25–59 (N)	13,778	25,223	71,280	143,560	199,755	245,430	255,929	309,330	411,884
APPRENTICE DATASET COVERAGE									
Share of apprentices observed (%)	30	31	53	69	79	72	73	76	18
Share of guilds observed (%)	13	21	30	36	66	65	66	68	16

Notes: Apprentices per annum is based on estimates discussed in appendix 2. The total for current apprentices assumes a term of seven years, with 75% reaching completion. The figure for former apprentices is the number of individuals who had started apprenticeships in the previous thirty years; this assumes that former apprentices' life expectancy at age twenty-four (the average age at the end of service) was thirty. This figure, which is several years shorter than the national estimates in Wrigley 1997, takes into account the impact of higher urban mortality. (a) Population estimates are from Barron 2000, 396; Boulton 2000, 316; Schwarz 2000, 650–51. (b) Estimates of twenty-five- to fifty-nine-year-olds are from Wrigley 1997, table A9.1, increased by 12% to adjust for the difference in the metropolitan age-structure demonstrated in Landers 1993, 180 (for simplicity, his ten-to-nineteen age group is divided by two to match Wrigley's format). For 1500, the 1541 figures are applied to the 2.2 million population estimate given by Broadberry et al. 2015.

males. Apprentices currently serving their indentures and registered within one of the city's gilds supplied roughly one in three of London's male workers. There were enough apprentices that the entire adult working population of the city—and more—could have once served one.

Early Elizabethan London was, in truth, a city built on apprentices.[19] Its workforce was flooded with migrants searching for opportunities. It is worth noting that the social and political importance of apprentices was rooted in this numerical heft.[20] Apprentices played a prominent part in popular protest in early modern London, forming a notorious mob that played an important role in events including the civil war. As a group, rioting apprentices could outnumber almost anything brought against them. The converse was that guild membership and urban citizenship were potentially nearly universal, as a result, even if that right would not be exercised by all. The expansion in guild apprenticeship tracked the economic and demographic expansion of London until around 1600. Much of the necessary stream of migrant labour that allowed the city to grow passed through the doors of the city's guilds when it arrived.

However, this relationship then started to break down. The city's rapid growth continued, but guild apprenticeship waned relative to the population from the end of the sixteenth century, as table 2.1 shows. It is unclear if the initial decline in the later seventeenth century onward was entirely due to a move away from guild apprenticeship in London, rather than a fall in the supply or demand for training, but a move away from guild apprenticeship seems likely to have played a large part.

The high level of guild apprenticeship in the sixteenth century was followed by a long process of *relative* decline in the weight of guild apprenticeship within the city's working population. It would not be wrong to say that the Statute of Artificers was passed in the 1560s at the point at which apprenticeship was most dominant within the metropolis. For all that the absolute number of guild apprentices would continue to grow for more than another century, their place in the city's workforce would never again be as great.

After 1700, former guild apprentices became a minority in the city's male workforce. By the mid-eighteenth century, one-quarter of the city's adult males may have served a guild apprenticeship. By the end of the eighteenth century perhaps only one-sixth had. Citizenship was now a minority activity increasingly linked to inheritance of privileges and wealth, as we will see in chapter 8. The shift from apprenticeship within guilds to apprenticeship to non-citizens marked the erosion of the economic and legal importance of guild membership to working life in London. The contrast with the sixteenth century is stark. One obvious implication is that the city's adult male workforce was no longer united in a shared experience of training within a common institutional framework. Another is that the threat of guild monopolies had lost most of its teeth. The final termination of guild involvement in apprenticeship in the nineteenth century was later than many have thought, but guilds had lost their hegemony around the end of the seventeenth century.

It is only right to note that each element of this narrative of London guild apprenticeship fits with one of the classic historiographical accounts. The all-encompassing scale of apprenticeship in the mid-sixteenth century sustains Rappaport's analysis of a city embedded tightly within its guilds.[21] George Unwin's classic account of the early decline of the guilds from the end of the sixteenth century matches the turning point in the relative importance of apprenticeship within London's society as a whole, as do Beier's estimates.[22] Kellet's and Kahl's suggestion that decline followed the Great Fire of 1666 broadly fits with the change in the absolute trend that we see at the end of the seventeenth century.[23] We can thus reconcile some of the main accounts of the development of the system, at least in outline.

What drove this change in guild apprenticeship? That the long and steady fall in the share of London's workforce who were guild apprentices, or who had completed one, began so early suggests that the roots lay in the spread of the urban area beyond the boundaries of the incorporated city of London. From the early seventeenth century onwards, an increasing number of masters worked in Westminster or the suburbs around London that fell outside the jurisdiction of the city's government. Many of them were no longer citizens of the city of London. These are the masters who come into sight first in the stamp tax records. The population of the corporate city made up just a quarter of the wider metropolis by 1700.[24] The area where the dictates of the Lord Mayor and Court of Aldermen and the guilds held strongest sway was encircled by an increasingly urbanised terrain notionally subject to other authorities where the city's orders might be ignored or contested.

This geographical trend predated any of the later legal or political changes that more directly struck the guilds' powers within the city—the civil war of the 1640s, the Great Fire of 1666, the quo warranto dispute, and the post-1688 weakening of royal prerogative that left guilds' legal advisors in doubt about their ability to discipline non-members.[25] These challenges to guild authority do coincide with the absolute nominal decline in apprenticeship. But by this point, guild apprentices were arguably already losing their importance compared to their position a century before.

Picking an apprenticeship with a guild member—the credential that meant that service would entitle a youth to access the guild's economic and political privileges—became an option, rather than a basic requirement. However, the fall in the scale of guild apprenticeship in the eighteenth century did not make these opportunities less valuable to those who pursued them. The price that apprentices and their families were willing to pay masters within the guilds of London to enter apprenticeships in most occupations remained constant or increased.

The sums that guild masters could command for apprenticeships rose in the first half of the century when the numbers entering guild apprenticeship declined most quickly. Between the 1710s and 1760s, premiums more than doubled in fifteen of the forty-four guilds for which an average premium can be calculated.[26] The largest increase was in several guilds in which low premiums had dominated at the start of the century, suggesting it was the lower end of the market that was declining most rapidly. The average premium in the Plasterers' Company rose from £8 to £45, and in the Cordwainers' from £9 to £26. Demand from families for this combination of human capital and legal and economic privileges remained robust, even as numbers shrank. After controlling for the differences between occupations and over time, citizen masters could charge around 30 per cent more as a premium than non-citizens, with the difference growing over the century.[27] Seemingly, guild apprenticeship moved up-market, with the associated corporate privileges becoming an attribute valued by the affluent middling sort. Access to the guilds became more closely linked to wealth, rather than an institution that cut across the city's social hierarchy.

The steep decline of guild apprenticeship did not mean that training overall in London dwindled as sharply. The records of the stamp tax show a fall from around 2,000 to 1,300 apprenticeships per year in London in the eighteenth century. Initially, many were still in guilds. In the 1710s, around 70 per cent of premium apprentices in London were trained by guild members. However, guild apprenticeships then collapsed to 45 to 50 per cent of premium apprentices in the 1750s and 1760s, and by the close of the century barely a quarter of masters taking premium apprentices in London were guild members. Training with London-based masters outside the guilds did not entirely fill the space left by the reduction in guild training; a smaller share of English apprentices trained in London in the 1700s. The erosion of guild power opened a greater space for those trained elsewhere to migrate into the city, potentially bringing a different mix of skills, and breaking the connection between teenage migration and training that had existed for centuries.

Training was more robust outside London. Figure 2.4 looks at the same provincial towns discussed earlier, but shows the number of apprentices

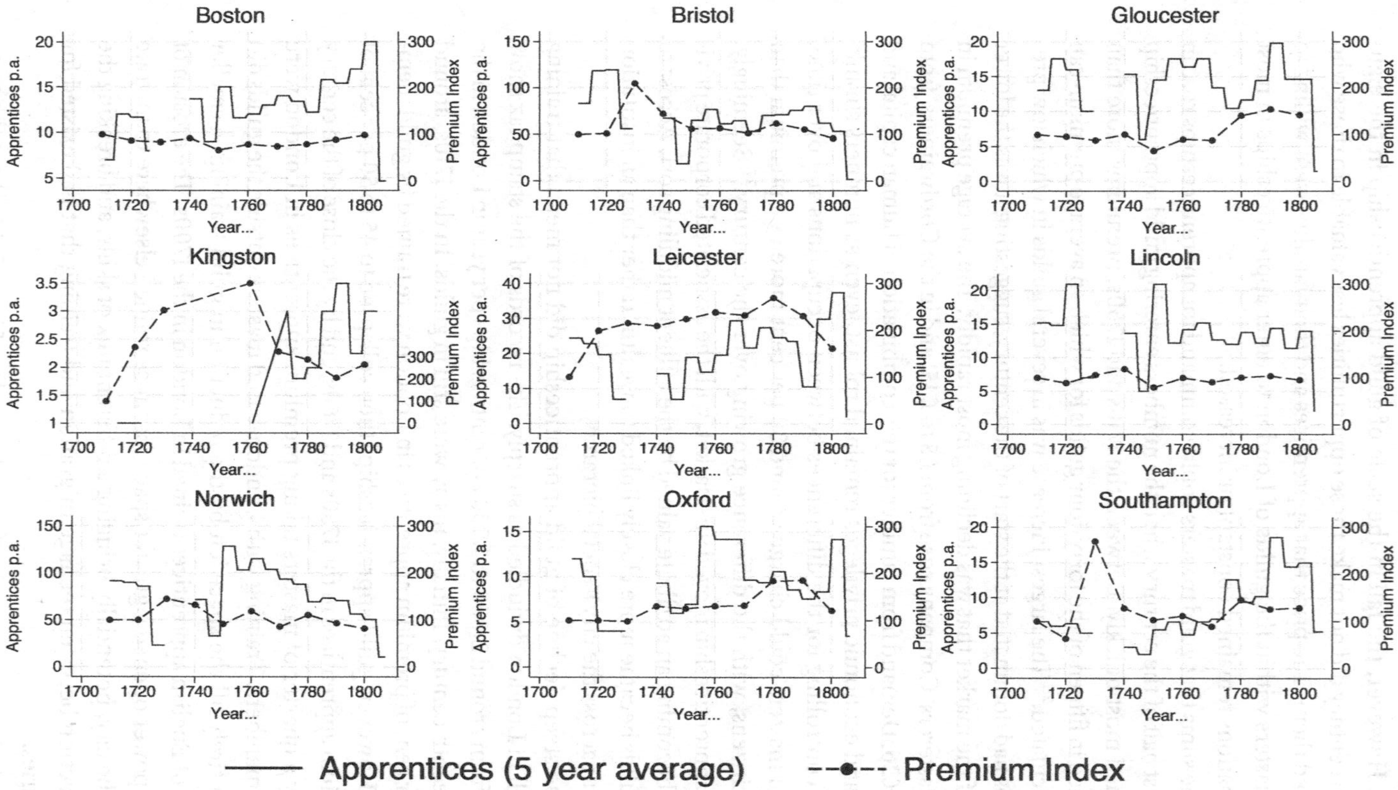

FIGURE 2.4. Premium apprentices in provincial towns and cities, 1710–1800. The figure reports five-year averages of the number of premium apprentices in each city in years with full sets of surviving registers. On the right-hand axis, it reports an index of average premiums per decade in that location, deflated to 1700 pounds using Robert Allen's CPI.

paying premiums and the average amount they paid to masters instead of the guild registration totals. In around half of the towns, the numbers of apprenticeships with premiums actually held up or increased, while the fees that families paid remained stable despite inflation.

Apprenticeships—as measured by levels of premium apprenticeship—was keeping its appeal even without the guilds. Apprentices were being trained, just not within English, particularly metropolitan, guilds and corporations.

The dynamic of guild apprenticeship's rise and fall was sharpest in London. The abundance of human capital fuelled the extraordinary demographic and economic rise of London. As Wrigley noted, a matching expansion in migration was essential for the city's rise and survival: London's rapid growth depended on a stream of youths arriving from across the nation and taking up new occupations.[28] This flow of human capital was positively selected for its willingness to migrate and actively choosing to invest in an array of expanding occupations. London's artisans, merchants, and traders were often migrants who had arrived for apprenticeships. They were then endowed with skills forged in the city by the artisans and traders of the previous generation who were prospering enough to attract trainees.

At a fundamental level, England's transition into a trading and manufacturing power depended on London's growth, and that depended on the sustained flow of betterment migrants that apprenticeship facilitated.[29] The experience of training that apprentices gained there was widely shared, with important consequences for the diffusion of knowledge and skills. Other factors mattered too, obviously, but apprenticeship was a key framework for the geographical and occupational mobility the metropolis relied upon and the spread of ideas and knowledge within and beyond this city at the frontier of the nation's economy.

Apprenticeship and Industrialisation in the Eighteenth Century

This section examines the distribution of training across the eighteenth century in greater detail, asking what this shows us about the connection between apprenticeship, economic specialisation, and—crucially—industrialisation.

A major disjuncture emerged between the fortunes of guild and private apprenticeship in the eighteenth century. As we have seen, training agreements registered in guilds and corporate cities did decline markedly. Although a few corporate towns avoided decline, such as Lincoln, most had

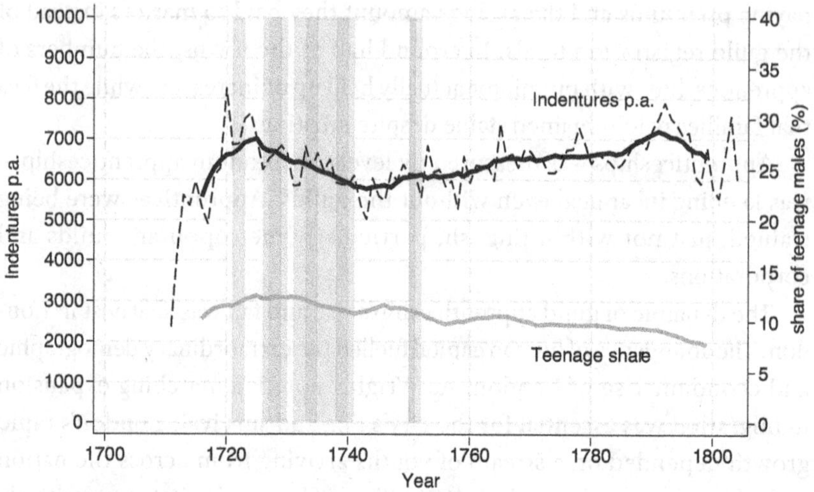

FIGURE 2.5. Premium apprenticeship in England, 1711–1804. Gaps in the series are interpolated using the average of apprentices per capita in the four years either side of the gap. The stamp registers are structured in two series (city and county). Light shading indicates a gap in one series; darker shading indicates gaps in both. For simplicity, any year affected by a gap is shaded, even if part of the register survives. The share of teenage males is calculated as the number of indentures divided by the number of sixteen-year-old male teenagers, estimated from Wrigley 1997, table A9.1, 134, 614–15. The number of indentures is adjusted down by 5% to exclude female apprentices and by 5% to exclude Scottish and Welsh apprentices; the shares of female and non-English apprentices are calculated from samples of the records. *Source:* TNA, IR1.

far lower levels of guild or civic registrations by 1800 than they had in 1600 or 1700. However, apprenticeship *outside* guilds remained robust across most of the century, including in the suburbs of London, and only saw a limited per capita decline in the latter part of the period.

The persistence of private apprenticeship can be seen in the number of apprenticeship indentures recorded by the stamp tax clerks between 1711 and 1804, shown in figure 2.5. In absolute terms, the scale of premium apprenticeship in the late eighteenth century was little different to that in the early eighteenth century, with 6,000 to 7,000 apprenticeships started annually, and what appears to be an upward trend from the 1740s until the 1790s. England's population was growing, but even expressed as the share of male youths, the long-term trend in training appears surprisingly robust, unlike the trend in guild apprenticeships. Between 10 and 12 per cent of teenage males entered premium apprenticeships until the 1790s.

We can see signs of a gentle decline in the share of male youths entering premium apprenticeships, particularly in the late 1790s, when the British population was growing rapidly and industrialisation was accelerating. At this point, the impact of the Napoleonic Wars on the economy may also have been affecting the demand for (and price of) apprenticeship in this period. Against this backdrop, it would be dangerous to infer that this was the beginning of a permanent absolute decline in apprenticeship. The lines in the figure end when the tax registers stop, not when apprenticeship ceases.

While the total number of premium apprentices remained largely flat, there was a geographical shift in apprenticeship. London remained the largest single centre of training in Britain in the eighteenth century, but its exceptionality was much reduced. The number of apprentices training in London drifted down over the century, while those training elsewhere rose considerably. In the 1710s, 34 per cent of apprentices paying premiums in England were indentured to London masters—whether they were guild members or not; London received three times the number of premium apprentices that its share of England's population (11%) would predict. By the 1790s, London trained just 15 per cent of premium apprentices, roughly one and half times the number that its share of the national population would predict. Given that London remained by far the largest and richest city in the nation, home to almost half of all England's residents of large towns even in 1800, this decline in its role in training is striking.[30]

Before 1700, apprenticeship outside incorporated towns is largely invisible in the historical record. With the evidence of premium apprenticeship provided by the stamp tax, we can finally say more. It reveals the remarkable penetration of apprenticeship into small hamlets and villages over the eighteenth century. Presumably, this continued a shift that must have begun soon after 1600. Even if the trend had begun earlier, it is clear that a radical spatial redistribution of apprenticeship occurred over the eighteenth century that led to premium apprentices training in villages and small towns where they were largely absent a generation before.

We illustrate the wider distribution of training across the eighteenth century in figure 2.6.[31] For 1710, it includes the locations of 28,082 apprentices, and for 1795, 34,818 apprentices (each is based on a six-year sample). The number of apprentices had risen by 24 per cent. The number of different places where apprentices are found had increased by 67 per cent, from 3,004 to 5,020 locations. The darkening of the map illustrates this proliferation of locations with apprentices. Most locations that appeared for the first time in 1795 were smaller places—including many villages and

FIGURE 2.6. The distribution of apprenticeships with premiums in England and Wales, c. 1710 and c. 1795. Locations where apprentices are trained are indicated by markers, with the size of the marker proportional to the number trained in that location.
Source: See appendix 1.

new townships—that soaked up youths who would have trained in London a century earlier.

Some of this diffusion of training reflected the transformative effect of industry and the expansion of cottage industry and industrial regions. In Lancashire, for example, the small hamlet of Hardshaw within Windle saw eleven apprentices in the 1790s, compared to none in the 1710s, as it was absorbed into the manufacturing and coal-mining town of St Helens (whose population would exceed 5,000 in the 1830s).[32] The growth of clock-making in the area is apparent from their trades: four joined masters who made watches or watch-parts; the rest were bound to a surgeon, a draper, a carpenter, a cooper, a saddler, and a joiner.[33] Half paid less than £10, and just two paid more than £20—those bound to the surgeon and the joiner. Similarly, Rainhill, a small township in the same county, saw three apprentices in the 1790s, against none in the 1710s. Two made watch-parts, and one became a saddler.

However, it was not industrialising England that attracted most premium-paying apprentices. Apprenticeships for which youths and their families paid were instead becoming increasingly concentrated in the backwaters of the English economy. One way to visualise this is to look at the number of apprentices per person by county, as shown in figure 2.7. Around 1700, apprenticeship is fairly widely spread. There is a perceptible doughnut-shaped shadow around London, where metropolitan opportunities lured in most youths. But only the northernmost and westernmost counties have relatively low rates of apprenticeship. By 1795/1801 there is a clear shift away from premium apprenticeship in the northern industrial counties. Now it is the largely agricultural counties of Norfolk with 1.26 apprentices per thousand and Leicestershire with 1.09 apprentices per thousand that vie for the top place if we rank counties by apprenticeships per person. Industrialising Lancashire (0.29 per 1,000) languishes at thirty-fifth place and Cheshire (0.27) at thirtieth of forty-two.[34]

The contrast is brought into sharp focus if we compare these geographical concentrations of premium apprenticeship with the diffusion of one of the classic macro-technologies of the Industrial Revolution: the steam engine. Figure 2.7 also shows the counties with the highest and lowest numbers of steam engines installed in the century or so up to 1830. Taking steam as one proxy for industrialisation (with the caveat that it is surely not a perfect one), the contrast between England's centres of industry and its centres for training in craft and trade skills is stark.

Much of England remained largely untouched by industrialisation in this period, and apprenticeship was increasingly concentrated in these quieter

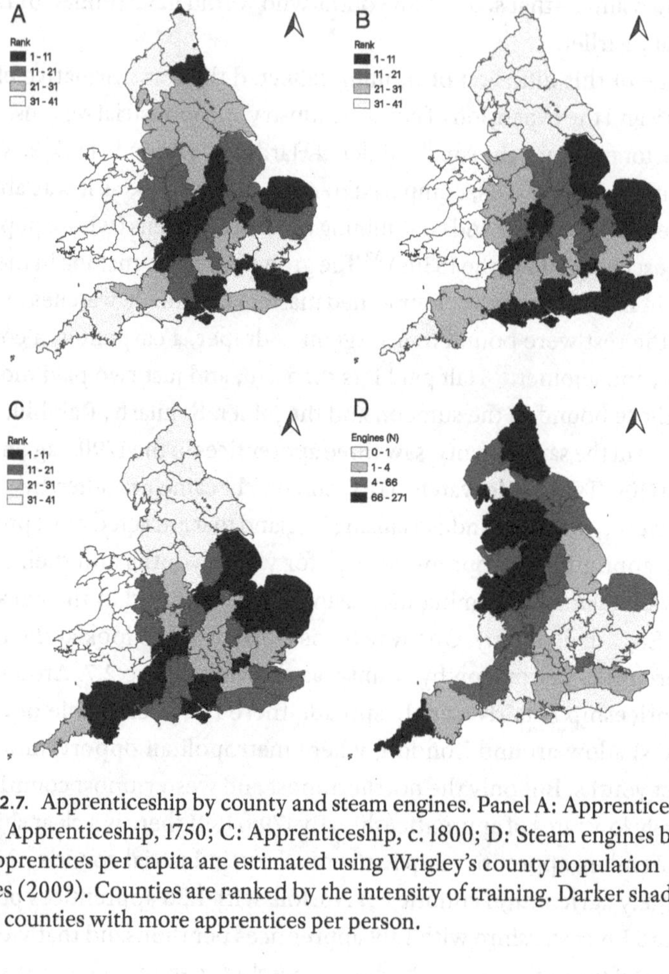

FIGURE 2.7. Apprenticeship by county and steam engines. Panel A: Apprenticeship, 1700; B: Apprenticeship, 1750; C: Apprenticeship, c. 1800; D: Steam engines by 1830. Apprentices per capita are estimated using Wrigley's county population estimates (2009). Counties are ranked by the intensity of training. Darker shades indicate counties with more apprentices per person.

areas. In Bedfordshire, it was small hamlets such as Old Warden, where the local carpenter Thomas Preston bound a youth for £6, and Ridgmont, where two cordwainers and a wheelwright each took an apprentice (for £5, £10, and £18, respectively), that saw apprentices bound for premiums in the 1790s, yet had seen none in the 1710s.

The trends in apprenticeship in Britain's large cities show the same tendency for apprenticeship to fade where industry was advancing most quickly, as table 2.2 shows. Britain's pre-eminent industrial city, Manchester, is distinguished by a persistently low number of apprentices relative to its population: 1.28 per 1,000 in 1700 and 0.25 per 1,000 in 1800, placing it thirty-fourth of thirty-eight English towns. Likewise, a number of the villages and small towns that would explode as nodes in the north's

TABLE 2.2. Urban apprenticeship, c. 1710 and c. 1795

	1710		1795	
City	Apps per 1,000	Rank	Apps per 1,000	Rank
Liverpool	8.75	1	0.61	25
Birmingham	6.29	2	0.91	18
Coventry	5.90	3	1.46	6
Worcester	5.69	4	0.73	21
Bristol	4.74	5	0.99	16
Leicester	4.19	6	0.89	19
Nottingham	4.19	7	1.04	14
King's Lynn	3.93	8	2.13	2
York	3.91	9	1.27	10
Chatham	3.67	10	1.00	15
Plymouth	3.61	11	1.30	9
Norwich	3.56	12	1.68	5
Portsmouth	3.37	13	0.32	32
Kingston upon Hull	3.33	14	0.97	17
London	3.25	15	1.06	13
Exeter	3.10	16	2.73	1
Leeds	3.03	17	0.52	28
Newcastle upon Tyne	2.94	18	0.38	31
Bath	2.78	19	1.14	11
Wolverhampton	2.67	20	0.67	22
Great Yarmouth	2.50	21	1.40	8
Chester	2.18	22	0.62	24
Ipswich	1.94	23	2.05	4
Oxford	1.75	24	0.44	29
Cambridge	1.52	25	2.10	3
Colchester	1.45	26	1.11	12
Shrewsbury	1.28	27	1.43	7
Manchester	1.28	28	0.25	34
Warrington	1.20	29	0.82	20
Sheffield	1.03	30	0.65	23
Greenwich	0.87	31	0.61	26
Carlisle	0.75	32	0.27	33
Salford	0.43	33	0.11	37
Sunderland	0.43	34	0.21	36
Bolton	0.23	35	0.54	27
Blackburn	0.13	36	0.44	29
Huddersfield	0.13	37	0.24	35
Yarmouth	0.07	38	0.01	38

industrial conurbations—Bolton, Blackburn, Huddersfield, Salford—had trivial quantities of premium apprenticeship in 1700 and 1800. But Liverpool and Birmingham begin the eighteenth century with high levels of apprenticeship: 8.8 per 1,000 and 6.3 per 1,000, respectively. In fact, they were the two large cities with the highest concentrations of premium apprenticeships per head, substantially ahead of London (3.2 per 1,000; ranked fifteenth). Yet both then saw a sharp fall in relative share and ranking. Liverpool has just 0.61 per 1,000 by 1795 (ranked twenty-fifth), Birmingham has 0.91 per 1,000 (ranked eighteenth).

The five cities with the highest concentrations of apprentices in the 1790s were Exeter, King's Lynn, Cambridge, Ipswich, and Norwich. These were slow-growing, economically peripheral towns and cities in the east or south where traditional forms of employment and business organisation still predominated. Many of the trades that youths entered in these locations were occupations servicing commercial agriculture: saddlers, blacksmiths, corn dealers, and so on.

Because the stamp tax only applied to premium-paying apprentices, it is possible that the diffusion of apprenticeship seen in table 2.2 and figure 2.7 reflects changes in the use of premiums, not apprenticeship itself. In 'hot' labour markets in industrialising regions, rising wages in new sectors may have made it impossible for masters to extract premiums as the opportunity cost of training rose, or their own need for apprentices to staff their workshops could have led to more of them offering places for free. This does not seem to have been the case: there was no decline in the average (real) premium in Lancashire or Derbyshire in the 1790s. Instead, families were paying more than they had in the 1710s or 1750s. The more likely explanation for falling numbers of apprentices is that larger firms and factories also brought in new routes to training—more informal systems of on-the-job traineeships—that would become replacements for apprenticeship in many occupations in the nineteenth century. Although there are few sources on this at the time, it was these new forms of training on the shop floors (shop floors that were themselves largely a new feature of the period) that had come to hold sway in many occupations by the nineteenth century when evidence again becomes clearer.[35]

Conversely, perhaps village boys in the rural south and east had been bound as often in the 1710s, but without paying fees. We cannot easily reject this hypothesis without evidence, which has not yet been found, on the frequency of rural apprenticeships without premiums. However, there is little sign that apprentices in places that saw training at both the start

TABLE 2.3. Premium apprenticeship by sector

Sector	Share of apprenticeships 1710s (%)	Share of apprenticeships 1790s (%)	Premium (mean) 1710s £	Premium (mean) 1790s £
Clothing	11.2	15.1	9.7	16.1
Footwear	7.7	13.3	6.2	8.6
Textiles	9.8	3.4	14.7	28.6
Iron & Steel	4.3	3.2	10.6	12.2
Machine & Tools	0.7	0.8	8.3	14.1
Construction	10.5	14.3	10.1	14.3
Manuf., other	26.6	27.9	16.1	21.1
Dealing & Retail	14.7	12.5	44.4	57.3
Service/Prof.	12.5	8.7	47.1	111.4
Transport	1.3	0.2	24.6	17.9
All			21.3	30

Source: See appendix 1.
Note: Table 2.3 reports the share of apprentices in non-primary-sector occupations in England in 1710–19 and c. 1790–99 in columns 1 and 2. Average premiums in current value (not deflated) are in columns 3 and 4. We exclude the primary sector, as apprenticeships were rarely used in those occupations.

and end of the century were paying much higher premiums in the later period, which we might also expect if changes in price were bringing rural apprentices into observation.[36] And the longer-term trends in the supply of urban apprenticeship are consistent with this pattern of ruralisation of training.

The erosion of apprenticeship in occupations most affected by industrialisation is also apparent if we look at how the occupations for which apprentices were paying premiums changed. This is no easy task: the stamp tax registers contain a myriad of different occupations, with an absurd array of spellings and terminology. Still, when grouped at a general level, some developments are clear. I adopt Wrigley's primary-secondary-tertiary schema to achieve comparability with other research on occupations. Table 2.3 shows the share of apprentices by occupation in the 1710s and 1790s in columns 1 and 2 and the average premium in columns 3 and 4.

Three clusters of occupations attracted substantially larger shares of premium apprentices at the end of the eighteenth century than at the beginning: clothing, footwear, and construction. Footwear consisted almost entirely of shoemakers (labelled either 'cordwainer' or 'shoemaker'). Clothing was split between tailors (52%), mantua makers (16%), and an array of smaller clothing-related trades. Construction was similarly mixed, with the major trade being carpenters (52%), followed by joiners (19%) and masons (6%).[37]

There were also big losers. Transport declined sharply, as did textiles, and the cluster of occupations under 'services and professions'. In transport, it is the near disappearance of mariners' apprentices that is responsible.[38] The largest occupation in textiles in both periods was weaving, although they decline from 64 to 48 per cent of masters.[39] The main occupations in the service/professional grouping are unchanged, with attorneys, surgeons, apothecaries, and barbers together taking the great majority of apprentices in 1710 and 1795, just in smaller numbers relative to the overall body of apprentices. That this did not equate to any decline in the appeal of these occupations is clear from the median premium, which rose from £47 to £111. In transport, by contrast, the median premium plummeted from £25 to £18 as numbers dwindled.

Apprentices to masters in machinery and tool-making (mainly millwrights) do become somewhat more common—from 0.7 to 0.8 per cent of all apprentices—suggesting some increase in industrial demand sparking investment in this critical aspect of human capital, as Joel Mokyr has argued.[40] Many of the artisans who constructed and maintained Britain's industrial and manufacturing machinery and tools would have been apprenticed. But the big winners visible from the composition of apprentices were occupations that are relatively traditional in their technical competencies, and associated with artisan communities who were famously defensive of their prerogatives and rights.[41] It was not until the Second Industrial Revolution of the later nineteenth century that mechanisation would transform clothing and shoemaking. The big loser, textiles, represented the occupations most affected by industrialisation. Iron, another focus of change, also fell.[42]

Of course, the occupational structure of the nation was not standing still in this period. To evaluate the significance of apprenticeship we ideally need to compare the number indenturing themselves to the number of workers entering each trade. In the absence of this, we are fortunate to have recent estimates of the occupational distribution of the male labour force around 1710 and 1817. Table 2.4 presents a simple thought experiment, showing the share of adult male workers in each occupation who had served apprenticeships, if all those training over the previous thirty-five years stayed in the occupations they first entered.[43] These figures are crude estimates, but they give a useful insight into the relative importance of premium apprenticeships in each sector.

TABLE 2.4. Estimates of workers who had served premium apprenticeships, c. 1710 and c. 1800

Sector	c. 1710 (%)	c. 1800 (%)
Clothing	28.3	42.5
Footwear	27.3	26.6
Textiles	12.4	3.2
Iron & Steel	14.3	10.5
Machine & Tools	6.4	8.3
Construction	21.1	18.6
Manuf., other	24.1	20.1
Dealing & Retail	42.2	44.9
Service/Prof.	21.5	9.1
Transport	2.1	0.3

Source: See appendix 1.
Note: Table 2.4 reports the share of adult male workers who could have been trained as apprentices if (i) the share of training that held in c. 1710–19 and c. 1800–1804 had been constant for the previous thirty-five years; (ii) all workers who entered a sector as apprentices remained in that area; (iii) life expectancy at age twenty-four was thirty-five years and 10% of apprentices died in training; and (iv) the 1817 occupational distribution held in 1800, but with numbers reduced in proportion to the difference in population between 1806 and 1816.

The comparison reinforces the strength of apprenticeship in clothing and footwear, where it suggests that a third or more of adults could have been apprenticed and that the share rose substantially over the century. If we take apprentices who did not pay premiums into account, it is easy to envisage that apprenticeship was close to universal in these trades. In clothing, the increase in apprenticeship coincides with a period in which tailors were apparently relatively successful at sustaining closed shops (given that these are premium apprenticeships, it is unlikely to be growing because masters were sweating apprentices).[44] Dealing and retailing (a heterogeneous group, with grocers, mercers, and tallow chandlers among its most numerous members) also relied heavily on apprenticeships, although given the higher average premiums we would not expect the numbers of apprentices without fees to be quite so large as in clothing and footwear. Construction and general manufacturing also had a substantial reliance on apprenticeship, though it would have been less universal, perhaps reflecting different mixes of skilled and unskilled labour.

If we turn to two of the core areas of work that were being affected by industrial change, textiles and iron and steel manufacturing, apprenticeship was less common than the share of the workforce would predict, in both 1710 and 1800. Textiles experienced a sharp relative decline; hand weaving in particular was experiencing a famously dramatic boom and bust.[45] The exception is the modest growth in machine and tool-making, where the role of premium apprenticeship grew slightly but still only accounted for fewer than one in ten adult workers. Overall, this exercise underlines the point that while apprenticeship survived, it did best in occupations and places with a conservative aspect that had not yet been affected by mechanisation.

To this extent, the evidence supports a traditional account that links industry to deskilling, or perhaps more accurately skill polarisation. Industrial work divided roles, intensified specialisation, and simplified tasks into more discrete elements. Workers in mills and factories began young, and many roles needed little or no preparation. Skills were learned on the job; the low incidence of premium apprenticeship in industrial cities was a natural consequence of this, just as illiteracy was rife and schooling neglected.[46] As factories and firms grew more common, they would grapple with developing systems of training that suited novel organisational structures that had few forbears before 1780. Some would employ apprentices, where the master was now a company; others developed alternative forms of on-the-job learning. Both options marked a move away from traditional apprenticeship.

In summary, apprenticeship remained robust in aggregate in the eighteenth century, but its focus changed, and there are clear signs that it would play a different role in many occupations within the industrial economy that was now developing. Families continued to use apprenticeship to pursue opportunities—Feldman and van der Beek have shown that new inventions attracted apprentices into the occupations they were enlivening, for example—but the tide was turning.[47] Significantly, apprenticeships for which premiums were paid began to fade away in the fastest industrialising regions of England. They remained most resilient in smaller towns and areas where trade and manufacturing operated in more traditional ways and on a smaller scale. While in most of the economy apprenticeship had not yet begun to beat its withdrawal, the first notes of the call for retreat could be heard clearly by the 1790s.

While apprenticeship undoubtedly played a major role in the structural change and diffusion of skills that characterised economic development in the period before industrialisation, it was increasingly displaced by alternative forms of training in many of the areas that were most directly affected by the new technologies and new forms of work organisation that characterised the Industrial Revolution.

Conclusion

At every point in the three centuries from 1500 to 1800, apprenticeship was the main focus of human capital investment in England. If we compare the importance of different types of training and education, apprentices substantially outnumbered students undertaking secondary schooling in grammar schools or the like.[48] The enduring importance of premium apprenticeship in the eighteenth century is equally evident from the financial investment it represented. If we look at the sums invested in premiums, in the 1710s, families of apprentices in England paid an average of £119,000 per year for premiums.[49] In the mid-1790s, they spent £177,000 per year; accounting for inflation, this was exactly the same as at the start of the century (£119,000 in 1700 pounds).[50]

Private expenditure on apprenticeship premiums was more than twice the amount spent on basic literacy in England at the start of the century, and still higher than spending on primary education by 1800. Reis's estimates of the direct cost of primary education (£2.4 per student) suggest that around 1700, something like £44,000 was spent on primary education, and by 1800 this reached £95,000.[51] Both at a national and individual-household level, spending on vocational training through apprenticeship substantially exceeded investment in basic schooling.[52]

The scale of the investment in human capital that went through apprenticeship is equally clear from the time spent in training and education. If we compare years spent in training within apprenticeships with de Pleijt's estimates that English males had less than two years of schooling on average in the eighteenth century, when averaged across the workforce, the number of years of vocational training would probably be slightly in excess of the average years of schooling (much depends on the share of apprentices quitting early). Conservatively, apprenticeship at least doubled the time spent on education and training by the English male workforce in the eighteenth century.[53]

The supply and demand for apprenticeship responded to shifts in economic opportunities, preventing them choking from a lack of skilled labour. The upsurge in training in London's guild economy reacted to and fueled the spectacular growth of the city's economy as a centre of trade, services, and manufacturing in the sixteenth and seventeenth centuries. The city offered riches, and the young came to seize them, bringing the human capital that would allow expansion to continue. Similarly, the rebalancing of the English economy away from London and the growth of rural industry in the eighteenth century saw apprenticeship grow in the countryside, sustaining new clusters of manufacturing and trade. The elasticity in the supply of skill this required is one of the key findings of Karine van der Beek's studies.[54]

Training was closely associated with large agglomerations of skill and industry. In most smaller towns, apprentices made up just 1 to 2 per cent of the population and were markedly less important to the labour supply for trade and manufacturing, just as these towns were less important to apprenticeship and the reproduction of skill between generations. Provincial workshops frequently lacked apprentices: the stylised image of master and apprentice was not the rule but the exception there.

Skilled workers were, in turn, less likely to have trained locally than we might have expected, especially before the eighteenth century. Many acquired their skills in one of a few major centres for training, principally London. The mobility of youths into training was followed by mobility after training, as we will see in chapter 8. The higher ratios of apprentices to adult workers seen in London, but also to some extent in other major cities such as Bristol, point to the ongoing movement of former apprentices to other locations. Signs of a system of mobile skill formation exist as early as the 1400s, and while the concentration of human capital formation within highly productive urban agglomerations peaked in the seventeenth century, aspects survived through the eighteenth century (and arguably continue to this day).[55]

The limited evidence that exists for the distribution of apprenticeships elsewhere in Europe suggests this connection between scale and training was a general pattern. Larger cities attracted more apprentices; Paris, Madrid, Vienna, Venice, and Amsterdam were all hubs of training as well as industry. In the Netherlands, fragmentary evidence suggests guilds in its larger cities recruited on a scale that would imply a higher degree of intensity than London.[56] In Paris in 1848–51, an inquiry found 19,000 apprentices, or around one in every seventeen workers, and about one in four teenagers.[57] By contrast, smaller cities such as Mainz, with 23,000 inhabitants, had just 257 apprentices in 1770—too few to replenish their own workshops.[58] Size might also be relative; Montreal in the late eighteenth century had only 12,000 people but was far larger than any other city in the region, and perhaps 60 per cent of teenage boys were apprenticed.[59] These imbalances were resolved by the movement of journeymen, which is well attested in much of continental Europe.

The changing contours of the relationship between apprenticeship and economic development in England should now be clear. Apprenticeship grew rapidly in early modern England, with training extraordinarily concentrated in London, and contributed critically to its rapid demographic and economic expansion and the larger process of commercialisation, structural change, and urbanisation that was reshaping the nation.

By the seventeenth century, the institutional framework was changing, particularly the connection between guilds and apprenticeship. Absolute 'decline' in apprenticeship appears to have been a phenomenon of the guilds, not of the number of apprentices or the share of young males in training, as historians have sometimes suggested. However, the share of young people entering apprenticeships did fall behind the expansion of manufacturing and services in the eighteenth century. Specialisation accompanied the growth of proto-industrial manufacturing and early industrialisation, and with it came changes in occupational training.

The decline in private apprenticeship in the eighteenth century was concentrated in the industrialising North of England. As new opportunities in less-skilled factory work emerged, firms offered different ways to accumulate skills or ways to work without formally training at all. The shift in the core of economic activity in Britain found no clear echo in the supply of (premium) apprenticeship as a whole, even though demand for training in individual trades was responsive to innovations.[60] If anything, apprenticeship was strongest in the counties that came latest to industry, if at all. Similarly, apprenticeship fell away most obviously in the occupations that were first affected by industrialisation, such as textiles and iron work.

These figures reflect behaviour in the aggregate labour force. Recently, Joel Mokyr and colleagues have underlined the importance of apprenticeship in training an upper tail of highly skilled workers—clockmakers, millwrights, machine makers, and the like—who would support the creation, maintenance, and improvement of machinery and other capital goods. They argue that Britain's abundance of skilled artisans was crucial to its capacity to implement industrialisation.[61] We can see evidence for this insofar as apprenticeship seems to have persisted among the 'small tail' of machine makers.

Numerically, the shift away from apprenticeship in what had been artisanal trades far outweighed the numbers who trained in this specialised sector. Economically, however, the importance of the skilled elite cannot be ignored. What they shared with the artisans and traders of England's small rural towns—where apprenticeship also persisted—was the small scale and complexity of their activities. The Industrial Revolution had a differentiated impact on apprenticeship, and human capital more generally, that defies any single narrative. Industrialisation brought a growth in occupational specialisation, the emergence of large enterprises, and the division of labour that led to a divergence in skill. With it came new mechanisms for training within the novel framework of the large firm. These would dethrone apprenticeship from its hegemonic position in trade and manufacturing.

3

Diffusing Skill and Innovation

Clock-making was one the most rapidly developing crafts of the early modern period. The falling cost and improving quality of clocks and watches gave a new sense of time to everyday life.[1] Exact time measurement was also essential to the development of new scientific knowledge. Clock-making is a rare example of a craft in which we can observe measurable improvements in both productivity and quality before the Industrial Revolution, through the falling price of clocks and watches and the growing precision with which time could be measured. We can also trace in detail parts of the process of innovation and diffusion that sustained these improvements.[2]

In the later seventeenth century, advances in European clock-making were largely being made in London, where natural philosophers such as Robert Hooke were working in collaboration with highly skilled artisans such as Thomas Tompion, George Graham, and William Clement to develop new types of escapement and spring that allowed for greater accuracy. It was Tompion who supplied the Royal Observatory with clocks that employed a new escapement, designed by Richard Towneley, that needed to be wound only once a year. Tompion also produced some of the first watches that used balance springs, devised by Hooke. His portrait (figure 3.1) shows him holding one of the elegant watches he produced. Tompion had been an apprentice—he had moved to London to train from a small village in Bedfordshire—and he would, in turn, indenture many of his own: he trained at least twenty-three apprentices in his workshop between 1673 and 1699.[3]

FIGURE 3.1. Thomas Tompion (1639–1713), English clockmaker. Mezzotint by John Smith. Image: National Portrait Gallery, London.

Thomas Tompion's combination of outstanding technical skill and abundant technical training offers one possible answer to the question addressed in this chapter: How did the training of apprentices affect the diffusion of new knowledge, high-quality skills, and technological developments in early modern England?

The diffusion of innovations is one of the great drivers of technological change and economic growth. It was a central element to the economic changes that occurred in early modern England, leading to the production of new kinds of manufactured goods, the adoption of new technologies and materials, and novel commercial and financial concepts; Tompion's own advances in clock-making were just one of a wide array of technological advances.[4] However, the connection between apprenticeship and the spread of new techniques and practices is not self-evident.

It is widely recognised that apprenticeship was about the transmission of skills and knowledge from one generation to the next, and the fundamental importance of this has been highlighted, most notably by S. R. Epstein.[5] The impact of teachers on students has been demonstrated powerfully in music by Borowiecki.[6] But the effects of this on the pace of diffusion and the type of skill and knowledge that was diffused depended on how apprenticeship was organised.

Consider the alternatives. It could be that apprentices were widely and evenly distributed, with one found in every workshop. This situation, if it existed, would match some traditional descriptions of the structure of artisanal enterprises, where masters kept small workshops in which an apprentice was a ubiquitous, necessary presence.[7] Another possibility was that apprentices were instead taken most often by profit-hungry masters who sought to exploit them as cheap labour while skimping on training. This was the classic bugbear of journeymen, and it is often associated with low-quality, high-volume sweatshops crowded with young workers who were locked into lengthy contracts that offered little skill in return for their labour.[8] Alternatively, most apprentices might instead find themselves places with skillful masters with relatively successful businesses that offered them the chance to learn trades from masters who had proven their abilities and would not treat them as low-cost labour. Perhaps not always a Thomas Tompion, but someone who was, like him, distinguished among his peers by his skill and knowledge.

The three scenarios just outlined each have different implications for the spread of knowledge, skills, and techniques in the workforce. At one extreme, if most apprentices are learning with masters who are primarily interested in sweating them as unskilled or semi-skilled labour, then the average skill level, and so the productivity, of the next generation of artisans and traders will be relatively low. In the middle case, if apprentices are evenly distributed across all workshops, then productivity will stay the same between generations. The capacities that each apprentice acquires will simply echo those of their master. Finally, if apprentices instead mainly train with the most productive masters, then we might expect the average productivity of the next generation to increase as they pick up the best techniques and learn about the most profitable products and business strategies. Two factors are at play here in determining how effective apprenticeship is as a training system: first, the way in which apprentices were distributed among different masters, and second, the variations in the relative skill and productivity between them.[9]

The argument of this chapter is simple: the provision of apprenticeship in England approximated to the third case. The distribution of training was uneven. The supply of apprenticeship was highly concentrated. Few of those who could have taken apprentices—because they had become a member of a guild or a citizen—would ever actually take one. Even among those artisans and tradesmen who did take apprentices, many took just one. The small group of masters who took many apprentices trained the majority of England's youths. Mostly, however, they did not take on large gangs of youths in the way that nineteenth-century factories would. Instead, they recruited a steady flow of apprentices, with a couple in their workshop or warehouse at any one time.

These masters were not simply specialists in training. Nor were they—at least for the most part—economically and socially marginal entrepreneurs targeting apprentices to exploit them as cheap labour (although this did occur, especially in the late eighteenth century). Instead, they were the most successful of their kind: those who held office in their guilds or cities; those with the largest families; those who gained the greatest wealth; and those with the best understanding of their craft or trade. Tompion represents an extreme exemplar of this pattern, a leader in his occupation, master of his guild, and trainer of many, who was so celebrated for his achievements that he was buried in Westminster Abbey. That his disciple George Graham would later be buried with him captures the idea. The skills, knowledge, and techniques these masters shared with their apprentices were the best of their generation.

The economic consequences of this pattern of training were profound for the diffusion of innovations and best practices, but the motive force behind it was simple: parents seeking to get the best start for their children. Just as today's families fret about the schools and universities that their children will attend, early modern parents invested considerable energy in identifying a good master for their son or daughter.[10] The motivation behind both searches is the belief that the quality of instruction and the richness of opportunity that a youth will receive varies between institutions and individual instructors. As Robert Campbell put it in his advice to parents, they should choose a master based on his 'Good-Nature, Sagacity, and Knowledge of his Business'.[11] Some masters were correctly perceived to be better than others, just as some schools are today, and parents sought to place their children with the best they could attain.

This search for quality by parents was limited by institutional constraints. Much as with places in the best schools in many parts of the modern world, apprenticeship in the most prosperous cities was subject to rationing: many guilds and some cities imposed quotas on the numbers of youths each master could take. Did this squeeze many youths into training with what we might style 'sink' masters—individuals seen as second-rate—just as today's parents sometimes fear their children are being forced into second-rate schools? Or was the number of able masters sufficient to accommodate most youths? The latter answer seems to be correct.

The pattern of concentrated training with high-quality masters uncovered in this chapter has powerful implications for the economic history of England, and plausibly other parts of Europe where the same processes of concentration seem to have occurred.[12] The spread of technology and innovation in premodern economies largely worked through the movement of skilled individuals.[13] Growth was, to some extent, positively correlated with mobility as a result. Institutions such as apprenticeship that could speed this up were 'critical in . . . the dissemination of new productive knowledge', as de la Croix et al. argue.[14]

Some of this movement of embodied knowledge occurred through the migration of journeymen, but in England apprenticeship was the key period of geographical movement across the labour market. It therefore matters greatly that the most successful firms trained the majority of apprentices, because this implied that the best practices, the newest innovations, and the most successful designs were diffused across each occupation. Unlike their modern successors, these youths were not destined for careers within the firm. Instead, they would serve their time and move on, taking their knowledge and skills with them. In short, apprenticeship was part of a virtuous cycle of diffusion of human capital and knowledge that ensured that valuable ideas spread widely across the economy.

Success and the Concentration of Training

It is much easier to ask the question of who trained apprentices than it is to answer it. In order to examine the training careers of masters, we have to first link together disparate individual records of apprentice contracts to a single master. To do this on any scale means addressing a series of problems, mostly centred on the potential for multiple masters to share the same or similar names. The ways in which this was addressed for London, Bristol, Gloucester, and Boston are discussed in appendix 7. The result of this rather laborious exercise was the creation of samples of nearly 21,000 London freemen in several guilds, 1,967 Bristol burgesses, 456 Gloucester freemen, and 771 Boston freemen for whom the set of apprentices they trained is known, at least insofar as they were recorded in the surviving guild or city records. In addition to this sample of masters, samples of guild members or urban citizens who did *not* appear in these registers as taking apprentices were constructed. The key point is that this group of individuals all had the ability to take apprentices, at least in contemporary legal and civic theory, but for some reason they did not.

Relying on urban and guild records in this way is unavoidable, but it does introduce a potential source of error: some masters may have chosen not to register every apprentice. Registration involved fees, albeit modest ones, as discussed in chapter 10. It also introduces selection bias: we lack information about whether training practices outside guilds were different, something that becomes increasingly important in the later eighteenth century as corporate regulation weakened in many settings.

The distribution of training across masters was also shaped in important ways by the guilds themselves. Guilds often set quotas on the number of apprentices that masters could take at any one time. Usually, ordinary freemen were permitted only one or two apprentices concurrently. London's guilds often rewarded more senior members with the right to an additional apprentice. Members of the livery, the tranche of more senior members with rights to vote in parliamentary elections and to participate in civic processions, usually had the right to bind another youth, while those selected into the Court of Assistants, the guild's governing court, might also be rewarded with a further apprentice. In London, for example, the Pewterers, Bakers, Carpenters, and Founders guilds all allowed one apprentice to freemen, two to liverymen, and three to assistants, while the Farriers and Tallow Chandlers set the base at two apprentices for ordinary freemen, with liverymen allowed one more.[15] For masters who sold training, these rights were attractive. Outside London, while quotas were normal, adjusting them to reward seniority was rare; three of Bristol's guilds did this (the Barber Surgeons, Glovers, and Tylers and Plaisterers), but none in any of the other towns and cities surveyed.[16]

Accusations that masters had broken their quota by secretly taking on additional apprentices, sometimes by conspiring with another master to bind them on their behalf, sometimes by simply failing to register indentures, do appear in guild and city records from this period. There is no good way of identifying how serious a problem this was.[17] Before assuming that it was a widespread issue, consider that this practice carried the risk that both apprentice and master would lose access to guild membership or citizenship. Youths and their families had good reason to ensure that their paperwork was in order, suggesting this may not have been commonplace. As will become clear, the more important effect of quotas may have been to moderate the tendency for training to become concentrated in the hands of a few masters, and thereby to slow the diffusion of knowledge and best practices. These

TABLE 3.1. Share of freemen taking apprentices

City	Period	Share taking apprentices %	Sample N
London*	1600–1800	43	17,772
Gloucester	1660–1800	21	1,184
Bristol	1720–1800	20	345
Boston	1670–1800	24	1,765

Note: London is for a sample of guilds, not citizens as a whole. See appendix 7 for the construction of the samples.

estimates thus perhaps under-identify the intensity of training, but evasion is unlikely to change the main conclusions.

The first and most striking observation that emerges from this body of evidence is that most freemen or urban citizens never bound any apprentices: fewer than half of guild freemen in London bound an apprentice in the forty years after they entered their guild (table 3.1). In Boston, Gloucester, and Bristol, the rates were even lower: just 20 to 25 per cent of burgesses and freemen in these towns took apprentices. For these provincial cities, the share may be under-estimated because increasing numbers of citizens lived outside their towns from the early eighteenth century. But even allowing for that, only a minority of resident citizens can have taken apprentices.

Second, even those people who did train apprentices usually bound only a few youths over their careers (table 3.2). In London, a third of masters who took an apprentice trained just one. Nearly two-thirds of masters recruited between one and three apprentices. Less than a quarter of masters took more than five apprentices.

Third, training large numbers of apprentices was very rare: just a tiny fraction of masters—1 per cent of freemen—took twenty or more. In Bristol and Gloucester, the figures were broadly similar, although in Bristol masters were even less likely to train large numbers than in London. In the small town of Boston, interestingly, somewhat more masters managed to take more than three apprentices during their career. The general pattern holds, however, and as in London and Bristol, very few of Boston's masters took more than ten. The norm among English urban masters was to have only a limited number of apprentices.

Fourth, although few masters took more than a couple of apprentices, the majority of apprentices were trained by that distinctive minority of freemen who did take apprentices in larger numbers, as table 3.2 also shows. In

TABLE 3.2. The distribution of training between masters

	London (1600–1800)		Bristol (1720–1800)		Boston (1670–1800)		Gloucester (1660–1800)	
No. of apps taken	Masters %	Training %	Masters %	Training %	Masters %	Training %	Masters %	Training %
1	34	9	44	15	20	4	17	4
2	19	10	22	15	15	7	18	9
3	12	10	11	11	13	9	18	13
4	8	9	7	9	9	8	16	16
5	6	8	5	8	10	11	6	8
6–9	13	27	8	18	22	35	21	38
10–19	6	21	3	15	11	27	4	11
20+	1	5	1	8	0	0	0	0
N	7,015	25,562	1,430	4,203	771	3,525	717	2,879

Note: See appendix 7 for the construction of the samples. The table reports the percentage of freemen training a number of apprentices over their careers in the column 'Masters'. Column 'Training' reports the percentage of apprentices in each city who were trained by masters who recruited that number of apprentices over their careers. The period for which data is reported is restricted to freemen who entered the guilds or cities in question in the years reported.

London, over half of all apprentices were trained by the one-fifth of masters who took more than five apprentices. More than a quarter were trained by the 7 per cent of masters who took ten or more. In Bristol, the distribution was slightly more even, but even so, 42 per cent of apprentices were taken by the 12 per cent of masters who took more than five over their career. In Boston, the split was stronger, with 62 per cent of apprentices trained by the 33 per cent of masters with more than five apprentices. Gloucester fell in between, with half of apprentices taken by masters with more than five apprentices. The impact that these relatively 'large' masters had on the supply of labour and the formation of the next generation of the workforce was entirely disproportionate to their own number.

The supply of training in English urban centres before 1800 thus had four central characteristics: first, few freemen or citizens took apprentices; second, most who did train took only a small number; third, almost no masters recruited very large numbers of apprentices—the category of masters with more than twenty recruits is almost empty; and fourth, the majority of apprentices trained with one of the minority of masters who did take apprentices repeatedly.

These larger masters who played such an important role in training were not operating proto-factories in which apprentices were hired in bulk. The hundreds of pauper apprentices working in some of the early textile factories offer a benchmark for what this might have looked like. In 1790, for example, Jeremiah Bury had 200 apprentices working in his cotton factory in Stockport, while William Toplis employed 600 apprentices in his worsted factory in Worksop in 1804.[18] There is no parallel to these factories in earlier guild records. Training was concentrated, rather than evenly distributed. But urban apprenticeship, at least, was not yet industrial in scale.

Learning from the Best

What type of master was taking apprentices? As we have seen, the majority of youths were crowding into a minority of businesses. These were certainly the most active firms in terms of training, but were they also the best? Numbers alone are not an indication of quality, but the evidence of apprenticeship premiums shows that families were willing to pay larger sums to masters who had already trained several apprentices: experience at training attracted a premium price, with the fourth apprentice a master recruited paying about 10 to 20 per cent more than the first.[19] This is the opposite of what we might expect of masters hiring youths to man a proto-production line. This section considers other indications of the quality of masters who trained most youths. It examines how training was distributed across masters differentiated by four different measures of success: external indicators of skill, office-holding, wealth, and family size. The short answer, at least, is that it was the most successful masters who provided the most apprenticeships.

Skill is perhaps the hardest of indicators to isolate historically. For most trades, the products have long since disappeared, and their consumers left no record of their opinions. However, in a handful of occupations—clockmakers, furniture makers, apothecaries, merchants—we can observe the training practices of those who were working at the pinnacle of their profession.

We began the chapter with Thomas Tompion, but he was not alone among leading clockmakers in his approach to training. If we focus on just the fourteen individuals who are named as among the most important innovators in clock- and watchmaking in classic studies, all but one trained apprentices, with the average (mean) being nine apprentices and the median six per master.[20] Tompion's twenty-three apprentices was the largest cluster, but George Graham—his partner late in his career—indentured sixteen and Daniel Quare bound fourteen. Like Tompion, these were the leaders in their field. Graham made several improvements to the pendulum clock and invented several astronomical instruments, as well as producing the mural quadrant at Greenwich Observatory for Edmond Halley.[21] Quare invented repeating watches and supplied clocks and watches to James II and William III.[22] Their workshops were large, but they were also hubs of innovation: Graham had learned from Tompion; his own apprentices included Thomas Mudge, who later invented the lever escapement that is still used today in almost all mechanical watches.[23]

What about other skilled crafts? Although we can rarely follow them as closely as clock-making, taking those who supplied the monarch and leading aristocratic families gives some confidence that they were highly skilled manufacturers and dealers. That the court and aristocracy were commissioning the finest artisans introduces a further challenge to testing this hypothesis: the latest designs and techniques from France, the Netherlands, and other places were often the products of immigrant artisans. For example, the artisans who produced furniture, wall hangings, and carvings for the English court in the seventeenth century include migrants such as the cabinetmaker Francis van Huissen and the upholsterer Jean Paudevin. These highly skilled individuals were rarely fully integrated into guilds, and so their training careers are invisible to us.

Even those migrants who do appear in the sources may have had careers that are censored because they migrated late. Take the cabinetmaker Jasper Bream, a Dutch immigrant who specialised in marquetry. Bream's abilities are well attested. One of his commissions was the Duchess of York's bed at Windsor Castle, which was to be inlayed 'with several coloured woods in Resemblance of flowers, leaves etc.', for which he was paid £33 6s 8d. His workshop hosted Jan van Meeckeren, later Holland's most famous marquetry craftsman. In a telling coincidence, he probably produced clock cases for Thomas Tompion. Bream trained four apprentices, which was already above the average. However, this may well be an under-estimate, as he entered the Joiners guild by redemption in 1676, by which time he was already established as an immigrant manufacturer of some skill (he arrived in London around 1661); any apprentices trained before he joined the guild are invisible to us.[24]

Nonetheless, among the eighteen elite furniture makers and upholsterers supplying the court and nobility who took apprentices, the mean number of apprentices they bound was ten, and the median was six.[25] These are largely

FIGURE 3.2. Temple Church reredos carved by William Emmett. Image: Steve Cadman.

prominent individuals, such as William Cleare, who worked on the carvings on the triumphal arch for Charles II's coronation, Badminton House, the Sheldonian Theatre, and the Divinity School at Oxford University, and William Emmett, who was sculptor to the Crown and worked on Whitehall Palace, Hampton Court, Kensington Palace, and Temple Church; some of his carving at Temple Church still survives (figure 3.2).[26] Cleare bound nine apprentices, Emmett took five. The scale of their undertakings may well have given them more use for additional hands, but those hands were employed on some of the most distinguished projects of the period.

Silversmithing is another skilled craft where some of the most able artisans can be distinguished. The painstaking work of David Mitchell and others has identified with a measure of confidence the silversmiths whose pieces survive in collections today.[27] The makers' marks stamped into each of these objects—a treasure trove of flagons, tankards, salvers, candlesticks, and other plate—identify who made them, and the guilds' records then tell us about their apprentices. I identified a small group of 113 individuals whose work was valuable enough to be preserved in museums, described in works of connoisseurship, and sold at auctions.[28] Overall, three-quarters of these silversmiths are known to have taken apprentices, almost twice the rate among freemen in general; those who did, bound an average of five apprentices (mean and median). Strikingly, those individuals for whom the most objects survive also trained more apprentices. Those with one surviving piece trained an average of three apprentices (median two); those with two to four objects in collections bound five (median four); those with five or more pieces bound seven. The most prolific producer by this measure—Edward Gladwin, whose mark survives on seventeen different objects—indentured eight apprentices. Similarly, those silversmiths who supplied the English royal household with objects that survive today in the royal collections, a partially overlapping but even smaller elite, bound an average of seven (median six) apprentices each.[29]

In medicine, too, the royal court recruited the best-known medical practitioners to serve the ruler and their household. Apothecaries supplied complex pharmaceutical preparations to doctors and patients, along with a range of other services. For the seventeenth century, nine royal apothecaries were active at the time for which guild records survive.[30] All of them took apprentices, and with at least fifty-three apprentices between them, they bound an average of almost six per person.[31] The largest number was accounted for by William Rowswell, who took twelve, while the apothecary to James I, Gideon De Laune (1565?–1659), shown in figure 3.3, bound at least eleven. A Huguenot migrant who was instrumental in the establishment of the Apothecaries guild as an independent institution in 1617, De Laune exemplifies the combination of skill and training; he supervised the production of the first official *Pharmacopoeia*, while much of his wealth derived from his own formulation of a popular medicine, Delaune's pill. He was also tremendously successful, able to donate the land on which the guild built its hall and elected (but disbarred because he was an alien) to the office of alderman, one of the city's governing elite.[32]

What about commercial skills? The rapid growth of overseas trade centred on London offered its most successful merchants the chance to gain enormous riches. Those at the pinnacles of their careers took roles as directors of the chartered companies, such as the Levant Company and East India Company, which governed many different parts of trade. If we look at a sample of merchant directors drawn from nine chartered companies with surviving records, plus the Bank of England, four out of five took apprentices.[33] On average, these leading traders took six apprentices apiece (the median was five), and one in four of them took more than eight apprentices.

FIGURE 3.3. Portrait of Gideon De Laune. Image: Wellcome Collection.

Some took many more. Matthew Craddock, who was unusual in holding a leading position in both the trade to the Mediterranean and Asia (he was elected a director of the East India Company in 1624 and the Levant Company in 1631) and the colonial trade to the Americas, bound twenty-eight apprentices between 1622 and 1641, often indenturing two a year in successive years.[34] Craddock was the first governor of the Massachusetts Bay Company and 'was among the leading figures in the Virginian and West Indian trades', according to Robert Brenner; he would be elected to the Short Parliament as one of the four representatives for London in 1640.[35] While his business no doubt demanded manpower to oversee the different branches of his enterprise, his apprentices thrived. Three of them, Benjamin Albyn (bound 1637), John Jolliffe (bound 1633), and Henry Spurstowe (bound 1632), would become directors in all three of the East India, Levant, and Muscovy Companies, while a fourth, Anthony Nicholets (bound 1638), became a director of the Levant Company.[36] As a further indicator of their success, Albyn, Jolliffe, and Spurstowe would be elected as aldermen of the city.[37] They also emulated their master in another way: Joliffe bound twenty-thee apprentices, Albyn eight, and Spurstowe thirteen. In short, like those of his peers among the mercantile elite, Craddock's counting-house was a commercial powerhouse and shaped many of the next generation of leading London traders.

High levels of skill were associated with high volumes of training, whether in crafts like silversmithing, furniture making, pharmacy, and clock-making, or in overseas trade. Taking apprentices was the norm amongst them: all the elite apothecaries, all but one elite clockmaker, and four-fifths of merchants and silversmiths bound apprentices, compared to just two-fifths of London's freemen. The average number of apprentices they trained was high. The median elite goldsmith and merchant took five apprentices, putting them in the top quartile of masters in the city. The median elite apothecary and clockmaker took six, and so was among the top fifth of masters. The median elite furniture maker took ten, and thus numbered in the top 1 per cent of masters. The leading figures in each of these crafts recruited heavily and trained prolifically. This allows us to reject with some confidence one possibility—that these innovative craftsmen and entrepreneurial traders shut their doors to outsiders to keep their secrets to themselves.

Detailed information on skill, success, and training is rare, and we have focused on the upper tail of the elite so far. Fortunately, other indicators show that the correlation between success and training held more generally.

Strong evidence that success and training went hand in hand can be found in the positions that large employers held in their guilds. Freemen who held senior offices in their guild were usually also major recruiters of apprentices; as we saw, the ability to bind more youths was one of the rewards for accepting office. In the Stationers' Company of London, for example, every single warden of the guild who was freed before 1650 took apprentices (wardens were the second-most-senior officers in the guild, responsible for its finances and property). So did more than 80 per cent of the company's liverymen, a larger group within the guild but one distinguished by wealth as well as seniority; joining involved paying a substantial fee of £10. By contrast, fewer than half of the remaining guild members, the 'yeomanry', would take apprentices, and those who did took relatively few. The largest numbers of apprentices were taken by the most senior guild members, with the peak—more than thirteen apprentices each, on average—occurring among the twenty freemen who reached the pinnacle of guild office, becoming master of the guild, and who were freed before 1600.

The members of the Stationers' guild were not unusual. Training was concentrated among the elite in other guilds in London. As in the Stationers,

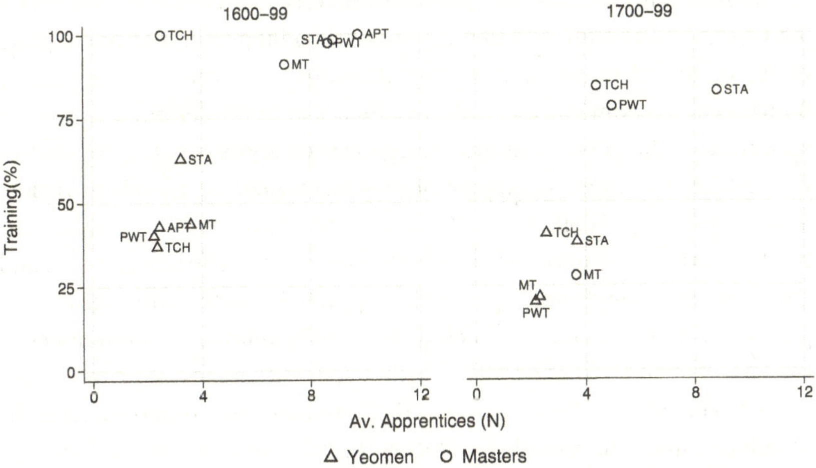

FIGURE 3.4. Guild status and provision of training. The figure reports the average number of apprentices trained over a career on the x-axis and the share of guild members in each category known to have trained apprentices on the y-axis. Masters were individuals who were masters of their guilds. Yeomen were individuals who did not progress to the livery or higher office. Key: APT=Apothecaries; MT=Merchant Taylors; PWT=Pewterers; STA=Stationers; TCH=Tallow Chandlers.

a step-like relationship between providing training and corporate promotion persisted across the board. In the Apothecaries, ordinary members who trained apprentices took 2.6 apprentices on average, liverymen took 5.8, assistants (liverymen who were co-opted into the guild's small governing Court of Assistants) took 7.5, while masters of the guild took 9.8.[38] The thirty-two masters of the guild took almost 20 per cent of all apprentices, while the 222 ordinary yeomen in this sample took around 33 per cent. Not a single freeman apothecary who held guild office—whether as master, warden, assistant, or liveryman—failed to take apprentices.

Figure 3.4 reports the share of guild members undertaking training, and the numbers of apprentices they took, for two groups: those who became masters of their guilds, its highest office, and those who remained ordinary yeomen. Panel A shows this for the seventeenth century, panel B for the eighteenth. The two groups of freemen had markedly different careers in all five of the guilds for which this information survives. For example, in the Tallow Chandlers guild, at least 84 per cent of the guild's masters in the eighteenth century took apprentices, compared to 40 per cent of other members, and on average, they took twice the number of apprentices (4.4) as other members (2.5) in the same period.[39]

Even among the most occupationally diverse guild of all, the Merchant Taylors, in the seventeenth century more than 90 per cent of the masters of the guild and 87 per cent of assistants took apprentices, compared to 44 per cent of yeomen. Again, senior officials in the guild took many more apprentices: the guild's masters averaged seven apprentices, compared to the 3.5 taken by those ordinary members who trained. The Merchant Taylors also show the rapid collapse of the association between training and office-holding in the eighteenth century: among its masters who entered the guild after 1750, not a single one registered an apprentice. In the same period, the guild—one that had once registered the greatest number of apprentices in the city—became a shadow of its former self, with almost no apprentices recorded being taken by members of the Merchant Taylors in the later eighteenth century. This remarkable shift in the behaviour of the guild's elite is visible in the second panel of figure 3.4.

The relationship between training and seniority was not just about an individual freeman's connection with their guild. Corporate advancement within a guild and success in business ran together: holding office brought costs, in the direct expenses of carrying out guild business, the time involved, and the expectation that senior members of a guild would make a greater financial contribution whenever necessary. In 1697, London's common council ordered that no one should be called to the livery who was worth less than £500 in most guilds and £1,000 in the Great Twelve, the politically most powerful guilds that supplied the city's aldermen.[40] Advancing within the guild also meant paying a fee to the organisation—often a substantial amount—when being elevated. Liverymen in the Brewers' paid nearly £7 when clothed in the seventeenth century; Coopers paid £15 from 1674, the same as the Apothecaries and Tallow Chandlers, while the Pewterers took £20.[41] In the larger, more mercantile guilds, livery fees were even higher. The Merchant Taylors took £25 from 1630, while the Drapers lifted their fee from £13 to £25 in 1695.[42]

The Stationers offer an unusually clear insight into the connection between wealth and training. Unusually, the guild ran a joint-stock enterprise called the English Stock to publish almanacs, an enormously popular genre for which it had obtained a corporate monopoly under a royal patent in 1603. For those who bought shares in the stock, we have a direct indication of their wealth.[43] Freemen who owned shares in the English Stock were almost twice as likely to take apprentices as those who did not (80% against 46%) and they took twice as many apprentices on average (6.7 against 3.8).[44] For the largest stockholders, inequality was even more pronounced. Before 1700, almost none of the freemen who held larger shares in the stock went without apprentices, and on average, they trained more than eight each. Wealth profoundly influenced the probability that freemen in the printing trades would take apprentices.

The strong association between wealth and training can be seen more generally in the households of Londoners who paid the 1691 poll tax. The listing drawn up reported the rental and stock value of each taxpayer, alongside a summary of who lived in their household, including servants and apprentices. This may well be an imperfect record of the numbers of apprentices within each household, but it is at the least suggestive. As can be seen in table 3.3, the tax record shows very clearly that it was the rich who took the most apprentices. Those with three or four apprentices were valued by the tax assessors as worth more than twice as much, paying around £7 each, as compared to the roughly £4 paid by freemen with just one apprentice or none; the values of their stock in trade and rents were even further apart, indicative of the relative scale of their businesses. While table 3.3 is based on the internal evidence of potentially flawed tax assessors, linking freemen to the tax record using their names and occupations gives the same result: those who paid higher rates of tax were more likely to be found taking apprentices. In a matched sample of 128 non-mercantile masters, 79 per cent of those paying £1 in tax, 92 per cent of those paying £11 or more, and 100 per cent of those paying £21 were matched to an apprentice in their guild record.[45] Just 12 per cent of matched taxpayers—inclusion by itself indicates they were better off—did not take an apprentice.

The poll tax record also makes clear that taking apprentices depended on possessing a certain level of resources. The tax listing distinguishes householders, who were usually lead tenants on a property, from lodgers. Householding mattered: 97 per cent of apprentices were found with householders, not lodgers, even though they made up only 68 per cent of those paying tax. Lodgers did often have domestic servants, but they rarely had apprentices. Clearly, apprentices and their families looked to find masters from among those with the capacity to maintain established and independent households, not the temporary arrangements that were the lot of many of the city's residents.[46]

There is a risk here that we are being confused by differences in longevity. Was it simply the length of their careers (and lives) in the city that meant that the most successful masters had the most apprentices as well as the highest offices? They had more years of work in which to take apprentices, and those years meant they were more likely to attain offices that were, in part, linked to seniority.

TABLE 3.3. Training and average wealth in London, 1691

Number of apprentices	Tax (£)	Stock (£)	Rent (£)	N
0	4.6	39	12.5	23,420
1	4.1	51	18	1,739
2	5.8	76.8	25.1	617
3	7.2	119.9	31.6	66
4	6.8	156.3	42.7	12

Source: J. Alexander, Poll Tax database, courtesy of Centre for Metropolitan History; see Alexander 1992.

This does not seem to be the case. The Stationers' records contain a level of detail that shows this best. For a small number of printers and stationers in the sample, the year of death is known. With this information, we can calculate the number of apprentices they took per year of their careers, making the reasonable assumption that this ran from their freedom to death. This controls for differences in longevity. Freemen who became liverymen were taking apprentices with a higher frequency than others in the print trade. In the seventeenth century they bound 0.21 apprentices per year of their careers against 0.11 for yeomen—one for every five years against one every ten years; in the eighteenth century they bound 0.16 apprentices per year, against 0.07 for yeomen.[47] Stationers with shares in the English Stock also took apprentices more frequently than those who did not. Success, not longevity, bred training, in short.

To summarise, training was concentrated among the most successful masters, whether measured by their output of high-quality products, guild office-holding, or wealth. This was a system in which training was biased towards the most productive and, by implication, the most creative masters—the Thomas Tompions who were producing new techniques and technologies, as well as reproducing artisans.

It is worth thinking about what this means for the reproduction of skill when taken cumulatively over the working careers of youths indentured into a trade. Roughly half of apprentices never became freemen. Upwards of four-fifths of freemen in provincial towns and cities and two-thirds in London never took *any* apprentices. Only half of those who trained apprentices took more than two. The chance that a new apprentice would one day indenture their own apprentices was very low, around one in ten. Only one in fifty apprentices would later stand among the ranks of those masters who took more than five apprentices—and who trained around half of all the apprentices in the next generation.

The Timing of Training

What did the connection between a master's success and their provision of training mean for those bound to them? Not all artisans and traders would take apprentices. For those who did, were the youths they bound integral parts of building their workshop or business—necessary labour to get a shop going—or did they come later, once their business and reputation were established and the benefit to an apprentice was obvious? This section considers what can we infer about the nature of training from how apprentices fit into the careers of masters.

These are hard questions to answer. English corporate records have a basic ambiguity lacking in much of Europe, because both waged journeymen and independent masters were required to become citizens or guild members and so possessed the same status. Nonetheless, some patterns are relatively clear. In London, only a minority of masters took apprentices as soon as they could. Roughly one in five freemen bound their first apprentice within twelve months of becoming a guild member; four out of five did not. This suggests that one possibility—that artisans only became guild members when they wanted to register an apprentice—was not a common phenomenon, though it may have mattered for a minority.

That said, starting the training of apprentices—when it occurred at all—was not long delayed. More than 60 per cent of freemen bound their first apprentice within five years. Only a small minority of freemen—around 15 per cent—indentured their first apprentice more than a decade after they took the freedom. On average, these late starters trained only a couple of apprentices.

The minority of freemen who played a principal role in training the next generation acted in a distinctive way early in their corporate careers. Catching up was hard in London. If many of the late starters were delayed because they were working as journeymen, as seems likely, then this also suggests that most new freemen had a small window of opportunity to achieve independence in business. Those who missed this struggled to set up on their own later in their lives.

In Bristol, for the most part, masters behaved in the same way as their peers in London: one in five took an apprentice within twelve months of becoming a citizen. They were slightly slower to train: only 49 per cent had their first apprentice in the first five years. In small-town Boston, masters were slower still. Just 13 per cent took their first apprentice in the year they became a citizen, and only 41 per cent had an apprentice in their first five years. Gloucester's masters were similar: 7 per cent in their first year and 48 per cent in the first five years. These quieter centres were more forgiving to late starters. In all three, around one-third of freemen would have a gap of a decade between becoming a citizen and taking their first apprentice.

City-level averages are somewhat misleading. Different occupations were organised in different ways: some favoured small shops, others had more work for additional hands. Even though London guilds contained a hodgepodge of occupations alongside their primary trades, something of this relationship can be seen in the variations in the time it took new freemen to bind their first apprentices. The connection between freedom and taking an apprentice was closest in the Apothecaries, where 39 per cent of those who ever trained bound an apprentice in the first year and 75 per cent in the first five years; running a workshop producing bespoke medicines while also visiting patients clearly put a premium on having help around to keep the doors open and the mortars and pestles moving at the same time. At the other end of the spectrum, in two guilds centred on retailing and wholesale dealing, only 53 per cent of mercers and 56 per cent of tallow chandlers who trained took their first apprentices within five years of becoming freemen. That production and apprentices need not go closely in hand is apparent from the pewterers, among whom just 11 per cent of those who ever took apprentices bound their first in the year after they were freed.[48]

In Bristol, Gloucester, and Boston, where masters' occupations are well-recorded, the varied needs of trades are clear. Apothecaries, again, stand out in taking apprentices quickly, with 35 per cent in Bristol having an apprentice within a year; at the other end of the spectrum, few tailors in either city recruited quickly—just 15 per cent in Bristol, 11 per cent in Gloucester, and 10 per cent in Boston had an apprentice within a year. Not all occupations behaved the same way in different cities, however, underlining an obvious but fundamental point about the local character of industries in this period. For example, cordwainers in Bristol recruited quickly, with 23 per cent having an apprentice within one year, while in Boston and Gloucester, just 4 per cent and 7 per cent did.

Apprentices were not an immediate or essential element to artisanal enterprises. Only a few families entrusted their children to the newest of masters, still wet behind their ears from own apprenticeships. Most masters took a few years to recruit an apprentice, with only around half having their first within the five years after attaining the status of guild or city freeman that qualified them to train. Training the next generation started when masters had demonstrated their ability to succeed in their business.

Once they had taken an apprentice, masters were generally hooked on the usefulness of the extra pair of hands. Training was continuous rather than intermittent in firms that undertook it. Most masters who took multiple apprentices bound them in overlapping sequences, often having two at a time.

In London, around nine out of ten masters who took more than one youth would bind their next apprentice within the seven years of taking their previous apprentice. Except in the Apothecaries, the median gap between apprentices was between twenty-four and forty-eight months in these guilds, with most recruiting when their apprentices reached the three-year mark. In the Clothworkers in the sixteenth and seventeenth centuries, the median gap was less than two years, implying either rapid turnover or an average of three apprentices in a workshop. The Apothecaries had a longer gap: more than four years. They also had the lowest limit on the number of apprentices that a freeman could train at one time: just one. Only liverymen could take more. The rest of the guilds allowed two (or sometimes more) apprentices per master, albeit with some restrictions on timing.[49]

Outside London, the same pattern of continuous training appears. Bristol had a median gap between apprentices of 2.2 years, and 87 per cent of masters recruited again within seven years. Boston had a median gap of 2.9 years, and 80 per cent recruited within seven years. In Gloucester the pace was slightly slower, four years and 71 per cent, but not greatly different.

Because we cannot be sure about which apprentices were replacing someone who had left early and which were truly additional bodies, these figures are not a direct estimate of the number of apprentices who worked concurrently. Yet, they certainly show that many masters who trained saw their apprentices as a useful and ordinary part of their operations. They also suggest that most apprentices entered a situation in which an older youth was present who had the capacity to assist, support, or exploit them, as far as the master permitted. The presence of these more experienced apprentices was itself a potentially useful source of training for a new entrant.

The character of training can be seen in figure 3.5, which shows the spread of apprentices taken over the career of six representative Bristol masters from different occupations. The figure represents the career of the master, with each apprentice represented by a bar that starts when their contract began. Each of these masters took the average number of apprentices for

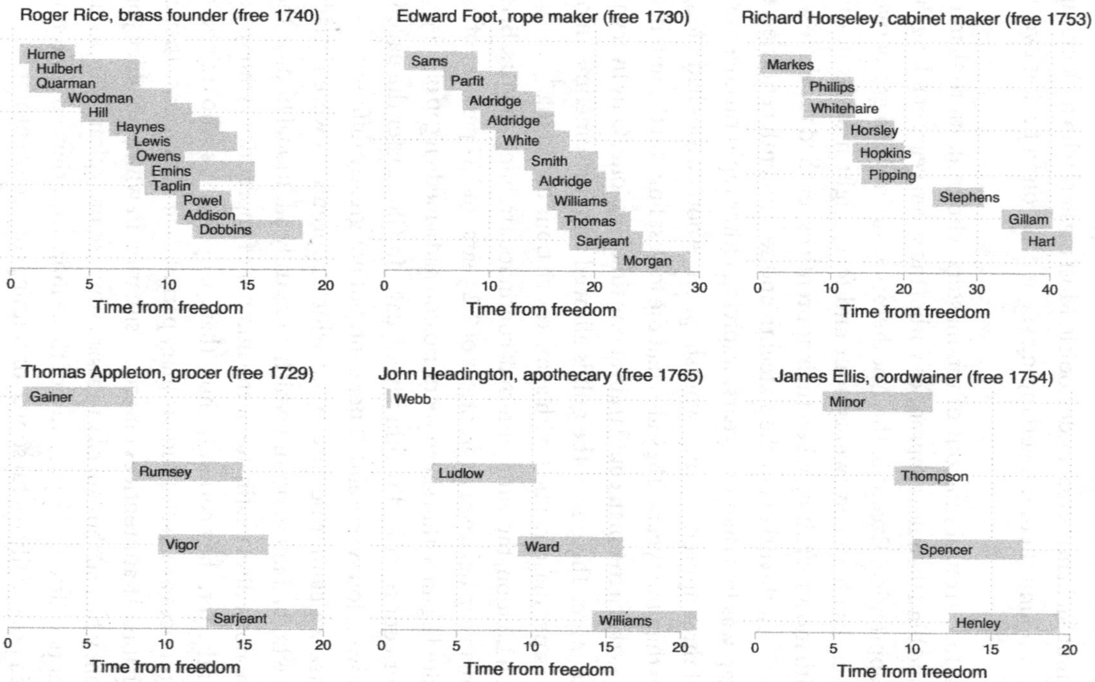

FIGURE 3.5. Training patterns, Bristol. Each apprentice taken by a master is represented by a horizontal bar located in the time since the master became a citizen.

their trade (because trades, not guilds, are reported in Boston and Bristol, I focus on these places).

The first three masters in the top row are from trades that took apprentices frequently and in large numbers; as one might anticipate, these were manufacturing occupations where scale was advantageous. The brass founder, Roger Rice, illustrates one extreme, taking thirteen apprentices over a relatively short career, with only brief breaks between them. Rice would often have had four or five apprentices working at the same time, probably acting as cheap labour in what appears to have been a substantial workshop. Rice is also interesting in taking three apprentices by turnover, including his first, John Hurne, while two of his last apprentices, Charles Powel and William Addison, would later be turned over to another master, probably because Rice had died; there was no such note on the record of his thirteenth and last apprentice, Thomas Dobbins, suggesting that he had already left his indenture early for some reason prior to Rice's death.

At the other end of the distribution are a grocer, apothecary, and cordwainer, all of whom took four apprentices over careers that lasted for around twenty years—roughly the same period in which Rice and Foot recruited many more youths. Even though their total of apprentices was lower, it was still common for two apprentices to overlap in these small firms. The apothecary John Headington, for example, maintained a tidy sequence of indentures in which the last year or two of each apprentice coincided with the arrival of a newcomer, presumably assigned to pick up the basics from their senior.

We can also see conflicts between masters and apprentices here. John Headington faced a problem with his earliest apprentice, Edward Webb, who was discharged by the city's Tolzey Court, a local civil court hearing actions from Bristol and its liberties, three months after his contract began, and he did not replace him for almost three years. For James Ellis, it was his second apprentice, George Thompson, who turned out to be trouble, running away at the end of two years. Ellis replaced him relatively quickly with his fourth apprentice, William Henley, who joined him eight months after Thompson fled, keeping him at a stable level of two apprentices in his workshop at the same time.

A similar set of figures can be drawn for Boston (figure 3.6), again taking the examples from masters who took high numbers and those who took the average number of apprentices. These careers illustrate the same patterns. The butcher, barber, and baker on the second row staggered recruitment, with one apprentice succeeding the other, with short overlaps or none. On

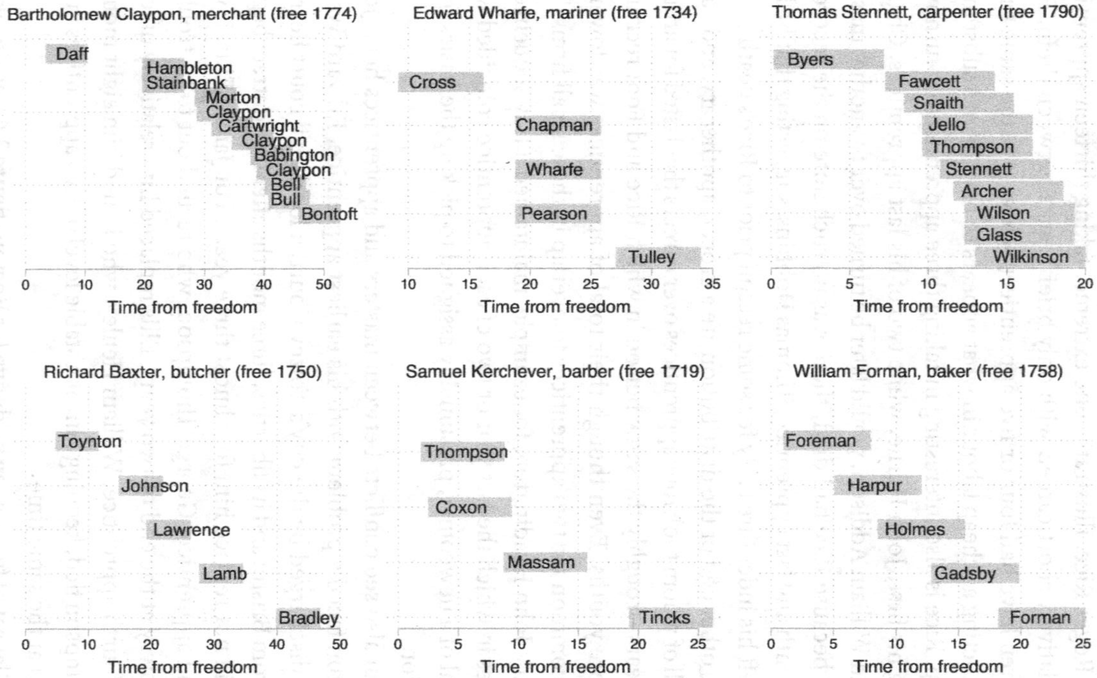

FIGURE 3.6. Training patterns, Boston. Each apprentice taken by a master is represented by a horizontal bar located in the time since the master became a citizen.

the top row, Bartholomew Claypon spread recruitment smoothly, while Edward Wharfe shows a pattern common among mariners of taking clusters of apprentices at the same time, presumably at the start of a voyage. Although mariners did not take the large numbers of apprentices found among merchants and carpenters, they did take them in groups.

We can also see a new extreme here: Thomas Stennett's carpentry business was taking apprentices on something like an industrial scale in his second decade as a freeman. The clerk's record of the indentures reflected this, describing the boys as bound to 'Stennett and Pearson', evidently a firm, not a single master. This clearly marked a shift from a much smaller initial enterprise, and—presumably not coincidentally—it was also occurring in the early 1800s, as the gospel of the factory became widely heard even in the most isolated of English towns.

Conclusion

The training of apprentices was mainly carried out by those who were economically (and socially) successful in early modern English towns and cities. Apprentices were clustered in the businesses of a minority of prosperous, skillful, and, sometimes, innovative masters who took relatively large numbers compared to most of their peers. Success and training were mutually reinforcing. It was the masters who had an abundance of business who could find the most use for an apprentice, and it was they who were the most attractive to those seeking training—from whom they could charge the highest fees. Their visible success drew in apprentices who, with the support of their families, were seeking the most advantageous position they could find in a broad training market.[50] Their apprentices, in turn, would absorb their skills, techniques, and knowledge, diffuse them across the industry and nation, and use them to lay the foundations of the next generation of businesses.

Not all apprentices experienced this: many masters took a solitary youth, if they trained at all, and many apprentices lacked the resources to access a leading master. But the masters who recruited the most apprentices and who trained the majority of the next generation were the most skilled and most successful; they were also the leaders of their guilds and the wealthiest members of their communities.

While they took the lion's share of youths, these large masters were not feeding them into sweated workshops in which apprentices were crowded onto a proto-production line. Instead, even those masters with the largest businesses mostly had only a few apprentices concurrently. In part as a result of guild rules that limited the scale of training and tied this to corporate seniority, apprentices were spread out over a master's career, and often staggered in ways that must have allowed the newcomer to learn from an advanced apprentice on the verge of leaving. Without these guild restrictions, concentration—and knowledge diffusion—may well have been faster. That said, limits on crowding may have helped maintain the quality of training. That youths were able to receive exposure to the full operations of the firm and training in its activities and areas of expertise seems a reasonable inference for these businesses in early modern English towns and cities. Moreover, chapters 6 and 7 discuss how apprentices who were unsatisfied had the ability to exit, and they used it, allowing them to respond directly to masters who did seek to take advantage of them.

The associations I identify here between success and training do not inform us directly about the quality of training an apprentice received. Nonetheless, the idea that there was no connection between the abilities of the master and the apprentices' opportunity to acquire the best technical knowledge and skill is hard to countenance. Apprenticeship involved a virtuous process of diffusion of skill, knowledge, and technique that spread an understanding of the production frontier from the workshops of the leading lights of each occupation to the rest of the economy. This was an important intensifier of the general effect of the concentration of apprenticeship in England's leading towns and cities, especially London. Families chased skill, and skill drove development. By focusing young workers' experience of labour and learning in the workshops and businesses of the wealthiest and most substantial masters, apprenticeship spread the best ideas across England.

4

Mobilising Labour

The Lee family of Godalming, a small market town in Surrey about 30 miles from London, were butchers—father, son, and grandson. The first Laurence (b. 1643) kept his butcher's shop at the Red Lion in the late seventeenth century. When his eldest son, also Laurence (b. 1668), was old enough, he left the local school and went to work for his father, perhaps without a formal apprenticeship, before setting up his own shop by the medieval market house in the town centre. His younger son, John (b. 1674), also spent time in school before being 'bound apprentice to his father'. On reaching twenty-one, 'father left his trade to him', and he kept a shop down the road from his elder brother. Laurence junior raised a large family that included another John, who would live and work as a butcher in Godalming until his death in 1757, and another Laurence, who took the bold step of setting up his butcher's shop in Milford, a village 3 miles to the south-west of the town.[1]

The idea that young people in premodern societies simply followed in their parents' footsteps, picking up their skills as they grew and joining the family trade, like the boys in the Lee family, has a long pedigree. Almost 150 years ago, John Stuart Mill argued that prior to industrialisation, jobs were 'almost equivalent to an hereditary distinction of caste', with 'each employment being chiefly recruited from the children of those already employed in it'.[2] In the world Mill described, opportunities would be narrowly channelled: society reproduces skills, but pays little attention to the interests or aptitudes of individuals, and there is not one labour market, but many, each kept separate from the others and unresponsive to changing demand. It is a world fixed in its path, revolving but not advancing. The butcher's son becomes a butcher, taking his father's job, perhaps along with his forename, as occurred in Godalming.

Mill's vision of sons ineluctably following the trades of their fathers is powerful. It resonates with common preconceptions about static premodern societies operating without markets, and some societies surely did operate much as he described, such as the caste systems of India that he mentioned.[3] De la Croix, Doepke, and Mokyr argue that in the absence of institutions such as apprenticeship that allow people to contract for training, training within the family—parents or elder relatives teaching children—will provide the basic mechanism for the intergenerational reproduction of skills across historical human societies, resulting in a narrow range of opportunities and the slow transmission of knowledge.[4]

However, as a description of England's past, Mill's account was sorely mistaken. Outside agriculture in the world of trade, industry, and services, work was anything but hereditary between the sixteenth and eighteenth centuries. This was an economy and society in flux. Cities and towns were expanding. Industry and services were growing. New types of work were appearing. For this to occur, sons—and daughters—could not simply take on the family trade.[5]

Apprenticeship was central to this process of change, allowing the supply of labour to adjust to the changes in demand that resulted from economic development. Apprenticeship, indeed, was conceptually the opposite to the training within the family that Mill envisaged. Contract replaced kinship. And one skill replaced another. In the great majority of cases, it was a way for a child to gain skills in a job *different* from their parents'. Moreover, it reallocated labour spatially. Apprentices were recruited from an array of towns and villages and a diversity of backgrounds into the different places and occupations where they would train.

Apprenticeship was not the only way in which labour was mobilised within the early modern labour market. The poor and unemployed or underemployed were a constant presence on the roads of England in the search for work or relief; young women moved long distances to find work in domestic service; some skilled workers and crafts were mobile.[6] But apprenticeship was one of the most important mechanisms for labour mobility, and without it, the scale and pace of change would have slowed. For some groups, particularly young men from the middling sort and elite, it was particularly significant, and this slice of the labour market brought financial capital as well as human capital from the countryside to the city. We saw evidence for the scale of this effect in the share of London's population that apprentices supplied, shown in chapter 2. This chapter looks more closely at the characteristics of the labour mobility that occurred within the framework of early modern English apprenticeship.[7]

It begins with the extraordinary geographical movement of apprentices, showing the relative importance of different training centres in youth migration and charting the emergence of narrower, regional migration fields over the seventeenth and eighteenth centuries, as England's economy rebalanced away from London. It then considers sectoral and occupational mobility. What kinds of families placed their children into apprenticeship, and how did this affect the jobs they could later take up?

The scope of labour mobility achieved through apprenticeship is striking, particularly in the sixteenth and early seventeenth centuries. It encompassed individuals from (nearly) all social classes and all sectors. This underlines apprenticeship's basic openness and accessibility, issues that are discussed in greater depth in the last part of the book. It was these qualities that made apprenticeship such an effective channel in the reallocation of labour, just as the way in which it was structured and practised made it an attractive option for families, as discussed in the next section of the book.

Not all young people were equally likely to find a place as an apprentice. The final part of the chapter asks what this great reshuffling of young workers into new places and trades meant for the prospects of those whose lives were caught up in it. Did these movements equate to social as well as geographical and sectoral mobility? The level of social mobility in premodern societies has attracted increasing attention as the limits to mobility in the present and recent past have become clearer. At least some evidence exists that suggests that English society—and other similar premodern societies—were characterised more by immobility than mobility over the long run: social status persisted strongly from generation to generation.[8]

To many of us, investments in training and education, such as apprenticeship, are intrinsically linked to the possibility that young persons can better themselves. Premodern apprenticeship certainly offered the possibility of advancement for some. However, when we look at the types of occupation young people entered, we see sharp distinctions by social class. The sons of the gentry were not working alongside the children of the poor. Far from it. One of the effects of apprenticeship operating as a market was that access to the fattest prospects came with the highest price tag. Wealthy families bought their children the chance to enter the most profitable lines of work by paying high premiums to masters. As Peter Earle noted, the best route to success was to begin with 'a rich father'.[9] Charity softened this at the margin, but this facet of apprenticeship—the way that price cleared the market for skill—helps us understand and explain this tendency for social immobility to persist over the long run.

Apprenticeship as a Response to Crisis

Before proceeding, however, we need to examine one implicit assumption that is being made here: families' choices about placing a child into an apprenticeship were usually strategic and forward-looking. It is possible to imagine a scenario in which apprenticeship was instead a response to crisis within the family, such as the loss of a parent. Was this the case in early modern England?

Family breakdown *could* lead to a youth's entry into apprenticeship, but this was not its usual prompt. Given the high rates of adult mortality in England, particularly its towns, teenage children frequently faced the death of one or both of their parents. Apprenticeship offered one way to manage the impact of this loss on the household. In the small port town of Rye, on the coast of the English Channel in East Sussex, formal apprenticeship was primarily a way to settle orphans and migrants into stable homes, Mayhew found.[10] But Rye appears to have been unusual. Apprenticeship was too extensive—and too expensive—to be explicable as just a method of crisis resolution. It is not clear, in fact, how useful it would be at achieving this; only a small share of children who lost a parent would be the right age for apprenticeship, underlining the importance of other means of caring for orphans.

In most cities and towns, only a minority of apprentices were orphans. In London, a quarter of apprentices enrolled between the sixteenth and eighteenth centuries had lost their fathers. Elsewhere, the share of orphans was similar. Bristol and Norwich recorded the highest shares of orphans, with 30 per cent having lost their fathers. Other provincial cities had slightly lower rates, but all were between 20 and 30 per cent.[11] These are roughly the levels implied by the adult mortality rates in this period. Between the ages of thirty (when a man could expect to have a child) and forty-five (when this child might enter service), male mortality was around 25 per cent nationally in the mid-seventeenth century. In London it was higher, about 32 per cent in the second quarter of the eighteenth century.[12]

Only Oxford had a system that mirrored Rye's for a period of time: 62 per cent of the locals who were apprenticed there in the 1540s and 1590s had deceased fathers, compared to 17 per cent of migrants. As Crossley notes, the city was registering relatively few locals in this period, and so it may be that other apprentices were less likely to be registered if the legal security of enrolment was seen as particularly important for youths who had been orphaned.[13] Elsewhere, the difference was small. In short, while many apprentices had suffered the loss of their fathers, there is no evidence that apprenticeship was strongly tied to such a family crisis.

Migration

When he reached fourteen, Thomas Bewick knew what he wanted for his future: 'any place where I could see pictures or where I thought I could have an opportunity of drawing them' was 'all I could think of', he later wrote. For the son of a tenant farmer who had grown up in rural Northumberland, this meant leaving the countryside behind, exchanging his much loved 'whinny wilds . . . the water banks, the woods' for Newcastle's densely packed streets.[14]

Bewick's move was a success, and he became one of the leading engravers of the late eighteenth century. Fittingly, given his passion for nature, it was his illustrations of animals in his *History of Quadrupeds* (1790) and *History of British Birds* (1797) that later secured his reputation.[15] Apprenticeship in early modern England was often about movement across space as much as between occupations. This was particularly true of apprentices in London, who came from across the nation. But it also applied, albeit to a lesser extent, to apprentices in other towns and cities, boys such as Bewick, whose journey of 12 miles along the Tyne to his master's workshop was not unusual among his peers moving from the land into urban crafts.

Two general features characterised the movements of migrant youths entering apprenticeships, summarised by quarter century in table 4.1. First, as we might expect, the bigger the city, the wider the area from which it drew apprentices. Youths travelled for hundreds of kilometres to enter apprenticeships in London. Even at the end of the eighteenth century, the average migrant youth had travelled more than 80 km. Smaller cities, such as Gloucester and Leicester, attracted youths from a much more modest 20 km on average—a comfortable day's journey by foot, if the roads were not too terrible.

Table 4.1 only covers apprentices in urban and guild records, but the evidence from the limited period in the 1720s to 1740s when the stamp duty clerks recorded a place of origin for apprentices shows that this held more generally. The average migrant youth joining a master based in a small

TABLE 4.1. Apprentice migration, 1525–1800

	1525–49 (km)	1575–99 (km)	1625–49 (km)	1675–99 (km)	1725–49 (km)	1775–99 (km)
Boston				41 (16–40)		48 (13–22)
Bristol	89 (34–126)	64 (27–83)	49 (17–55)	44 (17–53)	48 (23–56)	53 (17–65)
Gloucester			24 (10–31)	21 (11–25)	22 (11–24)	
Leicester			25 (8–20)	18 (10–25)	24 (10–26)	20 (8–22)
Lincoln				18 (12–23)	28 (14–40)	24 (10–32)
Liverpool					51 (16–61)	
London	216 (147–281)	169 (88–235)	134 (68–181)	122 (56–168)	98 (26–148)	81 (12–122)
Norwich	108 (25–208)	75 (18–91)	36 (16–36)	46 (24–54)		
Oxford	101 (22–148)	65 (14–96)				
Shrewsbury				46 (19–48)		

Note: Table reports the mean distance in kilometres travelled by a migrant entering apprenticeship in each quarter century in each town. The 25th and 75th percentiles are reported in parentheses. Distances are measured as the shortest direct route from place to place.

village or town with a population of less than 5,000 travelled 26 km, and only a quarter travelled more than 28 km. In the same sample, apprentices migrating to large centres of over 10,000 people (excluding London) travelled 39 km, and a quarter travelled over 50 km.[16] These averages don't distinguish between the sizes of the places the apprentices came from, but if we concentrate on apprentices who came from the countryside and small communities (less than 5,000 inhabitants), we find that those who migrated travelled 30 km to a master in a similarly sized place, 39 km to one in a town of 5,000 to 10,000, 42 km to one in a city of 10,000–50,000, and 93 km to a master in London.[17] In short, the pull of urban centres grew with their size, and the great gap in scale between London and its smaller rivals created a substantial step between their migration fields.

Second, the distance that young people travelled to enter an apprenticeship fell between the early sixteenth and the end of the seventeenth centuries, before stabilising.[18] Counter-intuitively, as communications and travel improved with literacy, market integration, turnpiked roads, and growing coastal shipping, youths became *less* likely to journey for hundreds of miles to enter training. Very long journeys, in particular, became rarer. Again, it was London that saw the most dramatic change. A quarter of youths in the early sixteenth century travelled over 280 km, literally moving from one end of the nation to the other. By the late seventeenth century, youths in the long-distance quartile travelled only over 120 km.

The enormous diminution in the field from which London's apprentices came is visualised in figure 4.1, which summarises migration for three quarter-century periods, each separated by around a century. The maps begin in the early seventeenth century, when the sample is large enough to cover a wide range of guilds, but as table 4.1 indicates, some concentration had already occurred.

Elsewhere, changes were more modest, in part because few were ever willing to travel far to train in more minor centres. Two smaller towns, Lincoln and Boston, even saw some growth in the distance that apprentices had travelled. But the contrast between the long distances moved by apprentices in Bristol and Oxford in the early sixteenth century, where youths were often moving well over 100 kilometres, and the shorter journeys seen a century or two later make clear that the hinterlands of towns in the middle tiers of England's urban hierarchy also diminished in a way that echoed London's narrowing.

The effect of this drawing in of horizons was a regionalisation of training and labour markets that is clearly visible by the eighteenth century. Figure 4.2 shows the origins of apprentices in Bristol, Gloucester, Lincoln, Liverpool, and Leicester between 1725 and 1749. By the second quarter of the eighteenth century, youths mainly sought apprenticeships in their local cities. Few 'by-passed' an opportunity in their region for one further away—unless they were travelling to London. Even Gloucester and Bristol, separated by only 50 km and linked by the great waterway of the Severn, had largely distinct migration fields.

As migration fields grew smaller over the seventeenth century, many more apprentices were recruited locally, drawn from the cities they were training in or their suburbs. Locals were a minority in the early sixteenth century: in 1525–49, Bristol supplied barely a third of its own apprentices, and locals made up 19 per cent of apprentices in Norwich, 13 per cent in Oxford, and just 12 per cent in London. Over the next 200 years, the

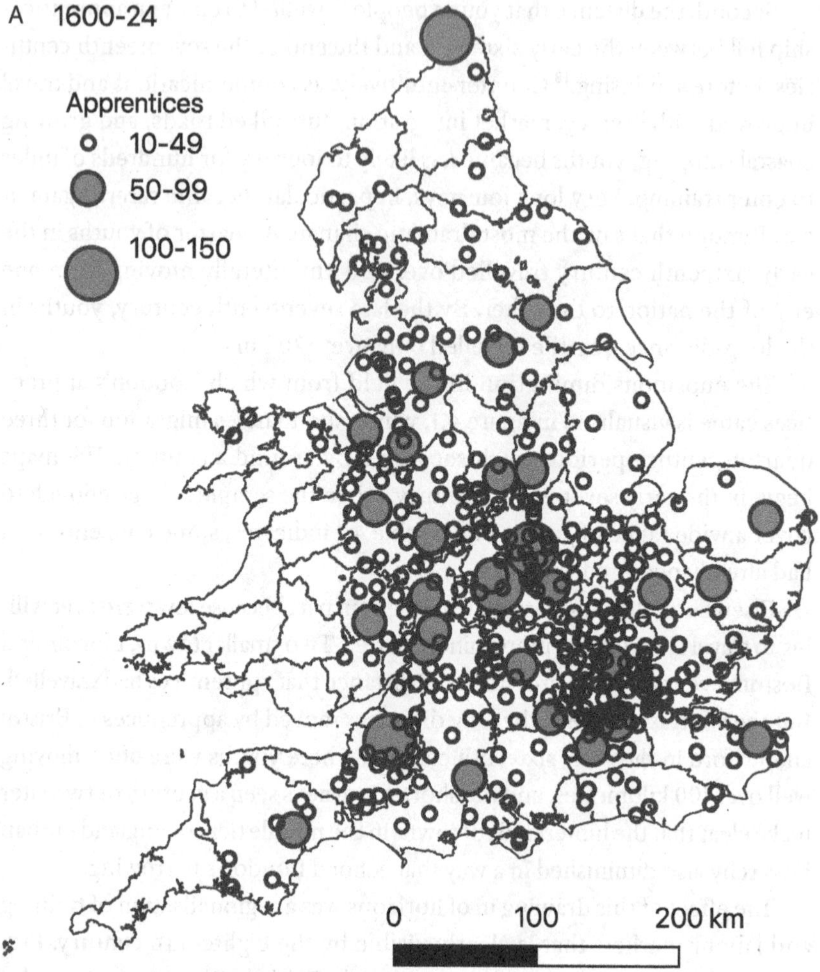

FIGURE 4.1. London's apprentice migration field, 1600–1800. Panel A: 1600–1624; B: 1700–1724; C: 1775–99. The maps report clusters of apprentices located by place of origin in the London livery company sample.
Source: Appendix 1.

balance shifted almost continuously towards local recruitment. Around one-half of apprentices came from the city or nearby in Bristol, Gloucester, Leicester, London, Norwich, and Shrewsbury in 1675–99. Over the eighteenth century, the share of locals crept up to three-quarters in Bristol and two-thirds in London. Some youths did still travel from further afield, but the average apprentice was now a local boy, not a migrant, marking a profound change in the structure of training and the link between

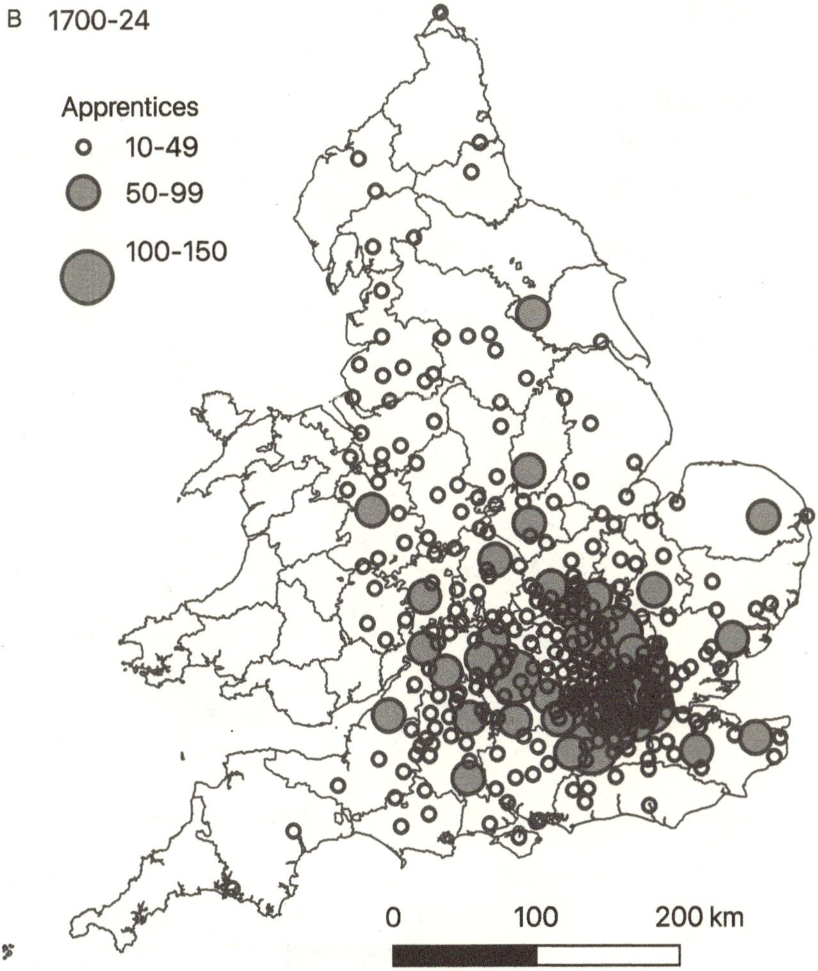

FIGURE 4.1. *(continued)*

apprenticeship, migration, and changes in the structure of the English economy.

Movement on the scale seen in the sixteenth and seventeenth centuries cost money, demanded access to information about opportunities, and even then, involved accepting risks. To travel meant overcoming the obvious requirements of paying for food and lodging while on the move, and perhaps for a place on a cart or horse if one was fortunate. It also meant having the resources to arrange a placement in a business from a distance—or having a friend or relative who could help a youth find a master once they arrived.

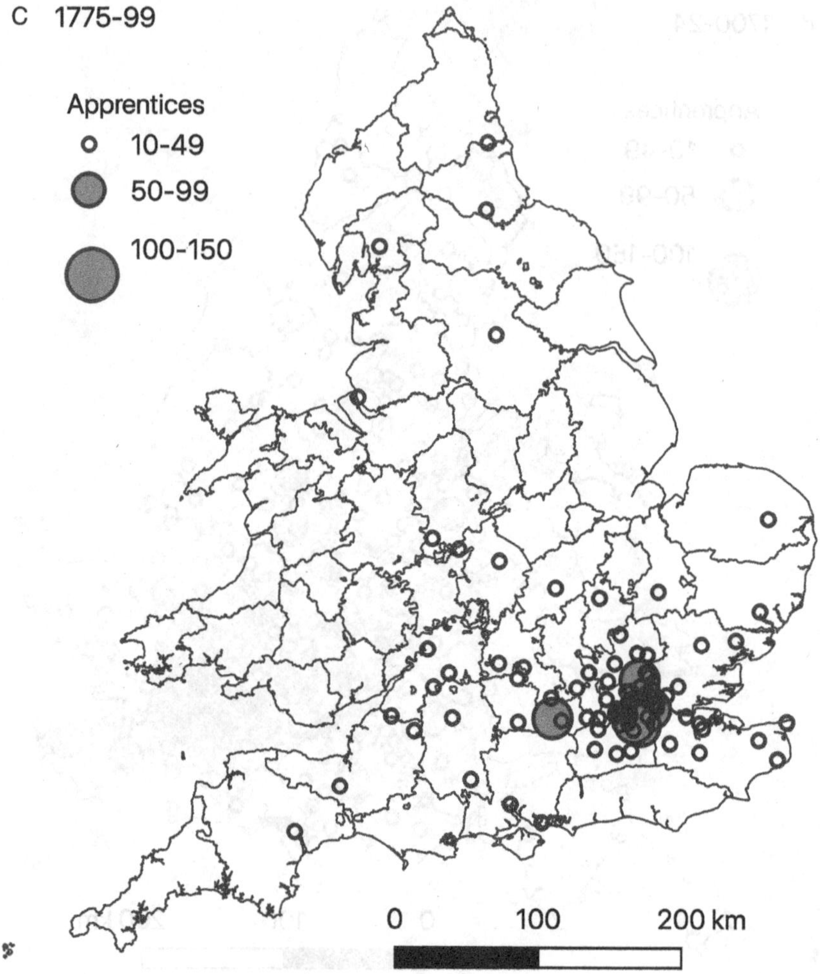

FIGURE 4.1. (*continued*)

As a result, it was mainly the wealthy who travelled the furthest. Gentlemen's sons, especially, came from far afield.[19] Husbandmen travelled shorter distances than yeomen. Even if locals are excluded, youths from urban crafts, such as tailors, came from locations that were substantially closer than youths from farming families. And the poor travelled least. Labourers' sons becoming apprentices in London moved on average 60 km in the seventeenth and 37 km in the eighteenth century. In other cities, most labourers' sons were from places within 5 to 10 km of the city they trained in. The average gentry son entering an apprenticeship in London moved more than twice as far as the average labourer's son. Those who travelled furthest were, unsurprisingly, those most likely to be entering the best positions.

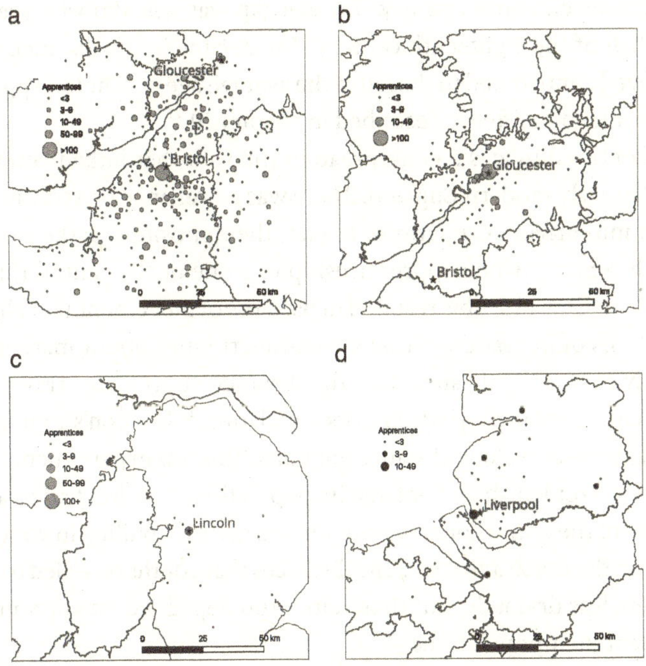

FIGURE 4.2. English urban migration fields, 1725–49. The maps report clusters of apprentices located by place of origin for a random 20% sample of Bristol apprentices and all apprentices in Gloucester, Lincoln and Liverpool.
Source: Appendix 1.

That this was fundamentally betterment migration is also apparent from the direction of movement: young people who were already in a well-established town or city with good opportunities did not move to another similarly sized urban centre. Less than a handful—just four—of the more than 300 eighteenth-century apprentices who left a substantial second-tier city such as Bristol or Norwich went to another city of similar size. Those who moved went to London (40% of migrants) or to a smaller, expanding city. The majority (1,111, or 78% of all apprentices from these centres) simply stayed where they were, well placed as they were.[20] If they migrated, youths generally moved up the urban hierarchy, drawn towards the brighter opportunities available in larger centres.

Migration also affected the point in their lives when youths migrated. Longer journeys were more often the preserve of older youths. Although there was some convergence over time, those who came to London from the furthest counties of Northern England were on average almost two years older than apprentices from the city and neighbouring Middlesex in the first half of the seventeenth century. The age gap was still almost a year in the second half of the eighteenth century. The decline in the distance apprentices moved contributed to the fall in the average age of London apprentices from seventeen to fifteen, described in chapter 10.[21]

Apprenticeship was a vital thread in the web that linked countryside and city in early modern England. There was no reliance on recruiting local children into urban occupations. In fact, the opposite was the case in the sixteenth century, when apprenticeship was one of the central threads of migration in England. This resulted in patterns of movement that align with expectations of migration within a well-functioning labour market—most obviously that, roughly speaking, the distance apprentices travelled to a town or city varies in proportion to its population.[22] London's apprentices in particular were often long-distance migrants. This was in part a demographic necessity: to replenish and enlarge its population, London had to attract a large slice of the entire country's population growth, pulling in youths from counties in the north and west. The distances that youths travelled to smaller cities were less dramatic, but those cities too depended on apprenticeship to maintain their populations.

The declining scale of movement of apprentices challenges preconceptions about how the integration of labour markets developed over the long run. Towns and cities recruited an increasing predominance of recruits from their own populations and areas nearby as England became better connected and wealthier over time. Better provincial opportunities meant that prospective apprentices no longer needed to travel. Elsewhere in Europe, youths tended to train near their families, allowing parents to support their children, and one imagines that English parents would have favoured this, too. Conversely, London was now able to supply more of its own apprentices, and it was increasingly accessible to skilled adult migrants.[23]

The distances involved in apprentice migration in the sixteenth and seventeenth centuries were extraordinary. The average London apprentice in the sixteenth century moved further than the average UK university student in 2014.[24] The ability to move long distances to become an apprentice was greatest among those from the wealthiest families, and it is clear that they were moving the furthest in pursuit of the best opportunities, often found in London. For those from less affluent backgrounds, resources constrained their choices to a narrower horizon.

That by the eighteenth century there had been a rebalancing, with more local movement, should not mislead us into thinking that apprenticeship was not still a key mechanism for migration. Rather, it reflects the moderation of the singular appeal of the metropolis and a few other cities, as a greater firmament of activity arose in the towns of the Midlands and North of England.[25] Now, young people were more likely to train in the region they came from and, in part because of that, to enter training earlier, increasing the supply of skilled labour. As a result of the quickening of economic growth outside London, the migration patterns of youths into apprenticeships in English cities was fundamentally different on the eve of the Industrial Revolution to that seen two centuries before, but apprenticeship remained central to the reallocation of labour.

Sectoral Mobility

What types of backgrounds did these highly mobile youths entering apprenticeship come from? The economic and social origins of youths entering apprenticeships between 1500 and 1800 in a number of England's towns and cities is summarised in figure 4.3.

The figure sorts apprentices' families based on the father's engagement in one of the three main sectors—agriculture, industry, or services—or his identity as a gentleman or labourer. London is shown by the solid black line, while the average for other centres is indicated by a broken line, with the variation in the underlying series shown in grey. The overall implication is that apprenticeship was socially broad, reaching from near the top—the gentry—to the labouring base of English society.

Like migration, however, apprentices' social origins were also changing between the sixteenth and eighteenth centuries. Three clear trends stand out across all these urban communities: the decline in the number of children from agricultural families, the growing importance of children from families in industry and services—families who might themselves train apprentices—and the rise and fall of genteel apprentices. There is also a fourth trend—a fall and rise in the share of labourers' sons among apprentices—although this is less strongly delineated.

Farming families were the dominant source of apprentices in the sixteenth century, supplying around half of apprentices in Oxford and London and a third in Bristol. Thereafter, the importance of agricultural families declined almost continually. By the late seventeenth century, around one in four apprentices were from farming families. By the late eighteenth century, in London and Bristol it was around one in ten, although some smaller centres such as Leicester and Lincoln saw higher shares.

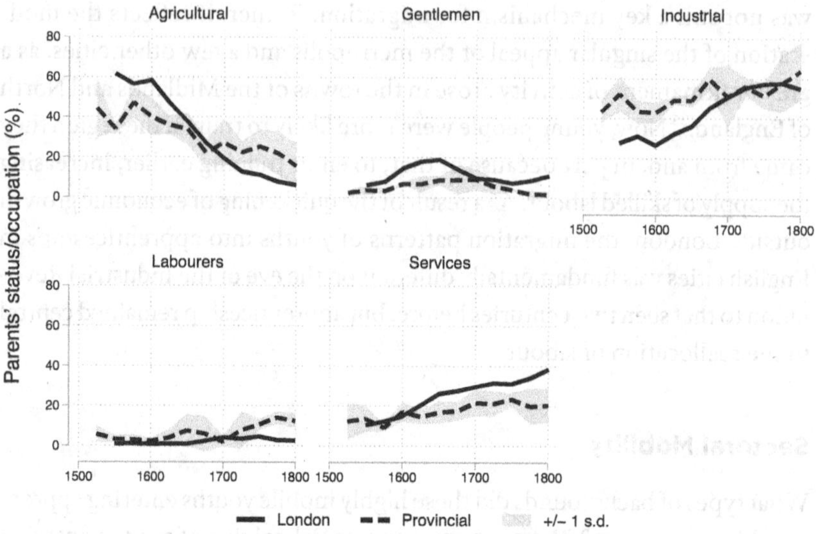

FIGURE 4.3. The status or occupational sector of apprentices' fathers in early modern towns and cities, 1500–1800. The shares for individual towns and cities are reported in appendix 5. London is shown by the solid black line. The provincial centres are Boston, Bristol, Gloucester, Leicester, Lincoln, Liverpool, Norwich, Oxford, and Shrewsbury, with the average indicated by the broken line.

A growing divide existed between London and the rest of the country by the 1700s: agriculture supplied almost twice as many apprentices outside London as it did within the city, as table 4.2 shows. Even compared to other towns and cities, the drop-off in youths from farming families training in London was sharper and steeper. Those families who did still send children into apprenticeships were increasingly drawn from the wealthier side of agriculture. Around 80 per cent of agricultural fathers were identified as husbandmen in early sixteenth-century Bristol and Oxford. By the late seventeenth century, yeomen outnumbered husbandmen, and by the late eighteenth century, husbandmen had all but disappeared from the lists of apprentices' fathers.

As fewer children came from farming families, their places were filled by boys from manufacturing and commercial backgrounds. London, in particular, saw the share of apprentices from families in service occupations almost triple between 1575 and 1775. Elsewhere, it was mainly families engaged in industry—usually artisanal crafts—whose children provided an expanding number of apprentices. Combined, the share of apprentices coming from families in industry and services reached around 80 per cent by the early

TABLE 4.2. The origins of premium apprentices, 1712–17

	Gentry (%)	Agriculture (%)	Industry (%)	Services (%)	Labourers (%)	N
Provincial	14	36	41	23	4	7,511
London	18	17	46	38	2	7,496

Source: Appendix 1. For this period, registers for both city and country survive, and apprentices' backgrounds are frequently recorded. In later periods, reports are too sparse to be reliably representative.
Note: Table reports the status or sector of the fathers of apprentices in the stamp duty registers in 1712–17, inclusive.

eighteenth century; these were children from occupations that recruited through apprenticeship entering apprenticeships of their own.

Even with this expansion, only a small share of those indentured in a trade were the children of their masters. It was not that apprenticeship excluded fathers training their own sons, just that the sons and daughters of masters were swamped by a flood of outsiders, as table 4.3 shows.[26]

Until the 1800s, youths explicitly recorded as being their masters' sons were most commonly found in smaller centres; the highest share of sons serving their fathers in the dataset was recorded in the market town of Shrewsbury, where almost one in three of the ninety-four guild apprentices were indentured to their own fathers in the eighteenth century.[27] But in most periods and places, father-to-son apprenticeships accounted for roughly less than 10 per cent of apprentices. In London, sons were least prominent: just 1–2 per cent of apprentices in London in the seventeenth century were bound to their fathers, depending on the measure used.

For the most part, in English towns and cities, eight or nine out of every ten apprentices were *not* the sons of masters. In its largest city, sons were even more of a minority: they supplied just two in every hundred London apprentices in the seventeenth century, underlining its role as a hub for training the young of the nation as a whole.

Compared to the fortunate children from the elite or middling sort, the sons of labourers rarely appear in urban or guild registers. In most cities, they were far outnumbered by the sons of gentlemen, a far smaller group in the population. Few places saw more than 5 per cent of guild apprentices coming from labourers' families. In London, they supplied just 1–2 per cent of apprentices. Similarly, on average, just 2 per cent of apprentices paying premiums in London were children of labourers, and 4 per cent of those in

TABLE 4.3. Apprenticeship within the nuclear family: Fathers and sons

	Kin tie stated (%)					Inferred from name (%)				
	1500–1599	1600–1699	1700–1799	1800–1899	All	1500–1599	1600–1699	1700–1799	1800–1899	All
Boston		13	9	0	6		11	25	.	20
Bristol	2	7	7	5	6	2	7	7	7	6
Gloucester	0	0	10	1	3	5	8	2	.	7
Leicester		11	8		9		13	8		10
Lincoln		6	4	5	5		6	5	4	5
Liverpool			2		2			2		2
London	0	1	6	11	3	0	2	8	14	5
Norwich	11	11	20		11	0	1	.		0
Oxford	0				0	1				1
Shrewsbury		18	33		21		18	30		21
Total		2	6		4	1	3	8	11	5
N (thousands)	2	268	153	7	471	20	246	169	18	246

Source: Appendix 1.

Note: The left-hand panel reports the share of apprentices with an explicit relationship stated in the original register; the right-hand panel reports an estimated based on apprentices whose fathers and masters had the same surnames and forenames.

the provinces. Poverty clearly had a substantial impact on the chances of children. Movement into (non-pauper) apprenticeship was relatively rare from labouring families. It needs to be emphasised that these are private apprenticeships; the share of pauper apprentices from labourers' families was likely to have been much higher.

Labourer might be an under-used label for the occupations of fathers, given that apprentices and their families had some control over the wording of how they were described in indentures, but there is no realistic adjustment to the numbers that could bridge the great gulf between the share of apprentices who were listed as labourers' children and the substantial numbers of labourers in the population. In 1688, King put 43 per cent of the population into his class of 'labourers, cottagers and paupers'; more precisely, Shaw-Taylor and his colleagues suggest that 24 per cent of workers were labourers around 1710.[28] These estimates are ten to twenty times higher than the share of labourers' sons appearing as apprentices in urban or guild records. Only Leicester, with its economy oriented to low-waged framework knitting to produce stockings and hose, recruited apprentices from this group in numbers that came anywhere close to their share of the population, with 22–23 per cent of its eighteenth-century apprentices being the children of labourers. That said, there are signs that labourers' sons had once had better chances of becoming apprentices in early sixteenth-century records from Bristol and Oxford, and that they were again emerging as a larger source of recruits in the later eighteenth century.

At the other end of the social spectrum, the importance of apprentices who identified themselves as being the sons of gentlemen may seem surprising given today's view of apprenticeship as a blue-collar phenomenon. But across England's towns and cities, there was a consistent pattern. In the records from Bristol and Oxford in the early sixteenth century, gentry sons appeared very rarely. Between the late sixteenth and early seventeenth centuries, however, gentry sons had become a normal feature in all these towns and cities. It was the largest cities that saw the most gentry children. In London, nearly one in five apprentices came from gentry families in the second quarter of the seventeenth century, and around the same share of metropolitan apprentices paying premiums described themselves as gentry in the early eighteenth century. This added up to an avalanche of genteel youngsters. More than 30,000 gentry sons entered apprenticeships in London in the seventeenth century alone. But even smaller centres received a number of apprentices hailing from elite backgrounds.

Were the 'gentlemen' in the apprenticeship registers really gentry? Historians have frequently been suspicious of these claims. Some conclude they were little more than socially aspirational large farmers—'parish gentry', in Brooks's words.[29] Grassby, for example, concluded that 'many of those [apprentices] described as gentlemen in the seventeenth century would not have been recognised as such in the sixteenth century'.[30] The sheer numbers of gentry families sending sons into apprenticeship suggest that some must have been on the margins of the group, perhaps with parents who were small landholders, attorneys, and other professionals. Gentry made up just 2.4 per cent of the population in the 1688 estimates of the early political economist Gregory King.[31] Across England, this would suggest there were around 1,000 male gentry sixteen-year-olds in the 1670s, in a period when in London alone around 500 new apprentices claimed to come from gentry families each year. Given that a great many gentry sons lived as landholders, or entered the church or army, many of the gentry apprentices must have come from families that did not fit King's tight definition.

Yet, for all that some claims to being gentlemen were dubious, there are large numbers of parents of apprentices whose gentility was indisputable. A considerable number of apprentices' fathers can be identified in lists of gentlemen having the right to display a coat of arms registered by the heralds in their visitations of England.[32] Those gentry could, in short, assert a credible claim before the officials whose role in life was to define the boundaries of gentility; they include members of Parliament and justices of the peace. The Surrey gentleman Arthur Onslow's eldest son, Richard, became chancellor of the exchequer in 1715; his fourth son, Henry, was apprenticed in the Grocers' Company in 1683. The same number of gentlemen's sons listed in the heralds' visitations entered apprenticeships as went to study at Oxford and Cambridge Universities, in fact. These were not future artisans, however. Many apprentices to merchants and wholesalers came from these wealthy and influential families. They were seeking careers in business where capital and connections mattered, not slaving away with their hands.

Apprenticeship witnessed a great inversion between the sixteenth and eighteenth centuries. In the sixteenth century, most youths who were indentured to a craft or trade were leaving agriculture, precisely the worry that consumed Parliament when passing the Statute of Artificers. Almost as soon as it became law, the purpose of the statute became increasingly irrelevant. Youths from farming families supplied an ever-smaller share of apprentices, in part because they made up a declining share of the populace after 1600.[33]

Two centuries later, apprenticeship had become a mechanism through which youths from manufacturing and industry followed the same broad road into a (usually different) craft or trade as their fathers had done before them. Apprenticeship also experienced a boom in popularity in the seventeenth and early eighteenth centuries, apparent in the surge of gentry families and the squeezing out of labourers' and husbandmen's sons, as well as in the willingness of families to pay premiums for good trades.

These flows of youths between sectors were a necessary part of the process of structural change occurring in the English economy in these centuries, helping the transition out of agriculture that occurred from the early seventeenth century, and the mercantile and commercial expansion that was most visible in the explosive increase in overseas trade through London. Neither would have been possible without the recruitment and training of youths from families that had relied on farming in earlier centuries.

England's reproduction of its workforce was not segmented between its different sectors. Although the rates of mobility between *sectors* through apprenticeship declined between the sixteenth and eighteenth centuries, as larger shares of new apprentices were drawn from families already engaged in industry and trade, there was never a great gap between the share of families active in each sector and the share of apprentices that emerged from them.

In the sixteenth century, when around 60 to 65 per cent of the nation's workforce were engaged in agriculture, a similar share of apprentices came from farming families. In most cities, the gap between the share of youths from farming families that we would expect to start apprenticeships if family background was irrelevant and the share that actually did was small—perhaps 10 to 20 per cent at most. By the eighteenth century, when around 40 per cent of the workforce was in agriculture, the gap had widened in some cities and was greatest in London, where just 13 per cent of guild apprentices in the second quarter of the century came from farming families. The second major trading city in the sample, Bristol, also received a low share from agriculture, at 15 per cent. But outside of London, the share of premium apprentices in the stamp tax records coming from farming families was 37 per cent in 1712–17, and in most smaller towns the share registered by the city or guilds was over 20 per cent. These are not far below the share we would see if family background did not matter.

The split in England's youth labour market between country and city grew somewhat in the eighteenth century, but a large share of youths still spilled out of the fields into work in craft and commerce. Much of the high levels of mobility between different sectors of the economy that is seen in early modern England was achieved within apprenticeship.

Urban Occupational Mobility

We have seen that there was no great gulf between city and country. Apprentices came from distant counties, different sectors, and many kinds of social status. For these youths, occupational mobility was often unavoidable and inseparable from migration into a town or city. However, even when we focus on people who we might expect to be the *least* occupationally mobile, apprenticeship still usually involved movement into a different trade. As the French political economist Richard Cantaillon recognised, 'The Craftsmen themselves do not make all their Children learn their own mystery: there would be too many of them for the needs of a City or a State; many would not find enough work'.[34]

Cantaillon's observation suggests that apprentices who came from the city would often be entering a different occupation to their father. This is exactly what happened in England. As table 4.4 shows, few youths from urban families were indentured to a master who followed their father's occupation. When they entered apprenticeship to someone other than their father, it was usually with a master in a different trade. Five out of six entered a different craft or trade to their father. Only a few towns ever saw even a third following the same occupations as their fathers, and then only sporadically.

These are, by definition, youths whose families are already invested in local, urban occupations. Many would have shops or businesses that their sons might work in or inherit. Most would have connections that could help build a career. Nonetheless, they chose—or were chosen by their families—to enter an apprenticeship outside their family.

Were the youths in this group exceptions? Did most youths fortunate enough to be born in an expanding town or city, and to survive to their teenage years, train within the family firm, where one existed? In short, did sons follow their fathers if they could?

Figure 4.4 reports estimates of the share of masters' sons bound to their own fathers for a cross-section of London's guilds, and citywide estimates for Bristol, Gloucester, Lincoln, and Norwich.[35] The message of figure 4.4 is clear: masters' sons were usually indentured to someone else. This is despite the fact that the share indentured to their fathers is overestimated (we miss

TABLE 4.4. Occupational persistence when training occurs outside the family

City	1500–1549 (%)	1550–99 (%)	1600–1649 (%)	1650–99 (%)	1700–1749 (%)	1750–99 (%)	All (%)	N
Bristol	18	20	21	18	14	12	16	15,338
Gloucester		29	33	35	18		29	2,218
Leicester			31	22	12	31	23	174
Lincoln				7		13	12	159
Liverpool					7		7	31
London		6	8	9	6	13	9	6,440
Norwich		36	15	24			22	324
Oxford	7	31					24	50
Shrewsbury				8			8	26
Total	18	24	21	17	13	12	16	24,760
N	584	524	4,410	7,452	4,903	6,887	24,760	

Note: The table reports the share of non-migrant apprentices whose fathers' occupations (in standardised spelling) match their masters' occupations, among apprentices bound to masters who were *not* recorded to be their fathers. All cells have twenty or more observations. The sample for London is largely from the Merchant Taylors (for most masters in London we only know their guilds, not their occupations); for other cities and towns, the samples are the same as in appendix 1. Apprentices trained by their fathers are excluded.

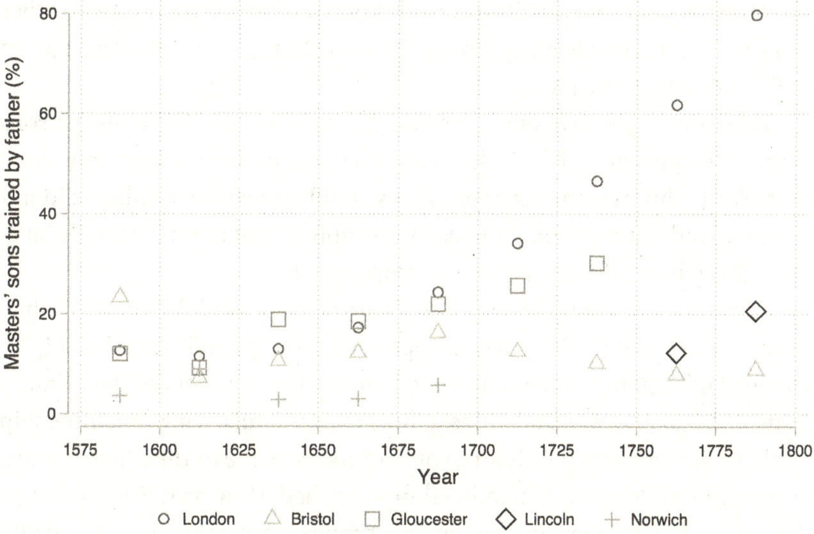

FIGURE 4.4. Share of masters' sons apprenticed to their own fathers. The figure reports city averages for (i) London citizens' sons and (ii) provincial cities' local youths whose fathers' occupations were commonly listed among the trades of local masters (minimum fifty times per half century). The sample reports guilds/cities for which eleven or more freemen/local masters bound their sons to themselves or other masters in each period.

sons indentured elsewhere, as well as those who did not become apprentices at all). In London, in the first quarter of the seventeenth century, only a small minority—less than one in five—of citizens' sons who became apprentices in the city were indentured to their own fathers. By 1700, around a third of sons trained with their own fathers. In Bristol, Gloucester, Lincoln, and Norwich the story is the same, although with no obvious trend. It was normal practice for a freeman to place his son in a different workshop in the sixteenth and seventeenth centuries.[36]

For the children of masters, this pattern of mobility through apprenticeship could and did change, as we see in London in the eighteenth century. There, in the same decades when the scale of guild apprenticeship declined sharply, youths were increasingly bound to their fathers. By 1800, if London masters' children became apprentices at all, then it was usually within their fathers' businesses. The emergence of this metropolitan pattern of apprenticeship endogamy is one of the sharpest changes in apprenticeship in this period and does not appear to have occurred in other centres. The timing suggests it reflects a shift in London towards seeing guild apprenticeship as a way to gain political rights, as well as growth in family firms.

Aside from this specific metropolitan development, apprenticeship in early modern England usually involved masters' offspring training with other artisans and traders; leaving their father's workshop was a standard option in English towns and cities.

These estimates have one important limitation: they only consider sons who were apprenticed formally. One other reason for the very low share of masters' children among apprentices could be that their fathers did not bother to indenture them. Perhaps they simply taught them the family business through an informal apprenticeship of sorts?

In most of Europe, the sons of masters were treated differently if they trained within their fathers' workshops, qualifying for guild membership by virtue of inheritance and not needing to prove they had served their time.[37] In most English towns and cities, guilds took a similar view: membership could be achieved by the children of masters by virtue of their 'patrimony', as their inherited right to membership was called. However, English law, in the Statute of Artificers, did not list inheritance among the routes to qualify for a craft or trade. It introduced an ambiguity, accepting that someone who had worked for seven years in a trade gained a right to use that occupation, but without the credentials provided by apprenticeship indentures, such claims were open to dispute.

The statute certainly mattered, reducing family training outside apprenticeships. In Oxford, Bristol, and London the share of freemen's sons enrolled as apprentices tripled or quadrupled after it passed. Still, some families surely ignored the legal risk and did not bother to formally apprentice children training at home. How common was this?

Direct evidence is limited. The best measure comes from the number of masters' sons joining guilds or claiming citizenship by patrimony who do not appear in apprentice registers. For seven London guilds in the seventeenth century, enough evidence on freedoms and apprenticeships survives to work this out.[38] In these guilds, 850 sons of guild masters joined their fathers' guilds after a registered apprenticeship, while 4,752 entered by patrimony. A few of those entering by patrimony may have been trained elsewhere,[39] and some may have been entering the guild to legitimate a business in a different trade. Even accounting for that, the figures suggest that fathers who trained their sons may have mainly done so informally, rather than within a formal apprenticeship. However, sons who trained informally with their fathers may still have been outnumbered by their siblings who trained with other masters; 6,262 sons of masters in these seven guilds were indentured in other guilds, even though records for some guilds are missing. In London at least, the flood of masters' children into other trades could well have outnumbered those training with their fathers until the eighteenth century.

Masters' sons were consistently massively outnumbered by apprentices from outside the guild, occupation, or city: there can be little doubt that the great majority of each generation of successful artisans and traders in English towns and cities had spent time as an apprentice. Even for the sons of local craftsmen or traders, their apprenticeships were usually with someone other than their fathers. Mobility was the norm, with apprenticeship providing the mechanism for intergenerational occupational changes within labour markets.

Unequal Opportunities: Mobility and Money

Apprenticeship encompassed the children of both rich and poor, townsmen and country folk, farmers and craftsmen. Judged on this simple metric, it was an open system that connected different parts of the labour market. To a large extent, recruitment on the scale apparent in these cities and towns necessitated this.

SOCIAL MOBILITY

While entry into apprenticeship was a possibility for everyone, the chances that children from poor labouring families would be placed in apprenticeships were much lower than for their better-off peers. And even if they were, the specific types of job that youths might pursue through apprenticeship were much more strongly defined by their backgrounds.

Poorer children largely ended up in the least prosperous trades, while merchants and the like took boys from families with considerable wealth. This can be illustrated easily by the occupations that each entered. Figure 4.5 shows the degree to which the sons of labourers and gentlemen were over- or under-represented among apprentices relative to their share of the sample of apprentices as a whole. These two groups stand in here for the two ends of the spectrum of wealth and connections. London apprentices are excluded in this analysis because the information on the occupations of masters is much more limited (most masters are labelled by their guild, not what job they did).

The destinations of gentry and labourers were quite different, as this simple indicator of bias illustrates. Gentry sons were concentrated in long-distance trade, wholesaling, and the respectable professions. There were more than four times more gentry sons among apprentice mercers and linen drapers, both profitable trading and mercantile occupations, than we would expect from the sample. Conversely, labourers were found disproportionately in manual crafts, becoming tilers, shoemakers, and, in an echo of Adam Smith's vison of deskilling, pin makers, two or three times more often than their share of the sample would predict.

While youths from particular backgrounds were crowded into trades that offered prospects commensurate with their families' wealth and status, it is their absences in other occupations that are even more telling. Consider pin-making: only a single apprentice from a gentry background was recorded entering pin-making, Mainard Peyton, who was bound to Anthony Barrett in Gloucester in 1738. There were roughly fifty times fewer gentry pinmakers than we would expect based just on the share of youths from a gentry family. Similarly, just two gentry sons were indentured to ropemakers, and four to tilers, twenty and ten times fewer than we would expect, respectively. For labourers, we see a similar story. Only one was bound to an apothecary and three to mercers, both around twenty times below the numbers we would expect based on the share of labourers' children in the sample; none at all were bound to a soap-maker. The number of youths who cross these divides

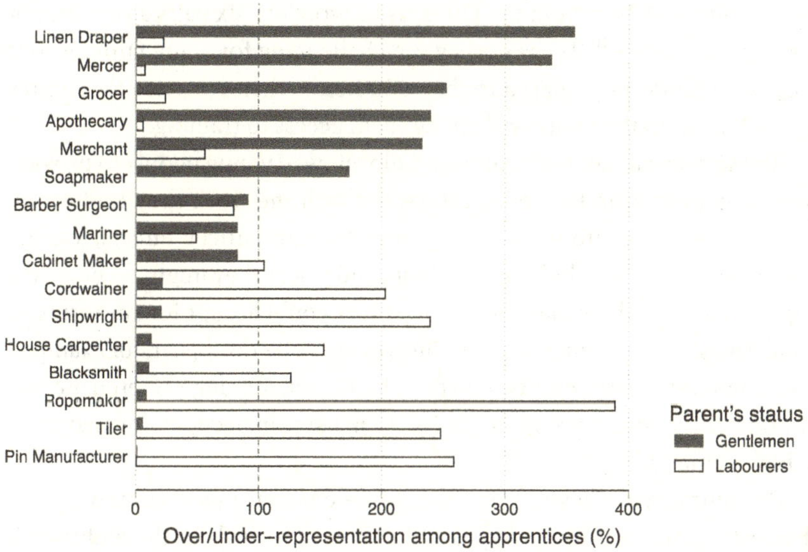

FIGURE 4.5. Bias in occupational entry by background. The figure reports the ratio of the share of entrants into each of the listed occupations who came from gentry and labourer families to the share of all apprentices from each of those backgrounds, expressed as a percentage. A value of 100% would indicate that the share of apprentices entering a specific trade matched the share of all apprentices from that background, implying no bias. Data is the sample of apprentices 1500–1800 in towns and cities outside London with information on parental background and master's trade, n=56,552.

is so small that they raise doubts about what was occurring here: Was Peyton's master Barrett running a factory rather than making pins himself, perhaps? Whatever the story behind such exceptions, the social and economic selectivity of occupations is clear. Children from particular backgrounds entered distinct constellations of work.

THE PRICE OF TRAINING

The opportunity to enter an apprenticeship was not evenly spread across society. Nor were all apprenticeships equal in the prospects that they brought. The root cause of this was money, not laws, rules, or customs.

Apprenticeship came with costs: it removed a pair of productive hands from a household, often at the point at which they were finally became valuable, and it took time and money to arrange. Youths needed a stock of clothing and travel money at the very least. John Cogg's shoes alone cost his mother almost £2 a year in the 1700s, as he wore out six pairs a year during his apprenticeship.[40] These costs were challenging for some families, but they were modest compared to the main item: whatever price the master set for taking on the youth and giving them access to training.

The service element of apprenticeship allowed young people to provide some compensation to their masters, through the work they undertook during their years with them. The value of the apprentices' efforts, less the cost of whatever food, lodging, clothing, and wages they might receive, was appropriated by their masters. Apprentices could accept longer terms to induce masters to accept them: bindings of ten years do appear, for example. Over the seventeenth century, however, families increasingly offered money, not time, by paying a premium, or fee, to masters in occupations that were in high demand.[41]

Premiums were never universal. Some occupations accepted a large share of recruits without a fee. Guild and civic records in the eighteenth century sometimes give an indication of the frequency with which premiums were paid, as clerks often noted the premium once it was recorded on the indenture as a result of the stamp tax. In London, only one-third of apprenticeships involved premiums.[42] In a sample of eight guilds, only three recorded a majority of apprenticeships requiring premiums—the Apothecaries (84% paying), the Grocers (53%) and the Turners (52%).[43] The majority of apprenticeships in several craft occupations such as plasterers, blacksmiths, and butchers required nothing. The probability of a family paying a premium was higher in occupations where premiums were larger, but even here, a third of apprentices training as druggists or grocers did not pay. Outside London, the share of indentures involving premiums in the records of towns was higher. In Oxford, 80 per cent of enrolled apprentices involved premiums.[44] In Gloucester it was 80–90 per cent, but in Leicester it was 46 to 64 per cent, more like London.[45]

Premiums were also lower than has sometimes been thought. Table 4.5 reports the fees charged in the most common occupations in the eighteenth century when they appear in stamp duty records. The median premium across all apprentices outside London was just £10 in the eighteenth century, and even in the city it was only £20. Many common manufacturing crafts, such as shoemakers and tailors, charged less than that.

Premiums, nonetheless, were a potent source of inequality. Premiums were a formidable challenge for poorer families when set against unskilled provincial wages of around £12 a year. Many of the most widespread occupations saw premiums at £5 to £10, close to a year's earnings. For the most

TABLE 4.5. Premiums charged for apprenticeships in eighteenth-century England

Occupation	Mean (£)	St. Dev. (£)	Med. (£)	P75 (£)	Max (£)	Prov. Med. (£)	London Med. (£)	Prov. P75 (£)	London P75 (£)
Attorney	119	91	100	158	844	100	105	150	200
Surgeon	80	64	63	105	1,000	63	100	100	158
Grocer	41	41	30	50	685	30	50	49	100
Milliner	28	15	30	40	200	26	30	35	42
Cabinetmaker	21	16	18	26	250	18	20	25	30
Saddler	20	18	17	25	525	16	21	21	32
Shipwright	18	17	14	21	600	15	10	21	20
Mantua-maker	16	11	13	21	223	10	20	20	26
Cooper	15	20	10	18	525	10	15	14	21
Joiner	14	14	10	18	600	10	12	16	20
Wheelwright	12	24	10	12	1,050	8	15	10	21
Baker	11	13	10	13	1,000	10	10	13	15
Butcher	11	12	10	13	630	10	10	12	20
Carpenter	11	10	10	14	432	9	10	13	20
Barber	10	13	9	10	420	8	10	10	13
Weaver	10	33	4	6	1,000	4	7	5	20
Tailor	9	9	7	10	500	7	10	10	20
Cordwainer	7	9	6	10	600	6	8	9	10
Blacksmith	6	8	5	7	300	5	10	7	15

Note: The table reports summary statistics for premiums in the stamp duty registers for England, 1711–1804. Columns 1 to 5 relate to the full national sample. Columns 6 to 10 distinguish between apprenticeships with masters in and outside London. The occupations reported appear more than 5,000 times in the full sample.

prosperous trades, particularly in commerce (merchants, mercers, drapers, grocers) and the professions (attorneys, surgeons, apothecaries), premiums might be far higher, excluding all but the children of the wealthy. These put substantial demands on parents. Individuals might be fortunate enough to inherit funds; London's Orphans' Court, for example, allowed guardians to spend inheritances on apprenticing heirs.[46]

The premiums that masters charged were not regulated in England. They were an important part of the price of the skill that masters sold, alongside their apprentices' labour. Premiums reflected the supply of and demand for human capital, as well as expectations about the future value of training.

They varied substantially within occupations, with individual masters able to charge different fees depending on their experience and success.[47]

The rich and those children whose personal connections allowed them to escape paying for training had an important advantage in the labour market. In this respect, 'insiders' such as masters' relatives did benefit. One of them was Joseph Blacket, whose brother, 'a ladies shoemaker in London, expressed a desire of taking me as an apprentice, on the most liberal terms; namely, to provide me with every thing for the space of seven years'.[48] Given that his father was a day labourer in a small village in North Yorkshire, Blacket would have had few other options. It was 'an opportunity which my parents lost not', and he was soon on his way south, a ten-day journey on a wagon, to enter his indentures. Outsiders—migrants and youths changing trade—tended to pay higher premiums; mobility had its price, perhaps because of the greater risk of contracts failing early.[49]

This direct financial barrier was more important than the statute law, guild rules, or exclusive artisanal norms in defining the prospects open to young people entering the skilled labour market in early modern England. The use of premiums undermined the way apprenticeship allowed individuals without access to capital to mortgage their labour to fund their training. The relationship between a family's economic position and the premiums it could afford to pay for its children meant that horizontal mobility was easier to achieve than upward mobility. Without capital markets that allowed young people or their families to borrow the funds to pay for training, premiums set boundaries on the aspirations of the young.[50]

APPRENTICE CHARITIES

Two things pushed against the exclusionary effects of premiums. First, the Poor Law led parish overseers to place pauper children in apprenticeships that gave them a chance to make a living independently. These were opportunities which their parents might not have been able to obtain for them, even if the parish generally did not provide youths with access to occupations outside the crafts and trades, such as weaving, shoemaking, and bricklaying, that employed large numbers of skilled, but rarely prosperous, men.[51] The scale of Poor Law apprenticeship across the country remains unclear, and the pool of youths who were placed was largely different to those entering private apprenticeships, but it was surely an important avenue into some skilled occupations.

The other avenue was charity. Large numbers of charities existed across England to help young people by contributing to the premiums they had to pay to enter apprenticeships.[52] Although they mostly centred on 'poor' children, they frequently excluded those whose families were supported by parish poor relief. The apprenticeships they funded tended to be among the most widespread crafts, and were often in the same occupations as the parents of the youths they assisted, so, like the pauper apprentices funded by the parish, they did not improve their conditions greatly.[53] That said, charitable funds could prevent a child whose parents had died or were struggling economically from missing the chance to enter a skilled occupation. While some were parsimonious, many offered premiums that were around the same as what families were paying privately.[54]

Supporting poor children who wished to become apprentices became a common object of charity in the late seventeenth and eighteenth centuries. Wigan, Lancashire, then a growing township, received eleven legacies totaling more than £600 between 1632 and 1761 to fund apprenticeships for poor children. Even the hamlet of Skelmersdale, 7 miles to the west, received two legacies, from Richard Moss in 1702 and Evan Smith in 1726, which generated a couple of pounds a year towards premiums. Some endowments were substantial. The lands that Sarah, dowager-duchess of Somerset, left to fund apprentices supported 2,456 boys from 1714 to 1838.[55] The timing of these gifts was significant, forming part of a wave of philanthropic action that washed across the nation.

Although some charities for apprenticing had been founded earlier, the bulk came in the later seventeenth and early eighteenth centuries, plausibly in response to the spread of premiums.[56] Figure 4.6 shows the growth in the number of charitable trusts concerned with apprenticing children, and the amount they could disperse each year, for three counties with very different economies: rural Gloucestershire, industrialising Lancashire, and diverse Warwickshire.[57]

These figures are only indicative of the trend. They exclude trusts without a reported date of foundation, ignore improvements in the value of assets, and—vitally—omit other important sources of charitable support including private gifts and funds from societies and organisations that were invisible to later Parliamentary enquiries.[58] On the other hand, some of these charities also had other aims (e.g., supporting or educating the poor as well as training them), and these could absorb funds that might have been dedicated to apprenticeships.

The importance of charity in allowing young people access to training is evident from the records of apprentice indentures that mention this. For some periods in the eighteenth century, a few city and guild clerks

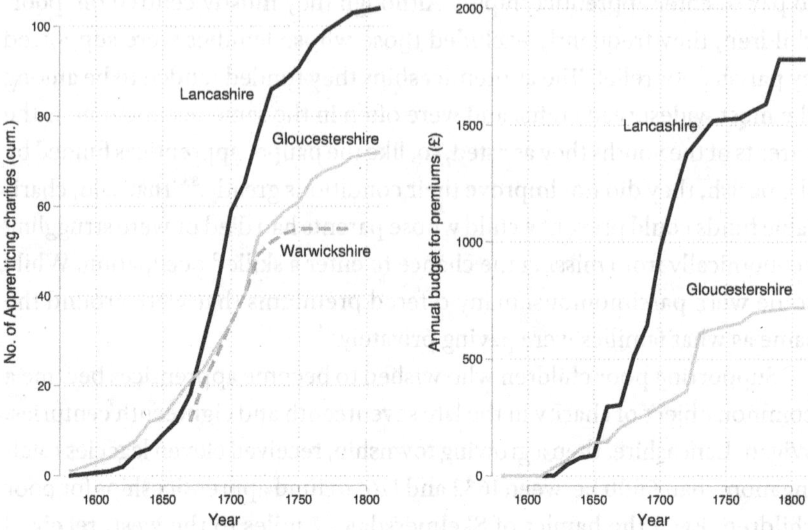

FIGURE 4.6. Charitable funding for apprenticeships. Counts of apprenticing charities in the left-hand panel allocate the charity to the date of probate of the will or the deed that created them. The annual budget in the right-hand panel is taken as either (i) its reported annual income in 1786–88; (ii) the income generated from the total legacy (assuming a 5% rate of return); or (iii) its annual income in the 1820s (for 7% of Lancashire charities and 41% of Gloucestershire charities) reported in the 1826 survey. To allow for the time to establish the trust, income is assumed to begin in the decade after foundation. No adjustment is made for inflation, as there is a mix of fixed and varying revenues.
Sources: Pinches 2000; United Kingdom. House of Commons 1816: XVI-A.1, XVI-B.1; United Kingdom. House of Commons 1826: vols. 12, 14, 16, 17 (Gloucestershire) and vols. 5, 11, 15, 19, 20, 21 (Lancashire).

consistently recorded premiums paid by charitable gifts when enrolling indentures. This was incidental to their main purpose, but enough evidence survives to allow us to illustrate the part that charity played in three provincial centres—Leicester, Oxford, and Gloucester—and in a subset of London guilds.

As table 4.6 shows, the share of apprentices benefiting from charities varied widely. In Leicester, where premiums were relatively rare and the sums given were smaller, 9 per cent were supported by the one charity mentioned, Mr Simon's charity.[59] In Oxford and Gloucester, half or more of apprenticeships with premiums were funded by charity. Most in Gloucester were by the Gloucestershire Society, established in 1657 by merchants from the county who lived in Bristol; as a society, it would not appear in the trusts counted in figure 4.6. In Oxford, the university gave the largest share, alongside an array of gifts from charities named after their founder or

TABLE 4.6. Premiums and charity funding for apprentices

	Paid premium %	Premium funded by: Charity %	Premium funded by: Private %	Supported by charity %	Median premium: Charity £	Median premium: Private £	N
Leicester							
1720s	52	13	39	26	5	6	109
1770s	40	6	34	14	5	8	81
All	46	9	37	19	5	7	190
Oxford							
1710s	82	53	29	65	10	10	91
1770s	79	37	42	47	10	15	79
All	80	46	35	57	10	11	170
Gloucester							
1750–74	87	44	43	50	7	16	147
1775–99	80	45	36	56	10	20	249
1800–1820	75	30	45	40	10	30	150
All	80	40	41	49	10	20	546
London guilds							
Blacksmiths	30	18	12	60	5	10	1,521
Clothworkers	36	8	28	22	5	21	5,513
Drapers	44	7	37	16	5	25	779
Founders	38	12	26	32	5	10	801
Grocers	62	11	51	18	7	84	227
Merchant Taylors	57	10	47	18	5	20	3,887
Plasterers	30	14	16	47	8	11	135
Stationers	42	9	33	21	5	25	5,318
Turners	53	19	34	36	5	10	844
Vintners	26	7	19	27	5	20	673
Total	42	10	32	24	5	20	19,698

Source: See appendix 1.

Note: Column 1 reports the share of apprentices bound with a premium; columns 2 and 3 report the share by source; column 4 reports the share of all apprentices with a charity premium. Columns 5 and 6 report the median premium paid.

location: Alderman Nixon, Alice Smith, Mr Bogan, Dr South, Dr Wall, Holywell Parish, Mrs Hoddy, Wallingford parish, and so on. In London, a quarter were charity-funded, but in some guilds the share was much higher. Dozens of charities existed in London. A few were particularly important, such as Christ's Hospital and Henry Dixon's charity, managed by the Drapers' Company. Each sponsored hundreds of apprentices over the century, a scale not seen elsewhere.

Selected urban figures of this kind offer no certainty about apprenticeships outside corporate towns and guilds. We can infer something of the scale of charitable support from the funding available in Gloucestershire and Lancashire. If we assume charities spent their annual incomes on paying the median private premiums observed in the stamp tax records (most charities in practice paid smaller premiums), we can get a rough lower-bound estimate of the numbers of apprentices who were supported.

In Lancashire in the 1710s, the charitable funding available each year from legacies alone (£1,189) would have supported 915 apprenticeships, almost equalling the 1,064 apprenticeships with privately funded premiums each year. From 1750 to 1800, when the stamp tax records are most complete, the number of charity apprentices was between 54 and 89 per cent of the number of private apprentices in most decades, with the share varying largely because the median private premium grew to £15 by the 1790s; if charity trustees kept to their more parsimonious norm of paying £5 to £10 premiums, numbers would have continued to almost match the number in privately supported apprenticeships. In Gloucestershire, there was less support: 439 charity-funded against 672 privately funded premium apprenticeships in the 1710s, and 731 against 1,160 in the 1780s. These estimates are deliberately conservative and represent only a subset of funding from charity. Even so, they confirm the importance of charity as a vital counterbalance to the exclusionary effects of premiums.

SET-UP COSTS

Finance did not matter only at the start of training. To make use of an apprenticeship as a merchant or wholesaler, a young person needed capital to establish a business afterwards. The sums needed to embark independently as an overseas merchant exceeded £500 even in the first half of the seventeenth century. By the later century, more than £1,000 might be required. Shopkeepers and dealers faced a lower bar, but even there, the cost of renting and stocking a shop might exceed £50 in the provinces and £100 in

London.[60] The crafts were similarly demanding, with Campbell estimating in 1747 that cabinetmakers needed £200 to £2,000 and mantua-makers needed £20 to £100 to set up as masters.[61] A few were less expensive—he thought buckle-makers might need just £5 to £10—but that was exceptionally cheap.

While waged work as a journeyman offered an avenue that avoided these capital requirements, it is clear that independence as a master was still an aspiration for many of those apprenticed. As Benjamin Bangs's mother warned him, he must choose a craft, not a trade, because 'it would be imprudent to put me to any higher Business, since a Stock would be wanted to set me up when I came out of my Time', and none could be promised with so many children to provide for.[62] Bangs would therefore become a shoemaker; wealth constrained young people's choices both at the entry and exit from training.

Conclusion

Labour mobility over space, sector, and occupation was one of the central contributions of apprenticeship in England. Apprentices were almost always drawn from outside the nuclear families. Only a small share were the sons of their masters; instead, masters' sons themselves often were apprenticed to different trades. Apprenticeships were served by the sons of artisans and traders, farmers and gentlemen, labourers and merchants alike. The movements they made followed the standard pattern observed in migration generally: youths travelled further to access positions in larger centres with better prospects. In provincial centres, apprentices tended to be drawn from distinct hinterlands that did not overlap. The scale of these apprentices' movements exceeded that seen in most other groups in the labour market at the time—or subsequently. Through the decisions of thousands of individual families seeking good futures for their children, workers were redistributed towards areas and occupations of demand, and the English labour market was effectively integrated across the boundaries of different occupations and sectors, town and country, periphery and metropolis.

Apprenticeship became a major driver of urbanisation and structural change, just as it spread knowledge out from the best workshops and traders. As Jane Humphries succinctly puts it, apprenticeship lowered 'transaction costs involved in transferring resources from agriculture to non-agriculture and facilitated the expansion of networks across sectors, which promoted trade and commerce'.[63] More than that, it incentivised those who possessed skill to transmit it to the next generation.

The great wave of geographical and occupational mobility through apprenticeship seems to have peaked in the seventeenth century and ebbed thereafter. Migration then declined. Regional labour markets became more distinct. Cities and towns supplied a larger share of their own apprentices. These apprentices also became younger, as the average age fell markedly.[64] Flows from the landed elite and rural middling sort into trade and industry slowed. The futures of children became more predictable over time; occupations became more strongly heritable. J. S. Mill's image of the past came into existence in the time of his own parents.

While movement was the norm, even before the eighteenth century, it was largely flat in economic and social terms. When we look at their occupational destinations, the young of English society moved within their own layers, as distinct as oil and water. The children of gentlemen and paupers may both have worn the same label of apprentice, but they did not sit shoulder to shoulder at the workbench. The occupations each pursued, and the journeys each would take, were powerfully shaped by the wealth and resources each possessed through their parents.

It was because apprenticeship was a market for skill that its direct effect on social mobility was limited. Fees for training, in particular, split access to training along the lines of family wealth, as they did elsewhere in Europe, even with the amelioration provided by charity.[65] Masters took those who had funds as well as ability rather than selecting apprentices by merit alone. That all families employed a common type of agreement for their children that allowed them to be labelled apprentices did not make this a social leveller any more than sharing the label of pupil bridged the gap between students at elite public schools and their impoverished peers at charity schools. Apprenticeship was a great engine for labour-market integration, but the mobility it induced was more horizontal than vertical.

PART II

A System of Training

5

Apprenticeship as Learning

Having examined some of the ways in which apprenticeship influenced English economic development between 1500 and 1800, it is now time to examine how this institution worked. The next four chapters describe premodern apprenticeship as a distinctive system of training. Distinctive from what? The main contrast I highlight here is with the form of apprenticeship and vocational training that emerged in the nineteenth century and became dominant in the twentieth century.

In the modern industrialised economy, apprenticeship combines workplace immersion with formal technical education outside; it is relatively stable, with high rates of completion in many places in the twentieth century; it often leads to long-term employment in the firm that provided the training; and employment problems are mainly dealt with between employers and apprentices, as the former is now usually a firm, not an individual.

Premodern training lacked much formal instruction. It was centred on immersion without technical education, as I show in this chapter. As the next chapter reveals, it was flexible, with high rates of non-completion, absences, and reassignments. It was overseen by a set of formal institutions—guilds and courts—that dealt with disputes and shaped their resolutions, which I discuss in chapter 7. And, as chapter 8 shows, when training ended, apprentices moved on, with some becoming independent masters, some waged workers, and some migrating.

Learning and Training

The meat of apprenticeship was, and still is, training. But what form did this training take? How did early modern apprentices learn? How did training adjust to shifts in knowledge or technology across the early modern period, if it adjusted at all? These questions are central to any understanding of apprenticeship as an institution embedded within particular historical or cultural contexts. They also determine how we interpret apprenticeship as part of the life experience of youths and masters and the cultural and social system that scaffolded premodern work.

The answers to these questions define where pre-industrial apprenticeship was positioned in a spectrum of possible forms of apprenticeship, many of which remain observable in parts of the world today. Although anthropologists and sociologists often discuss apprenticeship as a specific form of training, this is not helpful when considering the development of apprenticeship historically. For our purposes, apprenticeship is more usefully thought of as the arrangement within which training is delivered and funded.[1] From this perspective, the nature of the training that occurs within an apprenticeship depends on the balance struck between formal instruction, on the one hand, and experiential learning, acquiring skills by participating in production, on the other. The latter type of learning is sometimes thought of as 'apprenticeship', but in practice, apprenticeships can encompass elements of both.

Formal instruction here means teaching by the master, another worker, or an instructor.[2] This can take place within the workshop or another institution, such as a school or technical college. Today, formal instruction can absorb a considerable portion of an apprentice's time, with days or weeks spent studying in college, but even a few minutes sitting down with a journeyman to be shown how to make a cut or adjust an account would count.[3] One of the primary characteristics of formal instruction is that it breaks the connection between production and learning. While being taught, the apprentice becomes a cost, producing nothing for the firm, and is a recipient of an investment of time, money, and effort by the firm or master.

The other end of the spectrum is informal, experiential learning by participation in work. The apprentice is a (more or less productive) input into the creation of the business output at the same time as they gain in skill and knowledge. Learning by experience is characterised by emulation, imitation, and practice that occurs during work. Apprentices are watching, mimicking, copying—'stealing with their eyes', in one resonant phrase.[4] Some of this will occur even while they are carrying out unskilled work. Their productivity during this process can vary, as we will see. This form of learning was not costless: at the very least, apprentices used up materials, tied up tools, and occupied space less productively than skilled workers, and the price of their mistakes was absorbed into the firm's bottom line. On the other hand, experience can shade into exploitation if an apprentice is kept too long at a task once they have mastered it, rather than being exposed to other dimensions of a craft. However, it is the cost of formal instruction that moves the apprentice sharply from one side of the business's balance sheet to the other, and so the amount and intensity of periods of formal instruction most fundamentally shape the economics of an apprenticeship.

Despite more than a century of research into apprenticeship, we know little about how premodern apprentices actually acquired skills—that is, where they sat on the spectrum between experience and instruction (or exploitation).[5] Some analyses of apprenticeship, those focused on its operation as a credential or barrier to entry, pay little attention to this question. If access to economic privileges, not training, was the real intent of apprenticeship, the skills that apprentices gained were just the by-product of their growing experience in the workplace. Adam Smith considered that even the most advanced of arts, such as clock-making, might be acquired quickly:

> To explain to any young man, in the completest manner, how to apply the instruments and how to construct the machines, cannot well require more than the lessons of a few weeks: perhaps those of a few days might be sufficient. In the common mechanic trades, those of a few days might certainly be sufficient.[6]

The surviving evidence on how contemporaries perceived apprenticeship argues against this. Even Smith admitted in the same paragraph that 'the dexterity of hand, indeed, even in common trades, cannot be acquired without much practice and experience', suggesting this might be acquired while working for wages as a journeyman. The distinction that Smith, the academic, draws here might be reduced to the contrast between propositional knowledge and embodied or tacit knowledge, with the latter firmly consigned to the sidelines.[7]

Few researchers today would share Smith's confidence that skill takes nothing but time. The substantial body of scholarship on expertise might be reduced in newsprint to spending 10,000 hours on practice, but the importance of receiving support and guidance from teachers and experts carries equal weight in the literature.[8] Still, it is easy to appreciate why historians sometimes dismiss apprenticeship training, given the threadbare record of training that survives. Apprenticeship had no official curriculum, no set of examinations from which we might infer a course of learning, no manuals to support masters in teaching. It was almost deliberately obscure.

This chapter examines the surviving traces of how learning occurred within and around apprenticeship to lay out the basic characteristics of the system of apprenticeship. The first section analyses the nature of training within apprenticeship, drawing on legal disputes between masters and apprentices and autobiographical writings by apprentices. Despite their contrasting perspectives, a coherent understanding of learning was shared between both sources. The youth's agency in drawing on the opportunities that a workshop or firm presented to them was central, as was self-directed practice and the gradual absorption of unverbalised knowledge.

The experience early modern apprentices gained through participation in production dominated instruction. Formal education was almost entirely absent. Even the master's direct contribution might be almost imperceptible at times. It was closer to the structures of training that have been observed in modern anthropological research on apprentices in artisanal crafts in low-income countries than apprentices in industrial economies in the twentieth century, although all share a common reliance on situated learning. However, it was not equivalent to simply learning on the job, without any attention from the master to the apprentices' acquisition of skills. Instruction, while limited, was present.

The second half of the chapter considers how learning in the workshop connected to other forms of learning. I first examine and reject the argument that apprenticeship was actively intended to convey a specific set of cultural norms. I then look at other types of education and learning, in order to expose the sharp contrast between premodern training and the structures that developed from the later nineteenth century. These give modern apprenticeship in the twentieth and twenty-first centuries a financial link to the state and a level of general educational content that was not shared in earlier centuries.

Learning on the Shop Floor

What did masters think constituted training? A good place to start is the set of disputes between apprentices and masters that were brought to the Lord Mayor's Court of London in the seventeenth century. These lawsuits are discussed in detail in chapter 7, but for now, what matters is that they left a rare set of sources in which apprentices, masters and others discussed the content of apprenticeship training.[9] As failure to provide training was one of the legal grounds that apprentices could use to leave their master, the nature and quality of training were of vital importance.

A fine example of how training was conceived can be found in the way George Aston, a twenty-seven-year-old journeyman pewterer, recounted how John Hulls, a master pewterer, had treated John Walmesley, his apprentice: '[He] never employed the said complainant in any servile or domestic work not relating or usual in the Trade of a Pewterer but always put him as forward in the learning of his trade and gave him all the encouragement as possible might be'. Walmesley, he concluded, 'has as much instruction and understood his trade as well as most Apprentices for the time he was with' his master.[10] Similarly, in a dispute between an apprentice apothecary and his master, a witness testified that the master put his apprentice 'forward in the learning of his trade & did usually read Doctor's bills to him'. The apprentice was 'well instructed . . . during the time he was with him & understood the same very well'.[11]

This vocabulary of training—'putting forward', 'encouragement', and 'instruction'—appears in other suits.[12] As does the point about employing the apprentice in his trade, not 'in servile & domestic affairs', or 'drudgery work'. Somewhat surprisingly, even tasks taken on by journeymen might fall below some apprentices' lots: the apothecary James Cooke was accused of making his apprentice beat the mortar, 'which is many times performed by the journeymen & other sorts of servants'.[13] Whatever the truth here—and such statements were frequently contested—what matters is the insight they give into the essentials of apprenticeship. At the heart of this were opportunities to learn through work (whether positive or negative), encouragement in learning, and instruction, which formed a trinity of concepts that contemporaries identified as central to apprentices' learning.

'Instruction' explicitly had a place in training, but what did this amount to? Understanding in any detail the method, content, or intensity of teaching implied by instruction is challenging. Given the variety of trades and crafts that were acquired through apprenticeship, there can be no single answer. And even within a single craft, a detailed answer is elusive.

As a first step, we can be clear that contemporaries believed the intensity of instruction, at least, might be increased. This is explicit in Martha Drury's defence of her son Walter's treatment of his apprentice. Walter had instructed his apprentice James well, she argued:

> He was able to make plasters, caudles & most medicines & do many things as well as the defendant himself, & the defendant having no other apprentice & [James] being the 1st he took, did use the greater Time & Labour with him that he might be sooner capable of doing business than usually apprentices are wont to be.

As a result, James 'did often say & declare that he understood his trade' and 'was able to do things as well as those who had been three times longer at the trade than himself'.[14]

The converse—that intensity could be lowered if formal instruction was delayed—was also true. A good example of this is Thomas Hiat, an apprentice distiller, chemist, and surgeon who accused his master of sending him out of the room during important distillations. His master's reply was that the final year of training gave ample time to learn these secrets, and teaching them earlier would only encourage his apprentice to abscond.[15]

In both Drury's and Hiat's cases, formal instruction required the master's 'time and labour' and centred on propositional knowledge: recipes, formulae, 'secrets' of the trade. That the content and intensity of instruction could be changed has important implications. First, the master was not entirely passive; they were more than a model to be imitated. Second, stages of instruction in knowledge and skill were identifiable. This awareness and acceptance of an element of formal instruction distinguishes apprenticeship firmly from learning on the job. Knowledge could not *just* be 'stolen' by observation.

One other characteristic of early modern instruction needs to be emphasised: training and skills usually came from a broad range of sources, a workshop or craft community, rather than a single expert. Shaping the menu of experiences, challenges, and skilled individuals that an apprentice encountered was a central part of the master's role.[16] Exposure to different skilled workers and different parts of a business was therefore crucial.

If we look at who gave apprentices specific technical training, it is clear that this was often not their masters. This was implicit in various statements. One witness on behalf of Thomas Wallon, a wine cooper, asserted that 'if [the apprentice] wanted any instruction it was his own fault, for the Defendant kept several Journeymen, & had an Apprentice almost out of his time very well skilled in his trade, and that one or other of them were always at home'.[17]

The importance of journeymen was reflected in other cases, such as when a witness argued that the apothecary James Cooke's apprentice was not well instructed because his master 'kept divers outlandish [i.e., foreign] men as

Journeymen in his shop . . . whereby the complainant could not attain to any sufficient knowledge & experience in his trade'.[18]

Having apprentices work across the breadth of a firm to acquire the range of skills and insights that might blend into mastery was a distinction between traditional apprenticeship and learning on the job in industrial England that the economist Alfred Marshall noticed in the late nineteenth century: 'The employer binds himself to see that the apprentice is thoroughly taught in the workshop all the subdivisions of one great division of his trade, instead of letting him learn only one of these subdivisions, as too often happens now'.[19] Instruction might therefore be manifested by masters giving their apprentices responsibilities and tasks that demanded new skills, rather than allocating them to repetitive jobs that maximised their immediate output.

In its fullest form, masters advancing their apprentices might allow them to operate semi-autonomously within their firms. In trade, some experience of autonomy was widely seen as critical. Merchants' apprentices often combined their work as a factor or agent for their masters' firms with business on their own account. As Sir Peter Rich argued, 'Unless a Merchant's Apprentice be sent abroad as a factor he cannot be fully instructed in the way of Merchandize'.[20] In defence of another merchant, Elias Lambert, one of his former journeymen, emphasised that 'he sent [his apprentice] Lewis to fairs into the Country which is esteemed the most beneficial [experience] for an Apprentice both in respect of his gaining acquaintance & understanding his trade'.[21] Both Roger Lowe and William Stout finished their training as grocers running separate shops for their masters.[22] Similarly, the only regularly specified detail in Southampton merchant apprentices' indentures was that they should be dispatched abroad during their service, mostly to Spain or France, to learn a language and work as a factor.[23]

Not all types of commerce could give an apprentice the chance to act as their master's agent, but even so, the depth of their experience defined the quality of training. Size alone mattered. Defending the merchant William Barron's training of his apprentice, his partner highlighted the scale of their business: they had 'a considerable trade in way of merchandizing sufficient to instruct an Apprentice therein'.[24] In other trades and crafts, masters emphasised exposure to the different aspects of a business as a key element of instruction.

The merchant apprentice's travels had a counterpart within the shop, although the journeys through business papers that apprentices took were less exotic. In defence of John Brownrigg, a silk wholesaler, one witness emphasised that he 'let [the apprentice] have use & custody of all his

FIGURE 5.1. William Hogarth, *Industry and Idleness*, plate 4. Engraving by Thomas Cook after William Hogarth, 1795. Image: Wellcome Collection.

books both of buying and selling'.[25] Similarly, the druggist John Coningsby let his apprentice have 'as much freedom to resort to the Books & other matters relating to instruction therein as any Apprentice is wont to have'.[26] The books in question here were the business's account books. Unusually, Coningsby's books survive from a few years before the date of this dispute, when he was turning over more than £2,000 a year through a mix of retail and wholesale sales.[27] More than eighteen separate account books still exist, each devoted to recording different elements of the firm's activities. The freedom to roam these accounts was no trivial opportunity. As with assigning apprentices to different roles across a business, in permitting access to the firm's books, the master was privileging their apprentice's needs over commercial secrecy. This was a reward for progression, a position of trust exemplified in William Hogarth's *Industry and Idleness*, where Tom Goodchild is shown with his master's 'Day Book' and keys in his hands (figure 5.1).

Craft apprentices also frequently moved to different masters to gain exposure to technical skills and different products. After five years apprenticed to a tailor in Colchester, John Carter tried his luck in London, and on his return to Colchester 'I was considered to be a competent workman inasmuch as I had been working in London, which was thought to be the only efficient school for juvenile tailors'.[28] Periods working away were common for apprentices in a range of occupations. For example, Phineas Pett assisted two shipwrights in addition to his own master.[29] The apprentice surgeon George Benson was permitted 'travel for his better experience in his profession', having paid his master a fee to compensate him for his absence.[30] Alternatively, masters hired out their apprentices for wages, taking an income while also exposing them to different craftsmen.[31] Gaining a diverse range of skills required mobility, and James Watt's advice to youths seeking a career as a civil engineer envisaged precisely this: they should be 'put out to a Cabinet maker when he is 14 to learn to use his hands, and practice Geometry . . . at the same time he should work in a smith's shop to learn to forge and file'.[32]

Providing training involved exposing apprentices to a range of relevant skills and business processes and giving them opportunities to model and practise techniques and behaviours with increasing autonomy as they gained in ability. This might be achieved by witnessing different activities and workers within a workshop, or by time spent in other firms, sites, and spaces. It was more than simply time 'on the shop floor', in the way that any worker put to a job might learn.

Masters visualised high-quality instruction—for before the court, they all, of course, claimed to be exemplary masters—as navigating apprentices' voyages through a sea of opportunities. What distinguished this from simple experience was their direction: apprentices gained access and were put to tasks or dispatched into destinations in ways that would not have occurred if they were not undergoing apprenticeships.

Whether the apprentice actually learned much on the way was not the master's responsibility. Much of the onus for learning fell on the apprentice. Reflecting on how he might act if he was given his time again, John Dunton concluded that 'I'd endeavour to penetrate as far as possible into the Mysteries of my trade; for unless a Man looks well into the Nature of his Business, and see every Reference that it bears, he'll scarce make anything of it when he begins to depend upon his own Bottom'.[33] Perhaps the fullest expression of this philosophy was articulated by William Hutton, reflecting on the tribulations he and his brother had faced: 'As every human being wishes to be master of his own actions, the best mode of education is to guide without seeming to guide'.[34] In this Cook's tour of a trade, some soaked up the sights, others lingered at the bar.

Throughout their training, apprentices worked. Work was central to the acquisition of skills, providing the chance to practise techniques. It was also central to the economics of apprenticeship, in offsetting the cost of their training, subsistence, and any wage. And for this reason, not all of apprentices' work was skilled. Apprentices undertook a wide range of prosaic work that profited the master. John Carter's apprenticeship to a tailor started in 1805. He spent his first years sweeping the workshop, kindling fires, sifting coals, cleaning tools, collecting tools and materials, delivering cloth or clothes, and fetching beer for the tailors.[35] It was only after three years that another boy was taken on and relieved him of these jobs. More than two centuries earlier, Simon Forman's service in Sarum had started similarly: 'Being the youngest apprentice of four, [he] was put to all the worst, and being little and small of stature and young of years, every one did triumph over him'.[36] Maintaining a fair balance between these unloved but essential and productive tasks and the chance for advancement was one of the universal challenges of training.

One potential complement to this lengthy grind at the workbench or counter was book learning. Did books offer a supplementary or alternative route to skill for apprentices? Adam Smith believed so:

> There is scarce any common mechanic trade, on the contrary, of which all the operations may not be as completely and distinctly explained in a pamphlet of a very few pages. . . . In the history of the arts, now publishing by the French academy of sciences, several of them are actually explained in this manner.[37]

A century earlier, William Petty had the same hopes, arguing that an encyclopaedia of the crafts might teach youths 'the theory of their trades before they are bound to a master, and consequently [they] may be exempted from the tedium of a seven years' bondage'.[38]

For all Smith's bravado and Petty's faith in Baconian science, book learning does not seem to have existed in most occupations. The exception in some ways proves the rule. Merchant's manuals were published in very large numbers, forming a literary genre in their own right.[39] As a hodgepodge of legal information, accounting techniques, guides to commodities, market prices, and so on, they illustrate the potential of print to provide a short cut to knowledge and an *aide-mémoire*, but simultaneously reveal how little of the practice of commerce could be communicated in print. Where their authors tried to talk of trade itself, they were usually reduced to general moral injunctions, to the sensibilities and qualities of merchants, not their skills.[40] One of the earliest in England, John Browne's *Marchants Avizo*, incorporated a section on 'certain godly sentences necessary for youth to meditate upon', for example.[41]

Merchant's manuals have few equivalents in artisanal trades. Medicine, navigation, and accountancy are the only other sectors where print took on a crucial role, and much of the material that did appear in print or was circulated in manuscript was for the use of expert practitioners. Exceptions exist. The engraver Thomas Bewick was set to copying from 'Copeland's Ornaments' for a while after entering his business, but noted that this was 'the only kind of drawing upon which I ever had a lesson'.[42] A growing body of guides to drawing and design developed in the eighteenth century, but these were general skills, ideally acquired before learning a trade.[43]

The Baconian project to write histories of the trades aimed to make knowledge accessible to outside investigators and to advance technology, not to assist apprentices.[44] The diarist and naval administrator Samuel Pepys may have learned how to use a slide rule from a printed book, John Brown's *Description and Use of the Carpenter's Rule*, but one imagines that few carpenters did.[45] The earliest English manual on printing, Moxon's *Mechanick Exercises* (1683), was firmly aimed at the scholarly outsider.[46] In practice, the readers of the Baconian history and the merchant's manual often overlapped: both were wealthy and literate, and they were often gentlemen or prosperous leaders in urban society. Both could afford these texts.[47] Both possessed the general skills to utilise them. Neither bore much resemblance to the majority of apprentices.

Skill acquisition did not finish with the completion of apprenticeship. It was common for artisans to acquire advanced training in a centre of skill *after* completing their apprenticeships. This kind of learning by 'advancement', as More styled it in his study of nineteenth-century training, could be gained while hired as a journeyman, or, more rarely, through a contract for advanced instruction.[48] For instance, in 1688 the clock and instrument maker George Graham moved from an apprenticeship with an average master (Henry Aske) to working as a journeyman with one of the trade's leading innovators, Thomas Tompion.[49] Another example would be James Watt, who came to London in 1755 to advance himself as a mathematical instrument maker and arranged a year's instruction from John Morgan, for which he paid 20 guineas and his labour, to learn 'most branches of the business such as rules, scales, quadrants etc'.[50] The apprentice Thomas Bewick's master even left him in charge of the business while he went to London to take lessons in etching and engraving copper plates.[51] The many young artists who spent periods in Rembrandt's studio in Amsterdam offer a further example.[52] The benefits were clearly understood. In a final letter to John Dunton, then training as a bookseller, his dying father advised him that 'if you find not convincing reasons to the contrary . . . serve as Journey-Man for one Year; because I judge by that means you may gain more Acquaintance and Interest, and a further Insight into your trade'.[53]

Such peripatetic learning was widespread in premodern European crafts. It is innate in systems of tramping that led journeyman artisans through a series of workshops as they circulated between towns.[54] Even where tramping was not formalised, as in seventeenth-century England, artisans moved to learn. For example, the shoemaker Benjamin Bangs worked with two masters before deciding he understood his trade reasonably well and 'was a little ambitious in my mind to become master of it'. He left his second master and 'got into the company of the best workmen'.[55] A century later, Joseph Oxley followed a similar path. Having completed his apprenticeship with a clockmaker in Scarborough and 'being altogether ignorant of the watch-making branch, which I thought necessary to know',

> I went up to London, where I met my uncle Edmund, and by the interest he made, I got a place, though not so suitable as could be desired. My instructor was a good workman, and in many respects kind; but he was very much wanting in religion. . . . I was indented with this man for two years to learn to be a watchmaker, which I liked very well'.[56]

After a further period as a journeyman, Oxley eventually set up a small shop in Fakenham, Norfolk, all he could afford with the £30 he had as capital.

It is useful to distinguish journeymen's advancement from the initial period of training in the early stages of apprenticeship. Whereas the master curated the apprentices' training, journeymen identified their own needs and the way to supply them. And, unlike apprentices, they had the advantage of revealed aptitude—the sense of their ability and potential that both learner and teacher can recognise only *after* a youth has completed their early training.

Norms and Culture

Thus far, we have mainly focused on how apprentices learned skills—whether in their trade or more generally. But what about their broader moral, cultural, and religious formation?

A long-standing historical tradition holds that apprenticeship was intended to transmit culture as well as skill, integrating young people into urban society and guild life. This was central to early accounts of apprenticeship in which the paternal role of the master was identified as one of its key advantages. It was the master's guidance and concern that Dunlop and Denman contrasted with the unstructured experiences of youths in the late nineteenth century.[57] More recently, Christopher Brooks provided the fullest expression of this idea, arguing that apprentices were 'subjected . . . to an indoctrination about standards of behaviour as energetic as that experienced by any other social group in the realm'.[58] It is a position that finds much evidence in contemporary commentaries on the ideal household, which consistently emphasised the patriarchal and moral role of the master in this period.[59]

We can think of the role of apprenticeship in socialisation and cultural transmission in two ways. In its 'weak' form, apprenticeship is a period during which young people absorbed ideas, values, and norms from a range of sources in the workshop, city streets, and churches they attended. These norms were important. They included many of the modes of being—punctuality, self-control, accuracy, discipline—that might determine success in the long run. But they were gained passively as apprentices' work shaped their identities, as they soaked up values by watching their masters and others in the workplace, as their occupations repositioned them socially, and as they experienced everyday life.[60]

In its 'strong' form, socialisation was a specific responsibility and conscious concern of the masters as they fulfilled their patriarchal obligations and inculcated a specific set of urban or craft values. While it is hard to imagine that 'weak' socialisation did not occur, evidence for the strong form of socialisation, as envisaged by Brooks and earlier writers, is harder to identify.

If we look at apprentices' memoirs for evidence of masters fulfilling the role envisaged in the 'strong' account of socialisation, there is little sign that masters saw instilling norms and values as their responsibility.[61] The Quaker Samuel Bownas, for example, served a 'very honest Friend' Samuel Parrot and summarised their relationship simply: 'I had a very kind loving Master and Mistress, and I had Meat enough, and Work enough, but had little consideration about Religion, nor any Taste thereof'. Bownas's spiritual well-being was left to his own care—and he neglected it: 'On first-days I frequented Meetings, but the greater part of the Time I slept, and took no Account of Preaching, nor any other Benefit, than, being there, kept me out of bad Company'.[62]

Parrot was not alone among masters in focusing on craft skills, not cultural values. Henry Longden similarly lamented that he 'was not under greater moral restrictions in my apprenticeship'.[63] One nonconformist minister, James Clegg, worried about exactly this lack of moral guidance when he bound his son John to a Quaker master in Manchester in 1726: 'My conscience was not easy when I did it. I thought it not well to place him where no family worship was likely to be performed, but I suffered myself to be overruled by the advice of friends'.[64] Clegg would have preferred a religious household, but he placed the economic benefits of training above the spiritual and moral costs. In short, he accepted that apprenticeship might weaken his son's moral and religious socialisation.

Many memoirs of apprentices offered variations on the potent trope of moral decline arrested by the redemptive influence of divine grace. For example, William Devenport recalled that his master took them to church but had 'no further care of our Souls'. Devenport fell under the influence of a 'very wicked Fellow Apprentice' and 'through his Example, my own Corruptions and the Devil's Suggestions, I immediately arrived at that degree of Wickedness, for Swearing, Lying, Sabbath-breaking, and all manner of filthy and frothy Discourse, that I think few of my Age exceeded me'.[65]

However far the deeply religious Devenport actually fell from grace, what is striking is that it was the other apprentices or journeymen—those on the same tier of the workshop—who mattered most in his perception of his socialisation. His master remained at a distance. The same point is visible in other accounts: when James Lackington converted to Methodism, it was because his master's sons' discourses had 'created in me a desire for knowledge, that I might know who was right and who was wrong'; he followed them, not his master, to meetings.[66] The distance between master and employees could be protective: William Hart's 'master was an awful profane licentious character, whose conduct I used secretly to abhor'. However, far from emulating his teacher, Hart 'was respected for my steady and moral conduct by the many decent people in the town'; he would find employment afterwards based on the recommendation of a different cooper in the community.[67] As Paul Griffiths argued, too much attention to prescriptive literature, with its focus on the master as patriarch, can obscure the agency of the young. It also masks the importance of influences from outside the household.[68] Indeed, as workshops grew larger and apprentices became more likely to end up as journeymen, not masters, it would be the social world of the journeyman, not the citizen, that they would need to understand.[69]

Patriarchy was not the only model at play in apprenticeship. While apprenticeship fitted snuggly into contemporary hierarchical social models, it also had a powerful contractual element that specified obligations and set boundaries to the master's role in a way that contradicted the patriarchal ideal. In his study of Antwerp, De Munck suggested that 'apprentice contracts made relations between masters and apprentices more businesslike, regardless of any seemingly moral connotations in the terminology they contained'.[70] The aspects of the relationship that he cited to justify this—that the authority of masters to regulate apprentices was ambiguous and could be challenged, that the guilds played little role in shaping apprenticeship, and that ultimate authority remained with apprentices' parents—all apply in England.

Read in this light, the various, seemingly ineffective campaigns run sporadically by early modern guilds and cities to discipline the dress, behaviour, and clothing of apprentices are signals of urban authorities' anxieties about masters' lack of attention to patriarchal duties, or the limits to their authority. That would seem to be the message of complaints such as that by the London Clothworkers guild in 1548 that apprentices 'have so much of their will that they roam abroad and . . . their masters cannot rule and order them'.[71] Either way, these interventions offer little evidence that masters transmitted urban culture in the manner envisaged in the strong form of socialisation.

Finally, the idea of apprenticeship as 'strong' socialisation is equally hard to reconcile with what is now known about the age of apprentices. In the late sixteenth or seventeenth century, when apprentices were often eighteen or nineteen when they started and twenty-five or twenty-six years old when they finished, a great deal of their self-understanding and values must have been deeply embedded in advance of their indenturing as an apprentice.[72] If we take twenty-one as the age of adulthood, as has been suggested for this period, apprentices in the early seventeenth century would have been 'adult' for over half their terms. Two centuries later, when apprentices often started at fourteen, the roles of the master and his household were different: apprentices had become 'boys' rather than the 'lusty fellows' sought by Bartholomew Steer for the Oxfordshire rising.[73] Adulthood and completion of the contract now coincided.

Over the early modern period, apprenticeship labour increasingly *became* adolescent labour.[74] With this juvenilising of training, the importance of socialisation may have grown, but even in 1800 many apprentices would have spent years at work before starting their indentures. Timothy Claxton (b. 1790) had spent a year spinning wool, some time as a shepherd, and a period working in a market garden before being apprenticed at thirteen.[75] Frank Forrest (born c. 1817) worked six years in a mill in Dundee before being bound to a shoemaker.[76] A century earlier, Thomas Hutton spent his time from age eight to thirteen 'apprenticed' in a silk mill before starting a second proper apprenticeship to his uncle, a stocking maker.[77] Such youths hardly needed to be inducted into the disciplines of the workplace.

There is no doubt that apprenticeship was a formative period for the identities of the young. However, this seems largely incidental to the focus of the institution. Apprentices and masters understood their core concern was training in vocational skills.[78]

Specific and General Human Capital

It is worth recognising some of the forms of learning that were absent here. Apprenticeship in early modern England was *not* a mechanism by which youths were supplied with general academic skills.[79] The content of training was closely tied to the practice of a craft or trade. Aside from business skills and the disciplines of the workplace, nontrivial though those are, apprentices did not gain skills that might be applied in a range of domains. In this, premodern apprenticeship differed fundamentally from its twentieth- and twenty-first-century namesakes, which commonly combine training in general and specific skills.

Take two of the most fundamental general skills: literacy and numeracy. There is no evidence that these were part of the usual package of apprenticeship.[80] We can have some confidence in this precisely because of how they were discussed when they do—very occasionally—feature. For example, faced by an apprentice who 'could not write or cast accounts well', Isaac Barnard, a haberdasher, 'gave him leave near upon a year to go to school to learn the same'. Barnard paid for this, but he did not teach. The writing master involved, Richard Allen, received £2 for the twelve months in which he 'taught & instructed [the apprentice] in writing and accounts'.[81] Barnard, it should be noted, had received a premium of £100 with the youth: this was not his own investment, but covered by the apprentices' fee. The shoemaker's apprentice James Lackington used his own small allowance to pay his master's youngest son to teach him to read: 'For every three half-halfpence he taught me to spell one hour; this was done in the dark, as we were not allowed a candle after we were sent upstairs to bed'.[82]

Arrangements to put apprentices to their schoolbooks were rare. In Southampton, in a register of 650 indentures, only one master of a regular apprentice in the seventeenth century contracted to teach his apprentice 'to write and cipher', although a blacksmith taking a ten-year-old pauper apprentice also agreed to keep him at school for the first three years of his term.[83] Similarly, Simon Forman recalled that he had agreed to a long ten-year contract in the 1560s if his master would put him to school for three years.[84] Apprentices might sometimes gain these general skills, but they usually did so by being sent elsewhere to do so, and then only infrequently.

The absence of general human capital from apprenticeship training is easy to explain. For the most part, apprentices learned their letters and numbers—if they learned them at all—before beginning training. For this reason, in his 1747 guide for parents considering apprenticing their children, Campbell identifies trades that *require* literacy or ability in drawing, rather than those that will *teach* it. Similarly, schools anticipated that boys would remain until they found a place as an apprentice.[85]

Literacy was a part of earlier education. Schooling in reading and arithmetic occurred between six and fourteen years of age, whereas apprenticeships rarely started before youths reached fourteen to sixteen. Certainly, some people would learn these skills later, but this was more common among labourers, not skilled workers.[86] Numeracy, even accounting, was in the same category, taught in small mathematical and accounting schools in cities such as London by the sixteenth century.[87] As Campbell notes, those parts of education that 'are universally useful', such as reading, writing, arithmetic, and drawing, should be learned 'before [the apprentice] enters'. If they were not, 'it is seldom that he can find Time to acquire it till he is out of his Time; when he is far from being capable of making any Proficiency'.[88]

James Fretwell's education illustrates this clearly. The son of a timber dealer in Yorkshire, he was sent first to a boarding school. Then, his father,

> thinking that I had got as much of the learned languages as would be of any service to a tradesman, and indeed more than I have retained, thought it time to set me to learn something which more immediately related to the qualifying of me for business: therefore he sent me to Pontefract, to learn to write and accompt.

In Pontefract he gained 'most of the rules of vulgar arithmetic, and decimal fractions, with some little of practical geometry'. Then 'having now acquired as much learning as was thought necessary . . . my parents next care was to put me to some trade or business by which I might get an honest living in the world'.[89] His apprenticeship came next.

What about more advanced knowledge, such as natural philosophy? Where apprentices gained this, it was not from their masters. The few life histories and memoirs by apprentices who did study science, nature, and philosophy emphasise their *self-instruction*. Their own agency led these apprentices—admittedly an exceptional bunch—to gain knowledge beyond the specificities of their craft. Self-instruction took a range of forms, including reading books, talking to people, attending lectures, joining societies, and so on—the same *mélange* of sources employed by entrepreneurs and engineers.[90] They might be studying science while apprentices, but this correlation was not causal; this learning was occurring *outside* their training.

Self-instruction could be collective, in an associational, voluntary manner. For example, Charles Manby Smith, an apprentice printer in early nineteenth-century Bristol, heard about some youths who planned a club

> with a view to mutual improvement. The plan was, to hire a room for three-and-sixpence a week, and to stock it with books, papers, and drawing materials, each one contributing what he could. Subjects were to be discussed, essays written and criticised, the best authors read aloud, and their sentiments subjected to our common remark. I joined at once, without hesitation, and have congratulated myself that I did so to this day. . . . And thus, for six pence a week each, we had an imperfect, it is true, but still an efficient means of improvement at our command.[91]

Another illustration is offered by Charles Whetstone, an eighteenth-century shopkeeper's apprentice in Derby who found in his master's house

> a small library of books, to which I had free access. I read them all: but the work that most engrossed my attention, was 'Derham's Physico Theology, or a Demonstration of the Being and Attributes of God from his Works of Creation'. This very valuable and instructive work I perused with more pleasure and attention, and a greater number of times, than I had ever read any book before.[92]

Whetstone also befriended a surgeon's apprentice who 'was acquainted with several who at their leisure studied Geometry, Chemistry &c. and by borrowing and lending books, they mutually assisted each other'. However, because he 'had very few books to lend; I had less opportunity in the day time to partake of these advantages'. When he did manage to get one, 'I found more gratification in reading them, than I found in sleep'.[93]

One of the later founders of the Mechanical Institution, the whitesmith Timothy Claxton, describes how he sought knowledge beyond his trade. His master's workshop supplied a 'great variety of work', but gaining wider knowledge and skills depended on Claxton's own efforts. He spent his box money, the tips and gifts he received from customers and his master, on a 'good thick cyphering-book' to practise arithmetic. He took evening lessons from a journeyman carpenter who had 'several books full of examples in mensuration of superficies and solids, embracing the methods of measuring various kinds of artificers' work'. He spent his spare time 'in diverse curious experiments', building himself a clock. He never 'heard a lecture on anything, or read a book connected with the arts and sciences, save what I have mentioned, or a poor geography borrowed for a short time'.[94]

Claxton's experience parallels that of apprentice castor-maker Thomas Tryon in the 1650s, whose extensive studies in astrology, chemistry, and medicine were based on books he bought for himself from his extra earnings, and who crammed 'early and late' around his long days working for his master in London.[95] Similarly, Thomas Wright noted how it was in his leisure hours while apprenticed to a clockmaker in Northumberland in the 1720s that he applied 'close to study astronomy and spend all his money in Books'—although his ambitions were disrupted when his father 'by ill-advice think him mad [and] burn[ed] all the books he can get and endeavor to prevent [his] study'.[96] Claxton's reflections were likely coloured by his desire to encourage self-improvement, as were Tryon's, but they serve as a guide to his views about how artisans might gain advanced technical and scientific knowledge.

Masters were rarely involved in such wider learning. They may not have opposed it—Manby Smith's master apparently thoroughly approved of his evenings improving himself (the opposite, evenings of debauchery, was less appealing), but this was not his initiative.[97] Similarly, Claxton's master never objected when he spent his mealtimes preparing parts for his experiments—'in fact, he did not trouble himself about it'.[98]

These narratives highlight the significance of apprentices in constructing their own curriculums.[99] Manby Smith, Claxton, and the like were exceptional in their ardour for learning. Whether they represent a general fashion for self-improvement is hard to say.[100] These accounts also mainly date from the later eighteenth century, when books were cheaper and more accessible. The books the apprentices read were not didactic texts on craft skills. They studied learned, particularly scientific, knowledge in a period when natural philosophy was the focus of much enthusiasm and interest.[101] That we can describe in detail how they learned science from books—even for this handful of people—but cannot offer the same portrayal of how they learned their trade underlines the modest place that formalised propositional knowledge had in the training of apprentices.

Training beyond the Shop Floor: Academies and Technical Education

Apprenticeship can be a composite process of training, with instruction in the firm complemented by other sources of teaching. Learning in early modern workshops was not conceived of as an exclusive relationship between an aspirant youth and an expert master, as we have seen. But what role did organisations outside the workshop play here? Was training within workshops complemented by instruction from other bodies?

This possibility has been highlighted by Bert De Munck, who has discussed the establishment of a pair of teaching institutions in Antwerp in the seventeenth century—the Art Academy and the Medical College. These provided detailed instruction in specific skills using quite different pedagogical techniques—lectures, classes, and so on—to those seen in apprenticeship. De Munck identifies this with a shift in how skills are perceived, and particularly the increasing importance of 'an individualistic culture of humanistic elites'.[102]

Similar institutional innovations occurred across Europe, as cities created centres to teach surgery, pharmacy, art, and drawing, such as the Royal Academy of San Fernando in Madrid.[103] In England, elements of this appear in medicine, with hospital instruction following apprenticeships, and collective training in natural history through herbarising journeys.[104] In navigation, the Trinity House School in Newcastle provided instruction for mariners from 1712. William Richardson recalled studying there while an apprentice in the 1780s, making use of the winter period when his ship was laid up.[105] Yet, they never became common. Another potential channel of teaching, private schools for design, drawing, cookery, and similar skills, appeared in England in the later seventeenth and eighteenth century, but they served only a small share of those in related occupations.[106] These kinds of formal institutionalised instruction can productively coexist with apprenticeship, but they are dependent on different pedagogical strategies—and they may not be more effective or economical. In technical schools where training is disconnected from production, the vocational experience needed to gain artisanal skills is tremendously capital intensive and costly.

It was not until the nineteenth century that apprentices in England finally gained widespread access to technical training institutions.[107] From the 1820s, artisans, employers, and politicians were worrying about workers' capacity to understand the scientific principles involved in their work. This led to the creation of a number of important institutions, including the Mechanics' Institutes, the first in England being established in 1823. After the depression of the 1870s, efforts to expand training intensified. In 1879, the livery companies of London, now mostly propertied charities with limited involvement in trade, created the City and Guilds Institute to supply technical training and qualifications aimed at 'educating young artisans and others in the scientific and artistic branches of their trades'.[108] Then in 1889 Parliament passed the Technical Instruction Act, allowing local authorities to levy a modest tax (one penny on local rates) to fund technical education 'in the principles of science and art applicable to industries'; the act specifically excluded 'the practice of any trade'.[109]

This amounted to a major campaign to transfer high-level general skills to the workforce—that is, to create a generation of workers who could advance industrial production and to invest the state's resources in them. As Alfred Marshall recognised in 1890, 'Technical education has . . . raised its aims in recent years' and was now aiming 'at imparting artistic skill and knowledge, and methods of investigation, which are useful in particular occupations, but are seldom properly acquired in the course of practical work'.[110]

What stands out is not just the ambition of nineteenth-century schemes, but the mechanisms they used. First, this largely occurred outside the firm. Few employers offered to fund or supply instruction directly. As a result, instruction became supplementary to work. It took place through evening classes or weekend schools. Second, it was left to the youths to choose to train—which they did: perhaps a third of boys in the building trade, engineering, printing, and wood and furniture trades in London were taking classes at the end of the nineteenth century, although only 1 per cent of workers took any technical examinations each year.[111] Finally, it required collective action. The subsidies that made technical education financially feasible were drawn from charitable donations or general taxation. Youths on their own could not fund technical schooling, while most firms lacked the interest to provide it.

Formal institutions teaching advanced vocational skills or offering general or technical education were peripheral to the world of the craft or trade apprentice, outside of a few, select occupations, until the turn of the twentieth century. Medicine was one exception, but even there most training was via apprenticeship.[112] Art appears to be another.[113] As Klein observes of the institutions to train experts in mining and engineering that emerged in the eighteenth century, these were occupations that lacked guilds or apprenticeship.[114] Institutions offer a counterpoint and complement to apprenticeship. Students cannot fund their learning through their labour, so they need subsidies from taxation or charity—or access to credit. No wonder that these institutions often depended on wealthy, sometimes royal, sponsors.

Conclusion

Learning skills within premodern apprenticeship relied heavily on the energy of the apprentices, not the masters. The masters gave the youths the chance to observe, practice, and repeat; they provided access to tools and materials; they exposed them to norms, exemplars, and models. They curated the apprentices' encounters with a craft or trade. Much of the rest was left up to the apprentices' own interest in learning. For the learners to gain skills they had to undertake repetitive practice and embed themselves in a field of practice. What they learned was their trade, not general skills, science, or urbanity; it was 'knowledge how'. These characteristics of premodern learning match those identified in modern analyses of how humans gain embodied skills and acquire expertise.[115] This method of gaining skills by watching, copying, and repeating is found across a wide range of anthropological and historical studies of apprenticeship.[116]

Why was premodern apprenticeship structured as a chance to learn? Why not invest more in teaching apprentices, speeding their journeys to high productivity? In part, the reason is economic: the problem of contract enforcement. Apprenticeship was an unstable, fluid relationship; as we will see in the next chapter, many youths would leave their contracts early, and only a tiny number would work for their masters after finishing their indentures. A master who cannot force his apprentice to stick with his contract has little incentive to invest much in training. Whatever they do invest, they need to recover quickly, so productive and profitable work—even if it is unskilled—must feature prominently in the apprentice's daily existence. Even modern firms with high completion rates and the potential for long-term hiring tend to under-invest in training. Early modern production was organised on a small scale, with only a tiny share of workers engaged in long-term relationships to a firm or institution that might justify their employers investing in their abilities.

Another part of the reason is pedagogical, however. Acquiring embodied skills in crafts or trades depends on immersion. Theories of 'active learning' offer a compelling account of the importance of 'monitored participation' in this. As the anthropologist Esther Goody puts it, 'Routinized low-level participation acts to lay down a basic framework of implicit meaning and premises' that allows for mastering skills that 'cannot be taught, but must be learned'; 'the task of the master, in scaffolding this sort of learning has to be managed through the way in which tasks are assigned and monitored'.[117]

Listening to a master articulating how a particular process needed to be executed could only ever be a small part of the overall package of training. By definition, tacit knowledge cannot easily be articulated as guidelines, while learning about the qualities of materials depends on the accumulation of experience.[118] This is one reason why technical education today remains an expensive proposition, because the cost of the capital (tools, materials) tied up in lengthy periods spent at repetition is large. Moving beyond the premodern form of apprenticeship would require external investment by the state and/or firms, with realistic expectations that they were making long-term investments in future employees. In their absence, it was far better for these costs to be integrated into production.

The way that teaching and learning were organised in apprenticeship reflects the problem that transferring craft skills presents to instructors. It was not negligence. Apprenticeship was usually effective and functional, so far as we can tell. The tacit character of occupational skills means that transferring knowledge is slow and difficult. They are literally embodied in the person of the artisan.[119] While codified, academic, or propositional knowledge can be shared in print media, lowering the costs of dissemination between people and places (hence, the famously 'revolutionary' impact of print), acquiring tacit skills depends on a vocational pedagogy that is quite different to everyday pedagogies employed in schools teaching codified skills. Its features include a high volume of practice to instruction; long periods of working on the job at different skill levels; and circulating between workshops to acquire expertise through observation and immersion in different settings.

Printed texts and lessons taken at external institutions were largely absent from apprenticeship in England until the nineteenth century. Their arrival was one of the main shifts in the nature of apprenticeship training. Tacit knowledge was now supplemented with technical education that prepared young workers to engage with a changing economic landscape; firms ceded exclusive control over what apprentices learned to the state; and apprenticeship came to depend on government subsidies to sustain the higher direct cost of training.

6

The Flexibility of Apprenticeship

By nature lustful, and by drink made worse
Fierce over those he knew were bound t'obey,
Nero he seemed,—to us a greater curse,—
Whilst on our bones he furiously would lay,
A wretch so furious in his wrathful ire,
As filled us all with heat, and set our souls on fire.

Such was the wretch, so were his actions vile,
As worth proved of just reproach and shame,
As pushed me sooner to forsake my isle,
To be a stranger, and to merit blame;
Which might alas! My utter ruin been,
Had not Jehovah interposed between.

—GENT, *LIFE*, 26

The ninth of August 1710 found John Gent hiding in the hold of a ship tied up at the docks in Dublin. He had sixpence in his pocket, his best suit, and three loaves of bread to feed him during the voyage to Liverpool. For nearly four years he had served a 'tyrant' who 'cared for no servant, only for his work', as his verse account of his life recalled. Now he would escape. Gent's flight from Dublin took him first to Liverpool and then on to London. In the city, he was fortunate enough to find a new master, Edward Midwinter. Gent started a fresh apprenticeship on 2 October 1710. Where his first master had been 'severe beyond allowance', Midwinter 'like a parent unto me did prove'.[1]

The rules of apprenticeship were strict. The main clauses of English apprenticeship contracts were fixed by law. Apprentices served for a contractual term that was required to be at least seven years in length if it was to qualify them for guild membership, urban citizenship, or, most fundamentally, the right to work in a trade under the Statute of Artificers. During the terms of their contracts, apprentices were subject to the quasi-parental authority of their masters: their manners, entertainment, dress, appearance, and freedom to marry were limited. Their masters' right to chastise them—to beat them, indeed—was unquestioned, as Gent's master knew. Apprentices had no right to absent themselves without their masters' permission.

The legal and contractual framework set out by apprentices' contracts gives an impression of rigidity. In this chapter, I argue that the practice of apprenticeship as a system of training was often much more flexible than the bare terms of the indentures would suggest. To provide a way into the way apprenticeship worked, we will consider whether apprentices followed the most basic of these rules: Did they stay with their masters? If not, how often did they leave, as Gent had, and when?

Focusing on apprentices' persistence offers a powerful insight into how premodern apprenticeship worked. The patterns we can see cohere with the importance of accessing multiple sources of experience for young workers learning a craft, something discussed in the last chapter. Persistence and departures also offer a direct measure of contract performance and raise serious questions about the standard account of apprenticeship in which the master's investment in training was paid off subsequently through their apprentice's skilled work. If contracts were not enforced and apprentices left early, which we will see was often the case, how did masters recover their training costs? Equally, if masters could force out youths, then did apprenticeship really offer stability or serve to socialise youths into urban life?[2] Finally, it raises a question of equity. Which apprentices left their masters, and why? Entry to apprenticeship was relatively open, but insiders may have fared better during their training. If so, openness at point of entry could conceal deep inequalities in opportunity between privileged insiders and less-favoured outsiders which became visible only as the apprenticeship proceeded. As Steven Kaplan suggests, understanding 'success' in apprenticeship requires knowing 'at what point and why does an aspiring apprentice abandon the trajectory'.[3]

This evidence of how apprenticeship operated has implications for several debates about guilds, human capital formation, and premodern economic growth. A number of historians have pointed to specific elements of the institutional framework surrounding apprenticeship as critical to generating an abundance of human capital and transmitting skill and technology widely. In this analysis, guilds, in particular, maintained the stability of contracts in a way that permitted effective long-term exchanges of training and labour services.[4] From a rather different perspective, Sheilagh Ogilvie's interpretation of guilds as rent-seeking institutions also implies that completion rates should be high.[5] Why not finish if the main reason for apprenticeship was to gain the privileges that derived from completion? The persistence of apprentices within their indentures provides us with a test of both hypotheses, that of the contract-enforcing role of guilds and other urban agencies, and that of the centrality of guild rents from their corporate monopoly in justifying apprenticeship. Low levels of persistence cast both into question.

Absent Apprentices

Until recently, historians have known little about what happened to apprentices during their contracts. Memoirs and legal cases provided insights into the world of service, showing the enormous range of experiences that youths faced, from the truly awful to the deeply inspiring.[6] But it has been hard to generalise from these examples. The only quantitative evidence on the completion of apprenticeships that has been widely discussed is the proportion of apprentices later becoming freemen or citizens. This research showed that in many locations, fewer than 50 per cent of apprentices would achieve this status (see chapter 8 for a fuller discussion of this step).[7]

However, as everyone who has written on the topic has rightly acknowledged, data on apprentices becoming members of the guild or citizens provides only a weak guide to what happened during contracts. Former apprentices could have migrated to work elsewhere, or remained as journeymen operating semi-licitly with an unexercised right to the freedom, or they might have changed to another trade or simply died, as many did. It is usually impossible to tell whether apprentices left early, or if their completion of their contracts simply went unrecorded.[8] Becoming a master is a good measure of a former apprentice's success in one career pathway open to them, joining the local guild, but a poor test of how well apprenticeship contracts were honoured in reality since they ignore a wide range of the possible futures facing apprentices.

To understand the stability of apprenticeship contracts, we need to be able to observe who left and when they departed. Fortunately, we can come close to this by linking registers of contracts kept by cities and guilds with listings of the members of households, which were created occasionally, mostly to help raise tax revenues.[9] This process generates a snapshot of which apprentices were living with their masters at the time of the tax listing. Because apprentices began their contracts at different points in time, this evidence supplies an indication of what proportion remained with their masters across the duration of their contracts. For example, those whose contracts started five years before the tax assessment occurred form a cohort of apprentices in the fifth year of their indentures, and so on. Because the taxes tell us who was resident in a household, this method depends on the validity of one key assumption: that apprentices would be living with their masters if they were still serving them. This is the source of its greatest limitation: we cannot be sure if absences are temporary or permanent (or if the youth had ever actually started the contract in reality). And as we will see, apprentices did at times leave and then return.

One other concern is that because these records generally derive in part from taxation, they usually coincided with periods of political and economic conflict that pushed the state to search for new revenue. Much of the data discussed below is drawn from the 1690s. The main sample spans the Glorious Revolution of 1688 and coincides with the Nine Years' War (1688–97), which depressed trade and shipping.[10] By 1695, traders in one of the cities studied, Bristol, had lost 202 ships to the French. English exports to Spain and the Mediterranean had fallen to a quarter of their mid-1680s level.[11] Wartime taxation further pressured manufacturing and trade.[12] Uncertainty around the specie led to a recoinage in 1696 and economic crisis from shortage of coin.[13] Added to bad harvests, this produced high food prices, peaking in 1698, and lower real wages.[14] The situation in 1641, the date of another set of data, was potentially even more tense, with war in Scotland and turmoil in Parliament that would shortly lead to the outbreak of the English Civil War. It is certainly reasonable to expect that these conditions affected whether youths started apprenticeships. It is less obvious, however, that they would affect the main point of interest, the decision to remain in an apprenticeship, once families had invested time and resources in securing access to training in the first place.

What does this type of analysis tell us about the share of apprentices remaining in their contracts? Figure 6.1 shows the pattern of persistence in apprentices in three English cities, London, Bristol, and Shrewsbury, in 1695/6. While reading these, bear in mind that absence may be temporary as well as permanent. These synthetic cohorts will always display a lower

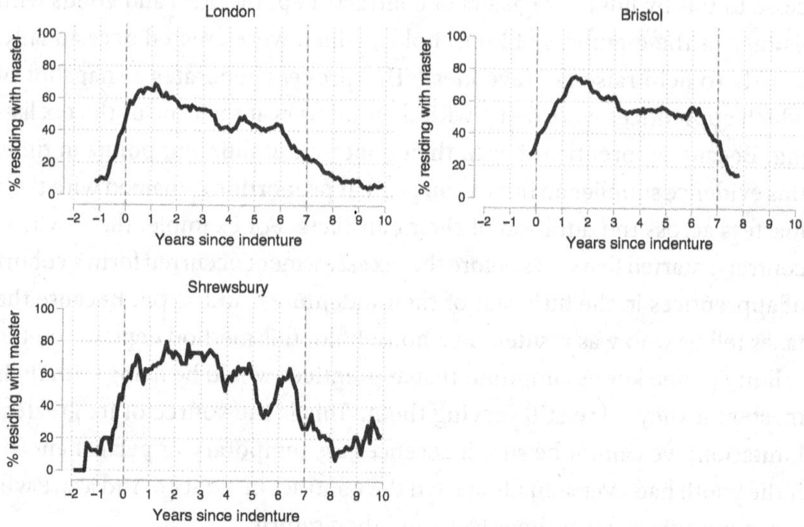

FIGURE 6.1. Apprentices' persistence in London, Bristol, and Shrewsbury, 1695/6. This figure reports smoothed eleven-month rolling averages of the share of apprentices present. For Shrewsbury, this exaggerates volatility as the total sample is small (n=223). For Bristol, this censors the period covered as the sample begins twelve months before the tax date. Note that these graphs are slightly different to those in Minns and Wallis 2012, as apprentices with a recorded turnover are included in the sample and the sample for London is larger.

share of persistence than if we had an accurate record of all the apprentices who had been present at one time or another.

All three cities show clear patterns of staged decline over apprentices' terms. Many apprentices left their original masters' households before their contracts were completed. Most departed in the first half of their terms. In London, the proportion of apprentices present peaked between the sixth and twenty-fourth month of service. It then declined sharply to a trough in year four. After small fluctuations, a final decline then began at the end of the sixth year. Bristol's experience looks broadly similar, although slightly more compressed than London's.[15] In Shrewsbury, much the smallest of the three cities, and the only one without a major share of its workforce tied to international trade and commerce, more apprentices were present with their masters, particularly in the first half of their terms. Nonetheless, even there, around 40 per cent of apprentices disappeared from their masters' households before the end of the seventh and (usually) final year of their contracts.

While the dominant impression in figure 6.1 is the decline in the presence of apprentices over time, it is also clear that the start of apprenticeship was

TABLE 6.1. Apprentices' presence with their masters around the time of binding

	Number of apprentices			Share present		
Period relative to date bound	London N	Bristol N	Shrewsbury N	London %	Bristol %	Shrewsbury %
12–6 months before	38	22	4	0	14	0
6–0 months before	33	82	5	42	17	20
0–6 months after	31	70	11	61	24	55
6–12 months after	46	91	12	70	41	67
1–6 years after	453	885	80	50	58	57

Note: Children bound to their own parents are excluded. Windows of observation are counted from the day before and day after binding.

not clear-cut in these cities. Some apprentices prefaced service with a trial period.[16] The rolling average used in figure 6.1 conceals much of this, but as table 6.1 shows, trial periods were common in London, where 42 per cent of apprentices were already living with their masters in the six months before they were formally bound. Trial periods were less common in Shrewsbury and Bristol, where 20 per cent and 17 per cent of apprentices were present, respectively. In these smaller cities, fewer youths travelled as far to train and costs were lower, allowing more youths to remain with their families while they got to know their masters and trades. Few trials in any location exceeded six months; these apprentices had not been working for long periods as servants in their masters' households before entering their contracts. Indenturing as an apprentice was not a reward for service or a formalisation of a longer-standing arrangement.

The slow arrival of many apprentices is even more striking. Apprentices' training apparently often began much later than the notional start date entered onto their indentures. In London, only around two-thirds of apprentices were present in their first year, with the proportion rising from 61 per cent in the first six months to 70 per cent in the second (table 6.1). Shrewsbury was similar, with the share present rising from 55 per cent to 67 per cent over the year. In Bristol the lag was even more pronounced: the proportion of apprentices present exceeded 50 per cent only a full year after contracts had technically begun. This was not because younger apprentices remained living in their family home while starting to work.[17] Instead, their late arrival in their masters' households reflected an adaptation to the burdensome extent of the seven-year term fixed by law and custom: the legal and effective dates of their contracts differed. That guilds and cities regularly allowed registration to occur up to a year after the contract date facilitated this. A few may even have been sent away to school for a period after the contract was registered.[18]

A great deal of the variation that existed between apprenticeships in different occupations and guilds is hidden by these aggregated trends. Striking differences appear when we focus on particular occupations.[19] This is clearly visible for Bristol, where masters' occupations are recorded (figure 6.2). The most dramatic divergences from the city average, presented in figure 6.1, were among merchant and seafaring apprentices and the building crafts. Merchants' apprentices might travel on behalf of their masters; indeed, their work as overseas factors was often the foundation of their later independent trading and formed an important element in the agreements between the apprentices' families and their masters. This service abroad could be determined formally. For example, the indenture of seafarer apprentice Thomas Garrard specified that 'at the end of three years [he was] to go to sea'.[20] That these apprentices were absent for so much of their service period underlines how in this field, training was centred on experience outside the master's household and immediate presence, but within the framework of his business and under his direction. For building crafts, we see something quite different: the high and stable share over the years suggests that guild control was particularly strong in this highly localised sector.

Focusing on occupations highlights another characteristic. In most trades, the decline in the second half of apprentices' terms was followed by resurgence in the year or so before completion. This end-of-term 'bump' may well be due to apprentices returning to their masters' workshops to regularise their service in the eyes of guild and city. Being present in the final year of their contracts would allow their masters to testify convincingly that they had completed their terms (figure 6.2).[21]

For London, apprentices can only be subdivided by type of guild, which matches occupation more loosely. Even this, however, reveals striking differences. As figure 6.3 shows, the proportion of apprentices present with their masters in the larger, less cohesive, and more mercantile guilds of the 'Great Twelve' falls more dramatically over their terms than in the smaller, more homogeneous other guilds. The level at which apprentices were present at the end of their terms is also higher outside the Great Twelve, suggesting greater concern with regulations. Although the Great Twelve were relatively rich and powerful, their sizes and occupationally varied memberships made monitoring apprenticeship and employment difficult.

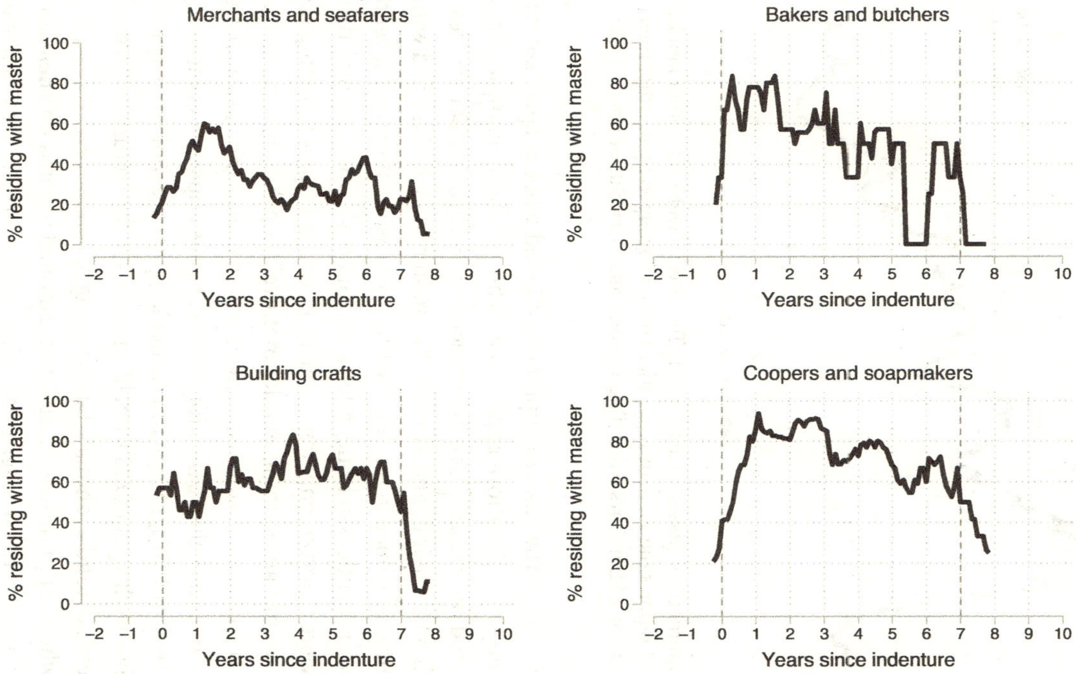

FIGURE 6.2. Apprentices' persistence by occupation, Bristol, 1696. Apprentices are clustered by master's occupation.
Source: See text.

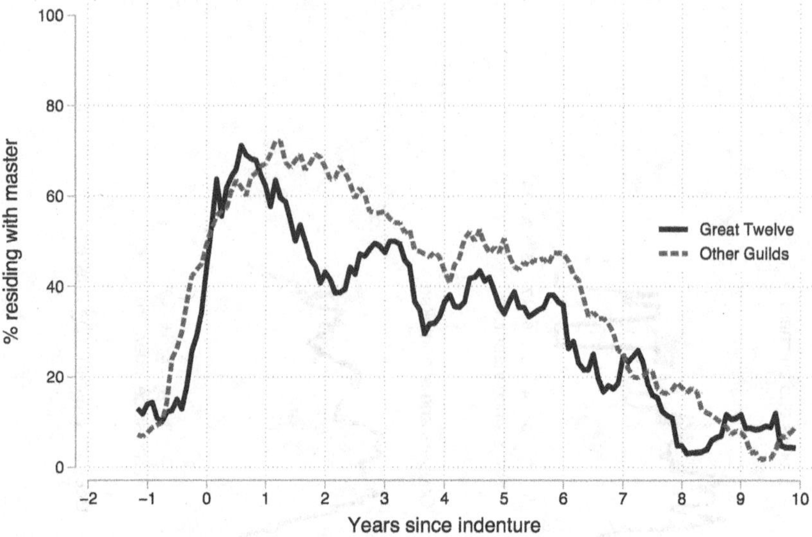

FIGURE 6.3. Apprentices' persistence by guild: The Great Twelve and other guilds, 1695. The figure reports the share of apprentices present grouped by whether their masters were in one of London's Great Twelve companies (n=590) or not (n=982).

One point where the rules of apprenticeship did work as specified was the end of the term. For those apprentices who got there, completion of their contracted time as an apprentice precipitated a firm break (or at least significant shift) in their connections to the masters they had trained with. Few apprentices remained in residence with their masters after their seventh year. Migrant apprentices in London left a little more slowly. However, their departures were deferred only temporarily. In general, apprenticeship did not often lead into an ongoing employment relationship, insofar as one is indicated through co-residence.[22] Even where it did, after seven years, apprentices often took the chance for a break. For example, on completing his term in the early 1780s, Joseph Brasbridge's apprentice took five weeks to see his family—with a gift of £15 from his master—before returning to work as his journeyman (and eventually bankrupting his employer).[23]

On the whole, apprentices more often trimmed months off their contracts than extended them. Laggards at the start of service, they departed precipitously at the end; the proportion present fell from the beginning of their seventh year, if not earlier. Guild records occasionally contain agreements allowing for an apprentice's early completion, sometimes in exchange for a gift or fee. For example, after he had served seven of his eight years, Rowland Bell's master, the London apothecary Thomas Laxton, was willing to 'give him the remainder of his time', and the guild agreed to admit him as a freeman for a £10 fee.[24] London's governors sometimes allowed apprentices to become citizens by redemption towards the end of their terms. In 1696, Richard Baron did this when his master William Poole died; Poole's executor was willing to remit the last year of his term and place Baron 'in his masters shop & trade', wrapping up two aspects of Poole's estate in one move.[25]

However, a far larger proportion of apprentices were absent during their final months of service than official records would indicate. This suggests contemporaries considered a satisfactory level of training was often achievable in fewer than seven years. Youths' time could be better spent elsewhere while they were technically fulfilling their contractual requirements, much as midshipmen in the English navy were entered on to ships' books while they remained at home to acquire notional sea time in the eighteenth century.

This delay in arriving with a master and exit in advance of the date at which the contract was completed had one obvious outcome: most English apprentices' actual period of service was substantially shorter than the seven years that the Statute of Artificers and many guild rules required. This matters for how we envisage the contrast between English apprenticeship and training in other parts of Europe, where terms of service were conventionally shorter. Apprentices systematically circumvented their formal obligations—and their masters must have connived at this for them to have been able to enter contracts and then depart for a period. Shortened terms do not imply that apprenticeship was not conveying sufficient training, however. Most continental European apprenticeships lasted less than seven years, and in England term lengths fell in the late eighteenth century. By trimming their terms, early modern English youths brought their experiences closer to those of their continental peers.[26]

The experience of apprenticeship varied between cities, between trades, and between locals and migrants. Some of this was linked to the nature of work in particular trades. Beyond this, the characteristics of apprentices' families or the masters they joined affected the probability they would remain with their master during their contracted terms.[27] Many of the apprentices who were absent had good prospects elsewhere, while those who remained often possessed local connections that improved their prospects in the city.

In short, at least some apprentices' absences were due to them bettering themselves. In London, for example, the sizes, quality, and locations of apprentices' networks and family resources affected completion. Citizens' sons were significantly more likely to be present with their masters.

Institutional factors also mattered: those whose masters lived within the city walls, where corporate controls were stronger, were more persistent.

It is hard to be sure about whether the experiences of apprentices in these three cities in the 1690s reflect what went on in other times and places. Useable evidence on the performance of apprenticeship contracts is scarce. For a few years in the 1570s, the London Carpenters' Company recorded what happened to apprentices in the margins of its account books. Between 1570 and 1573, 33 per cent were described as 'gone', 1 per cent were married, and 12 per cent had died during their terms. For another 12 per cent, nothing was reported. But only 42 per cent became freemen.[28] This figure of a third 'gone' needs to be read with an awareness of the lingering uncertainty that hangs over the timing of departure—if the alternative was becoming a freeman, perhaps some of those listed here had completed their time before they went. But the balance of outcomes is in line with what we observe in the 1690s, suggesting that the experience of sixteenth-century London apprentices was not dissimilar.

We can match another sample of apprentices against household listings made in London in 1641. The sample is quite large—1,889 apprentices entered contracts with masters identified in the listings between two years before and eleven years after 1641—and 477 apprentices were named among the servants and other residents of these households. Within the core seven years after binding, 409 out of 1,130 apprentices were still in place with their masters when the listing was drawn up. This lower overall level of presence seems to be the result of the tax records being less complete, and the impact of war and political strife may also be at play. However, the trend of persistence over time (figure 6.4) reveals a familiar pattern of late arrival and early decline.

Rural apprenticeship in the late eighteenth century also seems to bear comparison with urban patterns a century earlier. Faced with the looming threat of Revolutionary France, a list of all males aged between fifteen and forty-five who could serve in the militia was drawn up in Buckinghamshire in 1798.[29] For most communities, the list notes if those listed were apprentices or servants, as well as giving the occupations of most males. Buckinghamshire was a mainly agricultural area with a few small towns and villages; however, between 1790 and 1798, the stamp tax registers include 613 male apprentices taken by masters who lived in those parts of the county that were included in the militia list, and who paid tax on their apprenticeship premiums. This information means annual rates of persistence can be estimated.

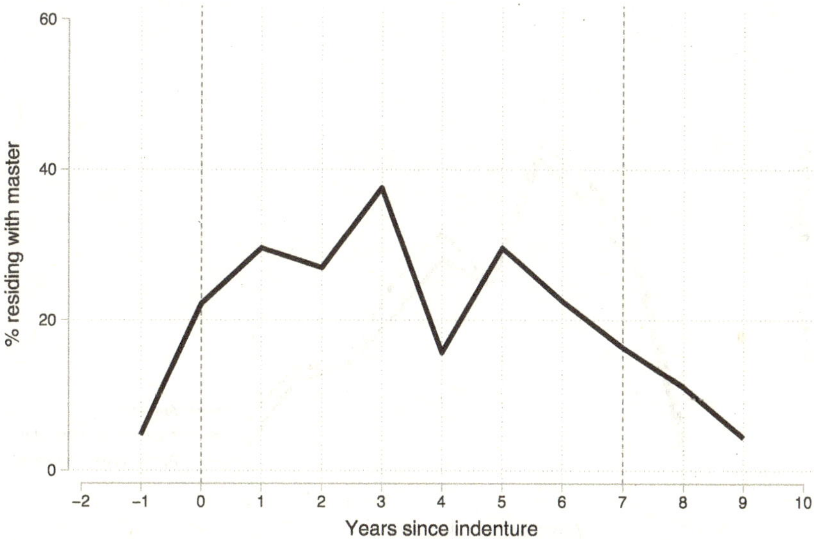

FIGURE 6.4. Apprentices' persistence in London, 1641.
Source: See text.

As figure 6.5 indicates, the share of youths found to be with their masters falls away in the middle of their terms in a way that is very similar to what is seen in England's largest cities in the 1690s.

Completion rates were also poor among London's parish apprentices in the first decade of the nineteenth century, according to evidence gathered by a parliamentary commission in 1815. These pauper youths were, as already mentioned, in many respects quite different to private apprentices in age and origin. Most were working in textile mills, again further distancing them from most private apprentices in artisanal and service occupations in cities. Nonetheless, it is striking that out of 1,486 pauper apprentices placed with masters in the country in the first decade of the nineteenth century, 17 per cent (246) had been turned over to a different master. Many of those studied by the commission were still serving their indentures, but of those who were not, just two-thirds (207) had served their time successfully, while a full third had either died (80), run away (166), or been sent back to their families (57).[30]

One contrary piece of evidence needs to be mentioned. In his seminal study of the eighteenth-century rural economy, Keith Snell argued that apprenticeship weakened markedly later in the century. The most concrete

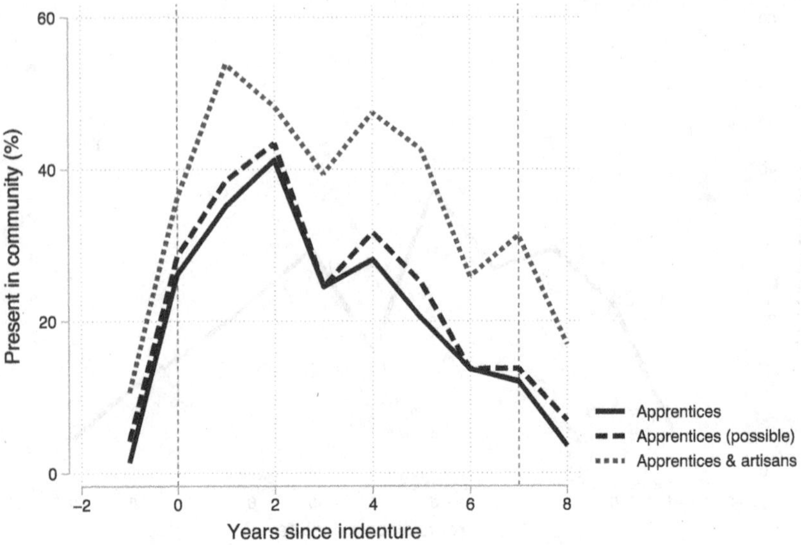

FIGURE 6.5. Apprentices' persistence in Buckinghamshire, c. 1790. The figure reports the presence of apprentices within the same communities as their masters, because the listings are organized by place, not household.
Source: See text.

symptoms were a fall between 1750 and 1795 in the time apprentices actually served, from 6.5 to under four years, and a rise in the share of apprenticeships that were illegal or that ended prematurely, from below 5 per cent in the 1750s to around 20 per cent from the 1780s. Both were observed among former apprentices subject to a settlement examination.[31] Snell interpreted this as a decline in the quality of apprenticeship; it amounted to a 'new found flexibility' in the system.[32] If this flexibility was in fact 'new found', this would contradict, or substantially complicate, the account given here. We would also need to explain why almost all settlement examinations report only completed apprenticeships until the 1760s, given the evidence from other sources that non-completion was common before then.[33] However, it is not clear that Snell's data captures a real change in apprenticeship. In the same period that settlement examinations start recording short and unfinished apprenticeships, justices of the peace were changing how they interpreted the right to settlement; this was the set of rules that defined who could claim poor relief in a parish, and was the reason for which these sources were produced.[34] In 1758, new legislation restated the rule (seemingly ignored before) that forty days of service as an apprentice, not the completion of indentures, provided apprentices with a local settlement.[35] It was soon after this legislation appeared that reported terms of service began to decline.

There is good reason to believe that, at a general level, the high rates of early departure apparent in London, Bristol, and Shrewsbury in the later seventeenth century were a feature of English apprenticeship in the early modern period. There was no great change to the other, less precise measure of persistence—rates of entry to the freedom—in this period, or indeed across several centuries before 1800, as we will see in chapter 8. Similarly, the institutional system of civic apprenticeship appears to have functioned stably: the strength of English guilds has been debated, but they continued to register apprentices and policed the number recruited.[36]

Although the levels of early exit visible in the sixteenth to eighteenth centuries appear high, it is likely that instability increased in the nineteenth century, following the abolition of the Statute of Artificers and the impact of industrialisation and ever greater urbanisation. In Durham, where a few guilds continued to register apprentices into the 1850s, the volume of turnovers and cancellations they recorded grew sharply in the nineteenth century. The share of apprentices affected doubled between the 1760s and 1820s and reached 32 per cent in the Barbers and 35 per cent in the Cordwainers guilds.[37]

Evidence from apprenticeship elsewhere in Europe suggests that early exits from masters were a general phenomenon of pre-industrial training. At least a third of apprentices in the silk industry in Lyon, France, in the eighteenth century would leave their contracts early, with 18 per cent cancelling their contracts, 15 per cent transferring to a different master, and 1 per cent dying. In several Dutch guilds in the eighteenth and early nineteenth centuries, between 42 and 53 per cent would quit and 11 per cent would transfer; these rates grew over time as the economy modernised.[38] Exactly the same distribution of absences seen in London and Bristol also occurred in these Dutch guilds: local youths, especially those with a link to the guild, were significantly more likely to remain. Family ties were the most powerful force affecting whether apprentices remained with their masters, though. These observations from Lyon and the Netherlands are lower and upper bounds, respectively, because of the types of sources that survive, but they suggest a broadly similar pattern.[39] They are not alone. In Vienna in the same period, the share of terminated contracts varied between 30 and 57 per cent, depending on guild and gender.[40] Half of the poor children apprenticed at Turin's Albergo di Virtù and between a quarter and a third of charity orphans in Lyon in the late eighteenth century left their places early.[41] Departures from masters were, it seems, a common feature of premodern apprenticeship across the continent.

Why Did Apprentices Leave?

What had happened to the one in two apprentices who were missing from their masters' homes? Why had they left? There are several explanations for apprentices' absences.[42] For some apprentices, absence reflected their exit from the trade as well as their master's household. Perhaps 10 per cent of apprentices died during their terms and more sickened—migrating into cities carried serious health risks.[43] To give one example, Isabella Harris's brother was forced to leave his apprenticeship to a cabinetmaker in the 1770s because of 'his health declining'.[44]

Less tragically, some apprentices simply dropped their trades because they disliked them or their employers, or they were ejected by their masters for disorderly behaviour (often drunkenness and violence), crime, marrying, or some other breach of their indentures. Examples of this abound. During three years apprenticed to his uncle, a Nottingham stocking-maker, Samuel Hutton, found the work so dull he 'ran away about ten times' before his final exit left him to find a makeshift living working for a butcher and later a mason in London and then Essex.[45] It would be five years before he returned to Nottingham. Samuel's brother William, who was apprenticed alongside him, also stuck at his work for three years before a quarrel with his uncle 'upon a mere trifle'—how hard they were working during the annual Nottingham races—'caused me to run away, blasted my views, sunk me in the dust, and placed me in a degrading point of view', as he later recalled.[46] Frank Forrest was ejected by his shoemaker master Isaac Dobson after composing a parody 'in which the weak and prominent points of Mr Dobson's character were rather ludicrously and painfully exposed'.[47] Samuel Hick (b. 1758) was dismissed when his master, the blacksmith Edward Derby of Healugh, Yorkshire, came downstairs earlier than usual one morning and found his daughter seated on Samuel's knee.[48]

For others, good fortune intervened. Gervase Disney had served four years of his apprenticeship with Martin Oglethorp, a silkman and merchant in Lombard Street, London, when the coincidence of the death of his eldest brother Cornelius and the outbreak of the Great Plague led his father, the country gentleman John Disney, to recall his now heir to the family home, Norwell Hall in Nottinghamshire. As Disney recalled, 'My Father prevailed with my Master, to give me leave to retire into the country, to him, during that Visitation. Accordingly, I came down in the Year 1665, to my Father's House'. He would never return: 'I presently was under Temptation to think that I must now carry it out, and live at the Rate of my Father's Eldest Son, and not as Mr. Oglethorp's apprentice and servant'. Instead of trade, he now practiced 'good Fellowship': 'I learned to drink and game and smoke Tobacco, and trifle' and 'could sometimes most wickedly triumph in my Ability to bear strong Drink'.[49]

The terms of apprentices' indentures could be broken by both parties of course, and problems on their masters' part feature prominently in apprentices' memoirs and court cases.[50] Probably the most common crisis was when the master's business failed. Arise Evans's service to a tailor in Westchester in the early 1600s ended after two years when 'my Master broke, and he sent me home to Merionethshire'. Evans was not disappointed, having found it a difficult place: 'I endured much hard usage, my Master not being a good husband and having a cross piece to his wife, made him worse'. He would eventually complete his term with his original master's father-in-law, Hugh Evans of Wrexham, 'until my Master was satisfied and I had my indentures'.[51] David Haggart's service with a firm of millwrights and engineers in Edinburgh ended with their bankruptcy, but he then fell into a career as a pickpocket and was eventually tried and executed for murder.[52]

Underlying these departures was a clear understanding that the contractual terms of apprenticeship were conditional. Apprentices need only continue to serve while their masters remained in a position to employ, maintain, and train them. At least in their own eyes, this extended to a right to fair treatment. In the aftermath of being beaten by his master 'for his mist[res]ses sake, herself being in fault', an outraged Simon Forman 'told his master flat that he had not performed his covenants according to promise and therefore he would give over the trade and go to his books again'.[53]

While it is easy to assume that apprentices' exits were rooted in conflict, at least some apprentices conspired with their masters to evade rules on citizenship, pretending to serve while actually following a different occupation or working independently. This 'colourable' service, as contemporaries styled it, allowed them to acquire the rights that came with completion of an apprenticeship without actually learning the trade. For example, in 1711, Thomas Blee was accused at the London Lord Mayor's Court of being 'turned over to . . . a Carman under colour of Service but never actually served him as an apprentice but hath ever since acted as a Porter'.[54] In 1677, Bristol's Tolzey Court had heard a similar accusation that Peter Harris's service to Roger Bagnall was

> a design to gain the freedom this City at the expiration of the said term Although the said Roger Bagnall doth not use or exercise the said trade of a Grocer or any way employ the said Apprentice who doth not live in the house or service of the said Roger Bagnall but resides with his father.[55]

Others negotiated terms that were shorter than their indentures stated. James Fretwell's brother, for example, 'was bound for seven years [in 1723]; but, by a particular agreement, was to be at liberty at Martinmas 1729'. The master he joined, Henry Abbey, a chandler and grocer in Doncaster, was no marginal figure and would be elected an alderman in 1731 and mayor in 1733.[56] Similarly, when James Lever bound his son James to Mr Ludlow of the London Coopers' Company, they agreed that James was 'to trade for himself in 4 or 5 years after he had been with him'.[57] Ludlow was probably a leading merchant, given the £400 premium Lever paid.[58]

As the last two examples indicate, not every departure from a master equated to an exit from the trade. Many absent apprentices continued to learn or practise the trade they had begun to learn when they were indentured to their masters. One London shoemaker's apprentice, Benjamin Bangs, quit after three years because he 'understood [his] business pretty well'; similarly, a Bristol weaver's apprentice, John Mayes, left after three years to work as a weaver in the countryside.[59] Both remained active in the trade they had been taught, but now kept their earnings for themselves, much as Lever had arranged for his son to do.

Those who left without permission from their masters might struggle against the suspicion of runaways and the risk of pursuit by their masters. Having quit Nottingham, William Hutton, an apprentice stocking-maker, was repeatedly refused work by masters elsewhere: 'Go about your business, I tell you, you are a runaway prentice', one told him.[60] The printer's apprentice John Gent, whose story we began with, was arrested by his former master 'for leaving my apprenticeship' when he returned to Dublin to visit his family, and had to flee the country again. It was not until 1717 that his parents managed to negotiate a discharge for him, at the cost of £5. 'Thus I became absolutely free, both in England and Ireland, which made me give sincere thanks to the Almighty from the inward recesses of my soul', Gent recalled.[61]

Runaways like Hutton and Gent tend to dominate the official sources—which are largely derived from legal disputes over contracts. However, it seems likely that this kind of contested exit represented the exception, not the rule. Halfway through his second contract, John Gent's master Midwinter gave him permission to 'work with whom you please'. Gent could stay if he wished, but as it was a quiet period for the firm, Midwinter suggested he 'make use of this opportunity by improving more with others', thus assisting them both.[62] Masters' changing need for labour meant that even permanent departures could be useful. If mutually agreed, departure normally occurred without any external record, concealing it from the institutional paper trail that we rely on as historians, and it need not mark an end to their training, let alone an end to their work in a trade.[63]

Apprentices who sought to leave their original masters permanently while continuing their apprenticeships had to be 'turned over' to other masters in the same craft. These transfers of contract were common and allowed apprentices to still qualify for civic and guild membership. Turning over was a response to an event that made the original agreement untenable, such as the death, sickness, bankruptcy, or retirement of the master. For example, when the calico-printer Richard Emery of West Ham in Essex gave up his business in the 1760s, his apprentice of five and a half years, Francis Joyce, was forced to find a different master. Joyce eventually joined one Mr Tallvin of Bromley by Bow for his last eighteen months of service.[64] Guild and urban authorities recorded turnovers inconsistently, missing many, perhaps most of them. Even so, in the well-organised London Apothecaries' guild in the seventeenth century, 17 per cent of apprentices were recorded as turned over to another master, the same share seen in the Dyers in the early eighteenth century.[65] Apprentices might experience both formal and informal turning over, complicating the picture. For example, Thomas Gibbs, a London baker's apprentice, served a different master for the first six years of his term 'but was not turned over to him according to ye Custom'. However, he was then formally 'turned over before ye Chamberlain to Joseph Golding of ye same Company & Trade with whom he completed the term'.[66]

Turnover is, in fact, under-represented in the direct evidence of persistence in London and Bristol the 1690s. Because we observe only apprentices whose masters were alive and still maintaining households, cases where a move would have been forced on a youth by the death, sickness, or failure of their master are excluded.[67] As a result, the absences visible in figure 6.1 under-estimate the share of apprentices who would have experienced a change of master or a forced exit from training. The 1690s sample offers some sense of the frequency with which apprentices were turned over to masters in the same city. Among the other people listed by the tax assessors as servants and apprentices in London masters' homes were sixty-five individuals, present as apprentices, servants, or lodgers, who had been indentured to a *different* master in the same guild during the previous seven years (of course, some may have been only temporarily absent from their original masters).[68] This category of mobile apprentices made up 14 per cent of the apprentices active in their businesses at any one time. In Bristol, similarly, movement to another master in the same trade and city might account for between 2 and 10 per cent of apprentices absent in 1695.

That absences were a mixture of turnovers moving apprentices to work in a different firm in the same trade and permanent departures from both occupation and service is also visible in the rates with which apprentices became citizens and freemen.[69] In both cities, masters had to swear that their apprentice had served his full indenture 'after the manner of an Apprentice' before they could be freed; the penalty for dishonesty was disenfranchisement for both.[70] Freedom rates thus offer an indication of the extent to which absence indicated a breakdown of service and training. Unsurprisingly, most of the apprentices who later became citizens were living with their masters.[71] However, a minority of those who were absent did later become citizens—33 per cent in London, 28 per cent in Bristol, and 7 per cent in Shrewsbury (we discuss the rate at which apprentices became citizens in greater depth in chapter 8).[72] This again implies that temporary periods of absence from their masters, and often their cities, were a common part of the experiences of apprentices, and that this was particularly normal in larger centres with more specialised economies that offered a wider range of other opportunities.

Conclusion

Looking at evidence of when and why apprentices continued to live and work with their masters shows us that the institution of apprenticeship was much more fluid than is traditionally understood. Early modern English apprenticeship was never 'inflexible'.[73] Instead of creating a rigid bond that fixed youths into years of subordination to their masters, it was often revised and adjusted. Apprentices frequently started late, often left temporarily or permanently after serving only part of their terms, and commonly finished early. This fits poorly with arguments for guild enforcement of contracts and for guild privileges as the motivation for apprenticeship.

Some departures took youths away from a trade. But those apprentices who permanently left service early were not necessarily training 'failures'. Often, they departed after three to four years—around the point at which many continental contracts would have finished. One consequence of this is that, in practice, English apprenticeship resembled the system of training used in France, Germany, and many other parts of Europe, in which comparatively short apprenticeships were followed by another few years of engagements as a journeyman, usually across a range of different towns and firms.[74] This was not the only similarity. Apprentices in England were more likely to exit when they lacked strong local ties and had good prospects elsewhere, while insiders stayed more often. Patterns of persistence among apprentices in the Netherlands and France reveal similar early exits and turnovers to those that seen in England.[75] For all that chance and conflict impact on young people's lives, there is a perceptible rationality to the decisions they took about their futures.

Even among the half of apprentices who did complete their terms, many had, in reality, served terms that were somewhat shorter than seven years, or were intermittent, consisting of a few years in residence followed by time spent working elsewhere. A large minority had served several masters in succession, whether the transfer of their contract was formalised or not. While apprenticed, they experienced significant mobility, gaining exposure to different workshops and businesses.

Some movements reflected the practicalities of operating a business—the variability of work, most obviously, meaning that masters sometimes needed more or fewer hands to assist them and used apprentices to balance these needs. Economic upturns and periods of depression must have played an important role in this. However, a substantial amount of mobility was intended to provide further useful training and experience to the apprentices. Flexibility was, at times, pedagogical, and the use of mobility for learning described in the last chapter was widespread.

This characteristic instability of premodern apprenticeship is another of the major fault-lines that separate it from its modern descendants. Few of the reasons that are sometimes proposed to explain why modern companies take apprentices, such as using the training period to gain information about employees' skills, or why apprentices remain in service, such as the chance to earn higher earnings in the firm after completion, could apply in this context.[76] Nor can we credibly envisage masters making investments in their apprentices' skills, with the expectation they can recoup them later on in their terms of service, as some standard accounts of training envisage.

With such high rates of departure, individual masters stood a high risk of losing their investments along with their apprentices. The numbers that most masters trained were too small for this risk to be amortised across a pool of trainees, while the fragmented organisation of production meant that there were large numbers of outside options open to apprentices. For this reason, those who were more likely to leave paid higher premiums.[77] From this observation comes one explanation for the longer duration of early modern training contracts and some of the core characteristics of learning in apprenticeship explored in chapter 5: masters expected a relatively high level of productive work from youths from the start of their indentures, even if it was in unskilled tasks, and they gave them relatively low levels of costly direct instruction, in part because they could not be sure they would stay and work later in their contracts.

Early modern apprenticeship generated slower training than some alternatives because of this instability. Modern firms can invest more heavily in training, as they can bear the risk and have a stronger position in the labour market, increasing the opportunity cost of quitting for apprentices.[78] But no real equivalent to today's large businesses existed before the 1800s. Early modern families could also train their own children more intensively at home, given the stronger hold parents had over their children's choices. But this option was not available for all, and it carried other costs and limited the range of opportunities for children.

We should also recognise that allowing failure, if that is how we should see apprentices' early exits, has its own value. It permitted individuals to change occupation and adjust to what they discovered about their aptitude for a craft or trade as they trained. Contracts that successfully lock in apprentices come at the price of committing them to a decision made early in their teenage years with limited information about themselves, the likely shape of the economy nearly a decade later, and their future resources.

The frequency of absences from apprenticeships means that most, presumably, were consensual. Still, qualitative sources indicate that at least some were not. This raises an obvious question: What were the organisations that were supposed to be monitoring and enforcing apprenticeship contracts doing? We turn next to the contribution that guilds, city governments, and rural magistrates made to the enforcement of apprenticeship in England.

7

Enforcing Apprenticeship

One Monday in high summer 1647, the assistants and master of the Barber Surgeons' Company of London gathered after lunch to hear a complaint by one of their guild brethren, a Mr Heydon. His apprentice—present in court but never named—was, he said, guilty of 'evil and stubborn behaviour towards him and frequent absences out of his service in Day time and in late houses at night'.[1] Heydon's apprentice gave an answer that was as troubling as the charge. The clerk recorded that he 'did rudely and most irreverently behave himself towards his said Master and the whole Court in saucy language and behaviour using several Oaths protesting That he will not serve his Master Whatever shall come of it'. Outraged, the court ordered 'the hair of the said Apprentice (being indecently long) to be cut shorter'. Whether or not the apprentice's provocative challenge to their authority reflected the heightened political temperature in the city—Cromwell had taken control of Parliament just two days before, and the Levellers were to publish their manifesto a few weeks later—is impossible to say.[2] Either way, the vignette captures one common view of the role guilds played in early modern apprenticeship: that they heard and resolved disputes between masters and apprentices, thereby enforcing apprenticeship contracts.

We can see a quite different response to apprenticeship troubles in the memoir of the London silversmith and cutler Joseph Brasbridge. After facing bankruptcy in the 1790s (Brasbridge attributed his failure to his journeyman—also his former apprentice—embezzling funds), he had scraped together enough to take a shop on Fleet Street, just one door down from his previous establishment.[3] When a Mr Horton came to him with a potential apprentice with a premium of 200 guineas, Brasbridge seized the opportunity to add to his capital.

'For a twelvemonth we went on very smoothly together', he recalled, but then 'the young man took it into his head that he would go to India, and began to play off a few airs of the nabob'. Things reached a crisis when Brasbridge asked him to go to a banker in the city, to which his apprentice replied

> that he did not choose to walk that way, but if I had anything to do towards the parks, he had no objection to going. 'Then it seems,' said I, 'that you are growing a great man; and that we are to have a fight for superiority, in which case the Chamberlain must be the umpire: I shall therefore go to him, and inform him of it'. 'You must be quick then', replied the young aspirant after oriental wealth, 'or I shall brush'. Accordingly, I set off, but on my return I found he had already brushed, as he termed it.

With the apprentice gone, Brasbridge went to Mr Horton and told him what had occurred, 'adding that as his ward had nothing to complain of, the apprentice-fee was forfeited in law, by his leaving me without cause'. Nonetheless, 'as honor and equity had far stronger claims upon me than any that the mere letter of the law could urge, I should do what I thought fair and just in dividing the matter, restoring one hundred and retaining one'. With this, 'both Mr Horton and myself were equally satisfied'.[4]

Brasbridge's account offers a rare glimpse of how problems in apprenticeship could be resolved informally in London. Brasbridge made no mention of calling on his guild, the Vintners. However, he did reference one of the city's other key institutions in apprenticeship when he invoked the city's chamberlain. Visible too are the city's norms about how to deal fairly with the premium when apprenticeship broke down. Brasbridge explicitly justified his restitution of half the premium as fair, because there was no cause for complaint. A similar idea of equity linked to contract performance was applied in the second of London's major institutions for supervising apprenticeship: the Lord Mayor's Court.

In this chapter I answer the question that emerges naturally from last chapter's description of the flexibility of apprenticeship, with its high level of absences and departures, including exits like that of Brasbridge's apprentice: What were the institutions that could have enforced apprenticeship contracts doing? Why didn't they prevent this? The answer can be found in the activities of the various formal institutions that oversaw apprenticeship and policed contracts and the behaviour of apprentices and masters in early modern England. Although the example of Brasbridge comes from the 1790s, the institutional framework I describe had been in place for centuries.

What the chapter shows is unexpected. Urban officials and city courts played a critical role in the practice of apprenticeship that has previously gone largely unnoticed, and this contributed significantly to legitimising the flexibility traced in the last chapter.[5] They even offered a mechanism to recover a portion of the premium, when masters were less generous than Brasbridge.

The presence of the chamberlain in Brasbridge's story shows one side of this: city officers could discipline and punish apprentices. However, more important was the approach the courts took to apprenticeship contracts. Both the scale of the courts' involvement and the way they rebalanced the asymmetries of power in master-apprentice relationships mattered.[6] Urban courts gave apprentices agency to defend themselves in disputes with their masters, as did rural justices of the peace. They allowed them a way to terminate or transfer contracts. In London, the courts' contribution was even more extreme. Many metropolitan apprenticeship contracts were deliberately executed in a way that permitted apprentices to exit at will. Where masters had large sums at risk in apprenticeship, however, central courts offered a counterbalance based on bonds that paralleled the main indentures.

The city and courts' work far outweighed the contribution of the guilds, such as the Barber Surgeons that Heydon appealed to. In arguing this, I depart from the line taken by many historians of apprenticeship. Cases such as that between Heydon and his apprentice convinced Dunlop that that the 'supervision of the gilds over their members, and, to a lesser extent, that of the municipal authorities over freemen, was a far greater protection to the boy against a bad master than was the then weak arm of the law'.[7] This idea was most fully articulated by Epstein, who suggested that premodern guilds' 'primary function' was 'to enforce contractual norms that reduced opportunism by masters and apprentices'.[8] It is an influential model that has been expanded upon by de la Croix, Doepke, and Mokyr; in their analysis, guilds improved on clan-based systems of contract enforcement and so increased the diffusion of productive knowledge in pre-industrial Europe.[9]

Epstein's analysis offers an optimistic interpretation of how guilds could sustain apprenticeship. More pessimistic accounts of guilds also exist. One line of thought is rooted in Adam Smith's critique of guilds as naturally self-serving bodies.[10] An implication is that guild supervision of apprenticeship contract performance will be biased towards their members—the masters—at the expense of their apprentices. Guilds might facilitate exploitation rather than acting as a neutral arbitrator. This kind of biased coercion of apprentices occurred in magistrates' courts during the nineteenth century.[11] Elements can be seen in the Barber Surgeons guild's imposition of a humiliating punishment on Heydon's apprentice: hair-cutting, an act of symbolic violence that restored the social hierarchy as much as offering justice.

This chapter begins by concentrating on London, where most urban apprenticeship occurred and the system was most developed. The first section tests the standard account of enforcement, by examining the role that London guilds played in monitoring and enforcing apprenticeship. It then turns to the role of London's central urban institutions, tracing the work of the city chamberlain and the Lord Mayor's Court, before looking at the way bonds offered a counterpart to the flexibility they provided. The final section considers evidence from other cities and towns and rural magistrates to see if the way apprenticeship worked in London was reflected elsewhere in England.

Guilds and Discipline

Most of the surviving primary evidence on English guilds' actions comes from London. London's records are extensive and detailed, allowing us to explore the everyday activities of guilds. Their survival also reflects their greater institutional capacity. Most London guilds were independently incorporated by royal charters, giving them a clear legal basis for overseeing the working lives of their members. Their members also trained the majority of English guild apprentices, as we saw in chapter 2. If any English city's guilds had the capacity and interest to monitor apprenticeship, it was London's. They offer the best test of the potential of guilds to enforce apprenticeship contracts.

There can be no doubt that guilds were a central institution in the regulation of apprenticeship in corporate towns. Their records are full of the registrations of new apprentices and the admissions of former apprentices as freemen. Guilds' governing bodies formed a court manned by established traders and craftsmen who could arbitrate disputes between masters and apprentices; guild ordinances often required members to bring disputes with another member to be heard by the guild before resorting to external courts, and they frequently banned masters from poaching apprentices from each other. Guilds also carried out searches of their members' businesses to identify badly made, underweight, or poor-quality products. Fault could be punished by the seizure of goods, periods of imprisonment, or corporal punishment.[12] During searches, which occurred regularly in the sixteenth and seventeenth centuries at least, poorly clothed, visibly abused, or ill-fed apprentices might be spotted.[13] And to back up their decisions, guilds could call on the support of local urban governments. These two capacities—to settle disputes and to inspect and rectify conditions—could have provided the foundations for a robust system of guild enforcement.

But did guilds actually match the attention they gave to registering apprentices' enrolment with a parallel effort at regulating what happened during apprenticeship? The answer can be found in the records of their governing bodies, the 'Courts of Assistants' that were both executives and tribunals. It is in their minute books that one would expect to see traces of any interventions and punishments, disputes and complaints.

To assess the part played in apprenticeship by London guilds between the early sixteenth and late eighteenth centuries, I examined the records of nine guilds. They include guilds dominated by overseas merchants and wholesalers in the Merchant Taylors and Grocers, finishers and exporters such as the Clothworkers, local service providers such as the Apothecaries, and several kinds of artisanal manufacturers including the Bakers, Brewers and Carpenters, serving local markets, and the Pewterers and Goldsmiths, with a wider audience. Four of the nine (the Grocers, Merchant Taylors, Clothworkers, and Goldsmiths) were among the large and powerful Great Twelve that provided the city's aldermen. Others were smaller and sometimes newer, with less political reach but potentially more internal cohesion.

Collectively, the guilds studied here were responsible for a substantial share of the city's apprentices. In the sixteenth century, they registered around a third or more of London apprentices. This fell to around one-seventh by the eighteenth century, as the Merchant Taylors, in particular, recorded far fewer indentures. Several, notably the Apothecaries, Brewers, Goldsmiths, and Pewterers, were relatively homogeneous, with most members involved in their trade, and an active and interventionist leadership. For each guild, I read the surviving records of their governing body for a continuous two- or three-year period, at half-century intervals. For some, I also reviewed the wardens' accounts if they recorded fines. In total, the sample covers the detailed record of meetings and actions over more than 120 years of guild activity.

The guilds' records reveal an illuminating absence of apprenticeship monitoring. There is a marked scarcity of complaints by masters or apprentices and a lack of interventions to resolve disputes.[14] This is not because of record keeping. Cases are present. For example, on 3 February 1577, the

Court of Assistants of the Goldsmiths heard from the 'friends' (including family) of John Pynkenam, apprenticed to Joseph Harryson, who requested that John

> might be well used of his Master & to be cleanly kept, the wife of the said Josephe Harryson being at this instant present, promised in her husband's behalf, that her said apprentice should be better looked unto for his keeping and also well used, or else her said husband should redeliver into his said friends' hands such money as he her said husband received of them with the said boy, always reserving such allowance for his meat and drink as shall be thought agreeable to reason.[15]

The cases that do appear are usually reported with great care; the need to maintain a record that could be referenced in future required nothing less.

Table 7.1 shows a count of the number of disputes between apprentices and masters that these guilds dealt with per year. These were all issues brought by a master or apprentice; none emerged from guild searches. Apprenticeship disputes turned up just once or twice a year in most guilds.

Disputes were more common in the sixteenth century, when the numbers of apprentices in each guild was lower. In the 1580s, the Bakers, Clothworkers, Goldsmiths, and Merchant Taylors were all dealing with around one dispute every two months or so. By the late seventeenth century, most guilds had lost any involvement in arbitrating or supervising the practice of apprenticeship. In the eighteenth century there were no cases at all.

Most of the disputes that guilds heard were about the conditions that apprentices experienced, the service they provided, and losses of money or goods: the usual themes were excessive 'correction' (physical punishment), poor food and drink, unlicensed absences or indolence, and theft and embezzlement. Only three disputes in our sample involved an apprentice explicitly stating that 'want of instruction' drove him to complain.[16] None touch on masters poaching each other's apprentices, despite the high mobility of apprentices described in chapter 6.

Guilds either heard the issue or they appointed arbitrators. Often, they sought to reconcile the master and apprentice, as when the master and wardens of the Clothworkers' Company instructed John Wells and William Este to 'go home with their said master, and do him faithful and true service, as good and true apprentices ought to do', with a warning to their master to feed and clothe them better in future—something he apparently failed to do afterwards.[17] The process often equated to voluntary arbitration. In the Carpenters, for example, John Hammond and his apprentice John Saunders

TABLE 7.1. Apprenticeship disputes per annum, selected guilds

Company	1530s	1580s	1630s	1680s	1730s	1780s
Apothecaries	n/a	n/a	1.3	0	0	0
Bakers	1.0	5.0	0.3	0	0	0
Brewers	0	0.7	0	0	0	0
Carpenters	0.8	1.7	0.3	0	0	0
Clothworkers	3.5	5.0	0.5	0	0	0
Grocers	n/a	0.5	0	0	0	0
Merchant Taylors	n/a	5.0	0.7	0	0	0
Pewterers	n/a	0.7	0	1.0	0	0
Goldsmiths	0.7	4.5	1	0	0	0
All (mean)	1.2	2.9	0.5	0.1	0.0	0.0
Apprentices per decade (N)	3,772	8,160	13,392	7,659	3,959	2,708
Share of London apprentices in sample (%)	39	32	35	18	14	14

Sources: Apothecaries: Society of Apothecaries Archive, 'Court Minutes' (1 Jan 1630–31, Dec 1644, Sept 1666–Sept 1670, Jan 1730–Feb 1733, Feb 1783–Feb 1786); Bakers: GL, MS 5117/1 (1536–38), 2 (1580–81), 4 (1630–33), 6 (1680–83), 7 (1729–32), 9 (1780–82); Brewers: GL, MS 5445/1 (1532–34), 7 (1582–84), 15 (1630–33), 22 (1676–79), 27 (1731–34), 31 (1780–82); Carpenters: Ainsworth et al. 1913–68, 4:16–34, 6:115–65, GL, MS 4329/3 (1635–38), 8, ff. 72r–90r, 15 (1729–31), 19 (1780–83); Clothworkers: LMA, CW/B/1/1 (1536–38), 3 (1581–83), 4, ff. 97v–125r, 10, ff. 536–606, 13, ff. 247–303, 15, ff. 45–67; Goldsmiths: Goldsmiths Company Archive, MS Court Minutes vol. C (1529–32), L2, ff. 271–376; Q f.133–R. f. 82, MS AF/2/3/1/8 (1679–82), 13 (1729–32), 45, ff. 90–253; Grocers: GL, MS 115881 (1579–81), 3 (1630–33), 5 (1680–82), 8 (1730–32), 8 (1780–82); Merchant Taylors: GL, MS 34010/2 (1574–76), MS 34017/4 (1630–33), MS 34010/10, ff. 30–170; MS 34018/6 (1679–82), MS 34010/12, ff. 268–92, 14, ff. 113–80; Pewterers: GL, MS 07090/1 (1581–83), 4 (1631–33), 9 (1732–34), 11 (1783–84).
Note: Disputes per year calculated based on coding of disputes for two- or three-year samples within each period; exact years vary because of source survival. Totals of apprentices per decade counts apprentices registered in these companies; the share of London apprentices is calculated using the total estimated in chapter 2.

appeared 'having mutually referred themselves to . . . this Court'.[18] Where master or apprentice had suffered losses, the guild might set compensation, ordering John Hammond's apprentice to pay his master 20s.

Very rarely, the guild's court ordered that the contract be ended.[19] The eight apprentices of Edward Bodye, who were found to have had 'good cause to complain' about their master 'misusing them in Correction as also for want of meat, drink, and apparel', were given the chance to move to a new master. The Clothworkers' court ordered that 'such as were most unwilling to tarry should be taken from him'. Three duly left, although it took the threat of imprisonment to force Bodye to produce their indentures.[20] The Brewers' court was more abrupt when ordering that the apprentice Richard P[ars]on[s] be discharged with 'his apron taken from him . . . and his Indenture burned', although we do not know his offence.[21]

More often, guilds simply registered discharges that had been agreed between apprentices and masters. For example, in 1613, the Merchant Taylors' heard from Charles Neale and his apprentice John Pavitt that

> upon certain controversies happening between them and also upon some dislike that the said apprentice had of the said trade [they] desired that a vacat might be made of the same indenture, and that the apprentice might not hereafter take any benefit thereby which vacat upon the payment of ten shillings to the said Neale was with all their consents accordingly made.[22]

Whatever Pavitt had done to incur the 10s cost was not mentioned, and the guild simply cancelled ('vacat[ed]') the agreement. Guilds offered little to those—whether apprentices or masters—who were in a dispute where one side was unwilling to acknowledge or address the problem; and it is not hard to envisage such situations, be they an apprentice's perception that his master had beaten him excessively, or a master whose apprentice had run off with goods or money.

Only three times in our sample—which covers more than a hundred years of guild life—did a guild impose corporal punishment. All three punished were apprentices, and all of the cases occurred in the sixteenth century. In 1582, the 'stubborn behaviour' and 'disobedience and misdemeanors' of Thomas Wilkenson led the Clothworkers to order him to be 'openly whipped'.[23] In 1576, the Goldsmiths ordered William Selbie to be 'openly punished in the parlor with whips for running away . . . & for taking up money due to his said Master . . . [and] misspending the same'.[24] The next year, in the Goldsmiths' court, two apprentices, Mathew Dayes and Thomas Snappe, were 'afore Master Wardens and divers young apprentices beat with rods to the example of others'. This unusual public punishment was for 'the said Mathew . . . calling his master false knave & Thomas . . . calling his said master fool and breaking his mistress's face with a salt'. A third apprentice, Jenks, was pardoned having showed himself penitent, in a display of clemency.[25]

One area where guilds were more effective was retrospective. Under their contracts, apprentices who left their masters prematurely owed them time to make up the period of service they had missed. Some guilds did stop former apprentices from becoming freemen and citizens until this debt was settled and their indentures fulfilled. The Merchant Taylors annotated its apprenticeship register in such cases, to prevent freedom being awarded without the debt being resolved. Arthur Thomas, for example, complained in May 1679 that his apprentice John Grimes had 'gone from [him] against his express command & [he] has not as yet heard of him', and the clerk noted: 'The apprentice not to be made free . . . until the master has notice'.[26] As a result, some apprentices made up for their absences. On 6 November 1616, Richard Morris appeared at Merchant Taylors' Hall and agreed to serve his master for two years 'in regard that he hath absented himself . . . without consent for so long term'.[27] Obviously, this affected only the minority of apprentices who sought to become freemen, and it relied on the guild's right to control who it admitted, a right that was largely unchallenged. In raising the price of defection, this did create a contract reinforcement mechanism for youths seeking a career within the city, the arena where the freedom mattered.

A few London guilds contemplated a fuller role. Some articulated this explicitly in their ordinances. The Merchant Taylors, for example, passed a rule requiring masters or apprentices to bring disputes to the company before other courts, so it could reconcile them or end the indenture.[28] The city chamberlain also occasionally attempted to use the guilds to settle conflicts. For example, he referred the dispute between Richard Bessey and his apprentice Edward Bludworth 'to the hearing examination and determination' of the master and wardens of the Bakers' guild. Yet, in an illustration of the limits guilds faced, the Bakers reported that Bessey 'doth refuse to refer the same to [their] ending and determination' and so they referred the dispute back to him.[29] Perhaps for this reason, the chamberlain passed only one other dispute to a guild in our sample period.

Guild arbitration of disputes appears to have been more important when freemen were in disputes with other freemen, not with their apprentices.[30] For its members, a guild offered an opportunity to settle issues of credit or reputation at a low cost and with some privacy. This had an obvious value when disputes might influence their future transactions with each other and their peers in the guild.

Freemen in several guilds actively used their guilds to settle disputes. Some guilds had ordinances that required their members to bring them any disputes with other members before suing them. The Merchant Taylors, the Clothworkers, and the Carpenters heard large numbers of disputes between freemen in the sixteenth century. In the 1530s and 1580s, more than fifteen disputes per year were brought to the Clothworkers court; the smaller Carpenters court heard around ten per year in the 1580s, up from four in the 1540s. The much larger Merchant Taylors heard more than forty per year in the 1580s. These cases were far more common than apprenticeship disputes, which supplied only a modest share of the conflicts heard by guilds.

Even at their most active, only a tiny percentage of enrolled apprenticeships generated a dispute that drew the official attention of their guild. The Merchant Taylors registered more than 300 apprentices a year in the 1580s, which implies that only around 1 per cent of contracts would generate a dispute in which the guild became involved.

It is possible that some kinds of intervention in apprenticeship are missing from the official record: clerks might have ignored 'minor' business; guild officers perhaps dealt with some disputes informally. In some larger guilds, subordinate junior organisations of 'yeomanry' existed, but their records rarely survive, so we cannot be sure if they had a role.

That said, there is little reason to believe that guild records did miss such activity. It is hard to understand why guild governors might record their arbitrations of disputes between freemen, but not between freemen and apprentices. Where guilds impose punishments, such as fines and corporal punishment, we would expect a record, given the potential for complaints to higher courts. Even if guild officials acted informally, we would expect this to be mentioned in the evidence about disputes between apprentices and masters given to the Lord Mayor's Court. There, witnesses frequently referred to informal arbitration and to the city's chamberlain, but in a sample of cases, not a single witness mentioned guild involvement.[31]

What London's guilds *were* doing was enforcing their own regulations on apprenticeship. Much of this work was bureaucratic and fiscal, the endless sequence of registrations of apprentices, turnovers, and freemen that allowed them to be sure that new entrants had served their terms and paid their fees. Guilds also enforced the quotas on apprentice numbers that most had established. In May 1580, for example, the Bakers' Company fined mistress Roop for having two apprentices 'above her stint', and Humfrey Walker was ordered to put away two of the five apprentices he had somehow accumulated.[32] Guilds took this aspect of their regulations seriously, stopping freemen from adding apprentices beyond the maximum permitted.[33] However, this should not be confused with enforcing the master's and apprentice's compliance with their contracts.

Masterpieces and Examinations

One final aspect of guilds' involvement in apprenticeship needs to be mentioned: the role they played at the end of the contract in ensuring that youths had received satisfactory training. The primary mechanism for this across early modern Europe was the production of the masterpiece, an object that demonstrated the apprentice's skill.[34] De Munck has shown that in Antwerp, some guilds utilised masterpiece tests relatively intensively, and judging from the few surviving examples, they demanded a high level of skill.[35] Masterpieces could offer a form of contract enforcement by confirming that the master had successfully trained their apprentice.

There is far less evidence for masterpieces in England than in Antwerp. In London, only a minority, twelve of twenty-six guilds in our sample of ordinances, formally required any examination for prospective freemen or householders.[36] Those that did ranged in complexity from the apothecaries, who were examined by both their guild and the College of Physicians, to the drapers, whose guild had a vague requirement that apprentices be tried by an 'experienced workman'. Most guild ordinances include some sense of what was required: clothworkers should show they could 'shear and work' cloth, feltmakers produced three proof pieces, and so on. Not all tests occurred immediately after the apprenticeship. In the Pewterers, Framework Knitters, and Clockmakers, the test was for journeymen who wished to set themselves up as independent masters. Tests were missing from some craft guilds, such as the Goldsmiths, where we would expect skill to be crucial.

Outside London, guild examinations for apprentices were even less common: just fourteen of sixty-two sets of provincial guild ordinances mention a test.[37] Only two, both shoemakers' guilds, mentioned making a proof piece. In Salisbury, this was a 'proof or praise boot, shoe or pantaffle to be allowed by the wardens'; in Carlisle, 'four pairs of shoes given him to work which shoes so by him wrought shall be showed to six of the ancient of this gild to be viewed and tried'.[38] Most ordinances were vaguely worded statements that an apprentice's skill needed to be approved by the guilds' senior members—'allowed to be a sufficient workman by the said Master Warden and Assistants', as Hull's Shipwrights put it.[39]

Even where a mastership test was mentioned in a guild's rules, it is not often clear that it was enforced. Trials and masterpieces are rarely visible in guild records. If masterpieces were applied rigorously, the process should leave a mark: examiners would need to be appointed; judgements might be disputed. This is what De Munck finds in Antwerp. In London there is very little sign of this. Instead, we find the opposite: freemen weavers complaining in 1627 that the Weavers guild was admitting people using other trades, 'Whereas none should be admitted before they make a proof of his workmanship'.[40] In a few cases, there is evidence that tests were applied. The examinations of apothecaries by the College of Physicians occurred regularly and do feature in their records.[41] But in the Bakers, Clothworkers, and Pewterers, all guilds which notionally had tests, their records are silent on the matter.[42]

Why were masterpieces not more prominent in London? Arguably, masterpieces sat awkwardly with the way the custom of London permitted members of guilds to use a wide range of occupations. Guilds that were populated by masters working in varied crafts and trades created two serious problems for testing skill. First, many apprentices were learning occupations in which their guild had no official interest. Second, guild officials were often engaged in other occupations, and so had little capacity to judge skills in the trade.

Guilds might circumvent the second problem by delegating testing. The Clothworkers proposed that at the end of their terms, apprentices 'of every handicrafts man' should be appointed to 'some honest and good workman of that Arte . . . to be assayed by the space of six or eight days at the least whether he be a good workman and can use his occupation sufficiently well and perfectly or no'.[43] Occasionally, guilds sought to address the first problem by regulating members of other guilds who were using their craft. In 1609, the city's Court of Aldermen proclaimed that all cordwainers, no matter what their guild, should make a masterpiece ('proof piece') at the Cordwainers' Hall, something the Cordwainers had been struggling to enforce.[44] But such campaigns seem to have been largely ineffective, and the heterogeneity of occupations within guilds presented a barrier to the serious use of examinations in London.

While specific English craft guilds managed to impose masterpiece tests on apprentices at times, this was rarely more than sporadic and certainly did not occur for the majority of apprenticeships. Guild contract enforcement did not function through retrospective tests on the skills that apprentices had gained.

The Chamberlain's Justice

Brasbridge's warning that he would take his apprentice to the city's chamberlain was no idle threat. The chamberlain of the City of London regularly heard disputes brought by masters or apprentices, offering summary justice for breaches of apprenticeship contracts. The chamberlain was one of the city's key officials, entrusted with managing the city's revenues. As part of this, he registered new apprentices and freemen. It was probably this role that had led to him hearing disputes over their behaviour.

Appealing to the chamberlain had three distinct advantages compared to the guilds. First, he could act on the complaint of just one party. Second, he could compel a freeman to appear by obtaining a warrant from the city's recorder. Third, he had the power to impose meaningful penalties: he could send a disruptive apprentice to Bridewell, one of the city's prisons, 'or otherwise punish him, according to the nature of his offence'; and he could 'relieve' an apprentice or give him leave to seek redress in the Lord Mayor's Court.[45] No doubt, punishment was what Brasbridge had in mind when he scolded his apprentice. Moreover, seeking the chamberlain's justice was cheap. Differences could be heard for a fee of 3 shillings (1 shilling for the summons; 2 shillings for the order).[46]

Unfortunately, no records survive of the chamberlain's activities in apprenticeship disputes before the late eighteenth century. From 1787, an incomplete series of 'complaint books' offer a window into the misdemeanours that troubled apprenticeships. Masters complained about apprentices' 'saucy behaviour', drunkenness, staying out late at night, leaving service without permission, working for their own profit, idleness, spoiling work, neglecting business, and disobedience. Apprentices reported masters who beat and kicked them repeatedly, failed to supply clothing or shoes, or employed them at domestic duties.[47]

The Chamberlain's Court was primarily used by masters, and its judgements were biased in their favour.[48] Apprentices supplied a minority of the complaints, just 14 per cent in the 1780s. While the chamberlain possessed a big stick with which to chastise recalcitrant youths, who could be sent to hard labour in Bridewell prison, he could do little more than admonish masters to reform their ways. As table 7.2 shows, more than two-fifths of apprentices who were brought before the chamberlain were 'committed' to Bridewell prison, often for more than a month.[49] The rest were reprimanded or forgiven on seeking their masters' pardon and promising to improve.

The results of apprentices' complaints were pathetic in comparison. Of the forty-five complaints brought by apprentices in 1789–90 for which a decision was recorded, 33 per cent were dismissed without adjudication, 56 per cent were dismissed with *both* master and apprentice being admonished, and just 11 per cent led to the master being ordered to remedy the

TABLE 7.2. Apprenticeship disputes in the Chamberlain's Court of London

Year	1789	1790	1831	1832	1833
Number of cases	183	166	159	123	111
Plaintiff					
Brought by master (%)	84	89	78	72	68
Brought by apprentice (%)	16	11	22	28	32
Outcomes					
Share of masters' complaints leading to imprisonment (%)	41	41	36	42	32
Share of apprentices imprisoned for < 1 month (%)	21	23	23	24	21
Share of apprentices imprisoned for 1–3 months (%)	13	13	5	7	1

Source: LMA, COL/CHD/AP/04/02/002; COL/CHD/AP/04/02/013.

problem by providing food or clothing or ceasing to beat his apprentice. Outcomes in the early nineteenth century were little different. In 1862, the city chamberlain Benjamin Scott reported that since 1826, his court had adjudicated 17,501 cases of grievances, resolving 14,000, with 1,044 ending in imprisonment.[50]

There is little reason to think that the chamberlain's role was much different in earlier centuries. As the municipal commissioners commented in 1837, 'We were told there had been no committal of a master for a century and a half'.[51] In interrogatories from the Lord Mayor's Court in the seventeenth century, a hearing before the chamberlain was mentioned in six of forty-nine disputes. Traces can be found in the records of Bridewell's Court of Governors.[52] For example, in February 1690/1 James Benwell, 'a Rebel Apprentice' who was a 'frequent drunkard', neglected his business, and behaved badly to his master, was committed by warrant from the chamberlain.[53] Eight months later, the chamberlain committed another disorderly apprentice, Richard Grainger, who was put 'to labor' for striking his master.[54]

The chamberlain acted as a citywide source of summary justice for complaints about contract performance by masters and apprentices. Although we lack direct evidence before the late eighteenth century, he features regularly in other accounts of disputes from earlier periods, unlike the guilds. The reason for his importance: unlike guild officials, he had the power to compel compliance and impose substantial punishments, including imprisonment.

The Lord Mayor's Court

If the chamberlain's willingness to punish disorderly apprentices at their master's behest fits comfortably with the view of early modern society as a hierarchically disciplined, patriarchal world, the same cannot be said of the other main part of London's government to intervene in apprenticeship: the Lord Mayor's Court.

Sitting in the outer chamber of Guildhall, the seat of London's government, with the city's recorder, its chief law officer, as judge, the court heard suits involving the city's customs, including many debt cases as well as apprenticeship suits. It also possessed an equity jurisdiction. But where the chamberlain could and did punish apprentices, the Mayor's Court allowed them to exit their contracts, almost at will.

The Lord Mayor's Court offered an accessible, quick, and cheap process to apprentices. Entering a petition to start a lawsuit cost just 4d, and a case could be brought to trial for 30s within a fortnight in the seventeenth century.[55] The court was predictable: in nearly every case, the apprentice would be discharged. Around a fifth of lawsuits never reached a judgement, but petitions from apprentices were dismissed only twice in the thousands of cases with surviving records.

The Lord Mayor's Court was open to apprentices from all backgrounds. The sons of citizens and locals appeared no more often than one would expect from apprenticeship registrations; female apprentices appear as well as males; and the sons of tailors, butchers, and weavers are among the ten most common groups using the court. To be sure, the sons of the gentry were more likely to turn to the court than poor husbandmen's sons, but the court was not the exclusive preserve of the rich, the connected, or the privileged.[56]

London's apprentices utilised the court with extraordinary vigour. The court's archive is fragmented, but from the 1610s to the 1720s 3 to 7 per cent of London apprentices entered petitions that still survive, as table 7.3 indicates. Given that many petitions were destroyed or lost, the original figure must have been substantially higher. Michael Scott's research suggests that between 18 and 65 per cent of petitions are missing.[57] If so, somewhere between one in twenty and one in ten London apprentices used the court.

Petitions to the Lord Mayor's Court were brought almost exclusively by apprentices. Discharge could be sought for a limited number of reasons. In his legal handbook, Emerson cited nine 'usual' causes that included breaches

TABLE 7.3. Actions by apprentices in the Lord Mayor's Court

Years	Petitions per annum N	Apprentices per annum N	Share in Mayor's Court %
1620–29	74 (6–108)	3,773	2 (0.2–2.9)
1630–39	115 (29–152)	3,803	3 (0.8–4)
1640–49	84 (34–135)	3,827	2.2 (0.9–3.5)
1650–59	159 (47–218)	4,359	3.6 (1.1–5)
1660–69	151 (73–201)	4,082	3.7 (1.8–4.9)
1670–79	203 (89–297)	4,687	4.3 (1.9–6.3)
1680–89	236 (159–311)	4,369	5.4 (3.6–7.1)
1690–99	155 (41–249)	4,088	3.8 (1–6.1)
1700–1709	186 (43–275)	4,285	4.3 (1–6.4)
1710–19	150 (59–183)	3,926	3.8 (1.5–4.7)
1720–29	110 (18–156)	3,325	3.3 (0.5–4.7)

Source: Calculated from Scott 2016. Column 2 reports the mean number of surviving petitions per decade with the range in parentheses. Column 3 uses apprentice estimates from chapter 2. Column 4 expresses the mean and range as a percentage of the number of apprenticeships per annum.

of city rules (e.g., bound under age or for short terms; not being enrolled) and breaches of contract, particularly mistreatment and failures in training.[58] In reality, four out of five petitions cited the same cause: non-enrolment, or failing to register the indenture with the city's chamberlain.[59]

The dominance of suits for non-enrolment gave a truly extraordinary character to apprenticeship cases in the Lord Mayor's Court. First, non-enrolment amounted to nothing more than a bureaucratic technicality. This was a failure of paperwork, not substance. Given how much of the debate about apprenticeship has been about how to enforce contracts, this is remarkable. If it seems incredible that the entire agreement could be undermined by such a trivial failing, then consider that it was entirely the master's fault, as he was responsible for enrolling his apprentice.

Second, a petition asserting non-enrolment brooked no opposition. As a result, most masters did not bother to defend themselves. Non-enrolment explains the monotonic outcome of cases in favour of the apprentices. Cases where other causes were asserted—particularly mistreatment—were more likely to inspire a defence from masters whose names were being tarnished.[60]

The lack of successful defences by masters does not imply they made no effort to maintain apprenticeships. As in debt cases, these suits often came late in a longer process of dispute.[61] Apprentices generally entered bills after they had left their masters' homes and workshops; the discharges regularised their situations and provided them with legal certainty, freeing them from the threat of pursuit for breach of contract. However, their relationships with their masters had often broken down gradually. Apprentices and masters regularly attempted to overcome problems informally. Numerous records of disputes mention masters accepting runaway apprentices back after parental intervention, or negotiating compensation for embezzlements. For example, one master's witnesses described how, when his apprentice returned after absenting himself, he 'did receive him kindly . . . in hope thereby to oblige him to be the more diligent in his business for the future'.[62]

Why would masters leave themselves in a position where they could not prevent their apprentices' departures? Certainly, this was not what the City of London advocated, at least in public. The city's government encouraged enrolment: it was mentioned in the citizenship oath, the fee was low (just 2s 6d), and masters who had failed to enrol an apprentice paid an additional 9s 2d fine if they later made them citizens. The city's printed guidance for new freemen warned that non-enrolment disturbed the balance of authority and hierarchy in the household and led to 'the Ruin of Hundreds of [apprentices]; for being sensible that it is entirely in their Power to leave their Service whenever they please, they too often presume upon it to behave in an unbecoming Manner to their Masters, to neglect their Business, and to take . . . bad Courses'.[63] Nevertheless, non-enrolment was widespread. We cannot estimate the level precisely, because of the loss of the city's records, but between one-quarter and a half of apprentices who became freemen from the mid-sixteenth to the early eighteenth centuries had not been enrolled.[64]

The explanation that contemporary city officials offered for non-enrolment was that masters wished to be able to eject apprentices at will, even if this came at the price of permitting their apprentices the same freedom to exit. Masters apparently believed that by avoiding enrolling their apprentices 'they have it in their Power to part with them if they should prove disorderly'.[65] The city's law officers vigorously denied the truth of this, but there are clear signs that masters and apprentices believed this. For example, in 1599 when the barber surgeon Thomas Jones refused to accept his apprentice Peter Phillips back into his service, he justified this on non-enrolment.[66]

Apprentices regularly accused their masters of having more nefarious plans. Several argued that their masters had encouraged them to quit, with the aim of appropriating the apprentices' premium. Richard Nest, for example, said his master neglected enrolment 'on purpose to give [him] occasion to sue forth his indentures thereby intending to keep himself the said fifty pounds'.[67] Worse, apprentices such as Joel Burford described his master beating him 'to force [him] . . . to quit his service but also to keep to his own use the said Thirty pounds'.[68] When reading these accusations, however, we need recognise that they were made to justify why the premium should be repaid to the apprentice's family.

Despite the risk that their masters might eject them, some apprentices and their families also preferred to avoid enrolment. Several masters asserted that it was the apprentice who had been 'unwilling to be inrolled'.[69] This may have reflected a view that enrolment removed a degree of freedom from an apprentice who was uncertain about their career or master. For example, James, the apprentice of clothworker Anthony Pearte, wanted to leave his trade and find a new master, but 'upon persuasion used towards him' by the guild's governors he agreed to remain with Pearte until Christmas next,

> and until then it was thought good by this Court that the said apprentice should not be enrolled, And as they like and agree together in the mean time so to continue forth the rest of his term, and if he cannot like then to be set over to some other of this company.[70]

Premiums explain the viability of non-enrolment. For the master, taking a premium meant that they had recouped some or all of the cost of feeding, lodging, and training a new apprentice at the outset. As we saw in chapter 4, premiums in many ordinary crafts and trades were equivalent to a year's wages for an unskilled worker. In the more profitable professions or trades, families paid multiples of that. Premiums were not universal—far from it—and a portion might be returned if an apprenticeship ended. But where they were used, they transformed the economics of apprenticeship, offsetting the master's costs and risk from an early end to the agreement.

For the apprentice, premiums meant that non-enrolment had a particular advantage. It strengthened their position when negotiating a transfer and gave them easy access to the court's equity side, where they could recover some of their money, a process discussed below. What we know about the pattern of non-enrolment supports the argument for apprentices' families contributing to the decision. First, non-enrolment increased over time, in parallel with the growing use of premiums (although the weakening regulatory influence of the city may have also lessened masters' concern). Second, non-enrolment was associated with larger premiums, implying that apprentices' families sought to protect larger investments.[71] Third, the odds of discharge increased among apprentices who were not enrolled: four-fifths of actions alleged non-enrolment, yet fewer than half of apprentices were not enrolled.[72] Given the scale of non-enrolment, it is hard to believe this was from ignorance or accident. It seems far more likely that non-enrolment was often a strategy agreed between the apprentice's family and the master.

The ease of exit possible in London because of non-enrolment may still seem inexplicable in the lack of friction around departure. However, as in a marriage, observing exactly whose behaviour was at fault in the privacy of a master's own workshop was hard, and proving fault might be reputationally costly. Lowering the standard of proof in the way non-enrolment allowed and stripping out any demonstration of serious fault was therefore a pragmatic response, one seemingly chosen by the contracting parties. Even then, some of the actions described in court records—masters sending apprentices out on an errand and shutting their doors to them—echo some of the 'proofs' of infidelity, such as pretences of adultery in a hotel, which are observed in settings where no-fault divorce is not permitted.[73]

The Lord Mayor's Court provided London's apprentices with a capacity to end contracts prematurely. The most obvious beneficiaries were the apprentices, who gained a freedom to exit their obligations, largely under a technical fault that was irrelevant to the performance of the contract. That said, although it was always an apprentice who initiated the petition, they might be coerced into this by a master who left them no alternative, by throwing them out of his house.

The ability to petition for discharge gave London's apprentices an escape hatch that freed them from the risk of pursuit and penalty by their masters—who could, as we have seen above, call upon the chamberlain to imprison runaways. It allowed them to defuse the financial risks created by bonds their parents and guardians may have entered. And it freed them to contract with another master. The greater rights the Mayor's Court gave to apprentices therefore went some way to reducing the risks of entering a long, costly apprenticeship contract with a master and in an occupation that were largely unknown in advance.

Equity and Recovering Apprenticeship Premiums

Apprenticeship involved investments of money as well as time. While being able to quit gave apprentices a measure of freedom, the premiums they paid to their masters acted as a commitment device, through both the financial loss that they would incur and the difficulty of raising further funding to contract with an alternative master. Here, too, London's institutions offered a solution. In addition to hearing petitions for discharge, the Lord Mayor's Court had an equity jurisdiction that gave it the power to decide what—if any—share of the apprentice's premium should be repaid when a contract broke down.

Apprentices less frequently brought suits to the equity side than petitioned for discharge. The records are incomplete, but they point to a minimum of twelve to sixteen suits each year in the 1670s and 1680s, compared to around 200 discharge petitions.[74] Equity cases were more socially selective than the petitions. Around a third of apprentices who brought equity cases were the sons of gentlemen and esquires, and many had started training for one of the higher-earning occupations. These were aspiring merchants, wholesalers and apothecaries. Most suits dealt with large premiums—over half were for £50 or more, a sum paid by just 13 per cent of London apprentices in 1711–21. Equity also involved much higher costs; legal costs were often awarded to the plaintiff, but not always, and at around £6, they were substantial.[75]

It seems clear that most apprentices would have sought to reach an agreement informally, rather than bring a suit. The threat of legal costs must have focused the minds of many masters. Previous deals over premiums are occasionally mentioned in equity cases. Nicholas Hanbury, for example, had already returned £17 of the £80 he had received with his apprentice Humphrey Babington.[76] Charles Bathurst's father even included this in the negotiation over binding his son: if his son left, two preselected referees were to redistribute his £200 premium.[77]

In several respects, the equity side of the Lord Mayor's Court mirrored its general apprenticeship business. Again, all suits were brought by apprentices.[78] And again, apprentices were generally successful: only twenty-six of 244 plaintiffs in our sample received nothing from their premium back, and just six cases were dismissed.[79] The share of the premium the court restored was quite predictable, as figure 7.1 shows, falling steadily as the time an apprentice had served grew.[80] The court apparently understood premiums not as compensation for the initial cost involved in training new apprentices, but as fees for access and living costs; no year was worth much more or less than another, despite the increasing value of apprentices' labour over time.

Where the two sides of the Lord Mayor's Court diverge is in the nature of the process. The discharge bills possess a sterile inevitability. In contrast, equity cases produced heated and contradictory accounts of exploitation

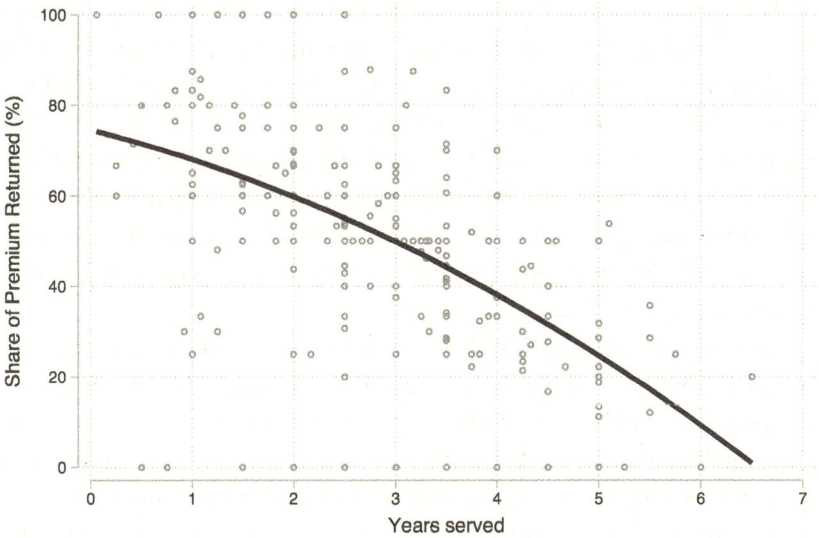

FIGURE 7.1. Share of premium returned by Mayor's Court by term served. The figure reports the share of premium returned for 232 cases with surviving information between 1668 and 1707.
Source: LMA, CLA/024.

and contractual failure. Although mostly discharged for non-enrolment, apprentices now reported a litany of abuses that explained the separation.[81]

For equity cases, fault mattered. Indeed, in one case, lack of fault meant that 'the court forbeareth to decree the cause for that no just cause appeareth against the defendant except want of enrollment'.[82] As Margaret Pelling noted, apprentices' and masters' stories are often impossible to reconcile.[83] To give one example from April 1691, Caleb Trenchfield's deponents told how, when he met his apprentice James Ellis for arbitration, Ellis asserted that 'now he had sued out his Indentures by which he was cleared from him the defendant . . . he would now make the best of his time to his own advantage urging it with a great deal of vehemency that he would not return again to the defendant'. Yet, Ellis's own deponents said that it was Trenchfield who had protested that 'he would not take [Ellis] again for an hundred pounds'.[84]

The litanies of faults that were put before the court reiterated, exploited, and reinforced the norms of apprenticeship in London. Both sides sought to convince the court that the other was (more) at fault. Each accusation linked ultimately to one of the clauses contained in London's apprenticeship contracts.

Within this framework, the court made a careful accounting. Apprentices' broken heads, bad diets, and paltry instruction were weighed against the unexplained absences and saucy words, thefts, and threats which they dealt to their masters. Worn-out clothes, absences, stolen shop goods, and medical treatment were all quantified and, if possible, priced; masters listed doctors' bills, garment prices, and the wages of journeymen employed in their apprentices' absence. Apprentices protested that no new master could be obtained without a premium, and that their masters had faced no great expense in keeping them.

The court adjusted financial liability according to culpability. The final settlement reflected the behaviour of each side. Central to this was why an apprentice had left: if voluntary, it weakened their case; if driven off, it weakened their master's. Although masters could simply turn apprentices away, for the purposes of the equity case, they preferred them to run away. As a result, any absence could be seized upon. In one case, an apprentice claimed that he had returned from the Lord Mayor's Show to find he was locked out.[85] Any evidence that the other side favoured dissolution mattered. Hence, John Walmesley's suit was undermined when one of his master's servants, Martha Bragg, recalled that

> she hath heard the Complainant several times say that he would not stay with the Defendant for that he had no mind to a handicraft trade and particularly the night before he went away [he] told this dept that he would and could go from the Defendant for that he was not enrolled & stayed out that night till past twelve of the clock on purpose (as this Deponent believeth) to give occasion for the Defendant to quarrel with him.[86]

More pungently, one witness for a master told how the apprentice had said he 'did not care a fart for living with his Master . . . & did not care a turd for the £25 his master had with him'.[87]

In the apprentices' evidence, the picture was inverted. Apprentices claimed they had been forced out 'by violence', as Weaver put it.[88] Browne, for example, claimed his master had 'called for his paring shovel and threatened to beat your orator down therewith and to charge your orator with a constable unless your orator would go out of his doors'.[89] For the same reason, apprentices consistently describe repeatedly submitting themselves to their masters and masters having 'offered to refer the said matter to any Indifferent persons', as Lovelace Apleford put it.[90]

The court's judgement reflected its view of these accusations. Figure 7.2 shows how the share of the premium that the court ordered to be returned

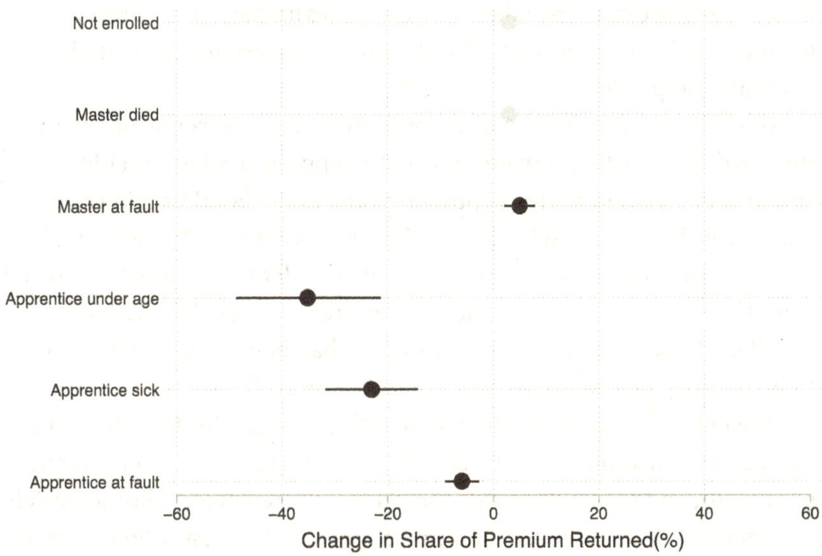

FIGURE 7.2. The impact of fault on the share of apprenticeship premium returned. The figure reports the percentile change in the share of the apprentice's premium that was returned predicted by a regression of the share of the premium returned on reported characteristics of each case, the term served, and the value of the premium. Full results in Wallis 2012, 813. All the characteristics reported in the figure are dummy variables. Those significant at the 10% level or higher are in black; others are in grey.

changed depending on the behaviour and circumstances of the master and apprentice it mentioned when making the decree, all else being equal. These adjustments for each specific fault were in addition to the effect of time served (shown in figure 7.1); for every year served, apprentices received around 12 per cent less back. Where apprentices had misbehaved, the amount they received fell by 6 per cent.[91] Similarly, when masters were at fault, they were ordered to return about 5 per cent more.[92] If apprentices had been sick, they received much less, having cost their masters money and earned little. Those bound under age also had less returned. In short, when apprentices or masters convinced the court that the other was at fault, they profited.

While the city offered to end contracts on demand, these financial reparations reveal a clear sense of the behaviour required from master and apprentice. In the court's view, apprenticeship still turned on an exchange of sufficient training for satisfactory service.

The equity side of the Lord Mayor's Court provided a means to resolve the financial consequences of the discharges executed by its common-law side, allowing discharged apprentices to recover a proportion of their premiums. The two sides of the court's activities meshed, providing a mechanism to resolve the contractual and financial uncertainties created when apprenticeship failed.

While most of the surviving records are from the seventeenth century, the Lord Mayor's Court oversaw London apprenticeship for at least five centuries. Hovland's study of apprenticeship in medieval London suggests that its role had emerged by the late thirteenth century.[93] In the fourteenth century many apprentices 'appeared only in order to be formally released from their apprenticeships', and in a quarter of cases they had not been enrolled.[94] The city's system of enrolment had been created only around 1300, not long before these cases began to appear.[95]

The court survived into the nineteenth century.[96] In the 1830s, parliamentary commissioners described it discharging apprentices, often for non-enrolment, and commented that the equity side remained 'almost entirely confined to bills of discovery and suits for compelling restitution of premiums to apprentices'.[97] The court thus predated the formation of most of the city's guilds and lasted after most had abandoned any aspirations to regulate training.

Apprenticeship Bonds and Central Equity Courts

The set of institutional arrangements discussed so far centred on the city's courts. However, London apprenticeship was not insulated from the Crown's courts, particularly the equity Courts of Chancery, Exchequer, and Requests. These had an important role in enforcing another mechanism in use for some elite apprenticeships: the bonds that were drawn up alongside the indentures.

Bonds 'for truth' provided additional security to masters, giving them recourse to a financial guarantor who accepted liability for losses or theft by apprentices. Legally, bonds operated in parallel with the apprenticeship contract: as counsel advised the London Coopers, 'masters may take security by bond and need not rely on the indenture'.[98] Bonds offer a further reason why masters might have entered what were essentially unenforceable contracts, thanks to the work of the Lord Mayor's Court, although their use was not limited to the capital.[99]

The exposure that parents and guardians faced from bonds could be substantial. In the early 1630s, John Gell entered a bond for £1,000 when he bound his son William to a London merchant, Mr Northey, and was forced to pay £470 to cover money that his son had embezzled and lost at dice and other games.[100] We know of Gell's losses only because he sought to recover them from the man he accused of corrupting his son in a separate case in the Court of Requests—the bond was never formally actioned; the threat was enough. Not all bonds were on this scale. When John Allen was apprenticed in 1665, for example, his father had to give a bond for £50 alongside a premium of the same amount.[101]

The sum Gell was committed to was large, but it was not out of the ordinary. The Merchant Taylors recorded bonds consistently between 1601 and 1684.[102] During that period, 5 per cent of indentures—over 2,000 apprenticeships—were accompanied by bonds. The average bond was £200; the largest was £1,200. They were agreed only by a select and elite minority of masters and families; 70 per cent were with masters who were drapers, mercers, merchants, or silkmen, and over half of the parents were gentlemen, esquires, or knights.

The Grocers' Company also registered bonds and reported slightly fewer (just under 900), but they had an even higher average value of £300 and a maximum of £2,000. One of the two apprentices with a £2,000 bond was Samuel Barnardiston, the third son of Sir Samuel Barnardiston. The younger Samuel was indentured to John Langham in 1639 and would gain substantial wealth as a Levant merchant, serve as a deputy governor of the East India Company, and sit in Parliament for many years. Within a year of his binding, he took part in the riots that followed the appointment of the royalist colonel Thomas Lunsford as lieutenant of the Tower of London in 1641.[103]

Bonds provided an important parallel mechanism for contract enforcement, largely used among elite apprentices. Like indentures, they relied on the courts, not the guilds. By protecting masters from losses, they alleviated a portion of the risk created by the low enforceability of contracts.

Beyond the Metropolis

How unique was London's system? The short answer is that urban guilds elsewhere in England seem to have been no more active than in London, while city courts heard cases about apprenticeship contracts across England and took much the same approach to discharge seen in London.

GUILD SUPERVISION OF APPRENTICESHIP OUTSIDE LONDON

Guilds in other English towns and cities behaved much like those in London. The volume of surviving provincial records is much more limited. Most provincial guilds were not independently incorporated and their records were lost after they were dissolved in the nineteenth century. No disputes between masters and apprentices were present in four provincial guilds: Bristol's Soapmakers guild, Shrewsbury's Weavers and Glovers guilds, and Newcastle's Barber Surgeons and Chandlers guild.[104]

Outside London, guilds were more, not less, reliant on the coercive powers of the town or city in which they were based. For example, when the Bristol Glovers learned that an apprentice had been bound colourably to one of its members while actually serving a non-freeman, they appealed to the mayor and aldermen, rather than summoning the culprits directly.[105]

Elsewhere in Europe, guild oversight of apprenticeship contracts was often similarly limited. Davids suggests Dutch guilds played little role in apprenticeship, implying that contract enforcement depended on individuals.[106] In Turin, the guilds lacked courts that could enforce contracts.[107] In the Southern Netherlands, contracts 'only seldom mention the guilds as an arbiter or judge in cases of breach of contract'; De Kerf's detailed study of the Antwerp Coopers turned up just one instance of the guild intervening in an apprenticeship dispute in the seventeenth century and ten in the eighteenth.[108]

Exceptions did exist. For example, De Bie argues that the Antwerp diamond cutters' guild mediated disputes.[109] The fullest study to date of a guild playing an active role in apprenticeship disputes, Caracausi's examination of the Woollen guild in Padua, shows how they might execute this role and reveals the bias they might show towards the master's interests.[110] If we turn to the other branch of guild regulation that directly touched on the quality of training, then, as Ogilvie shows, masterpieces were far from universal in Europe's guilds.[111]

APPRENTICESHIP TRIBUNALS IN INCORPORATED TOWNS AND CITIES

In most incorporated English towns and cities, the mayor and several officials served simultaneously as magistrates and as judges in urban courts. These courts had a well-established role in debt and contract disputes—including apprenticeship indentures—that dated to the foundation of the urban community.

Urban courts' actions echo London's process of hearing disputes and discharging apprenticeships. In Bristol, for example, the Tolzey Court heard apprenticeship cases. The turner William King complained to it in 1674 that his apprentice Samuel Giggs, 'being a disorderly servant & five times running away . . . is now run away with his Clothes'. Giggs had been previously sent to the House of Correction and 'admonished' by the city's aldermen to reform 'his life & manners'. Out of patience, the court 'ordered that the said apprentice be discharged from his said master and his said master be at liberty to take another apprentice unless upon notice the parents of the said Apprentice or the Apprentice himself show Cause to the Contrary at the next Sessions'.[112]

As in London, such cases came frequently. Between 1674 and 1678, the Tolzey Court judged fourteen apprenticeship disputes; more may have been dealt with informally.[113] Ten complaints came from apprentices, including six against masters who had left the city or quit their trade. The other four suits were brought by masters, complaining about apprentices who had left without permission, stolen, or been disorderly. The city's Quarter Sessions also heard apprenticeship cases. Both produced similar outcomes, as Ben-Amos showed, with most contracts being cancelled.[114]

Similar cases about runaways were brought to the Mayor's Court in Norwich, another of the largest cities, and, at the other end of the spectrum, to the borough court of the tiny town of New Woodstock.[115] To give one further example that illustrates the similarity to London, in 1797 the Borough Sessions at St Albans, Hertfordshire, settled the complaint made by Thomas Clark, an apprentice whitesmith, that his master Christopher Poulney refused 'to employ and teach him' or 'to provide his necessaries', by discharging him and ordering Poulney to repay 'the sum of five pounds and five shillings being one half part of the apprentice fee'.[116]

One thing that was missing in other English town courts was the extreme ease of exit offered by the Lord Mayor's Court in London. There is no evidence of discharge because of non-enrolment outside London.[117] Enrolment was required in only some boroughs, and even then, it was often patchy.[118] Nevertheless, urban courts showed the same willingness to revisit and cancel apprenticeship contracts and to restore a share of any premium.

APPRENTICESHIP AND JUSTICES OF THE PEACE

Outside the boroughs, the legal framework of apprenticeship was changed by the Statute of Artificers. This empowered justices of the peace to police apprenticeship and enforce contracts in a similar manner to urban courts (as a result, the statute had no meaningful impact on enforcement in incorporated boroughs).

The powers and duties of justices of the peace were extended and deepened in the eighteenth century to give them greater authority to apply summary justice at the lower end of the labour market.[119] From 1746, two justices could examine a master accused of 'Misusage, Refusal of necessary Provision, Cruelty or Ill-Treatment' and discharge his apprentices—so long as they had been placed by the parish or with a premium of £5 or less. Justices could also punish apprentices' 'Ill-behaviour' with a month of hard labour, much as London's chamberlain had long been doing.[120] Complaints about runaway apprentices led in 1765 to a further act that enabled justices of the peace to force them to serve the time they had missed.[121] From 1793, two justices could fine masters up to 40s for 'ill usage' or neglect of apprentices, with the fine given to the apprentice as 'recompence or compensation'. Both the 1765 and 1793 acts applied only to apprenticeships with a premium of £10 or less.[122] But by the eighteenth century, justices' guides generally suggested that they could order money to be restored 'for this, by an equitable Construction of the Statute, is a Power consequential upon their Jurisdiction to discharge'.[123]

What did this mean for contract enforcement? The surgeon James Clegg's diary contains a rare account of justices of the peace in action in the Peak District in 1735. On 2 July, Clegg 'Rid over to Tideswell and was terribly beaten by wind and rain; dined with Mr Kelsal, there appealed to the Justices about my apprentice, and they gave it on my side, I returned safe in the evening. Blessed be God!'. Nearly two weeks later, on 15 July, the business was concluded: 'I set out for the Sessions at Bakewell with Jos. Wood. . . . Retained Mr Cook for my counsel. Dined in the room with the Justices and went up to the Court, and after a brisk trial I carried my cause and got quit of the burden of an apprentice'.[124]

In the seventeenth and eighteenth centuries, provincial masters like Clegg appear regularly obtaining discharges from justices of the peace, as do their apprentices.[125] The complaint Elizabeth Parnell brought to the Hertfordshire quarter sessions, that her son Edward's master had set him to plough, cart, and harvest work instead of instructing him in his trade, mirrored the pleas brought to the Lord Mayor's Court, as does its conclusion: the magistrates ordered Edward discharged and £5 returned by his master to his mother.[126] Similarly, no London master would have been surprised that John Newman, a tailor in Shoreham, Sussex, convinced the justices to discharge his apprentice Henry Robinson for neglecting his service and behaving in a disorderly manner.[127] Many a London apprentice might, in turn, have echoed Thomas Wright's 'great joy' at being released from his master by three justices in October 1729, after he had run away because of 'very ill usage'.[128]

Justices of the Peace offered a process that was very similar to that seen in urban courts. Masters might call on the magistrates to discipline apprentices for idleness or running away, or they could seek to discharge apprentices for theft, gaming, refusing to obey lawful commands, or absence.[129] Apprentices could complain about their instruction, mistreatment, being turned away, or their master's own absence or bankruptcy.[130] And cases at Quarter Sessions show justices restoring premiums.[131] The one big difference from London was, as with other towns, the lack of a no-fault 'non-enrolment' plea.

Justices of the peace made regular use of their powers over apprenticeship contracts.[132] For Middlesex, where their jurisdiction covered large areas of London outside the boundaries of the old City, the press of apprenticeship business was so great that in 1752, the magistrates ordered that all petitions for discharge from apprentices needed to be entered before the end of the second day, as 'the Business of the Sessions at the Latter Part of the Sessions Week hath been very much hindered and retarded by hearing the Petitions for discharging Apprentices . . . preferred late in the Sessions'.[133]

Even so, the number of cases that Middlesex's magistrates heard was a shadow of that brought in the City of London. In 1690 and 1709, the Middlesex Quarter Sessions note twenty-four apprenticeship disputes in the nineteen months for which records survive. Around the same time, the Lord Mayor's Court was hearing nearly 200 cases a year, despite governing an area of similar or smaller population.[134]

In the nineteenth century, however, the justices' oversight of apprenticeship became folded into the wider set of master and servant laws that were used to limit the contractual freedom of a wide range of workers. The way in which employers used these laws to lock some types of apprentices into their positions has been ably uncovered by Marc Steinberg and Doug Hay.[135]

URBAN COURTS OUTSIDE ENGLAND

England's reliance on urban courts to adjudicate and enforce apprenticeship was not unique. Urban courts rather than guilds frequently played the primary role of enforcer in other parts of Europe.[136]

In Madrid, it was the city council and the Sala de Alcaldes de Casa y Corte (Hall of Mayors of House and Court—a title that echoes London's) that dealt with disputes over apprenticeship, and contracts specified that it, not the guild, was the formal tribunal.[137] In Venice, the Giustizia Vecchia registered apprenticeships and heard disputes for members of nearly all guilds.[138] In Turin, apprenticeship was regulated by the Consolato di Commercio, a city court for trade and business established in 1676 that also oversaw the guilds.[139] In Augsburg, the city's trade court heard disputes about apprenticeship.[140] In nineteenth-century France, after the abolition of guilds, city labour courts heard large volumes of apprenticeship cases.[141] De Munck concluded that in the Southern Netherlands 'none of the data indicate that craft guilds were disciplinary institutions' for apprenticeships; instead, disputes in Antwerp were addressed through the city's courts.[142] In the Northern Netherlands, similarly, surviving guild records 'are generally silent on contract enforcement'. Interestingly, the number of cases appearing in Dutch urban court records is also small, implying that private resolution was more important.[143] Problems with rural apprenticeships in Finland, where no guilds existed, were brought to the local courts.[144]

The approach taken by these tribunals seems to echo that taken in England. Turin's Consolato, for example, focused on balancing debts and obligations between apprentice and master, not compelling them to remain together.[145] The concentration seen in London on the contractual responsibilities between apprentice and master defined by the indenture is mirrored in disputes in Antwerp, which were 'without exception a business dispute' about 'breach of contract'.[146]

Conclusion

Historians have long debated how guilds affected premodern apprenticeship. For England, and possibly for much of Europe, this focus on guilds is mistaken. Guilds had only a modest role in overseeing and enforcing the contractual obligations that masters and apprentices accepted when they agreed contracts of apprenticeship. Some guilds did act as arbiters of apprenticeship sporadically in the sixteenth century, but this function disappeared in the middle of the seventeenth century, and they never came close to handling the volume of disputes brought to the Lord Mayor's Court. Instead, guilds largely confined themselves to a bureaucratic role.

Contractual performance may have benefited from guilds in two other ways. First, qualifying for guild membership gave youths an incentive to complete their apprenticeships. This influenced apprentices' behaviour in the final years of their contracts, as we saw in the last chapter. Second, guild examinations of apprentices who completed their terms might have provided a quality check on training. However, masterpieces and tests were far from universal, and they would have done little for the majority of apprentices who never sought entry to the guild. While not trivial, neither seem enough to sustain the larger claims made for guilds' contribution to apprenticeship.

Was this because English guilds were lax or weak, or because the central state had taken over, as some have posited?[147] One could suggest that England is an example of a precocious move to state enforcement. However, guilds were not absent. In the sixteenth or early seventeenth century, guilds were enforcing local monopsonies, settling other kinds of dispute between members, and effectively lobbying the monarch. Moreover, they continued to impact apprenticeship in other ways, extracting fees, defining their durations, and setting quotas. English guilds' absence from enforcement did not reflect a lack of power or capacity. It may, however, reflect their weakness relative to other urban institutions.

The crucial institutions in policing the system of apprenticeship in premodern England were the law courts and civic officers. Apprentices' indentures were legal contracts with their masters, and it fell to these legal tribunals to resolve disputes and enforce contracts, not to guilds. In London, several branches of city government had specific roles, including the Chamberlain's Court, Bridewell, and the Lord Mayor's Court. In other English cities and the countryside, town governments and magistrates performed similar functions. Although the role for the justices of the peace was created only in the 1560s, the urban court system had existed for centuries. In England's towns, there was no divide between the nature of enforcement in the medieval and early modern periods, just its extent.

Urban courts and officials played a vital role in resolving disputes where private arbitration had failed. This included imposing punishment—corporal and imprisonment—for misbehaviour and other breaches, largely those committed by apprentices. However, it also involved terminating contracts for cause. This latter function, supplying an affordable and equitable exit from apprenticeship indentures, is the most startling aspect of this system. It happened regularly, affecting a large number of apprenticeships—between 5 and 10 per cent in London. Ending apprenticeships did not necessitate a court's involvement if both parties could agree, meaning that the scale of discharges we see here are likely to have been outnumbered by those settled privately in the knowledge that this was an unavoidable outcome. In London, particularly, the ability to cite non-enrolment as a cause for ending an apprenticeship transformed indentures into agreements that could be terminated at will.

London's system was particularly favourable to apprentices, giving them a simple and effective way to leave positions if they wished, and it must have been one of the appealing features of training in the metropolis. The ease of exit in this institutional framework lowered the risk of entering and paying for an apprenticeship. The ability to eject unwanted and unproductive apprentices may also have encouraged masters to provide training, just as bonds reduced their financial risks. That both parties had access to credible threats if the contract was not performed properly must have improved its operation. This system reduced frictions around exit, but it did not remove all the costs. Premature exits meant abandoning the sunk costs of search and negotiation involved in arranging an apprenticeship, and the value of time an apprentice had already served to qualify for the freedom if a turnover could not be achieved. If they were managed badly, they risked damaging the apprentice's or master's reputation.[148]

The premodern answer to the problems of incomplete knowledge and risk of opportunism inherent in apprenticeship was to allow for exit. The consequences of this are visible in the flexible pattern of premature departures seen in the last chapter. If master and youth turned out to be ill-matched, apprenticeship could be a brief fling, not an enduring bad marriage.

Why did town and city governments take on these functions? Perhaps the most important reason was simply that they were there: urban courts were a facet of town government that predated craft and trade guilds (although some were intertwined with merchant guilds), and they heard a wide variety of contractual and commercial disputes. They were superior to the guilds in authority. These institutions were in place from the 1300s; this was no early modern novelty that developed as guilds declined.[149] Gaining the ability to offer legal services was a key reason for communities to obtain a charter of incorporation. To that extent, apprenticeship disputes were just one of several types of legal problem addressed by urban corporations seeking to ensure that markets functioned effectively.[150]

Arguably, urban authorities had two further compelling reasons to provide a fair and efficient source of contract enforcement and dissolution. First, the use of apprenticeship by urban families to place their children in different occupations meant that citizens, including the elite who governed the cities, would themselves benefit from this. Second, higher urban mortality meant that if towns and cities were unable to attract migrants, they would wither. Apprentices countered the demographic deficit.[151] This motivated communities to take oversight of apprenticeship contracts and to encourage recruitment by lowering the risks that families faced when sending their children from distant places, by allowing contracts to end.

The role of the town and city is missing in the sequence of enforcement institutions that de la Croix et al. sketch out in their influential recent model of training and innovation. Yet, the incorporated borough, town, or city is a better candidate than the guild to be a 'middle stage' between clan and national centralised state, sustaining training outside of families and generating the growth-enhancing effects their model envisages. It was local, more neutral to master and apprentice than a guild, and possessed legal powers of enforcement. Europe's urban governments and their courts are as ancient as its craft guilds—often, more ancient.[152] They share the characteristics that de la Croix et al. identify as critical to enforcement, having the ability to communicate and coordinate punishment. The effect of such a substitution is twofold first, to discard the idea that guilds sustained contracts, and second, to shift the contrast between pre-industrial and industrial apprenticeship. Both operate under formal systems of labour law. It was the scope of that law that changed, and the role of the large firm within it. Initially, in the nineteenth century, industrialisation led to a more coercive interpretation of apprenticeship law, as employers and magistrates colluded to constrain workers. Then, in reaction, came a move to a purely civil jurisdiction, with the wholesale revision of the law of master and servant in the last decades of the nineteenth century.[153]

8

Outcomes

> Despair not, there are better ways to Rise:
> Follow your Trades, and you may chance to be,
> Thought worthy of their Master's Pedigree:
> His pretty modest Daughter he'll bestow,
> Which you're acquainted with before, or so:
> To whom you've sung Ballad-obscenity
> The very Zenith of your Poetry.[1]

How to 'rise', as the anonymous author of this seventeenth-century poem put it, was the prime challenge facing all apprentices as they reached the end of their terms. It is little wonder that the idea of marrying the master's daughter resonated so strongly, promising the combination of security and resources that might allow a Dick Whittington–like ascension to fortune and success. The independence from servitude that came with the end of their indentures presented ex-apprentices with opportunities and risks. It demanded that they make decisions about the direction of their working lives. Freedom from the constraints of their masters' discipline also allowed for other possibilities. Completing his term during a contested parliamentary election where both candidates were attracting voters by offering generous hospitality, James Lackington recalled that 'I was at once . . . in the midst of a scene of riot and dissipation' and 'I had nearly sunk for ever into meanness, obscurity and vice'.[2]

One of the most distinctive features of the system of premodern apprenticeship was the inevitability with which each contract ended.

Apprenticeship was a delineated period in the life cycle of many youths that came to a predetermined close; its terminal date was known from the outset, even if many ended prematurely, as the last two chapters showed. Having looked in depth at the ways in which apprenticeship operated and the institutions that policed it and adjudicated disputes, this chapter explores what came next: What kinds of futures did apprenticeship lead to, and what factors influenced individual apprentices' destinations? These are questions that touch directly on the purpose, benefits, and openness of apprenticeship in early modern England, and the answers distinguish it from later forms of apprenticeship, rooted in longer-lasting employment.

Completing an apprenticeship brought with it several distinct sets of privileges. Through the Statute of Artificers, it gave a worker the right to work in most trades or crafts across rural and suburban England. That right was not tied to a specific place, but other elements of the institutional benefits of service were local. If it was served in one of many incorporated towns and cities, apprenticeship provided a qualification for local citizenship, which included the right to work in the place where they had trained, as well as other political and social rights and duties. If the apprenticeship was served with a member of a guild, it met one of the crucial qualifications for entry to the guild, giving the right to work in that guild's trade, to take apprentices, and to participate in the social, political, and economic community of the guild.[3] By providing a parish settlement, apprenticeship had already given the right to claim poor relief in the master's parish.

This set of economic and political rights offers one compelling answer to why apprentices served. They also suggest what would happen after they completed their terms: former apprentices should enter the privileged life of an urban citizen and guild member. Those who did not complete their terms were barred from setting up a business in the town or using their trade there, and lost the right (and burden) of participating in local and guild self-government. Formally, even skilled waged workers, journeymen, needed to have completed their apprenticeship and joined the guild, although the latter requirement was not always observed.[4]

We can see this as a test of the social and economic purpose of apprenticeship. If apprenticeship was primarily about gaining access to economic rents by achieving guild membership, then it is hard to understand why those who served would not wish to do just that. They may have to overcome further hurdles set by the guild, such as entry fees and tests of skill, but youths who could marshal the resources to achieve that would surely focus on joining their guild.

Some evidence that alternative opportunities could outweigh the potential benefits of urban and guild membership is provided by the distribution of early departures from apprenticeships analysed in chapter 6. The degree to which youths would become freemen of the guild and city they trained in, choose to return home, or migrate elsewhere, offer an even more robust test of the perceived significance of guild rents.

Alternatively, to the extent that apprenticeship was about gaining human capital—skills, knowledge, connections, experience—then one could imagine a more varied set of outcomes. Youths who sought to gain the most from their training would choose to take their human capital to the place where they could achieve the highest return from it. This would not always be the place where they trained (although they would sacrifice some place-specific knowledge and entitlements if they left). Former apprentices would be particularly likely to migrate if the economic rents from guild membership and urban citizenship were modest. Apprentices' movements after completing their training influence how effectively apprenticeship led to the diffusion of techniques and knowledge across a region or country. If few left the locations where they had trained, then ideas would have spread more slowly.

The connection between apprenticeship and citizenship also inflects how we evaluate the nature of urban society in this period. The corporate character of premodern cities and towns created a distance between them and the rural communities that made up the majority of the country. But how great was this distance? The local nature of premodern urban citizenship can be—and has been—interpreted as a source of strength in a society of orders, or, alternatively, as a deadweight cost that rewarded oligarchic elites at the expense of the rest of the population.[5] Tracing youths as they left apprenticeship reveals how exclusive these communities were in reality, and how far they advantaged their own descendants over outsiders.

The chapter looks at the outcomes of apprenticeship from three perspectives. The first section examines the formal process of entering the freedom of cities and guilds in England in order to identify the presence and size of barriers to entry and who they affected. This provides the baseline for the second section, which considers what share of apprentices did become freemen and what types of people took that path, and particularly what resources and connections of birth and marriage distinguished those who did from those who did not join their guild and city. The final section looks at those apprentices who did not stay in the places where they trained, exploring what share returned home to their places of origin.

As I show, formal barriers to becoming a guild member or citizen were relatively low in England. This was a relatively open system. Nevertheless, fewer than half of apprentices became citizens. Those who were better connected, better resourced, and better trained were more likely to do so, but the impact of these social and economic characteristics on apprentices' outcomes was modest. 'Outsiders' made it, and they supplied the majority of the next generation of citizens and freemen.

As importantly, entering the guild was not the only positive outcome from training: apprenticeship could be part of a circle of movement bringing skills back to one's place of origin, or a step in an onward movement to another place. The effect was to diffuse ideas and skills across the economy. In explaining the economic changes that occurred in England during these centuries, the former apprentices who departed matter as much as those who stayed. Former apprentices took with them the high-quality knowledge and techniques they had gained, and these allowed provincial centres and rural communities to diversify and grow, spreading structural change through the introduction of new occupations and manufactures out from London and the major cities and into the provinces.

Freedom

If we take the perspective of guild and civic officials, then early modern apprenticeship had but one natural end-point: becoming a freeman of a guild. The rules of England's guilds privileged apprenticeship to a master who was already within a guild as the central avenue into membership. The governors of a substantial number of English towns, particularly larger centres, viewed apprenticeship in much the same way: serving an apprenticeship to a local citizen was a way to qualify for citizenship. This ability to access citizenship and guild membership provided a powerful incentive to undertake apprenticeship. As Phil Withington has emphasised, from the perspective of those at the top of the urban hierarchy, apprenticeship was 'a regulative institution that demarcated urban freedoms even as it replenished them'.[6]

The extent and nature of citizenship and guild membership did change over this period. The formal abolition of one of the main institutional barriers tied to apprenticeship, with Parliament's removal in 1814 of the clauses from the Statute of Artificers that tied the right to work to a seven-year apprenticeship, provides us with the end-point of this study. Although important elements of urban and corporate economic regulation were in decline in early modern England, apprenticeship continued to be a source of meaningful legal qualification to that date and beyond.

Apprenticeship was not the only way to become a citizen or guild member. In London, sons of citizens and guild members could claim entry to city and guild by inheritance (termed 'patrimony'), and the status could be purchased for a fee; a few individuals were even gifted citizenship by the city's governors. Most major cities operated similar systems, but with some variation—marriage to a freeman's daughter in Bristol, for example, or holding certain plots of land.

Within London, the continued value of citizenship was attested by the large numbers of people purchasing it in the eighteenth century. Prosecutions for retailing without being a freeman continued into the 1830s. However, for some groups, notably merchants, the City abandoned its ambition to enforce the freedom in the later seventeenth century.[7] And from the mid-eighteenth century, non-free journeymen could be licensed to work in the City.[8] But for retailers and masters with workshops, working without the freedom continued to be risky, leaving them open to the risk of prosecution. A number of guilds, too, remained active for much of the century, and from the 1750s they made considerable efforts to assert control over their trades.[9] Moreover, for many artisans, the connection between apprenticeship, identity, and rights was firmly entrenched.

Elsewhere in England the situation varied. In some new or rapidly expanding towns, such as Manchester or Birmingham, guild and corporate regulation withered or was never established in the first place. In others, such as Shrewsbury or Beverley, it was not until the urban reforms of the 1830s that restrictions on unfree traders were lifted.[10]

Becoming a citizen was a public act enacted through oaths and public testimonials that incorporated the former apprentice into what Max Weber termed the oath-bound community of the city.[11] In London, the apprentice was first presented to the governing court of their guild. Their master testified that they had served their term of service and the court decided whether the apprentice should be admitted. The guild took its fees and required an oath to be sworn by the apprentice. For many apprentices, this was the first time they would have entered the guild's hall since their indentures were registered.

Next came citizenship of the city, for which the former apprentice, their master, and the guild's officers appeared between 12 A.M. and 1 P.M. at the Guildhall, the centre of London's government.[12] Their master again testified to their apprentice's service (false testimony could be punished by disenfranchisement),[13] and the former apprentice would take another oath, this time to the City, and pay more fees. Most guilds brought a cluster of new freemen to the Guildhall to enfranchise them together, making this their first public gathering with fellow guild members. Other English cities followed similar processes, with admission a formal event at the seat of the town's government, although most lacked the exclusive tie between guild freedom and citizenship found in London.

Unlike in much of continental Europe, in London journeymen were—at least in theory—expected to be members of their guild and citizens.[14] Guild rules often demanded that former apprentices be presented within a few months of the ends of their terms; wandering around the labour market was to be discouraged. In the most tightly governed guilds, freedom was essential; in the 1710s, for example, John Gent recalled that he had been discharged 'as a foreigner' for working as a printer's journeyman in London when 'I was not yet a freeman'.[15] Only a few London guilds demanded a period of journeywork before setting up shop.[16] In a few others, new freemen faced limits on the numbers of apprentices they could take; for example, between 1569 and 1655, the Carpenters banned freemen from taking apprentices in their first three years.[17] Once free, a former apprentice usually had much the same rights as any other member of their guild. Outside London, journeymen from other places were more likely to be officially tolerated, although they might still need to gain the permission of the guild or be examined before working.[18]

If entry to the freedom was not to be deferred, it was also not easily accelerated. Apprentices who sought to escape their contracts early might on occasion buy the last months or years of their terms from their masters. Sometimes masters might even remit a period as a gift. Several guilds were openly cautious about this practice. The Brewers' Company ordered that no one shall 'sell or pardon any part or parcel of the term of years of the same apprentice without license of the Chamberlain of London and of the Master and . . . Wardens'.[19] The Carpenters established a similar rule.[20] The basis for their caution was articulated most clearly by the Goldsmiths' Company in their 1478 Ordinances, when they banned the sale of apprentices' terms to any but a freeman

> because several members of the craft take apprentices who, as soon as they have a smattering of knowledge and have been entered in the craft and know its privities, buy their terms from their masters, and go to other cities, boroughs and towns where they work neither properly nor truly . . . to the great disgrace of the craft.[21]

Two hurdles could trip up an apprentice on the road to the freedom. The first was the requirement that apprentices be sufficiently skilled. However, as shown in chapter 7, masterpieces or other kinds of mastership test were not universal in England, and there is little evidence that they were strictly applied in most cases. The second was financial. London's fees in 1708 for freedom by servitude were 4s for the master and 1s for the apprentice, plus 2s 6d to the clerk. If the apprentice had not been enrolled, the master paid 13s 2d (the normal 4s plus a fine of 9s 2d).[22] If the apprentice was a pauper child who had been placed from Bridewell, they were admitted gratis.[23] As most of these charges were to be met by the master, it is perhaps unsurprising that occasionally masters refused to make an apprentice free.[24] Fees in other cities and towns were mostly at a similar—and similarly stable—level to those imposed in London, as can be seen in table 8.1, where they are expressed in cash and in the number of days of unskilled work that would be required to earn them.

Table 8.1 considers only the citizenship fees required by the town or city. Guilds' own fees were notionally fixed at an even lower level. Punitively high fees had been introduced by some London guilds in the fifteenth century. But in 1530, because of 'the great Hurt of the King's true Subjects putting their Child to be Apprentice', Parliament capped guild fees at 3s 4d for new freemen by apprenticeship; the same statute also cut apprenticeship fees.[25] Fees subsequently crept up in some guilds, but most remained below 10s until the mid- to late eighteenth century, when a few of the city's guilds began to demand more substantial sums—in the order of a pound for the Clothworkers, the Tylers and Bricklayers, and the Butchers. The most elaborate example was the carefully constructed tiers of fees established by the Merchant Taylors in January 1662, under which artisans such as armourers, hot-pressers, masons, and victuallers would pay 6s 8d, more prosperous trades paid 10s, most wholesalers such as drapers and mercers paid 13s 4d, and merchants trading overseas paid 20s.[26] Even so, only youths entering the wealthiest trades—for which they would need to possess substantial amounts of capital if they were to operate independently—were mulcted for sums over 10s.

In practice, guild charges might be higher, as additional 'gifts', administrative fees, and dinners were sometimes demanded.[27] The most common loophole used by London's guilds to top up freedom fees was to demand a 'gift' from the new freeman, most often a silver spoon worth 13s 4d, as in the Apothecaries, Poulterers, and Wheelwrights.[28] These additional costs were clearly not trivial, and various attempts were made to contain them.

TABLE 8.1. City fees for entry to freedom or citizenship

	Cash			Day Wages		
	1500–1599	1600–1699	1700–1799	1500–1599	1600–1699	1700–1799
Boston		3s 4d	3s 4d		3	3
Canterbury		4s 1d	7s 6d		9	6
Gloucester[1]		4s	4s		9	6
Great Yarmouth	6s 8d	6s 8d		16	7	
King's Lynn	0	0	0	0	0	0
Lancaster	26s 8d		26s 8d	64		20
Leicester		10s			10	
Liverpool[2]	6s 8d	6s 8d	6s 8d	18	11	6
London[3]	4s	4s	5s	7	2.4	2.3
Swansea[4]			5s			5

Sources: Bailey 1980–85, 1:290, 749, 4:445; Coy et al. 1993, 5:viii; Barlow 2001, xiv; *A Calendar of the Freemen of Great Yarmouth* (Hepworth 1910); *A Calendar of the Freemen of Lynn, 1292–1836* (1913); Hughes and Kendall 1935, v–vi; Hartopp 1927, xix; Hill 1956, 29, 80; Royal Commission on Municipal Corporations 1835, 2350, 2712; Twemlow 1912, 1:386; Muir and Platt 1906, 120; Alban 1982; Cowper 1903. Day wages are taken from Robert Allen's series. I use unskilled labourers for London for the London series, and for Oxford for all other locations.

[1] Plus an additional 5s 6d in officers' fees.

[2] Plus 10d fees and a breakfast or banquet (sixteen and seventeenth centuries).

[3] Plus 2s 6d in fees.

[4] Plus 1s in officers' fees.

In 1616, London's Court of Aldermen examined a complaint that various companies 'greatly surcharge such as are made free of their companies taking of them great sums of money or plate or imposing upon the Charge of keeping a dinner over and above the ordinary duties to be paid in that behalf'.[29] In 1622, they again worried that new freemen were being charged fees that were 'very great and heavy to poor men', prompting an investigation by the court.[30] The Drapers' Company's wardens were concerned in 1639 that people were deterred from entering the company because of the heavy charges incurred for dinners.[31]

Outside London, guild fees for membership give the general impression that direct costs were only a modest barrier to membership. The Gateshead Drapers imposed a remarkably high fee of 42s 6d in 1658, while in nearby Newcastle the Barber Surgeons expected 40s.[32] These seem to have been exceptional, however. In another seventeen guilds in Bristol, Lincoln,

Sheffield, Carlisle. and Hull, one charged 13s 4d, nine charged 6s 8d, five demanded 3s 4d, and the final two asked for just 2s 6d.[33] All were within the same range as the fees charged by London's guilds.

The fees that cities and guilds charged former apprentices for the freedom were more an annoyance than a major barrier in England once Parliament capped fees in 1530. Fees failed to rise with inflation in the sixteenth century, rendering them ever less significant as time passed. When we consider city fees against wages, as in the second panel of table 8.1, then with only a few exceptions, notably in Lancaster, they equaled a few days of wages for the lowest-paid male urban workers. The total fees charged by the City and an average London guild—including an additional 'gift' of a silver spoon—would have equated to about twelve to thirteen days wages for an unskilled building labourer in the seventeenth and eighteenth centuries. In the middle of the sixteenth century, before inflation took off, fees equated to, at most, around a month's income of an unskilled building labourer. Thereafter they fell substantially.[34] Provincial equivalents would probably have been similar, although there is too little information on any additional gifts to produce a precise estimate. Expressing fees in these terms deliberately overstates the real burden of fees for most of those who would have faced them: unskilled wages were substantially below the skilled wages that these former apprentices would have been earning, and in London, at least, part of this burden—the fee to the City—was paid out of the master's pocket.

Set against the charges imposed in other cities in Europe, English guild and city fees were low. Some guilds in Antwerp set fees that were more than six times higher—half a year of unskilled wages in the mid-seventeenth century. While Antwerp was exceptional even compared to most German, French, and Dutch guilds, fees were lower north of the English Channel.[35] In short, after 1530, English financial barriers to former apprentices joining guilds and cities were low in absolute and relative terms.

In England, entry fees were also structured in a way that did not create further inequities: they were fair, in short. Fees can be differentiated to give members of some preferred subgroup an advantage. This was common in some parts of Europe. In Paris, on average, guilds charged masters' sons entry fees that were less than half of what they extracted from former apprentices. Cities in the Southern Netherlands, such as Antwerp, usually halved fees for sons, as did Munich's guilds.[36] Discounts existed in the Northern Netherlands, but were smaller, around 20 per cent. In England, by contrast, the charges levied on apprentices were generally the same as those imposed on the sons of masters. In the city and guilds of London, both paid the same sums. Elsewhere, fees were also little different. The effect of this was to level the financial playing field between insiders and outsiders. The only group that faced truly penal costs to access guilds and citizenship in England, with fees often exceeding £10, were those who sought to enter by 'redemption', without either a claim through their father or time served as an apprentice to an existing member. Unsurprisingly, few joined in this way.

For most of the sixteenth and seventeenth centuries, these guild and city processes appear to have amounted to the totality of becoming a freeman. In the later eighteenth century, however, as the likelihood that they would become freemen and masters declined, journeymen in some occupations established their own trade societies separate from the guilds. These meant some former apprentices faced a different set of hurdles to access employment, not independence. By 1780, for example, the trade society of journeymen coopers demanded that a young man coming out of apprenticeship had to pay his 'footing': three gallons of beer, price 3s 6d, another gallon for each piece of work done for the first time, and an extra gallon for each different sort of timber. Fines amounting to 16s 4d were demanded (in beer) for work worth only 15s 9d.[37]

The openness of English cities and guilds to former apprentices is apparent in the share of freemen who qualified by servitude. From the sixteenth century to the close of the eighteenth century, the ranks of London's freemen were largely filled by former apprentices. Evidence for the city as a whole is scarce, thanks to the loss of the majority of London's registers of freemen in a fire in the 1780s, but in the 1550s nine out of ten new citizens qualified by servitude, and in the 1660s and 1690s, around four out of five.[38] In London, the centrality of apprenticeship to the admission of new citizens had emerged after a major reform in 1312 which gave the crafts control over who became citizens, replacing the 'free-for-all-who-would-pay' system of citizenship, as Caroline Barron describes it, in which access was usually bought not earned.[39] Shortly before that reform, fewer than three in ten new citizens had been former apprentices.[40] For several guilds, information on how freemen qualified in the sixteenth to eighteenth centuries does survive. As figure 8.1 shows, the share of apprentices among new freemen was declining slowly over time, but was rarely below 50 per cent before 1800. It was only in the nineteenth century that former apprentices became a minority in London's much diminished guilds.

Provincial towns and cities also drew heavily on local apprentices to fill out the ranks of their citizenry. Most were less dependent on this channel than the metropolis, as can be seen in figure 8.2, thanks to lower growth

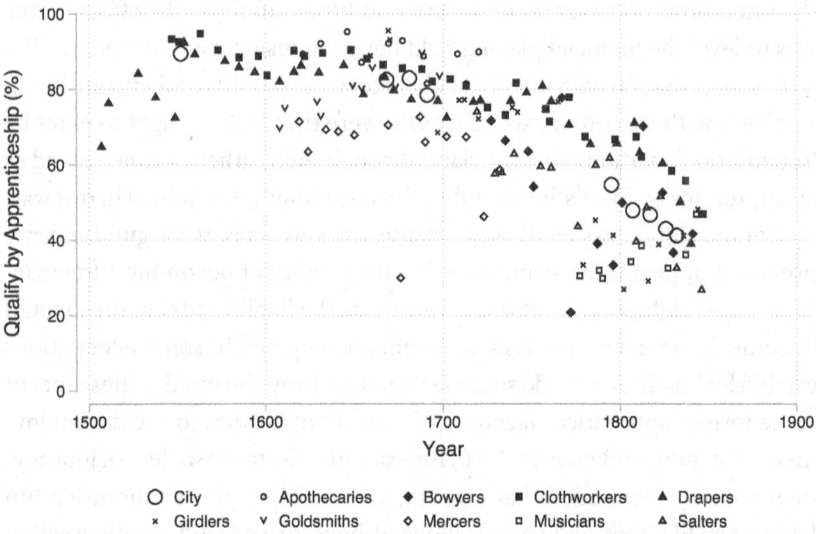

FIGURE 8.1. Share of new freemen and citizens by apprenticeship, London. The figure reports decadal averages of the share of new freemen entering by apprenticeship (servitude) from two categories of sources. The "City" figures are for all freemen from the surviving City of London records. The other figures are for nine individual guilds.

rates, healthier environments, and, in some places such as Bristol and Canterbury, the potential to enter through marriage to the daughter or widow of a citizen. Predictably, large and rapidly growing Bristol was closest to London, taking around two-thirds of new citizens through apprenticeship in the seventeenth century, while in Gloucester only around 40 per cent used this channel.

The degree to which apprenticeship and citizenship were entangled varied between places and over time. In Boston, Bristol, and Canterbury, apprenticeship was seemingly becoming more important in the decades around 1600. In York, however, it was already declining in significance, albeit from a very high level in the early 1500s. From around 1700 onwards, apprenticeship became less common as a route into the freedom in most cities except Boston.

The link between apprenticeship and migration meant that a period of urban growth of the kind seen in many towns in the sixteenth and seventeenth centuries was always likely to see a rise in the share of citizens entering through apprenticeship. However, the Elizabethan and Stuart boom in apprenticeship as a qualification that occurred in some of these

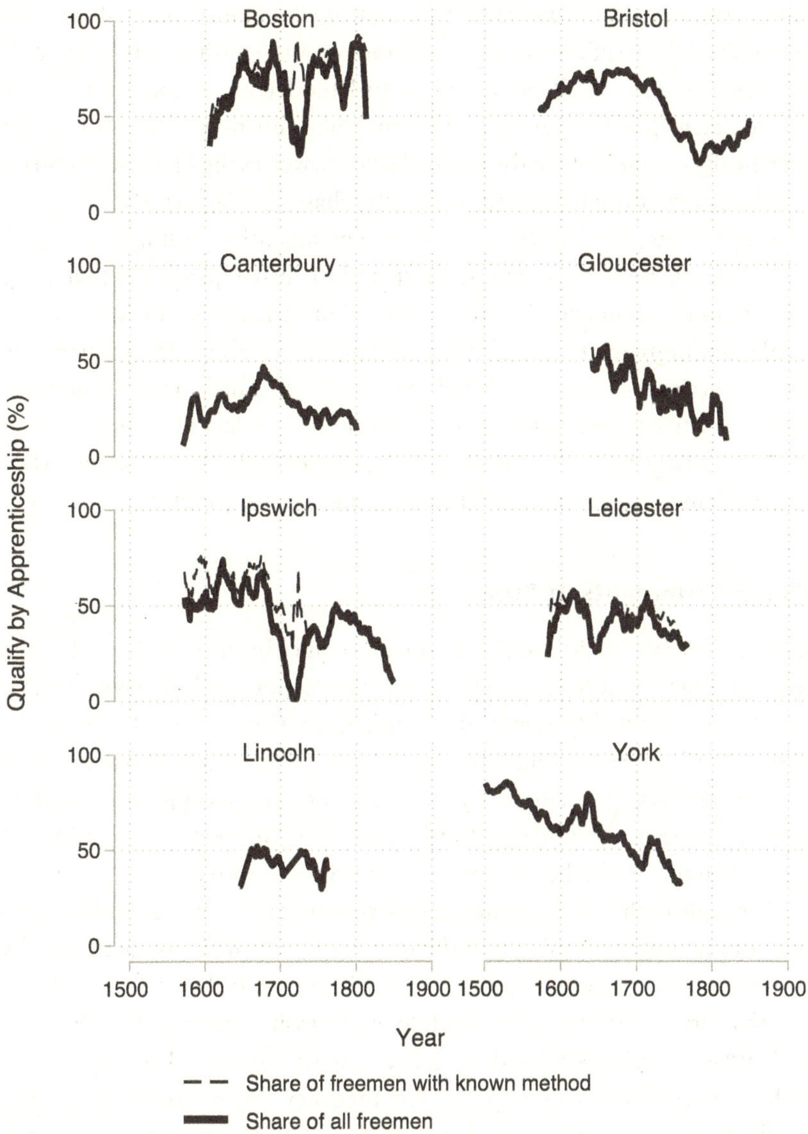

FIGURE 8.2. Share of new freemen by apprenticeship in provincial towns and cities. This figure reports the share of new freemen entering by servitude. For some cities, the method by which the freedom was entered is not known for all new freemen. For this reason, the figure also reports the share of freemen whose method of entry is known.

towns reflected central political intervention: the Statute of Artificers had generalised the requirement for apprenticeship and pushed youths towards its attractive mix of skill and privilege. Its later decline, in turn, reflects the weakening grip of the statute over journeymen and 'new' trades (those not specifically enumerated in the original law), as well as the increase in entries to urban citizenship by inheritance or purchase that occurred during contested parliamentary elections in the long eighteenth century.[41]

A close tie between apprenticeship and the urban privileges that came with guild freedom and citizenship existed in early modern England. This weakened in many, if not all, places during the eighteenth century. The formal barriers of money and skill that apprentices had to surmount were limited relative to some other parts of Europe. The effect of this can be seen in the very large share of urban residents who had gained their rights to live and work in a town or city through servitude as an apprentice.

The Determinants of Freedom

Large numbers of guild and city freemen had once been apprentices, but the reality for most youths was very far from the corporate ideal that saw servitude leading inevitably to citizenship and mastership. Despite low financial barriers and an urban community built largely from those who had served apprenticeships, only a minority of early modern urban apprentices would become freemen. Around two-thirds would not. This section asks what distinguished those who became freemen from those who did not.

The scale of the phenomenon can be summarised quite easily. The number of new apprentices dwarfed the number of new freemen qualifying by servitude in every London guild and English provincial city until the eighteenth century, indicating poor odds for a successful transition into the guild and citizenry. In the sixteenth and seventeenth centuries, London's guilds welcomed around two new apprentices for every one new freeman—a ratio similar to that observed in a wide range of cities and towns across Europe.[42]

Historians have long recognised that what Ilana Krausman Ben-Amos styled 'failure to become freemen' was the norm.[43] If anything, we have tended to understate the issue. Most estimates compare the number of new apprentices with the total number of new freemen, the measure used in the previous paragraph. But an important minority of freemen qualified through inheritance or purchase. To get a more accurate sense of the odds that apprentices faced, we can compare their numbers with the number of new freemen who entered through apprenticeship. The results for several London guilds, split by century, are given in table 8.2.

TABLE 8.2. Ratio of new freemen by servitude to new apprentices in London guilds

	1600–1699	1700–1799	1800–1899	N
Apothecaries	0.38	0.35		4,868
Bowyers		0.44	0.38	335
Clothworkers	0.38	0.50	0.55	31,239
Drapers	0.37	0.41	0.52	17,557
Girdlers	0.37	0.44	0.34	1,558
Goldsmiths	0.40			8,759
Mercers	0.35	0.36	0.11	4,004
Musicians		0.13	0.43	1,471
Salters		0.36	0.55	1,764
Tallow Chandlers			0.22	3,006
Average	0.36	0.38	0.45	31,239

Note: The table reports the ratio of apprentices to freemen qualifying by servitude in periods for which data for both is seemingly complete.

In most London guilds, around one new freeman was admitted by servitude for every three apprentices registered by the guild. In the seventeenth century, when guild apprenticeship was in full swing, there was surprisingly little variation between guilds. The situation became more mixed in the eighteenth and nineteenth centuries, but few guilds could be seen as offering odds that were particularly favourable to apprentices. Overall, these were poor chances indeed, if one defines success in this way.

Why did some apprentices become freemen while others did not? While this question cannot be answered fully, we can at least examine how the chance of successfully becoming a freeman was influenced by the background and choices that apprentices and their families made. Were all apprentices equally (un)likely to become freemen, or did some youths have better prospects than others?

We can examine the likelihood of apprentices becoming freemen for a large sample of over 100,000 apprentices across eighteen London guilds between the sixteenth and eighteenth centuries. The sample of guilds is larger than that used to calculate the ratio of apprentices to freemen because it incorporates additional guilds for which the full register of freemen is not in our dataset, just an indication of which apprentices were freed. Within this large sample, for around 17,000 apprentices in twelve guilds there is information about their masters' careers—the number of apprentices they took, the time since they became freemen themselves, and so on.

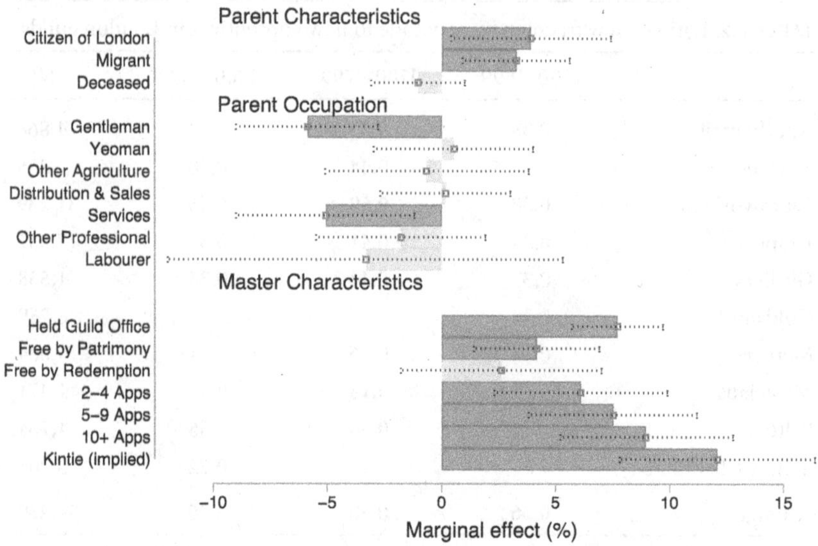

FIGURE 8.3. How apprentices' origins affected their chances of becoming freemen in London. The figure reports the marginal effect on the chance that an apprentice became a freeman for each of the listed variables, against an overall probability of 37% in the sample. Bars in dark grey are variables with statistically significant effects, at the 5% level or greater; bars in light grey do not meet conventional levels of significance. Whiskers report the confidence interval. The figure is based on model 10 in table A8.5: the reference group are non-migrant, non-citizen sons of living craftsmen training with masters who take a single apprentice.

The impact that apprentices' backgrounds and their masters' careers had on their chances of becoming freemen is illustrated in figure 8.3. This reports the marginal effect that various characteristics had on the probability of an apprentice becoming a freeman. The marginal effect can be thought of as the percentage point increase or decrease in the likelihood an outcome happened when compared to the chances faced by a reference group. The reference group in this case is made up of local boys born into craft families, whose fathers were not citizens and guild members themselves, and who trained with masters who took one apprentice; 35 per cent of the reference group became freemen. The full results are reported in appendix 8.

One striking feature of the analysis that is not visible in the figure needs to be emphasised first: none of the regression models explain very much of the variation in outcomes. All achieve pseudo-R-squared scores below 0.05. This means that most of the variation in the probability that an apprentice would become a freeman *cannot* be explained by those aspects of their background or training that are isolated and analysed here. The most likely reason for this is that apprentices made much of their own luck themselves.

The story that emerges from figure 8.3 is one in which social origins and networks had an important effect on entry to the freedom. Apprentices who were related to their masters—usually the masters' sons—were around 12 per cent more likely to become freemen than other apprentices. Wider connections to the corporate community of the city were less important. Migrants and sons of London citizens were both equally likely to become freemen, compared to Londoners who were not citizens' children,[44] and the advantage each group gained through their background was modest in real terms—they were only around 3–4 per cent more likely to become freemen than non-citizens' children.

Family resources also affected the chances of becoming a freeman. The reference category here are the children of artisans. Compared to them, gentry sons and those with parents in the service sector—cooks, innkeepers, victuallers, mariners, waggoners, and so on—and labourers' children were less likely to become freemen. This presumably reflects the availability and transferability of capital. That apprentices from families in distribution and sales were as likely as those from artisanal families to become freemen suggests similarly that shops and associated goodwill could be passed from father to son.

The choice of master also heavily influenced the paths apprentices took after they came to the end of their terms. Apprentices who trained with masters who bound multiple youths were significantly more likely to become freemen than those whose masters took just one. The increase in the chance of becoming a freeman was 7 per cent for those with masters training more than four apprentices, and 9 per cent for those training ten or more apprentices. Masters' own involvement in the guild was also strongly associated with their apprentices' outcomes. Masters whose own fathers had been guild members trained more apprentices who became freemen. Masters who led their guilds, taking offices in the governing councils, had apprentices who were 8 per cent more likely to become freemen than those without these guild roles. This evidence is consistent with the higher premiums that parents paid to masters who had trained multiple apprentices.[45] The master's experience and success lifted the chance their apprentice would themselves become free, and this effect further reinforced the role of large, successful masters in reproducing the skilled workforce discussed in chapter 3.

This was not just a metropolitan story. Carrying out the same exercise for a range of provincial towns and cities produces broadly similar results.

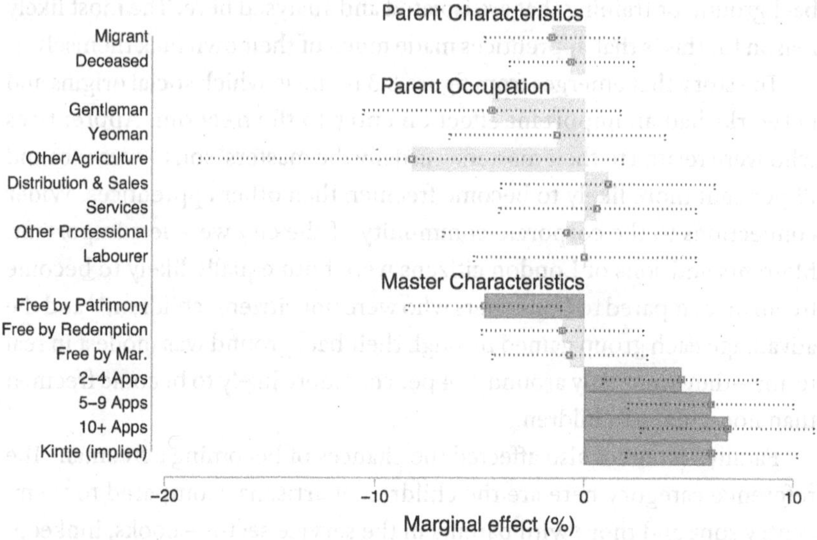

FIGURE 8.4. How apprentices' origins affected their chances of becoming freemen in provincial towns and cities. The figure reports the marginal effect on the chance that an apprentice became a freeman for each of the listed variables, against an overall probability of 44% in the sample. Bars in dark grey are variables with statistically significant effects, at the standard 10% level or greater; bars in light grey do not meet conventional levels of significance. The figure is based on model 8 in table A8.6: the reference group are local sons of living craftsmen training with masters who take a single apprentice.

For Bristol, Gloucester, Lincoln, and Boston, just over 25,000 apprentices can be traced in city records that record who became freemen. The process of linkage is summarised in appendix 8, along with the details of the underlying datasets. Bristol contributes the largest number of observations, with almost 11,000 apprentices identified in the city's freedom registers, while in Gloucester, just shy of 500 could be traced. Overall, 44 per cent of apprentices became freemen in these centres.

Figure 8.4 repeats the same approach to estimating the impact of different factors on the chance of apprentices becoming a freeman. Again, ties of kinship were important, lifting the likelihood of becoming a freeman for sons of masters by over 5 per cent. Resources mattered: apprentices whose futures might be affected by the lottery of inheritance in the countryside—gentlemen's sons and farmers—were less likely to remain, although these variables do not meet standard measures of significance. Interestingly, apprentices whose masters had entered their guilds by patrimony were less likely to become freemen in these settings. Most strikingly, our measure of master quality, the number of apprentices they took, influenced corporate success positively and substantially. The impact of the number of apprentices trained by the master was close to that seen in London.

One advantage of the provincial records is that they give us a guide to the occupations that youths were entering, not just their guild affiliations. Some of the occupations in which persistence during the apprenticeship contract was lower in the 1690s (discussed in chapter 7) were also occupations that tended to have lower chances of entering the freedom. Mariners' apprentices, whose fortunes lay in success in a risky enterprise that was the very definition of mobility, rarely became freemen.[46] Those entering rooted port trades with high local demand for their services—and three of these cities, Gloucester, Boston, and Bristol, were ports—such as coopers and carpenters, were more likely to become freemen.

To summarise, freedom followed apprenticeship for a minority of apprentices in both London and England's smaller towns and cities. It is important to be clear about what does *not* explain why some apprentices did not become freemen. This 'failure' was not because apprentices were squeezed out of places in guilds and cities by members of other groups, such as the sons of existing masters; none of these guilds or cities operated quotas on the numbers of members in the way that is found in Paris, for example. Nor were outsiders barred by high fees or exclusionary strategies of other kinds, as was shown in the previous section. Why some 'insiders' were more likely to become freemen cannot be explained by overt institutional decisions around rules and fees.

Three interlinked and overlapping factors were associated with a higher probability that an apprentice became a freeman: kinship, resources, and the master who trained them. Family connections, especially direct links, were powerful: masters' sons and their wider kin made it into the freedom more often than others.[47] In London, where this information was recorded, citizens' sons did better than sons of non-citizens. This is hardly surprising. Not only did citizens' sons have the help of direct connections, they also had longer experience and understanding of their trade, and a greater chance of inheriting an established business. The effect of resources was more subtle. Those whose fathers had wealth and (local) resources were more likely to end up as freemen than the children of poor labourers. Conversely, those with opportunities through inheritance elsewhere were less likely to stay and become freemen. With the shift towards local recruitment that occurred over the period described in chapter 4, more apprentices had these useful ties.

Finally, the role of the master was large: those serving successful masters who bound numerous youths and achieved prominence in their guilds were also more likely to make the next step into the freedom (that the master is picked by the family makes their characteristics in part a reflection of the apprentice's family and resources). Those who trained with masters on the margins of their guilds were likely to remain marginal. These are largely the same factors that influenced persistence, as shown in chapter 6, suggesting that these outcomes in part reflect decisions that were made before and during the course of training. Failure to become a freeman was not entirely the product of a post-apprenticeship choice between staying and going, or the consequence of commercial failure.

Ties, resources, and training mattered. Their effects combined to drive a wedge between different apprentices' chances of becoming freemen. Take London to illustrate this. For a youth born in London with all the disadvantages one can envisage—a dead, non-citizen father who had worked as a labourer, and a master who took just one apprentice and did not hold guild office—the predicted probability that he would become a freeman was 31 per cent; the equivalent migrant to London—the son of a dead provincial labourer, with the same type of master—had better odds, at 39 per cent.

Compare that with the opposite: a citizen's son, with a living father engaged in a craft occupation, and who trained with a relative who was a guild officer and taught more than ten apprentices over his career—their estimated chance of becoming a freeman was 70 per cent. The provincial equivalent would be the 35 per cent probability of becoming a freeman predicted for a migrant with a deceased labourer father, no kin tie to his master, and a master who trained one apprentice, compared to the 54 per cent probability of a local boy with a living father in distribution and sales, a kin tie to his master, and a master who trained more than ten apprentices. These gaps represent the extremes around an overall average probability of becoming a freeman of 43 per cent in our sample for London and 44 per cent in our sample for elsewhere.

Most apprentices had no kinship ties to their masters. That three out of ten of the most-favoured group—well-resourced insiders' sons—would not become freemen, while three out of ten of the least-favoured would, reveals an environment in which social and occupational mobility was possible, if not easy, success still depended on the individual, and—in a broad sense—'openness' to outsiders was the rule.

Setting aside sons of citizens who were bound to their own fathers, a group who supplied only a small share of apprentices, for most apprentices the odds of entry to the freedom fell somewhere around 40 per cent. For citizens' sons in London with all the other advantages cited above but who were *not* related to their masters, the probability of becoming a freeman fell to 58 per cent; in provincial centres, the probability of becoming a freeman without a kin tie fell to 46 per cent. That the odds in London were still almost twice the odds faced by their peers with the fewest advantages makes clear the inequality of opportunity that existed in early modern cities. On the other hand, among apprentices who were freed, 89 per cent had *no* kin tie, 86 per cent were *not* citizens' sons, 43 per cent were *not* from London, 68 per cent were *not* sons of craftsmen, and 61 per cent trained with masters who were *not* guild officers. Even among freemen, the advantaged were outnumbered by the less advantaged.

What about connections that were acquired through marriage, not inherited? Did these define apprentices' fortunes? Setting up as a freeman was linked to marrying and establishing a household. Apprentices were barred from marriage during their term by their contract. Not all observed this promise faithfully, to be sure, and unsurprisingly some were expelled from their contracts for breaking it.[48] But it was only with the end of servitude that marriage became a real possibility for most.

In fairy tales, it would be the master's daughter or widow who stood at the altar waiting for her groom. The economist Alfred Marshall noted the continued importance of this image in the nineteenth century:

> Many a youth has been stimulated to a brave career by the influence of ballads and tales which narrate the difficulties and the ultimate triumph of the faithful apprentice, who has at length been taken into partnership, perhaps on marrying his employer's daughter. There are no influences on national character more far-reaching than those which thus give shape to the aims of aspiring youth.[49]

A handful of famous examples, such as the prominent merchant Lionel Cranfield, achieved this dream. However, in reality, this was rarely the case.[50] For a modest sample of freemen, their marriage can be identified in the registers of marriage licences published for London. Just four of this sample of ninety-eight London apprentices from a range of guilds in the seventeenth century were marrying into their masters' families; all married their masters' daughters. This is almost exactly the same as the 4.8 per cent share found among a separate sample of 297 London Stationers' apprentices whose marriages can be traced.[51] Bristol's apprentices seem to have fared equally poorly in the eighteenth century, when 3 to 6 per cent wed brides with the same last names as their former masters.[52]

Although this degree of within-workshop marriage is greater than if former apprentices were finding brides at random, it is clear that marrying the master's daughter was an exceptional outcome. This should be no surprise: the chance that a master would have a child who survived to adulthood in early modern cities, London especially, was poor. Most apprentices were trained by masters who took multiple apprentices, increasing the competition for any surviving daughter's hand. Finally, the likelihood that a master would have a daughter of marriageable age at the same time as their apprentice sought a bride was low—this was particularly true for apprentices taken in the early years of their masters' careers, whose terms often started at the same time as the masters would be fathering their first children.

The opportunity to enter their father-in-laws' businesses seems to have been a modest factor in most former apprentices' marriages. Setting aside those who did marry into their masters' families, just four in fifty-seven London apprentices (7%) married daughters of men in the same trade or guild. Marrying a widow in the same trade was more common—four out of seventeen (24%) took this path—and guild regulations that punished widows who married someone outside the guild by stripping them of their residual right to operate in the trade encouraged this.[53] But most new London freemen were marrying spinsters, not widows.[54] Cumulatively, just 6 per cent of former apprentices in London chose an obviously strategically advantageous match.[55]

There is less information for Bristol, but there, too, widows played a marginal role. None of the apprentices who married into their masters' families were marrying their masters' widows. Only one in ten apprentices who later became citizens by marriage (one of the ways to qualify in Bristol) did so by marrying a widow, slightly below the 14 per cent among Bristol freemen by marriage overall.

With their freedom earned and marriage made, a former apprentice crossed the two key thresholds to full independence and identity as a citizen and householder. Insiders, however defined, did have an advantage: kinship ties made it more likely an apprentice achieved freedom; marrying into a master's family helped, but was very rare; training with one of the leading large masters increased the odds of corporate membership. These gave some a head start, but they did not stop others reaching the same point. While the odds of joining the group of freemen at the heart of the urban community were never high, this was still a realistic possibility for most apprentices, whatever their origins. This openness must have been one of the underlying reasons why so many early modern families were willing to choose apprenticeship for their children. But this left many apprentices who did not take this step into the citizenry. What did they do?

Returning Home

In 1793, the *Oxford Journal* ran an advertisement noting that Messrs Gee and Furnell had taken over from Mr C. Crease as coach- and harness-makers on the High Street in Marlborough, a small town in Wiltshire.[56] The business would survive into the 1820s, although Gee died in 1794 and was replaced by a Mr Tuck.[57] The Furnell in the business's name was one Thomas Furnell, who had been born around 1770 in Marlborough to Joseph, a cheesemonger and insurance agent, and his wife Elizabeth. Although he was born and spent much of his life working in Marlborough, Thomas had not trained there. Instead, on 21 October 1784 he had been apprenticed to John Forster, one of the members of the London Coachmakers guild. Thomas was one of the eight or so apprentices his master trained over his career, and although Thomas did not become a freeman, it seems likely he served his seven-year term, as it was ten years before he returned to his hometown to set up a business there, using the skills he had gained working for one of London's larger coachmakers.

That only a third or so of apprentices became freemen in the city in which they were trained leaves a large number of youths unaccounted for. One obvious possibility—at least for migrants—is that they returned home, as Furnell did. The idea that apprenticeship could provide the focus for this kind of circular migration, with young people voyaging to towns and cities in order to gain training and connections that they could use when they returned home, is intuitively plausible.

To see how common Furnell's story was, we need to trace the lives of apprentices after they left their masters. This is challenging, but possible for two groups: young people who came from parishes for which family reconstitutions exist, and youths with a claim to urban citizenship by inheritance. For the first, I use a sample of children born in one of the fifteen provincial and eight London parishes in which families have been reconstructed by the Cambridge Group for Population and Social Structure and the People in Place project.[58] Reconstructions link the different birth, marriage, and death records of a parish together into families, allowing us to trace the apprentices who emerged from these communities. Finding these communities' children among the apprentices in London's guilds and the stamp duty registers gives us three types of evidence about roughly 1,700 youths who took up apprenticeships in the seventeenth and eighteenth centuries: any marriage records of ex-apprentices, any evidence of burial in their parishes of birth, and any signs they started families within their parishes of birth.[59]

The share of apprentices who later reappeared in their home parishes' vital records is reported in table 8.3. Only one of these categories, establishing a family and baptising a child in the local church, offers incontrovertible evidence of continued residence or return. The other two are less definitive. A marriage might precede a further migration, or could simply be an apprentice returning to turn a childhood sweetheart into a bride who would then join him in another community. A death may reflect a youth who had come home when sick, or an adult who had returned in retirement to their place of origin. That said, at the very least, marriage and death records still indicate the persistence of strong connections with the community of origin, and some would reflect circular migration, as implied by having a family at home.

Just shy of a quarter of all provincial youths who had gone to London to train would appear in their home parish's records at some later stage: 12 per cent baptised a child or children there, our strongest measure, and as many as 17 per cent were buried at home. London was a much more 'sticky' destination than other places. Those provincial youths who left their home community to train, but did not go to the metropolis, were more likely to reappear in the place they were born, with 36 per cent present in at least one category, and 16 per cent baptising children.[60] This is much as one would expect: the distance and cost involved in finding a position in London were substantial, certainly higher than those faced by youths who found a place elsewhere in provincial England, and abandoning that investment must have been harder.

Table 8.3 also provides a baseline against which to compare the behaviour of apprentices born outside London who left home to train. Because some of our data comes from the stamp duty registers, it includes a group of 100 apprentices who came from provincial communities and who trained in their hometowns or villages. Among these 'locals', a quarter would marry in their parishes of birth and a third would be buried there. On our best measure of remaining active, later baptising children, 29 per cent of those who were apprenticed locally appear in their parishes of birth. This means that youths who trained locally were around twice as likely to appear in their parish

TABLE 8.3. Former apprentices active in their places of origin

Activity	Place apprenticed	Place of origin: Provincial %	London %	Total %
Married	Locally	26		26
	London	9	16	14
	Elsewhere	18		18
Buried	Locally	32		32
	London	17	7	10
	Elsewhere	3		30
Baptised child	Locally	29		29
	London	12	4	7
	Elsewhere	16		16
Any presence	Locally	44		44
	London	23	22	23
	Elsewhere	36		36
Sample		N	N	N
	Locally	100		100
	London	488	1,058	1,546
	Elsewhere	50		50

Note: The table reports the share of apprentices from provincial and London parishes who were identified in later parish records being married or buried or baptising a child. The final rows report the share with any kind of later presence.

records as adults as those who went to train in London. Youths who left their parishes for apprenticeships but did not go to London fell between the two.

The second column of table 8.3 suggests one initially surprising observation: youths who were born and raised in London were much less likely to reappear as adults in their home parishes than youths from provincial parishes. Just a fifth reappeared in any form, and only 4 per cent baptised children in their home parishes. However, this was probably a consequence of the city's many parishes being small, which meant that a move of a few hundred feet could mean leaving the parish. The high levels of mobility between lodgings and homes within the city, as well as peculiarities of the city such as the popularity of non-parochial marriage at the Fleet and other liberties, all challenge reconstructions. It is not, in short, necessarily a measure of outmigration by Londoners leaving the metropolis, even though some surely did that.

What might make apprentices return home? A key factor appears to have been the survival of their birth families. Apprentices who were orphans behaved in a markedly different way to those who had left living parents for training. Orphans were much less likely to reappear in their home parishes; it was those whose parents were alive when they entered training who tended to reappear in their home parishes later in their lives. Among provincial apprentices who went to London, 41 per cent who had two living parents when they were bound would reappear in their home parishes' records compared to just 10 per cent of those whose parents were both dead when they started training.[61] Even London-born apprentices who stayed in the capital differed, with 43 per cent of those with two living parents reappearing compared to 32 per cent of orphans.

We lack enough information about the timing of apprentices' returns to be able to distinguish between apprentices who were responding to the availability of an inheritance following the death of a parent and those who returned to living parents. However, at least 20 per cent of apprentices returned before their last surviving parent died, indicating that inheritance is at best a partial explanation. In general, the relationship between the survival of a parental household and the return of its children to their parish of birth suggests that returning apprentices were drawn back by the advantages presented by the continuing presence of the social capital and economic resources of their parents, as we would expect in circular migration.

There is a second group of former apprentices who can be traced: youths who came from a corporate town or city to train in London. Rather than looking at their marriages, families, and deaths, we can instead see how many of them later established themselves as citizens of their hometowns, not the metropolis. This group were doubly privileged: their apprenticeships allowed them to become guild members in London, while their births gave them the right to claim citizenship by inheritance in their hometowns. The survival of urban registers of freemen, often from as early as the thirteenth century onwards, allows us look at which apprentices appeared as citizens for eleven towns and cities across England.[62] Over 1,000 apprentices in London in the sixteenth to eighteenth centuries came from one or another of these cities. As table 8.4 shows, many would choose to return home and take the citizenship of their hometowns, drawing on their local birth rights, not their privileges gained by migration and service.

TABLE 8.4. Former London apprentices who later became citizens in their place of origin

City	Number of apprentices	Weak link (%)	Medium link (%)	Strong link (%)
Boston	36	6		
Bristol	168	7	5	5
Canterbury	155	14	12	10
Chester	81	6	2	
Exeter	27	11	11	4
Gloucester	22	14	14	9
Ipswich	115	10	9	1
King's Lynn	39	8		
Leicester	183	16	16	7
Lincoln	48	10		
Newcastle upon Tyne	13	38		
Norwich	155	7	6	1
York	104	18	16	12
Total	1146	11	10	6

Note: The table reports apprentices indentured in London before 1800 who are observed as citizens in their towns or cities of origin. A weak link is a link based on the apprentice's forename and surname; a medium link adds the father's forename and surname; a strong link also adds the father's occupation. Cities without the necessary data are excluded from the medium and strong link counts.

Eleven per cent of London's apprentices who came from these cities can be found in their hometowns' citizenship registers.[63] In several cities, such as York, Leicester, and Canterbury, an even greater share would exercise their right to citizenship in their places of birth by inheritance. The shares based on more restrictive matching criteria reported in columns 3 and 4 are demanding tests, as city records do not consistently include evidence on new citizens' parents' names and occupations, generating false negatives, and even when they do, this information may not appear in the same format used in London's apprenticeship registers.[64] But where data was better kept, as in Canterbury or Leicester, the rates are very close to those found in the weaker links reported in column 2.

Many of the apprentices who later resurfaced in their origin communities were returning to settle and establish themselves, as can be seen from the timing of their entries to the citizenry.[65] Figure 8.5 shows how long

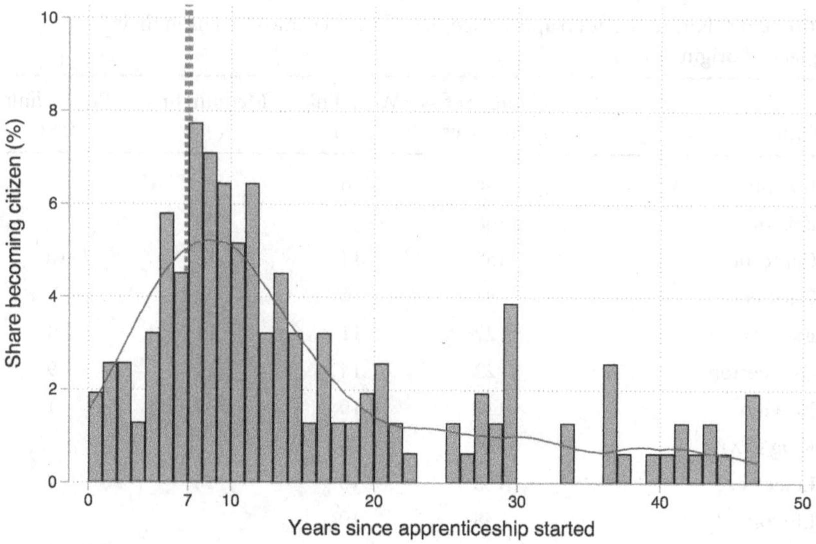

FIGURE 8.5. Time from apprenticeship to citizenship in hometown.
Source: See text.

apprentices took to obtain their citizenship back home. The clock begins when they entered their apprenticeships in London. Some left early, as one might expect, given the share who left their masters (seen in chapter 6). However, a clear peak is apparent at seven or eight years, the point when their contracts as apprentices would have finished. This is followed by a slow decline in the share returning over time.

A handful of urban returnees moved home later in life, some after twenty or thirty years in the metropolis. Thomas Wenman became a freeman in Norwich in 1693, thirty-one years after taking his freedom in the Drapers guild of London. Wenman took at least one apprentice of his own in London, binding Peter Thaker in 1663, and so would appear to have had an active career in the city. But most circular migrants seem to have come to London, trained, and gone home soon after, perhaps with a few years as journeymen in the city. For some, this may have reflected a failed attempt to set up independently in the metropolis; 37 per cent of those traced had also become members of their London masters' guilds.[66] Whether they turned up at home with their tails between their legs or bushy with confidence from their exposure to the cutting edge of the nation's economy, they brought with them the skills, knowledge, and techniques of trade and business in London, and a set of connections that further integrated the nation's markets.

Apprentices who returned to their places of origin account for a minority of those who migrated to train. Between one in ten and one in five London apprentices returned home to rural parishes or incorporated towns and cities, on top of which were an unknown number who returned but did not appear in the surviving records. As around a half or more of youths did stay in London to build futures as freemen or non-guild workers, this implies that returnees accounted for somewhere between one-fifth and one-half of apprentices who left London—a frustratingly wide estimate. At the least, we can be sure that circular migration was a common occurrence, and that it was not the dominant trajectory among those who did not remain.

There were many other options for former apprentices of course: other towns and villages within Britain to settle in, the chance to emigrate to the growing colonies in the Caribbean and Americas, fortunes to be grasped at in Asia and elsewhere. Even settling in other incorporated towns or cities was possible for former apprentices, but only if they were willing to pay the high fees demanded of those who had not been born or apprenticed there. Once out of their time, artisans in particular had skills that were highly portable. James Lackington's account of his travels after finishing his service to a shoemaker in Taunton, Somerset, began first with a different master in Taunton before he moved to find work in Bristol, where he lodged with John Jones, a twenty-one-year-old shoemaker who made 'women's stuff shoes: which he sold by the dozen to warehouses'. After around a year in Bristol, he and Jones together travelled to Bridgewater, where they worked for a Mr Cash, whose 'pretty and very amiable' daughter later married Jones. When work in Bridgewater dried up, Lackington moved on. He tried Exeter, where he couldn't find work, but then learned that a Mr John Taylor of Kingsbridge, a small market town 40 miles away, wanted a hand. Lackington went there and was very gladly received 'as he never treated me as a journeyman, but made me his companion'.

In a small way, Lackington made his own contribution to the spread of skill:

> I was the first man he ever had that was able to make stuff and silk shoes, and it being also known that I came from Bristol, this had great weight with the country ladies, and procured my master customers . . . and I was looked upon by all to be the best workman in the town.[67]

Accounts like this are rare, and there is no way to estimate how many former apprentices took any of these chances with any confidence. Nonetheless, set alongside the evidence that many youths found their way home after serving their indentures, they underline the way in which apprenticeship fitted into a system of work and training that circulated skill and knowledge around the nation.

Conclusion

The focus of this chapter has been on the choices apprentices made as they completed their training. In particular, how important was accessing corporate privileges compared to their other opportunities? Privilege there undoubtedly was. Apprenticeship offered the right to access a set of institutions that claimed monopolistic control over various lucrative areas of the economy. For those who finished their terms of service, there were few barriers left to achieving this. The formal transition from apprentice to guild member meant crossing a reasonably low bar in England. Tests of skill were rare. Fees were set at levels that were surmountable by all, and they were not structured in a way that privileged particular groups of insiders.

The outcome of this for the cities and guilds of the country was that apprenticeship served as the dominant mechanism by which new citizens were made. This was particularly true of the largest cities, while mid-sized towns were more evenly split between those who claimed citizenship by inheritance and former apprentices. This formal openness undoubtedly provided one of the motivating forces for entry into apprenticeship in the first place.

However, even though apprentices accounted for most freemen, only a minority of apprentices eventually became freemen. We might expect that this pathway was the preserve of the well-connected, just as the best-paid professions tend to be the preserve of the children of the wealthy today. Yet, the impact of youths' origins and resources on the chance that they became freemen was limited, aside from those with direct kinship to their masters. Marriage, too, was rarely part of a strategy to gain access to urban networks. Urban freedom and guild membership were relatively open to all apprentices, whether or not they possessed close ties to the guild, substantial resources, or local connections, or married a master's daughter. In short, compared to some other parts of Europe, England's urban communities were relatively open-access regimes in practice as well as in principle, for those who could overcome the—low—barrier to entering apprenticeship in the first place.[68]

What about those who did not take up the freedom or become citizens? While we may never know what happened to many former apprentices, a substantial number returned home. For them, apprenticeship was a process of circular migration, ending—possibly as was always intended—with return to their places of birth. Their actions make it clear that former apprentices' absences from the lists of guild freemen or urban citizens were not necessarily failures. Rather, the choices that apprentices made when they finished their training contained a thread of rational decision-making, one also evident in James Lackington's pursuit of the opportunities he could find in the region near Bristol.

Apprenticeship did not just replenish the skilled workforce of the nation's towns, and it was not motivated just by the chance to access guild rents. The pathway into onward migration meant that apprenticeship also diffused skills and knowledge across the nation and beyond. It provided some of the human capital that fuelled the spread of manufacturing and services outside England's major cities, one of the major features of the nation's economic development in this period. The institutional structures that were put in place by the Statute of Artificers may well have helped encourage this, by turning apprenticeship into a source of legal privilege in occupations outside agriculture that was valid nationally, not just locally. In this, it brought non-corporate England into line with practices in the Low Countries and Germany, where apprenticeships served in one town were recognised in others. As importantly, servitude in an incorporated centre gave an apprentice an option to settle that they could exercise on completion if they wished, encouraging aspirational families to place their children in major centres, despite the costs of migrating at an early age.

The migratory decisions made by the youths after they completed their training—whether to stick in the cities where they had trained or not—are comprehensible based on the mix of opportunities, rights, and resources they possessed as a result of their servitude. Those with substantial social capital in their places of origin were more likely to return; those who had invested the most in their exits were more likely to remain where they trained.

The economic implications for England are clear: apprenticeship was structured in way that encouraged concentration of training and then diffusion of skills. Knowledge spilled out from the cities into the countryside and villages, techniques spread, and a web of personal and commercial connections emerged between town and country as young people sought to find their places in the world.

PART III

Apprenticeship and the Enemies of Opportunity

9

Laws, Rules, and Barriers to Skill

Limiting access is one of the most obvious ways in which the system of apprenticeship that existed in premodern Europe could become unfair and inefficient. If only some members of a society are allowed to access the training that they need to take up skilled occupations, then they will reap an unwarranted advantage.

The injustice of this is blindingly obvious. But its economic impact is also pernicious. Two forces will be at play, cutting away at the conditions of those left outside. First, if pitched narrowly enough, closed labour markets bring economic rents—higher incomes earned through the exclusion of competition—to insiders at the expense of those excluded from those markets. Second, human talent is wasted. The match between the abilities of individuals and the demands of the economy will be less successful than if every person had the same chance to put their talent to its best use. The economy will simply operate less efficiently than it could.

The penalty that limited-access regimes impose on premodern economies has long been emphasised by historians, just as it has attracted the critical scrutiny of economists studying modern economies.[1] To give just two examples, the broad institutional evolution sketched out by North, Wallis, and Weingast focuses precisely on the shift from closed to open-access orders, though their focus is primarily on markets for political power.[2] Conversely, Ogilvie's analysis of the pernicious impact of guilds highlights the limits they placed on who could enter particular occupations.[3]

The forces that can act to limit access—the enemies of opportunity—take several forms. The formal laws and regulations that define who is permitted to access specific parts of the labour market are the most clearly visible in the written record. The implementation of laws and regulations, the way they are put into practice, can serve to enhance or ameliorate whatever was stated in the statute book or civic ordinances. Social structures and cultural norms can also be forces for inclusion or exclusion, irrespective of the actions of the state.

The four chapters in this section discuss the ways in which the opportunities young people had to access apprenticeship, and through this, to enter the skilled workforce in industry and trade, were constrained by these enemies of opportunity in premodern England. This chapter and chapter 10 focus on the laws and regulations that were instituted to limit who could become an apprentice, and the extent to which these had the practical effect that their creators had intended. Chapter 11 looks at the way in which cultural norms shaped who entered training, particularly ideas around gender and birth order. Finally, chapter 12 examines the degree to which access to apprenticeship was reliant on families' social networks, and the effect this had on the options that were open to aspiring apprentices.

Laws, Rules, and Barriers

Apprenticeship in England was valuable. It was also regulated. The laws and ordinances that structured apprenticeship in England explicitly aimed to control who could access training. That efforts were made to circumscribe entry to apprenticeship is not surprising. Early modern England was an ordered society in which an individual's rank, social status, gender, age, and nationality all defined their freedom of action and treatment before the law. How this logic of social discrimination affected a youth's ability to start an apprenticeship has a fundamental importance for our understanding of way opportunity was limited by the formal rules that structured apprenticeship.

This chapter examines the laws and ordinances that defined access to apprenticeship in early modern England from the start of the sixteenth century until 1814. It identifies where these rules incorporated exclusionary elements, who was excluded by them, and where the impetus to exclusion in one set of rules might be counterbalanced by the effects of other laws and customs—particularly in relation to the Poor Law—that were established for different purposes. It also considers how the framework of regulations developed, particularly the extent to which judicial decisions frayed the force of statute law over the long eighteenth century. While elements of the law were whittled away, much of the core remained. There was no Whiggish trajectory towards a free labour market. In law (if not always in practice), the final end of statutory regulation came suddenly; it was not the terminus of a long period of erosion.

The conclusion I reach about the formal regulatory framework of apprenticeship in England is, perhaps, a surprising one. England's system was relatively restrictive, at least on paper. Exclusionary rules restricting access to apprenticeship based on *individual* characteristics, such as gender, race, or religion, were relatively uncommon in English cities and guilds. Nationality, however, was the basis for restrictions on access. Potentially much more limiting were nationwide rules established by Parliament in the Statute of Artificers that linked occupations to the location and wealth of a youth's parents. These set out a framework based on wealth, status, and geography that was, in principle, more restrictive than in other parts of Europe.

The rule that would matter most was the new general restriction on access to skilled labour markets unless a seven-year apprenticeship had been served. This onerous obligation was introduced by the Statute of Artificers with the aim of reducing the number of young people leaving farming for other occupations. Its effect, however, was to raise the value of apprenticeship by making the completion of training a basic requirement for work in many manufacturing and service occupations wherever they were practised. The rule, designed to keep workers in agriculture, had the paradoxical effect of raising demand for apprenticeship in services and manufacturing by increasing the returns that could be earned from fulfilling this formal qualification to access skilled work. If the barriers established by the Statute of Artificers shifted the calculus around apprenticeship for the middling sorts, for the poorest, England's welfare system pulled in another direction and created a path into apprenticeship that might, in principle, allow their children a way to access training and its associated privileges.

To organise this material effectively, this chapter moves from the general to the more local. It first surveys national laws on apprenticeship and the linked legislation on the Poor Law that intersected with it. It then discusses customary and local regulations in London, and finally England's provincial towns and cities. The focus here is very much on law and regulation, and the critical questions of enforcement and the presence of informal barriers are left to the next chapter.

The State and Laws of Apprenticeship

Limiting opportunities was exactly what the government set out to do in the principal piece of legislation on apprenticeship in early modern England. The Statute of Artificers, passed by Parliament in 1562, was a conservative attempt by the Crown to regulate the labour market in general, and to 'advance husbandry' in particular. It obliged labourers to accept employment, limited worker mobility, specified working hours, gave magistrates the power to fix wages and settle employment disputes, and prevented employers from short-term hiring, alongside several other measures that tied workers to prescribed patterns of employment. In many of these provisions, it incorporated or extended laws dating back to the fourteenth century that supported landowners and farmers.[4]

It is ironic, then, that in an attempt to maintain the rural labour supply, the Statute of Artificers introduced an important novelty in the entirely new requirement that a seven-year long term of apprenticeship be served before anyone could 'set up, occupy use or exercise any craft, mystery or occupation' anywhere in the realm.[5] In its original formulation, *all* skilled workers in all crafts—whether employed as journeymen, hired by the day, or setting up an independent workshop—had to have served apprenticeships.[6] As Deakin and Wilkinson observe, in principle, the statute 'made capitalist forms of employment unlawful in the regulated trades'.[7] This rule was, in its spirit, close kin to existing English town regulations that made apprenticeship the principal way for outsiders to qualify for entry to many guilds and town citizenship. Yet, the statute's scope was much wider and its consequences necessarily greater. By erecting a protective barrier to artisanal labour markets, it also created a major incentive for entering and completing apprenticeships—precisely the opposite of its authors' intent.

The rest of the statute's provisions for apprenticeship were less radical, but would still have wide repercussions. In part, it generalised existing norms rather than inventing new ones, requiring that all apprentices be bound 'after the Custom and Order of the City of *London*' and contracted with written indentures that would run until they were twenty-four years of age, at the least; like the seven-year term, this echoed London's existing rules.[8] As well as homogenising the form of apprenticeship, it instituted a new level of oversight, by giving English magistrates, the justices of the peace, the power to grant writs against apprentices (and other servants) who had fled their occupations, to examine disputes between masters and apprentices, and—where appropriate—to discharge them from their contracts. These were powers that urban governments had long exercised through city courts, but now justices of the peace exercised them across villages and smaller, unincorporated towns, and this had important repercussions for the way apprentices and masters dealt with each other. Perhaps the least notable clause, both in terms of the numbers of masters affected and the notice taken of it, was a partial limit on apprentice numbers: clothmakers, fullers, shearmen, weavers, tailors, and shoemakers were to keep one journeyman for every apprentice they took beyond three.[9]

The statute's mechanisms to restrict social and occupational mobility were mainly contained in a series of clauses that erected boundaries around who was allowed to enter specific trades, based on location and wealth. Artisan householders living in an incorporated town or city could apprentice the children of artisans who also lived in an incorporated town, but not the sons of labourers or those 'occupying husbandry'.[10] In turn, artisan householders living in *unincorporated* market towns could only take the sons of people who also lived in a market town in the same county; again, no labourers or husbandmen's sons could be trained.[11] Prosperous mercantile, manufacturing, and retail work was specially limited. Only people with land worth 40 shillings a year could apprentice their children to a 'Merchant . . . Mercer, Draper, Goldsmith, Ironmonger, Imbroiderer or Clothier' living in an incorporated town or city; in a bid to concentrate trade in larger centres, to place a child with those merchants and the like who lived in a market town, parents needed to have even more—£3 a year in property.[12] To ensure these requirements were applied, the value of the land was to be certified under the hand and seal of three justices of the peace and enrolled when the apprentice was registered.

On the other hand, in another group of occupations, the 'Son of any Person' could be apprenticed so long as the apprentice's family held *no* property. These essential but low-status trades were distinguished by being as important to agriculture as industry: 'Smith, Wheel-wright, Plough-wright, Mill-wright, Carpenter, Rough Mason, Plaisterer, Sawyer, Lime-burner, Brick-maker, Bricklayer, Tyler, Slater, Helier, Tyle-maker, Linen-weaver, Turner, Cooper, Millers, Earthen Potters, Woollen Weaver weaving Housewives or Household Cloth only and none other Cloth, Fuller, otherwise called Tucker or Walker, Burner of Ore and Wood-Ashes, Thatcher or Shingler'.[13]

Finally, weaving, the great proto-industrial employer of the countryside, was to be closed off to the rural poor, except in the fringes of the country. Weavers based outside incorporated towns or market towns could take only their own sons or the children of families with property of £3 a year, a wealth bar clearly intended as prohibitive.[14] Keeping rural children working on the land was not a new ambition.[15] These clauses echoed earlier labour laws, and they operated in parallel with existing laws banning foreign craftsmen from taking any but English subjects as apprentices.[16]

The Statute of Artificers was motivated by anxieties about vagrancy and under-employment, and the potential for violence and rebellion they generated. At the same time, its authors intended to constrain the flow of labour from agriculture into industry, to prevent 'such a decay of husbandry that masters cannot get skillful servants to till the ground without unreasonable wages', and to ease the landed elite's and yeomanry's difficulties when recruiting farm workers.[17] To help deal with the reluctant workers, the statute gave justices of the peace the authority to compel people to enter an annual contract in husbandry or any other trade, and to put them to apprenticeships.[18] Any farmer who wanted a youth to serve them as an agricultural labourer could appeal to the justices to force someone into a contract.[19] Again, this was not a new idea: vagrant children between five and fourteen could already be ordered to be bound apprentice by the justices of peace, and acts passed during the reigns of Henry VIII and Edward VI had extended this until age twenty-four for men and twenty for women.[20] The tenor of the state's involvement in apprenticeship was focused on restricting occupational and geographical mobility, maintaining an orderly labour market, and ensuring a supply of agricultural labour.

THE POOR LAW

The Statute of Artificers attempted to lift a drawbridge between field labour and artisanal crafts, but it had the accidental side effect of providing a new incentive that drew people in the opposite direction. The Tudors' other great social policy initiative, the Poor Laws of 1598 and 1601, gave a more direct encouragement to apprenticeship, motivated by much the same concern with poverty and its associated sins of idleness and independence.[21] The Poor Laws made the apprenticeship of poor children one of the strategies for relief available to local parishes, who could now spend parish rates to remove pauper children from their families and place them into apprenticeships.[22] With this, the parish could at one stroke reduce the number of dependents it supported through its poor rates and—ideally—give the child a set of skills and habits of industry and thrift that might allow them to avoid indigence as an adult.

Pauper apprenticeship differed from its private sibling in several key elements. The first, most obviously, is that pauper children and their parents had little agency in their destinations, or indeed in the decision to be apprenticed in the first place. The householders with whom they were placed might have little desire to receive them, although parish officers seem generally to have preferred to place (and pay) masters and mistresses rather than use their powers to assign apprentices.[23] The second is that pauper apprentices might be bound to activities, such as housewifery or agricultural service and husbandry, that were not trades or crafts within the terms of the Statute of Artificers. In such cases, their service brought no privileges in the labour market, though it might, of course, give them some basic skills. The third is that the age and duration of pauper apprenticeships differed: they could begin far younger—fourteen was the *maximum* age of binding until 1696—and so they might serve for much longer than private apprentices before reaching the age of twenty-four (for boys) or twenty-one (for girls), when their contracts ended.[24] The result was that an unfortunate pauper child could face a decade or more of grinding unskilled labour in an unwelcoming household.

Nonetheless, at least in theory, pauper apprentices might find themselves in situations indistinguishable from private apprentices, and they could earn the same legal privileges to use an occupation. Similar attempts to provide training for the children of the poor, including allowing them entitlements to join guilds, were created in towns and cities across Europe.[25] Depending on how parish officials and justices used their powers, pauper apprenticeship had the potential to contradict and undermine the socially exclusionary elements of the Statute of Artificers.

ADJUSTMENTS IN LAW: DECLINE?

The core elements of this system of formal rules remained in place until the end of the eighteenth century. However, there were some changes. The adjustments that were made reflected a rumbling debate about the value of the requirement that those working in crafts and trades had served a seven-year apprenticeship.

At the level of statute law, most interventions in apprenticeship regulation sought to reinforce or overturn the basic requirement for a seven-year apprenticeship to work in a specific field. These laws were generally passed in response to petitions from different trades. Acts to reinforce apprenticeship (and often, to limit the numbers of apprentices a master could take) were obtained at various times by hatmakers, skinners, printers, and weavers.[26] Reinforcement found approval in Parliament mostly in the seventeenth century, but even at the end of the eighteenth century some petitions were successful. In 1772 Parliament passed a statute limiting London silk-weavers to two apprentices, and in 1781 an act requiring the registration of apprentices in Coventry.[27] Derogations from the seven-year rule do appear in some statutes passed in the eighteenth century. They were few in number, however, and were granted to only a few trades, such as distillers, dyers, and, in 1779, London's bakers.[28]

Apprenticeship rules were also relaxed by Parliament to help several groups whose means of support had been removed. From the 1650s onwards, former soldiers and sailors who had started but not finished apprenticeships were exempted from the seven-year apprenticeship requirement by a series of acts.[29] In 1777, hatmakers were exempted from apprenticeship requirements. In 1785, former licensed hawkers, now barred from their old trade, were permitted to take up a trade in their place of residence. Industrialisation quickened this. In 1795, wool-combers were allowed to use any trade, as their old craft had been replaced by machinery; the same liberty was granted to all those who had served apprenticeships in woollen manufactures in 1809.

This deliberate fraying of the edges of the statute by Parliament reflected a wider turn among the elite against restrictive economic policies, apparent in the views of Adam Smith and other economists who were increasingly influential in this period. This was most significant in the way it seems to have encouraged judges to interpret the scope of existing laws in narrower terms. Indeed, the most serious challenges to the Statute of Artificers came through the courts, where a body of case law that emerged from the late seventeenth century developed the new interpretation that its requirement for a seven-year apprenticeship applied only to trades that were 'exercised at or prior to the passing of the act . . . and not any art or mystery since invented' and which require 'skill and experience'.[30] This narrowing of the law created a space in which 'new' occupations could operate without regard for the apprenticeship requirements that applied elsewhere, which covered an ever-expanding slice of the economy as new products and processes that had been unknown in the 1560s were developed or introduced.

The statute was increasingly interpreted narrowly by the courts, particularly from the mid-eighteenth century.[31] In a case in 1699, it was decided that using a trade in a country village was not within the statute.[32] In several cases soon after, judges took the view that following a trade for seven years without a formal indenture could be sufficient to qualify as a lawful workman.[33]

The application of the statute to individuals hiring workmen in a trade but not using the craft themselves was also challenged.[34] Legal counsel advising guilds increasingly advised caution in enforcing apprenticeship rules before courts that viewed restrictions on trade with suspicion.[35] The right of urban corporations to prevent non-citizens from engaging in trade in a town was also vulnerable.[36] The application of the statute to journeymen also came into question; in 1773, the Butchers' Company was advised that a journeyman might work without completing his service, as they 'did not exercise the trade for his own benefit'.[37]

There was no consensus around ideas of free labour, however. Many craftsmen and journeymen fought hard to defend the principle that apprenticeship should be a requirement for using their occupation. In fact, in the end, it was in part an attempt by journeymen to revitalise the apprenticeship requirement that led—to their horror—to the final demise of the apprenticeship clauses of the Statute of Artificers in 1814.[38] Abolition was, it should be emphasised, in no way a foregone conclusion or the consequence of some overbearing economic logic of liberalism. Other elements of labour law were being strengthened in the same period, and the emerging law of master-servant tightened discipline around employees in the nineteenth century, reinforcing their subordinate position.[39] In the German lands, apprenticeship requirements were widely retained and revived within a corporatist system.[40]

After 1814, a seven-year apprenticeship was no longer a legal requirement to set up in a trade in England. This was a final, fundamental break in the connection between law and apprenticeship that removed the general nationwide privilege that the Statute of Artificers had created 250 years earlier. However, the repeal did not abolish the rules of London and other cities by which service for a particular term could be required to gain access to urban labour markets.[41] And of course it did not end the need for human capital, for skill itself. Rather, the abolition freed up apprenticeship legally to take different forms—now any person could take an apprentice, and they could set the term themselves—and other, less structured forms of learning could take its place in occupations where formal apprenticeships fell out of favour.

PROTECTION OF APPRENTICES

Although the central question here is about how pre-industrial English labour markets might be restricted by formal institutions, we cannot ignore the ways in which the state gradually developed an alternative role in protecting poor children at work as apprentices. Pauper apprenticeship in particular was refined under statutory interventions over the two centuries following 1600.[42] Many of these acts were, essentially, protective, and they grew in frequency from the late eighteenth century as concerns about the conditions of children increased. In 1766, parishes were required to pay a minimum of £4 2s as a premium to the masters of pauper apprentices, and the minimum age for completion was cut to twenty-one years for parish apprentices from London.[43] The 1802 Health and Morals of Apprentices Act, passed in the teeth of opposition from factory owners whose businesses employed numerous pauper apprentices, aimed to improve the health and morals of apprentices by fixing standards for cleanliness, ventilation, working hours, clothing, and medical care. The act even required that apprentices receive basic religious instruction and education in reading, writing, and arithmetic.[44] The same year, parishes were required to keep a register of those bound as pauper apprentices.[45] In 1816, a further act set a 40-mile limit on the distance youths could be sent from their parish, to prevent their estrangement from their families and allow parish officials to monitor their placements.[46] These protections might seem paltry sops in the context of children being forced into apprenticeship, yet there can be no doubt that they marked the first small steps towards the state protecting workers.

Poor relief also intersected with apprenticeship in another way. Under the Poor Law, the right to claim poor relief was local. Each parish supported its own paupers and after 1662 was empowered to dispatch those from elsewhere back to their own parishes.[47] In a society characterised by high levels of migration, identifying who qualified as a resident became an important issue. Apprenticeship became one of the ways in which people could acquire a new settlement and with it, rights to welfare. From 1691, apprentices who were bound were 'settled' in their masters' parishes after forty days of service.[48] Settlement rights thus added another powerful incentive to become an apprentice.

Pulling youths into apprenticeship was a deliberate aim in one other strand of state interventions in this period. In order to secure a sufficient supply of skilled mariners for the navy, Parliament passed a series of laws encouraging and regulating apprenticeship at sea.[49] In the same year it passed the Statute of Artificers, Parliament established specific rules for mariners, fishermen, shipwrights, and sea-gunners in the 1562 Maintenance of the Navy Act. Apprentices were to be bound for a maximum of ten years or less, following the custom of London: they must be at least fourteen years old and indentured in writing, with their contract enrolled in a corporate town, for which a fee of no more than 12d could be charged by the city officials.[50] A short-lived exception came in the eighteenth century, when pauper boys were allowed to be bound from ten years of age, in order to further increase the supply of seamen for the navy.[51] But this was rapidly revised to thirteen years of age with a further caveat that they were 'fitly qualified both as to Health and Strength of Body for that Service'.[52] Thames fishing apprentices were to be registered by the company of fishermen.[53] To the same end, a series of laws (that appeared in accelerating numbers during the Napoleonic Wars) obliged fishing and trading ships to carry a *minimum* number of apprentices depending on their size.[54]

Urban Law and Custom

The 'custom of London' that the Statute of Artificers spread to the country as a whole was a set of legal and customary norms that had evolved over several centuries. It defined the terms of apprenticeship contracts, but was set within a wider complex of rules about access to training set by cities and guilds. This section discusses the formal barriers to entry set by city and guild in London and in other incorporated towns and cities.

Within London, two clusters of institutions had the greatest impact on apprenticeship regulations. The first were the city's hundred or more livery companies, as its guilds were known. The second cluster was the city's central authorities, which were made up of the Lord Mayor and Court of Aldermen (drawn from members the Great Twelve livery companies) who acted as the city's executive, and the Court of Common Council, elected by the entire body of city freemen, which met less frequently.

Apprenticeship was a prominent concern for these organisations in part because of its role in qualifying youths for citizenship and guild membership—becoming 'freemen', in the language often used. Both cities and guilds were corporate bodies whose full members had a potentially valuable set of rights, including the exclusive right to certain kinds of work, as well as political privileges (including voting for parliamentary representatives in towns and cities) and social benefits, alongside the commensurate obligations of contributing to the costs of the institution, accepting the burden of local government and guild offices, and keeping their rules.[55] They also defined the terms under which new members would join them, discussed in chapter 8.

In other English towns and cities, guilds were generally less independent. Most provincial guilds depended on the governments of their towns or cities, which were usually drawn from the wealthiest residents and oligarchic in organisation, to approve their existence and sign off on their rules. Most of London's companies had bought charters from the Crown directly, giving them an independent corporate existence and somewhat greater autonomy. This was much rarer elsewhere. Apprenticeship was also not always as central to provincial urban structures as it was in London, with its role as a qualification for citizenship limited or absent in some towns. However, while the balance of powers varied across the country, the practical differences were limited: in most urban communities both guild and city could set rules to limit who might become apprentices.

Like the Crown, for the City of London, the main focus of its regulations was on defining who could access apprenticeship and who could supply it. Nationality was the key barrier in London. Apprentices were required to have been born in the king's domain. Faced by growing migration from the continent, the City tightened this rule further in 1574 with the demand that apprentices should also be the sons of 'Englishmen born', accusing the sons of aliens of undermining the community by colouring (selling as their own) the goods of strangers and apprenticing foreign children rather than English youths.[56] By English, in practice the City meant English or Welsh, although with expanding colonisation in the seventeenth and eighteenth century, the scope of the king's domain grew. Scottish youths, however, remained in an uncertain legal position between the accession of James I and the Act of Union.

Age limits added a further set of restrictions to apprenticeship. In 1556, in what it presented as an attempt to reduce the 'great poverty, penury and lack of living' that was the fruit of 'overhasty marriages' by young people as soon as they finished their apprenticeships, the City ruled that apprentices' terms should last until they were at least twenty-four years old, and that no one was to become a freemen by apprenticeship or redemption under that age.[57] Earlier rules had already established that apprentices in London should be at least fourteen years old when they were bound, and no older than twenty-one.[58] For some trades, age limits were higher. The Thames Watermen Act of 1603 required apprentices to be eighteen years old at least and to serve seven years.[59] In addition, apprentices were to be unmarried—and remain so throughout their term.[60]

One consequence of these age rules was that apprentices were legally minors when they entered their contracts. Though they took the apprentices' oath themselves, they needed to be presented by a parent or guardian. That their terms of service ran on past the age of twenty-one, at which point they became legal adults, raised questions about the enforceability of their contracts. It was not until 1809, however, that the Court of King's Bench ruled that an apprentice had a right to void his indentures on reaching maturity, reversing the earlier convention that apprentices' indentures held even once they had reached their majority.[61]

What about other formal exclusions based on identity? One of the central charges levelled against early modern corporations and cities by some historians is that they excluded entire sections of the population from apprenticeship or membership based on their gender or creed.[62] In London, aside from the nationality requirements, such restrictive ordinances were largely absent. Gender was not a formal bar to apprenticeship. Female apprentices faced the same formal rules and restrictions as males in London: they had to be at least fourteen years old and should serve for seven years or longer.[63] If they served a female master, whom the indenture named depended on their master's marital status. As one summary of the City's rules from 1722 stated, 'If an Exchange-Woman or Sempstress, who hath a Husband, shall take a Maid Apprentice, such Maid must be bound to the Husband . . . and shall be made Free at the end of her Term', while a 'Widow of a Freeman may take a Maid Apprentice, and Inroll her'.[64] But there is no doubt that women were legally permitted to become apprentices and did so—albeit in small numbers, as discussed in chapter 11—throughout the early modern period. The only companies that appear to have been exceptions to this were the Weavers, who passed an ordinance in 1577 that no one was to 'teach, instruct or bring up in the use . . . of the same arte of weaving any maid damsel or other woman whatsoever', and the Broderers, who instituted a similar ban in 1609.[65] Nor was religion a basis for an explicit formal barrier to apprenticeship in the sixteenth or seventeenth century, when apprenticeship in London was at its height.

London did introduce some identity-based exclusions into its legal codes in the eighteenth century. In the 1780s, Jews, even those who had renounced their faith and been baptised, were excluded from the freedom of the city, and so, by implication, from apprenticeship.[66] Race also became a barrier to apprenticeship in the eighteenth century. In 1731, a Black apprentice, John Satia, petitioned to be freed by servitude on the basis of his service to William Attery, a citizen and joiner. Satia's problem was that he had no evidence that he was born in Barbados, within the king's dominions, as the City's rules required. All he had was hearsay: he swore that 'he hath often heard Mr Gerrard a Merchant since deceased say that he brought him from Barbados when he was about two years old & that he was born there. And that the said Mr Gerrard put him out as an apprentice'. The Court of Aldermen admitted him as a freeman. However, they then ordered that 'for the future no negros or other blacks be suffered to be bound apprentices at any of the companies of this City to any freeman thereof' and none were to be made freemen likewise.[67]

Although the city could have constrained access to training on the basis of ethnicity earlier, there is no evidence that this occurred before the eighteenth century. This was not because the city stood for diversity; it did not. More likely, there was simply no occasion to consider the question.

What did the guilds add to these city regulations? London's companies did expand on the City's restrictive requirements to some extent. In a few rare cases, they added measures to ensure apprentices possessed sufficient ability to operate in the trade. The Apothecaries examined the learning of prospective apprentices and expected them to have some Latin.[68] The Goldsmiths had required apprentices to be literate since 1469, and the Barber Surgeons also required literacy.[69] That none others did underlines the distinction between book learning and occupational skills in premodern apprenticeship, in contrast to the complementary relationship that would develop from the nineteenth century onwards. To the extent they articulated criteria for apprentices at all, most guild rules echoed and intensified the city's tone. Apprentices should be English.[70] They should be free-born. And they should not be lame, deformed, or disabled. Disability was a particular concern of guilds in the late fifteenth and early sixteenth centuries, but it is never mentioned in seventeenth- or eighteenth-century rules.[71] At times, some companies also demanded terms that exceeded the City custom of seven years. Again, this was more common in earlier ordinances. The Goldsmiths required a term of ten years in 1370, as did the Ironmongers in 1498, while the Pewterers established a nine-year term in 1582, although they cut it back to seven years in 1607.[72] In extending these barriers, the companies were not entirely autonomous: guild rules had to be approved by justices of the peace or the chancellor.[73]

The importance of these formal guild rules on entry to apprenticeship should not be overstated. Nationality and freedom of birth were redundant, given the City's rules. And more importantly, few companies set rules limiting entry based on characteristics. To obtain a sense of the spread of different rules, I reviewed the ordinances of twenty-six London guilds.[74] Nationality was mentioned by only five; disability and disease or freedom by birth by just six. Only one of the fifteen companies that specified term lengths exceeded seven years: the Apothecaries, who required eight years. More significant was the simple expectation incorporated into most companies' practices, and often their formal rules: none were to instruct anyone in their trade *other* than an apprentice, unless it was their child.[75] Apprenticeship was to be the sole legal route to skill for those who were not the sons of masters.[76]

Even the advantaged position of masters' sons was, in fact, contentious. In the eyes of the city and most guilds, they were a privileged group, able to enter the freedom by right, so long as they had been born after their fathers became freemen and could pay the modest fees involved. They were not required to have served apprenticeships. Instead, the underlying assumption was that they had been trained by working within the household. Occasional exceptions—such as the Merchant Taylors' rule forbidding masters from employing their children without apprenticing them—illustrate the rule. Yet, there was no parallel exemption for craftsmen's sons within the Statute of Artificers, and the custom of London that freemen may use any occupation was judged not to offer an exemption from apprenticeships in 'manufactures or handicrafts', just in trade.[77]

What of guilds outside London? The tenor of London's rules about apprenticeship was echoed in most other towns and cities across England. Formal bars on gender, faith, or race seem to have been largely absent. Norwich's mid-fifteenth-century ordinances required that apprentices be of free birth, but such concerns had evaporated by the sixteenth century.[78] Nationality was occasionally mentioned—particularly in the northern town of Carlisle, which banned Scottish apprentices (and almost any other involvement with the Scots).[79] Managing the characteristics of prospective apprentices en masse was seemingly less of an issue outside the metropolis.

In fact, guilds in provincial cities and towns rarely gave much thought to who could become apprentices. I surveyed sets of ordinances for forty-six guilds from eleven of England's towns and cities.[80] A few set rules about age that echoed those in London: a minimum age of fourteen was specified by three guilds in Carlisle (Merchants, Shoemakers, and Glovers) and one in Norwich, while the Sheffield Cutlers finally set a minimum age at twelve in 1728; finishing at twenty-four years was required by Salisbury's Butchers and Shoemakers and Hull's Cordwainers.[81] However, thirty-two guilds' rules included nothing on age. Even fewer mentioned place of origin. Only six guilds passed rules barring apprentices because of where they came from: four limited access to English youths, including Bristol's Hoopers, whose 1439 ordinances barred aliens or any 'rebel of Ireland'.[82] Another two required youths to be local: Bristol's Weavers (1346) expected apprentices to be born in the city, unless special permission was granted, as did Hull's

Joiners (1598). No guild ordinances in our sample dated after 1600 contained a rule on nationality or place of origin.

What about the other criteria that occasionally appeared in London's guild rules? Not a single provincial guild in our sample bothered to establish a requirement that apprentices met any standard of learning, physical ability, or legitimacy. Just one guild set a rule about religion: Carlisle's Merchants ordered that no Quaker's son was to be accepted as an apprentice in 1703. Elsewhere, however, Quakers actively recruited and trained apprentices with no sign of impediment.[83] Moreover, every guild specified the same length of training: seven years was universal, including in the eight sets of ordinances dating from before the Statute of Artificers where a term was mentioned.

One final formal mechanism of exclusion needs to be mentioned: financial barriers. Both cities and guilds had the power to charge apprentices fees to register their contracts. Without registration, contracts might be declared void or might not count towards membership of the guild or city. Fees were commonplace. They provided a useful source of income for guilds and cities and their officials. Charging a registration fee is not necessarily an intentional bar (although for the truly indigent, *any* financial requirement would present a challenge). Fees would not add substantially to the more basic limits that poverty placed on opportunity, if they were low relative to the private costs of apprenticeship such as the charges a family might face to clothe a youth when they began work, to raise a premium (a fee agreed privately) to attract a master, and to travel to town to identify a place. Yet, fees could be set at levels that precluded access for all but the rich. Or they could be structured in ways that obviously advantaged one group over others, as discussed in chapter 8. Examples of guilds in Antwerp that charged very high fees for outsiders while offering deep discounts for the sons of guild members illustrate how this might work, irrespective of the motive.[84] In short, the exclusionary effect of fees depends on their level, and this along with the implementation of rules on access more generally is the subject of the next chapter.

Conclusion

Between 1562 and 1814, England's nationwide legal framework for apprenticeship was distinctive. Elsewhere in Europe, apprenticeship rules were largely fixed at the level of city and guild. The three key contributions made by the English state were, first, to create an exclusive right to skilled work for those who completed apprenticeships, providing a clear nationwide incentive for training; second, to fix a high price for training by setting a long minimum term for indentures; and third, to establish a tribunal for disputes and discipline, giving oversight of contracts to justices of the peace, as discussed in chapter 7.

The state's legal interventions in apprenticeship had little practical impact in the incorporated towns and cities that housed the majority of trade and industry in the sixteenth century because in those places, lengthy seven-year apprenticeships were *already* standard, for the most part. Apprenticeship had long been linked to economic privileges through urban citizenship. Similarly, borough courts had already had oversight of contracts between masters and apprentices. For this reason, Lane's suggestion that the act 'was administered almost entirely by local guilds' fundamentally misreads the statute's implications.[85] Guilds had no need of the statute, at least until the late seventeenth century, when their own monopolistic powers to discipline non-members and prevent them working in the locality came into question. It was only as the tide of corporate privileges receded that the statute gained the symbolic and legal importance that led eighteenth- and nineteenth-century artisans to hymn its benefits.[86]

It was *outside* of corporate, urban England that the statute's main impact on the rules of apprenticeship was first felt. The Statute of Artificers generalised urban norms about apprenticeship and craft work into the small towns and villages where the great majority of the English population lived. It created the framework for a single, national approach to training in occupations outside of agriculture. It gave young people and their families a clear incentive to consider apprenticeship as a route into the adult world, by linking service to a privileged position in the labour market, although from around 1700 judicial decisions reduced the importance for those who would spend their lives as journeymen, not masters, and created occupational enclaves that were outside the scope of the statute. A completed apprenticeship now created a legal entitlement to operate in a craft or trade by excluding those who had not served their time, guild or no guild. This pull into apprenticeship to access rents was further strengthened by the Poor Law, which gave local government a mechanism to place youths into apprenticeship and created a further reward to service by making it a way to acquire the entitlement to welfare.

These new incentives to apprenticeship were embedded into a set of rules about who could access apprenticeship that aimed to exclude, not encourage, training. These mainly concentrated on several social and economic dimensions: the occupation, wealth, and residence of a youth's family.

To these, city rules added constraints on the nationality of apprentices. Beyond this, formal restrictions on access to apprenticeship based on other characteristics did exist, but they were far from ubiquitous. Rules excluding youths with a visible disability were apparent in some London guild ordinances in the fourteenth century, but were silently dropped in later editions of regulations. Rules barring youths based on race and religion appear to have been introduced only in some cities, notably London, in the eighteenth century. Gender bars were largely absent, as were prohibitions on illegitimate children.

Put in comparison with some other parts of Europe, the formal boundaries around apprenticeship in England were substantial, in particular its long obligatory minimum term of service and the connection between social and economic status and access to trades, but they were less closely tied to ascribed characteristics.[87] On the continent, while gender and religious bars were present in some cities and guilds, wealth qualifications and rules on nationality were rare, and minimum terms were generally far shorter.[88] In short, England's unique national system of apprenticeship regulation was, at least on the surface, further from an open-access regime than those in most parts of Europe. However, the real test for the impact of the English regime on the opportunities of the young is the degree to which these rules were implemented, and it is that which we turn to next.

10

Exclusion in Practice?

THE EFFECTS OF RULES ON APPRENTICESHIP

England's national laws and urban and guild regulations on access to apprenticeship principally set barriers to opportunity on two criteria: status and geography. As we saw in the last chapter, they obliged the authorities to ask if families met criteria of status—defined variously by income, wealth, and paternal occupation—and location that permitted them to place their children into specific occupations. Apprenticeship was also limited by age, and its burden was extended by the long minimum term of seven years that was universalised in 1562. Though weighty for the individual and their family, age and term restrictions were faced by all; they lifted the costs of training, potentially excluding those with limited resources, but did not discriminate based on inherited characteristics, unlike the rules on status and wealth.

This chapter considers the actual impact of England's body of laws and urban and guild regulations on access to training, asking which were applied and how their effects changed over time. This speaks to two of the ways in which formal rules can limit people's ability to gain skills and move freely in the labour market. The first is by formally excluding some people from opportunities because of who they are. In this regard, our primary concern is with the impact of the rules tying wealth to access to specific occupations, the bar on agricultural labourers and workers in husbandry, and the statute's convoluted requirements about place of birth (incorporated town, market town, or countryside). Each of these creates invidious divides between youths on the basis of their birth and family.

The second way these rules could limit opportunity is by increasing the cost of training. This will distort demand for training and eventually the labour supply, by shifting the relative returns to different careers, and generate economic rents for those who are on the other side of the process, such as masters and skilled workers. The direct costs from England's rules about the timing and duration of training were borne by apprentices and families; indirectly, they would have wider effects on welfare. To understand their impact, we need to consider how closely legal and customary expectations were followed in setting contracts: Were terms always at least seven years? Were youths always fourteen or older? And, to the extent we can, we need to ask how far they deviated from the level that would have been set without these laws. And we also need to be aware that their effects may have changed over time.

It is important to be clear that this chapter focuses on the rules around *access* to apprenticeship, not the implementation of what was the most important aspect of the Statute of Artificers: the restriction of work in crafts and trades to people who had completed a seven-year apprenticeship. That legal limit in the market for skilled labour in industry and services was a critical ingredient in the English system of apprenticeship.

We are fortunate to have compelling studies of the implementation of the seven-year rule by T. K. Derry and Margaret Davies. As they showed, prosecutions under the Statute of Artificers against artisans who were using a trade without having served a seven-year apprenticeship abound in court records. These were brought largely by professional informers who sought to profit from the fines imposed, and as a result, nearly all were against independent craftsmen, who were more likely to be able to pay, not journeymen who worked for wages. Enforcement was not so strict that it prevented anyone working who had not served an apprenticeship, particularly if they were employed by someone, but prosecution was certainly a real risk, and it increased as an artisan established themselves more fully.[1]

There are two main sources for information on how the statute affected access to apprenticeship. The records of the courts that would hear cases about breaches of the statute offer one avenue.[2] Another is the set of records of apprenticeship that survive. The impact of England's formal barriers on access can be traced in the records of apprenticeship. These reveal whether the laws and customs of pre-industrial English apprenticeship had a meaningful impact on who actually became apprentices. If the statute worked as intended, then it would have limited who started training in particular occupations. Perhaps the most obvious question to ask is, simply, *were* these barriers implemented, or were they dead letters?

The chapter begins with the evidence of the implementation of apprenticeship rules in the English courts, then turns to the evidence that exists of who became apprentices, to see if they met or broke the rules that the state and urban elites had created.

Implementation

If we take court records first, the simple answer is that the statute's exclusionary rules around the status, occupation, or place of origin of apprentices were rarely the basis for prosecutions. In fact, the result was so poor that the efficacy of the mechanism through which the Statute of Artificers was to work has attracted some criticism from historians.[3] Offenders were punishable by a fine of 40s for each month they breached the law.[4] This was no trivial penalty. Yet, there was no state-led registration or enforcement mechanism, after a few attempts to develop a system in the early seventeenth century failed.[5] Outside corporate towns, where guild and city governments often maintained registers of apprentices, there was no organisation with oversight over who was being admitted as an apprentice.[6]

This is not to argue that the Statute of Artificers did not matter. It did, and parts of the statute had a real impact, including the rule requiring a seven-year apprenticeship, as Derry and Davies showed. But surveys of court records all reach the same conclusion: very few prosecutions were made under the property and occupational clauses restricting apprenticeship. Nor is there much sign that justices of the peace were often asked to attest to apprentices' family property assets, as the statute required. Davies did uncover a few certificates from justices in Chester that reported parent's status.[7] But there is no evidence of a body of suits against unqualified youths becoming apprentices on the grounds of wealth or place of birth. Elsewhere in Europe, when apprentices were required to produce evidence to prove that they met requirements such as being born within wedlock, certificates survive, along with records of youths being excluded because they had not produced the right paperwork.[8] England's guilds' lack of an equivalent paper trail suggests that no great heed was ever paid to these rules.

When we turn to the records of apprentices in England's towns and cities, there is equally little evidence that these legal barriers to training were implemented. First, it is worth highlighting an important gap: the Statute of

Artificers explicitly excluded from its remit London and Norwich, the two largest cities in the country and the biggest concentrations of apprenticeship; they already had local rules that covered much of the same ground, but they lacked any equivalent to the wealth test contained in the statute. The result? In the forty years that followed the passing of the Statute of Artificers, 2,400 husbandmen's sons and 160 labourers' sons appear in our sample of London's guild records, making up a substantial share of the 15,000 apprentices with information on their parents' occupations in that period, and a great many had grown up in villages. Norwich registered fewer apprentices, and the record is sporadic before the late 1570s, but ninety of the 428 apprentices enrolled before 1603 were husbandmen's sons, and another nine were labourers' children.[9] That sons of labourers and husbandmen both appear in London's guild records, as do numerous children from families living in villages in the countryside, highlights a major loophole in this superficially restrictive regime.

What about communities where the Statute of Artificers did apply? Because unincorporated towns and rural communities did not generally have the infrastructure or need to produce registers of apprentices, we lack any easy way to learn if masters from market towns limited themselves to children from market towns, or rural cloth weavers took only the offspring of well-to-do families, as the statute required. By the eighteenth century, however, there is no sign that these rules had any traction. In the 1710s and 1720s, for example, the children of labourers were being bound to rural weavers in considerable numbers, and paying a premium for the privilege. Of the 276 new apprentices bound to weavers working in villages scattered across England who appear in the stamp duty in these decades, forty-two were the children of labourers.[10]

A number of incorporated towns such as Gloucester, Oxford, and Bristol have left records from the late sixteenth and early seventeenth centuries, soon after the statute was passed. In theory, the statute specified that apprentices in these towns were to be drawn from other incorporated towns. Yet, each received large numbers of youths from rural villages and small market towns in the late sixteenth century, and continued to do so until the end of the eighteenth century. Each accepted the children of rural labourers and husbandmen placed in craft and trade apprenticeships, groups explicitly barred from apprenticeship by law. Between 1600 and 1610 in Gloucester, to take one example, labourers' sons were apprenticed to coopers, glaziers, vintners, glovers, wire-drawers, clothiers, bakers, and cordwainers—all trades that were theoretically closed to them.[11] And while some of the youths did come from the city itself, others came from small villages such as Tirley, Blaisdon, Twyning, and Bulley. Ten years before, Oxford's apprentices had come from villages such as Cumnor, Deddington, and Doddershall, as well as smaller corporations such as Chipping Norton and Tewkesbury, and agricultural labourers' sons had been indentured by glovers, weavers, painters, haberdashers, joiners, and chandlers.[12] While similar records survive for only a handful of towns, there is no evidence that the statute's attempts to limit the migration of the young into England's cities were anything more than a dead letter, coming at the start of a sustained period of urbanisation that drew thirstily upon the offspring of families in the countryside.

Whether or not the property and wealth requirements in the statute were ever taken seriously is difficult to say. On the one hand, the 40s and £3 per year wealth requirements were so low as to be of limited relevance for middling farming families; having been set shortly before a substantial rise in land rents, these equated to holdings of six to nine acres by 1600, a small share of an average farm.[13] The urban trades that the statute mentioned specifically were occupations in which the premium a master might demand, or the capital needed to establish a business, were both much larger barriers to entry than a parental income requirement of £3 a year in property, even before inflation undermined the size of such a requirement.[14] As we discuss in chapter 4, the premiums that merchants were asking by the early seventeenth century were substantial; even for provincial traders, capital requirements were an order of magnitude greater than the £3 set out in the statute.[15]

The Poor Law offered a potential counterweight to the ambitions of the statute to keep the poor for agriculture. Was it as ineffective? The answer seems to be no. At least some parishes chose to place pauper youths in apprenticeships that would qualify them to work in a craft under the statute. This could require a substantial investment, and premiums for pauper children entering trades were at a similar level to those for private apprentices in similar occupations.[16] In 1631, for example, St Clement Danes, in London, paid £4 to bind George Blunt to a roper in Clerkenwell and £4 to bind William Bellamye to William Kinge, a citizen and member of the Merchant Taylors' Company, who worked as a cutter in Newgate Market.[17] Bellamye was duly enrolled for an eight-year term at the Merchant Taylors' Hall on 3 November 1631. This was an urban metropolitan parish, so such a destination made sense, but the idea of placing paupers in crafts, as well as service and husbandry, was widespread. Indeed, Lord Keeper Bacon encouraged judges who were monitoring pauper apprenticeship to 'cherish manufactures, old and new, especially draperies'.[18] As Steve Hindle has shown, even in rural areas, placements for pauper children in crafts and shopkeeping were common.[19] Pauper children are recorded entering indentures in a number of towns and cities—although this kind of contextual information is rarely consistently recorded. Churchwardens are explicitly noted in city records as placing children with artisans such as ropemakers and cordwainers in Boston, with basket-makers, cordwainers, framework knitters, and wool-combers in Leicester, with masons, bakers, blacksmiths, and (again) cordwainers in Lincoln, and with tailors and shoemakers in Liverpool.[20]

Over the eighteenth century, pauper children were notoriously dispatched in ever larger numbers into apprenticeships in industry, particularly in the new textile factories of the north. But even in London, large numbers of paupers were still placed into traditional craft apprenticeships with masters who were guild members. The London Blacksmiths' Company, for example, recorded substantial numbers of apprentices with premiums paid by parish Poor Law authorities.[21] Similarly, a number of poor boys from Bridewell Hospital, one of London's major institutions addressing poverty and disorder in the metropolis, are known to have been bound apprentice in the Weavers' Company (and later freed) between 1689 and 1697, when this information was appended to the register.[22] Bridewell Hospital itself expected that the youths it placed into apprenticeships would be freed into the city once they completed, and noted this in its records.[23] Woolnoth Smith, a 'parish boy', and by his forename probably a foundling, of the parish of St Mary Woolnoth, London, was bound to the citizen and salter Edward Bracebridge, 30 March 1744, and later freed into the guild in 1754, illustrating the path from pauper to freeman that the Poor Laws opened.[24]

By European standards, the Statute of Artificers created an unusually exclusionary set of rules that limited apprenticeship to the children of parents who met a complicated set of property and wealth requirements. Aimed at preventing migration from agriculture to urban occupations, they appear to have been disregarded from the outset. Even before inflation eroded their bite, they left no sign in the apprenticeship registers that exist from the 1560s onwards. The Poor Law, by contrast, did succeed in placing at least some poor children into apprenticeships that gave them the same occupational and legal privileges as their more fortunate peers. Similar initiatives to provide training for poor children that would allow them to access skilled work in industry were created in a range of European cities and towns, particularly in the late seventeenth and eighteenth centuries.[25]

Nationality

While wealth, parental occupation, and place of origin within England appear to have been moot, nationality—defined by birth in the domain of the English monarch—does appear to have provided a firm boundary to apprenticeship flows. English apprentices were not just English. London's guilds record a small but steady stream of youths from Wales entering apprenticeships, making up 2 per cent of guild apprentices in the sixteenth to eighteenth centuries. Later, youths from English colonies in the Americas and the Caribbean appeared as apprentices.

Apprentices from France, the Netherlands, or other parts of mainland Europe are almost entirely absent, however. Most significantly, even after 1604, youths from Scotland are exceptionally rare in the records of London and other cities. Scots make up only around 0.2 per cent of apprentices in London in the seventeenth and eighteenth centuries. It would be easy to object that such a barrier was insignificant given the distances involved; migration fields were relatively limited aside from London. Yet, apprentices reached the metropolis from across the Atlantic in the seventeenth and eighteenth centuries; the North Sea was hardly a barrier, in comparison. In the fifteenth and early sixteenth centuries, journeymen from the Low Countries, Germany, and France had played an important role in bringing new trades into England.[26] The Low Countries were in many ways more accessible from London than Lancashire or Cheshire on the distant west coast, and strong commercial ties linked communities across the English Channel. As Jelle van Lottum has shown for a later period, migrants into the Netherlands came from many more distant countries via ship, while the migration fields of England's major cities largely ended at the coasts of the island.[27]

The impact of the prohibition on foreign apprentices was most onerous for the children of the large numbers of religious migrants from the continent who settled in England during the sixteenth and seventeenth centuries. Skilled migrant adults, if working in a trade, were allowed to accept English youths as apprentices.[28] But their children were barred from apprenticeship, even though they were living in England already. The legal inability of religious migrants to serve apprenticeships and thereby gain the right to work in a craft was repeatedly a source of harassment and prosecution, despite religious refugees having royal permission to settle and work.[29] In 1571, Dutch Strangers petitioned Parliament about being prevented from working 'for not having bin seven years an apprentice in England . . . although they well know that a stranger by the Law may not be an Apprentice in England'.

Much the same complaint would come in 1612 from the Walloons settled in Norwich.[30]

In reality, some alien children did enter apprenticeships, but the numbers were limited, particularly after 1574, when even the children of aliens born in England were barred from apprenticeships in London, extending the restriction to the second generation. In 1593, a survey of alien householders in London recorded them as having 389 English apprentices but just twenty-five alien apprentices, largely fulfilling the government's ambition that their skills should be spread into the native population.[31] In the later seventeenth century, the Weavers' Company in London recorded just a dribble of alien apprentices—193 among the almost 9,000 youths they enrolled between 1662 and 1694, despite the importance of textiles, and particularly silk-weaving, among Huguenot immigrants, thousands of whom were working in that industry in the city in these decades.[32] Similarly, the Goldsmiths' Company recorded just seventy-nine Huguenot youths training with Huguenot masters in the eighty-four years between 1693 and 1777. Among them was Augustine Courtauld, the son of a merchant from the Île d'Oléron near La Rochelle in France, who was bound to Samuel Pantin, another Huguenot goldsmith, in 1701, and whose work is still displayed in the Courtauld Institute, endowed by one of his descendants. Courtauld himself would take three Huguenot boys as apprentices over his career, along with six English apprentices.[33]

It is hard to say whether or not removing the legal barrier to foreigners entering apprenticeships would have opened a substantial flow of youths from the continent into English apprenticeships. In other parts of Europe where rules around nationality did not apply, apprentices did cross state borders: Antwerp drew youths from outside Brabant in the 1500s, Munich from beyond Bavaria in 1848, and Vienna from outside the German lands in 1750–1848; Barcelona and Madrid both saw occasional apprentices from outside Spain in the sixteenth to eighteenth centuries; and Venice recruited youths from Spain, France, Germany, and Austria in the sixteenth and early seventeenth centuries.[34] However, the numbers making these journeys were not large, if only because of the distances involved. Most of the long-distance migration seen into the Netherlands occurred slightly later in the life cycle, among adult labourers and journeymen.

England's training system was isolated from the continent and Scotland by the legal requirement for apprentices to be born in the king's dominion. The reverse was not true: immigrants were allowed, even encouraged, to provide training. From the perspective of the opportunities available to

Europe's young people, however, the largest impact was probably felt by children from refugee communities who were already in England.[35]

Fees

What about the direct financial barriers to apprenticeship that guilds and cities established in the form of the fees that they charged for registering contracts? Apprentices to citizens of London had to register twice—first with the guild, then the city. In London, the median fee taken by a guild between the mid-sixteenth and late eighteenth centuries was 2s 6d, around a day's wage for a building craftsman in the middle of the seventeenth century.[36] Only a couple of guilds charged much less than this. The lowest fee in our sample was the Tylers and Bricklayers', which charged 10d from 1680, when the decision to open access to construction work in the city after the Great Fire must have been sharply reducing interest in apprenticeships with guild members. Equally few charged much more, however. The highest fees were the Clothworkers' (c. 1800) and Coopers' (1741), which both took 5s, despite the notional cap set in 1530.

The official charge levied by the guild for its collective use was not the totality of the fees that youths faced, however. On top of the company's own demands, the various officers whom it employed were often allowed to extract fees, and from 1695 every enrolment was subject to a tax of 2s 6d imposed to help pay the city's debts from its mismanagement of orphans' estates.[37] In the Clothworkers, by 1800, the 5s the company received was dwarfed by the 4s 2d taken by the company clerk for the enrolment, the extra 3s 4d to 7s 2d the clerk charged for attending the stamping, the 1s paid to the upper beadle, and the 6d to 16s 6d paid to the under-beadle. The total cost of enrolment was between £1 6s 8d and £1 10s 10d, depending on the premium paid, and most of it was fees to officers.[38] This was exceptional, but in most cases where we can identify these additional fees, they amounted to between a third and two-thirds of the total cost of registration, increasing the real fee substantially beyond the level visible in guild accounts.[39]

In effect, guilds were funding their bureaucracy, such as it was, through fees for services, a common approach in the period. To this, the City—motivated by similar reasons—added a fee of 2s 6d for enrolment by the chamberlain, plus 4d to the clerk; this was notionally paid by the master but presumably often funded by the apprentice.[40] Even with officers' fees accounted for, however, the financial costs of registration were a modest addition to the sums needed to pay a premium or even to furnish a youth with the wardrobe they needed. Cumulatively, fees at this level were in the order of less than a week's wages for a building labourer in the city in the middle of the seventeenth century—certainly not trivial, but not prohibitive either.[41] Fees had been higher in the fifteenth century in some guilds, and the sums of 30s to 40s cited as the reason for passing the 1530 law that capped guild fees suggest that barriers might have been substantial for early modern apprentices if levels had not been restrained by the state's intervention.[42]

Outside London, the story was similar, as table 10.1 shows. The fees that apprentices were charged to start their training appear to have been modest for the most part. Charging a fee at all became more common as enrolment was implemented better in the late sixteenth and early seventeenth centuries. But even then, they were rarely substantial; much more attention was paid to entry to freedom or citizenship than to a master taking another youth as an apprentice. Several guilds charged a shilling or less.[43] Others hovered around the level of 2s 6d or 3s 4d seen in various London guilds.[44] Clerks' fees and other incidental charges seem to have added to the cost in a similar manner to what we see in London.[45] On average, the median provincial apprentice fee was equivalent to the earnings from two days of work for an unskilled building labourer, and the mean was 4.2 days' work.

A few exceptions suggest what could have occurred. In the seventeenth century, the Butchers' guilds in both Salisbury and Carlisle set lower fees for apprentices who were the sons of citizens or guild members, respectively. Their fees were not so large in either case, so the 30 to 50 per cent difference was probably more of an irritation than impediment. But from 1740, Carlisle's Butchers went further, demanding £5 from each new apprentice.[46] At this level, access equated to around two months' income for a building labourer.[47]

The case of the Carlisle Butchers points to the way entry fees could have been exploited to restrict entry to training, either by giving a substantial advantage to 'insiders' or by setting prohibitive demands that would dissuade most entrants, as London's guilds had before 1530. At the same time, that the Butchers were unusual underlines the fact that in practice, formal financial barriers were low in England, as they were in several other areas of Europe.

We can usefully benchmark fees by comparing them to the wages of an unskilled urban labourer.[48] In Paris, guild apprenticeship fees were at the same level, averaging two days' wages in the sixteenth and seventeenth centuries. In the cities of the Southern and Northern Netherlands, sons of guild members were often advantaged, paying low fees—on average, half

TABLE 10.1. Provincial guild apprenticeship registration fees

City	Guild	Date	Type	Fee (money)	Includes clerk's fees?	Fee (days)
Bristol	Barber Surgeons	1652	All	12d		0.7
	Glovers	1670	All	2s 6d		1.7
	Soapmakers	1630	All	2s 6d		2.1
Carlisle	Glovers	1665	All	3s 6d	y	2.3
	Merchants	1624	All	6d		0.5
	Merchants	1656	Foreigners	4s	y	2.7
	Merchants	1656	Members' sons	3s 6d		2.3
	Shoemakers	1595	All	2s 1d	y	2.1
	Smiths	1562	All	6d		0.6
	Butchers	1665	All	6d		0.3
	Butchers	1740	All	£5		50.0
Devizes	Merchants	1614	All	2s 4d	y	2.3
Hull	Barber Surgeons	1714	All	2s 6d		1.4
	Coopers	1598	All	6d		0.5
	Coopers	1681	All	30d	y	1.7
	Glovers	1499	All	12d		2.0
	Joiners	1598	All	6d		0.5
	Shipwrights	1682	All	3s	y	2.0
	Tailors	1553	All	6d		0.7
Salisbury	Bakers	1675	All	4s 6d	y	3.0
	Barber Surgeons	1675	All	3s	y	2.0
	Butchers	1614	Citizens' sons	4s 10d	y	4.8
	Butchers	1614	Foreigners	5s 10d	y	5.8
	Butchers	1614	Members' sons	3s 11d	y	3.9
	Town	1612	All	12d	y	1.0
Shrewsbury	Barber Surgeons	1787	All	2s 6d		1.0
	Glovers	1614	Members' sons	2s	y	2.0
	Glovers	1614	Members' sons	3s	y	3.0
	Tailors	1610	All	20s		20.0

Sources: Parker 1922, 173–78; BRO, MS 08018, 10 June 1670; Matthews 1940, 43; Ferguson and Nanson 1887; Kite 1858; Lambert 1891, 165–69; Haskins 1912; Leighton 1881, 268–75; SRO, MS 6001/4275, MS 6001/5837. The wage used is Allen's southern England building labourer, because his northern England wage series is incomplete over this period. The southern wage was 5% higher in the seventeenth century and 11% in the eighteenth century, so the difference is slight.

a day's wage in the seventeenth century and two days' in the eighteenth, and sometimes nothing at all. But even migrants would pay only two or three days' wages in fees in cities such as Alkmaar, Amsterdam, Arnhem, Haarlem, Rotterdam, Utrecht, and Leuven. Guilds in a few cities, such as Antwerp, pushed fees higher, to a month's wages, and then usually in periods of financial distress in the eighteenth century. England's fee regime was in line with those seen elsewhere in Northwestern Europe and presented a low barrier from the 1530s onwards.

Age

The rules around the age at which young people could be apprenticed varied more than most other aspects of the institution. For pauper children being placed into apprenticeship by a parish or justice of the peace, age was an upper limit; until 1696, their service needed to begin before they reached fourteen and could not end after a terminal point at twenty-four or twenty years, depending on gender, and while it is not clear how strictly these were enforced, there is abundant evidence of pauper children under ten being placed into apprenticeships.[49] For guild apprentices in London, the city set a minimum age for entering apprenticeship of fourteen and a maximum of twenty-one, to which a 1556 order set a minimum age of completion of twenty-four years.[50] The city authorities remained clear into the nineteenth century that apprentices had to be under twenty-one years old when bound; this was part of the freeman's oath, and as late as 1812 they disenfranchised Richard Pallet, a scale-beam maker in Leadenhall Street, for binding two apprentices above this age.[51] The Statute of Artificers set no minimum, but with a seven-year term lasting until twenty-four, it encouraged a later start.

What impact did these formal age regulations have? Unfortunately, the actual age of apprentices is rarely recorded in early modern records. The little direct information that survives from London in the sixteenth and early seventeenth centuries suggests that the age limits set by the city were well below the age of most apprentices. Evidence of new apprentices' ages contained in the records of the Carpenters' Company from 1572 to 1594 indicates an average age of 19.5 years; only seven of 1,317 youths were younger than fourteen when they began their training (four were twelve and three were thirteen). However, sixty (4.6%) were older than twenty-four years, suggesting that the upper age limit was more vulnerable to being breached than the lower one.[52]

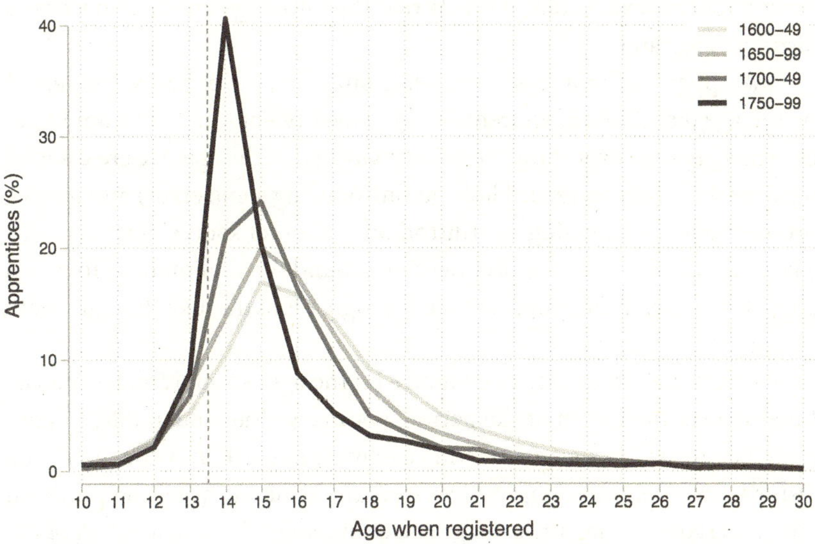

FIGURE 10.1. The ages of London apprentices, 1600–1799. The dashed line indicates the legal minimum in London of fourteen years.
Source: Wallis et al. 2010.

Fortunately, for a large sample of London apprentices bound between the 1580s and 1800s, we are able to estimate ages by linking baptismal records to indentures.[53] This evidence shows that the ages at which apprentices were bound in London fell markedly over these two centuries, drawing ever closer to the boundary set by the city's rules. At the end of the sixteenth century, apprentices were, on average, verging on eighteen years old when bound. By the start of the nineteenth century, they were only around fifteen and a half years old. The median age of apprenticeship fell even further, from 17.4 in the 1590s to 14.7 in the 1800s. At the same time, the spread of ages at which youths were bound narrowed substantially, with a large spike in fourteen-year-olds, as figure 10.1 shows.

Despite this move towards a younger start for training, the effect of the rules on age remained strongly in evidence in London. The proportion of apprentices who were in breach of the regulations for being very young remained fairly constant and low. In 1600–1649, 4 per cent of apprentices were under thirteen years old, and 9 per cent were under fourteen, and hence in breach of city rules. Most apprentices were older, and only 11 per cent were actually fourteen. In 1750–99, 3 per cent of apprentices were under thirteen years old, and 12 per cent were under fourteen. These are similar shares to those 150 years earlier, except now, 41 per cent of apprentices were exactly fourteen years old; it seems that the lower age limit had become a distinct constraint.

The upper age limit was broken less often and never had a clear effect on the age distribution; apprentices aged over twenty-one fell from 12 per cent to 5 per cent over the same period. Given that the ages we are discussing here are based on record linkage (introducing some error) and may be prone to under-estimating age (introducing another source of error), such a large break in entry to apprenticeship around the minimum of fourteen indicates the persistent impact of the age regulations through the eighteenth century.[54]

We lack the same body of evidence on the ages of apprentices outside London over the length of the period. For many cities and guilds, it is not clear that formal rules on a starting age were in place. In Gloucester and Oxford, however, most apprentices were the same age as in London, with fifteen to sixteen being the average age of binding.[55] For the first half of the eighteenth century we can identify the age of around 4,200 apprentices with premiums in the stamp duty records who entered contracts with provincial masters. Their average age when they were bound was 15.6 years, just under a year below the 16.5 years that was the average age in London in that period.[56]

When we look at the share of younger teenagers taken by masters in provincial incorporated towns, 11 per cent were under thirteen and 26 per cent were under fourteen years old. Outside these towns and boroughs, more apprentices were younger: 15 per cent were under thirteen and 30 per cent were under fourteen. The substantial difference between incorporated towns and other areas in the share of under-fourteens indentured suggests that urban regulations affected the age of youths entering training in provincial towns and cities, just as they did in London.

It is clear from this comparison that London's rules did matter. The share of younger apprentices outside corporate centres was substantially higher than in London's guilds at the same time: there were five times more new apprentices aged under thirteen and three times more aged under fourteen in unincorporated areas than in the metropolis. Some of this difference will have been a consequence of the status, migration, and occupations of the apprentices and their masters—both the wealth of apprentices' families and the distances they travelled were positively associated with an older age of binding. Even accounting for that effect, it is clear that corporate rules did limit entry to apprenticeship.

In other large European centres, apprentices generally started their training at around the same age as in England. The difference was that they were bound over a wider span of ages, including more who were younger than fourteen.[57] In early modern Madrid, apprentices were on average fifteen, so little different, but 27 per cent were under fourteen in the seventeenth century.[58] Similarly, the average age was 14.4 years in Venice in 1582–1665, but 39 per cent of apprentices were bound before they reached fourteen.[59] In the census of Turin taken in 1802, 16 per cent of male apprentices were still under fourteen when observed. Most German apprentices began between thirteen and fifteen.[60] In 1761, French apprentices were actually often older when they began—seventeen on average—but their ages ranged from twelve to over thirty years of age. By the early 1800s, however, youths were markedly younger, typically thirteen years old when indentured in France.[61]

In short, age regulations, notably in London, did constrain access to training by preventing earlier entry into training. The rules affected all youths, and so did not obviously generate inequalities between them. They did, however, distort the economy, slowing young people's training in some locations and delaying their entry into the skilled workforce. Such rules can be protective, keeping children from exploitation and ensuring they receive an education. This is unlikely to have been the effect in this period. Entering service outside the family did not usually mark the beginning of work. Humphries and Horrell's examination of the age at which children started work within the family in the early nineteenth century suggests this could occur around the age of ten, while by 1851, census data suggests that 46 per cent of thirteen-year-old and 68 per cent of fourteen-year-old children were in employment.[62]

Industrialisation had already changed employment substantially by the mid-nineteenth century, and we lack equivalent figures for the seventeenth and early eighteenth centuries, but a range of sources indicate that youths started working well before the age at which they entered indentures. Apprenticeship regulations prevented apprenticeship, not work. However, we should not exaggerate the impact of the age restriction; even in areas without this rule, the average apprentice would have been fourteen years old—or older—before they started their indenture.

The Seven-Year Term

The long term of service required of English apprenticeships is one of its best-known features. Present from the earliest extant regulations, a contractual norm of seven years—or more—was one of the defining elements of the customary framework articulated in most guild ordinances and civic rules.

This rule, above all, was a fixture in early modern apprenticeship before the eighteenth century. Not all apprentices served their full terms of service. In fact, a great many did not, as we discussed in chapter 6. Their contracts would end prematurely as they left the trade or moved to a different master. However, the terms they had agreed to in their indentures still mattered in defining the final boundaries of the agreements. During their term of service, any move to a different employer or exit might need to be negotiated or resolved before one of the institutions that oversaw contracts in England, particularly the urban courts and county magistrates.

The evidence we have from English city and guild records makes clear that the fame of this requirement is justified. Seven years was the shortest term for enrolled apprenticeships in corporate England. For London, Gloucester, Lincoln, Norwich, Oxford, and Shrewsbury, the terms survive for just short of 137,000 apprentices bound before 1800, mostly in the seventeenth and eighteenth centuries. Over 99.99 per cent of contracts were for seven years or longer. This figure is kept below 100 per cent by occasional exceptions, numbering just seventy-four in this sample. However, these seem mostly explicable as cases where turnovers of apprentices (transfers of the remainder of a youth's period of service to a different master) are recorded without an explanation given in the register; they are clerical errors, not real variations in term length.

The only city with records in our sample where this near universal seven-year minimum term of service does not hold is Liverpool, where in the early eighteenth century around 17 per cent of indentures were for less than seven years. Reflecting Liverpool's position as an expanding port, these contracts were largely, but not universally, for mariners' apprentices being bound to serve on ships. Their terms were often three or four years. This is something we also observe in the records of apprenticeship disputes brought to the Lord Mayor's Court in London in the seventeenth century, where 177 of the mariners' apprentices who petitioned for discharge reported contracts of less than seven years; most had been contracted for five years instead.[63] Mariners were, however, a distinct group with a specific legal framework that differed from the Statute of Artificers in setting a maximum but not a minimum term, as we saw in the previous chapter.[64] In short, these exceptions reinforce the impression of the force of law and custom on age.

If anything, the customary minimum seven-year term became *more* important over the sixteenth and seventeenth centuries. Figure 10.2 shows that the seven-year term increased from being the most common of a range of terms in the later sixteenth century to being nearly universal by the start

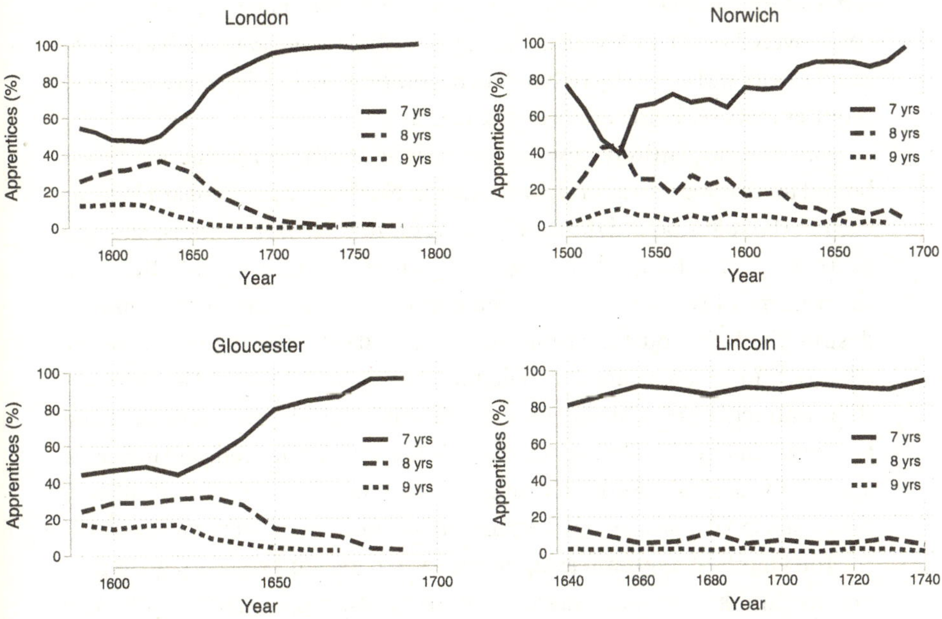

FIGURE 10.2. The rise of the seven-year term in corporate towns. The figure reports the share of indentures with each of the three most common term lengths by decade.

of the eighteenth.[65] Longer agreements of eight or nine years (or more) accounted for around half of apprenticeships in Elizabethan London and Gloucester and a quarter in Norwich. They disappeared over the next century. Apprenticeship became standardised, with the legal minimum becoming the norm. Terms shortened on average. In effect, this meant that the opportunity cost of apprenticeship fell. It is unlikely to be coincidence that this occurred at a time when the direct cost, in the form of the share of youths paying premiums, appears to have grown. In England's incorporated cities and guilds, apprenticeship terms had essentially converged to their legal minimum of seven years by 1700.

What happened to apprenticeship terms in the eighteenth century? This century saw a judicial weakening of the Statute of Artificers, questioning its application in country villages or to journeymen hired by masters. Outside corporate settings, the eighteenth century saw a significant decline in the duration of apprenticeships, essentially continuing the trend towards shorter average terms visible in figure 10.2. By 1783–90, the average term set in indentures for male apprentices outside incorporated towns was 6.1 years, and 39 per cent of male apprentices had terms shorter than seven years.[66]

A decade on, in 1800–1804, this had fallen to 5.7 years, and over half—54 per cent—were bound for less than seven years. Away from England's incorporated towns and cities, by 1800 it had become normal to disregard the term requirements set in the Statute of Artificers.

This was not entirely new: as early as the 1660s, Benjamin Bangs was bound for five years to a rural shoemaker in Norfolk, while Leonard Wheatcroft in the 1680s bound three of his sons for four years, five years, and two years, respectively, and his daughter Elizabeth for four years.[67] But such short terms of service had not been common at the start of the century, despite the 1699 court decision that the statute did not apply in country villages.[68] In Lincolnshire and Wiltshire, the mean duration of apprenticeship contracts agreed for males bound outside incorporated towns had been 6.96 years in 1710–19, almost exactly what the statute required, and in Sussex it was 6.5 years.[69] By 1800–1804, average terms in these settings had fallen to 6.23 years in Wiltshire, 6.02 years in Lincolnshire, and 5.70 years in Sussex.

The length of apprenticeship terms for female apprentices paying premiums shrank even more sharply. By the 1780s, three-quarters of female apprentices agreed to serve less than seven years, and the average term was just 4.4 years. From this point, terms seem to have been reasonably stable, and only fell slightly to 4.2 years in the 1800s.

Apprenticeships in incorporated towns and cities did adhere more closely to the statutory seven-year term over the eighteenth century—this is the setting that we observed in our city and guild series in figure 10.2. Apprenticeship was still connected to local citizenship rights as well as to the general privileges set out in the Statute of Artificers, and those local rules which often demanded a seven-year term remained in place. However, even in incorporated towns, 33 per cent of contracts with premiums were shorter than seven years by 1800–1804. Seven years remained by far the most common term specified in urban contracts, but an increasing number specified three to six years of service. Where we can observe change, most of the decline in terms occurred after 1750. By necessity, all these shorter contracts occurred outside the oversight of the local city or guild authorities.

Not all occupations saw the same developments. From the stamp tax, we know the contract duration agreed for almost 18,000 apprentices with premiums in the first years of the nineteenth century. Figure 10.3 reports the distribution of term lengths in eight of the most common trades, distinguishing between those agreed in incorporated towns and cities and those agreed elsewhere. In some, such as tailors, shoemakers, and carpenters, custom remained dominant, especially in incorporated towns, perhaps reflecting

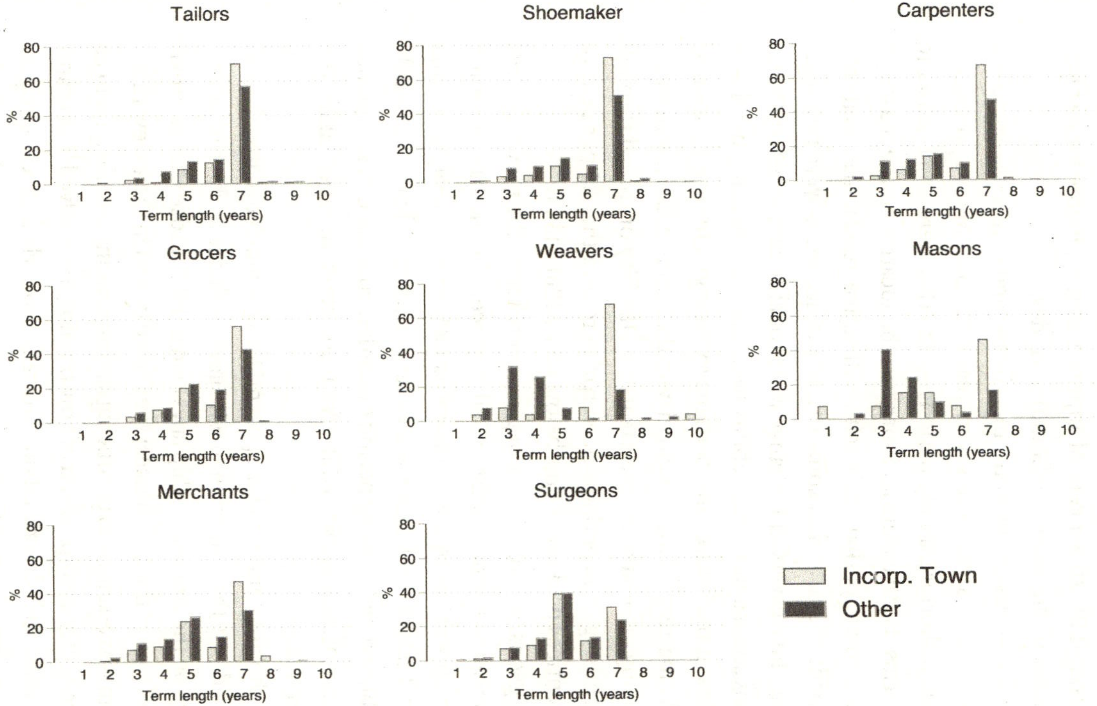

FIGURE 10.3. Contracted terms, 1800–1804. The figure reports the percentage of apprentices bound with premiums and paying stamp duty from 1800 to 1804 inclusive, by term length in years. Masters are assigned to an incorporated town or city based on the location reported in the register, not their individual status as citizen or guild member. Occupations are standardized and clustered where appropriate (e.g., cordwainers are included in shoemakers). In total, the dataset contains 7,326 apprentices across these occupations. The smallest sample is of masons (366) and the largest is shoemakers (1,732).
Source: See Appendix 1.

the sustained strength of local guilds in these trades. And in all but one occupation, seven years remained the modal term for male apprentices. However, alongside those whose contracts met the requirements of the Statute of Artificers were another 30–40 per cent of apprentices bound for less than seven years. These were not all small reductions in the expected term either: around 10–20 per cent of apprentices were bound for just four or five years, even in the most hidebound of trades.

Several trades—weavers, masons, merchants, and surgeons—stand out for their marked move away from seven-year contracts. Many apprentices now served much shorter training periods—ones that were much closer to continental norms. For weavers and masons, the location of the master in an incorporated town, perhaps one with still active guilds, mattered substantially. Outside them, and to some extent inside, terms were markedly shorter. Among the weavers, this change was probably connected to declining expectations about apprentices' ability to secure their own independence as small masters in the future, and perhaps to their greater exploitation as cheap labour by masters.[70] This coincided with the boom in handloom weaving that was being generated by the greater availability of thread through mechanical spinning; it is perhaps no surprise to find that 85 per cent of weavers' apprentices paid premiums below £5 by 1800–1804.

Among surgeons, and to a lesser degree, merchants, the move towards shorter terms was not connected to a fall in price. The median premium for surgeons' apprentices by 1800–1804 was £84, a world away from that of the weavers. Instead, for surgeons, shorter contracts did not necessarily equate to an abbreviated training period but rather could fit into a sequence of different stages of learning with different instructors, such as walking the wards in a hospital.

The use of shorter contracts for apprentices was much discussed—and heavily criticised—by the journeymen who gave evidence to the parliamentary committee on the apprenticeship laws held in 1812. Those who gave evidence were far from neutral witnesses; they were united in their view that a seven-year term was essential to producing skilfull artisans. But the practices they condemned offer an impression of how training had evolved. For example, Frobisham Mitchell described one Graves, 'formerly a cheesemonger, [who] was afterwards articled for four or five years to Mr Smith, a coachmaker in Swallow Street', while John Glass Paradise suggested that among goldsmiths it was now the 'general practice of those illegal masters . . . to bind persons for short terms, namely three, four or five years, employing them to make only one particular article'.[71] Shorter periods of training were often tied to narrower skill sets, the witnesses suggested, and sometimes to apprentices receiving wages, and so it seems they were spending more time on lower-skilled production than acquiring advanced skills. A number of witnesses claimed that these 'illegal' apprentices were often older and had previously been engaged in another trade; at least some were shifting from one occupation to another, a practice the witnesses condemned fiercely, whether it occurred at the level of business owners, masters, journeymen, or apprentices.[72]

For all the examples that these witnesses presented of defections from the statutory norm, the basic continuities in the term lengths and approach to training are as striking. Seven years retained its normative force, as the stamp duty records also indicate. Even when written contracts dropped this, masters and apprentices remained reliant on them; although the service brought no legal rights under the statute, masters and apprentices were still signing formal indentures, and some were still paying premiums. Indeed, one witness, a leather finisher, actually produced a batch of short-term indentures before the committee.[73]

Did shorter terms equate to less-well-trained apprentices? To the extent that skill usually increases with experience, the answer is obviously yes. There is no way to counter the argument put by the witnesses defending mandatory seven-year apprenticeships at the 1812 commission, given that they were all willing to embrace the idea that a worker never ceased to gain knowledge over time. As one the millwright put it, theirs was 'a business that is never learned; it requires a long servitude; a man can never come near to perfection; it is impossible to be perfect in it; there are new things coming forward every day'.[74] The more important question, however, is whether these shorter apprenticeships were ending before the point at which the youths were sufficiently skilled that they no longer needed to engage in the exchange of training for labour, or, alternatively, whether the content of their training was being watered down or narrowed to such an extent that they were unable to find work subsequently. In considering this, it is important to recognise that seven years of apprenticeship was not usually taken by contemporaries as essential to achieving high levels of human capital *outside* Britain; a move away from this distinctively long formal term length may therefore not have equated to deskilling or imply a decline in earning power.

The force of the seven-year term across these three centuries is clear. It remained the normative length of an apprenticeship to 1800 and beyond, and was always the required minimum term for masters with citizenship in corporate towns and cities. Even outside those privileged enclaves, only a few occupations saw terms move entirely away from seven years before the nineteenth century. However, it is equally clear that the impact of the legal and customary rule shifted as terms declined overall, initially converging towards seven years and then slipping below that in the later eighteenth century. Despite the campaigns of some artisans, the most famous element of the Statute of Artificers had been eroded and weakened by the time of its abolition.

This had three important effects for how we think about human capital in England in the early Industrial Revolution and before. First, the opportunity cost of training declined, widening access to skilled work. Second, England converged towards the European norm of apprenticeships lasting three to five years. Third, it had become cheaper for workers to acquire skills in rural, unincorporated parts of England than in its towns, which helps to explain the growth in apprenticeship in the countryside that we observed in chapter 3, and the rise in rural proto-industry that occurred in the long eighteenth century.

Conclusion

England's rules on access to apprenticeship were a distinctive but not always effective feature of its training system between the sixteenth and early nineteenth centuries. That is, they were distinctive in the nationwide scope of the legal provisions established by the Statute of Artificers, a state-authored statutory system that was not found elsewhere in Europe, but not always effective in that several of the barriers established by law had little practical impact. As has been observed for a range of European settings, rules 'were more a reference than a reflection of reality', and they were 'often dead letters'.[75]

This was, in practice, a largely open-access regime in which institutional barriers based on ascriptive characteristics of gender, wealth, status, and religion had little consequence for young people's ability to obtain training. Only the rules around nationality had teeth, isolating the English training market from Scottish and continental youths, including the children of religious refugees. Real barriers to opportunity from law and regulation were far lower than they appeared on paper.

Family background and resources did still impose a binding constraint on the choices that youths might realistically make about their futures. But this was mainly because of the funds they needed to possess to carry the opportunity costs of servitude, especially the long terms of service, the premium paid to a master, and the working capital they would need for a craft or trade. These are the costs we discussed in detail in chapter 4. City and guild fees added to this, but they were a small—if surely unwelcome—part of the financial pressures youths faced. For the English, at least, the market for apprenticeship was little different, then, to the situation one would observe in an open, unregulated labour market. The main driver of inequality of opportunity was existing social and economic inequality, not exclusionary institutions.

Some rules did matter. In towns and cities with civic and guild rules, age and term length came to matter more over time, in fact. These were also the areas where rules existed in most other parts of Europe. Practice, in short, stripped the main distinctive features away from the English system, reducing it to much the same skeleton of regulations found across the continent. In both age and term length, boundaries that had been at the base of a range came to be cliff edges in corporate England by the later seventeenth century. Fourteen years of age moved from being a minimum to a norm for starting an apprenticeship. Seven-year terms evolved from a commonplace to a near universal. This bunching of contracts at the threshold of legality, and the subsequent erosion of these rules in occupations and areas outside corporate oversight over the eighteenth century, indicate that the rules imposed greater friction over time. As they distorted the market, they increased the costs of training and provided rents to those who were supplying it.

The direction of movement in bargaining around apprenticeship was towards younger teenagers serving shorter terms of service. Were the limits on age and term length that slowed this drift economically important? We have no good counterfactual that would allow us to estimate their effect on the overall flow of young people into skilled crafts and trades. Some would presumably have been put off. Others may have been encouraged by the rents that completing apprenticeship might bring. But to put this question in some kind of context, the fall in the average age of starting apprenticeship from eighteen to fifteen years old expanded the size of the nation's skilled workforce by perhaps 10 per cent between 1600 and 1800, as apprentices' graduation into the ranks of journeymen and masters occurred at an earlier age.[76] At the same time, it shifted a larger slice of children's labour from unskilled work in and around the domestic economy to semi-skilled and skilled work in the market. It seems plausible that this was, in part, a response to the decline in children's real wages in the sixteenth century, as well as to the demand for skilled labour.[77] The average length of contracts also fell, adding to this increase in labour supply.

In the absence of the rules on age and term length, this process of starting younger and training for a shorter period would have advanced even more quickly in England, expanding the supply of skilled labour in these two centuries of profound structural change. While there are some obvious limits to when training could usefully have begun, each extra year of work an individual could provide after their training is completed increases the skilled labour supply by around 3 per cent. Regulations, in short, did impose a real, but not a large, deadweight cost on productivity in pre-industrial England.

11

Cultural Barriers

Investments in apprenticeship and other kinds of training and education reflect a society's set of cultural values about what types of people should have certain kinds of skills or carry out particular occupations and roles. Ideas about gender, race, religion, age, class, appearance, and other characteristics enhance or constrain opportunities historically, as they still do today. Some are articulated in the laws and customs created by a society, and chapters 9 and 10 explored aspects of this in the way regulations were constructed in early modern England to filter entry to apprenticeship by nationality, age, and status. Others are internalised and visible only in the actions people take. The ways in which early modern English families' decisions about placing their children into apprenticeship were limited by a 'cage of norms' is the focus of this chapter.[1]

That culture shapes economic behaviour is a fact more easily stated than demonstrated empirically. For this reason, I concentrate on two areas where the effect of social norms can be seen reasonably directly in the surviving evidence. First, what impact did gender have on young people's access to apprenticeship? And second, how did the decision to put a child into an apprenticeship relate to the order in which they were born, especially relative to the eldest son, who was usually the primary heir? In effect, we are looking at the impact a child's characteristics had on their family's choices about how to educate and train them. Where the effects of laws and regulations are often apparent in the differences in the opportunities that existed *between* families, differences *within* families can help us to understand norms and culture. Both, however, affect the openness and accessibility of apprenticeship and will therefore contribute to the way opportunities through apprenticeship are limited.

Neither legal statute nor guild ordinances in England usually imposed access restrictions based on the gender or birth order of a youth. Formal rules on who could be apprenticed therefore do not explain why girls were twenty times less likely to be apprenticed than boys, or why it was the younger and not the elder sons from rural farming or gentry households who would be sent to be indentured in London. In each case, it is likely that economic potential was wasted and individual preferences and happiness were frustrated.

Before interpreting the under-representation of girls and eldest boys as solely the product of the destructive power of norms on the opportunities of young people in early modern England, it is important to recognise the wider institutional framework. The way in which gender and birth order shaped the opportunities of young people certainly shows us how cultural values shaped decisions about training, but values on their own were not the only force at work here.

Formal institutions are also an important part of this story. Gender and birth order were important criteria within English laws and urban regulations around inheritance, marriage, and labour-market access, affecting what those who had served apprenticeships in early modern England might do later in their lives and creating strong incentives for parents to select particular children for apprenticeship.[2] Laws were, of course, shaped by norms, particularly elite norms, so any separation of formal and informal is somewhat artificial. However, the slow pace of legal evolution, even in a common-law system, and the narrow cross-section of interests represented when Crown and Parliament set laws, meant that formal rules and informal norms could diverge (or from the perspective of some groups, had never agreed). This made the law a partially independent factor. The critical point to keep in mind is that one consequence of England's formal institutions was that the rational allocation of training would not necessarily approximate to an even or random distribution between children.

Gender

Gender was arguably the most powerful determinant of an individual's social position in early modern England. It is no surprise to find that the largest 'missing' group among apprentices were defined by their gender, not their wealth. This was not because of laws or regulations that specifically prevented girls from accessing training. Laws that banned female apprentices were almost non-existent in England.[3] Other rules did matter, though. In London, the largest centre for training, a husband's freedom or citizenship encompassed their wife, allowing married women to evade the requirement to serve an apprenticeship in order to use a trade; on the other hand, marriage extinguished any independent rights that women had previously gained by apprenticeship.[4] These formal institutions around marriage and their effect on economic rights combined with expectations about gender roles to lower the incentive for parents to make formal investments in their daughters' human capital through an apprenticeship.[5]

This has led some historians to suggest that female apprenticeship either never occurred, or was little more than a form of domestic service when it appears in the records.[6] There is a grain of truth in this. Young girls from poor families were commonly placed by parishes in pauper apprenticeships, and a substantial share of these contracts were to learn 'housewifery', as happened to Jane Joyce when the overseers of St Botolph's Aldgate in London bound her to Sarah Pluckrose of Wanstead, Essex, in 1803 at the age of six.[7] Numerically, these pauper apprentices were undoubtedly the largest group of female apprentices. Girls made up a substantial share—albeit still a minority—of the children placed into apprenticeships by their parishes. Around a third of pauper apprentices in Snell's sample of southern parishes were female, as were 42 per cent of the London pauper apprentices studied by Levene.[8]

Yet, as Snell and others have shown, early modern parish apprenticeships also placed girls in a wide range of other occupations, including in manufacturing and services; they were not all being dispatched to domestic service.[9] These girls learned skilled trades and would later practice them. Although the range of occupations narrowed over the eighteenth century, they included many that are often thought of as 'male' jobs, such as blacksmiths, shoemakers, tailors, weavers, butchers, and clockmakers.

Private apprenticeships of women into other crafts or trades were rarer than parish apprenticeships, but they did occur, as recent work by Amy Erickson and Laura Gowing has shown to great effect. Female apprentices even appear in English guilds. Unlike in France, there are no known female guilds in England and only a few guilds in which women were present in very large numbers—the Merchant Taylors of York, in which almost half of apprentices and many freemen were female in the middle of the eighteenth century, and the Glovers and Pinmakers in London, in which female apprentices peaked in the late seventeenth century.[10] Where female apprentices appear in other guilds, they are scattered needles among a haystack of males. In London, roughly 1 per cent of apprentices registered by early modern guilds were female, with a peak of 2 per cent in the last quarter of the seventeenth century.[11]

There are some signs that female apprenticeship was more common when the supply of apprentices was lower. Female apprentices were more frequent in earlier centuries.[12] Bristol's city records contain a relatively high share of female apprentices—4 per cent—in the early sixteenth century, the period in which masters also offered greater end-of-service rewards, such as tools or clothing, to encourage youths into placements, but numbers dwindled thereafter.[13] Female apprentices had disappeared from Bristol's records by the eighteenth century, suggesting the possibility that women, like labourers' children, were squeezed out as apprenticeship became more attractive and the price of training rose. On the other hand, in Leicester, which was distinguished by its large number of poor apprentices in the eighteenth century, 2 to 3 per cent of apprentices were female. The significance of such cycles is overshadowed by the general absence of female apprentices in civic and guild records. In Boston, Lincoln, Oxford, and Liverpool, not a single female apprentice was identifiable in our sample of city records. Gloucester had just one.

City and guild records under-estimate the true rate of private female apprenticeship, however. The stamp tax records offer a (marginally) more optimistic account. Each year in the eighteenth century, several hundred young women were indentured as apprentices with premiums in England, as figure 11.1 shows. Nine per cent of apprentices in London paying premiums in the eighteenth century were female—a similar share to the 10 per cent identified by Hovland in city records in the fourteenth and fifteenth centuries.[14] Outside London the share was lower, at just under 5 per cent.

All of the provincial cities that were just discussed did contain female apprentices whose families paid premiums in the eighteenth century. These girls were simply not registered with the city's authorities. In Gloucester, for example, eighty-five female apprentices were bound to masters or mistresses with premiums that were registered in the stamp duty records.[15] None appear in the city's records. Indeed, none of the fifty-three masters who took them, including the twenty-two male masters, appear in the city records taking any other apprentices either, with one possible exception: Elizabeth Barton, mantua-maker, who may be the Elizabeth Barton, 'plumber and glazier' who bound Seth Kitchen with a £10 premium in 1774—this inconsistency might be explained if the city clerk entered her husband William's

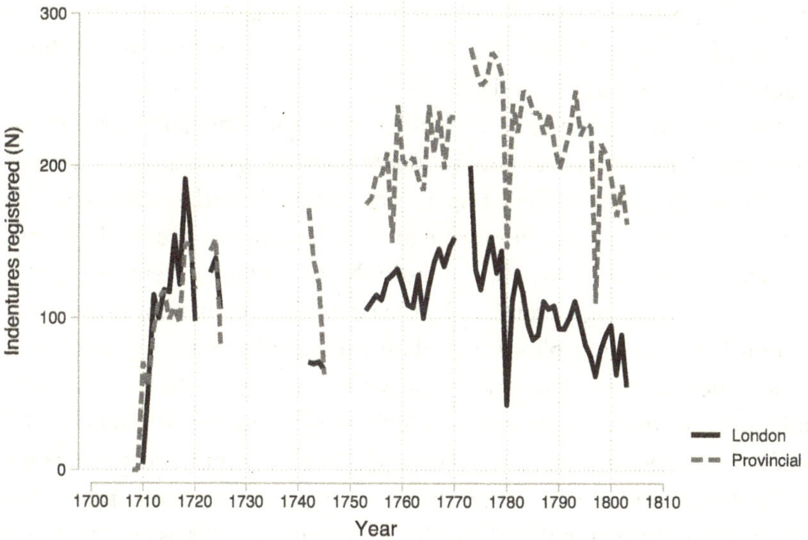

FIGURE 11.1. Female apprentices with premiums. The figure reports annual totals for female apprentices registered in the stamp duty records (Appendix 1) for years in which the registers exist for city and country.

trade rather than her own in that instance, perhaps because it was the root of her rights in the city.[16]

The gap between corporate registration and the use of private apprenticeship was growing over the eighteenth century, as was shown in chapter 2. Almost all female apprentices seem to have fallen into this space, and it seems that their masters were also largely operating outside the corporate framework. In part, this reflected the way in which women were indentured. As Amy Erickson has noted, female apprentices were more likely to be bound for less than seven years, as meeting the requirements set in the Statute of Artificers was less important to them.[17] This meant they might not be able to have their contracts registered by their city or guilds because they did not meet local rules and customs about minimum terms of service; this shirking of corporate registration would also save on fees, of course, but at the price of losing eligibility for guild membership.[18] Nonetheless, it did not mean that they could evade the taxman, and their indentures' validity at law depended on having the appropriate stamps attached to show that any duty owed on the premiums had been paid. This explanation gains credence from the fact that there is clear evidence for shorter terms in the female indentures recorded in the stamp duty. The length of the apprenticeships of female apprentices paying premiums fell sharply over the eighteenth century, from an average term of 5.7 years in 1720–50 to an average of 3.5 years for those indentured between 1790 and 1804.[19]

Even taking into account this avoidance of urban and guild institutions, there can be no doubt that young women were far less frequently apprenticed than young men.[20] The stamp duty records indicate that only about one in twenty English apprentices were female. To estimate the total number of female apprentices, we need to multiply the number of female apprentices recorded paying a premium by the ratio of premium to non-premium apprentices. The multiplier is based on evidence for male apprentices in trades where a parallel guild record survives, which show that one in three indentures involved premiums. While there is no obvious reason to think that families found it easier to place girls than boys into apprenticeships without a premium, and the premiums they paid were comparable, it is important to underline that the estimate depends on this assumption and needs to be interpreted with caution.

This calculation suggests that around 1,000 girls per annum, give or take a few hundred, started private apprenticeships each year in eighteenth-century England. More would have been apprenticed by their parishes, but there are no reliable figures for that. Apprenticeship absorbed about 1.5 to 2 per cent of the nation's teenage girls, a fraction of its importance to the training of teenage boys.[21]

Girls who were bound as apprentices were placed mainly in a limited number of trades, particularly millinery or clothing production, although occasional female apprentices can be found in most occupations, and they were particularly prominent among the small share of apprentices in agricultural occupations.[22] Table 11.1 summarises the occupations of the masters and mistresses of female apprentices found in the stamp tax records for four periods across the eighteenth century where the sample years are complete. It shows that what Snell styled the 'relative dominance of needlework occupations'—mantua-makers and milliners, haberdashers and dressmakers, occupations that were seen as more appropriate for girls—increased substantially over the century.[23] By the 1790s, over two-thirds of female apprentices were entering these trades, compared to fewer than one in five in London and one in three elsewhere in the 1710s.

Training was highly specialised and segregated by gender, even within the clothing trades: female tailors, for example, almost disappeared between the early and the late eighteenth century. Several of the trades that women trained in were almost exclusively female. Both dressmakers and spinners

TABLE 11.1. The trades of female apprentices

	London					Provinces				
Master occupation	1711–18 %	1741–56 %	1767–71 %	1791–98 %	All %	1711–18 %	1741–56 %	1767–71 %	1791–98 %	All %
Mantua-maker	24.3	40.8	30.3	44.7	34.1	15.9	40.1	41.3	41.5	37.6
Milliner	11.4	19.7	35.6	27.2	24.8	16.4	13.8	26.1	25.7	21.9
Haberdasher	1.2	1.6	7.6	5.2	4.3	0.2	0.1	0.7	2.0	0.9
Seamstress	7.3	3.2	0.1	0.2	2.5	5.3	1.9	0.7	0.7	1.6
Schoolmistress	0.7	0.4	1.1	4.8	1.6	0.0	0.0	0.5	2.1	0.8
Weaver	1.2	2.6	0.7	0.4	1.1	1.5	3.3	2.1	4.4	3.0
Glover	2.4	1.2	0.7	0.0	1.1	5.3	4.4	3.2	2.2	3.5
Stay-maker	1.0	0.6	1.1	1.0	0.9	0.2	2.0	1.0	1.3	1.2
Tailor	3.1	0.4	0.2	0.2	0.9	10.8	6.8	2.1	2.2	4.4
Cordwainer	1.4	0.8	0.0	0.2	0.5	1.1	1.0	1.4	1.3	1.3
Other	46.1	28.8	22.6	16.3	28.1	43.4	26.6	21.0	16.6	24.0
Total	100	100	100	100	100	100	100	100	100	100
N	588	503	857	523	2,471	530	884	1,317	1,178	3,909

Note: Table reports the ten most common occupations entered by female apprentices in the stamp tax sample for four sample periods with full samples for provincial and metropolitan apprenticeships.

took only female apprentices. All of the 336 dressmakers' and 204 spinners' apprentices listed in the stamp tax records were female. Almost all mantua-makers' and milliners' apprentices registered in this period were female—98 per cent of the more than 12,000 apprentices in these occupations. Indeed, this may well be an under-estimate, as Francis was the most common 'male' forename among the rest, and it can be used for both genders. The same cannot be said for the Isaacs, Matthews, and Daniels who were bound to mantua-makers, suggesting this was not an absolute split by gender. In other trades, however, female apprentices were present as a minority amidst a preponderance of males, with girls supplying 20 per cent of haberdashers', 7 per cent of weavers', and 6 per cent of coachmakers' apprentices over the period.

At least some families invested substantial sums in their daughters' human capital. The £15 median premium for female apprenticeships in the eighteenth century was actually higher than the £10 median for males; this was largely because of higher fees in London, where the median was £20 for females. The top quartile of female apprenticeships cost more than £31 each. There was a small, but not insubstantial, number of girls in this high-paying group—around 5,000 across the century in the records that survive. As one might expect, it was girls entering commercial and shopkeeping trades or professions whose families paid more: median premiums for milliners, haberdashers, and schoolmistresses were around £30. Crafts were more affordable: apprentices to mantua-makers paid £13, dressmakers, spinners, and tailors all paid £10, and glovers paid £6. Weavers' apprentices paid their masters just £4 on average, and a quarter paid less than £2 10s.

This raises the question of what kinds of families were investing such sums of money to dispatch their daughters into apprenticeships. Snell, for one, has suggested that female apprentices paying premiums came largely from middling families, and 'as the social status of family of origin rose . . . their likelihood of participating in any occupation fell relative to boys'.[24] Warnings by contemporaries about the risk of ruin faced by young women, largely from 'the many Snares laid for them by designing Men', might have been expected to reinforce caution.[25] On the other hand, Amy Erickson has tracked a cluster of respectable families apprenticing their daughters into prosperous trades in London, principally as milliners, in the early eighteenth century with premiums of £30 to £60.[26] These female apprentices in London guilds had fathers who were gentry, clerks, or prosperous tradesmen. Erickson argues that this represents a largely obscured channel of investment in young women's training by middling and genteel families, as does Laura Gowing in her meticulous reconstruction of female apprenticeship in London.[27]

The evidence from the stamp tax supports Erickson's and Gowing's argument. Premium apprenticeships indicate a strong interest among elite families in training girls.[28] The sex ratios of apprentices drawn from different family backgrounds give us a clear signal about this. Daughters made up 6 per cent of apprentices from fathers identified as gentry, clergy, or merchants, compared to 3 per cent of apprentices from families in a broad range of manufacturing trades. For families involved in widespread but less profitable crafts, the share of daughters among the children they placed into apprenticeships was even lower: just 4 per cent of weavers' and 2 per cent of tailors' children who became apprentices were daughters, for example.

If anything, higher-status families appear to have been more willing to invest in their daughters' occupational skills. This perhaps reflects these families' greater resources, as they were less likely to have to ration money for premiums between their children, and it certainly argues against a disengagement with apprenticeship among the gentry and middling sort. It may also be a response to the possibility that these women would not marry, given the rates of singletons in this period.[29] That said, occupations are recorded for apprentices' parents in the stamp duty registers only in the 1710s and 1720s, and so this may have changed with the century if the gender division of labour grew stronger within higher-status families, as Snell argues.[30]

Gender norms still limited the chances given to the young women in these families and shaped their parents' decisions. This is particularly obvious if we look at how brothers and sisters in the same families were treated. The stamp duty records include at least seventy-one early eighteenth-century families who paid premiums to place both male and female children with masters and mistresses.[31] On average, the premiums paid with daughters were worth 86 per cent of the premiums given with boys. There were exceptions: nine families invested the same amounts for daughters and sons, and fourteen gave more with their daughters. However, two-thirds of families invested less in daughters than sons. It was parents like the London haberdasher William Grooby, who gave £30 with his son William in 1723 but just £15 with his daughter Anne a year later, who were in the majority.

Anne Grooby was indentured to Elizabeth Ducy, a draper, and like her, many female apprentices would train with female masters, often alongside other female apprentices.[32] The milliner Bridget George, of Bath, registered nine female apprentices paying premiums between 1784 and 1800, and all but one paid £50 for the privilege of training with her. Her main competitors in the town, Penelope Gay and Jane Davy, bound sixteen female apprentice milliners to their partnership between 1779 and 1787, all at similarly high fees. Neither took any male apprentices. These female-headed firms were based in England's most fashionable leisure town, and their fees reflected the opportunities it offered for someone who could be 'a perfect Connoisseiuer in Dress and Fashion'.[33] But similar patterns can be seen elsewhere. In Speenhamland, the parish that would become synonymous with the grinding rural poverty that its Poor Law system sustained, the mantua-maker Mary Gale took five female apprentices in the 1790s and early 1800s.[34]

In all, more than 60 per cent of female apprentices paying premiums in the eighteenth century were bound to female masters. Many of the remainder were bound to both a master and his wife, with both parties named, a practice that was almost never observed in contracts for male apprentices and that indicated that the master's wife was taking the apprentice as her own.[35] To put this another way, around 16,000 contracts out of 378,000 recorded in the surviving stamp duty registers named female masters, and 12,000 of these were to take female apprentices. It seems evident that a small but coherent group of skilled female workers were well placed to reproduce themselves in this period; female apprentices were common enough that some printers started to produce indentures without gendered pronouns.[36] Unfortunately, similar evidence is missing on the period before 1711, when the stamp duty began, but Laura Gowing argues convincingly that at least in London, a swelling stream of girls were becoming apprentices from the 1650s, reflecting both 'an increased interest in the education and training of middling sort girls' and the specialisation of female fashions and dress, while the Bristol records studied by Ilana Krausman Ben-Amos suggest something similar for the sixteenth century in that city.[37] To these reasons we should add the expansion of consumer demand for less-durable textiles and clothing, particularly linens, new draperies, and cottons, which all increased the demand for skilled workers with the sewing skills that were characteristically associated with female work.[38] For these girls, indentures offered the same framework of legal and contractual protections that they offered to their male peers.

Gender strongly shaped access to apprenticeship. The effect was at least threefold. First, female apprentices were far less common than we would expect if gender norms had not raised barriers to women's opportunities, but they were not absent. English law and custom did not prevent the apprenticeship of women, but other rules gave it a distinctive format and hedged in the work that followed an apprenticeship with restrictions tied to marital status. Women's training and work was, as Laura Gowing put it, 'above all, contingent' and conditional in a way that it was not for men.[39]

Second, few female apprentices were registered by guilds. This disengagement reflects the limited and conditional nature of the benefits of corporate membership for women, given the loss of privileges that they experienced when they married, relative to the costs of the longer terms of service needed to meet guild rules. Operating outside guild oversight meant that female apprentices entered shorter contracts. They avoided some of the burden borne by male apprentices, but also sacrificed their entitlement to become members of the guild and the privileges this brought.

Third, female apprentices, like adult women, clustered in a specific group of occupations. Some of these trades were almost exclusively female. Their roles were constrained by gendered assumptions about what kinds of work were appropriate for women. The way that women were squeezed into specific roles must have reduced their incomes by artificially increasing the supply of labour. That said, some of these occupations still offered reasonable livings to women. Successful female businesswomen were able to sell training in the same way as their male counterparts in other trades. These mistresses attracted middling and well-off families who paid considerable amounts for their daughters' training and were more likely to invest in their daughters' human capital than poorer families, even if the sums they put in were, on average, lower than they spent on their sons' apprenticeships.

Birth Order

When we think about social mobility, we tend to assume that all children were treated equally. Yet, in a society organised by primogeniture, this assumption is flawed.[40] The choices families made about which child to apprentice illustrate this clearly, as figure 11.2 shows. This reports the way birth order affected the chance that male children would become apprentices in London. If opportunities are distributed equally, the likelihood that any individual son would be apprenticed should not be affected by whether they are the eldest or the youngest child, or anywhere in between. Figure 11.2 shows the difference between the share of children observed as apprentices and the share expected if opportunities had been distributed randomly between the children in the sample.

Four broad types of families appear here. The first is a set of London families who were living and raising children in the city itself. They are the consummate insiders. The second is families living in the countryside or small

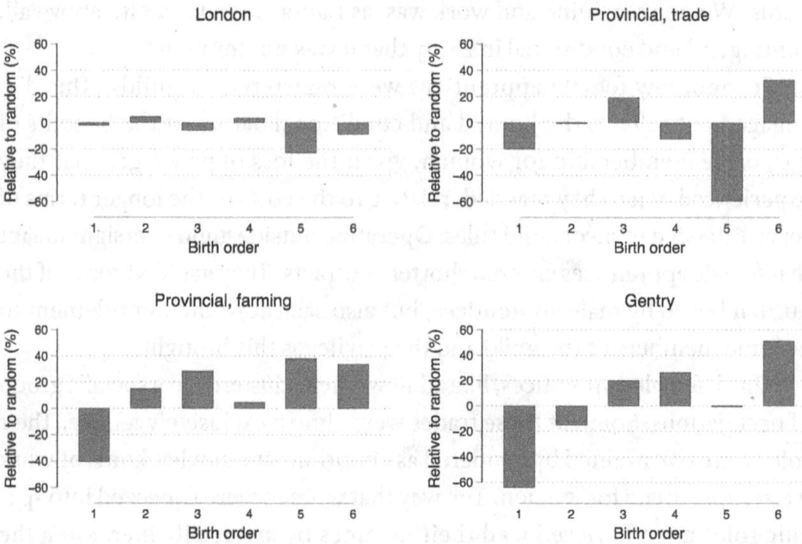

FIGURE 11.2. Birth order and apprenticeship. The figure reports the difference between the observed and predicted shares of apprentices in each place in the birth order as a percentage of the predicted share. Observed is the share of male children identified among London apprentices. Predicted is the share expected if birth order had no effect. Birth order is censored at the sixth son, as the numbers observed beyond that become small. Note that because the sample includes families with different numbers of sons, and some apprenticed multiple sons, the shares observed and predicted at each position in the birth order are different. All families included had (i) two or more sons who survive beyond aged five and (ii) at least one linked apprentice son. Samples are from London reconstitution (top left, n=1,249) and provincial reconstitution samples (top right, n=899, and bottom left, n=236), both described in Klemp et al. 2013. The gentry sample (bottom right, n = 737) is described in Wallis and Webb 2011.

towns, such as Banbury, who make a living in manufacturing or services. The third is families in the same provincial communities, but their focus is farming. Finally, a sample of gentry families from the heralds' visitations for Bedfordshire, Somerset, Surrey, and Westmoreland in the seventeenth century, is shown in the bottom right panel. They represent a group of elites, largely defined by status but normally in possession of substantial landholdings, who are sometimes thought to have spurned 'trade' altogether.

Each type of family took a different strategy. Strikingly, for children born into families based in London, birth order appears to have had no meaningful impact on the likelihood that they would become apprentices; the observed and predicted shares of sons apprenticed are nearly parallel from the eldest to the fourth son. Odds then decline a little for fifth and sixth sons, who are much rarer (the sample contains only thirty-six and twelve, respectively). Apprenticeships were spread between different sons in a manner that is close to random in London families.

This aligns with what is known about the transfer of resources between generations in London. Urban inheritance was often partible, equally split between children. It also fits with the social capital they inherited, as their families' resources and networks were already tied to crafts and trade. Many had fathers who would have been apprenticed. For children of the urban middling sort, norms about birth order mattered little in defining the broad category of work they would enter. If we look at the poorest groups, such as labourers, eldest sons were in fact substantially more likely to be apprenticed, suggesting that families were directing opportunities towards eldest sons.[41]

That urban families placed children into apprenticeships largely independent of birth position suggests that the child's ability and enthusiasm—conditional on the families' resources and ties—were allowed to play a larger part in defining who trained outside the home and who might follow other pathways. Contemporary advice for parents certainly espoused this approach. For example, Robert Campbell's guide for parents emphasized the importance of matching the 'Genius and Temper' of children to their careers.[42] Indeed, as Ben-Amos has shown, youths of all backgrounds usually had a voice in choosing their careers. [43] Apprenticeships usually started with a trial period of a month or so, in part to accommodate this. Adam Martindale (b. 1623), for one, returned to school to prepare for university after having spent a few weeks as an apprentice in trade, as his father had seen 'which way my mind still went'.[44]

In provincial families, the prospects of children were different. Rural farming families, headed by yeomen or husbandmen, clearly favoured apprenticing their younger sons. The large gap in figure 11.2 between observed and predicted apprenticeships for sons at the top of the birth order indicates that they were much less likely to bind an eldest son into a craft or trade. For these families, the chances of elder sons inheriting the farm trumped migration into more urban occupations.[45] Still, some eldest sons from farming families *did* enter apprenticeships, indicating that this could be an appealing prospect. The husbandman John Barwell of the parish of Austrey in Warwickshire placed his eldest son Thomas with Richard Malibar, a London cordwainer, in December 1666, and it went well enough that he also bound his third son John to the same master in July 1669.[46] While relatively few first sons from farming families were apprenticed, more junior sons were favoured, indicating the draw of a metropolitan apprenticeship.

Even for families in the provinces where the head of the household made their living outside agriculture, a London apprenticeship was less likely than chance would suggest for eldest sons, and also for the youngest. The (smaller) gap between the share of eldest sons apprenticed and that predicted by the number of surviving sons implies that an inheritance effect still mattered for eldest sons in provincial craft and services families.

The trend among gentry families is even more striking, and underlines how powerful norms about birth order could be. Gentry apprentices were almost exclusively younger sons, and most often the youngest sons of large families. To give one example, Oliver Carew, bound to Thomas Lawley of the London Drapers' Company in May 1629, was his father Nicholas's fifth and final son. His four elder brothers had all been sent to Oxford University and the Inns of Court, instead.[47] Oliver's indentures were not the result of genteel poverty. His father had once been troubled for money—he had written begging for £200 from his father-in-law in the early 1600s, complaining that 'if I cannot have I must leave my country, and my wife and children to the parish'. However, from the 1610s, Nicholas's position had reversed as he inherited the manor of Beddington and a £400 annuity and acquired the office of chamberlain of the exchequer.[48] The choice to put Oliver into trade may have been shaped by the connections of Nicholas's second wife, Susan Bright, as she was the widow of Henry Butler, a merchant and member of the Drapers.[49]

For gentry sons, as Oliver's case exemplifies, the odds of apprenticeship increased linearly with each step (except the fifth) down the birth order until the sixth son, as figure 11.2 shows. Very few eldest sons would be apprenticed, as one would expect in a situation in which substantial landed wealth (and status) was transferred through primogeniture. Instead, families normally invested in legal education at one of the Inns of Court in London or a period at Oxford or Cambridge University as preparation for a life as a landed gentleman. Almost all gentry families in which a younger son was apprenticed had sent the eldest brother to the Inns or university.

Conclusion

The point, and the desirability, of apprenticeship varied between families, depending on their occupation, wealth, and location. As we have seen in this chapter, this does not exhaust the ways in which the opportunities of youths were channelled and constrained by their backgrounds. Their gender and their position in the birth order mattered greatly in defining the opportunities for training that were given to young people in early modern England.

Norms meant that when deciding which child to apprentice, most families chose the boy. Gender was a profoundly important determinant of access to apprenticeship in England, as it was elsewhere in Europe. Far fewer women were bound as apprentices than we would expect if they had had the same opportunities as their brothers, and almost none were enrolled with guilds. Equal access would have meant a twentyfold increase in female apprentices in England. But even at its actual level of participation, England, like parts of France, was more open to female apprenticeship than some other regions of Europe, where, as Ogilvie and others have shown, girls could be entirely excluded from formal systems of training.[50]

The scarcity of formal apprenticeships for women did not mean that such training was restricted to the poor or marginal. While female apprentices were largely concentrated in, even crowded into, a limited group of occupations, upper- and middle-class families with abundant resources were willing to make substantial investments in apprenticing their daughters into 'good' trades for women, such as millinery. And as they did, they made use of female traders' looser relationship to urban institutions to write shorter contracts, gaining a measure of flexibility from this. That apprenticeship was emerging as a desirable option for better-off families further underlines the degree to which women's opportunities were restricted by cultural norms. Most families did not make the same choice for their daughters as they did for their sons, but this reflects not a gender barrier within the structure of apprenticeship itself, but rather the effect of perceptions about appropriate work, the way that the value of skills and the ability of women to exercise economic rights intersected with marriage, and the decision to allocate scarce resources to male children in preference to their sisters.

When choosing which boy to train, different structures of inheritance and forms of capital meant that family strategies varied greatly by wealth, status, and occupation. Among the landed elite, apprenticeship was an avenue for the youngest siblings, presenting them with a future very different to the heir's, or even to the career in the law, the military, or the church that their elder brothers were offered. Among English farmers, similarly, elder sons were more likely to be kept to the land they would inherit than sent to the city to tread a different path.

For urban families, who formed an increasingly important share of the population, birth order had little discernible effect. With partible inheritance and no farm to maintain, apprenticeship was an investment of equal utility to all sons and an opportunity that was allocated reasonably equally. Stripped of a legal imperative to structure training around birth order and inheritance, urban families were able to set this enemy to opportunity to one side. In short, it was the intersection between apprenticeship, norms about work, and the institutions and laws that defined inheritance and labour-market rights that shaped the way in which families employed this mechanism to train their children. Opportunities were conditioned by each youth's context, not just their characteristics.

12

Social Networks and the Search for Opportunity

John Dunton was a disappointment to his father. Reverend Daniel Dunton was the rector of Graffham, Huntingdonshire, and a former fellow of Trinity College, Cambridge. The son and grandson of clergymen himself, Reverend Dunton had put John into a school at Dungrove for nine years to prepare him for a career in the church. But the fourth generation of this clerical family was less inclined to theology. John had failed to learn Greek, instead falling in love, and he struggled with philosophy. 'Father's hopes began now to dwindle very sensibly . . . so that he began to take up a Resolution to dispose me some other way', Dunton recalled, and 'seeing my Inclinations did not lead me to Learning, he would put me out an Apprentice'.[1]

How could the priest of a rural parish find a suitable place for his child? The bare bones of the search were simple: 'My Father made Application to his very intimate Friend Mr. Sands'. Sands then identified a potential master and 'recommended Mr. Tho. Parkhurst as a religious and a just Man', and 'upon this Information my Father (after giving me his Blessing) sent me to London' and John 'bid a Joyful Farewell to Letters'. Dunton's recollections illustrate one model of how parents found opportunities for their children, by using their social network of family, friends, and associates as a source of information about potential masters.

Dunton's career choice was a success: he would become a successful bookseller and publisher with a business at the Sign of the Raven, near the

Royal Exchange in London, and learnt to love books despite his struggles at school. However, his initial start was difficult. After a few days on trial with Parkhurst, he 'could not reconcile my Mind to confinement' and so took a horse and rode home. His father helped him realise his 'folly' and wrote to Parkhurst asking for John to be accepted again. But while he was away, another boy, John Laurence, had 'stepped into my Room upon Trial'. Dunton was unable to rejoin his master until Laurence's trial ended and so lodged with his cousin, Mr. John Child, a grocer in Stocks-Market.[2]

Dunton's cousin's appearance in the story points to another way in which social networks could have shaped access to training: social ties could have provided a necessary connecting thread between masters and apprentices, allowing each to credibly commit to the arrangement. But Dunton did not become Child's apprentice, even though Child had both experience of training and the right to take him.[3] Dunton was able to become a bookseller, not a grocer; his career options were wider than they would have been if it was the opportunities available within his extended family that defined his future.[4]

Although social networks are important in both, these two models of how apprentices found their masters have quite different outcomes for opportunity. One defines the set of possible matches that an apprentice or a master could make narrowly; in the other, their social network widens a youth's opportunities by connecting them with more people. At its narrowest, the first restricts young people to the shallow array of opportunities offered by their extended family, as de la Croix, Doepke, and Mokyr have emphasised.[5]

It is easy to imagine why families might look first within their social networks for masters. There were obvious advantages when apprentices and their families shared a 'strong tie' with the masters. Their connections meant they had information about each other in advance. Their ties would help sustain the contract. Studies of employment in England and America in the nineteenth and twentieth centuries have found that many people found their first job through their families or neighbours.[6] Similarly, research on premodern artisans in India shows that most recruitment was within the immediate or extended family.[7]

The argument gets only stronger if we consider that apprenticeship contracts were long and involved young people, often leaving home for the first time, who were vulnerable to exploitation and also to vice and distraction. Masters surely had their own worries: apprentices were entering their homes, sharing their tables, accessing their possessions, learning their techniques, befriending their clients, and influencing their profits. These are exactly the conditions that would in theory incline them to seek out the benefits that strong ties promise—foreknowledge, contract enforcement, mutual interest in preserving the relationship, and easier monitoring.

However, strong ties also impose constraints that can make them an enemy to opportunity if a society depends on them to reproduce skill. Individuals possess meaningful and strong connections to only a limited number of other people. If strong ties formed through kinship, profession, or social origin were necessary for apprenticeship, the ability of young people to access a full range of opportunities would be restricted. They could struggle to find the best match between their talents and aptitudes and the options available to them.[8] Their geographical and occupational movements would be limited, reducing the pace and scale of structural change and the responsiveness of the labour market to shifts in demand. In the longer term, depending on strong ties would also hinder the spread of skills and ideas, hampering the adoption of new technologies and products.

This chapter asks how often strong ties can explain apprentices' matches with their masters in England. I show that strong ties between master and apprentice were of only modest importance in determining who young people trained with in early modern England. Contracts crossed lines of kinship, geography, and occupation. Most apprentices in London and other cities and towns in England trained with masters who were outside their immediate networks. They were not connected by family, place of origin, or a common trade.

As Dunston's case shows, this does not mean that apprentices' and masters' social networks were unimportant. Networks provided information, not placements. In this, early modern apprenticeship drew on the strength of weak ties and the enormous scope of our social links at three or four degrees of separation.[9] The last section of this chapter uses diaries and memoirs to flesh out the process by which apprentices found their masters. This substantiates the claim that families were willing to take up opportunities with previously unknown masters. It also shows how families exploited their networks of strong ties to discover information about potential placements. Friends and relations searched out positions, researched likely masters, negotiated terms, and gave ongoing support to youths once they were in their positions.[10] Information, not informal enforcement, was the contribution that premodern networks made to sustaining apprenticeship.

Measuring Ties between Masters and Apprentices

Studies of English and European apprenticeship suggest that several kinds of social connections could matter for recruitment. The most direct of these connections would be close ties of kinship between apprentices and their masters, who in extreme cases could restrict training to their sons. Such an autarkic world of closed family workshops in which the secrets of a trade were passed from father to son was never dominant in early modern European apprenticeship. Although reliance on the nuclear family was rare, discussions of apprenticeship frequently emphasise the importance of more distant degrees of kinship. Specifically, historians have often suggested that extended family networks facilitated entry to apprenticeship.[11]

Other types of connections that could facilitate access to apprenticeship include institutional links between parents and masters through membership of the same guild, and geographical ties based on common origin or residential propinquity.[12] These networks would often overlap in practice: guild members will generally live in the same town, for example, so identifying whether it was knowing one's neighbour or one's guild brother that mattered can be hard to distinguish in such a case.

The balance between different types of ties varies in studies of guilds across Europe. Late eighteenth-century Parisian apprenticeship was dominated by local apprentices, though guild connections between masters and those presenting youths (typically, fathers or their surrogates) do not seem especially common.[13] In contrast, in Wildberg (Württemberg), geographical ties appear to have been a by-product of guild membership, as the vast majority of new masters were the sons of existing masters who also, by default, were locals.[14] Apprentices' places of origin are also thought to have mattered for their training in subtler ways. For example, Steve Rappaport highlights the importance of 'trade routes between London and other towns' in the placement of apprentices into different crafts, as youths might build on connections acquired through participating in the supply chain that linked provincial English counties and the metropolis.[15]

Four potential sources of connection stand out in these studies: ties of kinship, geography, guild, and occupation. Chapter 4 showed that occupational ties were of necessarily limited importance in England, because intergenerational mobility between sectors and occupations was the norm. Ninety per cent of apprentices were training in a different occupation to their father; even among urban artisans and traders, most of their children were bound into a different trade. But a world in which children pursued a different trade to their father could be one in which other kinds of connection are even more important in managing the uncertainty of acquiring a novel skill set and entering a different type of career.

In order to evaluate the importance of ties of kinship, geography, and guild in securing an apprenticeship in early modern England, I pursue two strategies in this chapter. The first is a direct assault on the apprenticeship registers to estimate the share of apprentices in different towns who possessed one or another of these types of connections with their masters. This section mainly uses evidence from London, Bristol, and Gloucester. The underlying data is described in appendix 1; ties of kinship and guild, if any, are directly visible in most apprenticeship registers. Identifying geographical ties requires identifying the masters' own place of origin, using the records of their apprenticeship and, where possible, guild admissions of freemen and urban citizenship lists.

Kinship

When Richard Gines left the small village of Compton nestled in the Wiltshire Downs to take up a place as an apprentice in London, his destination was a silversmith's workshop in Southwark, just south of the Thames, run by one Robert Munday. Gines was bound to Munday on 12 January 1687/88 for nine years, on the same day that Munday's son Thomas also entered his father's service. Gines would take his freedom in 1698 and set himself up as a working goldsmith and later as a goldsmith-banker in Lombard Street.[16] Gines's bank, at the Rose & Crown, Lombard Street, survived him and passed into his own son's care before finally falling into bankruptcy in 1781. Gines's family's decision about who might train him was not accidental: there were strong ties between them and his master. Robert Munday's own path to London had started from the hamlet of Coombe, just 2 miles down the river Avon from the Gines family farm in Compton, and his sister Margaret Munday had been born there around 1645 before she made her way up the valley to marry Gines's father John.

That Gines's master was his uncle and had been a near-neighbour of his family before migrating to London underlines how youths seeking apprenticeships could have found a place with a relative. The combination of a large share of families working in agriculture, low levels of urbanisation, and low life expectancy made this the only option for many youths: few had parents who could offer them an apprenticeship. Gines also highlights the difference in the roles kinship played for apprentices who were bound to their fathers and for those who came from outside their master's nuclear family. The former is an example where strong ties lead to immobility; in the latter, strong ties sustain some degree of social, geographical, or economic mobility. As we saw in chapter 4, masters' sons supplied only a small proportion of apprentices in England. Youths training outside of their immediate families were the predominant group of apprentices. How many were the nephews, cousins, or more distant kin of their masters?

A person's wider family was an important source of connections in early modern England. While studies of the European marriage pattern have emphasised the dominance of nuclear families in England, work on social networks, credit, and family has underlined the persistence and strength of the wider fabric of kinship. For youths seeking apprenticeships, their extended family had a greater chance of containing a potential master who could take them on. For masters, conversely, hiring brothers, cousins, nephews, or more distant relations as apprentices had the obvious advantage that the pool of potential youths was much wider. Crucially, these relatives were more likely to be the right age for training than their own children in the first decades of a master's career.

Unfortunately, these types of more distant familial relationship were not usually noted in guild or city records. The family ties that do find a mention in guild registers were almost always fathers and sons, with a scattering of brothers and grandchildren. This reflects the purpose of the registration system: masters' sons had rights—they could usually seek to enter a guild by inheritance rather than apprenticeship. Noting their connections made institutional sense. But there was no equivalent reason where the father was not the master, and so town and guild clerks generally did not bother.

With no direct measure available, surnames give us a proxy for a family relationship. When masters and apprentices shared the same surname but the master's and father's forenames did not match, we can take this as a sign of a more distant kinship tie.

Judged by this measure, masters and apprentices rarely shared family ties other than the close parent-child tie that existed within the nuclear family in early modern England. As table 12.1 shows, just 3 per cent shared a surname—just 6,575 of 193,719 apprentices in this sample. There was little variation over time or space: the maximum, 16 per cent, found in Durham in the second quarter of the seventeenth century, was based on only thirty-seven observations, and so may simply be chance. Most of the time, just 2 to 4 per cent of apprentices in early modern English towns and cities shared a surname with a master who was not a parent.

TABLE 12.1. Apprenticeship within extended families

	1525–49 %	1575–99 %	1625–49 %	1675–99 %	1725–49 %	1775–99 %	All %	N
Boston				2		3	3	213
Bristol	2	3	4	4	4	2	4	26,975
Durham			16	6	8	2	6	564
Gloucester			3	4	6		4	2,043
Leicester			3	0	6	3	4	500
Lincoln			8	4	4	2	3	1,004
Liverpool					3		3	167
London	1	3	3	3	4	5	3	159,915
Norwich	0	2	3	2			2	1,724
Oxford	3	2					2	391
Shrewsbury				5			5	223
All	2	3	3	3	4	4	3	
N	3,218	16,828	57,283	61,424	31,968	22,998		193,719

Note: The table reports apprentices whose fathers have the same surname but *not* the same forename as their masters. The sample is restricted to bindings for which information on surnames and forenames is available. Cells with fewer than ten observations are omitted. All surnames are included, because the sample size is too small for provincial cities otherwise. As a result some matches are likely to be coincidences.

The obvious limit to taking common surnames as a proxy for family connections is that the share of kin who bear the same surname falls rapidly outside the nuclear family. This is one of the obvious lessons of the example of Richard Gines, where it was his mother Margaret's surname that reveals the connection. Ignoring the complicated (but probably small) effect of half-siblings and remarriages, then on average our shared surname test will capture all of a master's unmarried siblings, half his nephews and nieces, and a quarter of his cousins. Once they married, a master would acquire a new crop of relations with whom they did not share a surname. If we group blood relatives and in-laws, for a married master, half of their siblings shared a surname, as did a quarter of their nephews and nieces, and a bare one-eighth of their cousins. The problem only gets larger if we define the net of kinship more widely. No easy rule can resolve this, as there is no clear, conventional boundary beyond which relationships lose their significance. Friendship and ties of blood and marriage were as extensive as each party allowed them to be.[17]

We can, however, make a little progress. Masters' wives' maiden names give us an indication of the importance of relatives through marriage among apprentices. This information is difficult to collect, and we draw on four samples from London and Bristol. The share of apprentices with a surname link to their master's wife was uniformly low. Overall, just 1 per cent of 4,721 apprentices bound to masters in our sample had the same surname as their master's wife. Interestingly, Richard Gines was one of those whose own training showed no signs of such ties via marriage—none of the six apprentices he later took bore the surname of his wife, Emma Kannigator. In every sample, apprentices sharing the master's wife's surname were much less common than apprentices sharing their master's surname, even after excluding masters' sons, appearing only a third as often.[18]

The scarcity of apprentices connected through the master's spouse suggests a structural weakness in kinship ties created by marriage. When masters did take relatives of their wives, they were often indenturing their close kin, not members of their wives' more distant family. For the Stationers, there is enough information on the backgrounds of eleven masters' wives and apprentices to assess the kinds of relationships that existed. To give one example, the Joane Brent of St Paul's Covent Garden who married the stationer Adiel Mill in April 1674 was probably the Joane Brent, daughter of Daniel and Joane, who had been baptised in 1653 at St Martin Ludgate. Seven years after their marriage, in 1681, Mill bound George Brent, who was described as the son of Daniel, gentleman, of Covent Garden. It seems likely that George was Joane's brother, given that both were children of Daniel Brent, and came from the same part of London, Covent Garden. In six of the eleven cases where families can be tracked back in this way, the apprentice who bore the same surname as the master's wife seems to have been her brother, and so the master's brother-in-law. Another two apprentices were probably nephews. The other three apprentices were almost certainly not brothers, but the relationship (if one actually existed, and these were not just coincidences) cannot be pinned down. These figures are small, but suggestive of the limited reach of family connections made through marriage.[19]

In Bristol, too, brothers-in-law were visible: Francis Baugh, for example, was indentured to Walter Ellis on the first of March 1777, just four months after Ellis had married Mary Baugh, his sister. Because the city of Bristol allowed men to become burgesses by marrying a burgess's widow, masters also bound new sons-in-law. Of thirteen apprentices in Bristol who shared a surname with their master's wife, three were being indentured to their step-fathers and four were joining their step-brothers. Just two were nephews entering the businesses of their uncles. The nature of any connections to the other four is unclear, and two—Owen Jones and James Curtis—had common enough names that the matching surnames were possibly coincidental. In short, masters were mainly apprenticing members of their wives' close family—sons, brothers, and nephews. And in a number of cases, as in London, these look like indentures that provided places (and formalised relationships) for children who were left vulnerable by the deaths of their fathers and the remarriages of their mothers.

What about more distant family connections? For Bristol, the maiden names of the mothers of a number of masters can be identified, revealing the effect of local city connections through the maternal line; this is possible for a group of masters whose fathers had become citizens (burgesses) of the city through marriage to existing citizens' daughters.[20] How many of those forty-seven masters took an apprentice who bore their own mother's maiden name? Just one. And even that may not have reflected a tie by kinship, as the name that the apprentice and the master's mother shared was Smith, the most common surname in England.

This is only one piece of evidence, to be sure, but it aligns with other indications that the kinship ties that mattered were the closest ones, and that ties through the male line were more important than those through the female line. In such a situation, the number of potential kinship ties would be lower than one might imagine from the initial sketch of the exponential growth in related, but differently named, kin that existed outside the nuclear family. If the most important connections were those between a master and his wife and their own siblings and nephews and nieces, this would suggest multiplying the same-name proxy by four to account for unobserved kinship ties. This indicates that roughly 16 per cent of apprentices in early modern England had family ties to their masters. If correct, apprentices with family ties who came from outside the nuclear household would have been equalled in number by apprentices who were their masters' sons, despite the fact that masters could—if they possessed them—take on other kin throughout their careers, while the steady pace of biology meant their own sons were only reaching the age of apprenticeship in the later stages of their lives.

Kinship mattered. But only a minority of apprentices were linked to their masters through extended family connections. The family tie that mattered most was between masters and sons. Families did find masters among their wider networks of relations, particularly if this was a tie of blood, not marriage, but this was relatively uncommon. Richard Gines's contract with his uncle was the exception, not the rule. A few years later, Gines's own younger brother Thomas was bound to a seemingly unconnected master in the Haberdashers' Company, Richard Bramwell.[21] Like Thomas, the vast majority of apprentices had no family ties to their masters at all.

Occupation and Guild

Only a small share of apprentices entered the same occupations as their fathers, and the majority of apprentices were migrants. This meant that, for the most part, connections forged within urban guilds had little relevance for apprentices seeking masters. Guilds were basically local institutions, despite sporadic attempts to establish and maintain wider powers.[22] Apprenticeship was a regional and national system, by contrast.

Yet, guilds could still matter for the few prospective apprentices who did have connections to one; these were the sons of existing or deceased masters. We have seen that in London at least, the sons of masters increasingly tended to be apprenticed to their fathers in the eighteenth century. But in the seventeenth century, the majority of freemen's sons were apprenticed *outside* their nuclear families. Did they stick to the same guilds as their fathers, perhaps helped into a place by the connections between their masters and their fathers that shared membership of a corporation provided?

Looking at the share of apprentices from London citizen families who trained within their fathers' guilds shows that most freemen's sons were placed with masters from *other* guilds if they were leaving the family firm. Excluding sons training with their fathers, only 19 per cent of freemen's sons in London stayed within their fathers' guilds in the seventeenth century and 17 per cent in the eighteenth century. This was similar across most of the city's guilds throughout the seventeenth and early eighteenth centuries, as figure 12.1 shows.[23] There was a small trend towards staying within one's father's guild, a trend that mirrors the rise in apprenticing within the family. However, it was less pronounced: even in the last quarter of the eighteenth century, most masters' sons who did not join their fathers entered different guilds.

This level of intergenerational persistence within the same guild is higher than we would expect if apprentices were distributed at random across the city's many guilds. But it is hardly a strong signal that keeping a connection to the guild mattered greatly for families who could not, or did not wish to, apprentice their sons themselves. One of the two exceptions in the early seventeenth century was among youths with fathers in the Merchant Taylors' Company: in 1600–1624, 62 per cent of Merchant Taylors' sons were apprenticed to other Merchant Taylors, if not to their own fathers.

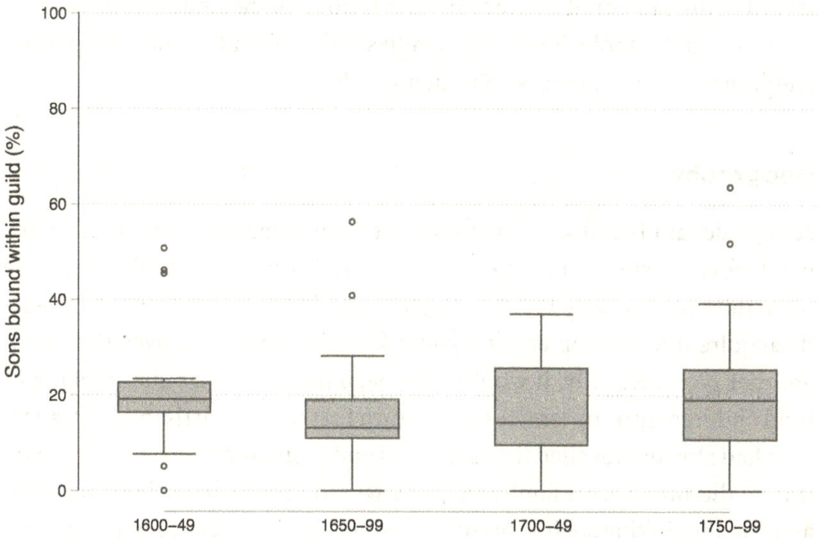

FIGURE 12.1. How frequently did sons stay in their fathers' guilds? For each London guild, the share of freemen's sons bound to different masters in their fathers' guilds or to masters in different guilds (excluding sons bound to their fathers) is calculated. The number of guilds in observation in each half century from 1600–1649 onwards is twenty-six, forty, forty, and thirty-six. Guilds in which fewer than ten apprentices were reported to be sons of freemen in each period are excluded.

This would seem to be the exception that proves the rule that occupation trumped guild. The Merchant Taylors was the largest and most occupationally diverse guild in the city; in such a big tent, occupational mobility could be achieved without stepping outside the guild. Families were able to exploit connections without paying the price of losing occupational choice. But no other guild equalled the Merchant Taylors.

The great majority of families within the city chose between two strategies: either they kept sons within the family (and so, within the guild) or they diversified by dispatching them to a different occupation, which meant a different master who would usually be in a different guild. For this reason, networks based on common institutional membership or derived from occupational relationships played only a minor role in the London apprenticeship market. Outside London, the sources largely report the occupations of apprentices' fathers, not their guilds. However, occupation and guild naturally had a relationship, and this offers a similar test for the part institutions might offer in finding a place for a youth. The levels of occupational persistence—reported in chapter 5—show that only a few local children stayed in the same trades if they did not train with their fathers: 16 per cent across our full sample. Implicitly, families were not finding masters for their children from their peers within their guilds.

Geography

Alongside family links, connections between neighbours are perhaps the most obvious source of strong ties. Often, both master and apprentice were migrants in early modern England, and the master could more easily acquire information about a youth from his own birthplace than from another place. Equally, it would have been natural for families seeking to send children into apprenticeships to turn first to those artisans and traders who had already travelled the same road and found success in the city. Even if they did not share a family tie, they would know each other's relatives and friends. Taking such apprentices would meet expectations about helping family friends and neighbours. Regional specialisation could also affect apprentices' opportunities, as Knotter and van Zanden have argued with regard to Amsterdam.[24]

If local ties affected who apprentices could train with, then migrant apprentices would be found serving masters who had come from the same place. A number of historians have emphasised the importance of local connections in various trades and cities.[25] The contribution of geographical ties can be examined by comparing the places of origin of masters (taken from their own apprenticeship registrations) and migrant apprentices for several cities.[26] To remove some of the confounding effects of kinship ties—as family members would probably also live in the master's place of origin—masters and apprentices who share a surname are excluded, however common it may be. Because some related apprentices had different surnames, these figures provide an upper bound on neighbourly ties.

Ties through common places of origin mattered a bit to apprentices seeking places, but not that much. Just 5 per cent of migrant apprentices in London were trained by an unrelated master from their place of origin; in Bristol, only 3 per cent were.[27] Even in Gloucester, only 9 per cent of apprentices bound to unrelated migrant masters were trained by someone from their home community. If apprentices who shared their masters' surnames are included, the share of apprentices with a place tie rises to 8 per cent in London and Gloucester and 5 per cent in Bristol.

What about masters? It might still be that for migrants who succeeded in becoming masters, training a youth from their place of origin was an expectation. This does not seem to be the case. Only 8 per cent of migrant masters in London, 9 per cent in Bristol, and 14 per cent in Gloucester ever trained a non-relative from their place of origin. Including apprentices with the same names—and so, encompassing all those apprentices whose recruitments might have been shaped by ties channelled through place or kinship ties—only lifts the share of masters with a connected apprentice to between 13 and 15 per cent.

Even those masters who took just one or two apprentices in their careers were not much more likely to have been taking 'connected' apprentices. Just 3–6 per cent of masters in London, Bristol, and Gloucester who took only one apprentice recruited a youth with a different name from their place of origin. Ties of place do not seem to have pushed masters to take apprentices they did not want. Conversely, there is also little sign that masters who took many apprentices favoured apprentices from their own places of origin. Fewer than one in five of the 'large' masters who took more than ten apprentices during their careers recruited a youth from their own hometown.

The scattered geography of settlement outside towns in early modern England means that a substantial number of apprentices came from places that were too small to have produced a master in the previous generation. Apprentices from these villages and hamlets could not have sought out a master from their community. In this case, the 'same place test' is too severe. The county of origin offers an alternative unit of analysis, with the share of youths who were apprenticed to someone from their own county offering some measure of the importance of geographical networks.[28]

The change in scale from thousands of places to forty or so counties inevitably meant that more migrant apprentices joined masters from the same county. Some 15 per cent of migrant apprentices in London, 35 per cent in Bristol, and 74 per cent in Gloucester joined masters with a different name from the same county. To put this in context, we can estimate what share we would expect if apprentices were assigned at random: these figures are significantly higher than the 2.3 per cent rate that would occur with random matching in London, or the 39 per cent in Gloucester.[29] However, Bristol's rate was actually lower than the 44 per cent that we would expect with random matching.

Migrant masters were also more likely to take apprentices from the same county, with 31 per cent in London, 54 per cent in Bristol and 49 per cent in Gloucester doing so over their careers. These figures are an upper bound on the importance of geographical ties, as they include kinship ties where surnames are different. The wider focus offered by the county roughly doubles the share of youths whose common place of origin may have given them a connection to their master. It also complicates the process by which this operated, introducing indirect lines of contact between a master and an apprentice's family, who may have been put in touch by mutual friends within the county rather than have had a personal relationship.

While ties of place mattered to some, four-fifths of migrant apprentices in London and two-thirds in Bristol were indentured to masters from a different county, suggesting that extended as well as narrow geographic networks had only a limited role in large centres for training. The higher rates of county ties in Gloucester, where only a quarter joined a master from a different county, suggests that ties mattered more in smaller centres, but this needs to be read against the smaller distances that apprentices travelled to Gloucester (discussed in chapter 4), making the county a particularly crude measure of neighbourliness in that city. Critically, for our assessment of whether apprenticeship was constrained by the need to possess strong ties with a master, these figures indicate clearly that possibilities for migrant apprentices were not limited by the absence of masters from their places or regions in particular trades.

Searching for a Master

If entry to apprenticeship in the towns and cities of England operated largely outside the strong networks of kin, guild, occupation, and geography that tied people together, how did apprentices find masters? Given the personal and economic costs of apprenticeship, one would expect that families investigated possibilities thoroughly. Families needed to know the quality of training and supervision on offer, while masters needed a sense of their prospective apprentices.

This was, to be clear, a search. Masters who might take apprentices were scattered across towns and cities, not aggregated into large firms. Even the masters who trained the most apprentices rarely took more than one or two youths a year: they did not enter the market often. Identifying a master who might have a place for a youth was therefore the first challenge, and there could be vigorous competition. As we saw at the start of the chapter, Dunton nearly lost his chance to another applicant. James Fretwell's family eventually gave up, 'being disappointed in the choice of one or two whom they had pitched upon as a master for me'. He would instead train with his father: 'This I've often lamented, for I think they did not duly consider which way my genius tended'.[30]

Little is known about how individuals and masters found each other. Two possible avenues can be ruled out. Only a tiny proportion of apprenticeships were advertised. John Houghton, the London apothecary, publisher, and natural philosopher, offered himself as a broker for apprenticeships in his newspaper in the 1690s. But Houghton's enterprise was unusual and found only a few echoes in other, later newspapers. Similarly, there is little sign that guilds regularly took on the role of broker, although this may have occurred occasionally.[31] The guilds' records of apprenticeship start when the master presented the apprentice, an event that usually followed a trial period of weeks or months.

It seems that most knowledge about youths seeking places and masters offering apprenticeships spread via informal channels. Parents' personal knowledge of London may have helped: around one in six English people spent part of their life in London.[32] Although the numbers entering apprenticeships in other towns and cities were much smaller, as we saw in chapter 2, their hinterlands were smaller too, increasing the likelihood that parents and masters might find each other through mutual connections.

Families hunted for apprenticeships for their children through search efforts that utilised third parties. It is this that shows the importance of networks in supplying information. Provincial apprentices relied on their parents' connections in London and other cities to locate masters.

Most would-be apprentices and families who have left records of the process used friends, acquaintances, and kin to find masters.[33] For example, Bartholomew Adsworth's 1688 apprenticeship to a cooper was arranged by Adsworth's cousin, George Fox, a citizen and vintner of London.[34] It was Graves Baker's brother, Thomas, who placed him with his master, a gold and silver wire-drawer.[35] Once Leonard Wheatcroft's son was established in London, he wrote to his parents that 'he lived so well, and that he had a mind to have his brother John to come up to him, and that he would provide him a master to which I and my wife gave consent to his journey'; John duly left in April 1681 and 'had a very good journey thither, and was well entertained both of his uncle and brother and other friends. So after a little trial he bound himself'. Although John's master's name was not given, he was neither John's uncle nor his brother, who had made the match for him.[36]

Similarly, Daniel Clarke of Tring, Hertfordshire, arranged his son Francis's apprenticeship in London in the 1690s with the help of 'friends', probably including Francis's uncle, who together sought a 'freeman & one that dealt Considerably in his way of trade & was a fair dealing man'.[37] Unfortunately, the master they found proved to be abusive.[38] Around the same time, George Long of Ludlow similarly arranged for friends to make a 'diligent enquiry' for a 'fit person' for his son.[39] When Joseph Oxley's relatives were choosing a place for him with a clockmaker, they found a master, Robert Henderson, in Scarborough, because his uncle was in the same town.[40] For William Hart, a century later, it was his grandmother's nephew John Sapwill who assisted, telling him about 'a man in Luton of the name of Wingrave a Cooper who was in the habit of taking apprentices'; armed with information, Hart 'wrote a letter to him and sent it by John Sapwill'.[41]

While it seems that it was family that provided the most agents, others exploited different types of connection. When George Bewley reached the age of fourteen and was 'fit to go Apprentice', it was Gershon Boat, a Quaker minister from Ireland who was lodging with Bewley's parents in Ivegill, Cumberland, who offered to help. Bewley recalled that Boat proposed to send

> me to Dublin, in which City he thought he could readily provide me a Place; they consented, and I was satisfied therewith, and soon after the Return of said Friends to Ireland, a letter came from Edward Webb, a Linen-draper in Dublin (to whom Gershon Boat had spoken concerning me) desiring my Father to send me over as soon as he could; accordingly I went over in the sixth month 1698.

Boat's matchmaking succeeded and Bewley would complete his term with Webb, despite the temptations of the city that left him 'at times too free in discourse and jocularity'.[42]

These examples suggest that apprentices' family connections might matter greatly in finding an apprenticeship. But the strong ties were between the apprentice's family and the person whom they trusted to search and negotiate for a place on their behalf. The presence of these agents would make it possible for apprentices to acquire placements with masters with whom they were not directly connected. There is no way to tell if there was a prior relationship between the urban contact and the master selected, but it is certain that the person with whom the apprentices' family had a strong tie usually did not become the master.

It seems unlikely that prospective apprentices in London were restricted to matches made through indirect ties, or that any use they made of such connections seriously limited their opportunities.[43] Indeed, the Clarke and Long cases emphasise that the matches were to be determined by the prospective masters' professional attributes, and there is no mention of the masters having connections to the apprentices' families or to their London contacts. These examples may be exceptional—we know about some of them because the indentures broke down, and they may therefore reflect unusually weak apprenticeship arrangements. They do suggest, however, that the primary role played by an aspirant apprentice's contacts in the city was to identify potential placements and provide information about prospective masters rather than to take on the apprentice themselves.

Conclusion

Strong ties between individuals and families offer a mechanism to strengthen contracts and commit both parties to the performance of a lengthy, potentially onerous agreement. Ties can also provide a reason for masters to accept an apprentice, if it was a reciprocal obligation to their friends and neighbours. Despite this, connections played a limited part in defining possible matches between masters and apprentices in early modern England. Apprentices' families mainly used their networks to help search out opportunities with masters they did not know directly—and presumably they used the same connections to monitor how the apprentices were treated once their contracts had started. The majority did not seek to place their children with masters within their own networks.[44] Social networks supported identifying opportunity in this system, they did not restrict it.

This chapter has looked across a range of potential connections between master and apprentice: kinship, occupation, guild, and place. Many inevitably overlap, meaning that some apprentices possess more than one of these ties. We are able to gross them up, so to speak, to estimate the share of migrant apprentices who possessed at least one potential link to their master. If we do, we find that only 15 percent of migrant apprentices to London and Bristol and 33 per cent in Gloucester shared a potential family tie with their master, were from the same place, or had a father in the same occupation. If the definition of geographical ties is extended to the county level, the share with an observable tie rises to 20 per cent in London, 45 per cent in Bristol, and 85 per cent in Gloucester. There is still uncertainty about how well this measure captures family ties, given its reliance on surnames as indicators. As a rough estimate of the missing kin with different names, we might quadruple the rate of family ties. This lifts the estimated share of migrant apprentices with strong ties to their masters to 35 per cent in London, 36 per cent in Bristol, and 92 per cent in Gloucester.[45]

On either measure, the average apprentice in a large English city had no direct connection to their master. In smaller centres connections were more common, and so plausibly more important in finding an opportunity in these narrower markets for training. London's dominance in training before the eighteenth century, however, means that English urban training was characterised by a lack of ties between apprentices and masters.

How does the English case compare to elsewhere in Europe? Summarising a wide set of studies for seventeenth- and eighteenth-century Europe, Farr concludes that 'the sons of masters were not categorically staying in their father's trade, but many, and in some place most, new masters were sons of masters of other guilds within the same locality'.[46] Existing studies of cities such as Milan, Württemberg, Antwerp, and Nordlingen do identify exclusive behaviour by early modern corporate communities in continental Europe.[47] Zucca Micheletto concluded that in Turin, 'family ties played a crucial role in training offspring'.[48] However, this is not a universal pattern, and exclusive behaviour was often associated with economic downturns. We might see parallels here with Gloucester's narrower channels of recruitment. London and Bristol, in contrast, were undergoing unprecedented, if not always unproblematic, economic and spatial growth.[49]

Apprenticeship was accessible to youths from outside the master's close social network. Individuals entered into long-term training contracts with counterparties with whom they had no prior connection and from whom they were separated by significant distance and travel costs. Compared to credit markets, which were embedded locally, training markets were much more open, despite the risks of opportunism and the sums involved.[50] This suggests contemporaries had a high degree of confidence in both the operation of apprenticeship contracts, even though contracts were not always fully performed by either apprentice or master, and the institutional framework of enforcement described in chapter 7. It also helps explain why those formal institutions played such an important role in allowing apprentices and masters to renegotiate or exit unsatisfactory contracts, given that these relationships were not rooted in strong ties.

That apprentices and masters were matched in this way had important consequences. The preponderance of relatively open apprentice recruitment implies that youths could find places that suited their resources, aptitudes, and interests, increasing their productivity as adults. They could choose trades for which they had 'a natural Liking, or Turn of Mind', as Campbell advised, and from which he believed flowed success: 'The greater Affection he discovers for it, the greater Application he gives to it, the sooner his Labour will be over; for a Tradesman no sooner becomes possessed of the Mystery of the Craft, than the uneasy laborious Part of it vanishes'.[51]

Dunton's case illustrates this, but he was not alone. Ebeneezer Fox's mother kept him at home 'until you are old enough to learn a trade, and then choose one for yourself', and at thirteen he was sent to Boston with his brother 'to choose our trades and seek our employers'.[52] Similarly, Timothy Claxton recalled how 'my father gave me the choice of being a carpenter or a whitesmith'.[53] These choices could be made only because young people could look beyond the limited pool of masters with whom they had strong ties. The result was critical: craft skills could diffuse widely through the English economy, and families and communities far from the main training and trading centres were able to establish connections to urban trades and support the movement of their children into towns and cities.

13 Conclusion

The nominal end date for the system of apprenticeship that I describe in this book is 1814, when the apprenticeship clauses of the Statute of Artificers were removed by Parliament. This was the result of decades of conflict between employers and journeymen over the employment of workers who had not served or completed apprenticeships.[1] It did not mark a sudden change. In some sectors the battle for 'closed shops', which only hired journeymen who had served apprenticeships, was already lost. Equally, in others, apprenticeship would remain commonplace through the nineteenth century, as Jane Humphries has shown, and the 1814 decision followed an active campaign by skilled workers to see the clauses strengthened and extended.[2] Even in the 1920s, government inquiries found over 300,000 apprentices in Britain.[3]

Nonetheless, the abolition of the statute's apprenticeship clauses was a legal and parliamentary watershed in the history of British apprenticeship. We might ask why it mattered at all. Most of the apprenticeship clauses in the statute that sought to limit entry to apprenticeship had never had much force, as we have seen. Yet, the one rule that did have teeth was the requirement that people serve a seven-year apprenticeship to practice most non-agricultural skilled occupations, and it was the removal of this rule which counted.

Major economic and ideological shifts lay behind this institutional change. Defined initially by the urban commercial and artisanal elites of medieval cities to restrict entry to their privileged ranks, and then generalised nationwide in 1562 by Elizabethan statesmen seeking to hold onto rural workers, the seven-year term had become an object of opposition for their successors. Shifts in economic organisation meant that an increasing number of England's governing elite now identified as employers of a separate class of permanent waged workers, while changes in economic ideas led them to oppose restrictions to laissez-faire on principle. Now, it was the skilled waged workers who undertook the ultimately futile defense of the part that long apprenticeships played in their 'property in skill'.[4] As the artisans petitioning Parliament in favor of stronger enforcement of the apprentice laws declared, they had a right to 'the quiet and exclusive use and enjoyment of their several and respective arts and trades, which the law has already conferred upon them as a property, much as it has secured the property of the stockholder in the public funds'.[5]

The growth of the chorus against the seven-year term coincided with the arrival of a new actor, the firm, into a space that had previously been defined by the relatively symmetrical power relationship between masters and apprentices' families. Initially, these firms were still usually small partnerships led by masters who employed relatively limited numbers of journeymen and other workers. They were not greatly dissimilar to larger workshops that had appeared in some trades in earlier centuries. Bigger firms would not come to dominate employment until the twentieth century.[6] Differences in the relationship between employer and apprentice were widening, however, as proprietors came from outside the craft, separating the person who contracted with the apprentice from the skilled individual they would learn from, and the path from journeyman to independent master narrowed, with the emergence of more complex hierarchies of employment and proto-managerial grades.

It would be the firm that changed apprenticeship most fundamentally in the nineteenth and twentieth centuries, just as it transformed other dimensions of employment. In some contexts, it gave apprentices a new incentive—the prospect of a lifetime career in the firm—to complete their contracts. This allowed firms to recoup training costs from former apprentices over long periods and incentivised some firms to commit to training, setting up technical schools and creating demanding training schemes. Not all firms chose to invest in training, however, leaving this to workers' own initiative through out-of-hours vocational courses, or their ability to gain skills informally on the job. Taking apprentices became a strategic decision that was inseparable from a firm's wider approach to hiring and retention.[7] The emergence of the firm increased the asymmetry in power between apprentice and employer. Apprenticeship now separated skilled workers and managers, where before, it had united masters and journeymen.

Industrial organisation, as much as the Industrial Revolution per se, disrupted the structure of apprenticeship that had dominated in medieval and early modern Europe.[8] The content of apprenticeship was also changed, however. This was more clearly the effect of a different aspect of industrialisation: the acceleration of technological change and the partnership of science and industry. Highly skilled work now commonly required a direct engagement with codified academic knowledge and techniques, such as mathematics, some of which was embodied in the growing physical capital of machinery that firms now deployed. The early signs of this were evident in the way engineers and medical practitioners were incorporating formal institutions into training before 1800. When generalised across the manufacturing sector, as in Germany from the late nineteenth century, the effect was the gradual restructuring of training schemes to incorporate instruction away from the shop floor.[9] This introduced a new and different pedagogy alongside the embedded process of learning through observation and practice that formed the core of learning in premodern apprenticeship. Some of the costs of this technical element were borne by local or central government, giving the state a new role in co-funding and regulating the content of apprenticeship in coordination with organisations of employers.

In Britain since 1814, vocational training through apprenticeships has never been as well integrated and stable as it became in Germany, Denmark, and Switzerland in the twentieth century, despite a series of attempts to create national provisions for apprenticeship. Employers in many parts of British manufacturing under-invested in training. The state and business jointly failed to create a credible system of certification that would reward investment in training by apprentices, leading to negative selection and a lack of credible commitment to contracts as trainees quit for better-paying work elsewhere. In some industries, and for some privileged grades of apprentices, British firms did offer effective training. But many of those who were classified as apprentices did not receive a wide and deep education.[10] In those occupations that became the professions, particularly medicine and law, national laws created exclusive skills-based entry criteria enforced by occupational organisations that generated the most durable form of closed shops. Stripped of the label of apprenticeship, but with many of the same qualities, professional training avoided the crisis around skills that affected many less powerful and lower-status occupations.[11]

'Modern' apprenticeship, where it survives, is thus quite different to the early modern system of training that it evolved from.[12] Apprenticeship now actively involves a triangle of actors: firms, young people and their families, and the state. Training combines a mix of classroom and workplace teaching, linked to explicit curricula and certification. It is often subsidised by the state. Apprentices are salaried employees, with private lives outside their employers' control. In successful systems, completion rates are high and continue seamlessly into long careers in the firms that offer training. In Britain, as in a number of other countries, substantial sectors of the economy no longer engage with apprenticeship, either because they have reformulated occupational training in partnership with higher education, as is common in the professions, or because they lack a defined structure for training beyond on-the-job experience and perhaps a scattergun array of short courses and specific qualifications. In some other developed countries, such as Germany and the Netherlands, apprenticeship thrives in more areas of the economy, but even so, its scope is narrowed.[13]

Both the structure and content of modern apprenticeship in industrial economies are substantially different to the system of premodern apprenticeship that I have described here. We can identify multiple points of contrast. Premodern apprenticeship was a bilateral legal agreement between master and the apprentice and their family: a contract to purchase training, not an agreement for employment. Training was embedded learning, with little teaching, no curriculum, and no certification. The long minimum term of service was an anchoring concept that placed time, not quality, at the heart of apprenticeship. Apprentices generally lived with their masters. Completion rates were low. When apprenticeships ended, former apprentices potentially became competitors to their masters, not their employees, entered a highly mobile, waged labour force, or moved to different locations. Their service was rewarded with a package of diverse economic, political, and social rights, depending on where they trained. Apprenticeship, moreover, was utilised in a very broad set of occupations outside of agriculture, giving members of both the urban and rural elite an interest in it as participants and parents as well as employers. In anachronistic terms, employers had an interest in how well the system served employees.

Without firms and the central state, what institutions set the rules for premodern apprenticeship? We can reject one possible explanation. Premodern apprenticeship was not necessarily part of a 'guild system'.[14] Premodern apprenticeship did not depend upon the guilds and functioned effectively in their absence; the same is true of urban corporate regulation.

Apprenticeship could thrive as a training system in the period before and after guilds emerged in urban centers, and in areas and occupations outside their governance.[15]

This is not to say that guilds did not matter. Where they took root, they affected this and many other aspects of their members' activities. Where guilds paid attention to apprenticeship by their members—which was not inevitable—this affected the contractual structure, especially the duration of training agreements and the concentration of training, through quotas on the numbers of apprentices a master could train. In some settings, they gave a reason to complete apprenticeships that surely influenced behaviour. We can see the impact of this on recruitment by individuals, where it artificially produced scarcity, reflected in higher fees, and put a constraint on the pace of dissemination of knowledge. We should also acknowledge that it may have served to avoid some of the abuses of the system that could occur where masters were able to hire en masse and treat apprentices as cheap labour.

Apprenticeship was about gaining skill in an occupation and a place. However, the popularity and performance of apprenticeship was supported by two features of the system that we have seen throughout the book: first, the set of incentives linked to completing apprenticeships that rewarded workers who acquired skills through this form of training; and second, the flexibility produced by the institutions responsible for enforcing contracts that lowered the risks of entering apprenticeship contracts.

If we begin with incentives, apprenticeship gives access to a set of complementary, interlocking privileges. In some cities and towns across Europe, the connection between completing apprenticeship and entering a guild or becoming an urban citizen provided a reward for completion that encouraged people to start apprenticeships and helped to stabilise their operation. In England, this local privilege became increasingly secondary to the more powerful and general inducement created by the Statute of Artificers, which linked apprenticeship to practising that occupation anywhere in the country. The statute affected apprentices and artisans working outside incorporated towns and cities, and it retained greater legal and economic force than guild privileges from the later seventeenth century. In addition to skills, English apprenticeship provided a nationwide licence to enter an occupation and, from 1598, a right to claim welfare. Before 1562, only the first had existed, and then only in certain towns and guilds.

These same factors encouraged apprentices to enter indentures in the first place, and they explain the popularity of apprenticeships once urban growth and the expansion of manufacturing and trade began. With no parallel system of restriction for agricultural work, and entry to many occupations effectively limited after this point in the life cycle, at least having a go at an apprenticeship made sense.

This package of incentives emerged gradually. Several of the key innovations in England occurred in the sixteenth century and combined to make apprenticeship particularly attractive. This surely explains some of the enormous growth in training that followed. In short, English families' decisions to make these investments in human capital were shaped by the political choices of the English state and its cities and guilds.

Put another way, England was an environment in which partial occupational closure gave an economic advantage to people who completed an apprenticeship. Closure raised the cost of defection, by limiting access to outside options during and after training.[16] It provided a payoff to apprenticeship that went beyond the skill and knowledge that were acquired. It is important to add that in England, closure was never complete, meaning that partial training could still have value, especially for waged work, and it did not cover all occupations, meaning that outside options in other lines of work were always available; keep in mind that large share of apprentices who did not complete their contracts.

The set of incentives present in early modern England were not the only possible package that could achieve this effect. Craft unions and journeymen's organisations in England perpetuated closure in some jobs after the abolition of the statute. In labour markets with thick information and collective norms that value trustworthiness, including those in premodern societies, the cost of reputational damage from breach of contract alone could induce a sufficient measure of compliance to stabilise and reward apprenticeship, especially in smaller communities.[17] Modern apprenticeship systems provide the same incentives through certification or job hierarchies. Professions have done an even better job, arguably, through national licensing.

The size and distribution of the economic rents that actually flowed to those who completed apprenticeships is unclear, as are the welfare costs they imposed on the rest of the population; what we know of the wage premium for skilled work suggests they were modest, but that evidence is limited in scope and captures only one potential outcome.[18] Apprenticeship today is associated with wage compression, not high skill premiums, in Germany. What is clear is the extraordinary scale and metropolitan concentration of demand for apprenticeship in the sixteenth and seventeenth centuries, as this system was instituted and operated most fully. Far from keeping workers in agriculture, as its authors intended, England's apprenticeship system helped initiate an extraordinary period of structural change and urbanisation.

What about the second point, the institutions for contract enforcement? The argument I have made is that apprenticeship needs to be understood as a flexible legal contract that could be adjusted and terminated early. Because of this, the formal institutions that were critical to enforcement were the courts, especially the local courts of towns and cities that developed their own distinctive customs.[19] The court system, and the mix of customary and urban law it enforced, varied somewhat between locations.

One side of this—the power to discipline and punish disorderly youth—has long been recognised by historians. What has been missed is the counterpart that balanced this. The availability of courts and law officers with the power to enforce, adjust, or *discharge* contracts was central to the operation and success of apprenticeship. The pinnacle of this was reached in London's Lord Mayor's Court, which was the opposite of the relationship-sustaining institution that many suggest was needed to maintain apprenticeship, in enabling apprentices to exit contracts with little cost or effort. Instead of destroying apprenticeship, it sat at the center of the largest concentration of training in the nation.

To understand why this was possible, we need to revise how we think about contract enforcement in apprenticeship. The measure of enforcement is frequently taken as the degree to which contracted terms of service were completed; at its simplest, the issue becomes whether or not apprentices were prevented from early departure.[20] Without that, the argument goes, theory suggests that training will be under-produced.

There are two major flaws with this analysis. As an interpretation of training, first of all, it identifies the most rapid method of training, in which time and effort is invested in instruction initially and the now-skilled worker repays this investment subsequently, as being the only method of training. As I argue, early modern employers could and did lower their risk of loss from investing in training their apprentices by limiting the amount of direct (and costly) instruction they gave, widening the period over which instruction was given, ensuring that apprentices paid their way through low-skilled work, bargaining for fees from parents, and demanding bonds for any wider business risks that apprentice malfeasance could threaten. Moreover, this form of training, emphasising the youth's learning rather than the master's teaching, was characteristic of a wide array of forms of apprenticeship outside industrial settings.

Second, as an interpretation of enforcement, it is too narrow. Opportunistic exits are only one element of contract performance, which encompasses both parties' compliance with the requirements of the contract and their capacity to do so. The enforcement system in England provided a way to resolve poor matches and poor performance that were unobserved until training started, and to address the challenges to training that were created by the high risk of failure that all businesses faced in the volatile economy of this period. Responding to asymmetric information and uncertainty about what would happen during the indentures was the focus of the system, more than opportunism.

Apprenticeships were major investments of time and money made by families into the human capital of their children. Both masters and apprentices utilised trial periods to alleviate some of the uncertainties they faced, and the system allowed for consensual exits, but these were only a partial solution to this problem. What the legal framework added to this was a mechanism that allowed premodern families to make these investments in the knowledge that they and their children had a way to revise their decision if they were not satisfied with the quality of the training or their treatment, or if either their own circumstances or the capacity of the master to provide training changed.

If this interpretation of the work of the courts sounds unduly considerate and sympathetic to the interests of apprentices, recall that their masters profited from fees as well as unskilled work in this system of training, limiting their losses from an apprentice's exit, and that these apprentices' families were not just the blue-collar manual workers we associate with apprenticeship in the industrial cities of the twentieth century, but included many members of the landed and commercial elite, gentlemen, landowners, major merchants, and urban officials. No doubt these parents also possessed the resources to navigate the institutions of enforcement most effectively. But the system that was created in their interest benefited apprentices from all social backgrounds.

What were the consequences of apprenticeship for technological and economic development in England? Two variables were critical: the knowledge young workers gained and its diffusion. Apprenticeship was, at its core, a system for reproducing knowledge about a craft or trade. It could do this poorly if apprentices were exploited, or it could mechanically transfer the mix of knowledge each generation of masters possessed. In England, at least, training was instead concentrated in the workshops of the most successful and most skillful and innovative masters. Apprenticeship spread best practice.

The beneficiaries of this were not only the towns or cities where apprentices trained, but the nation as a whole. Apprenticeship replenished urban populations, but it also formed part of circular migrations that took young people back into the small towns and villages with the knowledge they absorbed from their masters. These movements were anticipated before and during training; they were not just the consequence of failure to succeed in the urban labour market. As a result, apprenticeship promoted structural change and the growth of rural industry and commerce.

The scope and inclusiveness of apprenticeship intensified this effect, allowing young people to choose a trade that suited their interests and abilities. Rules that could and should have segmented England's labour market by status, occupation, and geography were ignored from the outset. The social breadth of apprenticeship mattered. It encompassed the children of rich and poor, of city and country, of farm and counting-house, of church and meeting house. The social openness of apprenticeship mattered, too. Apprentices and masters were not usually drawn from the same backgrounds or connected by strong social ties. Finally, the cultural openness towards apprenticeship mattered. Norms about who could train did not exclude women from apprenticeship, though they drastically narrowed the types of work they undertook, nor did they define which child should be trained, except where expectations about the inheritance of land through primogeniture divided opportunities between siblings.

Opportunities were not equal. The market for training meant masters set a price for entry that reflected the value of the skills they could offer, to which guilds and cities added their own demands. Access was only open to those whose families could afford it. Nor was everyone welcome. Access was still limited by nationality, excluding immigrant children, and later by race and religion, excluding Black and Jewish apprentices. But the characteristics of apprenticeship in England were closer to offering the 'broad based economic opportunities' Acemoglu and Robinson argue are central to prosperity than some traditional images of a premodern society of orders might suggest—images that reflect the narrower pools of recruitment apparent in some more restrictive regions of Europe.[21]

The focus of this book was on apprenticeship as it operated in early modern England, but the wider European practice of training was broadly similar. A wave of recent studies has highlighted many of the same features seen in England in other regions: similar forms of learning; similar openness to migrants and those from outside the craft; similar patterns of flexibility and adjustment during terms of service; and a similar reliance on urban courts instead of guilds to enforce contracts.[22] Differences were present. The Statute of Artificers was unique to England in establishing closure across the nation based on the seven-year apprenticeship. Elsewhere, terms of service were shorter, lowering entry barriers. Contracts were written in several different ways, some more bespoke and costly in the notarial systems seen in France and the Southern Netherlands, others simpler oral agreements. Guilds paid more or less attention to training, but generally had a similar impact to their equivalents in England's urban areas. To me, the similarities outweigh these differences, but we still have no good comparisons of the quantity, quality, and price of human capital generated by the different variations on apprenticeship across Europe.

This system of European apprenticeship possesses several features that approximate, within certain limits, to what North, Wallis, and Weingast describe as an 'open access' order, the form of economic and political organisation they identify with development and growth. Entry was largely open.[23] The principal urban organisations were perpetual corporations. Participants possessed—or acquired—citizenship that provided them with a voice in local legislative processes, including oversight over the behaviour of the courts that enforced the contracts they participated in as employers and parents.

Forged initially in the distinctive setting of premodern European citizenship, apprenticeship benefited from the impersonal operation of local urban courts that developed distinctive systems that applied a flexible approach to apprenticeship contracts.[24] In this way, Europe's cities produced a system of labour regulation that sustained extensive training markets, plausibly because they were in competition with each other for labour and human capital. There is an obvious parallel with the process Oscar Gelderblom identified by which cities competitively reshaped their legal, commercial, and financial institutions to enhance their commercial connectivity and attract flows of long-distance trade.[25]

The existence of apprenticeship helps explain some of the dynamic changes seen in late medieval and early modern Europe. I have suggested that the way that apprenticeship integrated markets in training and labour helped facilitate several of the major economic changes seen in England in the centuries before industrialisation: the growth of towns; the shift from agriculture to industry and services; the growing variety, range, and quality of manufactured goods; and the geographical shift in economic activity. These were common features in the sequence of what Goldstone usefully describes as 'efflorescences'—periods of relatively rapid, concentrated economic growth, often around a cluster of major cities, that occurred across the continent, as in Renaissance Northern Italy and Holland, over a period of several centuries before we see these similar changes affecting England.[26] Each of these occurred in a setting where apprenticeship was present and actively used to recruit and train labour. The hypothesis—and for now, it is no more than that—is that this was not coincidental. Apprenticeship provided an important mechanism that flexibly linked urban and rural labour markets, allowing the rapid expansion of human capital as demand grew.

This constructive set of apprenticeship institutions persisted successfully while urban demographic imbalances needed to be settled by large-scale internal migration, and while a relatively equal balance of interest and influence existed between employers and apprentices. Although relatively stable for several centuries, the institutions were not locked in place, but were contingent and vulnerable to revision as power and economic interests shifted. Elements of this were already visible in the eighteenth century. In the nineteenth century, there is strong evidence that in England, the system of apprenticeship was increasingly captured and manipulated by the interests of employers, who used the law of master and servant to tie apprentices into contracts on pain of extended periods of imprisonment.[27] It was not until the late nineteenth century that labour relations were rebalanced to give greater protection again to workers.

Apprenticeship played an important part in many of the critical economic developments that occurred in England between 1500 and 1800 and in other periods of rapid growth in premodern Europe. Each of these can be linked to industrialisation. Can we say more—can apprenticeship help explain the Industrial Revolution?

To the extent that industrialisation depended on a supply of highly skilled artisans able to implement innovations in a creative partnership with enlightened inventors, apprenticeship was certainly a supporting institution. The upper tail of the workforce that Joel Mokyr has highlighted was composed of artisans who had served apprenticeships, and we can trace the existence of dynasties of talented and innovative individuals whose capabilities were formed during their training in this system, such as the clockmakers Graham and Townley.[28] A potentially compelling contrast can be drawn between Europe's systems of apprenticeship and training in other regions of the world, as de la Croix, Doepke, and Mokyr have suggested.[29] Where European apprenticeship integrated markets in labour and diffused knowledge, in India occupational training was segmented and divided as endogenous guilds kept skills to their own extended families, and in China craft skills and commercial activity were usually restricted within extended lineages.[30]

We get less help from apprenticeship in answering the question of why industrialisation took hold first in Britain. Apprenticeship in England and the rest of Europe was similar enough in structure that it is hard to identify distinctive features that generated a greater abundance or quality of skilled workers which might enable industrialisation on the one side of the English Channel and not on the other.[31] If anything, England was converging ever closer with practices elsewhere in Europe in the eighteenth century, as the force of the Statute of Artificers was curtailed, terms were shortened, and the extreme concentration on London as a site of training reduced. Measures of the relative price of skill constructed by van Zanden show a low and stable wage premium across Western and Central Europe from the fifteenth century to the nineteenth.[32] Plausibly, any abundance of artisanal skills in what would turn out to be propitious areas for industrialisation, such as metalworking and clock-making, may be the fortunate effect of patterns of specialisation in particular branches of manufacturing. As Rosenberger and Hanlon suggest, England's industries may simply have been concentrated in areas that would become the focus of the inventive technological advances of the First Industrial Revolution.[33]

Premodern apprenticeship contributed to creating the initial conditions for modern economic growth, but the organisational and technological changes that accompanied industrialisation would lead to its transformation. We should not let that obscure the significance of the system of training that existed before. It was shaped to fit a very different world. Masters were building tiny businesses in the face of dramatic economic and demographic volatility. Families faced enormous uncertainty about the choices they were making for their children, choices that would send them to distant places and unfamiliar jobs. In the face of this, apprenticeship linked together places, trades, and generations in a market for skill that allowed workers, ideas, and techniques to move and improve. It did so because the institutions and actors enabled flexibility and adjustment, and because barriers to entry—and exit—were low. Opportunities could be seized and aspirations realised. As John Carter, the Essex tailor we began the book with, described, once he had an independent workshop in Colchester, 'a youth . . . offered himself as an apprentice. He was a very industrious, clever, attentive lad, and soon made an excellent workman'.[34] And so the cycle continued.

APPENDIX 1

Apprenticeship Registration Records

Much of the work presented in this book depends on digitized lists of apprenticeship records taken from guild, urban, and national records. Without the work of countless individuals who have extracted these from the original manuscripts, and in particular the heroic contribution of Cliff Webb for London, this project would have been impossible.

Records of London Guild Apprenticeships

For London, I use indentures from the records of eighty-two London livery companies. These records were kept by guilds in a variety of manuscript formats and are separate from the city's own records, which are now largely lost. The numbers of observations and the date ranges of the series are given in table A1.1.

The records are taken from Webb (1994–) for all guilds with the exceptions of (i) the Bowyers, Clothworkers, Drapers, Founders, Girdlers, Goldsmiths, Mercers, Musicians, Salters, and Tallow Chandlers, which were digitized by the Records of London's Livery Companies Online (ROLLCO) project and can be accessed at https://www.londonroll.org/; (ii) the Merchant Taylors, from Scott (2019); (iii) the Watermen, created by Docklands Ancestors (Cottrell n.d.); (iv) the Bakers, Barbers, Carpenters, Coopers, Leathersellers, and Shipwrights, for which I use samples taken by Webb for four counties; and (v) the Apothecaries, from Wallis (2000).

TABLE A1.1. London guild records of apprenticeship in the dataset

Company	Apprentices (N)	Start year	End year
Apothecaries	6,329	1618	1800
Armourers	3,505	1607	1800
Bakers	650	1632	1798
Barbers	782	1658	1799
Basketmakers	1,384	1639	1824
Blacksmiths	13,254	1594	1800
Bowyers	626	1680	1877
Brewers	6,019	1531	1800
Broderers	886	1673	1800
Brown-bakers	657	1615	1646
Butchers	9,680	1585	1800
Cardmakers	509	1675	1760
Carmen	2,444	1668	1800
Carpenters	999	1572	1799
Clockmakers	7,410	1631	1928
Clothworkers	31,244	1597	1897
Coachmakers	3,390	1644	1800
Comb-makers	42	1744	1750
Cooks	3,073	1654	1800
Coopers	1,294	1587	1799
Cordwainers	8,867	1636	1802
Curriers	2,740	1628	1800
Cutlers	6,412	1443	1800
Distillers	1,752	1659	1811
Drapers	21,063	1289	1898
Dyers	1,932	1703	1746
Fan Makers	43	1776	1805
Farriers	3,709	1619	1800
Feltmakers	4,628	1669	1800
Fishmongers	8,313	1614	1800
Fletchers	119	1739	1808
Founders	3,691	1610	1860
Framework Knitters	229	1725	1730
Fruiterers	169	1750	1815
Gardeners	136	1764	1850
Girdlers	2,328	1654	1936
Glass Sellers	915	1665	1812
Glaziers	1,684	1693	1800
Glovers	1,055	1671	1804
Goldsmiths	9,847	1573	1802
Grocers	10,965	1629	1800

TABLE A1.1. (*continued*)

Company	Apprentices (N)	Start year	End year
Gunmakers	1,828	1656	1800
Haberdashers	26,311	1600	1800
Horners	154	1731	1800
Innholders	1,519	1642	1800
Ironmongers	2,830	1655	1800
Joiners	13,058	1641	1721
Leathersellers	429	1629	1798
Longbowstring Makers	298	1604	1717
Loriners	472	1718	1800
Masons	1,881	1663	1805
Mercers	6,117	1339	1890
Merchant Taylors	65,392	1490	1800
Musicians	1,578	1624	1877
Needlemakers	1,502	1664	1801
Painters	3,917	1655	1800
Pattenmakers	1,321	1673	1805
Paviors	952	1527	1800
Pewterers	5,200	1608	1800
Pinmakers	343	1690	1723
Plasterers	3,031	1597	1800
Plumbers	1,797	1571	1800
Poulterers	1,429	1685	1800
Saddlers	195	1657	1666
Salters	3,350	1600	1900
Scriveners	11	1580	1621
Shipwrights	100	1692	1793
Skinners	10,622	1492	1800
Spectacle Makers	832	1652	1800
Stationers	19,061	1542	1830
Tallow Chandlers	6,600	1629	1867
Tin Plate Workers	1,983	1666	1800
Tobacco-pipe Makers	8	1795	1800
Turners	7,380	1596	1800
Tylers	3,712	1612	1800
Upholders	1,318	1704	1772
Vintners	19,034	1609	1800
Watermen	41,338	1692	1822
Wax Chandlers	1,130	1666	1800
Weavers	17,578	1607	1800
Woolmen	616	1665	1828
Wyre Drawers	1,263	1693	1837
Total	462,264	1289	1936

Records of Provincial Urban and Guild Apprenticeships

To examine apprenticeship outside London I use a range of sources, primarily urban registers that capture enrolled contracts brought by citizens, using all occupations and guilds. The exceptions are Durham and Shrewsbury, which are drawn from surviving guild records. Therefore, despite its smaller size, the provincial sample is more complete for some places than the London sample.

TABLE A1.2. Provincial urban and guild apprentices in the dataset

City	Apprentices (N)	Start year	End year	Sample structure
Boston	2,902	1663	1903	All
Bristol	58,555	1532	2009	All
Durham	3,814	1599	1939	10 guilds
Gloucester	6,557	1595	1834	All
Leicester	570	1637	1770	1637–50; 1676–81; 1716–22; 1767–70
Lincoln	2,917	1633	1866	All
Liverpool	701	1701	1748	All
Norwich	5,873	1490	1749	All
Oxford	400	1530	1594	1530–40; 1590–94
Shrewsbury	411	1681	1725	5 guilds
Total	82,700	1490	2009	

Sources

Boston: A transcript of the town records was kindly supplied by the Lincoln Family History Society and contains both bindings and freedoms.

Bristol: This is based on the two major digitized editions produced by the Bristol & Avon Family History Society, for 1532 to 1724 (published 2019) and 1724 to 2009 (published 2012).

Durham: The records of ten guilds—the Barbers, Barkers, Cordwainers, Curriers, Dyers, Joiners, Masons, Mercers, Plumbers, and Weavers–are included, drawn from the calendar published online by Durham University Library at https://reed.dur.ac.uk/xtf/data/pdf/DCGApprtce/DCGApprtce.pdf.

Gloucester: Jill Barlow generously shared the data published by the Bristol and Gloucestershire Archaeological Society in her edition of the city's registers (2001,2011).

Leicester: Samples were drawn from the material included in Hartopp (1927).

Lincoln: A transcript of the city records was kindly supplied by the Lincoln Family History Society.

Liverpool: Data is from Power et al. (1998).

Norwich: Data is from Rising and Millican (1959).

Oxford: Manual samples were taken from Crossley (2012).

Shrewsbury: Data is derived from SRO, MS6001/126 (Glovers); 6001/4263 (Mercers); 6001/5837 (Tailors); 6001/3360 (Weavers); and 6001/4583 (Smiths).

The Stamp Tax Records

For the eighteenth century, records from the stamp duty come from the index to the registers recently produced by Ancestry.com and indexes prepared by the Society of Genealogists, with their kind permission.

Notionally, the tax records contain all indentures for which a premium was paid, unless it was funded by charity or parish welfare. By law, the master was required to pay tax within one year after making the contract. However, in practice, the lag between binding an apprentice and paying the tax could be substantial, and the state offered several amnesties over the eighteenth century to encourage those who had not paid the tax within the required time to do so.[1]

The Stamp Office kept two series of registers. The 'city' registers record tax payments made directly at the Stamp Office in London. For this series of registers, the dates when the register was in use and the dates of tax payment are identical. The 'country' registers record the details of tax payments made by masters to commissioners outside London.

Because commissioners sent batches of records to London, there was often a gap of several months between the date the tax was paid and the date that the Stamp Office recorded the payment into their office register. For this reason, the dates during which the country registers were in use do not coincide perfectly with the dates of the tax payments they recorded. For example, a country register that started in June 1750 might report indentures for which the tax was paid in November 1749, given the time it took the local commissioners to dispatch their records to London for registration.

TABLE A1.3. Breaks in the stamp tax series of apprenticeship premium registers

Registers around break	Last date of register	First date of next register	Length of break (days)	Length of break (years)
CITY REGISTERS				
8–9	26-8-1721	7-1-1723	499	1.37
11–12	4-3-1727	16-3-1730	1,108	3.03
13–14	2-8-1733	5-4-1735	611	1.67
15–16	7-10-1738	6-10-1740	730	2.00
18–19	29-12-1749	27-4-1752	850	2.33
Total			3,798	10.40
COUNTRY REGISTERS				
48–49	13-1-1726	6-11-1728	1,028	2.81
49–50	2-11-1731	9-4-1741	3,446	9.43
50–51	14-12-1745	16-10-1750	1,767	4.84
Total			6,241	17.09

Source: Rice 1922, xxii–xxiii.
Note: Years are reported in new style.

Neither series of registers survives in its entirety. Although the modern archival numbering created by the National Archives is sequential, there are significant breaks, particularly in the first half of the eighteenth century. The timing and duration of the gaps are reported in table A1.3. The gaps amount to ten years in the city series and seventeen years in the country series. The losses are concentrated between 1720 and 1753.

APPENDIX 2

Estimating the Number of Apprentices in London's Guilds, 1500–1850

How many apprentices were indentured to members of London's guilds? Little of the city's own records of apprentices survive, and livery company records are patchy. Many guilds have lost their earliest records, and not all maintained registers, particularly before the late sixteenth century. A few sources provide snapshots of the stock of apprentices or freemen, but these do not give much of a sense of trends between the mid-sixteenth and late seventeenth centuries. The estimates presented here fill this void and are based on a very large sample of surviving London guild records, supplemented by other sources.

I first present the sources used to estimate apprentice numbers and then describe the estimation method.

Guild Records

For much of 1600 to 1850, counts of apprentices enrolled in guild records described in appendix 1 can be constructed. This is my preferred starting point. It is not a full measure of all apprenticeships in London, of course: not all masters were members of guilds, and registration was evaded by some who were, either to duck fees, to escape quotas, or simply because they did not see it as important. The latter becomes a particular risk in the latter part of this period, where some fading guilds saw their freemen drift away. However, as a measure of corporate apprenticeship, it is the best indicator that exists.

I measure apprenticeship by decade. There is a pragmatic reason for this: it allows Rappaport's counts of apprenticeship in a number of guilds in the mid-sixteenth century to be included. It also dampens the impact of annual volatility in numbers and short breaks in data series. Where individual observations from detailed guild records exist, I first calculate annual totals, and then decadal totals and average apprenticeship rates per year for each guild and decade.

Some individual guild records have gaps in coverage. Others include years in which zero apprentices are registered. This may be because the records are incomplete, but it may also be because there were actually no new entrants in that guild.

Where gaps or zero counts exist, I estimate a total number of enrolments for the decade. To do this, I multiply by ten the average annual apprenticeship rate for that decade, calculated from years with apprentices recorded, to give a decadal total. I include estimates for guilds where apprenticeships were registered for at least six out of the ten years in a decade. To avoid inflating apprentice counts, I assume that years with zero apprentices reflect years without registrations—zeroes, not absences—if the average of apprentices registered per year in that decade in years with recorded apprentices is at or below three per year. The impact of using alternative thresholds for zeroes is minimal.

Taking this approach provides direct counts of apprentices for a rising share of London's guilds. In the early sixteenth century only 10 to 20 per cent of guilds are in the sample, but this rises steadily to around half of active guilds by the second half of the seventeenth century and more than three-quarters of the eighty-five or so guilds active across the eighteenth century, as figure A2.1 shows. Cliff Webb's listings largely end in 1800, and so the sample of guilds falls markedly in the nineteenth century. The simple counting of guilds understates the extent to which the sample covers training, as nearly all of the larger guilds that took the most apprentices are in the dataset throughout the seventeenth century.

Freedom Samples

In order to estimate the numbers of apprentices in guilds for which enrolment records are missing, I use benchmark years for which good measures of the related process of admitting freemen survive. I generate benchmarks for apprenticeship rates in the mid-sixteenth and mid-seventeenth centuries using the information available on the numbers of people becoming freemen in the fragments of the city's records that survive for 1551–53 and 1667–68 based on bivariate regressions between the average number of apprentices

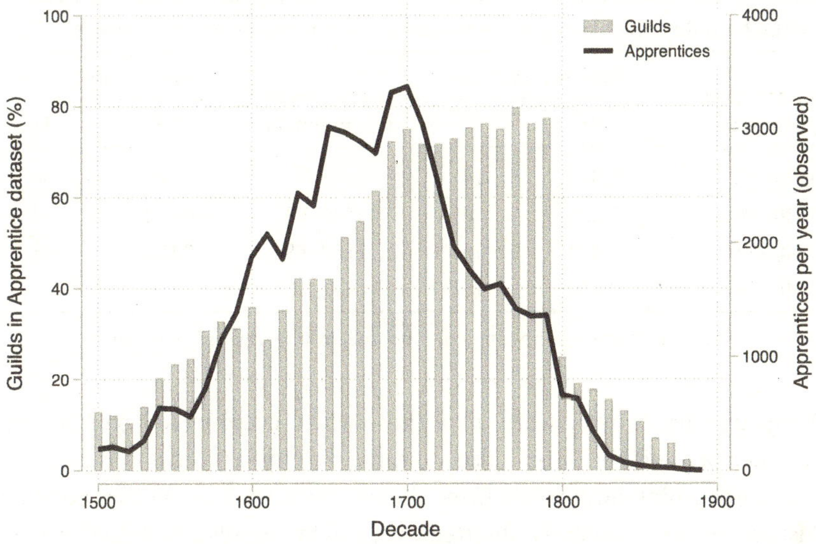

FIGURE A2.1. London guild sample coverage and apprentice totals by decade, 1500–1900.

per annum observed in surviving guild records and the number of new freemen enrolled by the city from those guilds. I experimented with combinations of different sample periods for the number of apprentices in order to identify whether the fit was better with a sample preceding or overlapping the count of freemen.

Table A2.1 shows the number of observations and the R-squared for each model, indicating the goodness of fit. For the mid-sixteenth century, the best fit was obtained using the average of apprentices per annum for the preceding period 1530–49. For the mid-seventeenth century, the best fit was the overlapping period 1650–69, probably due to the effect of the civil war on recruitment in the 1640s. In both periods, freedom rates are strongly associated with apprenticeship levels, each explaining more than 90% of the variation in the other.

The city registers include freedom entries in 1551–53 for members of fifty-eight livery companies.[1] The implication is that no freemen were admitted into the other five companies thought to have been active during this period (the Brown-Bakers, Glaziers, Longbowstring Makers, Loriners, Plumbers). The surviving record is for a short period and admissions are clustered by guild, so there may be some omissions. However, it is unlikely that a guild that was admitting large numbers of freemen would not appear at all. As

TABLE A2.1. Results of bivariate regressions of apprentices on freedom entries

Apprentices per annum in:	Freemen 1551–53		Apprentices per annum in:	Freemen 1667–68	
	R^2	N		R^2	N
1530–49	**0.902**	**14**	1640–59	0.861	34
1530–59	0.856	16	1640–69	0.862	44
1540–59	0.820	16	**1650–69**	**0.925**	**43**
1540–49	0.820	16			

Note: The model is structured with apprentices per annum as the dependent variable.

Rappaport has shown, nearly all of those who are known to have become freemen of a guild in 1551–53 also appear in the city's record in this period.[2] And some guilds did enrol small numbers of freemen: four guilds presented just one person, six guilds admitted two, and five guilds admitted three. In estimating numbers of apprentices in guilds where apprenticeship records are missing, I therefore assume that the six guilds that recorded no freemen were recruiting the average number of apprentices per year observed in guilds that registered a single freeman in 1551–53.

The extract from the register in 1667–68 includes records from seventy-three companies of seventy-seven that are thought to have been active in this period.[3] As occured a century before, small numbers of entries are not uncommon: three guilds admitted a single freeman, and two guilds each admitted two, three, or four freemen that year. The four guilds without any freemen in this period are all minor players: the Cardmakers and Soapmakers were both small; the Tobacco-pipe Makers had its charter restored only in 1663; the Musicians had been stripped of their charter in 1632. As before, I assume that these guilds recruited the average number of apprentices observed in the three guilds admitting a single freeman.

Orphans' Duty

For the eighteenth century, a new central city record of apprenticeship numbers exists, the orphans' duty registers. The orphans' duty registers give a reasonably effective and speedy way to obtain totals of apprentices from companies. The orphans' duty was imposed in 1694 to help the city repay its debts to orphans who were its wards. Among other duties, a fee of 2s 6d was paid for every apprenticeship. Companies kept records of these fees, which were separate from their existing records, and the sums raised

TABLE A2.2. Orphans' duty records of apprenticeship in London

	1699–1700	1730–31	1760–63	1790–93	1820–23
Guilds with apprentices in sample (N)	83	43	43	46	75
Active guilds without apprentices in sample (N)	1	41	42	39	10
Apprentices p.a. (N)	3,805	1,605	1,081	1,203	1,173

were paid on an annual or biannual basis to city collectors, whose books of accounts survive.

The orphans' duty registers give some indication about which companies were still actively registering apprentices in the eighteenth and early nineteenth centuries. The totals of apprentices they record are imperfect if treated as annual totals, as companies tended to pay the city less frequently than this. To address this, I took samples from the accounts for 1699–1701, 1731–32, 1760–62, 1790–92, and 1820–22.[4] These samples give an indication of the proportion of active companies and the distribution of apprentices between companies over this period.

As one would expect, where companies made duty payments, the counts are very close to counts derived from guild records. I produce annual estimates of apprentices per year paying orphans' duty and then estimate the decadal total. I treat this as a lagged count of the previous decade's entries, to allow for late payment. The correlation coefficient between the decadal totals in the guild series, where observed directly, and the orphans' duty registers is 0.89 ($p=0.000$).

As table A2.2 shows, there was a substantial decline in the proportion of companies paying orphans' duty in the middle of the eighteenth century. However, the number of companies making duty payments increased again in the early nineteenth century. A similar story emerges if we look at the numbers of apprentices being bound in London: by 1760 they had tumbled rapidly to just over a quarter of the level in 1700, but numbers then stabilised and remained roughly constant into the early nineteenth century.

Estimation Process

Although the direct coverage of apprentices from guild records is considerable, it is not sufficient to give a citywide total. Estimating totals for the numbers of apprentices in London's guilds requires finding a plausible way to fill in the many blanks in the guild record where no records of guild enrolments survive. I proceeded as follows.

First, for the sixteenth and seventeenth centuries, where information that allows the estimation of guild-specific apprenticeship levels directly survives, I do this. So, for guilds thought to have been active in the 1550s and 1660s but which have no apprentice records, I use the freedom records to provide an estimate of apprentices in 1540–49 and 1660–69, respectively. This provides estimates of apprentices for forty-three of fifty-six guilds in the 1540s and thirty-eight of seventy-eight guilds in the 1660s.

Second, I use the orphans' duty data to provide direct estimates for the eighteenth and early nineteenth century where guilds made duty payments. I use the counts of duty paid from the start of each decade as estimates of decadal totals in guild records for the previous decade, so the annual average of apprentices per year in entries for 1730–33 is the basis for a decadal total for 1720–29. This accounts for the problem of late payments of duty that is observable in the records: the tax payments lagged apprenticeship, essentially.

The orphans' duty overlaps with a period in which guild records are relatively abundant, and so most guilds are observed directly from their own registers, but nonetheless, I use this source for twenty-three of eighty-five guilds in 1690, seven in the 1720s, eight in the 1750s, and eleven in the 1780s. In the 1810s, the orphans' duty gives figures for sixty of eighty-four guilds, as it occurs after Webb's series of transcriptions finish.

This set of estimates and direct totals gives a skeleton of data that needs filling out. Even with these added estimates, few guild series start before the 1550s, and many end prematurely. A large number have a substantial break between the 1550s estimate from the City's freedom register and the start of count data from the guild's own records. And for some nothing exists between the two estimates for the 1550s and 1660s.

To resolve this, I used the available evidence on apprentices per decade to estimate an OLS regression with apprentices per decade as the dependent variable. The main explanatory variables are a simple time trend and a quadratic time trend to account for the non-linearity of the series. I also include dummy variables for each guild. I explored alternative models, but use OLS for simplicity of interpretation.

This model predicts apprenticeship numbers per decade for each guild, giving estimates of the predicted proportional change in apprenticeship in each decade over the period. These predictions capture the common time trend in recruitment in the sample as a whole. I took the predicted rate of

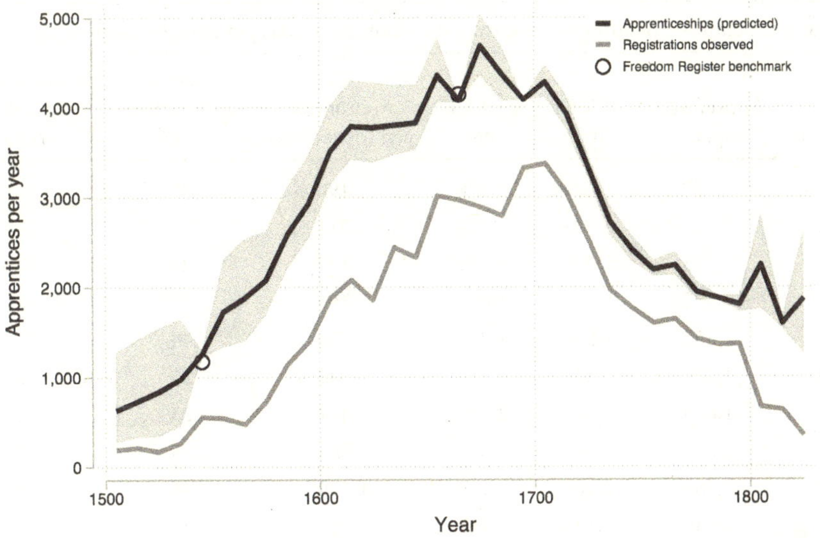

FIGURE A2.2. Guild apprenticeship in London, 1500–1820.

growth or decline for each decade and used this to project the data series backwards from the earliest and forwards from the latest observations in the dataset for each guild. The key assumption here is that patterns of growth and decline in each individual London guild followed those observed in the dataset as a whole. For out-of-sample prediction, this appears a conservative assumption.

Where periods include breaks in the guild data series, I interpolated using the predicted proportional change over each gap, but weighted the change to align with the observed counts at the beginning and end of each gap. Essentially, this adjusted the predicted rate of growth or decline in apprenticeships to bridge smoothly between the numbers observed in each guild's records.

This approach generates a series of apprentice counts for all guilds thought to be active between 1500 and 1900. The degree to which this London total of apprentices relies upon estimation varies from period to period. In the sixteenth century, 71% of decadal counts for individual guilds are estimated, and in the nineteenth century it is 80%. In the seventeenth century only 44% are estimated, while in the eighteenth century estimates make up just 21% of the total. The estimates are reported with error bounds in figure A2.2.

Focusing on the share of guilds is, fortunately, slightly misleading, as many of the largest guilds are in the dataset. Table A2.3 reports estimates

TABLE A2.3. Number of apprentices enrolled by London guilds per decade, 1500–1829

Decade	Apprentices p.a.	95% CI, min	95% CI, max	Apprentice p.a. (observed)	Share of apprentices observed (%)	Share of guilds observed (%)
1500	627	276	1,278	190	30	13
1510	727	331	1,424	211	29	11
1520	835	340	1,551	170	20	10
1530	975	459	1,643	266	27	12
1540	1,257	1,230	1,305	550	44	78
1550	1,729	1,336	2,319	542	31	21
1560	1,880	1,396	2,545	474	25	22
1570	2,074	1,692	2,627	723	35	27
1580	2,584	2,204	3,119	1,139	44	28
1590	2,930	2,548	3,470	1,390	47	27
1600	3,512	3,141	4,030	1,876	53	30
1610	3,787	3,424	4,302	2,079	55	24
1620	3,773	3,384	4,281	1,859	49	30
1630	3,803	3,475	4,254	2,439	64	35
1640	3,827	3,523	4,259	2,328	61	37
1650	4,359	4,061	4,777	3,019	69	36
1660	4,082	4,055	4,108	2,972	73	85
1670	4,687	4,355	5,035	2,891	62	48
1680	4,369	4,081	4,675	2,791	64	54
1690	4,088	4,083	4,094	3,324	81	87
1700	4,285	4,115	4,483	3,376	79	66
1710	3,926	3,753	4,131	3,045	78	64
1720	3,325	3,205	3,459	2,520	76	71
1730	2,731	2,577	2,905	1,969	72	65
1740	2,416	2,281	2,571	1,763	73	67
1750	2,193	2,117	2,296	1,596	73	74
1760	2,239	2,132	2,389	1,639	73	66
1770	1,943	1,850	2,062	1,424	73	70
1780	1,874	1,854	1,903	1,358	72	77
1790	1,803	1,722	1,904	1,366	76	68
1800	2,246	1,753	2,811	661	29	22
1810	1,597	1,537	1,667	629	39	79
1820	1,873	1,255	2,631	344	18	16

for apprentices per year, along with the share observed and the share of active guilds observed. For much of the sixteenth century, around one in three apprentices are observed directly. Even in the decade with the most limited coverage, one in five are observed. For the seventeenth century, direct observations are never less than half of apprentices, and often two-thirds or more.

HOW CREDIBLE ARE THESE ESTIMATES?

There are a number of scattered individual estimates of apprentices that exist in the literature. For 1550, Rappaport estimated around 1,500 apprentices per year, which is not far from the central estimate of 1,729 and falls within the 95% confidence interval, an unsurprising finding given that these new estimates rely heavily on his data.[5] The estimates of around 3,500 apprentices per annum for 1600 also strengthen Schwarz's doubts that Brodsky Elliott's estimate of 4,000 to 5,000 bound per year at that point was implausibly high.[6]

One useful test possible for the latter part of the period is to compare the number of apprentices bound to the number of freemen in the city. The earliest figure for freemen is for 1668–69, and counts from financial records of the number of fees paid continue (with some gaps) into the 1820s.[7] Initially, freemen by patrimony and servitude (apprenticeship) are indistinguishable. From the 1780s, they are separated. Patrimony accounts for a relatively small share of entries until the later eighteenth century, however.

If we use average apprentice numbers a decade earlier to give the size the pool of potential freemen, then this suggests that up to 46% of apprentices (including some who were freemen's sons by patrimony) could have become freemen in the 1660s. Thereafter, as figure A2.3 shows, the average share of apprentices and sons becoming freemen fluctuates around 30% to 40%, with one spike in the 1780s. In the late eighteenth century and early nineteenth century, freedom rates by servitude alone were between 20% and 30%. These rates are in line with other estimates of freedom rates, from guild records and other urban centres. This offers substantial reassurance about the quality of the estimates from the middle of the seventeenth century.

These figures also suggest that the model is not substantially undercounting apprentices in the mid-seventeenth century. Lower estimates of the total number of apprentices for the mid-seventeenth century would

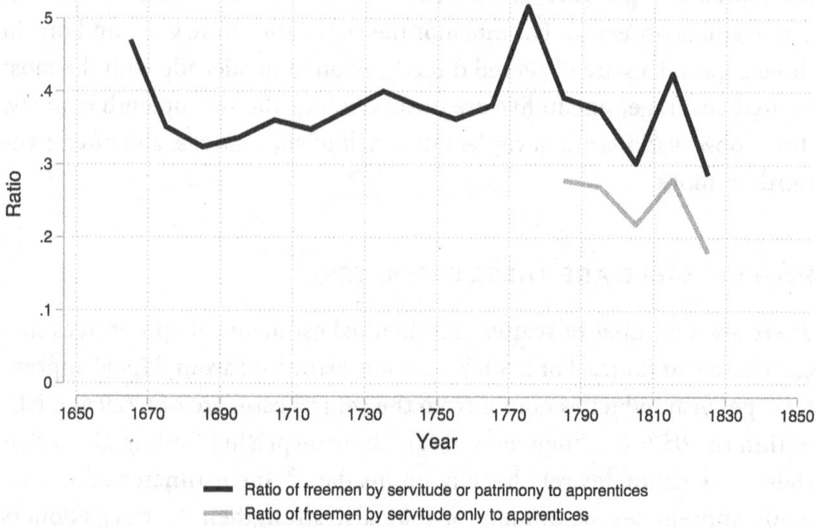

FIGURE A2.3. Share of apprentices becoming freemen, from London citizen counts. The figure reports estimates of the share of apprentices becoming freemen, calculated by dividing the number of new London citizens in the city records by the estimated number of apprentices enrolled in the previous decade.

produce implausibly high freedom rates: if 3,000, not 5,000, apprentices were being bound in the 1660s, then city freedom rates would be around 60%, which would far exceed the rates observed in individual guilds.

COUNTS FOR GUILDS OUTSIDE THE MAIN DATASET

Not all the guilds are in the dataset. For some I use counts drawn from existing sources that are not yet digitized. Many are Orphans Duty Books, which are name lists of apprentices indentured in the company that indicate the total sums owing to the city for the orphans' duty (2/6 per apprentice) and are countersigned by the city collectors to indicate receipt.

Bakers: Annual count from 1694 from the orphans' duty records: Orphans Duty Books, GL, MS 5184/3, 6–7 (1694–1729; 1729–95; 1795–1841).

Barber Surgeons: Annual count for 1690 onwards from the orphans' duty records: Orphans Duty Books, GL, MS 5274/1–3.

Carpenters: For 1654–94, Ainsworth et al. (1913–68, 1:1–4), http://www.british-history.ac.uk/report.aspx?compid=46225. From 1694, annual counts from the Orphans Duty Books, GL, MS 4337/4.

Coopers: Annual count for 1694 onwards from the orphans' duty records: Orphans Duty Books, GL, MS 5629/1.

Leathersellers: Counts of annual enrolments from the guild register of bindings for 1629–1705: Leathersellers' Company Archive, Mem/7/1: register of apprentices 1629–77; and Mem/7/2: register of apprentices 1686–1707. For 1706–1883, counts from the guild records of its orphans' duty payments Mem/7/3.

APPENDIX 3

Estimating the Incidence of Apprenticeship in England

How many apprentices were there in early modern England? Data on the number of youths entering private apprenticeships is fragmentary. I approach this in two ways. First, I construct estimates for urban apprenticeship in incorporated towns and cities and in other urban centres for 1500, 1600, 1700, and 1800. Second, I construct national estimates for private apprentices paying premiums around 1700 and 1800.

Table A3.1 reports estimates for the number of youths starting apprenticeships each year in England for several categories of city, town, and borough. Columns 1 to 4 give estimates of the numbers of youths entering guild or city-registered apprenticeships in towns and cities of different sizes around 1500, 1600, 1700, and 1800.[1]

Table A3.1 is restricted to towns that were incorporated by a royal charter at some point in this period. Chartering often followed a period in which corporate and guild governance was in place, and so I assume that towns that were first formally chartered during these centuries could have 'guild' apprentices throughout. I also assume that guild apprentices could be taken even when urban registration ceased, as town records are partial and individual trades may have maintained expectations about apprenticeship even without formal registration.

How close would the figures in table A3.1 be to an estimate of urban apprenticeship in England? Before 1700, most large towns were chartered. However, in the eighteenth century, some new and expanding centres, such as Birmingham and Manchester, were not yet incorporated. They lacked the infrastructure to record apprenticeships. As a result, corporate apprenticeship registration becomes less meaningful at a national level after 1700. In table A3.2 I report estimates of the numbers of apprentices who might have

TABLE A3.1. Annual entries to guild/urban apprenticeship in England, 1500–1800

	Apprentices in incorporated cities			
	c. 1500	c. 1600	c. 1700	c. 1800
London	627	3,512	4,285	2,246
Towns >10,000	346 (246–471)	503 (358–685)	1,152 (819–1,567)	1,721 (1,532–3,943)
Towns 5,000–10,000	145 (109–206)	208 (155–294)	378 (282–535)	55 (43–75)
Small boroughs	113 (82–155)	161 (116–222)	379 (274–522)	673 (598–1,530)
Total	1,232 (712–2,111)	4,384 (3,770–5,230)	6,194 (5,490–7,107)	4,694 (4,419–7,795)

Note: Towns in the sample include Bath, Bristol, Cambridge, Canterbury, Carlisle, Chester, Coventry, Derby, Exeter, Ipswich, King's Lynn, Kingston upon Hull, Leeds, Leicester, Liverpool, Newcastle upon Tyne, Norwich, Nottingham, Oxford, Plymouth, Portsmouth, Preston, Reading, Salisbury, Sheffield, and Shrewsbury.

been trained in large towns and cities that were *not* chartered if training occurred at the same frequency per capita as in incorporated cities (note that in practice, these locations also lacked some of the legal and political incentives for entering apprenticeship). On this assumption, until 1700, these towns would have seen a trivial share of apprentices, relative to the total in all large urban centres. Most were too small to meet the 5,000-inhabitant population threshold, in fact, and so were allocated zero apprentices. By 1800, however, all had over 10,000 inhabitants, and they might have contributed about a fifth to the total number of apprentices in larger urban centres in England.

These estimates for guild apprenticeship (and non-incorporated urban apprenticeship) for 1500 to 1800 are based on the following methodology. I construct town-level estimates for the twenty-seven English incorporated towns and cities that would at some stage become large enough to feature in De Vries's 1984 study of urban populations. First, I distinguish between London, large towns with 10,000 inhabitants or more, and small towns with fewer than 10,000 inhabitants. In 1500, in addition to London, England had four cities with more than 10,000 inhabitants (Norwich, Bristol, Exeter, and Newcastle) and six incorporated towns with 5,000 to 10,000. By 1600,

York's population also exceeded 10,000. By 1700, nine cities exceeded 10,000 inhabitants, and thirteen had 5,000 to 10,000 inhabitants.[2] By 1800, nineteen had broken the 10,000 threshold and only two were still below it.

Second, I calculate the numbers of apprentices per inhabitant at various points between 1600 and 1700 for cities where data exists on enrolments and urban populations. These are Boston, Bristol, Coventry, Gloucester, Ipswich, King's Lynn, Leicester, Lincoln, Liverpool, London, Northampton, Norwich, Oxford, Southampton, and St Albans. For small towns (less than 10,000), a median of 4.15 apprentices were indentured per thousand people with an interquartile range of 3.1–5.9. For large towns (10,000+), mainly based on Norwich and Bristol, the median is 8.7 (6.2–11.8) apprentices per thousand people. These are based on city registers, and not all youths registered their indentured, so it will be an undercount. The number of observations for some categories of town is limited, and so I pool all observations between 1600 and 1700 and use them to estimate a rate for 1500, 1600 and 1700. Reassuringly, there is no clear trend over time in these estimates. This gives twenty-one observations for small towns and seven observations for larger towns. For 1800, I use the observations in each category between 1750 and 1800, giving us a median of 3.2 (2.5–4.4) for smaller towns and 3.0 (2.7–6.8) for larger towns.

Third, I multiply the median rate of apprentices per inhabitant by the population estimates for all towns in each category (London, large towns, and small towns) to give estimated totals of apprentices enrolled in all the urban centres of each size. I also report the totals if the 25th and 75th percentile rate of apprentices per inhabitant is used instead. I report the total of apprentices for towns in each category that were incorporated boroughs (table A3.1) and for other urban centres (table A3.2).

This method excludes a host of smaller chartered boroughs (232 places in England had been incorporated by 1830). A number of these were very small (the median population was around 3,000 in 1830) and most did not use apprenticeship as an admission method to local citizenship (only fifty-five mentioned this in evidence gathered by a parliamentary commission in 1830). Not all can be dismissed, however. This large category extends from Abingdon to Yeovil. Many were already important centres, such as Durham, Bath, Canterbury, and Lancaster. Others, such as Bradford and Wigan, would expand rapidly. Although individually small, they formed an important tier of England's urban hierarchy, carrying out many of the political and economic functions that distinguish towns. For these small centres, I assume that apprentice numbers were equal to 22% of the total in the

TABLE A3.2. Annual entries to urban apprenticeship outside incorporated centres

	Apprentices in non-incorporated cities			
	c. 1500	c. 1600	c. 1700	c. 1800
Towns >10,000	0 (0–0)	0 (0–0)	87 (62–118)	1,282 (1,142–2,938)
Towns 5,000-10,000	21 (16–29)	21 (16–29)	108 (81–153)	0 (0–0)
Share of urban apprentices (%)	1.5 (2–1.3)	0.5 (0.4–0.5)	2.9 (2.4–3.5)	19.6 (18.9–24.5)
Total (*corporate and non-corporate*)	1,324 (779–2,238)	4,536 (3,881–5,441)	6,700 (5,856–7,805)	6,526 (6,051–11,985)

Note: Table A3.2 reports estimates of apprentices in Birmingham, Blackburn, Bolton, Bradford, Chatham, Colchester, Deptford, Greenwich, Huddersfield, Manchester, Oldham, Salford, Stockport, Sunderland, Warrington, Wenlock, Wigan, and Wolverhampton, based on de Vries's population estimates (1984) and the methodology and apprenticeship rates set out in the text.

twenty-seven larger urban centres. This is the share of premium apprentices in the 1710s who trained in the 139 small, chartered boroughs that would exceed 1,000 inhabitants in 1832.

From 1711 the stamp-tax records allow the production of separate estimates. Table A3.3 reports counts of these fee-paying apprentices for the 1710s and 1790s. These cover only one-third to one-half of apprenticeships in which the master received a premium: as a rule of thumb, doubling these numbers will give a reasonable estimate of the number of apprentices. But they extend over the entirety of the country, allowing us to examine both rural and urban apprenticeship.

These estimates are based on six-year samples (for 1712–17 and 1792–97), assigned to locations within England; part of the underlying data was kindly shared by Karine van der Beek. Urban populations are derived from de Vries (1984) and Langton (2000).

In the text, I compare apprentice estimates to the number of teenage males, and the share of teenage males working outside of agriculture. These estimates of sixteen-year-old males outside agriculture are derived from Wrigley's work.[3] For 1500, I assume the same share of the population are sixteen as in 1541—the earliest year for which Wrigley et al. (2018) provide an age structure—and the population was 2.2 million.[4] The structural share estimates are based on the following assumptions. For 1600, 65% of

TABLE A3.3. Private apprenticeships involving premiums in England

	Apprentices paying premiums	
	c. 1710	c. 1790
Urban		
London	1,961	1,019
Towns >10,000	405	865
Towns 5,000–10,000	539	280
Small boroughs	651	742
Urban subtotal	3,556	2,906
Rural subtotal	2,227	3,746
Total	5,783	6,652

the male population is employed in agriculture.[5] For 1500, 1700, and 1800, I use Broadberry et al.'s figures of 68%, 46%, and 36% of males in agriculture.[6] Estimates of the share of non-agricultural workforce outside towns assume that all urban workers are non-agricultural, and define the urban population as the share living in towns with populations over 5,000 per Wrigley (1985, 688).

APPENDIX 4

Guild Ordinances

The discussion of guild rules is based on a sample of ordinances for forty-six guilds from eleven of England's towns and cities outside London, described in table A4.1. The sample for London, which covers a broad cross-section of thirty-one guilds, is described in table A4.2.

TABLE A4.1. Ordinances of provincial guilds used in analysis

Place	Year	Source
BEVERLEY		
Bakers	n.d.	Dennett 1933
Butchers	1596	Dennett 1933
Carpenters	1596	Dennett 1933
Drapers	1596	Dennett 1933
Merchants & Mercers	1596	Dennett 1933
BRISTOL		
Barber Surgeons	1652	Parker 1922
Barbers	1418	Bickley 1900
Cobblers	1346	Bickley 1900
Cordwainers	1408	Bickley 1900
Dyers	c. 1460	Bickley 1900
Glovers	1670	BRO, MS 08018
Hoopers	1439	Bickley 1900
Mercers & Linendrapers	1658	BRO, MS 06157, ff. 40–45
Smiths, Farriers, Cutlers, & Lockyers	1403	BRO, MS 06157
Soapmakers	1603	Matthews 1940
Tailors	1381	BRO, MS 06157
Tylers & Plaisterers	1671	BRO, MS 06157, ff. 66–74
Weavers	1346	Bickley 1900
Weavers	1490	Bickley 1900
CARLISLE		
Butchers	1665	Ferguson and Nanson 1887, 244–46
Butchers	1797	Ferguson and Nanson 1887, 257–60
Glovers	1665	Ferguson and Nanson 1887, 211–18
Merchants	1624/56	Ferguson and Nanson 1887, 94–95
Shoemakers	1595	Ferguson and Nanson 1887, 172–84
Shoemakers	1735	Ferguson and Nanson 1887, 193–97
Tailors	1607	Ferguson and Nanson 1887, 145–50
Weavers	1679	Ferguson and Nanson 1887, 119–20
DEVIZES		
Merchants	1614	Kite 1858, 165–69
EXETER		
Bakers	1438	Toulmin-Smith 1870, 208–10
HULL		
Barber Surgeons & Perukemakers	1714	Lambert 1891, 357–65
Brewers	1558	Lambert 1891, 224–27
Bricklayers, Tilers, Wallers, Plasterers, & Pavers	1599/1665	Lambert 1891, 272-81

TABLE A4.1. *(continued)*

Place	Year	Source
HULL		
Carpenters	1598	Lambert 1891, 258–61
Coopers	1598/1681	Lambert 1891, 290–98
Cordwainers & Shoemakers	1564/1624	Lambert 1891, 315-24
Glovers	1499	Lambert 1891, 215–17
Goldsmiths, Smiths, Pewterers, Plumbers, Glaziers, Painters, Cutlers, Musicians, Stationers, Bookbinders, & Basketmakers	1598	Lambert 1891, 264-68
Joiners	1598	Lambert 1891, 251–56
Merchants	1499	Lambert 1891, 157–59
Shipwrights	1682	Lambert 1891, 341–50
Tailors	1553	Lambert 1891, 236–39
Tailors	1680	Lambert 1891, 240–49
Weavers	1490	Lambert 1891, 204–7
Weavers	1673	Lambert 1891, 208–13
LIVERPOOL		
Tailors	1559	Twemlow 1912, 1:113–19
NEWCASTLE		
Barber Surgeons & Wax & Tallow Chandlers	1671	Tyne & Wear Archives, GU/BS/1
NORWICH		
Worsted Weavers	1511	Hudson and Tingey 1906, 2:376–78
SALISBURY		
Bakers	1675	Haskins 1912, 254–59
Barber Surgeons	1675	Haskins 1912, 364–68
Butchers	1614	Haskins 1912, 254–59
Merchants, Mercers, Grocers, Apothecaries, Goldsmiths, Linendrapers, Milliners, Vintners, Upholsterers, Embroiderers	1675	Haskins 1912, 52–54
Shoemakers	1613	Haskins 1912, 221–25
SHREWSBURY		
Barber Surgeons, Wax Chandlers, Tallow Chandlers, Apothecaries	1662	Leighton 1881,268–75
Weavers	1584	SRO, X6001/16/2/3359 6001/Fiche 1–8
WORCESTER		
Joiners & Carpenters	1692	Toulmin-Smith 1870, 208–10

TABLE A4.2. Ordinances of London guilds used in analysis

Guild	Year	Source
Apothecaries	1617	GL, MS 8205
Armourers & Brasiers	1570, 1709	Glover 2008
Bakers	1507, 1582, 1666, 1746	GL, MS 5197, MS 5197A, MS 5198
Barber Surgeons	1530	Furnivall and Furnivall 1888
Basketmakers	1569	Bobart 1911
Blacksmiths	1641	Hey 2010
Brewers	1482, 1580, 1639, 1714	Ball 1977; GL, MS 5496, MS 5435
Butchers	1607, 1638, 1752	Pearce 1929; GL, MS 6460
Carpenters	1486–87, 1607	Jupp and Pocock 1887; Ainsworth et al. 1913–68, 1: 5–13
Clockmakers	1631/32	GL, MS 3949; Atkins 1931
Clothworkers	1531/32, 1587, 1639	Clothworkers Company 1881
Coopers	1420, 1507, 1561, 1741	Firth 1848; GL, MS 5633A, 5633B
Curriers	1605	Mayer and Adamson 2000, 182; GL MS 6117.
Cutlers	1606	Welch 1919–23, vols. 1–2
Drapers	1418, 1455–56, 1541–60, 1576,	Johnson 1914–22, 1:app. 9, 10, 2: 284–92, 309–24
Farriers	1678	Robson 1949, 34–49
Felt-makers	1669	Weinstein 2004
Founders	1489, 1615	Hibbert 1925, 183–84, 289–90
Framework Knitters	1664, 1745	Mason 2000, 232–33, 234–36
Girdlers	1682	Barker 1957, 89–93
Glass Sellers	1664	Howard 1940, 124–41
Glaziers	1749	Ashdown 1919, 130–46
Glovers	1681	Waggett 2000, 103–8
Gold and Silver Wyre Drawers	1700	Stewart 1891, 67–73
Goldsmiths	1478, 1513, 1729	Reddaway and Walker 1975, 210–74; Prideaux 1896–97, 1:39–40
Grocers	1345, 1525, 1687, 1690, 1711	Kingdon 1886; GL, MS 11639, MS 39801, MS 11640
Horners	1638	Fisher 1936, 100–112
Merchant Taylors	1507,1613, 1662	GL, MS 34005, MS 34006
Stationers	1562, 1678	Blagden 1960; Greg 1928, 395–425
Tylers & Bricklayers	1571	GL, MS 04323, 31–38
Weavers	1577, 1589, 1737	GL, MS 4647, MS 10596

APPENDIX 5

Social Origins of Apprentices in England

The discussion in chapter 4 reports the social origins of apprentices in a range of cities by sector in graphical form. This appendix reports the underlying statistics for each location by half century between 1500 and 1799 in table A5.1.

TABLE A5.1. The status or occupational sector of apprentices' fathers in early modern towns and cities, 1500–1800

City	1500–1549	1550–99	1600–1649	1650–99	1700–1749	1750–99	All
				GENTLEMAN			
Boston				9			9
Bristol	3	6	7	9	8	4	7
Gloucester		6	6	5	5		5
Leicester			2	0	5	0	2
Lincoln						3	3
Liverpool					15		15
London		8	17	17	9	8	13
Norwich		3	9	9	4		7
Oxford	1	3					2
Shrewsbury				22			22
				AGRICULTURAL			
Boston		27			27		
Bristol	34	31	35	28	16	15	25
Gloucester		46	46	35	28		37
Leicester			36	32	21	20	25
Lincoln						34	34
Liverpool					38		38
London		57	52	32	17	10	32
Norwich		39	32	24	20		33
Oxford	55	53					54
Shrewsbury				10			10
				INDUSTRY			
Boston				54			54
Bristol	47	50	46	49	57	60	52
Gloucester		40	43	52	59		51
Leicester			51	56	61	70	61
Lincoln						44	44
Liverpool					35		35
London		31	30	41	53	58	43
Norwich		51	50	57	60		52
Oxford	39	39					39
Shrewsbury				69			69

TABLE A5.1. *(continued)*

City	1500–1549	1550–99	1600–1649	1650–99	1700–1749	1750–99	All
				SERVICES			
Boston				19			19
Bristol	19	18	19	23	26	25	23
Gloucester		15	11	13	13		12
Leicester			13	12	18	10	13
Lincoln						22	22
Liverpool					27		27
London		12	18	27	30	33	26
Norwich		10	18	19	20		16
Oxford	6	8					7
Shrewsbury				22			22
				LABOURER			
Boston				6			6
Bristol	3	2	1	1	2	9	3
Gloucester		2	3	3	6		4
Leicester			10	18	23	13	16
Lincoln						14	14
Liverpool					2		2
London		1	1	2	4	4	2
Norwich		2	2	1	0		2
Oxford	8	5					6
Shrewsbury				1			1

Source: Appendix 1.
Note: The percentage of apprentices in each period whose fathers were identified with this status or occupation is reported; we exclude apprentices whose fathers have no reported occupation.

APPENDIX 6

Apprentice Migration and Family Background

Chapter 4 discusses the relationship between apprentices' social origins and the distances they moved to enter apprenticeships, as part of a consideration of the way mobility and resources intersected. The analysis needs to take into account the confounding effect introduced by characteristics of the town or city to which apprentices migrated. To control this, I used a simple OLS analysis, reporting the results here.

Table A6.1 presents the results that regressing the distance that apprentices had migrated has on their social origins for apprentices from a subset of well-identified and differentiated backgrounds, relative to that of a migrant craftsman's son (identified as having an industrial occupation, except weaving). In each case, it is the apprentice's father's status or occupation that is being observed. The distance between the apprentice's place of origin and their destination is calculated as a straight line.

The analysis includes migrant apprentices training in London, Bristol, Gloucester, Leicester, Lincoln, Liverpool, Norwich, and Oxford between 1500 and 1800. Column 1 reports a simple model without fixed effects. Columns 2 and 3 add destination fixed effects and time fixed effects, respectively. The estimated coefficients remain stable across the three models.

Table A6.2 repeats the exercise using data in the stamp duty for which the apprentice's place of origin is reported (mostly early in the eighteenth century). Because these apprentices were moving to a range of destinations, communities are grouped according to the best available estimates of their population c. 1700 in De Vries (1984) and Langdon (2000). Towns are separated into: (i) communities with no population estimate, usually villages; (ii) small towns with fewer than 5,000 inhabitants; (iii) towns with 5,000–10,000 inhabitants; (iv) towns with 10,000–50,000 inhabitants; and

TABLE A6.1. Regression results: Distance and origin, guild sample

	(1)	(2)	(3)
	Distance	Distance	Distance
Husbandman	23.28***	25.72***	10.79***
	(−0.88)	(−0.83)	(−0.81)
Yeoman	30.18***	28.55***	16.65***
	(−0.62)	(−0.59)	(−0.59)
Tailor	24.67***	21.00***	8.48***
	(−1.15)	(−1.1)	(−1.09)
Clerk	19.32***	15.98***	11.53***
	(−1.11)	(−1.06)	(−1.07)
Weaver	18.65***	21.22***	14.29***
	(−1.55)	(−1.46)	(−1.45)
Gentleman	32.43***	27.57***	22.33***
	(−0.7)	(−0.68)	(−0.68)
Labourer	−23.41***	−20.81***	−13.98***
	(−1.21)	(−1.18)	(−1.15)
Destination F.E.	N	Y	Y
Time F.E.	N	N	Y
Constant	97.71***	33.04***	113.12***
	(−0.39)	(−0.51)	(−13.01)
R-squared	0.03	0.12	0.16
N	151,695	151,695	151,526

Source: Appendix 1.
Note: The table reports the coefficient with the standard error in parentheses. All standard errors are robust.
* $p<0.05$
** $p<0.01$
*** $p<0.001$

(v) towns with over 50,000 inhabitants. It follows the same approach in introducing location and time fixed effects. The coefficients are largely similar to those we observe in the guild sample after controlling for the size of the destination, with higher-status families (gentlemen, yeomen) sending children further and lower-status families (labourers, husbandmen) sending them shorter distances, although there are some differences.

TABLE A6.2. Regression results: Distance and origin, stamp duty sample

	(1)	(2)	(3)
	Distance	Distance	Distance
Husbandman	−11.93***	2.91	2.56
	(2.76)	(2.55)	(2.55)
Yeoman	−1.16	12.22***	11.91***
	(1.89)	(1.78)	(1.78)
Tailor	−4.84	−7.57*	−7.61*
	(3.55)	(3.56)	(3.55)
Clerk	29.27***	30.20***	30.55***
	(3.91)	(3.44)	(3.45)
Weaver	−4.49	−0.85	−0.76
	(4.28)	(4.15)	(4.15)
Gentleman	25.59***	23.22***	23.37***
	(2.11)	(2.02)	(2.02)
Labourer	−13.84***	−5.26*	−5.41*
	(2.80)	(2.62)	(2.60)
Urban population F.E.	N	Y	Y
Year F.E.	N	N	Y
Constant	44.08***	16.92***	500.29**
	(1.05)	(1.40)	(164.06)
R-squared	0.04	0.15	0.15
N	8962	8962	8950

Source: Appendix 1.
Note: The table reports the coefficient with the standard error in parentheses. All standard errors are robust. The reference category is other craft (industry) occupations.
* $p < 0.05$
** $p < 0.01$
*** $p < 0.001$

APPENDIX 7

Reconstructing the Training Careers of Masters

In order to analyse masters' careers as trainers of apprentices, I constructed samples of masters whose contracts with their apprentices were recorded in city and guild records from London, Bristol, Gloucester, and Boston. The basic principle for each of the samples was the same.

For London, I started by constructing a list of freemen based on existing printed or digital sources. This allowed the pool of individuals who were able to take and register apprentices in those guilds to be identified (individuals who were not guild members are excluded by definition). The pool was then limited to individuals whose names were unique in the forty years before and after they became freemen. To avoid missing variant spellings, names were converted into phonetic codes using Gill Newton's Double Metaphone algorithm and the initials of their surnames before identifying duplicates. This avoided having multiple masters in the dataset who were potentially actively recruiting apprentices in the same period. Removing freemen whose names were duplicated left a list of uniquely named freemen active in a well-defined period.

I next constructed a sample of apprenticeships recorded in each guild. The apprenticeship series was restricted to begin before the start date of the freedom sample, to avoid missing the start of a master's training career. It also ran for at least forty years after the last recorded freedom, to avoid censoring apprentices taken late in the master's career. Naturally, only apprenticeships for which the master's name was fully recorded were linkable.

The masters for all apprenticeships were collated into a single list with the date of each apprenticeship. This included masters who received apprentices by turnover for guilds in the London roll dataset, but for other series it is restricted to masters who took the apprentices at the start of their indentures.

I then ran a cartesian match between the pool of masters who had taken apprentices and the list of uniquely named freemen who had been freed into the guild in the previous forty years. This created a list of apprenticeships with masters who were connected to single freemen; this provides the set of freemen acting as masters, as those apprenticeships were now all connected to unique individuals. It also identifies the set of freemen who did not take apprentices.

To account for freemen with long careers, I searched the set of unlinked apprentices for those who could be associated with unique freemen up to fifty-five years after their entry to the freedom, extending the span of possible careers by an additional fifteen years.

Relying on algorithms and phonetic matches to construct links in this way introduces some risks of both false positives and false negatives. There were a handful of exceptions where the manual linkages made by individual researchers who had explored company records in detail could be used. This gave larger, robust samples from the Stationers, Clockmakers, Apothecaries, and Pewterers guilds in London. In order to strengthen the quality of the sample, I selected a subsample of masters with forenames that were common and usually consistently spelled, but not so ubiquitous that they were often part of duplicates: James (3.2% of masters), Henry (3.2%), and Edward (3.7%) were used in London. By selecting on forenames, I ensured that most of the masters had distinct names. I then manually reviewed all apprentices taken by masters with these names to check the clusters linked to individuals. This reduced false negatives and false positives.

The information on who could take apprentices is for the freemen in a group of London guilds. Freemen were full members of the guild who were qualified to take apprentices and register them with the guild. Their apprentices could, in time, join the guild if they wished. Table A7.1 reports the full size of the sample of apprenticeships and freemen for the guilds in the dataset included in the linkage process.

The linkage process shrinks the sample substantially by removing potential duplicates. The linkage method means that freemen fall into three groups: those who cannot be identified in the list of masters who took apprentices; those who are identified securely as masters recruiting apprentices; and those whose name is shared (in its phonetic form) with one or more other freeman who could have been active during the same time, making it impossible to distinguish their careers reliably.

TABLE A7.1. Apprentices and freemen in London sample

	Apprentice sample (N)	Freemen sample (N)	Start year	End year
Apothecaries	2,637	1,199	1618	1679
Bowyers	305	259	1724	1833
Clothworkers	30,916	15,626	1607	1856
Drapers	17,520	8,957	1506	1859
Founders	1,271	1,110	1744	1859
Girdlers	2,230	1,547	1655	1859
Goldsmiths	4,283	2,222	1616	1667
Mercers	5,331	3,598	1408	1849
Merchant Taylors	56,829	22,258	1584	1708
Musicians	1,529	1,912	1731	1836
Pewterers	4,970	792	1573	1788
Salters	1,814	1,264	1714	1859
Tallow Chandlers	2,323	1,462	1710	1826
Total	131,958	62,206	1408	1859

Note: The sample of Mercers is interrupted between 1489 and 1619, and Drapers between 1520 and 1604.

TABLE A7.2. Freemen masters, final sample, London

Guild	1400–1499	1500–1599	1600–1699	1700–1799	1800–1899	All
Apothecaries	0	0	140	0	0	140
Clockmakers	0	0	607	882	181	1,670
Clothworkers	0	0	949	589	250	1,788
Drapers	0	21	526	274	244	1,065
Girdlers	0	0	0	84	89	173
Goldsmiths	0	0	230	0	0	230
Mercers	53	0	163	87	38	341
Merchant Taylors	0	96	2,006	64	0	2,166
Pewterers	0	125	2,856	2,125	85	5,191
Stationers	0	647	3,687	3,376	0	7,710
Tallow Chandlers	0	0	0	125	39	164
Total	53	889	11,164	7,606	926	20,638

Note: The table reports the number of individual freemen identified taking apprentices or not training, by guild and century of entry to the freedom. In the chapter, the analysis is restricted more strictly by period.

Bristol

For Bristol, more finely grained information about masters exists, because the record gives both the master's occupation and their wife's forename. I therefore began by grouping apprentices by master based on phonetic coding of the master's surname and forename using Gill Newton's Double Metaphone system. Matches were constrained such that masters had the same initial letters of their surnames and the apprentices were taken within a forty-year window.

Potential clusters were then cleaned manually in two waves. In the first, clusters associated with masters who had one of four common but not ubiquitous forenames (James, Edward, Henry, and George) were examined manually, as in London. In the second, clusters associated with masters whose names (in phonetic form) appeared only once in the city's burgess records were examined manually. The final sample includes 8,242 apprentices linked to a unique master, of whom 5,987 were with one of 1,967 masters whose record of entry as a burgess was identifiable. Although the records span the eighteenth to twentieth centuries, 69% of apprentices were with a master who took their first apprentice in the eighteenth century.

In order to securely identify a pool of masters/burgesses who did not take apprentices, I manually rechecked all masters named James, Edward, Henry, and George with surnames beginning with *A* or *B* who had not been identified with a burgess against the list of burgesses to identify any possible matches. On the strong assumption that the burgess and apprentice record is complete, this gives a sample of 587 burgesses with no apprentices.

Boston

Numbers of apprenticeships in Boston are sufficiently low that I relied on manual linkage throughout. I used the calendar of Boston's apprenticeship and freedom records from 1663 to 1903 produced by the Lincolnshire Family History Society. Apprentices were grouped to masters by matching text strings containing their surnames and forenames, and then checked manually to ensure coherence between occupations and that bindings fall within a forty-year window. Masters were then matched to the records of new freemen (n = 3,245), based on surname and forename. Matches were restricted to masters whose first apprentice was recorded within thirty years of the freedom entry. Duplicates were manually differentiated where possible, based on occupation, and excluded otherwise.

The final sample contains 2,902 apprentices, of whom 2,029 (70%) were bound to a master who was strongly identified as taking a cluster of apprentices, 427 were linked to a master with whom the link between masters was potentially complicated by a potential duplicate or similar, and 446 were bound to a master who could not be confidently identified (usually because multiple masters in different occupations shared a name, or because multiple freemen shared that name). For 1,789 apprentices bound to 472 masters, I securely identified the masters' freedom entry based on name, date, and occupation. Between 1700 and 1800, 377 of the 1,398 new freemen took apprentices. I therefore have a substantial pool of freemen who are known not to have trained, and only a limited share are likely to be because of false negatives due to matching errors.

Gloucester

I used the calendar of Gloucester apprentices produced by Jill Barlow, who kindly shared this in the form of a database. Apprentices were grouped to masters by matching text strings containing the master's surname and the initial three letters of the surname across apprenticeships. As with Boston, clusters were then checked manually to ensure that masters' occupations matched across all apprentices in the group and that the chronological spread of training across the apprentices was no greater than forty years.

Masters with surnames beginning with letters *A–C* were then matched by hand to Ripley and Jurica's (1991) record of Gloucester citizens to allow cases to be identified in which more than one master with a similar name had been freed in the period before or during which the master trained; any potential duplicates were then excluded. The final sample of apprentices linked to masters who were identifiable contained 1,417 apprentices bound to 456 unique masters between 1595 and 1830.

APPENDIX 8

Identifying Apprentices as Freemen

The analysis in chapter 8 relies on accurate identification of apprentices who achieved corporate 'success' by becoming freemen of London or citizens of provincial cities. Fortunately, linkages between apprentices and freemen have been made by hand by earlier researchers for several London guilds, or existed in the original records. Where this information exists, I utilized it.[1] However, because guild and city records rarely integrated this information into a single record, in other cases this required linking series of apprenticeships with separate registers of freemen or citizens.

The linkage was organized as follows: I only match individuals for whom their forename, surname, and year of indenture (in the apprentice list) and year of freedom (in freedom, citizen lists) survives; and I exclude individuals with names that appear twice in either the apprentice or freedom record, because of uncertainty about whether these are duplicate entries (which sometimes feature in these records) or two individuals with the same name.

The matching process operates within the set of each city or guild's records. A cartesian match is made between the phonetically coded forenames and surnames of all apprentices and all freemen in a specific city or guild's records. Unique one-to-one matches are retained. I also keep the best match of a set of one-to-many matches based on proximity of the name (measured by string distance); the presence of a match on the master's name in the apprentice and freedom record where it was given in both; the freeman's method of entry to freedom (preferring those who enter through servitude); and the time that had elapsed between the date of their indenturing as an apprentice and their entry to the freedom.

Matches are limited to individuals who became freemen or citizens between 4 and 39 years (inclusive) after the year of their indenture. Links from apprentices to freemen entering by patrimony are restricted to apprentices whose fathers were reported as being citizens (and so meet that qualification).

This linkage approach is deliberately cautious. For the London sample, most (85%) linked individuals are unique in both apprentice and freeman/citizen lists, and so are one-to-one linkages. The majority match exactly on surname and forename (87%). In addition, 67% have information on the apprentice's master in both indenture and freedom record. In the provincial sample, 84% match exactly on name and forename. Variation in string distance between names is limited to allow at most two different characters between the spellings, and this is restricted to matches with either (i) supporting information on the master's name in both apprentice and freedom records and/or (ii) a gap of less than eight years between the freedom and the time when a former apprentice would qualify for admission (set at seven years after registration).

The linkage procedure gives positive results only for apprentices who become freemen/citizens. To understand how common this was, we need to identify the pool of apprentices who did *not* become freemen/citizens. These are individuals who could have been linked with confidence, if they had become freemen/citizens. This required defining a pool of apprentices whose names were unique in the period in which information on freedoms exists. I defined uniqueness by coding names into phonetic versions, to address variance in spellings. I excluded apprentices whose names matched another apprentice bound in the fifty years before or after the year they were indentured. I then identified which were linked to freedom entries and which were not, producing the sample.

Errors will no doubt exist in the linkage. Some will be due to problems in the original manuscript records: apprentices or freemen who are missed out of the register and those whose names are written differently in their two entries are the obvious issues. The linkage itself is, no doubt, imperfect. The method is designed to avoid false positives, and will generate false negatives because of a lack of certainty about which person became a freeman when there are M:1 matches. I expect estimates to be attenuated by this.

A subset of the sample of apprentices who became freemen were linked to additional information about the masters who trained them for a number of London guilds and three out of four provincial cities. For this subsample, information was obtained on contextual factors that may have influenced their futures, such as the number of apprentices their masters trained over their careers, any guild offices taken by their masters (for masters in some London guilds), and the way their masters qualified for the freedom. The size of the sample was limited because linkage was limited to the manually checked sample of apprentice-master links to reduce the addition of errors into the dataset at this stage. The number of observations in this subsample is given in the column 'Master data' in tables A8.1 and A8.2.

TABLE A8.1. London apprentices with information on entry to freedom

Guild	Freedom data N	Master data N	Start date	End date
MANUAL LINKAGE				
Apothecaries	1,227	154	1612	1680
Butchers	1,466	0	1740	1780
Clockmakers	6,280	1,438	1640	1888
Curriers	2,314	0	1653	1800
Mercers	172	7	1395	1860
Merchant Taylors	63,100	3,963	1533	1780
Stationers	14,501	12,791	1552	1846
Upholders	1,186	0	1699	1764
Watermen	30,538	0	1582	1780
Wyre Drawers	451	0	1688	1726
Subtotal	121,235	18,353	1740	1888
LINKAGE BY ALGORITHM				
Apothecaries	962	79	1612	1680
Bowyers	170	0	1719	1860
Clothworkers	15,042	1,177	1540	1869
Drapers	11,091	760	1470	1860
Founders	571	0	1739	1946
Girdlers	918	100	1689	1860
Goldsmiths	3,294	227	1595	1659
Mercers	2,935	245	1395	1860
Musicians	983	0	1738	1860
Pewterers	2,815	0	1636	1759
Salters	1,036	0	1712	1861
Tallow Chandlers	3,366	141	1659	1860
Subtotal	43,183	2,729	1739	1946
Total	164,418	21,082	1395	1946

Note: Some guilds (Apothecaries and Mercers) include periods of manual and periods of algorithmic linkage, and so appear in both panels of the table.

TABLE A8.2. Provincial apprentices with information on entry to freedom/citizenship

City	Freedom data	Master data	Start date	End date
Boston	2,866	1,073	1663	1891
Bristol	21,822	5,317	1533	1899
Gloucester	1,064	212	1639	1788
Lincoln	2,826	0	1661	1866
Total	28,578	6,602	1533	1899

The sample of apprentices becoming freemen outside London is constructed in a similar fashion.

The Likelihood of Becoming a Freeman

Chapter 8 discusses the characteristics that are associated with an apprentice being more likely to become a freeman or citizen. The analysis is based on the sample of apprentices described above.

It utilizes a set of variables derived from each apprentice's indenture records, which generally contain information on their family of origin, revealing whether they were a migrant to London (defined here as having a father living outside Middlesex or those parts of Surrey that were described by contemporaries as being in London), whether their father was a citizen of London, and whether their father had died by the time they were indentured.

The indenture also provides information on the apprentice's father's occupation or status. This was coded using the CAMPOP PST system and grouped into clusters for gentlemen, yeomen, other agricultural workers, craftsmen, distribution and sales, services, professions, and labourers. In addition, potential family links between apprentices and their masters were identified based on either stated connections, as when the master is explicitly recorded as the father, or implied connections, when the apprentice and master have the same surname. Because of apparent under-reporting of explicit kin ties, I rely on the 'same surname' variable in the main analysis.

For the subsample including other information on the master's career, variables capture the master's own method of entry to freedom, whether by servitude, patrimony (inheritance), or redemption (purchase). For three guilds in London, information survives on roles they took within their guild, such as warden, assistant, and master of the guild. These are captured in a single variable, office-holding. Information on whether masters entered their guilds' liveries exists for a smaller group and is less consistent (some office-holders are not recorded as liverymen, which is unlikely given the sequence of advancement in guilds in this period). I therefore rely on company office-holding in the main analysis and report this as an alternative specification here. For some provincial masters, information survives on their occupation or trade, not their guild. The analysis of masters' occupations is approached in two ways. The first matches the categories used to examine apprentice persistence, defined around Bristol and first deployed in Minns and Wallis (2012). The second is defined to reflect the main clusters of work across the provincial towns.

Finally, the dataset includes information on the total number of apprentices taken by masters. This is grouped into four categories rather than included as a continuous variable, because of the asymptotic structure of the data. In the London sample of masters, 27% trained a single apprentice, 40% trained two to four apprentices, 24% trained five to nine apprentices, and 9% trained ten or more. In the sample of apprentices, 8% trained with a master who took just them, 27% were with a master who trained two to four, 35% with one who trained five to nine, and 29% with one who trained ten or more. The figures were similar for provincial cities. Clustering is particularly important given the presence of outliers, such as the Bristol shipbuilder James Martin Hilhouse, who registered 258 apprentices in the late eighteenth century to work in his expanding dockyard where large numbers of naval ships were constructed during the Napoleonic Wars.

The summary statistics for the sample are set out in tables A8.3 and A8.4.

The basic model is a probit model

$$y_i = \beta_0 + \beta_1 X_i + \beta_2 G_i + \beta_3 T_t + \epsilon,$$

where y is a binary variable which equals 1 if an apprentice became a freeman, X is the set of explanatory variables, G is guild or city dummies, and T is period dummies for each half century. The analysis is limited to the period 1500–1800, where evidence is most abundant. This largely avoids the impact of periods where the dataset is dominated by a single guild or influenced by the development of firms.

The results of the analysis for London are set out in table A8.5. In the main text I concentrate on model 10, which has the richest set of results. The full set of models is presented here to give the reader confidence about the robustness of the analysis.

The first set of models (1–4) examine the largest sample, for which information survives only on the apprentice, not the master's career. Models 5–10

A8.3. Summary statistics, London sample

Variable	N	Mean	S.D.	Min	Max
Apprentice freed	164,418	0.31	0.46	0	1
Gender	128,184	0.01	0.10	0	1
Migrant	164,418	0.46	0.50	0	1
Parent characteristics					
Parent deceased	131,756	0.25	0.43	0	1
Parent citizen	107,908	0.14	0.34	0	1
Non-migrant citizen	164,418	0.09	0.28	0	1
Non-migrant non-citizen	164,418	0.13	0.33	0	1
Gentleman	105,292	0.16	0.37	0	1
Yeoman	105,292	0.24	0.42	0	1
Agriculture, other	105,292	0.07	0.26	0	1
Craft	105,292	0.31	0.46	0	1
Distribution, sales	105,292	0.12	0.32	0	1
Services	105,292	0.05	0.22	0	1
Professional	105,292	0.05	0.21	0	1
Labourer	105,292	0.01	0.11	0	1
Master characteristics					
Master name match	163,950	0.08	0.28	0	1
Master kin tie	164,418	0.01	0.11	0	1
Apprentices trained	21,093	7.93	6.59	1	50
Years since master freed	21,055	13.52	10.66	0	50
Free by servitude	20,097	0.84	0.37	0	1
Free by patrimony	20,097	0.11	0.31	0	1
Free by redemption	20,097	0.05	0.22	0	1
Liveryman	11,690	0.36	0.48	0	1
Assistant	11,690	0.19	0.39	0	1
Guild master	14,384	0.13	0.34	0	1
Guild office	14,384	0.37	0.48	0	1

TABLE A8.4. Summary statistics, provincial sample

	N	Mean	S.D.	Min	Max
Apprentice freed	28,578	0.44	0.5	0	1
Gender	27,606	0.00	0.02	0	1
Migrant	28,578	0.29	0.45	0	1
Parent characteristics					
Parent deceased	25,752	0.27	0.44	0	1
Gentleman	28,578	0.04	0.19	0	1
Yeoman	28,578	0.07	0.26	0	1
Agriculture, other	28,578	0.03	0.16	0	1
Craft	28,578	0.40	0.49	0	1
Distribution, sales	28,578	0.06	0.23	0	1
Services	28,578	0.08	0.27	0	1
Professional	28,578	0.04	0.20	0	1
Labourer	28,578	0.07	0.25	0	1
Master characteristics					
Master name match	28,518	0.10	0.30	0	1
Master kin tie	28,578	0.06	0.23	0	1
Apprentices trained	10,123	13.19	37.78	1	245
Years since master freed	6,784	14.01	10.48	−1	50
Free by servitude	6,602	0.60	0.49	0	1
Free by patrimony	6,602	0.15	0.35	0	1
Free by redemption	6,602	0.12	0.32	0	1
Master occupation match	20,873	0.17	0.37	0	1
Master occupation					
Barber Surgeon	28,578	0.01	0.11	0	1
Joiner	28,578	0.02	0.15	0	1
House Carpenter	28,578	0.02	0.13	0	1
Baker	28,578	0.03	0.16	0	1
Cooper	28,578	0.02	0.16	0	1
Grocer	28,578	0.02	0.13	0	1
Merchant	28,578	0.06	0.23	0	1
Weaver	28,578	0.01	0.08	0	1
Seaman	28,578	0.02	0.12	0	1
Observations	28,578				

TABLE A8.5. Entry to the freedom, London

	1	2	3	4	5	6	7	8	9	10
Gender	–0.323**	–0.324**	–0.323**							
	(–0.022)	(–0.022)	(–0.022)							
Migrant	0.024**		0.025**	0.025**	0.035**	0.034**	0.033**	0.031*	0.035**	0.033**
	(–0.004)		(–0.004)	(–0.004)	(–0.01)	(–0.01)	(–0.01)	(–0.013)	(–0.012)	(–0.012)
Parent deceased	–0.014**	–0.016**	–0.014**	–0.016**	–0.011	–0.012	–0.013	–0.012	–0.009	–0.01*
	(–0.003)	(–0.003)	(–0.003)	(–0.003)	(–0.008)	(–0.009)	(–0.009)	(–0.012)	(–0.01)	(–0.011)
Parent citizen of London	0.014*		0.016**	0.023**	0.03*	0.026	0.029	0.04*	0.04*	0.039*
	(–0.006)		(–0.006)	(–0.006)	(–0.015)	(–0.015)	(–0.015)	(–0.019)	(–0.017)	(–0.018)
Parent gentleman	–0.014**	–0.014**	0.106	–0.016**	–0.039**	–0.04**	–0.039**	–0.064**	–0.061**	–0.059**
	(–0.005)	(–0.005)	(–0.074)	(–0.005)	(–0.013)	(–0.013)	(–0.013)	(–0.017)	(–0.015)	(–0.016)
Parent yeoman	0.015**	0.017**	0.136	0.015**	0.009	0.011	0.014	0.003	0.004	0.005
	(–0.004)	(–0.004)	(–0.074)	(–0.004)	(–0.013)	(–0.013)	(–0.013)	(–0.019)	(–0.017)	(–0.018)
Parent other agriculture	0.001	0.002	0.121	0.002	–0.011	–0.011	–0.008	–0.007	–0.011	–0.007
	(–0.006)	(–0.006)	(–0.074)	(–0.006)	(–0.017)	(–0.017)	(–0.018)	(–0.024)	(–0.022)	(–0.023)
Parent distribution and sale	–0.008	–0.005	0.115	–0.012*	0	–0.002	0	–0.012	–0.001	0.002
	(–0.005)	(–0.005)	(–0.074)	(–0.005)	(–0.012)	(–0.012)	(–0.013)	(–0.016)	(–0.014)	(–0.015)
Parent service	–0.028**	–0.03**	0.091	–0.03**	–0.052**	–0.054**	–0.051**	–0.058**	–0.055**	–0.051
	(–0.007)	(–0.007)	(–0.074)	(–0.007)	(–0.017)	(–0.017)	(–0.017)	(–0.022)	(–0.02)	(–0.02)
Parent other professional	0.014*	0.015*	0.133	0.011	0.001	0	–0.007	–0.01	–0.01	–0.018
	(–0.007)	(–0.007)	(–0.074)	(–0.007)	(–0.016)	(–0.016)	(–0.017)	(–0.021)	(–0.018)	(–0.019)
Parent labourer	–0.029*	–0.032*	0.089	–0.03*	–0.026	–0.027	–0.028	–0.028	–0.035	–0.033*
	(–0.013)	(–0.013)	(–0.075)	(–0.014)	(–0.038)	(–0.038)	(–0.038)	(–0.048)	(–0.044)	(–0.044)
Same name as master	0.064**			0.063**	0.118**	0.108**	0.104**	0.128**	0.118**	0.121**
	(–0.006)			(–0.006)	(–0.017)	(–0.017)	(–0.017)	(–0.023)	(–0.021)	(–0.022)
Master Great Twelve company	0.097**	0.1**	0.1**	–0.016	–0.117**	–0.111**	–0.056	–0.32**	–0.316**	–0.321**
	(–0.024)	(–0.024)	(–0.024)	(–0.012)	(–0.039)	(–0.04)	(–0.046)	(–0.066)	(–0.065)	(–0.066)
Parent citizen Londoner		0.002								
		(–0.005)								
Parent non-citizen Londoner		–0.023**								
		(–0.004)								

Kin tie to master			0.094**							
			(−0.012)							
2–4 apps.					0.046**					0.061
					(−0.015)					(−0.019)
5–9 apps.					0.074**					0.075
					(−0.015)					(−0.019)
10+ apps					0.09**					0.09
					(−0.015)					(−0.019)
10–19 yrs						0.021*				
						(−0.009)				
20–29 yrs						0.04**				
						(−0.011)				
30–39 yrs						0.017				
						(−0.015)				
40+ yrs						0.101**				
						(−0.026)				
Master, free by pat.							0.025*			0.042
							(−0.012)			(−0.014)
Master, free by red.							0.023			0.026
							(−0.017)			(−0.022)
Master was liveryman								0.103**		
								(−0.011)		
Master held guild office									0.085**	0.077
									(−0.01)	(−0.01)
Time F.E.	Y	Y	Y	Y	Y	Y	Y	Y	Y	Y
Guild F.E.	Y	Y	Y	Y	Y	Y	Y	Y	Y	Y
N	102612	102717	102717	104098	17215	17177	16449	9419	11865	11175

Note: The table reports marginal effects estimated at means with standard errors reported in parentheses.

* $p < .05$

** $p < .01$

*** $p < 0.001$

TABLE A.8.6. Entry to the freedom, provincial

	1	2	3	4	5	6	7	8	9
Gender	−0.262	−0.273*	0.036	−0.033	−0.039		−0.009		−0.013
	(−0.164)	(−0.164)	(−0.224)	(−0.293)	(−0.292)		(−0.286)		(−0.287)
Migrant	−0.018**	−0.017**	−0.019	−0.02	−0.02	−0.012	−0.017	−0.018	−0.02
	(−0.008)	(−0.008)	(−0.014)	(−0.017)	(−0.017)	(−0.009)	(−0.017)	(−0.016)	(−0.017)
Parent deceased	−0.026***	−0.026***	−0.014	−0.005	−0.003	−0.027***	−0.001	−0.007	0
	(−0.007)	(−0.007)	(−0.013)	(−0.015)	(−0.015)	(−0.008)	(−0.015)	(−0.015)	(−0.016)
Parent gentleman	−0.011	−0.011	−0.041	−0.045	−0.045	−0.018	−0.032	−0.044	−0.038
	(−0.017)	(−0.017)	(−0.028)	(−0.032)	(−0.032)	(−0.019)	(−0.033)	(−0.031)	(−0.032)
Parent yeoman	0.023*	0.021*	0.009	−0.015	−0.017	0.026*	−0.013	−0.012	−0.015
	(−0.013)	(−0.013)	(−0.023)	(−0.027)	(−0.027)	(−0.014)	(−0.027)	(−0.027)	(−0.027)
Parent other agriculture	−0.031	−0.033	−0.083**	−0.089*	−0.089*	−0.02	−0.097*	−0.083	−0.098*
	(−0.022)	(−0.022)	(−0.04)	(−0.052)	(−0.052)	(−0.024)	(−0.053)	(−0.052)	(−0.052)
Parent distribution and sale	0.022	0.024*	−0.003	0.012	0.012	0.03**	0.022	0.012	0.018
	(−0.013)	(−0.013)	(−0.023)	(−0.027)	(−0.027)	(−0.015)	(−0.028)	(−0.026)	(−0.027)
Parent service	−0.016	−0.019	−0.014	0.002	−0.001	−0.011	0.008	0.002	0.004
	(−0.012)	(−0.012)	(−0.02)	(−0.024)	(−0.024)	(−0.013)	(−0.025)	(−0.024)	(−0.024)
Parent other professional	−0.027*	−0.029*	−0.027	0.003	0.002	−0.023	0.019	−0.006	0.008
	(−0.016)	(−0.016)	(−0.026)	(−0.031)	(−0.031)	(−0.017)	(−0.032)	(−0.03)	(−0.031)
Parent labourer	0.005	0.002	−0.002	0.011	0.008	0.003	0.004	0.001	0.002
	(−0.013)	(−0.013)	(−0.022)	(−0.027)	(−0.027)	(−0.014)	(−0.027)	(−0.027)	(−0.027)
Same name as master	0.119***		0.088***	0.063***	0.054**	0.084***	0.061***	0.059***	
	(−0.011)		(−0.017)	(−0.021)	(−0.021)	(−0.015)	(−0.022)	(−0.021)	
Kin tie to master		0.12***							0.068**
		(−0.014)							(−0.03)

2–4 apps	0.062***				0.038**	0.046**	0.038**
	(−0.015)				(−0.019)	(−0.019)	(−0.019)
5–9 apps	0.1***				0.053**	0.061***	0.054***
	(−0.016)				(−0.021)	(−0.02)	(−0.021)
10+ apps	0.072***				0.061***	0.071***	0.06***
	(−0.017)				(−0.022)	(−0.021)	(−0.022)
10–19 yrs		−0.028*					
		(−0.015)					
20–29 yrs		−0.03*					
		(−0.017)					
30–39 yrs		−0.024					
		(−0.026)					
40+ yrs		−0.039					
		(−0.046)					
Master, free by pat.			−0.059***		−0.044**	−0.049***	−0.049**
			(−0.019)		(−0.02)	(−0.019)	(−0.019)
Master, free by red.			−0.015		0.001	−0.013	−0.006
			(−0.021)		(−0.021)	(−0.02)	(−0.021)
Master, free by mar.			−0.009		0.014	−0.006	0.012
			(−0.019)		(−0.02)	(−0.019)	(−0.019)
Master, same occupation as parent				0.017			
				(−0.012)			
Shoemaker				−0.001	−0.002		
				(−0.019)	(−0.031)		
Shipbuilder				−0.043***	−0.03		
				(−0.014)	(−0.03)		

(*continued*)

TABLE A.8.6. (*continued*)

	1	2	3	4	5	6	7	8	9
Carpenter						0.014	0.035		
						(–0.015)	(–0.028)		
Merchant						–0.079***	–0.016		
						(–0.019)	(–0.031)		
Leather						0.011	–0.033		
						(–0.021)	(–0.038)		
Baker						–0.01	–0.001		
						(–0.024)	(–0.043)		
Cooper						0.026	0.025		
						(–0.016)	(–0.032)		
Tailor						–0.042	–0.023		
						(–0.027)	(–0.043)		
Joiner						–0.003	0.062*		
						(–0.023)	(–0.037)		
Barber						–0.037	–0.043		
						(–0.023)	(–0.039)		
Surgeon						–0.028	–0.074		
						(–0.029)	(–0.047)		
Dist./Sales						0.013	–0.029		
						(–0.013)	(–0.022)		
Service						–0.24***	–0.265***		
						(–0.029)	(–0.048)		
Prof.						–0.123***	–0.11**		
						(–0.026)	(–0.045)		

Other						–0.2*	0.092		
						(–0.108)	(–0.139)		
Barber Surgeon									–0.063
									(–0.054)
Joiner									0.07
									(–0.046)
House Carpenter									0.118**
									(–0.048)
Baker									–0.003
									(–0.048)
Cooper									0.071*
									(–0.037)
Grocer									–0.066
									(–0.049)
Merchant									–0.029
									(–0.026)
Weaver									–0.021
									(–0.115)
Mariner									–0.241***
									(–0.048)
Number of observations	24,780	24,800	9,666	6,500	6,341	19,251	6,341	6,596	6,341

Note: The table reports marginal effects estimated at means with standard errors reported in parentheses.

* $p < 0.05$

** $p < 0.01$

*** $p < 0.001$

examine the effect of adding information on the master's career. The main results are highly consistent across all the models. The parent occupation variables gain or lose significance in some models, but with the exception of the 'other agriculture' group, they retain the same sign.

To evaluate our variable choice, in model 2, when the data is split between locals who are sons of citizens and those who are not, it is clear that immigrants and sons of citizens were not significantly different; it was local non-citizens who faced poorer odds. Model 3 shows that the effect of family links between masters and apprentices is the same if the alternative measure of an explicitly stated kin tie is used.

This larger sample allows gender to be considered (the share of female apprentices is too small to discuss in the subsample). Female apprentices were more than 30% less likely to become freemen than male apprentices. This result is consistent with the literature.

The second set of models examines the smaller but richer subsample for which evidence on masters' careers exists. Model 5 examines the effect of the master's career stage, measured in decades since they were freed. Model 6 uses my preferred measure, apprentice recruitment. Model 7 examines the impact of the master's mode of entry to freedom. Model 8 explores the less consistently reported measure of guild success, entry to the livery, and model 9 presents guild office-holding on its own. Model 10 incorporates the preferred measures into a full model and is presented visually in chapter 8.

The results for provincial centres are set out in table A8.6.

To match the discussion of London, I present the fullest equivalent model (model 8) in the main text. The series of models we present here offer an indication of the robustness of the results and areas where additional data exists.

The first model concentrates solely on the apprentices' family origins. The key difference to London is that migrants are significantly less likely to become freemen than locals. Note that the provincial data does not distinguish between local citizens and local non-citizens, however. Model 2 shows that using the alternative measure of reported kin ties produces consistent results. Models 3 and 4 incorporate measures of masters' success. While apprentice training has strong positive effects, longevity is much weaker and has opposed effects. Entry by patrimony is associated with a lower probability of entry to the freedom, again in contrast to London. Models 6, 7, and 9 examine the relationship if master occupations are included. As can be seen, these have strong associations, as we discuss in the main text, with mobile occupations such as mariners seeing lower rates of entry than occupations where cities offered strong local-market opportunities.

NOTES

Chapter 1. Introduction

1. Brown 1972, 105. Note that contractions in original manuscripts are silently expanded and spellings modernised in this and subsequent quotations.

2. Coy 1989; Thelen 2004.

3. These ideas permeate many works. The set I summarise here are drawn from Lane 1996, 1–2.

4. The quote here is from a British politician, John Hayes MP, '"The craft so long to lerne": Skills and Their Place in Modern Britain', oral statement to Parliament, Royal Society of Arts, 26 October 2010.

5. In treating apprenticeship as a market, I follow important work by Hamilton 1996; Justman and van der Beek 2015.

6. The limited role of human capital before industrialisation is central to Galor's theory (Galor 2011).

7. The seminal work for England was Mitch 1993. Note that Kunnas's estimates suggest human capital was already a high share of wealth in 1770 (Kunnas 2016, 233).

8. The categories I use here draw on Mokyr 2002; Polanyi 1966.

9. Autor et al. 2020; Katz 2007. The original metaphor is Tinbergen's, as they note.

10. Marshall 1890, bk. 4, chap. 12. Marx noted a similar diminution of skill, and with it, apprenticeship (Marx 1906, chap. 17, sec. 3, para. 54). Direct observation of this process is rare, but see Atack et al. 2019.

11. For evidence of the latter, see Franck and Galor 2022; Goldin and Katz 1998, 2008. Differential changes in human capital are identified in de Pleijt and Weisdorf 2017; de Pleijt et al. 2020. Earlier evidence is surveyed in Acemoglu 2002. Note that if capital is complementary to skill, wage differentials need not fall.

12. Cummins 2020; Clark 2007.

13. Galor and Weil 1999; Galor 2011.

14. It is worth noting that apprenticeship also delayed marriage for men (and some women) and constrained fertility, forming one of the ingredients of the European marriage pattern (EMP). Rightly, work on the EMP mainly focuses on late female marriage, but the pool of available husbands also affects fertility via nuptiality and the share of never marrieds.

15. For a classic statement, see Goody 1989, 243–44.

16. Interestingly, the loss of opportunity due to a decline in apprenticeship was a central concern of the earliest economic histories of apprenticeship (Dunlop and Denman 1912; Tawney 1909).

17. North et al. 2009, 114.

18. Acemoglu and Robinson 2019, 142–46.

19. Smith 1776, bk. 1, chap. 13, pt. 2.

20. Smith 1776, bk. 1, chap. 13, pt. 2. For recent analyses that follow Smith, see Ogilvie 2004, 2019; Earle 1989, 85; Swanson 1989, 115–16.

21. For a useful review, see Bills 2003.

22. The background and particularly the role of labour market studies is well described in Teixeira 2014.

23. Becker 1962, 13.

24. These issues are excellently outlined in Mokyr 2020, 25.

25. Important contributions focusing on training in imperfect labour markets include Acemoglu and Pischke 1999; Stevens 1994. For a useful survey, see Smits and Stromback 2000.

26. See, for major contributions, Soskice and Hall 2001; Thelen 2004; Streeck 2011.

27. Important analyses include Epstein 1998, 2008; Humphries 2003; de la Croix et al. 2018. A related debate on enforcement in North America is critically reviewed in Hamilton 1995.

28. The most important voice in challenging Epstein has been Ogilvie, in a series of important works: Ogilvie 2004, 2008, 2007, 2019.

29. For some key statements, see de la Croix et al. 2018; Kelly et al. 2014; Mokyr 2009.

30. Burn 1831, 174–75.

31. Bentham 1823, chap. 16, sec. 3–4, n. 77.

32. The form of the earliest surviving contracts is discussed in Epstein 1991, 73–79.

33. The distinction is clear with farm servants and indentured colonial servitude. See Kussmaul 1981; Whittle 2017; Wareing 2017.

34. Dunlop and Denman 1912, 55. For an alternative interpretation of premiums as gifts, see Ben-Amos 2008, 288–89.

35. Unlike for other servants, embezzlement by apprentices was not a felony under 21 Hen 8.

36. The premium was taxed from 1709 onwards—and from that point, indentures needed to be stamped and registered by inspectors.

37. Wages were illegal in London, but they do appear to have been paid at times and they became more common in the eighteenth century, especially outside London, as living in declined (Lane 1996; Dunlop and Denman 1912).

38. So, parallel covenants to an indenture agreeing that an apprentice would serve only five years of their term were judged an offence. LMA, CLRO Rep. 104, f. 202 (1700). Few indentures from London survive from before the 1680s, when the earliest files of admissions to the city exist. These contain the indentures. Printed forms were in use in Gloucester by 1604 (Barlow 2001, xiii).

39. See chapter 7 on the nineteenth century. On apprenticeship and slavery, see Richards 2018; Anderson et al. 2020; Ryan 2016; Anderson 2022, 765; Drescher 2002, 145–59.

40. Kahan and Klausner 1997.

41. Kaplan 1993. Similarly, Genoa, Montreal, and some Southern Netherlands contracts were notarial (Epstein 1991; De Munck 2007; Hamilton 1996).

42. Hamilton 1996.

43. Dunlop and Denman 1912.

44. Lane 1996; Brooks 1994; Humphries 2010; Pelling 1994; Gowing 2021.

45. The sample and sources are presented in appendix 1.

46. Some of the findings are available in Prak and Wallis 2019; Kaplan 2023; Bellavitis and Sapienza 2023.

47. Some earlier records exist for a handful of London guilds and cities. See Hovland 2007, and more generally, Hanawalt 1993.

48. Two landmark studies redefined the field: Ben-Amos 1994; Griffiths 1996.

Chapter 2. The Rise and (Partial) Fall of Apprenticeship

1. Key contributions to the debate on the decline of apprenticeship include Unwin 1963; Dunlop and Denman 1912; Kahl 1960; Kellett 1957–58; Brooks 1994; Walker 1986; Snell 1985; Humphries 2010.

2. The 'guild' series counts two types of registered apprentices. Those with guild members (mainly London) and those registered by urban citizens (other towns). In both cases, apprenticeship was linked to access to local economic rights to work in an occupation and political rights in the local urban community. The extrapolation of national totals from surviving series is described in appendices 2 and 3.

3. From 1711, the stamp duty registers record the receipts from a 2.5–5% tax imposed on the premiums (fees) paid to masters for apprenticeships. The tax was due for all apprenticeships, not just those made by masters in guilds, but omits those without any fee or funded by parish welfare or charity. See appendix 1.

4. Detailed information on the apprentice estimates are in appendices 1 and 2. Earlier estimates include Brooks 1994; Humphries 2003. For London, see Rappaport 1989, 232–33; Elliott 1978, 214–15; Kitch 1986; Beier 1986, 157–59. For Bristol and York, see Ben-Amos 1994, 84–51, 264–65. Recent figures for the eighteenth century are in Ben Zeev et al. 2017.

5. Allen 2003.

6. Wallis et al. 2018; Kelly et al. 2014.

7. Note that contemporary complains in the textile industry from the sixteenth century onwards often suggest a large share were trained outside apprenticeships (Gendron 2023, 132–36).

8. Broadberry et al. 2015; Wrigley et al. 1997, 134, 614–15, tab. A9.1.

9. Taylor et al. 2007, xxxi.

10. Sacks 1991.

11. For Gloucestershire, 8,248 are observed in London, while 4,699 trained in Gloucester. Counts of Oxfordshire apprentices in surviving London guild records exceed 100 per year on occasion in the seventeenth century; not all guild records survive.

12. Guild and city rules are discussed in chapter 9.

13. Withington 2005; Archer 2000, 241–46; Innes and Rogers 2000, 538.

14. Brooks 1994.

15. 5&6 Wm IV, c. 76. See Keith-Lucas 1952. See also Keith-Lucas 1980; Prest 1990.

16. Haupt 2002.

17. The estimates assume a 75% survivorship rate to take into account those apprentices who left service early. As chapter 6 shows, slightly over half of apprentices were present with their original master at the end of their indenture, having left at a varying rate over their period of indentures. To this, the shares who would have changed master and completed, and who remained active in London with partial training, need to be added. Against that, return migration reduces the total.

18. On the number of apprentices per capita registered in guilds with records from the fifteenth century, see Hovland 2007, 229; Leach 2017, 280.

19. Rappaport 1989, 52–53.

20. Smith 1973; Harris 1987.

21. Rappaport 1989.

22. Unwin 1963; Beier 1986, 157–59.

23. Kellett 1957–58; Kahl 1960.

24. Harding 1990, 123.

25. Ashton 1979; Ward 1997; De Krey 2005; Knights 1997; Halliday 1998.

26. Average premiums per company were calculated per decade (1710–19, etc.) and exclude companies where fewer than thirty observations survive per decade. Company members are defined as masters whose occupation is in the form of "Citizen & X" where X matches the name of an extant livery company (e.g., Citizen & Grocer). This cannot be calculated after the 1760s, as the dataset rarely records the status of master as citizen.

27. In an OLS regression of deflated premiums against citizenship, with occupation and time fixed effects, the coefficient on a variable indicating the master was a citizen was 12.16 (s.e. 0.66) and the constant 37.80 (N = 58,984, R^2 0.33). The sample was restricted to the fifty-six largest

occupations (>500 observations). Premiums deflated to 1700 values using Robert Allen's new London CPI.

28. Wrigley 1967.

29. From very different perspectives, urban centres play a key role in Allen 2003; Acemoglu et al. 2005; Zahedieh 2010, chap. 3.

30. Estimates calculated using de Vries's and Langton's figures for English large cities in 1800 (defined as population >= 10,000), with Langton's more recent figures used where available. De Vries 1984; Langton 2000. Cities with no population estimate for 1700 are assumed to have had 5,000 residents. The massive size of London means that the estimates are not particularly sensitive to missing information. If we instead assumed those missing cities had 10,000 residents London's share of England's large city population would fall from 61 to 57%.

31. Inevitably, not all locations of masters can be matched to identifiable places. However, the share matched includes 96% of English apprentices for the 1710s and 1790s.

32. In this paragraph, the 1710s and 1790s are six-year samples for 1712–17 and 1792–97, respectively.

33. On training and clock-making, see Cookson 2018, 78–85; Cummins and Ó Gráda 2022.

34. The estimates of apprentices per 1,000 people are for 1795 (mean number of apprentices per year 1792–97, inclusive) relative to the 1801 county population.

35. More 1980; Knox 1980.

36. Judicial decisions had also removed the requirement for a seven-year apprenticeship to trade in a country village in the mid eighteenth century (1 Ventr. 51; 2 Keb. 583).

37. Distributions are for master's occupations in the 1795 sample.

38. In Transport, 88% (n 410) of apprentices in the 1710 sample are mariners; in 1795, they make up 52% (n = 38).

39. Counting all occupations in which 'weaver' is stated (e.g., weaver, broad weaver, silk-weaver).

40. Mokyr 2009; Kelly et al. 2023.

41. The shoemaking industry was changing in organisational structure with the rise in the Northamptonshire industry.

42. This coheres with the findings of Kelly et al. on iron and Minolleti's work on weaving. Kelly et al. 2023; Minoletti 2011, 223.

43. The comparison is tentative at best, assuming, as it does, stable ratios of skilled and unskilled work in each sector, stable age distributions among workers, stable propensities to pay premiums among apprentices, and the continuity of definition of sectors over a century of structural change, specialisation, and process and technological innovation, not to mention the seventeen-year gap that separates the 1800 sample and the second benchmark.

44. Schwarz 1992.

45. Bythell 1969.

46. Humphries 2010; de Pleijt 2016; Mitch 1993.

47. Feldman and van der Beek 2016.

48. De Pleijt 2018.

49. Average of the annual total paid for English indentures, 1712–19 (the initial year of the tax records is affected by under-recording).

50. Premiums are deflated using Allen's new London CPI to 1700 values.

51. These figures infer primary education from male literacy rates of 43% c. 1700 and 56% c. 1800 and cohorts of 43,000 and 70,000 youths, respectively. Reis draws his estimate of costs from several sources for 1700–1730 (Reis 2005, 215). In taking literacy to indicate primary education I follow de Pleijt 2016. I do not adjust the figure for 1800 for inflation, but this would not change the conclusion. Reis also estimates the opportunity cost of primary education. I exclude this for

simplicity here, but this would only increase the investment in apprenticeship, given the older age of youths who were training.

52. De Pleijt 2016, 108–11. Higher education was also far outstripped, with around 1,000 students p.a. admitted in England's two universities at the highpoint in the 1620s and 1630s, equivalent to, at most, one-quarter of the number apprenticed in London alone (Stone 1975, 6, 12). A full accounting of national investment in apprenticeship would need to incorporate funds provided by charities and legacies, where apprenticeship was a major recipient. In the two counties with estimates of funds available, Gloucestershire and Lancashire, charitable trusts would have added around another one-quarter to one-third to the moneys spent by families.

53. If 30% of English males served seven-year apprenticeships then, averaged over the whole male population this would be 2.1 years per person. If half left early at 3.5 years and half completed, this would be 1.6 years per person.

54. Feldman and van der Beek 2016; Justman and van der Beek 2015; Ben Zeev et al. 2017.

55. The early period is excellently presented in Hovland 2007.

56. Around 1700, these nine large cities had a total population of around 460,000, about 100,000 smaller than London in the same period, and would have been recruiting around 1,000 more apprentices. These totals are extrapolated from averages for twelve guilds out of 296 in these cities, so the margin for error is wide (Schalk 2019, 192).

57. Crowston and Lemercier 2019, 283.

58. Stöger and Reith 2019, 142; Pfister 2020, 43.

59. Hamilton 2000, 1996.

60. Feldman and van der Beek 2016; Ben Zeev et al. 2017.

61. Kelly et al. 2023; Kelly et al. 2014; Meisenzahl and Mokyr 2012; Mokyr 2009.

Chapter 3. Diffusing Skill and Innovation

1. Thrift 2009.

2. Kelly and Ó Gráda 2016. See also Kelly and Ó Gráda 2022.

3. Tompion's career is well summarised in the *ODNB*, s.v. 'Thomas Tompion'. Tompion's training career is reconstructed from the guild records.

4. Mokyr 1990. See also Berg 2002; Luu 2005; Harris 2020.

5. Epstein 1998. See the essays collected in Prak and van Zanden 2013.

6. Borowiecki 2021.

7. An alternative version of this, with similar implications, is where apprentices are recruited to fill in gaps in the family labour supply, for example because of the absence of a son (Goody 1989: 243–45).

8. For a useful discussion of these approaches, see De Munck and De Kerf 2018, 38–40. On sweating, usefully and critically, see Riello 2012; Blackburn 2006.

9. These questions parallel the important macro analysis of training systems, comparing clans, guilds and markets, in de la Croix et al. 2018.

10. See chapter 12. More generally, see Ben-Amos 1994; Brooks 1994, 52–55.

11. Campbell 1747, 312

12. For preliminary evidence on the Netherlands, Flanders, and Spain, see Stabel 2007, 173; De Munck and De Kerf 2018, 39–40, 53–55; Sánchez 2022. An important early study for London is Feldman 2014. Cookson notes clusters among engineers (Cookson 2018, 100–102). Hamilton considers the question of master quality, but does not find an effect in her sample for Montreal (Hamilton 1996: 513–54).

13. Epstein 1998, 2004; Pfister 2008; Reith 2008; de la Croix et al. 2018; Garrioch 2022.

14. De la Croix et al. 2018, 3.

15. See appendix 4 for ordinances.

16. See appendix 4 for ordinances.

17. For the Goldsmiths, 5% of apprentices who petitioned in the Mayor's Court did not have a guild entry (Chaffin and Wallis 2023, 13).

18. Honeyman 2007, 104; Chapman 1965, 541.

19. Minns and Wallis 2013, 348.

20. The fourteen were drawn from Britten et al. 1986; Turner 2008; and Landes 1983. They were John Arnold, Josiah Aspinall, William Clement, John Ellicott, Ahaseureus Fromantel, John Fromantel, George Graham, Joseph Knibb, Thomas Mudge, Daniel Quare, Thomas Tompion, Samuel Watson, Joseph Williamson, and Henry Wynne

21. Britten et al. 1986; Turner 2008, 272–73, n. 25.

22. *ODNB*, s.v. 'Quare, Daniel'; Britten 1894.

23. Britten et al. 1986.

24. Bristol and Avon Family History Society 2019, s.v. 'Bream, Jasper'.

25. The sample of manufacturers used here contains fifty-six individuals selected from the British and Irish Furniture Makers Online dataset (Furniture History Society n.d.) on the criteria that they were active from 1650 to 1700 and are known to have supplied the Crown or an aristocratic household, or produced distinguished work. They were linked to London guild records, primarily the Joiners. The Joiners' apprenticeship records begin in 1641, however their freedom records appear to be incomplete and we are unable to safely identify masters who did not train among the larger sample of distinguished makers.

26. Crook 1965.

27. Mitchell identified objects in a range of sources. See Mitchell 2017.

28. This is a subsample of those Mitchell identified based on taking their freedom between 1600 and 1670, so allowing their training careers to be observed in the guild's records. The linkage between marks and makers is not certain, but based on expert judgement.

29. This is a sample of fourteen individuals identified by Mitchell as a producer of silver plate from the seventeenth century in the royal collection. Most surviving plate post-dates the civil war, so this group is clustered in the 1660s–1690s and their apprentice numbers may be censored by the end of that dataset in 1700.

30. The sample was drawn from information in Furdell's study, linked to the records of the Society of Apothecaries which begin in 1617. Furdell 2001; GL, MS 8200/1–2.

31. The total is brought down by the single youth registered to Paul L'Obell in 1619; the records of the Grocers' Company do not allow me to reconstruct his earlier career as a master.

32. *ODNB*, s.v. 'Gideon Delaune'; Furdell 2001.

33. The sample of 438 merchant directors was constructed by Aske Brock 2017. Estimating the share training is complicated for this group by the range of guilds and the limits to information on potential duplicate masters. We can link 161 merchant directors with some confidence to freedom entries in guilds with good apprenticeship and freedom records; 128 (79.5%) bound apprentices. Another seven probably took apprentices, but have obvious risks of duplication with other individuals of the same name.

34. Brenner 1993, 137–40.

35. Brenner 1993, 137.

36. Spurstowe took his freedom in the Clothworkers by patrimony in 1644.

37. Woodhead 1965: s.v.

38. Based on a sample of 377 apothecaries with manually constructed training careers who took their first apprentice prior to 1650. The training careers were reconstructed manually for 1617 to 1670.

39. Based on a sample of 1,128 guild freemen (freed 1700–1799) of whom sixty-four served as master of the company. These training careers were reconstructed by clustering masters

by name and period; name variations and duplicates mean that not all careers can be fully reconstructed.

40. GL, MS 22169.

41. Brewers in GL, MS 5442/7, 5442/8; Coopers in GL, MS 05633A, #8; Pewterers in GL, MS 22188/1; Tallow Chandlers in GL, MS 6174/2; Apothecaries in GL, MS 8200/2, f. 38v.

42. Merchant Taylors: GL, MS 34,048/15; Drapers: Johnson 1914–22, 3:432.

43. Blagden 1955, 168.

44. Average apprentice numbers calculated for freemen with at least one apprentice.

45. For this exercise, linkage was restricted to strong ties based on an exact string of name and occupation, with duplicates excluded.

46. On lodgers, see Boulton 1987, 17; McEwan 2011.

47. These figures are calculated for freemen grouped according to the century they entered the freedom: for 1600–99, n = 94; for 1700–99, n = 340.

48. In the seventeenth century. The Pewterers' 1702 ordinances barred members binding youths in their first year after becoming freemen (GL, CLC/L/PE/A/029/MS07116). Earlier rules required freemen to gain guild approval before setting up a shop and taking apprentices, separately from their freedom. GL, CLC/L/PE/A/009/MS07115 (1564); GL, CLC/L/PE/A/028/MS07117 (1607).

49. The Pewterers allowed the second apprentice to start only when the first was within two years of the end of their term (GL, MS 07117, ff. 7r, 38). Requests around this were regularly made in the 1680s. GL, MS 22180/7, 24 Mar 1681, 23 June 1681, 11 Aug 1681.

50. Matching and concentration offers an alternative mechanism to that modelled in de la Croix et al. 2018, where apprentices cannot observe masters in advance and the key variant is the size of the pool of masters that is defined by the scope of enforcement.

Chapter 4. Mobilising Labour

1. Jenkinson 1914, 5, 14.

2. Mill 1848, 1:462–63.

3. Note that artisanal organisation in India may be better described as an endogenous guild, reliant on family connections, than as a caste as such (Roy 2013, 2010).

4. De la Croix et al. 2018.

5. All the data analysed in this chapter except the section on masters' sons includes both male and female apprentices. Female apprentices account for only a small percentage of those included, and they are discussed in greater detail in chapter 11.

6. Beier 1985; Hubbard 2012; Clark 1979.

7. Important discussions on particular centres include Sacks 1991, 105–27; Brooks 1994. On London, see Kitch 1986; Schwarzberg 2016.

8. Clark and Cummins 2015; Boberg-Fazlić and Sharp 2018. Contrast with the emphasis on other forms of mobility in Collins 1991.

9. Earle 1989, 141. Similar caution is voiced by Brooks 1994.

10. Mayhew 1991. See also Pelling 1994, 1998.

11. The rates reported in this paragraph are drawn from the sample of city and guild records, which contain this information. I exclude entries that lack information on the father's location, in order to retain only records with fuller evidence on family background and limit the impact of under-recording.

12. Wrigley 1997, 291; Landers 1993, 172.

13. Crossley 2012, xxxi.

14. Bewick 1862, 51–52.

15. *ODNB.*, s.v. 'Bewick, Thomas'.

16. These distances are estimated based on 49,208 apprenticeship records with information on parent and master place in the stamp duty register, TNA, IR1. The majority of these (91%) date from 1711 to the 1740s. Populations are imputed from a range of standard secondary sources.

17. N = 9,361.

18. See Stone 1966, 31–32.

19. This paragraph summarises the results of a regression of distance on parental background with city and period dummies reported in appendix 6.

20. Based on the sample of stamp duty apprentices between 1711 and 1749 for whom both a place of origin and master's location can be identified (N = 49,233). Urban and guild records for earlier periods show a similar lack of recruits from other major towns.

21. The overall average age fell because of compositional effects (highlighted here) and because apprentices coming from a given location were also getting younger (Wallis et al. 2010, 387–89).

22. Ravenstein 1885, 198–99.

23. This may also reflect improving changes of survival for urban children.

24. The 2014 student figure was 146 km. https://www.theguardian.com/news/datablog/2014/aug/18/students-travel-average-91-miles-home-university.

25. Urban growth in the north and west was largely based on migrants from surrounding areas (Redford 1926, 65–67, 183–84).

26. This information was not universally recorded, and so family relationships are inferred from names as a cross-check, assuming that if the apprentice's father and their master had the same forename and surname, then they were probably being bound to their own father.

27. In Boston, forenames for both father and master were recorded for 473 of 1,479 apprentices enrolled in the eighteenth century. The main gap was for fathers' names: just 33% had forenames recorded. It is plausible that this was more common when the father was also the master.

28. Cited in Broadberry et al. 2013, 19.

29. Brooks 1994, 61.

30. Grassby 1995, 143.

31. King 1936. I take his categories of knights, esquires, and gentry collectively. On King's estimates, see Arkell 2006, 51–52.

32. Wallis and Webb 2011.

33. Wallis et al. 2018.

34. Cantillon [1730] 1959, pt. 1, chap. 7.

35. For London, we can only estimate the share who were trained by their own father or another master, as there is a lack of good information on the destinations of all children from a family. That said, the records of multiple guilds allow the identification of instances when masters' children were trained in a different guild. The number of London guilds in the dataset increases substantially over time, meaning that the error should be greatest in the early seventeenth century and lowest in the late eighteenth century. For other cities, as citizenships or guild memberships were not recorded in the registers, the exercise cannot be replicated. The best approximation for these centres is taking the pool of local apprentices whose fathers worked in crafts or trades into which substantial numbers of apprentices (at least fifty) were recruited.

36. It is easy to imagine masters who train their own sons operating as a closed group, keeping knowledge, resources, and opportunities to themselves. However, this was not the case. Few (one in ten masters in Bristol and Gloucester, one in fifty in London) bound their sons as their *only* apprentices. There was a strong positive correlation between the chance that a master would take his own son and the number that he trained overall.

37. For example, López Barahona and Nieto Sánchez 2019, 67–68; Crowston and Lemercier 2019, 285.

38. The guilds in the sample are the Apothecaries, Clothworkers, Drapers, Goldsmiths, Mercers, Merchant Taylors, and Tallow Chandlers.

39. I searched the apprenticeship dataset for those entering by patrimony and could identify just 4% among apprentices.

40. Beloff 1942, 45. On the costs of training, see Ben-Amos 1994; Ben-Amos 2008, 22–24.

41. There is no systematic data on the use of premiums in earlier periods. The premiums recorded in the stamp duty were similar to those Ben-Amos observed in Bristol a century earlier. However, in sixteenth-century Oxford, contracts often included payments from masters to apprentices at the ends of their terms, suggesting lower demand (Ben-Amos 1994, 87–92; Crossley 2012, xxii). End-of-term payments were also common in Venice (Colavizza et al. 2019, 124–25). In Madrid, payments by both apprentice and master sometimes occurred (López Barahona and Nieto Sánchez 2019, 61–62).

42. Minns and Wallis 2013, 343–44. A comparison of 2,128 stamp duty and London guild registrations indicated that only 6% of guild registrations failed to record a premium when one was taxed.

43. The other guilds were the Blacksmiths (23%), Plasterers (28%), Stationers (46%), Vintners (30%), and Clothworkers (36%).

44. Two samples (1714–16, 1775–79) from Graham 1987.

45. The range reflects the share if non-reported premiums are treated as zero or omitted (Barlow 2001, 2011; Hartopp 1927).

46. Carlton 1974.

47. Minns and Wallis 2013; Justman and van der Beek 2015; Ben Zeev et al. 2017.

48. Blacket 1811, 3. James Lackington was offered a place as a shoemaker's apprentice without a premium, having already worked for his father in shoemaking for a period (Lackington 1793, 72).

49. Minns and Wallis 2013.

50. Early modern England did, of course, have a great deal of borrowing, but mostly for shorter terms. See Muldrew 1998.

51. The occupations in which pauper apprentices are placed are covered in Sharpe 1991; Honeyman 2007, 129–49; Snell 1985, 278–90; Levene 2010, 926–34; Chivers 2006, 113–16. More generally, see Crawford 2010.

52. Jordan 1959, 268–70; Pinches 2000; Lane 1996; Hanley 2005; Briggs 1954; Payne 2008, 184–90.

53. The Foundling Hospital, for example, largely placed children in occupations that matched those of the groups whose children were left to its care (Levene 2010; Berry 2023; Briggs 1954, 50–52).

54. Hanley 2005, 69.

55. Carter 2020, 2. An even larger £3,000 endowment had been left by the Duke of Somerset in 1676 for apprenticing (Hurley et al. 1996, 2).

56. Jordan identifies an initial surge in the 1590s and 1620s to 1640s, but sums remain relatively small in the period he covers (Jordan 1959, 269–70).

57. These three counties were roughly in the middle of the distribution of English counties in the share of charity devoted to apprenticeship in 1877, the first time that is reported (United Kingdom. House of Commons 1877, 17–18).

58. The date of foundation is missing for 17% of Gloucestershire and 24% of Lancashire charities.

59. Other apprenticing charities existed in the borough, suggesting under-reporting is an issue here.

60. Grassby 1995, 82–84.

61. Campbell 1747, 336. Campbell's estimates are tested against other sources and shown to be valid in Justman and van der Beek 2015.

62. Hobson 1757, 11.

63. Humphries 2003, 74. See also Ben Zeev et al. 2017, 1196.

64. See chapter 10.

65. Premiums were similar in German, French, and Dutch records. Stöger and Reith 2019, 143–45; Kaplan 1981, 283; Crowston and Lemercier 2019, 287; Schalk 2019, 197–98.

Chapter 5. Apprenticeship as Learning

1. Lancy 2012, 113.

2. This distinction echoes that in Akinnaso 1992, 77–78, but without the necessity of institutionalisation.

3. Fuller et al. 2005, 56–59, 65–66.

4. Steffens 2001. See also Singleton 1998, 14; Marchand 2001, 138.

5. The main recent contributions on training are Gowing 2021, 150–71; Smith 2022, chap. 5; De Munck 2010, 336–39; Earle 1989, 96–102; More 1980, 137–52; Wallis 2008; Epstein 2013.

6. Smith 1776, bk. 1, chap. 13, pt. 2. The same critique was echoed in Spanish political economy in this period (López Barahona and Nieto Sánchez 2019, 45).

7. The distinction is explored more fully by Polanyi (1962), and in a somewhat different way by Mokyr (2002).

8. See, for example, Ericsson 2006, 689, 699.

9. The evidence discussed here is from the records of the Lord Mayor's Court of London, equity side, formerly in the Corporation of London Record Office now in the LMA. The references are to the CLRO catalogue. The court's actions are discussed by Wallis (2012) and Pelling (1994). Gowing explores the evidence for female apprentices specifically (2021, 153–77). De Munck has discussed similar evidence for Antwerp (2007, 53–58).

10. CLRO MC6/526A (1691).

11. CLRO MC6/525B (1691).

12. For example, CLRO MC6/521B (1691); MC6/529A–B (1691); MC6/506B (1689).

13. CLRO MC6/547 (1672/3); MC6/477B (1687).

14. CLRO MC6/552A (1673).

15. Pelling 1995, 258–59.

16. Grassby 1995; Gauci 2001; Zahedieh 2010.

17. CLRO MC6/488A (1688).

18. CLRO MC6/477B (1687).

19. Marshall 1890, bk. 4, chap. 6, n. 82.

20. CLRO MC6/503A (1689).

21. CLRO MC6/553 (1673).

22. Winstanley 1994, 41; Stout 1967, 25.

23. Merson 1968, xxii–xxiii.

24. CLRO MC6/508A (1689); MC6/500A (1689).

25. CLRO MC6/551A (1673). See also MC6/503A (1689).

26. CLRO MC6/506B (1689).

27. Wallis 2002, 200–202.

28. Brown 1972, 109.

29. Ben-Amos 1994, 114.

30. GL, MS 5257/3, f. 45. See also GL, MS 5257/4, f. 41; Hobson 1757, 12–13.

31. Ben-Amos 1994, 127–28; Ainsworth et al. 1913–68, 6:124; BRO, MS 08018, 'Ordinances for City Companies', f. 56; Bird 1795, 35–36; GL, MS 5257/5, f. 170; Gregg and Boswell 1930, 61–62.

32. Cited by Mokyr 2009, 120.

33. Dunton had not been so diligent: '[Had] I not been over-born with Head-strong Passions, both to my own ruine and the loss of time, I might have made considerable Improvements in so good a Family' (Dunton 1974, 40, 55–56).

34. Hutton 1872, 36.

35. Brown 1972, 106–7.

36. Forman 1849, 6.

37. Smith 1776, bk. 1, chap. 13, pt. 2.

38. Petty 1647; Webster 1975.

39. Glaisyer 2006; Rabuzzi 1995; Finkelstein 2000.

40. Rabuzzi 1995.

41. Browne 1590, 55ff.

42. Bewick 1862, 57. He is referring to Matthias Lock and Henry Copland, *A New Book of Ornaments* (London, 1768).

43. Craske 1999, 190–91.

44. Bertucci and Courcelle 2015, 165–66.

45. Brown also sold him the slide rule (Glaisyer and Pennell 2003, 13).

46. Maruca 2003, 326–27.

47. The impact of cost on reading choices is well illustrated in the one study of an apprentices' reading that I am aware of—Colclough 2000. Nieto Sánchez also notes the lack of manuals in apprenticeship in Madrid (Nieto Sánchez 2022, 146).

48. More 1980, 108–17.

49. *ODNB*, s.v. 'Graham'.

50. *ODNB*, s.v. 'Watt'.

51. Bewick 1862, 58.

52. Prak 2008.

53. Dunton 1974, 45.

54. Epstein 1998, 2004; Reith 2008; Groot and Schalk 2022. Aspects of mobility are central in Hilaire-Pérez 2007; Klein 2017; Garrioch 2022.

55. Hobson 1757, 7.

56. Oxley 1836, 5:209.

57. Dunlop and Denman 1912.

58. Brooks 1994, 76. Also, Yarbrough 1979, 67.

59. This literature is well surveyed in Griffiths 1996, 72–78; Smith 1973, 152; Houlbrooke 1988; Crawford 2010, 13–22.

60. This issue has been the focus of considerable anthropological and sociological discussion. The connection between work and identity is discussed usefully in Venkatesan 2010. The significance of hierarchy and youth experiences in a range of contemporary observations of apprenticeship (linked to delaying knowledge transmission) is underlined in Dallos 2021; Lancy 2012, 120–21.

61. In addition to the cases discussed here, Ben-Amos provides a much fuller analysis of the varieties of youths' experiences and their relationship with their masters (Ben-Amos 1994).

62. Bownas 1756, 3.

63. Longden 1837, 20.

64. Kirke 1899, 31.

65. 'An account of the work of grace upon Will. Devenport of London, written by him, and given to me March 1698', in Doe 1700, 1. Other examples include Melhuish 1805, 8.

66. Lackington 1793, 84–104.

67. Hudson and Hunter 1981, 151.

68. Griffiths 1996, 12–14. Smith offers an interesting survey of external moral sources, including songs and ballads (1973, 152–55). Yarbrough similarly notes religious writers securing a distinctive role in spiritual guidance apart from the master (1979, 72).

69. Eisenberg 1991, 510–12.

70. Davids 2007, 220.

71. LMA, CW/B/1/1, f. 39v. The efforts by city authorities to remedy this are surveyed in Griffiths 1996, 222–33.

72. Ben-Amos 1994, 85.

73. Quoted in Walter 2007, 110.

74. Rahikainen 2004, 12–13; Cunningham 1990, 118, where childhood is taken as ending at fifteen.

75. Claxton 1839, 5. More generally, Horrell and Humphries 2019.

76. Myles 1850, 66.

77. Hutton 1872, 32.

78. Smith 1973, 151.

79. The relevant distinction here is between academic and technical skills, not general and specific human capital in a Beckerian sense, as the apprentice gained craft/trade skills that were applicable in a variety of firms.

80. Yarbrough 1979, 69. Hamilton finds provision for schooling more often in Montreal in the late eighteenth century, but even then, only 16% of contracts included this (Hamilton 1996, 501).

81. CLRO MC6/505A (1689). See also CLRO MC6/479A (1687). In 1682, George Marshall's family spent £1 on his 'writing master' while he was an apprentice (Derbyshire Record Office, D258/45/10/46).

82. Lackington 1793, 72.

83. Merson 1968, xxii. See also Briggs 1954, 48.

84. Forman 1849, 6. Another case of a master receiving a premium linked to allowing his apprentice to send him to school is described in Ben-Amos 2008, 289.

85. Simonton 2004, 372; 2000, 196–97.

86. Galenson 1981, 823.

87. Charlton 1965, 264–65, 268; Schulz 1943. Offers of courses specific to business also developed, e.g., Watts 1722, 64.

88. Campbell 1747, 19–20. The same argument is made in Gordon 1777, 2–3.

89. Jackson 1877, 187–88. For a similar sequence, Buckley 1909, 171.

90. Jacob 2007.

91. Manby Smith 1853, 15. Frank Forrest formed a similar society as a journeyman shoemaker in the 1830s (Myles 1850, 77–78).

92. Whetstone 1807, 76.

93. Whetstone 1807, 76–77, 84.

94. Claxton 1839, 7–16.

95. Tryon 1705, 19–25.

96. Buckley 1909, 171.

97. Manby Smith 1853, 15.

98. Claxton 1839, 13.

99. Marchand 2010, 59.

100. An idea epitomised in Smiles 1866.

101. Mokyr 2009; Jacob 2014.

102. De Munck 2010, 356.

103. De Munck 2010, 334, n. 8; Pevsner 1940; Tkaczyk 2017; López Barahona and Nieto Sánchez 2019, 53; Davids 2007.

104. Wallis 2019, 161; Pelling 2019; Cunningham 1974, 168–70, 206–10.

105. Richardson 1908, 6. See also Mackenzie 1827, 443–45.

106. Craske 1999, 206

107. See Dearle 1914; Knox 1980, 228–79; More 1980, 198–225; Walker 2013. A similar expansion in technical education followed industrial expansion in France (Diebolt et al. 2019).

108. Floud 1982, 159; Gay 2000.

109. Floud 1982, 160, 162–63.

110. Marshall 1890, bk. 4, chap. 6, sec. 4.

111. Knox 1980, 255; More 1980, 207.

112. Pelling 2019.

113. De Munck 2010.

114. Klein 2017.

115. Ericsson 2006.

116. The key anthropological statements are Goody 1989; Ingold 2001; Coy 1989. Specific applications include Argenti 2002, 507–9; Herzfeld 2004; Venkatesan 2010, esp. S168–S171; Dilley 1999, 41–45. Earlier literature is surveyed in Wallis 2008, 849–50.

117. Goody 1989, 274; Lave and Wenger 1991. Illustrations of the process include Venkatesan 2010; Nielsen 2008.

118. Polanyi 1962, 49; Ingold 2001, 21–22. On skilled perception, see Sennett's idea of 'material consciousness' in Sennett 2009; and Marchand 2010, 260–61.

119. Epstein 1998; Hilaire-Pérez and Verna 2006.

Chapter 6. The Flexibility of Apprenticeship

1. Gent 1832, 2, 25–26.

2. On apprenticeship for security, see Lane 1996, 2. On socialisation, see Brooks 1994, 73–83; Smith 1973. More generally, see Kaplan 1993; De Munck 2007, 201–5; Farr 2000, 20–21.

3. Kaplan 2007, 212.

4. Epstein 1998, 687; de la Croix et al. 2018. See also Humphries 2003, 84–85; van Zanden 2009, 139–40.

5. Ogilvie 2004, 302–14; 2008, 177–78; 2007, 16–30. Similar implications can be drawn from De Munck's study of Antwerp apprenticeship (2007, 118–19).

6. For examples, see England: Griffiths 1996, 330–35; Ben-Amos 1994.

7. An extensive array of evidence on completion rates is surveyed in Wallis 2008, 838–39, 855; Ogilvie 2019, 406–7.

8. A few sources do record the termination of contracts but do not state when termination occurred: Ben-Amos 1991, 166–67; Steidl 2007, 145–50 (although see also 135, n. 12); De Munck 2007, 190–91.

9. The details of the linkage process can be found in Minns and Wallis 2012 and Schalk et al. 2017. The analysis here draws on an expanded London sample (n = 1,951) which includes a further fifteen guilds (Bakers, Barbers, Carpenters, Clothworkers, Coopers, Cordwainers, Drapers, Goldsmiths, Haberdashers, Joiners, Mercers, Merchant Taylors, Tallow Chandlers, Watermen, Weavers).

10. See, on the 1690s, Waddell 2015, 2022.

11. Jones 1988, 130–31, 159; Rose 1999, 126–28.

12. Brewer 1989, 89, 95–100, 114.

13. Rose 1999, 137–40; Horsefield 1960, 14–17; Jones 1988, 20–21.

14. Clark 2004, 41–124; Clay 1984, i, 52.

15. Bristol apprenticeships were for seven years, with three exceptions in this period bound for eight years.

16. Dunlop and Denman 1912, 162. This was common elsewhere (Hamilton 1996, 498).

17. If this occurred, we would expect more migrants to be present in year one. This was not the case.

18. Ben-Amos 1994, 112, 173; GL, MS 5257/5, f. 131.

19. Occupational effects in Shrewsbury cannot be discussed meaningfully because the sample size is too small; the largest occupation is tailoring, with sixty-eight observations, and even then, only one year has more than ten observations. For most occupations fewer than five apprentices appear in each year cohort.

20. BRO, 04353/2, f. 243 (20 Aug 1696).

21. The resurgence does not appear to be a cohort effect, due to demographic or economic factors. The timing of the bump is similar in London and Bristol, though the tax listings that are the basis of the observation differ by a year. Second, the difference between local and migrant resurgence suggests that endogenous rather than exogenous factors drive that pattern.

22. Cf. Levene 2008, 192.

23. Brasbridge 1824, 74.

24. 6 November 1670. Bell had been bound in December 1663.

25. LMA, COL/CA/05/02, s.v. 'Baron, 1690'; 'Batty, n.d.'; 'Chase, c. 1688'; 'Corbett, c. 1670'.

26. Evidence from Vienna suggests that effective terms in that city were also shorter than prescribed by law (Steidl 2007, 143–45).

27. This paragraph summarises findings in Minns and Wallis 2012.

28. Ainsworth et al. 1913–68, vols. 4 and 5. I sampled 172 apprentice entries between 1570 and 1573 inclusive.

29. Beckett 1985.

30. United Kingdom. House of Commons 1815, 4. Another eighty-six had enlisted in the army or navy, but there is no information on whether this was before or after the completion of their contracts.

31. Snell 1985, 236, 253–54, percentages taken from figure 5.8. The share rose again in the 1810s. Payne applied the same methodology to a sample of London examinations, finding 63% completed their terms (2008, 201–2).

32. Snell 1985, 261 (quotation).

33. Snell's explanation for decline builds from an expansion in the numbers of apprentices that masters took in the middle of the century in response to shifts in demand, followed by a growth in early departures by apprentices during the slump that followed. However, the evidence for this expansion in numbers is limited, and it has no visible effect on the numbers of apprentices paying premiums or the premiums paid, which we would expect if a major glut in training occurred (Snell 1985, 242–43). The sharp decline in real wages in the late eighteenth century that is apparent in Phelps-Brown and Hopkins's series and which sustains Snell's view that apprentices faced increasingly precarious futures is much less visible in more recent real wage series (Clark 2005).

34. Although the letter of the law had specified that forty days of service as an apprentice secured settlement in a community, not all justices of the peace appear to have accepted this; indeed, Snell himself suggests that the law was 'frequently ignored' (Snell 1985, 258). Others disagree: see chapter 9.

35. 31 Geo II, c. 11.

36. On guilds' powers, see Walker 1986; Schwarz 1992, 210–11; Berlin 2008; Kellett 1957–58.

37. Durham University Archives, 'Durham City Guild Records: Index to Apprentices', http://reed.dur.ac.uk/xtf/data/pdf/DCGApprtce/DCGApprtce.pdf.

38. Schalk 2015, 2016.

39. Schalk et al. 2017, 141.

40. Steidl 2007, 133–57.

41. Zucca Micheletto 2019, 100; Gutton 2003.

42. Rich discussions of the issues involved in apprentices' exits include Griffiths 1996, 323–44.

43. Schwarz 1987, 18–22; Pelling 1994.

44. Harris and Harris 1869, 14.

45. Hutton 1872, 35.

46. Hutton 1872, 127

47. Myles 1850, 75.

48. Everett and Hick 1856, 33.

49. Disney 1692, 31–32.

50. LMA, Repertories, v. 63, f. 91, v. 88, f. 1b, v. 91, f. 65; v. 94, f. 45; Evans 1652, 4–5; BRO, JTOL, J/2/1, pp. 513, 514, 516, 531, 533, 543, 546–55. On reasons for departure, see Griffiths 1996, 299–313, 324–41; Ben-Amos 1994: 103–8, 213–15; Steidl 2007, 147–50; Stabel 2004, 201–3.

51. Evans 1652, 4–5, 7.

52. Haggart 1821, 7.

53. Forman was hardly innocent in this: when his mistress tried to beat him for having lost some flax (which he denied), he 'thrust her up behind a door, and put the door on her, whereupon she durst not meddle with Simon again' (Feldman 2014, 10).

54. LMA, COL/CA/05/02, A–C, 22 Jan 1711; see also s.v. 'Clarke, n.d.' Numerous contemporary complaints exist about this practice: GL, MS 5257/3, f. 39; 5257/5, f. 239; LMA, Repertories, 61/258b, 63/171; 63/373, 64/73, 66/209, 66/291; BRO, J/Tol/2/1, pp. 506, 504, 497–96, 470, 439; BRO, MS 08018, p. 27; McGrath 1952, 38, 40, 49; Pelling 1998, 212–13.

55. BRO, JTOL/J/2/1, p. 504 (2 Mar 1677).

56. Jackson 1877, 199.

57. Lever 1891, 14.

58. TNA, IR1/3, 61.

59. Ben-Amos 1991, 170. See also Nicholas 1995, 1125.

60. Hutton 1872, 134–36.

61. Gent 1832, 50–51, 67.

62. Gent 1832, 11–12.

63. Ben-Amos 1991, 167.

64. Webb 1994–, s.v. 'Joyce Francis (19 Oct 1771)'. Tallvin paid for him to be lodged nearby, rather than living in, adding to the uncertainty of the measure.

65. Wallis 2002, 146; Feldman 2014, 42. On illicit intercompany transfers, see Schwarz 1992, 218.

66. LMA, COL/CA/05/02, D–K, s.v. 'Gibbs, c. 1718'.

67. In Bristol, fifty-three apprentices (twenty-two of whom were present) were bound to masters who died before 1696 and whose widows maintained their households.

68. The linkage was restricted to apprentices bound from 1688 to 1695 who were not found with their own masters and who did not possess a common name (e.g., John Smith, Thomas Powell). The sixty-five people matched to apprentices were with forty-six different masters. The initial linkage was on forename and surname using Double Metaphone, followed by manual checking.

69. For London, this is based on freedom records for eighteen companies with 674 apprentices in the sample: the Masons, Clockmakers, Curriers, Tylers, Carmen, Ironmongers, Blacksmiths, Painters, Fishmongers, Distillers, Stationers, Apothecaries, Butchers, Turners, Vintners, Innholders, Cooks, and Grocers. For Bristol, see Bristol & Avon Family History Society 2004.

70. For certification, see LMA, COL/CHD/FR/12/048, s.v. 'Cheale 1766'. Disenfranchisement was enforced; see, for example, LMA, Repertories, v. 70, f. 19b; v. 87, ff. 199b, 206b, 210; v. 91 f. 98; v. 92, ff. 103, 215; LMA, COL CHD/FR/12/048, s.v. 'Ansley (1720)'. Some disenfranchisement cases, including untrue declarations by masters, are indexed at LMA, COL/CHD/FR/12/005.

71. The proportion of apprentices later freed who were present in 1695 was 67% in London and 72% in Bristol. Both city differences have high levels of statistical significance, with t-statistics above 7.

72. The proportions of absent apprentices later freed are London 25%, Bristol 31%.

73. Cf. Lane 1996, 2.

74. Studies of contracts show much variation within trades and shorter terms. De Munck 2007, 43–49, 63; Kaplan 1993, 450–51. On journeywork, see Reith 2008; Ehmer 1994.

75. Schalk 2016; Schalk et al. 2017; Van den Wyngaert 2021, 173–211.

76. Acemoglu and Pischke 1999; Smits and Stromback 2000.

77. Minns and Wallis 2013.

78. See, for example, Cappelli 1996; Bednarz 2014; Mohrenweiser and Backes-Gellner 2010.

Chapter 7. Enforcing Apprenticeship

1. GL, MS 5257/5, f. 404 (9 Aug 1647). Several freemen of the guild were named Haydon/ Heydon in this period.

2. On politics within guilds in this period, see Carlin 1994, 228.

3. The charges against (and conviction of) Ashforth are detailed in a pamphlet, Brasbridge 1796 (ESTC N048463). Surviving bills from his business held in the British Museum note his address: 'No.100 Fleet St. Removed from 98' (Heal, 67.35, dated 1805), https://www.britishmuseum.org/collection/term/BIOG213018. There is no record of Brasbridge binding Ashforth in the Vinters' company registers.

4. Brasbridge 1824, 108–9. Brasbridge does not name the apprentice, but it was probably Charles Farebrother, who was bound for that sum on 6 February 1799. Webb 1994–, Vintners' Company, s.v. 'Farebrother'; TNA, IR1/37, f. 225.

5. Important discussions of apprentices in courts include Griffiths 1996, 303–12; Smith 1973, 152–53.

6. Cf. Ben-Amos 2008, 324–25.

7. Dunlop and Denman 1912, 174. See also Lane 1996, 4; Archer 1991, 216–19; Rappaport 1989, 209, 234.

8. Epstein 1998, 685, 687.

9. De la Croix et al. 2018.

10. Smith 1776; Ogilvie 2019, 354–437; Caracausi 2017, 108; De Munck 2011.

11. Hay 2004; Steinfeld 1991.

12. Wallis 2002.

13. Archer 1991, 125–27.

14. Cf. Archer 1991, 217.

15. Goldsmiths' Company Archive, Minutes of the Court of Assistants, MS L2, f. 364.

16. GL, MS CL/B/1/3 (Clothworkers' Company, Court Minutes), f. 27r (30 July 1583). The other cases were Goldsmiths' Company Archive, Court Minutes, MS Q2, f. 152v (15 Jan 1629), Farmer v Scarborough; L2, f. 344 (18 Nov 1577), Norrys v Shakleton.

17. GL, MS CL/B/1/3, f. 14r, 26 Jun 1582, f. 15v (12 Sept 1582). Orders can be identified for thirty-eight disputes brought before guilds in our sample; twelve were simply told to continue.

18. GL, MS 4329/3, f. 4 (6 Dec 1636).

19. GL, MS 4329/3, f. 4v (6 Dec 1636).

20. GL, MS CL/B/1/3, ff. 15r, 15v (4, 18 Sept 1582).

21. GL, MS 5445/7, n.f. (15 Jan 1583). Parsons had been bound to Maurice Waide on 28 November 1581. Webb 1994–, Brewers, s.v. 'Parsons'.

22. Scott 2019, s.v. 'Pavitt'.

23. GL, MS CL/B/1/3, f. 16r (9 Oct 1582).

24. Goldsmiths' Company Archive, L2, f. 271 (6 July 1576).

25. Goldsmiths' Company Archive, L2, f. 370 (3 March 1577).

26. Scott 2019, s.v. 'Grimes'. Merchant Taylors' Company Archive, MS Apprenticeship Registers, 16, f. 183 (14 May 1679). Grimes had been bound 7 April 1674. Grimes did become a freeman

on 21 June 1681, suggesting he had little time (if any) to make up. The Merchant Taylors' registers include fifty-two annotations of this kind from 1603–1740, a period in which they registered almost 49,000 apprenticeships.

27. Scott 2019, s.v. 'Morris'. Merchant Taylors' Company Archive, MS Apprenticeship Registers, 4, f. 247. Morris had been bound on 7 October 1605.

28. Clode 1875, 225 (1613).

29. GL, MS 5177/4, 164r (6 Nov 1632).

30. Guild courts in the sixteenth century are discussed in detail in Rappaport 1989, 201–13, 234–35.

31. LMA, CLA/024/05/15 (1687–90), 16 (1691–1710).

32. GL, MS 5177/2 (3 May 1580).

33. Archer 1991, 127–28.

34. In Madrid, unusually, as well as guild tests for journeymen seeking to become masters, separate examinations for apprentices were organised privately and written into indentures, with both the apprentice's family and the master appointing an examiner (López Barahona and Nieto Sánchez 2019, 50).

35. De Munck 2007.

36. See appendix 4.

37. See appendix 4.

38. Haskins 1912, 221–25 (1613); Ferguson and Nanson 1887, 172–84 (1595).

39. Lambert 1891, 290–98 (1682).

40. GL, MS 4647, f. 182.

41. Wallis 2002.

42. At least during the sample years mentioned in table 7.1

43. Clothworkers' Company 1881, 70 (1587 ordinances).

44. LMA, Rep. 29, f. 24 (1609).

45. Bohun 1702, 339 (quote). Also Greene 1708, 207. Bridewell's own pauper apprentices were more strictly regulated, with evidence of many disciplined for running away. Bridewell Royal Hospital, 'Apprenticeship Indentures and Disciplinary Cases', LL ref: GLBRIA200000031 (http://www.londonlives.org).

46. City of London. Court of Common Council 1680, 254; Greene 1708, 208.

47. LMA, COL/CHD/AP/04/02/002 (Jan 1789–Sept 1793).

48. Hay 2004.

49. These penalties were frequently reduced or forgiven. Bridewell's General Prison Committee never reported more than one apprentice incarcerated at any one time in its surveys of prisoner numbers in the mid-1790s, whereas the records would suggest far higher numbers should have been present. See, for example, Bridewell Royal Hospital, 'Minute Books of the General Prison Committee', 14 Aug 1793, LL GLBRMB201020062 (http://www.londonlives.org). As Griffiths shows in his study of Bridewell, its court dealt with very few apprentices directly (Griffiths 2008, 384).

50. Scott 1863, 186.

51. Royal Commission on Municipal Corporations 1837, 101.

52. Only around a third of those committed to Bridewell in the seventeenth century were recorded in the court records (Dabhoiwala 2006, 806). See also Shoemaker 1991: service disputes (including but not exclusively apprentices) made up 7–8% of Middlesex and Westminster committals in 1660–1720. In the eighteenth century, a separate cell was kept for apprentices. It was ordered that the cell be repaired in 1784. Bridewell Royal Hospital, 'Minutes of the General Prison Committee', 14 July 1784. LL ref: GLBRMB201000024 (http://www.londonlives.org). Lists of prisoners noting numbers of apprentices are recorded on 14 August 1793, 26 September 1793, 13 November 1793, 20 February 1793, 20 February 1794, 30 October 1794, 5 February 1795, and 1 October 1795.

53. Bridewell Royal Hospital, 'Minutes of the Court of Governors', 13 Feb 1690/1: LL ref: BBBRMG202010129 (http://www.londonlives.org).

54. Bridewell Royal Hospital, 'Minutes of the Court of Governors', 12 Sep 1690. LL ref: BBBRMG202010109 (http://www.londonlives.org).

55. City of London. Court of Common Council 1680, 5–6.

56. Wallis 2012.

57. Scott compared attorneys' records and surviving petitions and found that 65% of records of actions made by the attorneys lacked bills, suggesting very large losses, while surviving records of warnings to masters to appear in court suggest that (at most) 82% of petitions survive (Scott 2016, table 8).

58. Emerson 1794, 66–67.

59. Enrolment with the guild had no equivalent significance, and it was widespread.

60. Excessive chastisement, in particular, led masters to respond vigorously; although cited by barely 1% of bills, this led to 13% of jury trials. Whereas 86% of cases citing non-enrolment produced a discharge, just 54% of cases alleging excessive chastisement did.

61. Muldrew 1998, 199–203.

62. LMA, MC6/495A.

63. Barnard n.d., 23. This text is undated, but internal evidence on the statutes cited dates it to between 1746 and 1765. The British Library copy has a manuscript note on the frontispiece: 'Given me before the Chamberlain at the taking of my freedom'.

64. Wallis 2012.

65. Barnard n.d., 23. See also Bohun 1702, 340–41; J. M. 1750, 152.

66. GL, MS 5257/3, f. 11v (13 Feb 1598/9).

67. LMA, CLA/024/07/62 (Nest). Also CLA/024/07/62 (Tayler v Spicer), CLA/024/07/63 (Anderton v Fountain), CLA/024/07/63 (Audley v Greene), CLA/024/07/63 (Hatt v Botley), CLA/024/07/63 (Thornecomb v Taylor), CLA/024/07/88 (Prouting v Lawford), CLA/024/07/89 (Abbingdon v Peacocke), CLA/024/07/01 (Richards v Blanchard), CLA/024/07/02 (Smart v Woodstock); Griffiths 1996, 317; Gowing 2021, 178–79.

68. LMA, CLA/024/07/88 (Burford v Apleford). Similar charges are common, e.g., CLA/024/07/02 (Chapman v Roberts), CLA/024/07/02 (Power v Foster), MC6/502, MC6/504B.

69. LMA, CLA/024/07/62 (Sutton v Woodrow). See also LMA CLA/024/08/84 (26 Mar 1687), MC6/518.

70. GL, CW/B/1/1, f. 3 (5 Sept 1581).

71. Premiums are only available for equity cases (see below); this omits apprentices without premiums and biases the sample to apprentices with large premiums. The mean premium in equity cases citing non-enrolment was £83 against £69 for other causes (n = 243). However, the difference is not statistically significant at the 10% level (t = 1.25).

72. Conversely, easier exit may also have encouraged departure, as the City warned.

73. Kha 2017, 123; Langhamer 2006, 98–99.

74. None of the major record series for the equity side are complete, and this figure is estimated from linking interrogatories, bills, and decrees (Wallis 2012, 808–9).

75. Kearsley 1786, 75. Higher costs were noted occasionally: £9 14s 8d in 1684 LMA, CLA/024/08/82 (Gerey v Sykes).

76. LMA, CLA/024/07/89 (Babington v Hanbury). See also CLA/024/07/01 (Okeover v Withers), CLA/024/07/02 (Smart v Woodcock), MC6/525B, CLA/024/05/016 (Edmonds v Braylsford), MC6/494, MC6/478A.

77. LMA, CLA/024/08/72 (7 Apr 1668). See also MC6/503B (redistribution on apprentice's death).

78. In a sample of forty equity bills, seventeen were initiated by apprentices' fathers, nine by their guardians, six by their mothers, and only eight by apprentices independently. LMA, CLA/024/07/01–02, 63, 88–89.

79. One case where master undertakes to find apprentice a new position: LMA, CLA/024/08/84 (6 Mar 1687).

80. Note that figure 7.1 and subsequent statistics exclude any clothing given with apprentices, as this is valued in only thirty-nine decrees.

81. The proportion of equity cases mentioning non-enrolment (68%) is almost identical to the proportion of discharge bills for non-enrolment in 1690–1720 (66%).

82. LMA, CLA/024/08/074 (24 Oct 1671).

83. Pelling 1988.

84. LMA, MC6/521A.

85. LMA, MC6/433A–B.

86. LMA, MC6/526A. See also MC6/527A.

87. LMA, MC6/552A.

88. LMA, CLA/024/07/62 (Weaver v Feathers)

89. LMA, CLA/024/07/62 (Browne v Brerewood).

90. LMA, CLA/024/07/88 (Burford v Apleford). For apprentice submissions, see LMA, CLA/024/07/88 (Anderton v Hancock), CLA/024/07/88 (Whitchurch v Sambrooke).

91. 'Apprentice faults' include embezzlement (41), running away (24), and general misbehaviour (16).

92. 'Master faults' include turning away apprentices (25), leaving off their trade for various reasons (22), failure to train (12), failure to provide necessaries (10), excessive correction (12), and other ill-usages (5).

93. Hovland 2007, 129–32, 158–59, 164–65; Sutton 1998, 138, n. 76.

94. Hovland 2007, 130. Another third had masters who had left trading or the city; a third cited instruction; about 5% cited excess correction.

95. Hovland 2007, 154.

96. Dalton 1742, 142–43; Bird 1795, 29–30; Kearsley 1786, 75.

97. Royal Commission on Municipal Corporations 1837, 60, 127.

98. GL, MS 05633A/1: 26 (c. 1650–60).

99. Seaver 1989, 50–56; Ben-Amos 1994, 210–12; Ben-Amos 2008; Horwitz and Cooke 2000, 135, 276. No London exchequer cases in published samples focus on premiums (Horwitz and Cooke 2000, 7). Damages were written into some Montreal contracts (Hamilton 1996).

100. Derbyshire Record Office, D258/20/4/1. A larger bond, of £3,000, was suggested in 1676 by David for an apprenticeship in his partnership (Roseveare 1987, 432).

101. Worth 1886, 243–44. On bonds, see Ben-Amos 1994, 87.

102. Scott 2019.

103. Seemingly, it was Barnardiston's haircut that drew the first use of the term 'roundhead', when the queen noted him in the crowd and commented on 'what a handsome young Round-head is there' (de Rapin 1759, 9:410, n. 2).

104. Matthews 1940; Shrewsbury Glovers: SRO, SBR 6001/16/2/126; Shrewsbury Weavers: SRO, SBR 6001/16/2/3359, 6001/16/2/3350 (sampled 1609–14, 1664–71, 1725–58); Newcastle Barber Surgeons: Tyne and Wear Archives, GU.BS.

105. BRO, JTOL/J/2/1: 506 (27 Oct 1677). The Sievemakers guild made a similar complaint in 1678 (p. 497–96, 20 January 1678), the Coopers in 1680 (p. 470, 30 June 1680), and the Ironmongers in 1682 (p. 439, 6 November 1682). The mayor and aldermen had made an order seeking to prevent colourable service in February 1672 (BRO, MS 06157: 27).

106. Davids 2007, 66–70; Schalk 2019, 205–6. See also Stabel 2007, 175. Humphries also draws attention to characteristics that could induce commitment to contracts in the absence of guilds (Humphries 2003, 87–92).

107. Zucca Micheletto 2019, 91.

108. De Munck et al. 2019, 233; De Kerf 2014, 249–50.

109. De Bie 2014, 293.

110. Caracausi 2017, esp. 104.

111. Ogilvie 2019, 411–14.

112. BRO, JTOL/J/2/1, 11 (18 Apr 1674).

113. BRO, JTOL/J/2/1, 1–50, 432–548. See also Ben-Amos 2008.

114. Ben-Amos 2008, 322–23.

115. Hudson and Tingey 1906, 2:179; Taylor 2002, 10.

116. Hertfordshire Record Office, SBR/456/6, 7.

117. Personal communications from C. W. Brooks and Craig Muldrew.

118. Clark 1979, 61–62; Pelling 1998, 216–17. Carlisle's oath required enrolment (Ferguson and Nanson 1887, 51). Norwich required enrolment in 1512 (Hudson and Tingey 1906, 108), and Beverley in 1728 (Dennett 1933, 93).

119. Many appear to have believed that they could summarily punish idle and disorderly apprentices and servants under the Vagabonds Act of 1609 (7 Ja I, c. 4, s. 5). Hay and Craven 2004, 77. Marshall finds several examples of justices appearing to act on apprentices under this law (Marshall 2013, 267).

120. 20 Geo II, c 19, s. 3. Level raised to £25 in 4 Geo 4, c. 29, s. 1.

121. 6 Geo III, c. 25.

122. 33 Geo III, c. 55.

123. Barlow 1745, 34. This power was tested and settled gradually. Kearsley 1786, 81–83; Comyns 1800, 552; Salkeld 1773, 67–68.

124. Kirke 1899, 57.

125. 5 Eliz I, c.4, s. 35. Rushton 1991, esp. 96–98; Ben-Amos 1988, 55; Lane 1996, 214–27; King 2004.

126. Le Hardy 1931, 115.

127. Burchall 2008, no. 185.

128. Buckley 1909, 171.

129. Greene 1708, 29.

130. The bankruptcy of the master became a cause for discharge under 6 Geo IV. c. 16, s. 49.

131. Cases in which a share of premiums is returned can be seen in examples from three counties. Le Hardy 1905, 2, 19, 20, 25; Le Hardy 1931, 92, 115, 133; Le Hardy and Reckitt 1939, 7, 10, 18–19.

132. The scale of justices' involvement is difficult to estimate, as not all their involvement in apprenticeship occurred at sessions (Marshall 2013, 264).

133. Middlesex Sessions, 'General Orders of the Court', 20 Feb 1752. LL ref: LMSMGO556020514 (http://www.londonlives.org),

134. Samples of cases taken for 1690 and 1709 (Le Hardy 1905). For population estimates, see Harding 1990, 112.

135. Steinberg 2006; Hay and Craven 2004.

136. Stabel 2007, 161.

137. López Barahona and Nieto Sánchez 2019, 51.

138. Colavizza et al. 2019, 109–10.

139. Zucca Micheletto 2019, 91–92. More generally, see Cerutti 2002, 1491–520.

140. Stöger and Reith 2019, 157–58.

141. Crowston and Lemercier 2019, 290–91.

142. De Munck 2007, 16; De Munck 2010, 4–5, 16–19.

143. Schalk 2019, 204–6, quote at 206.

144. Uotila 2019, 175.

145. Zucca Micheletto 2019, 92–95.

146. De Munck 2007, 216–17.

147. Ogilvie 2019, 521, 530, 537–40, 557–59; de la Croix et al. 2018, 17–18.

148. Humphries 2003.

149. One possibility suggested by de la Croix et al. 2018, 17–18.

150. Gelderblom 2013; Gelderblom and Grafe 2010.

151. An alternative often associated with China is to draw recruits from a specific rural place into a defined urban occupation. This is observed in Europe in a few cases (glass making, terrazzo). It does not seem widespread, and the system comes at the cost of preventing families from matching their resources and their children's abilities to their future occupations.

152. The sequence of institutional arrangements in this account might look somewhat different. Where de la Croix et al. envisage a sequence of family > clan > guild > state, or family > guild > state, Europe might be closer to clan > family > state, with the 'family' stage coexisting with the development of corporative institutions, such as urban and manorial bodies, that allowed cooperation among non-kin and so made nuclear families viable. The early existence of independent cities is noted by de la Croix 2018, 60.

153. Hay and Craven 2004; Frank 2010; Naidu and Yuchtman 2013; Deakin and Wilkinson 2005.

Chapter 8. Outcomes

1. University of Oxford [1681] 2011.

2. Lackington 1793, 127.

3. In the City of London, journeymen were required to be full guild members, i.e., masters. From 1750, the City introduced a system to license the employment of non-free journeymen by citizens. At least in theory, free journeymen still possessed a priority in hiring.

4. Ogilvie 2019, 87–93.

5. Prak 2018. Growth in oligarchy linked to this is discussed in Clark and Slack 1972, 20–24; Brooks 1994. For a classic illustration of citizenship and oligarchy, see Friedrichs 1975.

6. Withington 2005, 29.

7. The Court of Aldermen and Common Council had complained that the chartered merchant companies were accepting non-freemen from the early seventeenth century onwards, and it sought to address this via charter reform and other strategies into the 1660s. LMA, Rep. 43, f. 5v (1628), 60, f. 63 (1649); 67, f. 198 (1660); LMA, JCC, 38, f. 103r (1638).

8. Permissions to take non-free journeymen prior to 1750 suggest the bar possessed at least some meaning before that date. John Lee, goldbeater, was allowed to take foreign journeymen to help him in some work for the king. LMA, Rep. 44, f. 354 (1630). Other licences: LMA, Rep. 91, f. 131b (c. 1685); Rep. 108, f. 91 (1703); Rep. 110, f. 195v (1706); Rep. 126, f. 33 (1721); Rep. 133, f. 258 (1729); Rep. 153, f. 327 (1749). The need for unusual skills justified exceptions on several occasions. In 1717, Harding's petition was because 'he could get no freemen capable of doing his business, being engine work of new inventions'. LMA, Rep. 121, f. 349, 358 (1717). In 1729, Greaves was allowed to employ a foreigner to finish 'some ceilings done in a sort of work called Stuckoe work that no freeman is capable of performing the same'. LMA, Rep. 133, f. 310 (1729). A petition to allow foreign journeymen to be employed on building the mayor's residence, Mansion House, was rejected, and at least one of the artisans was arrested for not being free. LMA, Rep. 144, f. 264 (1740), Rep. 145, f. 205 (1741). In the sixteenth century the Bakers had a general exemption, being allowed to employ foreigners 'for they cannot otherwise serve'. This was abolished in 1623 after a dispute with the free journeymen. GL, MS 5195, f. 52v, 60v–61v.

9. Berlin 1997, 2008.

10. Proceedings preventing former apprentices becoming burgesses in Beverley and non-burgesses from trading can be found in the 1810s (Dennett 1933, 119, 122–23, 131, 141).

11. Weber 1966.

12. The requirement that the wardens of the company attend and declare that the prospective citizen is a freeman of their company was restated in an order of 1687 (LMA, Rep. 92, f. 221) and later revived, having been 'greatly neglected', in 1717 (Rep. 122, f. 177 [1717]).

13. Greene 1708, 209–10. In 1729, the Court of Aldermen approved a master who had retired to the country supplying an affidavit to his apprentice's service: LMA, Rep. 134, f. 187 (1729). And again in 1733: Rep. 138, f. 101 (1733).

14. Evidence on the mobility of journeymen in England is limited, though widespread in parts of Europe. Fragmentary evidence, largely from the eighteenth century, is collated by Leeson, but in many guilds there is clear evidence of effective prohibitions. See Leeson 1979; Hobsbawm 1964.

15. Gent 1832, 17.

16. The Weavers, Clockmakers, and Horners all required two years of service as a journeyman before establishing a shop. See appendix 4.

17. Carpenters' ordinances. Similar bars existed in the Goldsmiths and Coopers (for first two years), Pewterers (first year), the Tylers and Bricklayers (first four years). The Clothworkers limited new members to one apprentice for the first two years, the Apothecaries limited freemen to one apprentice during first three years (1617–36). See appendix 4.

18. Requirements for examination by the guild's governors were in the rules of Hull's Weavers (1490, 1673) and Cordwainers (1564); Salisbury's Shoemakers (1613), Bakers (1675), Butchers (1614), and Barbers (1675); Devizes's Merchants (1614); and Carlisle's Shoemakers (1595) and Glovers (1665). In Bristol, they needed permission from the mayor: Tylers & Plaisterers (n.d.), Barber Surgeons (1652).

19. GL, MS 05496, ff. 10–11.

20. Ainsworth et al. 1913–68, 1:5–13.

21. Reddaway and Walker 1975, 230.

22. Greene 1708, 210.

23. LMA, Rep. 21, f. 385b (1587); reiterated in Rep. 26.2, f. 356v (1604), Rep. 58, f. 29v (c. 1642, index only).

24. In these situations, the chamberlain could order him to appear and show cause for his refusal. City of London. Court of Common Council 1680, 257; Greene 1708, 206.

25. 22 Hen VIII, c. 4 and 28 Hen VIII, c. 5 banned additional fees for setting up shop, etc. On apprenticeship fees, see chapter 9.

26. GL, MS 34006, ff. 57r–60r.

27. Company officials might also extort additional fees for services. In 1633, the beadle and porter of the Drapers were forbidden to demand fees beyond those allowed by the ordinances for binding or making free. They had been demanding 1s from those entering by apprenticeship and 2s from those entering by redemption or patrimony, rather than the 4d allowed (Johnson 1914–22, 3:192, n.2).

28. Wallis 2002; Dowling 1889, 40; Scott 1961, 15. The Needlemakers charged 10s (London Needlemakers Company 1876, 31); the Basketmakers spoon was to be worth 10s (Bobart 1911, 107).

29. LMA, Rep. 32, f. 366 (1616).

30. LMA, Rep. 37, f. 214v (1622).

31. Johnson 1914–22, 3:193.

32. Ferguson and Nanson 1887, 183.

33. BRO, MS 08018; Matthews 1940; Hill 1956, 80; Unwin 1995; Lambert 1891, 174, 195, 217, 238, 251–56, 290–98; Ferguson 2000, 94–95, 101, 211–18, 244–46.

34. Wallis et al. 2015, table 3.

35. Wallis et al. 2015, 25.

36. Wallis et al. 2015, 25; Stabel 2007, 160.

37. Elkington 1930, 160. His sources are not clear, though. In some trades, journeymen imposed entry fines at a firm level, as Benjamin Franklin discovered when 5s for drink was demanded from him on joining a London printing house (Franklin 1894, 41).

38. Figures for the 1550s (89.5%) are from Rappaport 1989, 292 n. 8. For the 1660s, see LMA, Col/CHD/FR/01/003 (1668–69).

39. Barron 2004, 205.

40. Sutton 1998, 138–39; Barron 2004.

41. Rogers 1989, 287–88.

42. An extensive literature is usefully summarised in Ogilvie 2019, 406–7. The gap narrowed in the eighteenth century, but this was because of a growth in the share of freemen qualifying by inheritance and purchase, not because apprentices became more likely to make the step.

43. Ben-Amos 1991.

44. See appendix 8. There is no significant difference between migrants and sons of citizens.

45. Minns and Wallis 2013.

46. The marginal effects for master occupations are presented in appendix 8.

47. See also Stabel 2007, 175.

48. Grassby 2000, 45.

49. Marshall 1890, bk. 4, chap. 12, para. 7, n. 144.

50. Grassby also recognises this rarely occurred but does not report his totals as a share of businessmen for whom he had an identified master (2000, 51).

51. Calculated from M. L. Turner, *The London Book Trades: A Biographical and Documentary Resource*, http://lbt.bodleian.ox.ac.uk/mediawiki/index.php/Main_Page.

52. These figures are based on two things. (1) The first is linkage between burgesses of Bristol entering by apprenticeship (for whom the register includes their masters' names) and marriage records. Links were identified when (i) surname and forename (in Double Metaphone) match; (ii) the initial letters of the surname also match (to reduce the risk of false positives in Double Metaphone); (iii) the occupation of groom and apprentice match. N = 94 (free 1700–1799), 5.3% marry a bride with their master's surname. Exact string matches on name and occupation produce N = 74 (free 1700–1799), of whom 5.5% marry a potential relative. (2) The second is linkage between apprenticeship records for Bristol and the burgess records (as used above). 212 apprentices were identified among burgesses admitted by marriage in 1700–1799. Among this group, 3% married a bride whose father had the same surname and forename as their master. In 1800–1899, only 1% of the 154 apprentices linked to burgesses by marriage married their master's daughter. Sources: Apprentices and Citizen record, as in section 1; marriage records: Price 2015, 2014, 2014; Bristol & Avon Family History Society 2004, 2008.

53. Grassby 2000, 53.

54. Overall, 23% of marriages in our two London samples were to widows (n = 222), but only 11% of marriages (n = 127) that occurred in the two years prior or the four years after the groom became a freeman were to widows.

55. These figures are relative to the pool of 186 marriages with information on whether the bride was in the master's family or the bride's father shared their occupation or guild.

56. *Oxford Journal*, 27 April 1793. I am grateful to Melanie Winterbottom for sharing her research into Furnell which revealed this story.

57. *Gloucester Journal*, 4 August 1794.

58. The Cambridge Group reconstitutions are described in Wrigley 1998 and Wrigley et al. 2018. The People in Place project was led by Vanessa Harding and the data are Baker et al. 2020. Not

all of the parishes analysed by Wrigley et al. have the names of parishioners digitized. I matched apprentices to children born in these parishes based on name, gender, common place, and (where available) occupation. Links were restricted, so the age at binding was between twelve and thirty years, and excluded potential duplicates in either parish or guild records. Names were linked initially using the Double Metaphone algorithm and then checked.

59. An earlier version of these results was published as Klemp et al. 2013. The sample size here is larger (1,696 vs. 1,362 observations).

60. The apprentices identified baptising children do not all overlap with those identified marrying: forty-four of ninety-seven who baptised children have no associated marriage record, indicating marriage occurred elsewhere.

61. The differences reported for provincial apprentices in this sentence are both statistically significant at the 1% level. The differences for London apprentices are not statistically significant at conventional levels.

62. Linkages were made by hand based on name and supplementary information on father's name and occupation, where given. Links were rejected where name data conflicted, where the claim was based on service (local apprenticeship), and where more than fifty years separated binding and entry to citizenship (allowing an age range of c. sixteen to c. sixty-six). Reliability was coded based on the amount of evidence for the link, with weak being just a name match, medium a name and father's name, and strong a match on the name, father's name, and father's occupation. Boston's freedom register was searched for apprentices indentured 1605–1800 (Boston Borough Council n.d.); Bristol's burgess register was searched for 1558 onwards (Bristol & Avon Family History Society 2004); Canterbury's register runs from 1392 (Cowper 1903); Chester's register runs from 1392 (Chester 1904–5, 1906–7); Exeter runs from 1266 (Rowe and Jackson 1973). Gloucester's survive from 1641 (Ripley and Jurica 1991). Ipswich runs from 1320 (McCurrach 1997), King's Lynn from 1292 (*Calendar of the Freemen of Lynn* 1913), Leicester from 1196 (Hartopp 1927), Lincoln from 1642 (Lincolnshire Family History Society n.d.), Newcastle upon Tyne from 1539 (Dodds 1923; Oliver 1926), Norwich from 1548 (Millican 1934, 1952), and York from 1559 (Freemen 1900).

63. A few—eight—were accepted as citizens of their hometown before becoming apprentices.

64. Shifts between status (e.g., alderman) and occupation (e.g., merchant) are a particular issue here.

65. Some may have claimed citizenship to acquire the right to vote without taking up residence. This certainly occurred in the eighteenth century, as poll lists with addresses make clear. However, the effect seems limited, and the share returning in 1600–1650, when elections were less common and votes less valuable, was similar at 10%.

66. Twenty-eight of seventy-six London apprentices identified as citizens of provincial cities. They were freed into seven London guilds—the Drapers, Goldsmiths, Mercers, Merchant Taylors, Musicians, Salters, and Stationers—between 1600 and 1800. Most (fourteen) were observed in 1600–1649.

67. Lackington 1793, 175–76.

68. Barriers have been extensively surveyed by Ogilvie; note here that we are considering openness as a relative characteristic, compared to other parts of Europe, and in a society in which many forms of economic and migratory choices were restricted. See Ogilvie 2019, chap. 3.

Chapter 9. Laws, Rules, and Barriers to Skill

1. The discussion dates to the earliest work in political economy. In Smith's work it was mainly the impact on consumers, but later studies emphasised the impact on other workers. Smith 1776; Walker 1876, pt. 2, chap. 17. Modern literature on rents from closed labour markets through licensing is surveyed in Kleiner 2006.

2. North et al. 2009; see also Acemoglu and Robinson 2019.

3. Barriers to training are discussed extensively in Ogilvie 2003, 96–99, 131–33; 2019, 354–437; 2011.

4. The origins of the statute are discussed in Woodward 1981. For earlier laws, see Putnam 1908; Palmer 1993. More generally, see Cohn 2007.

5. A similar requirement had been imposed in 1555, for weaving and cloth manufacturing (2 & 3 Ph. & Mary, c. 11). Earlier laws had applied seven-year terms to specific trades: a law limiting the use of worsted shearing in Norwich to those who had served seven-year apprenticeships in 1495 (11 Hen 7, c. 11) was overturned in 1503 by a law that claimed that the limit had been used 'to inhance the Price of Shearing of Worsteds' (19 Hen 7, c. 17).

6. A few specific exclusions were included for Norwich worsted makers and weavers (s. 34), London and Norwich (s. 40), and Godalming (s. 41)

7. Deakin and Wilkinson 2005, 56. For the textile industry specifically, see Gendron 2023.

8. Note that a reference by Lane (1996, 5 n. 16) to an act (8 Geo III c. 28) that supposedly lowered the age of completion to twenty-one is spurious; I have identified no act of this kind that applies to private apprentices.

9. 5 Eliz 1, c. 4, s. 33. Rules on apprentice numbers had been included in earlier acts (11 Hen 7, c.11; 14 & 15 Hen 8, c. 3, s. 8).

10. 5 Eliz 1, c, 4, s. 26.

11. 5 Eliz 1, c. 4, s. 28.

12. 5 Eliz 1, c, 4, s. 27, 29.

13. 5 Eliz 1, c. 4, s. 30.

14. 14–15 Hen VIII, c. 2 (1523); 5 Eliz 1, s. 32. Weavers of Frizes, Cottons, and Housewifes Cloth in Cumberland, Westmorland, Lancashire, and Wales were excepted.

15. Apprenticeship had been restricted to the children of parents worth 20s in land or rent in 1405 (7 Hen IV, c. 17). In 1495, Norwich citizens were allowed to apprentice the son of any person, and in 1496 this was extended to all worsted weavers in Norfolk (11 Hen 7, c. 11; 12 Hen 7, c. 1).

16. See 1 Ric 3; 14 & 15, Hen VIII, c. 2; 33 Hen. 8, c. 4. Aliens faced limits on taking apprentices under 32 Hen 8, s. 3, 8, and this remained an issue (Luu 2005: 202–5). There was no equivalent national ban on English masters taking alien apprentices, but urban rules were in place for some periods.

17. 'Considerations delivered to the Parliament, 1559', in Tawney and Power 1924, 1:325–30.

18. 5 Eliz I, c. 4, s. 4, 7. The act is ambiguous in that it gives the justices the right to force people into service (s. 4) but also allows those who refuse to 'be an Apprentice, and to serve in Husbandry, or in any other Kind of Art' when required to by any householder to be imprisoned (s. 35). It was interpreted as allowing the justices to compel people into apprenticeship.

19. 5 Eliz I, c. 4, s. 35.

20. 27 Hen VIII, c. 25; 1 Ed VI, c. 3.

21. 39 Eliz I, c. 3; 43 Eliz I, c. 2. The language of the acts is essentially identical on this point. A 1609 act set out regulations on how parishes should use charity funds for binding apprentices (21 Jas 1, c. 3).

22. On earlier uses of apprenticeship for paupers, which had been anticipated for beggars' children in earlier statutes, see McIntosh 2013, 31. Generally, Hindle 2004, 191–223; Crawford 2010, 213–18.

23. The authority of parishes to impose apprentices was questioned throughout the seventeenth century until 1696–97, when statute law specifically gave them this power (Hindle 2004, 198–202). That at least some masters were compelled by the parish to take apprentices is implicit in the 1780 act that stated that the Guardians of the Poor, who were now placing paupers, had

the same power to impose apprentices as the churchwardens had previously exercised (20 Geo III, c. 36).

24. 39 Eliz I, c. 3 (fourteen-year cap); 43 Eliz 1, c. 2 (age at end); 8 Anne, c. 9 (sixteen-year-old cap). The young age of pauper apprentices is apparent in surviving records (Hindle 2004, 214; Levene 2010). Institutional charities were in a middle ground (Berry 2023).

25. López Barahona and Nieto Sánchez 2019, 51–53; Zucca Micheletto 2019, 95–101; Schalk 2019, 191; De Munck et al. 2019, 226–28.

26. Hatmakers: 8 Eliz. C.11 (1566), 1 Jas I, c. 17 (1603), 5 Geo II, c. 22, s. 7 (1731), 16 Geo III, c. 55 (1776); Skinners: 3 Jas I, c. 9 (1605); Printers: 14 Chas II, c. 33, s. 13 (1662); Norwich weavers: 14 Chas II, c. 5, s. 15–18 (1662).

27. Silkweavers: 13 Geo III, c. 68 (1772); Coventry: 21 Geo III, c. 54 (1781).

28. The bakers act is from Dobson 1980, 114. Deakin and Wilkinson date the first as the clothworkers in 1733 and the hatters in 1777 (Deakin and Wilkinson 2005).

29. 1654 act: 12 Chas II, c. 16; 10 William III, c. 17; 6 Geo II, c. 37, s. 3; 1777 17 Geo II, c. 55, s. 5; 24 Geo III, s. 2, c. 6.

30. Bird 1795, 19. Earlier, a number of cases had led to judgements in which apprenticeship was not required where trades (upholsterer, tallow chandler) did not require any skill (Derry 1930, 54–61).

31. This process is best surveyed in Deakin and Wilkinson 2005, 54–58.

32. Dunlop and Denman 1912, 119; Derry 1930, 67–69. The exemption was not fully established though.

33. Dunlop and Denman 1912, 119; Derry 1930, 65–68. The Brewers received legal advice to this effect in 1700 and 1719 (GL, MS 07294).

34. Deakin and Wilkinson 2005, 54–57.

35. Dunlop and Denman 1912, 120–21.

36. Dunlop and Denman 1912, 124.

37. Pearce 1929, 120.

38. 54 Geo III c. 96, s. 2. See Derry 1950; Rule 1981.

39. Hay 2004; Deakin and Wilkinson 2005, 61–71, 106–7.

40. Thelen 2004, 42–47.

41. A written contract was still required if the apprenticeship was to provide the basis for settlement under the Poor Law and if the agreement was for more than a year, because of the Statute of Frauds, 29 Car II, c.3 (Burn 1831, 159). Note that Marshall finds one justice of the peace who decided that a period of service without an indenture could be taken as one (2013, 25–26).

42. Honeyman surveys the statutory framework for pauper apprenticeship (2007, 47–54).

43. 7 Geo III, c. 39 s. 14–15 (1766). The lower age limit was applied to parish apprentices nationwide in 1778 (18 Geo III, c. 47). Note that this act applied only to parish apprentices, not to all males at twenty-one, as Dunlop and Denman and Lane mistakenly suggest (Dunlop and Denman 1912, 167, n. 1; Lane 1996, 5; Simonton 1990, 235).

44. 42 Geo III, c 73. For a detailed discussion, see Innes 2002, 30–55. Paupers bound to chimney sweepers were the subject of an earlier protective act in 1788 (28 Geo III, c. 48).

45. 42 Geo III, c. 46.

46. 56 Geo III, c. 139.

47. 14 Chas II, c. 12 (1662).

48. 3 Wm & Mary, s. 8 (1691). Even before 1691, binding poor apprentices to masters in other communities had been interpreted as a device to shift settlement (Hindle 2004, 199). From 1757, apprentices gained settlement even if their contract was not indented, so long as it was stamped (31 Geo II, c. 11, s. 1). Historians have disagreed on the length of service required. Snell suggests that justices of the peace often demanded completion of apprenticeship in practice (Snell 1985,

258). Others find forty days being applied (Humphries 2003, 77; Marshall 2013; Ely 1986, 8–9). Parishes sought to resist settlement rights being obtained in various ways (Snell 2006, 148–49).

49. Laws encouraging ships and marine trades to take apprentices appeared regularly over this period. For example: 2 Geo III, c. 15, s. 22 (1762) (protected from impressment); 15 Geo III, c. 31, s. 22 (1775) (one apprentice per 50 tons burthen on newfoundland fisheries ships); 37 Geo III c. 73, s. 4 (1797) (one apprentice per 100 tons burthen on West Indies ships). They were accompanied by laws encouraging putting paupers to sea as well (Thomas 1977, 154).

50. 5 Eliz 1, c. 5, s. 12 (1562).

51. 2 & 3 Ann c. 6., s. 1 (1703).

52. 4 & 5 Ann c. 19, s. 16 (1705).

53. 9 Ann c 2. s. 6 (1710/11). Earlier restrictive rules on the numbers of apprentices that Thames Watermen could take were abolished in 1705 by 4 & 5 Ann, c. 3. The City had approved similar rules in the 1630s. LMA, Rep. 52, f. 140 (1638).

54. Whale fishery: 28 Geo II, c. 20, s. 5 (1755); 26 Geo III, c. 41 (1786), 29 Geo III, c. 53 (1789), 32 Geo III, c. 22 (1792). General fisheries: 37 Geo III c. 73, s. 4 (1797). The requirement for ships to carry apprentices was abolished only in 1849 (Withall 2014, 171).

55. A substantial literature on guilds can be usefully accessed via Ogilvie 2019. The specifics of English and London's guilds and citizenship are discussed in Withington 2005; Archer 1991; Rappaport 1989.

56. LMA, JCC, J. 20.1, f. 176b (1574), also J. 20.1, f. 239 (1575); LMA, Rep. 18, f. 256. A precept to the companies ordering that this bar by nationality be enforced was issued in 1575 and reissued in 1582. LMA, Rep. 18, f. 406, Rep. 20, f. 360. One master Stationer who broke the rule had to print 200 copies of the precept at his own expense as part of his penalty. LMA, Rep. 20, f. 380 (1582). See also Luu 2005, 166. The rule against alien apprentices was written into the oath of a new freeman and was still being enforced in the eighteenth century. City of London. Court of Common Council 1680, 252; LMA, Rep. 139, f. 293 (1735).

57. LMA, JCC, J. 17, f. 16 (1556); LMA, Rep. 13.2, f. 423 (1556). The rule was repeated in later orders. J. 16, f. 6b (3 Mar 1). In 1815, redemptioners were required to present a certificate of birth following a disenfranchisement for being admitted too young. LMA, Rep. 219, f. 786 (1815).

58. See LMA, JCC, J. 1, f. 42 (discharge for apprenticing minor). Age rules were reiterated in the eighteenth and nineteenth centuries. Greene 1708, 27; Barnard n.d., 24; LMA, Rep. 216, f. 398 (1812).

59. 1 Jas I, c. 16. (sons could be apprenticed at sixteen if trained to the oar).

60. See for example, the apprentice discharged for being an 'ancient married man'. LMA, Rep. 37, f. 115v (1622).

61. LMA, Rep. 218, f. 58 (1813), Eden v Gaubert.

62. Ogilvie 2019, 93–120, 266–71, 432–34.

63. City of London. Court of Common Council 1680, 47–48.

64. Greene 1708, 34.

65. GL, MS 4647, no. 12; Gowing 2021, 66. Conversely, in 1569 the Drapers restated the century-old practice that a woman might be bound an apprentice and enjoy the freedom, so long as she did not marry (Johnson 1914–22, 2:198).

66. Committee to enquire how Jews have become freemen and to prevent it: LMA, JCC, v. 58, f. 73b (1737). Order barring baptised Jews from entering the freedom: LMA, Rep. 190, f. 143 (1786). Applied in Rep. 190, f. 143 (1786); Rep. 198, f. 231 (1794); Rep. 209, f. 194 (1805); Rep. 220, f. 478 (1816); Rep. 231, ff. 16, 839–44 (1817). The city's ability to exclude Jews was accepted in a case at King's Bench in 1821, reported in Rep. 224, f. 354 (1820). The order against baptised Jews was rescinded in 1827 by Rep. 232, f. 312 (1827). The bar on Jews was maintained in Rep. 235, f. 164 (1831).

67. LMA, Rep. 135, f. 475 (1731). The printed order is LMA, COL/SJ/27/509. Similar rules did not exist in other towns (Chater 2007, 79).

68. Wallis 2002.

69. Reddaway and Walker 1975, 261–62 (1478).

70. Stated in the ordinances for the Butchers, Goldsmiths, Grocers, and Merchant Taylors (appendix 4).

71. Similar clauses about apprentices' bodies were included in ordinances for the Brewers (1482, 1579), Carpenters (1486), Clothworkers (1531/32), Coopers (1507), Grocers (1525), Merchant Taylors (1507), and Barber Surgeons (1530). See also Dunlop and Denman 1912, 44, on the Leathersellers, Skinners, and Mercers, who have similar rules in ordinances from this period. These clauses tended to disappear in ordinances from the seventeenth century onwards.

72. Prideaux 1896–97, 1:9; Nicholl 1851, 121; Welch 1902, 1:290 (nine years, 1582).

73. 15 Hen VI, c. 6; 19 Hen VII, c. 7.

74. The ordinances are listed in appendix 4.

75. Goldsmiths: Reddaway and Walker 1975, 248; Merchant Taylors, 1507 Ordinances, 139–40; Weavers, 1737 Ordinances, GL, MS 10596, f. 45; Gold and Silver Wyre Drawers: Stewart 1891, 71. In an unusual exception to the privilege of sons training without indentures, the Hat Act (1603) required sons to be indentured for seven years (1 Jas. 1 c. 17, para 5).

76. Not all groups agreed. Merchants, in particular, tended to try to evade City regulation. The City's 1638 charter from Charles I required merchants to take apprentices for a minimum of seven years, and to enrol them with the City's chamberlain.

77. The City failed to find evidence to support the custom in Bagshawe's case. His defense in King's Bench, against a suit brought under 5 Eliz I, was that the custom meant that a freeman 'may lawfully at his pleasure use and exercise as well that art mystery manual occupation and faculty whereof he is free as any other art mystery or manual occupation . . . albeit every such freeman was never brought up in the same'. The City's own counsel's report found this right extended only to 'merchandizing and trades'. LMA, Rep. 48, ff. 66r–v (1634).

78. Hudson and Tingey 1906, 2:291.

79. Ferguson and Nanson 1887, 66; Neville 1996, 433.

80. See appendix 4.

81. Carlisle Merchants (1624/56), Shoemakers (1735), and Glovers (1665): Ferguson and Nanson 1887, 94–95, 193–97, 211–18. Norwich Worsted Weavers (1511): Hudson and Tingey 1906, 2:376–78. Salisbury Shoemakers (1613) and Butchers (1614): Haskins 1912, 221–25, 254–59. Hull Cordwainers and Shoemakers (1564/1624): Hey 1991, 140; Lambert 1891, 290–98.

82. As did Hull's Glovers (1499), Norwich's Worsted Weavers (1511), and Carlisle's Shoemakers (1595).

83. Sahle 2018, 228–29; Mortimer 1971; Palmer 1989, 371.

84. De Munck et al. 2014.

85. Lane 1996, 3.

86. Rule 1989.

87. Ogilvie 2019; Wallis et al. 2015, passim.

88. López Barahona and Nieto Sánchez 2019, 70–71 (Spain); Nieto Sánchez and Llorente 2016 (Madrid); Zucca Micheletto 2019, 84–85 (Turin); Colavizza et al. 2019, 113 (Venice); Stöger and Reith 2019, 141, 149; De Munck et al. 2019, 230, 233–34 (Southern Netherlands); Schalk 2019, 189, 194–95 (Northern Netherlands); Kaplan 1993, 455–56.

Chapter 10. Exclusion in Practice?

1. Davies 1956, 18–22, 77–107; Derry 1930.

2. Davies 1956; Derry 1930.

3. Davies 1956, 6; Derry 1930.

4. The fine was limited to £24, or twelve months, in 1589 (Davies 1956, 24).

5. Several proposals for central registries were made between 1573 and 1619, but the only patent granted (in 1619 to Sir James Spence) operated for less than a year before being struck down. Davies 1956, 33–37; Derry 1930, 35–37.

6. Occasionally, contracts are registered at Quarter Sessions, but this was rare.

7. Davies 1956, 8, n. 28.

8. Söderlund 1949, 398.

9. See appendix 1 for sources.

10. TNA, IR1.

11. Barlow 2001.

12. Oxford, 1590–1600: Crossley 2012.

13. Using the 1600–1609 England rental price: Clark 2002, 297.

14. Minns and Wallis 2013.

15. Shepard and Spicksley's survey of statements of worth suggests average levels well in excess of £3 by 1600 for most groups above labourers (Shepard and Spicksley 2011, 517).

16. Expenditure on pauper apprenticeship is apparent in a range of studies: Kent and King 2003, n. 60; Hindle 2004, 216–17; Sharpe 1991, 256; Turner 1883, 98–99, 103.

17. Westminster City Archives, St Clement Danes Overseers' Accounts, B24 (1631); Scott 2019, s.v. 'Bellamy, William'. There is no reference to the parish in the binding record by the guild.

18. Hindle 2004, 198.

19. Hindle 2004, 215–16.

20. Boston Borough Council n.d., s.v. 'Watson, Edward (1676)', 'Cleasby, Roger (1676)', 'Sleight, John (1665)', 'Halliday, Richard (1676)', 'Tingcombe, John (1665)', 'Barke, Samuel (1665)'. Information on consent for binding is only recorded occasionally. Hartopp 1927, passim; Lincolnshire Family History Society, n.d.; Power et al. 1998.

21. Webb 1994–, s.v. 'Blacksmiths' Company'.

22. GL, MS 2886/5; Webb 1994–, s.v. 'Weavers' Company'.

23. Bridewell Hospital, 'Minutes of the Court of Governors'. References to apprentices becoming freeman are common in petitions relating to Lock's Gift (a capital fund the hospital managed to help them set up in business), for example BBBRMG202030041 or BBBRMG202030049 or BBBRMG202030731. See Hitchcock et al. 2012.

24. Webb 1994–, s.v. 'Salters' Company', 'Woolnoth Smith'.

25. López Barahona and Nieto Sánchez 2019, 51–53; Zucca Micheletto 2019, 95–101; Schalk 2019, 191; De Munck et al. 2019, 226–28.

26. Luu 2005.

27. Van Lottum 2011.

28. The numbers affected were not trivial. In 1593, a survey of aliens in London reported the presence of 244 sons and 245 daughters born abroad, with 1,393 sons and 979 daughters born in England (Luu 2005, 132). Estimates of migrant numbers vary, but from 1550 to 1600, perhaps 10,000 Londoners were immigrants from the continent, and another 40,000 settled elsewhere in England (Pettigree 1986).

29. These tensions were of long standing, of course (Lambert and Pajic 2016).

30. Luu 2005, 127–28; Moens 1887, 269–70.

31. Luu 2005, 128–29. Alien apprentices were more common in earlier surveys from the 1520s and 1540s (Kirk and Kirk 1900–1908, 3, 5, 27, 60, 70–71).

32. Luu 2005, 203.

33. Luu 2005, 247.

34. De Munck 2007, 170–71; Stöger and Reith 2019, 150–51; López Barahona and Nieto Sánchez 2019, 60–61; Colavizza et al. 2019, 116–21.

35. England was linked to the circulation of skilled journeymen from the continent, particularly before the Reformation. See Luu 2005; Lutkin 2016; Ormrod et al. 2018.

36. I surveyed fees between 1550 and 1800 for eleven London companies: the Bakers, Brewers, Butchers, Carpenters, Clothworkers, Coopers, Drapers, Grocers, Merchant Taylors, Pewterers, and the Tylers and Bricklayers. A statutory limit of 2s 6d had been set on apprentice enrolment fees in 22 Hen VIII, c. 4 (1530).

37. Wm & Mary, c. 10, s. 6 (1694).

38. Clothworkers Company 1840, 15.

39. Taking fees and costs for sixteen points in time for seventeen different London companies, in ten cases, the fee is between 33% and 67% of the total cost.

40. Fee level recorded in City of London. Court of Common Council 1680, 42, and in eighteenth-century publications. Fees had been increased at times in the fifteenth century by the city to defray debt (Leach 2017, 137–38).

41. Allen 2001. Using the 20d per day figure for c. 1650

42. Rappaport 1989, 47–49. How long high fees had been in place is unclear. The Carpenters, for example, raised fees from 12d to 3s only in 1508 (Leach 2017, 137).

43. Carlisle Glovers (1665) and Butchers (1665); Bristol Soapmakers (1580) and Barber Surgeons (1652).

44. Salisbury Butchers (1614) and Barber Surgeons (1675); Shrewsbury Barber Surgeons (1662); Bristol Glovers (1670).

45. Fees made up 14–51% of the total cost of entry. Note that this information was only obtained for four provincial guilds: Salisbury Bakers (1675), Butchers (1614), Barber Surgeons (1675), and Carlisle Shoemakers (1595).

46. Ferguson and Nanson 1887, 249.

47. Using the 12d per diem wage reported in Allen 2001 dataset for Northern England.

48. The fees reported here are in Wallis et al. 2015. Ogilvie's sample overlaps in part, but differs on Paris and England (Ogilvie 2019).

49. Levene 2010.

50. Rappaport 1989, 323–25. See also Dunlop and Denman 1912, 134–35, 258–59; Le Hardy 1930, 2:326.

51. LMA, Rep., 216, f. 398 (2 Jun 1812), 217, f. 70 (1 Dec 1812).

52. Rappaport 1989, 295–96.

53. N = 14,647. Details of the underlying data are in Wallis et al. 2010.

54. The ages discussed here are based on baptismal dates in parish records (which lag birth to some extent) and the date of registration of indentures (which often anticipate a later start date), so some of the thirteen-year-old apprentices are likely to have been fourteen when they started service.

55. Based on linkages of small samples of apprentices to parish records (Barlow 2001, xvii; Crossley 2012, xviii).

56. For comparison, Snell's exploration of provincial apprenticeship found that the mean age of entry among those later examined under settlement regulations rose, with a mean age of 14.0 years in 1700–1760, 14.1 in 1761–80, and 14.3 in 1781–1815 (Snell 1985, 236, 323–31).

57. Information on the range of ages is scarce for the Netherlands. However, the average age in the Northern Netherlands was also around fourteen, and the few contracts in Antwerp give an average of 15.6, but with the caveat that they may not be representative (Schalk 2019, 191; De Munck 2007, 178).

58. López Barahona and Nieto Sánchez 2019, 55.

59. Colavizza et al. 2019; age distribution calculated from their dataset of contracts available at https://doi.org/10.5281/zenodo.2652855.

60. Stöger and Reith 2019, 147.

61. Crowston and Lemercier 2019, 287–88.

62. Humphries 2010, 176–77; Horrell and Humphries 1995; Cunningham 2005, 213. See also Honeyman 2007, 45–47.

63. Only 211 youths mentioned contracts of less than seven years, out of 14,032 petitions with a term reported (Scott 2016). On marine apprenticeship more generally, see Fury 1998, 55–83.

64. Withall 2014, 173. Parliamentary data on mariners' apprentices in the 1830s indicates that these apprentices were roughly evenly split between those bound for terms less than four years and those bound for longer (United Kingdom. House of Commons 1861). Occasional cases of mariners' apprentices with short terms appeared at the Lord Mayor's Court of London, e.g., five-year terms in Antroby v Burrish, LMA CLA/024/08/92 (26 July 1698), and Crouch v Boucher LMA CLA/024/08/96 (11 May 1703).

65. The London data in figure 10.2 are drawn from several guilds. The distribution of terms is almost exactly the same if we instead use the indentures challenged at the Lord Mayor's Court of London, which are drawn from a wide cross-section of guilds. There, seven-year terms account for 50 per cent of indentures in the 1580s and 90 per cent after 1700 (calculated from Scott 2016).

66. Calculated from the stamp duty records (TNA, IR1).

67. Hobson 1757, 11; Kerry 1899, 44, 45, 46, 60.

68. See chapter 9.

69. Lincolnshire calculated from Lincoln City Apprentices, Li/5/1, Li/5/4/1, Li/5/4/2. Contracts restricted to males indentured in identifiable trades within Lincolnshire. For 1710–1804, n = 4,047 (incorporated boroughs) and 6,045 (other locations). Wiltshire calculated for a sample of 100 entries in Dale 1961. Sussex calculated for a sample of 100 entries in Rice 1922.

70. Bythell 1969.

71. United Kingdom. House of Commons 1812–13, 11.

72. United Kingdom. House of Commons 1812–13, 8, 11, 13, 34.

73. United Kingdom. House of Commons 1812–13, 19.

74. United Kingdom. House of Commons 1812–13, 16–17.

75. Nieto Sánchez and Llorente 2016, 266. Similar conclusions are reached by Swanson 1988; Stabel 2004, 205–9; Ogilvie 2004, 292–94.

76. Life expectancy at age twenty-five was 58.9 in 1780–89 (Wrigley 1997, 290). If we assume that apprentices were skilled workers after seven years' service, then the number of skilled working years if apprenticeship had started at 17.88 (the median in 1580–89) would be 34.02 years; if apprenticeship started at 14.77, the skilled career is 37.13 years. If the training term was four years, the skilled career is 40.13 years.

77. Horrell and Humphries 2019.

Chapter 11. Cultural Barriers

1. Acemoglu and Robinson 2019.

2. Gowing 2021, esp. 61–67, 80–83, 125–27.

3. That said, some guilds and cities did have exclusionary rules; see chapter 9. It was the failure of an attempt to secure legislation to exclude women in clothing production by tailors in York, Norwich, Oxford, Newcastle, Bristol, Exeter, and several other towns in 1702 that led to their inclusion in the Merchant Taylors of York (Smith 2005, 119).

4. Generally, see Erickson 2005; Gowing 2021, 60–68, 209–42. The problems the Statute of Artificers presented to single women who had not served apprenticeships are set out in Froide 2005, 93–94.

5. Cocula 1993, 429.

6. The older literature on this is well summarised in Snell 1985, 270–72, although, as he notes, female apprenticeship was recognised in the core texts, e.g., Dunlop and Denman 1912, 150–54.

7. Data from Alyssa Levene, personal communication; Simonton 2004, 374.

8. Snell 1985, 278–87; Levene 2010, 921. Simonton finds similar figures for Staffordshire and Essex, while Withall's slightly later sample (1750–1870) found that 46% were female (Simonton 2004, 378; Withall 2014, 59).

9. Snell 1985, 278–87. The range of occupations for parish apprentices is also shown in Simonton 2004, 378–79; Withall 2014.

10. Smith 2005, 107; Gowing 2021, 74–76, 88. On female apprenticeship and participation in guilds in Europe more generally, see Crowston 2008; Ogilvie 2003.

11. Erickson 2011, 150; Froide 2005, 90–91; Gowing 2021, 73–74.

12. Hovland 2007.

13. The figures from the longer period confirm the trend identified in Ben-Amos 1991, 229.

14. Hovland 2008.

15. I use the stamp duty dataset, filtered to female (by forename) apprentices to masters in Gloucester, and compared this manually to Barlow 2001 to allow a variety of possible matches to be identified. The sample included eighty-five female apprentices—twenty-eight bound to twenty-two male masters, fifty-seven bound to thirty-four female masters.

16. Barlow 2001, s.v. Barton, Elizabeth.

17. Erickson 1993, 55.

18. Gowing 2021, 220–21.

19. Median reported. N = 1,260.

20. Estimates based on city-level observations are usefully summarised in Froide 2005, 91.

21. The stamp duty registers record 6,000 to 7,000 apprentices per annum across the century. Overall, 5.6% were female (based on forenames), which equates to 330 to 390 girls a year. The number of sixteen-year-old females in England was around 48,000 in 1710 and 70,000 by 1790. The figure in the text assumes that one in three private indentures attracted a premium, as found for males.

22. Froide 2005, 91; Snell 1985; Simonton 2004, 379–80; Birt 2021. This discussion builds on Snell's observations from samples of the stamp duty up to 1760, extending them across the century beyond his end-point of 1760 (Snell 1985, 291–96). Masters identified in agricultural occupations are rare in the stamp duty records (just 2,440 in the sample), but female apprentices supplied 31% of the 435 bound by husbandmen, 16% of the thirty-eight bound to graziers, 19% of the 300 bound to farmers, and predictably, eighteen of the nineteen bound to dairymen.

23. Snell 1985, 293. The concentration is very clear in London, as Gowing's study shows (2021, 144–47). The extent to which this was an even longer running process, as suggested by Ben-Amos, remains unclear (Ben-Amos 1991, 234).

24. Snell 1985, 294.

25. Campbell 1747, 228.

26. Erickson 2011. Similarly large premiums were paid in York, for girls training in millinery and haberdashers in the Merchant Taylors (Smith 2005, 104).

27. Erickson 2011; Gowing 2016, 453; and more generally, Gowing 2021.

28. Erickson 2011, 142. See also Ben-Amos 1991, 230–31; Birt 2021.

29. De la Croix et al. 2019.

30. Snell 1985, 311.

31. Apprentices were clustered into families based on the name, occupation, and location of their father. All clusters were checked manually. Limits to the information recorded mean that families were identifiable between 1711 and 1743.

32. Similarly, in York, 70% of female apprentices joined a female master (Smith 2005, 107). See also Froide 2005, 105–6; Ben-Amos 1991, 237.

33. Campbell 1747, 207.

34. TNA, IR1/27, 71; IR1/36, f. 210; IR1/39, f. 20; IR1/68, f. 62; IR1/69, ff. 30, 182; IR1/70, f. 213.

35. London's customs required girls to be indentured to both husband and wife, even if they were to learn the wife's trade. Ricard, *Maire of Bristowe*, cited in Snell 1985, 302.

36. Gowing 2016, 464. Snell notes that pauper indentures in the nineteenth century moved to having male pronouns, in contrast to gender-neutral eighteenth-century printed contracts (1985, 290).

37. Ben-Amos 1991; Gowing 2016, 450.

38. Styles 2007; de Vries 2008.

39. Gowing 2021, 242.

40. This focus on the type of investment is related but distinct from the choice about the relationship of the level of investment to birth order, family size, and educational and economic outcomes (Black et al. 2005).

41. Information about social origins and birth order is in Klemp et al. 2013. See also Cooper 1992, 293–94.

42. Campbell 1747, 17.

43. Ben-Amos 1994, 66-67.

44. Martindale, *Diary*, in Bagley 1975.

45. Klemp et al. 2013.

46. Apprenticeship records Webb 1994, s.v. 'Cordwainers' Company'; Wrigley et al. 2018. Richard Malibar does not appear to have been a relative: when apprenticed in 1640, he was described as the son of 'Richard Mallabare' of St Dunstan-in-the-West, London.

47. Bannerman 1899, 214. See Foster 1888–91, s.v. 'Nicholas Carew', 'George Carew', and 'Edmund Carew'; Cooke 1878, 149, 155.

48. Hasler 1981, s.v. 'Nicholas Carew alias Throckmorten'. Carew's home still stands, known as Carew Manor, and is currently used as a school.

49. See Boyd 1939, D.R. 66 (Henry Butler). Butler died in 1615, and Susan married Carew in 1616.

50. See in particular Ogilvie 2003, 2004.

Chapter 12. Social Networks and the Search for Opportunity

1. This and the next paragraph are drawn from Dunton 1974, 16–17, 33–34.

2. Dunton was eventually bound to Parkhurst on 30 November 1674 and was freed in December 1681. Dunton's father was living at Aston Clinton, Buckinghamshire, at this point, not Graffham.

3. Child enrolled apprentices in 1652, 1653, 1656, 1672, and 1679. During Dunton's search he had at most two apprentices indentured, and his guild ordinances allowed members to take up to three apprentices.

4. His relative was plausibly the same John Child in the Grocers' Company of London who bound apprentices George Salter and John Bird (both gentry children) in 1672 and 1679. Child's exact connection to Dunton is not clear.

5. The problem of restricting training within a lineage or clan is discussed in de la Croix et al. 2018.

6. Granovetter 2017; Montgomery 1991, table 1.

7. Roy 2013, 72–75.

8. Growth economists argue that matching talent to opportunity affects macroeconomic outcomes, with economic mobility both a cause and consequence of technical change. See Murphy et al. 1991; Galor and Tsiddon 1997.

9. The richest discussion of the variety of networks relevant is Ben-Amos 2008. For an overview of information connections, see Schnettler 2009, esp. 172–73. The classic discussion of weak

ties is Granovetter 1983. The process described here is akin to circular migration using connections for information, not employment. A general model explaining this process is Barr 2009. For evidence on this process, see Fontaine 2007; Wegge 1998; Wilson 2020; Hatton 2010, 947, 960.

10. Ben-Amos 2008, 52–53, 322; Ben-Amos 2008, 321–22.

11. Rappaport 1983, 120; Clark 1972, 135; Clark 1987, 271–72; Yarbrough 1980, 115.

12. Much work has focused on identifying the proportion of new masters whose fathers were existing masters. Such studies offer only limited information about access to apprenticeship recruitment more generally. Shephard 1986, 123; Ogilvie 1997, 162–79; De Munck 2007, 161–68; Stabel 2007, 170; Dambruyne 1998, 47–51. Other relevant work includes Dolan 1989, 186–88; D'Amico 2000; Cavallo 2007, 139–40; Farr 2000, 244–47; Farr 1988, 21–23. On geographic ties, see also Wareing 1980, 247; McKenzie 1961, 299.

13. Kaplan et al. 2009, 18. Vienna was similar (Ehmer 1994, 185).

14. Ogilvie 2004, table 4. See also Shephard 1986, 122–24; Dolan 1989, 186–88.

15. Rappaport 1983, 102. See also Ben-Amos 1988, 48; Yarbrough 1980, 115; Clark 1987, 273; Kitch 1986, 247; Lovett et al. 1985, 330.

16. Scott 2019, s.v. 'Guines'. I am grateful to Melanie Winterbottom for the information on which this paragraph is based.

17. Archer 2000; Tadmor 2001.

18. The number of apprentices bearing the same surname as their master was 2.8% (excluding sons), compared to 1.0% bearing their master's wife's surname. The individual sample averages of apprentices with their masters' wives' surnames were, for London, 0.9%, 0.7%, and for Bristol, 1.0% and 1.4%.

19. For a similar example, see Gowing 2021, 28–29.

20. I first link the father's citizenship record (by marriage) to their sons, to connect the generations and identify their wife/mother's surname. I then link sons who become citizens to their apprentices. After excluding potential duplicates, the sample contains 507 apprentices bound to 263 masters. This sample is biased by construction, as all the wife/mothers came from local Bristol citizen families.

21. Bramwell does not appear in the Haberdashers' apprenticeship records and so is likely to have entered via patrimony, as a son of a London citizen. Gines's family tree includes no connection via his father's family to any Bramwell. Richard himself did train another of his brothers, George.

22. Gadd and Wallis 2008. The exception are guilds with multiple occupations.

23. This is not affected by whether the apprentice's father is alive or dead at the time when they were bound. López Barahona and Nieto Sánchez observe a similar pattern in Madrid, where roughly 80% of masters' sons go to different guilds (López Barahona and Nieto Sánchez 2019).

24. See De Munck 2007, 172 for a summary in English.

25. Wareing 1980, 247; Keene 2000, 109–10; Lovett et al. 1985, 330; McKenzie 1961, 299.

26. This analysis excludes apprentices from London and Middlesex. Place of origin is drawn from the origin of the apprentice and his family recorded in the original indenture. In many cases it is equivalent to their parish of origin, but for urban apprentices from towns with several parishes, it is usually the case that only the name of the town was recorded.

27. Figures are for the share of migrant apprentices. Data for London is 1600–1799; 1724–99 for Bristol; and 1614–1731 for Gloucester.

28. A shared county is a rough proxy for common region of origin, whose utility varies with county size, topography, and the individual's proximity to county boundaries.

29. Calculated as the sum across counties of the product of masters from all counties and migrant apprentices' shares for each county: $p_{random} = \sum_c \%masters_c * \%apprentices_c$, where c is a county index.

30. James Fretwell, 'A Family History', in Jackson 1877, 188.

31. In the Coachmakers, large numbers in the 1670s were bound to a single member, William Watson, and then turned over to freemen who were active in the trade, but members of different guilds (Coachmakers Company 1937, 63–64). This may have been linked to finding a place. Alternatively, this may be due to unspecified institutional concerns about enrolling contracts.

32. Wrigley 1967, 221.

33. Ben-Amos 1994, 62–67; Houlbrooke 1988, 182–90.

34. LMA, MC6/500A (Sept 1689).

35. LMA, MC6/520B.

36. Kerry 1899, 45.

37. 'Friends' can indicate kin or non-kin connections.

38. LMA, CLA/024/07/81, #4.

39. LMA, CLA/024/07/81, #5.

40. Oxley 1836, 208.

41. Hudson and Hunter 1981, 151.

42. Gough 1750, 10–11, 14.

43. Limited quantitative evidence from modern labour markets indicates that 'long chains' of contact between employees and employers that one would associate with the use of indirect ties are relatively uncommon. For example, Granovetter finds that fewer than 20% of employer-employee matches were separated by more than one degree (2017, 57).

44. Ben-Amos 2008, 322.

45. For London, N = 2,191 (migrant apprentices in London, 1500–1800, with information on master's place, occupation, and name), for Bristol N = 860, and for Gloucester N = 190. The estimate assumes the same degree of overlap existed between differently named kin and place and occupation that is observed for same name-based ties.

46. Farr 2000, 250.

47. Friedrichs 1975, 24–49; D'Amico 2000; Ogilvie 1997, 162–79; De Munck 2007, 90–96; Stöger and Reith 2019, 148–49.

48. Zucca Micheletto 2019, 101.

49. Boulton 2000.

50. Muldrew 1998, 95–99, 148–72.

51. Campbell 1747, 313. Much the same point was made in other works, such as Powell 1631. Campbell's ideas link to a wider contemporary literature on the importance of identifying vocation that allowed agency to young people (O'Day 2000, 34–41).

52. Fox 1838, 42.

53. Claxton 1839, 6.

Chapter 13. Conclusion

1. Derry 1950; More 1980, chap. 2. On earlier disputes, see Dobson 1980.

2. Humphries 2010, 262.

3. More 1980, 46.

4. Rule 1989.

5. Quoted in Derry 1950, 78.

6. Bennett et al. 2019.

7. This point is central to the political science literature on training, and it is made effectively in the US historical context in Jacoby 1991. More generally, Culpepper and Thelen 2008.

8. The extent of organisational change in areas that were not affected yet by technology is emphasised in Sabel and Zeitlin 2002.

9. Thelen summarises this effectively, but for Britain, see Floud 1982.

10. Thelen 2004, 133–47; Childs 1990. This was still better than the US experience. Elbaum 1989; Elbaum and Singh 1995; Jacoby 1991.

11. Only a small share of the classical learned professions had been trained at universities. Most had been apprentices. Pelling 2019; Corfield 1995; Holmes 1982; O'Day 2000.

12. I focus here on commonalities, but there has been extended debate on the varieties of vocational education and their wider economic and political implications in recent decades, see Streeck 2011; Iversen and Soskice 2001; Thelen 2014.

13. The contrast between liberal and coordinated economies drawn in the literature on the varieties of capitalism, and by its critics, has a heavy focus on manufacturing—particularly engineering, one of the new occupations created through industrialisation—that can overshadow this issue.

14. This is a common founding assumption in sociological interpretations. See Streeck 2011, 323.

15. This was not a uniquely English feature. See Haru Crowston 2005; Nieto Sánchez and Llorente 2016, 255; Davids 2007; Hamilton 1996, 498.

16. A vivid illustration of the effect of the removal of these incentives in the Netherlands is in Schalk 2016.

17. These are mechanisms highlighted by Hamilton 2000; Humphries 2003.

18. Van Zanden 2009. Who bore the cost is the question raised and explored by Ogilvie, notably in 2003, 2019.

19. The centrality of contract is also emphasised in Nieto Sánchez and Llorente 2016, 255–56; De Munck 2010, 4.

20. Epstein 1998; Wallis 2008.

21. Acemoglu and Robinson 2019; Ogilvie 2019. A robust historiography on hierarchy, identity, and deference exists, notably Wrightson 1994; Shepard 2015, chap. 1.

22. See the essays collected in Prak and Wallis 2019; Schalk et al. 2017.

23. Significant limits did exist around gender, religion, and other characteristics in some parts of Europe (Ogilvie 2003, 2004, 2019).

24. Prak 2018, 29–31.

25. Gelderblom 2013.

26. Goldstone 2002. The timing echoes de Vries's list of consumer revolutions (2008).

27. See in particular Steinfeld 1991; Steinberg 2016.

28. Meisenzahl and Mokyr 2012.

29. De la Croix et al. 2018.

30. Roy 2010; de la Croix et al. 2018; Moll-Murata 2013. Note that Pomeranz's brief comparison of structures of apprenticeship highlighted considerable similarities in term lengths and lack of a final test (Pomeranz 2013, 108–11).

31. For this argument, see Ben Zeev et al. 2017; Mokyr 2009; Kelly et al. 2014.

32. Van Zanden 2009, 153–66.

33. Rosenberger 2022.

34. Brown 1972, 114.

Appendix 1

1. By the later eighteenth century, 94% of masters paid the tax within the required twelve-month window (calculated using samples of city and country registers from the 1780s and 1800s).

Appendix 2

1. Rappaport 1989, 92.
2. Rappaport 1989, 28.

3. LMA, Col/CHD/FR/01/003 (1668–69). Two guilds, the Tanners and Tapissers, are noted making freemen in 1551–53, but appear to have disappeared by this point. The Tapissers may have been absorbed by the Broderers. The Tanners may simply have been a group within the Curriers. Working from freemen to apprentices does not work for three organizations that were not able to admit freemen but did take apprentices: the Carmen, Woodmongers, and Watermen.

4. LMA, COL/CHD/0A/12/1: 6th and 7th accounts; 12/3: 38th and 39th accounts; 12/4: 66th to 69th accounts; 12/5: 97th–99th, 127th accounts; 12/6: 128th and 129th accounts.

5. Rappaport 1991, 258–59.

6. Schwarz 1987, 18–19; Brodsky Elliott 1978.

7. LMA, Col/CHD/FR/01/003; Col/CHD/FR/10/1/1, 4, 9, 12, 15; Royal Commission on Municipal Corporations 1837, 65. See also Kellett 1957–58, 389.

Appendix 3

1. These are, by definition, an under-estimate, as official registers are known to under-record the actual numbers of apprentices (Pelling, 1998). See also Barlow 2001, xxxi; Merson and Willis 1968, xvv–xvi, lxxiv.

2. De Vries 1984; Wrigley 1985, 686.

3. Wrigley 1997, 614–15, 134.

4. Broadberry et al. 2015.

5. Wallis et al. 2018, 862–903.

6. Broadberry et al. 2013, 24.

Appendix 8

1. Manual linkages by the author and others were as follows: (1) the Butchers, Curriers, Upholders, and Wyre Drawers are in Webb 1994–; (2) the Watermen is in the Watermen dataset in Cottrell, n.d.; (3) the Merchant Taylors is from Scott 2019; (4) the Clockmakers is based on a linkage between Daniels 1984 and Atkins 1931; (5) the Apothecaries is described in Wallis 2002; (6) the Stationers is derived from Michael Turner's London Book Trades database; and (7) the linkage for Gloucester was also made by hand, as the sample was small.

REFERENCES

Acemoglu, Daron. 2002. "Technical Change, Inequality, and the Labor Market." *Journal of Economic Literature* 40 (1): 7–72.

Acemoglu, Daron, Simon Johnson, and James Robinson. 2005. "The Rise of Europe: Atlantic Trade, Institutional Change, and Economic Growth." *American Economic Review* 95 (3): 546–579.

Acemoglu, Daron, and Jörn-Steffan Pischke. 1999. "Beyond Becker: Training in Imperfect Labour Markets." *Economic Journal* 109 (453): F112–F142.

Acemoglu, Daron, and James A. Robinson. 2019. *The Narrow Corridor: States, Societies, and the Fate of Liberty.* New York: Penguin.

Ainsworth, John Francis, Bower Marsh, and Annie Mary Millard, eds. 1913–68. *Records of the Worshipful Company of Carpenters.* 7 vols. Oxford: Oxford University Press.

Akinnaso, F. Niyi. 1992. "Schooling, Language, and Knowledge in Literate and Nonliterate Societies." *Comparative Studies in Society and History* 34 (1): 68–109.

Alban, J. R. 1982. *Calendar of Swansea Freemen's Records from 1760.* Swansea: Swansea City Council.

Alexander, J. 1992. "The City Revealed: An Analysis of the 1692 Poll Tax and the 1693 4s. Aid in London." In *Surveying the People: The Interpretation and Use of Document Sources for the Study of Population in the Later Seventeenth Century,* edited by T. Arkell and K. Schurer, 181–200. Oxford: Leopard's Head Press.

Allen, Robert C. 2001 "Data—Wage and Price History." https://www.nuffield.ox.ac.uk/people/sites/allen-research-pages. Accessed 10 February 2012.

——— 2003. "Progress and Poverty in Early Modern Europe." *Economic History Review* 56 (3): 403–443.

Anderson, Richard. 2022. "Abolition's Adolescence: Apprenticeship as 'Liberation' in Sierra Leone, 1808–1848." *English Historical Review* 137 (586): 763–793.

Anderson, Richard, Henry B. Lovejoy, Allen M. Howard, Andrew Pearson, Chris Saunders, Daniel B. Domingues da Silva, Érika Melek Delgado, Inés Roldán de Montaud, José C. Curto, and Katelyn E. Ziegler. 2020. *Liberated Africans and the Abolition of the Slave Trade, 1807–1896.* New ed. Rochester Studies in African History and the Diaspora 86. Rochester, NY: Boydell & Brewer.

Archer, Ian W. 1991. *The Pursuit of Stability: Social Relations in Elizabethan London.* Cambridge: Cambridge University Press.

———. 2000a. "Politics and Government 1540–1700." In *The Cambridge Urban History of Britain,* vol. 2, *1540–1840,* edited by Peter Clark, 235–262. Cambridge: Cambridge University Press.

———. 2000b. "Social Networks in Restoration London: The Evidence from Samuel Pepys' Diary." In *Communities in Early Modern England,* edited by Alexandra Shepard and Phil Withington, 76–94. Manchester: Manchester University Press.

Argenti, Nicolas. 2002. "People of the Chisel: Apprenticeship, Youth, and Elites in Oku (Cameroon)." *American Ethnologist* 29 (3): 497–533.

Arkell, Tom. 2006. "Illuminations and Distortions: Gregory King's Scheme Calculated for the Year 1688 and the Social Structure of Later Stuart England." *Economic History Review* 59 (1): 32–69.

Ashdown, Charles Henry. 1919. *History of the Worshipful Company of Glaziers of the City of London.* London: Blades, East & Blades.

Ashton, Robert. 1979. *The City and the Court, 1603–1643.* Cambridge: Cambridge University Press.

Atack, Jeremy, Robert A. Margo, and Paul W. Rhode. 2019. "'Automation' of Manufacturing in the Late Nineteenth Century: The Hand and Machine Labor Study." *Journal of Economic Perspectives* 33 (2): 51–70.

Atkins, Charles Edward. 1931. *Register of Apprentices of the Worshipful Company of Clockmakers.* Frome: Privately printed.

Autor, David, Claudia Goldin, and Lawrence F. Katz. 2020. "Extending the Race between Education and Technology." *AEA Papers and Proceedings* 110: 347–351.

Bagley, J. J., ed. 1975. *Lancashire Diarists: Three Centuries of Lancashire Lives.* London: Phillimore.

Bailey, John F. 1980–1985. *Transcription of Minutes of the Corporation of Boston.* 5 vols. [Boston]: History of Boston Project.

Baker, Philip, Mark Merry, and Gill Newton. 2020. People in Place: Families, Households, and Housing in London, 1550–1720. [Data collection.] 10.5255/UKDA-SN-5791-1. Colchester: UK Data Service. https://beta.ukdataservice.ac.uk/datacatalogue/studies/study?id=5791.

Ball, Mia. 1977. *The Worshipful Company of Brewers: A Short History.* London: Hutchinson.

Bannerman, W. Bruce, ed. 1899. *The Visitations of the County of Surrey Made and Taken in the Years 1530 by Thomas Benolte; 1573 by Robert Cooke; and 1623 by Samuel Thompson, Harleian Society.* Vol. 43. London: Harleian Society.

Barker, T. C. 1957. *The Girdlers' Company, a Second History.* London: Girdlers' Company.

Barlow, Jill. 2001. *A Calendar of the Registers of Apprentices of the City of Gloucester, 1595–1700.* Vol. 14. Gloucester: Bristol and Gloucestershire Archaeological Society.

———. 2011. *A Calendar of the Registers of Apprentices of the City of Gloucester, 1700–1834.* Vol. 25. Gloucester: Bristol and Gloucestershire Archaeological Society.

Barlow, Theodore. 1745. *The Justice of Peace: A Treatise Containing the Power and Duty of That Magistrate.* London: J. & P. Knapton; John Nourse.

Barnard, John. n.d. *Some rules for the conduct of life: to which are added, a few cautions for the use of such freemen of London as take apprentices.* [London].

Barr, Tavis. 2009. "With Friends Like These: Endogenous Labor Market Segregation with Homogeneous, Nonprejudiced Agents." *American Journal of Economics and Sociology* 68 (3): 703–746.

Barron, Caroline. 2000. "London 1300–1540." In *The Cambridge Urban History of Britain*, vol. 1, *600–1540*, edited by D. M. Palliser, 395–440. Cambridge: Cambridge University Press.

———. 2004. *London in the Later Middle Ages: Government and People, 1200–1500.* Oxford: Oxford University Press.

Becker, Gary S. 1962. "Investment in Human Capital: A Theoretical Analysis." *Journal of Political Economy* 70 (5): 9–49.

Beckett, Ian F. W., ed. 1985. *The Buckinghamshire Posse Comitatus 1798.* Buckinghamshire Record Society No. 22. Chippenham, Wiltshire: Antony Rowe for the Buckinghamshire Record Society.

Bednarz, Alice. 2014. *Understanding the Non-completion of Apprentices.* Occasional paper, National Centre for Vocational Education Research, Australian Government Department of Industry. 12 June 2014. https://apo.org.au/node/40068.

Beier, A. L. 1985. *Masterless Men: The Vagrancy Problem in England 1560–1640.* London: Methuen.

———. 1986. "Engine of Manufacture: The Trades of London." In *The Making of the Metropolis: Essays in the Social and Economic History of London, 1500–1700*, edited by A. L. Beier and Roger Finlay, 141–167. London: Longman.

Bellavitis, Anna, and Valentina Sapienza. 2023. *Apprenticeship, Work, Society in Early Modern Venice*. London: Routledge.

Beloff, Max. 1942. "A London Apprentice's Notebook, 1703–5." *History* 27 (105): 38–45.

Ben-Amos, Ilana Krausman. 1988. "Service and the Coming of Age of Young Men in Seventeenth-Century England." *Continuity and Change* 3 (1): 41–64.

———. 1991a. "Failure to Become Freemen: Urban Apprentices in Early Modern England." *Social History* 16: 155–172.

———. 1991b. "Women Apprentices in the Trades and Crafts of Early Modern Bristol." *Continuity and Change* 6 (2): 227–252.

———. 1994. *Adolescence and Youth in Early Modern England*. New Haven, CT: Yale University Press.

———. 2008. *The Culture of Giving: Informal Support and Gift-Exchange in Early Modern England*. Cambridge: Cambridge University Press.

Bennett, R. J., Harry Smith, and Carry van Lieshout. 2019. *The Age of Entrepreneurship: Business Proprietors, Self-Employment and Corporations since 1851*. New York: Routledge.

Bentham, Jeremy. (1789) 1823. *An Introduction to the Principles of Morals and Legislation*. New ed. corrected by the author. London: W. Pickering.

Berg, Maxine. 2002. "From Imitation to Invention: Creating Commodities in Eighteenth-Century Britain." *Economic History Review* 55 (1): 1–30.

Berlin, Michael. 1997. "'Broken all in pieces': Artisans and the Regulation of Workmanship in Early Modern London." In *The Artisan and the European Town*, edited by Geoffrey Crossick, 75–91. Aldershot: Scolar Press.

———. 2008. "Guilds in Decline? London Livery Companies and the Rise of a Liberal Economy, 1600–1800." In *Guilds, Innovation, and the European Economy, 1400–1800*, edited by S. R. Epstein and Maarten Prak, 316–342. Cambridge: Cambridge University Press.

Berry, Helen. 2023. "The Occupational Distribution of Foundling Apprentices during the English Industrial Revolution." *Social History* 48 (2): 259–283.

Bertucci, Paola, and Olivier Courcelle. 2015. "Artisanal Knowledge, Expertise, and Patronage in Early Eighteenth-Century Paris: The Société des Arts (1728–36)." *Eighteenth-Century Studies* 48 (2): 159–179.

Bewick, Thomas. 1862. *A Memoir of Thomas Bewick, Written by Himself*. Newcastle upon Tyne: Longman.

Bickley, Francis B. 1900. *The Little Red Book of Bristol*. Bristol: W. Crofton Hemmons.

Bills, David B. 2003. "Credentials, Signals, and Screens: Explaining the Relationship between Schooling and Job Assignment." *Review of Educational Research* 73 (4): 441–469.

Bird, James B. 1795. *The Laws Respecting Masters and Servants*. London: W. Clarke and Son.

Birt, Sarah. 2021. "Women, Guilds and the Tailoring Trades: The Occupational Training of Merchant Taylors' Company Apprentices in Early Modern London." *London Journal* 46 (2): 146–164.

Black, Sandra E., Paul J. Devereux, and Kjell G. Salvanes. 2005. "The More the Merrier? The Effect of Family Size and Birth Order on Children's Education." *Quarterly Journal of Economics* 120 (2): 669–700.

Blackburn, Sheila. 2006. "Between the Devil of Cheap Labour Competition and the Deep Sea of Family Poverty? Sweated Labour in Time and Place, 1840–1914." *Labour History Review* 71 (2): 99–121.

Blacket, Joseph. 1811. *The Remains of Joseph Blacket, Consisting of Poems, Dramatic Sketches, the Times, an Ode, and a Memoir of His Life*. London: Sherwood, Neely, and Jones.

Blagden, Cyprian. 1955. "The English Stock of the Stationers' Company." *Library* 10 (3): 163.

———. 1960. *The Stationers' Company: A History, 1403–1959*. London: George Allen & Unwin.

Bobart, Henry, ed. 1911. *Records of the Basketmakers' Company*. London: Dunn, Collin.

Boberg-Fazlić, Nina, and Paul Sharp. 2018. "North and South: Long-Run Social Mobility in England and Attitudes toward Welfare." *Cliometrica* 12 (2): 251–276.

Bohun, William. 1702. *Privilegia Londini; or, the laws, customs, and priviledges of the city of London*. London: D. Brown and J. Walthoe.

Borowiecki, Karol Jan. 2021. "Good Reverberations? Teacher Influence in Music Composition since 1450." *Journal of Political Economy* 130 (4): 991–1090.

Boston Borough Council. n.d. *Boston Borough Council Apprenticeship Registers 1663–1903; Register of Freemen 1545–1903*. Lincoln: Lincolnshire Family History Society.

Boulton, J. P. 1987. *Neighbourhood and Society: A London Suburb in the Seventeenth Century*. Cambridge: Cambridge University Press.

Boulton, Jeremy. 2000. "London 1540–1700." In *The Cambridge Urban History of Britain*, vol. 2, *1540–1840*, edited by Peter Clark, 315–346. Cambridge: Cambridge University Press.

Bownas, Samuel. 1756. *An account of the life, travels and Christian experiences in the work of the Ministry of Samuel Bownas*. London: Luke Hinde.

Brasbridge, Joseph. [1796]. *In the King's Bench: Brasbridge v. Ashforth. Sittings before Lord Kenyon Guildhall, London, June 29, 1796*. ESTC N48463. London: Printed at the Philanthropic Reform.

———. 1824. *The Fruits of Experience; or, Memoir of Joseph Brasbridge, Written in His 80th Year*. London: For the Author.

Brenner, Robert. 1993. *Merchants and Revolution: Commercial Change, Political Conflict, and London's Overseas Traders, 1550–1653*. Cambridge: Cambridge University Press.

Brewer, John. 1989. *The Sinews of Power: War, Money and the English State, 1688–1783*. London: Unwin Hyman.

Briggs, W. G. 1954. "Records of an Apprenticeship Charity 1685/1753." *Derbyshire Archaeological Journal* 74: 43–61.

Bristol & Avon Family History Society. 2004a. *Bristol Burgess Books*. Vols. 1–21, *Index & Transcripts 1557–1995*. Bristol: Bristol & Avon Family History Society.

———. 2004b. *Index to the Avon Marriage Registers*. Vol. 8, *Bristol Diocese Parishes 1813–1837*. Bristol: Bristol & Avon Family History Society.

———. 2008. *Index to the Avon Marriage Registers*. Vol. 9, *Bristol Diocese Parishes 1754–1812*. Bristol: Bristol & Avon Family History Society.

Britten, Frederick. 1894. *Former Clock & Watchmakers and Their Work*. London: E. & F. N. Spon.

Britten, Frederick, Cecil Clutton, and G. H. Baillie. 1986. *Britten's Old Clocks and Watches and Their Makers: A History of Styles in Clocks and Watches and Their Mechanisms*. 9th ed. London: Bloomsbury.

Broadberry, S. N., Bruce Campbell, Alexander Klein, Mark Overton, and Bas van Leeuwen. 2015. *British Economic Growth, 1270–1870*. Cambridge: Cambridge University Press.

Broadberry, Stephen, Bruce M. S. Campbell, and Bas van Leeuwen. 2013. "When Did Britain Industrialise? The Sectoral Distribution of the Labour Force and Labour Productivity in Britain, 1381–1851." *Explorations in Economic History* 50 (1): 16–27.

Brock, Aske Laursen. 2017. "The Company Director: Commerce, State and Society." PhD diss., University of Kent.

Brodsky Elliott, Vivien. 1978. "Mobility and Marriage in Pre-industrial England." PhD diss., University of Cambridge.

Brooks, C. W. 1994. "Apprenticeship, Social Mobility and the Middling Sort, 1550–1800." In *The Middling Sort of People: Culture, Society and Politics in England, 1550–1800*, edited by Jonathan Barry and C. W. Brooks, 52–83. Basingstoke: Macmillan.

Brown, Arthur Frederick James, ed. 1972. *Essex People, 1750–1900, from Their Diaries, Memoirs and Letters.* Chelmsford: Essex County Council.

Browne, John. 1590. *The marchants auizo. Verie necessarie for their sonnes and seruants, when they first send them beyond the seas.* London: Thomas Orwin.

Buckley, James. 1909. "The Journal of Thomas Wright: Author of Louthiana (1711–1786)." *Journal of the County Louth Archaeological Society* 2 (2): 165–185.

Burchall, Michael J. 2008. *The Sussex Poor 1, 1661–1800.* Edited by the Sussex Family History Group. Waterlooville, Hampshire: Parish Register Transcription Society.

Burn, Richard. 1831. *The Justice of the Peace, and Parish Officer.* 26th ed. London.

Bythell, Duncan. 1969. *The Handloom Weavers: A Study in the English Cotton Industry during the Industrial Revolution.* Cambridge: Cambridge University Press.

A Calendar of the Freemen of Lynn, 1292–1836. 1913. Norwich: Norfolk and Norwich Archaeological Society

Campbell, Robert. 1747. *The London Tradesman, being a compendious view of all the trades, professions, arts, both liberal and mechanic, now practised in the cities of London and Westminster.* London: T. Gardner.

Cantillon, Richard. [1730] 1959. *Essai sur la nature du commerce en general: Edited with an English translation and other material.* London: Frank Cass.

Cappelli, Peter. 1996. "Youth Apprenticeship in Britain: Lessons for the United States." *Industrial Relations* 35 (1): 1–31.

Caracausi, Andrea. 2017. "A Reassessment of the Role of Guild Courts in Disputes over Apprenticeship Contracts: A Case Study from Early Modern Italy." *Continuity and Change* 32 (1): 85–114.

Carlin, Norah. 1994. "Liberty and Fraternities in the English Revolution: The Politics of London Artisans' Protests." *International Review of Social History* 39: 223–254.

Carlton, Charles. 1974. *The Orphans' Court.* Leicester: Leicester University Press.

Carter, Barbara J. 2020. *Broad Town Charity Apprentices.* 2nd ed. Devizes: Wiltshire Family History Society.

Cavallo, Sandra. 2007. *Artisans of the Body in Early Modern Italy: Identities, Families and Masculinities.* Manchester: Manchester University Press.

Cerutti, Simona. 2002. "Nature des choses et qualité des personnes: Le consulat de commerce de Turin au XVIIIe siècle." *Annales: Histoire, Sciences Sociales* 57 (6): 1491–1520.

Chaffin, W. LaJean, and Patrick Wallis. 2023. "Unmaking Apprenticeship in Early Modern London: Goldsmiths' Apprentices and the Lord Mayor's Court, 1597–1720." *London Journal* 48 (2): 99–121.

Chapman, S. D. 1965. "The Transition to the Factory System in the Midlands Cotton-Spinning Industry." *Economic History Review* 18 (3): 526–543.

Charlton, Kenneth. 1965. *Education in Renaissance England.* London: Routledge & Kegan Paul.

Chater, Kathy. 2007. "Black People in England, 1660–1807." *Parliamentary History* 26 (S1): 66–83.

Chester, Bennett John Henry Elliot. 1904–1905. *The Rolls of the Freemen of the City of Chester.* Part 1, *1392–1700.* Record Society of Lancaster and Cheshire Series, no. 51. Chester: Record Society of Lancaster and Cheshire.

———. 1906–1907. *The Rolls of the Freemen of the City of Chester.* Part 2, *1700–1805.* Record Society of Lancaster and Cheshire Series, no. 55. Chester: Record Society of Lancaster and Cheshire.

Childs, Michael J. 1990. "Boy Labour in Late Victorian and Edwardian England and the Remaking of the Working Class." *Journal of Social History* 23 (4): 783–802.

Chivers, Janet Mary. 2006. "'A resonating void': Strategies and Responses to Poverty, Bath, 1770–1835." PhD diss., Bath Spa University.

City of London. Court of Common Council. 1680. *Lex Londinensis; or The City Law.* London: Henry Twyford.

Clark, Gregory. 2002. "Land Rental Values and the Agrarian Economy: England and Wales, 1500–1914." *European Review of Economic History* 6 (3): 281–308.

———. 2004. "The Price History of English Agriculture, 1209–1914." *Research in Economic History* 22: 41–124.

———. 2005. "The Condition of the Working Class in England, 1209–2004." *Journal of Political Economy* 113: 1307–1340.

———. 2007. *A Farewell to Alms: A Brief Economic History of the World.* Princeton, NJ: Princeton University Press.

———. 2014. *The Son Also Rises: Surnames and the History of Social Mobility.* Princeton, NJ: Princeton University Press.

Clark, Gregory, and Neil Cummins. 2015. "Intergenerational Wealth Mobility in England, 1858–2012: Surnames and Social Mobility." *Economic Journal* 125 (582): 61–85.

Clark, Peter. 1972. "The Migrant in Kentish Towns 1580–1640." In *Crisis and Order in English Towns 1500–1700*, edited by Peter Clark and Paul Slack, 117–63. London: Routledge.

———. 1979. "Migration in England during the Late Seventeenth and Early Eighteenth Centuries." *Past & Present* (83): 57–90.

———. 1987. "Migrants in the City: The Process of Social Adaptation in English Towns 1500–1800." In *Migration and Society in Early Modern England*, edited by Peter Clark and David Souden, 267–291. London: Hutchinson.

Clark, Peter, and Jean Hosking. 1993. *Population Estimates of English Small Towns, 1550–1851.* 2nd ed. Leicester: Centre for Urban History, University of Leicester.

Clark, Peter, and Paul Slack. 1972. *Crisis and Order in English Towns, 1500–1700: Essays in Urban History.* London: Routledge & Kegan Paul.

Claxton, Timothy. 1839. *Hints to Mechanics, on Self-Education and Mutual Instruction.* London: Taylor & Walton.

Clay, C. 1984. *Economic Expansion and Social Change: England, 1500–1700.* 2 vols. Cambridge: Cambridge University Press.

Clode, Charles M. 1875. *Memorials of the Guild of Merchant Taylors of the Fraternity of St. John the Baptist.* London: Harrison and Sons.

Clothworkers Company. 1840. *Selection from the Rules and Orders of the Clothworkers, together with the Ordinances.* London: Clothworkers Company.

———. 1881. *The Ordinances of the Clothworkers Company, together with Those of the Ancient Guilds of Fullers and Shearmen.* London: Clothworkers Company.

Coachmakers Company. 1937. *A History of the Worshipful Company of Coachmakers and Coach Harness-Makers of London.* London: Chapel River Press.

Cocula, Anne-Marie. 1993. "Contrats d'apprentissage du XVIIIe siècle: Quelques enseignements d'une moisson aquitaine." *Revue d'histoire moderne et contemporaine* 40 (3): 423–435.

Cohn, Samuel Kline. 2007. "After the Black Death: Labour Legislation and Attitudes towards Labour in Late-Medieval Western Europe." *Economic History Review* 60 (3): 457–485.

Colavizza, Giovanni, Riccardo Cella, and Anna Bellavitis. 2019. "Apprenticeship in Early Modern Venice." In *Apprenticeship in Early Modern Europe*, edited by Maarten Prak and Patrick Wallis, 106–137. Cambridge: Cambridge University Press.

Colclough, Stephen M. 2000. "Procuring Books and Consuming Texts: The Reading Experience of a Sheffield Apprentice, 1798." *Book History* 3 (1): 21–44.

Collins, James B. 1991. "Geographic and Social Mobility in Early-Modern France." *Journal of Social History* 24 (3): 563–577.

Comyns, John. 1800. *A Digest of the Laws of England.* 4th ed. London: A. Strahan.

Cooke, William Henry. 1878. *Students Admitted to the Inner Temple 1547–1660.* London: W. Clowes and Sons.

Cookson, Gillian. 2018. *The Age of Machinery: Engineering the Industrial Revolution, 1770–1850.* Woodbridge: Boydell Press.

Cooper, Sheila M. 1992. "Intergenerational Social Mobility in Late-Seventeenth- and Early-Eighteenth-Century England." *Continuity and Change* 7 (3): 283–301.

Corfield, Penelope J. 1995. *Power and the Professions in Britain 1700–1850.* London: Routledge.

Cottrell, Rob. n.d. *Company of Watermen & Lightermen Binding Index 1692–1949.* Edited by Trueflare Genealogy. Longfield, Kent: Trueflare Genealogy.

Cowper, J. Meadows, ed. 1903. *The Roll of the Freemen of the City of Canterbury from 1392 to 1800.* Canterbury: Cross & Jackman.

Coy, Betty, Sheila Hill, and Vera Sharpe. 1993. *Transcription of Minutes of the Corporation of Boston.* Vol. 5, *1717 to 1763.* Boston: History of Boston Project.

Coy, Michael William. 1989. *Apprenticeship: From Theory to Method and Back Again.* Albany: State University of New York Press.

Craske, Matthew. 1999. "Plan and Control: Design and the Competitive Spirit in Early and Mid-Eighteenth-Century England." *Journal of Design History* 12 (3): 187–216.

Crawford, Patricia. 2010. *Parents of Poor Children in England 1580–1800.* Oxford: Oxford University Press.

Crook, J. Mordaunt. 1965. "The Restoration of the Temple Church: Ecclesiology and Recrimination." *Architectural History* 8: 39–51.

Crossley, Alan. 2012. *Oxford City Apprentices, 1513–1602.* Oxford Historical Society, n.s. 44. Woodbridge: Boydell and Brewer.

Crowston, Clare Haru. 2005. "L'apprentissage hors des corporations." *Annales: Histoire, sciences sociales* 60 (2): 409–441.

———. 2008. "Women, Gender and Guilds in Early Modern Europe: An Overview of Recent Research." *International Review of Social History* 53: 19–44.

Crowston, Clare Haru, and Claire Lemercier. 2019. "Surviving the End of the Guilds: Apprenticeship in Eighteenth- and Nineteenth-Century France." In *Apprenticeship in Early Modern Europe*, edited by Maarten Prak and Patrick Wallis, 282–308. Cambridge: Cambridge University Press.

Culpepper, Pepper D., and Kathleen Thelen. 2008. "Institutions and Collective Actions in the Provision of Training: Historical and Cross-national Comparisons." In *Skill Formation: Interdisciplinary and Cross-national Perspectives*, edited by Karl Ulrich Mayer and Heike Solga, 21–49. Cambridge: Cambridge University Press.

Cummins, Neil. 2020. "The Micro-evidence for the Malthusian System: France, 1670–1840." *European Economic Review* 129 (19): 103544.

Cummins, Neil, and Cormac Ó Gráda. 2022. "Artisanal Skills, Watchmaking, and the Industrial Revolution: Prescot and Beyond." *Northern History* 59 (2): 216–238.

Cunningham, Andrew. 1974. "Aspects of the History of Medical Education in Britain in the 17th & Early 18th Centuries." PhD diss., University College London.

Cunningham, Hugh. 1990. "The Employment and Unemployment of Children in England c. 1680–1851." *Past & Present* 126: 115–150.

———. 2005. "How Many Children Were 'Unemployed' in Eighteenth- and Nineteenth-Century England? Reply." *Past & Present* 187: 203–215.

Dabhoiwala, Faramerz. 2006. "Summary Justice in Early Modern London." *English Historical Review* 121 (492): 796–822.

Dale, Christabel. 1961. *Wiltshire Apprentices and Their Masters, 1710–1760.* Devizes: Wiltshire Archaeological & Natural History Society.

Dallos, Csilla. 2021. "Is There More to Human Social Learning Than Enhanced Facilitation? Prolonged Learning and Its Impact on Culture." *Humanities & Social Sciences Communications* 8 (1): 1–10.

Dalton, Michael. 1742. *The Country Justice*. London: William Rawlins and Samuel Roycroft.

Dambruyne, Johan. 1998. "Guilds, Social Mobility and Status in Sixteenth-Century Ghent." *International Review of Social History* 43 (1): 31–78.

D'Amico, Stefano. 2000. "Crisis and Transformation: Economic Organization and Social Structures in Milan, 1570–1610." *Social History* 25 (1): 1–21.

Daniels, George. 1984. *Freemen of the Worshipful Company of Clockmakers, 1631–1884*. Isle of Man: George Daniels.

Davids, Karel. 2007. "Apprenticeship and Guild Control in the Netherlands, c. 1450–1800." In *Learning on the Shop Floor: Historical Perspectives on Apprenticeship*, edited by Bert De Munck, Steven L. Kaplan and Hugo Soly, 65–84. New York: Berghahn.

Davies, M. G. 1956. *The Enforcement of English Apprenticeship, 1563–1642: A Study in Applied Mercantilism, 1563–1642*. Cambridge, MA: Harvard University Press.

Deakin, Simon, and Frank Wilkinson. 2005. *The Law of the Labour Market: Industrialization, Employment and Legal Evolution*. Oxford: Oxford University Press.

Dearle, Norman Burrell. 1914. *Industrial Training, with Special Reference to the Conditions Prevailing in London*. London: P. S. King & Son.

De Bie, Annelies. 2014. "The Paradox of the Antwerp Rose: Symbol of Decline or Token of Craftsmanship?" In *Innovation and Creativity in Late Medieval and Early Modern European Cities*, edited by Karel Davids and Bert De Munck, 269–293. Farnham: Ashgate.

De Kerf, Raoul. 2014. "The Early Modern Antwerp Coopers' Guild: From a Contract-Enforcing Organization to an Empty Box?" In *Innovation and Creativity in Late Medieval and Early Modern European Cities*, edited by Karel Davids and Bert De Munck, 245–267. Farnham: Ashgate.

De Krey, Gary Stuart. 2005. *London and the Restoration, 1659–1683*. Cambridge: Cambridge University Press.

De la Croix, David, Matthias Doepke, and Joel Mokyr. 2018. "Clans, Guilds, and Markets: Apprenticeship Institutions and Growth in the Preindustrial Economy." *Quarterly Journal of Economics* 133 (1): 1–70.

De la Croix, David, Eric B. Schneider, and Jacob Weisdorf. 2019. "Childlessness, Celibacy and Net Fertility in Pre-industrial England: The Middle-Class Evolutionary Advantage." *Journal of Economic Growth* 24 (3): 223–256.

De Munck, Bert. 2007. *Technologies of Learning: Apprenticeship in Antwerp Guilds from the 15th Century to the End of the Ancien Regime*. Turnhout: Brepols.

———. 2010a. "Corpses, Live Models, and Nature: Assessing Skills and Knowledge before the Industrial Revolution (Case: Antwerp)." *Technology and Culture* 51 (2): 332–356.

———. 2010b. "From Brotherhood Community to Civil Society? Apprentices between Guild, Household and the Freedom of Contract in Early Modern Antwerp." *Social History* 35 (1): 1–20.

———. 2011. "Gilding Golden Ages: Perspectives from Early Modern Antwerp on the Guild Debate, c. 1450–c. 1650." *European Review of Economic History* 15 (2): 221–253.

De Munck, Bert, Karel Davids, and Ellen Burm. 2014. "Beyond Exclusivism: Entrance Fees for Guilds in the Early Modern Low Countries, c. 1450–1800." In *Innovation and Creativity in Late Medieval and Early Modern European Cities*, edited by Karel Davids and Bert De Munck, 189–224. Farnham: Ashgate.

De Munck, Bert, and Raoul De Kerf. 2018. "Wandering about the Learning Market: Early Modern Apprenticeship in Antwerp Gold- and Silversmith Ateliers." In *Navigating History: Economy, Society, Knowledge, and Nature*, edited by Pepijn Brandon, Sabine Go, and Wybren Verstegen, 36–63. Leiden: Brill.

De Munck, Bert, Raoul De Kerf, and Annelies De Bie. 2019. "Apprenticeship in the Southern Netherlands, c. 1400–c. 1800." In *Apprenticeship in Early Modern Europe*, edited by Maarten Prak and Patrick Wallis, 217–246. Cambridge: Cambridge University Press.

Dennett, John, ed. 1933. *Beverley Borough Records, 1575–1821.* Yorkshire Archaeological Society Record Series no. 84. Wakefield: Yorkshire Archaeological Society.

De Pleijt, Alexandra M. 2016. "Human Capital Formation in the Long Run: Evidence from Average Years of Schooling in England, 1300–1900." *Cliometrica* 12 (1): 99–126.

De Pleijt, Alexandra, Alessandro Nuvolari, and Jacob Weisdorf. 2020. "Human Capital Formation during the First Industrial Revolution: Evidence from the Use of Steam Engines." *Journal of the European Economic Association* 18 (2): 829–889.

De Pleijt, Alexandra M., and Jacob L. Weisdorf. 2017. "Human Capital Formation from Occupations: The 'Deskilling Hypothesis' Revisited." *Cliometrica* 11 (1): 1–30.

De Rapin, Paul. 1759. *The History of England.* Translated by N. Tindal. 5th ed. 12 vols. London: Mr Knapton.

Derry, T. K. 1930. "The Enforcement of a Seven Years Apprenticeship under the Statute of Artificers." DPhil thesis, University of Oxford.

———. 1950. "The Repeal of the Apprenticeship Clauses of the Statute of Apprentices." *Economic History Review* 3 (1): 67–87.

De Vries, Jan. 1984. *European Urbanization 1600–1800.* London: Methuen.

———. 2008. *The Industrious Revolution: Consumer Behavior and the Household Economy, 1650 to the Present.* Cambridge: Cambridge University Press.

Diebolt, Claude, Charlotte Le Chapelain, and Audrey-Rose Menard. 2019. "Learning Outside the Factory: A Cliometric Reappraisal on the Impact of Technological Change on Human Capital Accumulation." *European Journal of the History of Economic Thought* 26 (4): 775–800.

Dilley, Roy. 1999. "Ways of Knowing, Forms of Power." *Cultural Dynamics* 11 (1): 33–55.

Disney, Gervase. 1692. *Some remarkable passages in the holy life and death of Gervase Disney, Esq. to which are added several letters and poems.* London: Jonathan Robinson. Early English Books Online. https://search.proquest.com/docview/2248511783.

Dobson, C. R. 1980. *Masters and Journeymen: A Prehistory of Industrial Relations, 1717–1800.* London: Croom Helm.

Dodds, Madeleine Hope, ed. 1923. *The Register of Freemen of Newcastle upon Tyne from the Corporation Guild and Admission Books.* Vol. 3. Newcastle upon Tyne: Newcastle upon Tyne Records Committee.

Doe, Charles. 1700. *A collection of experience of the work of grace.* London: Printed for Charles Doe.

Dolan, Claire. 1989. "The Artisans of Aix-en-Provence in the Sixteenth Century: A Micro-Analysis of Social Relationships." In *Cities and Social Change in Early Modern France*, edited by Philip Benedict, 174–94. London: Routledge.

Dowling, J. L. 1889. *The Charter of the Worshipful Company of Poulters, London.* London: W. H. and L. Collingridge.

Drescher, Seymour. 2002. *The Mighty Experiment: Free Labor versus Slavery in British Emancipation.* Oxford: Oxford University Press.

Dunlop, Olive Jocelyn, and Richard Douglas Denman. 1912. *English Apprenticeship & Child Labour.* London: T. Fisher Unwin.

Dunton, John. 1974. *The Life and Errors of John Dunton.* New York: Garland.

Earle, Peter. 1989. *The Making of the English Middle Class: Business, Society and Family Life in London, 1660–1730.* London: Methuen.

Ehmer, Josef. 1994. "Worlds of Mobility: Migration Patterns of Viennese Artisans in the Eighteenth Century." In *The Artisan and the European Town, 1500–1900*, edited by Geoffrey Crossick, 172–199. Aldershot: Scolar Press.

Eisenberg, C. 1991. "Artisans' Socialization at Work: Workshop Life in Early Nineteenth-Century England and Germany." *Journal of Social History* 24 (3): 507–520.

Elbaum, Bernard. 1989. "Why Apprenticeship Persisted in Britain but Not in the United States." *Journal of Economic History* 49 (2): 337–349.

Elbaum, Bernard, and Nirvikar Singh. 1995. "The Economic Rationale of Apprenticeship Training: Some Lessons from British and U.S. Experience." *Industrial Relations* 34 (4): 593–622.

Elkington, George. 1930. *The Worshipful Company of Coopers: With Notes and Recollections, 1872–1930.* Margate: W.J. Parrett.

Ely, James W. 1986. "The Eighteenth-Century Poor Laws in the West Riding of Yorkshire." *American Journal of Legal History* 30 (1): 1–24.

Emerson, Thomas Attorney. 1794. *A concise treatise on the Courts of Law of the City of London.* London: J. Nichols.

Epstein, S. R. 1998. "Craft Guilds, Apprenticeship, and Technological Change in Preindustrial Europe." *Journal of Economic History* 58 (3): 684–713.

———. 2004. "Labour Mobility, Journeyman Organisations and Markets in Skilled Labour in Europe, 14th–18th Centuries." In *Le technicien dans la cité en Europe occidentale 1250–1650,* edited by Mathieu Arnoux and Pierre Monnet, 251–269. Rome: École française de Rome.

———. 2008. "Craft Guilds in the Pre-modern Economy: A Discussion." *Economic History Review* 61 (1): 155–174.

———. 2013. "Transferring Technical Knowledge and Innovating in Europe, c. 1200–c. 1800." In *Technology, Skills and the Pre-modern Economy in the East and the West,* edited by Maarten Roy Prak and J. L. van Zanden, 25–67. Leiden: Brill.

Epstein, Steven A. 1991. *Wage Labor and Guilds in Medieval Europe.* Chapel Hill: University of North Carolina Press.

Erickson, Amy Louise. 1993. *Women and Property in Early Modern England.* London: Routledge.

———. 2005. "Coverture and Capitalism." *History Workshop Journal* 59:1–16.

———. 2011. "Eleanor Mosley and Other Milliners in the City of London Companies 1700–1750." *History Workshop Journal* 71:142–172.

Ericsson, K. Anders. 2006. "The Influence of Experience and Deliberate Practice on the Development of Superior Expert Performance." In *The Cambridge Handbook of Expertise and Expert Performance,* edited by K. Anders Ericsson, Neil Charness, Paul J. Feltovich, and Robert R. Hoffman, 683–704. Cambridge: Cambridge University Press.

Ericsson, K. Anders, Neil Charness, Paul J. Feltovich, and Robert R. Hoffman, eds. 2006. *The Cambridge Handbook of Expertise and Expert Performance.* Cambridge: Cambridge University Press.

Evans, Arise. 1652. *An eccho to the Voice from heaven, or, A narration of the life and visions of A. Evans.* London: For the Author.

Everett, James. 1832. *The Village Blacksmith; or, Piety and Usefulness Exemplified in a Memoir of the Life of Samuel Hick.* London: Hamilton, Adams.

Farr, James R. 1988. *Hands of Honor. Artisans and Their World in Dijon, 1550–1650.* Ithaca, NY: Cornell University Press.

———. 2000. *Artisans in Europe, 1300–1914.* Cambridge: Cambridge University Press.

Feldman, Naomi E., and Karine Van der Beek. 2016. "Skill Choice and Skill Complementarity in Eighteenth-Century England." *Explorations in Economic History* 59: 94–113.

Feldman, Roger. 2014. "Dyeing and the London Dyers' Company: Membership, Craft, and Knowledge Transmission, 1649–1829." *London Journal* 39 (1): 37–58.

Ferguson, Dean T. 2000. "The Body, the Corporate Idiom, and the Police of the Unincorporated Worker in Early Modern Lyons." *French Historical Studies* 23 (4): 545–575.

Ferguson, R. S., and W. Nanson. 1887. *Some Municipal Records of the City of Carlisle.* Carlisle: George Bell and Sons.

Finkelstein, Andrea. 2000. "Gerard de Malynes and Edward Misselden: The Learned Library of the Seventeenth-Century Merchant." *Book History* 3 (1): 1–20.

Firth, James Francis. 1848. *Coopers' Company, London. Historical Memoranda, Charters, Documents, and Extracts from the Records of the Corporation and the Books of the Company.* London: Arthur Taylor.

Fisher, F. J. 1936. *A Short History of the Worshipful Company of Horners*. Croydon: George Becker.

Floud, Roderick. 1982. "Technical Education and Economic Performance: Britain, 1850–1914." *Albion* 14 (2): 153–171.

Fontaine, Laurence. 2007. "Kinship and Mobility: Migrant Networks in Europe." In *Kinship in Europe*, edited by David Warren Sabean, Simon Teuscher, and Jon Mathieu, 193–210. New York: Berghahn.

Forman, Simon. 1849. *The Autobiography and Personal Diary of Dr. Simon Forman, the Celebrated Astrologer, from A.D. 1552, to A.D. 1602, from the Unpublished Manuscripts in the Ashmolean Museum, Oxford*. Edited by J. O. Halliwell-Phillipps. London: Richards.

Foster, Joseph. 1888–91. *Alumni Oxonienses*. 8 vols. Oxford: Oxford University Press.

Fox, Ebenezer. 1838. *The Revolutionary Adventures of Ebenezer Fox*. Boston: Munroe & Francis.

Franck, Raphaël, and Oded Galor. 2022. "Technology-Skill Complementarity in Early Phases of Industrialisation." *Economic Journal* 132 (642): 618–643.

Frank, Christopher. 2010. *Master and Servant Law: Chartists, Trade Unions, Radical Lawyers and the Magistracy in England, 1840–1865*. Farnham: Ashgate.

Franklin, Benjamin. 1894. *Autobiography and Letters of Benjamin Franklin*. London: Ward, Lock, & Bowden.

Freemen, Collins Francis, ed. 1900. *Register of the Freemen of the City of York, II: 1559–1759, Surtees Society, no. 102*. Durham: Surtees Society.

Friedrichs, Christopher R. 1975. "Capitalism, Mobility and Class Formation in the Early Modern German City." *Past & Present* (69): 24–49.

Froide, Amy M. 2005. *Never Married: Singlewomen in Early Modern England*. Oxford: Oxford University Press.

Fuller, Alison, Heather Hodkinson, Phil Hodkinson, and Lorna Unwin. 2005. "Learning as Peripheral Participation in Communities of Practice: A Reassessment of Key Concepts in Workplace Learning." *British Educational Research Journal* 31 (1): 49–68.

Furdell, Elizabeth Lane. 2001. *The Royal Doctors, 1485–1714: Medical Personnel at the Tudor and Stuart Courts*. Rochester, NY: University of Rochester Press.

Furniture History Society. n.d. British and Irish Furniture Makers Online. https://bifmo.furniturehistorysociety.org/.

Furnivall, Frederick James, and Percy Furnivall, eds. 1888. *The Anatomie of the bodie of man, by T. Vicary*. Vol. 53. London: Early English Text Society.

Fury, Cheryl A. 1998. "Tides in the Affairs of Men: The Social History of Elizabethan Seamen, 1580–1603." PhD diss., McMaster University.

Gadd, Ian Anders, and Patrick Wallis. 2008. "Reaching beyond the City Wall: London Guilds and National Regulation, 1500–1700." In *Guilds, Innovation, and the European Economy, 1400–1800*, edited by S. R. Epstein and M. R. Prak, 288–315. Cambridge: Cambridge University Press.

Galenson, David W. 1981. "Literacy and Age in Preindustrial England: Quantitative Evidence and Implications." *Economic Development and Cultural Change* 29 (4): 813–829.

Galor, Oded. 2011. *Unified Growth Theory*. Princeton, NJ: Princeton University Press.

Galor, Oded, and Daniel Tsiddon. 1997. "Technological Progress, Mobility, and Economic Growth." *American Economic Review* 87 (3): 363–382.

Galor, Oded, and David N. Weil. 1999. "From Malthusian Stagnation to Modern Growth." *American Economic Review* 89 (2): 150–154.

Garrioch, D., ed. 2022. *The Republic of Skill: Artisan Mobility, Innovation, and the Circulation of Knowledge in Premodern Europe*. Leiden: Brill.

Gauci, Perry. 2001. *The Politics of Trade: The Overseas Merchant in State and Society, 1660–1720*. Oxford: Oxford University Press.

Gay, Hannah. 2000. "Association and Practice: The City and Guilds of London Institute for the Advancement of Technical Education." *Annals of Science* 57 (4): 369–398.

Gelderblom, Oscar. 2013. *Cities of Commerce: The Institutional Foundations of International Trade in the Low Countries, 1250–1650*. Princeton, NJ: Princeton University Press.

Gelderblom, Oscar, and Regina Grafe. 2010. "The Rise and Fall of the Merchant Guilds: Rethinking the Comparative Study of Commercial Institutions in Premodern Europe." *Journal of Interdisciplinary History* 40 (4): 477–511.

Gendron, John. 2023. "Changes in Textile Regulation in Early Modern England, 1550–1640." PhD diss., Texas Tech University.

Gent, Thomas. 1832. *The Life of Mr Thomas Gent: Printer of York*. London: Thomas Thorpe.

Glaisyer, Natasha. 2006. *The Culture of Commerce in England, 1660–1720*. Woodbridge: Boydell.

Glaisyer, Natasha, and Sara Pennell. 2003. Introduction to *Didactic Literature in England 1500–1800*, edited by Natasha Glaisyer and Sara Pennell, 1–18. London: Ashgate.

Glover, Elizabeth. 2008. *Men of Metal: History of the Armourers and Brasiers of the City of London*. Huddersfield: Worshipful Company of Armourers and Brasiers.

Goldin, Claudia, and Lawrence F. Katz. 1998. "The Origins of Technology-Skill Complementarity." *Quarterly Journal of Economics* 113 (3): 693–732.

———. 2008. *The Race between Education and Technology*. Cambridge, MA: Harvard University Press.

Goldstone, Jack A. 2002. "Efflorescences and Economic Growth in World History: Rethinking the "Rise of the West" and the Industrial Revolution." *Journal of World History* 13 (2): 323–389.

Goody, Esther N. 1989. "Learning, Apprenticeship and the Division of Labor." In *Apprenticeship: From Theory to Method and Back Again*, edited by Michael William Coy, 233–266. Albany: State University of New York Press.

Gordon, William. 1777. *The Universal accountant and complete merchant*. 4th ed. Edinburgh: A. Donaldson and J. Reid.

Gough, James, ed. 1750. *A Narrative of the Christian Experiences of George Bewley . . . deceased. Written by himself.* Dublin: I. Jackson.

Gowing, Laura. 2016. "Girls on Forms: Apprenticing Young Women in Seventeenth-Century London." *Journal of British Studies* 55 (3): 447–473.

———. 2021. *Ingenious Trade: Women and Work in Seventeenth-Century London*. Cambridge: Cambridge University Press.

Graham, Malcolm, ed. 1987. *Oxford City Apprentices 1697–1800*. Vol. 31. Oxford: Oxford Historical Society.

Granovetter, Mark. 1983. "Weak Ties." *Sociological Theory* 1: 201–233.

———. 2017. *Getting a Job: A Study of Contacts and Careers*. 2nd ed. Chicago: University of Chicago Press.

Grassby, Richard. 1995. *The Business Community of Seventeenth-Century England*. Cambridge: Cambridge University Press.

———. 2000. *Kinship and Capitalism: Marriage, Family, and Business in the English-Speaking World, 1580–1740*. Woodrow Wilson Center series. New York: Cambridge University Press.

Greene, John. 1708. *The priviledges of the Lord Mayor and Aldermen of the City*. London: Charles Harper.

Gregg, W. W. 1928. "The Decrees and Ordinances of the Stationers' Company, 1576–1602." *Library* 8 (4): 395–425.

Gregg, W. W., and E. Boswell. 1930. *Records of the Court of the Stationers' Company, 1576 to 1602, from Register, B*. London: Bibliographical Society.

Griffiths, Paul. 1996. *Youth and Authority: Formative Experiences in England, 1560–1640*. Oxford: Clarendon Press.

———. 2008. *Lost Londons: Change, Crime and Control in the Capital City, 1550–1660*. Cambridge: Cambridge University Press.

Groot, Piet, and Ruben Schalk. 2022. "Journeymen Migration and Settlement in Eighteenth-Century Holland." *Continuity and Change* 37 (2): 199–232.

Gutton, Jean-Pierre. 2003. "L'insertion sociale des enfants recueillis par la Charité de Lyon au XVIIIe siècle un bilan provisoire." In *Lorsque l'enfant grandit: Entre dépendance et autonomie*, edited by Jean-Pierre Bardet, Jean-Noël Luc, and Isabelle Robin-Romero, 929–939. Paris: Presses de l'Université de Paris–Sorbonne.

Haggart, David. 1821. *The Life of David Haggart: Alias John Wilson, alias John Morison, alias Barney M'Coul, alias John M'Colgan, alias Daniel O'Brien, alias the Switcher*. 2nd ed. Edinburgh: W. and C. Tait.

Halliday, Paul D. 1998. *Dismembering the Body Politic: Partisan Politics in England's Towns, 1650–1730*. Cambridge: Cambridge University Press.

Hamilton, Gillian. 1995. "Enforcement in Apprenticeship Contracts: Were Runaways a Serious Problem? Evidence from Montreal." *Journal of Economic History* 55 (3): 551.

———. 1996. "The Market for Montreal Apprentices: Contract Length and Information." *Explorations in Economic History* 33 (4): 496–523.

———. 2000. "The Decline of Apprenticeship in North America: Evidence from Montreal." *Journal of Economic History* 60 (3): 627–664.

Hanawalt, Barbara A. 1993. *Growing Up in Medieval London: The Experience of Childhood in History*. Oxford: Oxford University Press.

Hanley, Hugh. 2005. *Apprenticing in a Market Town: The Story of William Harding's Charity, Aylesbury, 1719–2000*. Chichester: Phillimore.

Harding, V. 1990. "The Population of London, 1500–1700: A Review of the Published Evidence." *London Journal* 15 (2): 111–128.

Harris, Isabella, and Mary Ann Harris. 1869. *Family Memorials: Chiefly the Memoranda Left by Isabella Harris; with Some Extracts from the Journal of Her Mother, etc.* London: E. Barrett and Sons.

Harris, Ron. 2020. *Going the Distance: Eurasian Trade and the Rise of the Business Corporation, 1400–1700*. Princeton, NJ: Princeton University Press.

Harris, Tim. 1987. *London Crowds in the Reign of Charles II: Propaganda and Politics from the Restoration until the Exclusion Crisis*. New York: Cambridge University Press.

Hartopp, Henry. 1927. *Register of the Freemen of Leicester, 1196–1770*. 2 vols. Leicester: Corporation of the City of Leicester.

Haskins, Charles. 1912. *The Ancient Trade Guilds and Companies of Salisbury*. Salisbury: Bennett Brothers.

Hasler, P. W., ed. 1981. *The House of Commons 1558–1603*. London: H.M.S.O.

Hatton, Timothy J. 2010. "The Cliometrics of International Migration: A Survey." *Journal of Economic Surveys* 24 (5): 941–969.

Haupt, Heinz-Gerhard. 2002. *Das Ende der Zünfte: Ein europäischer Vergleich*. Kritische Studien zur Geschichtswissenschaft 151. Göttingen: Vandenhoeck & Ruprecht.

Hay, Douglas. 2004. "England, 1562–1875: The Law and Its Uses." In *Masters, Servants, and Magistrates in Britain and the Empire, 1562–1955*, edited by Douglas Hay and Paul Craven, 59–116. Chapel Hill: University of North Carolina Press.

Hay, Douglas, and Paul Craven. 2004. *Masters, Servants, and Magistrates in Britain and the Empire, 1562–1955*. Studies in Legal History. Chapel Hill: University of North Carolina Press.

Hepworth, Methold. 1910. *A Calendar of the Freemen of Great Yarmouth, 1429–1800. Compiled from the Records of the Corporation of That Borough, etc.* Norwich: Norwich Archaeological Society.

Herzfeld, Michael. 2004. *The Body Impolitic: Artisans and Artifice in the Global Hierarchy of Value*. Chicago: Chicago: University of Chicago Press.

Hey, David. 1991. *The Fiery Blades of Hallamshire: Sheffield and Its Neighbourhood 1660–1740*. Leicester: Leicester University Press.

———. 2010. *The Worshipful Company of Blacksmiths*. Lancaster: Carnegie.

Hibbert, W. N. 1925. *History of the Worshipful Company of Founders of the City of London*. London: Worshipful Company of Founders.

Hilaire-Pérez, Liliane. 2007. "Technology as a Public Culture in the Eighteenth Century: The Artisans' Legacy." *History of Science* 45 (2): 135–153.

Hilaire-Pérez, Liliane, and Catherine Verna. 2006. "Dissemination of Technical Knowledge in the Middle Ages and the Early Modern Era: New Approaches and Methodological Issues." *Technology and Culture* 47 (3): 536–565.

Hill, J. W. F. 1956. *Tudor and Stuart Lincoln*. Cambridge: Cambridge University Press.

Hindle, Steve. 2004. *On the Parish? The Micro-politics of Poor Relief in Rural England c. 1550–1750*. Oxford: Clarendon Press.

Hitchcock, Tim, Robert B. Shoemaker, Sharon Howard, and Jamie McLaughlin. 2018. *London Lives, 1690–1800: Crime, Poverty and Social Policy in the Metropolis*. http://www.londonlives.org.

Hobsbawm, E. J. 1964. *Labouring Men*. London: Weidenfeld & Nicolson.

Hobson, Joseph. 1757. *Memoirs of the Life and Convincement of that worthy Friend B. Bangs mostly taken from his own mouth by Joseph Hobson*. London: Luke Hinde.

Holmes, Geoffrey. 1982. *Augustan England: Professions, State and Society, 1680–1730*. London: George Allen & Unwin.

Honeyman, Katrina. 2007. *Child Workers in England, 1780–1820: Parish Apprentices and the Making of the Early Industrial Labour Force*. Aldershot: Ashgate.

Horrell, Sara, and Jane Humphries. 1995. "'The Exploitation of Little Children': Child Labor and the Family Economy in the Industrial Revolution." *Explorations in Economic History* 32 (4): 485–516.

———. 2019. "Children's Work and Wages in Britain, 1280–1860." *Explorations in Economic History* 73: 101272.

Horsefield, John Keith. 1960. *British Monetary Experiments, 1650–1710*. London: G. Bell & Sons.

Horwitz, Henry, and Jessica Cooke, eds. 2000. *London and Middlesex Exchequer Equity Pleadings, 1685–6 and 1784–5: A Calendar*. London Record Society 35. London: London Record Society.

Houlbrooke, Ralph A. 1988. *English Family Life, 1576–1716: An Anthology from Diaries*. Oxford: Basil Blackwell.

Hovland, Stephanie R. 2007. "Apprenticeship in Later Medieval London, c. 1300–c. 1530." PhD diss., Royal Holloway, University of London.

———. 2008. "Girls as Apprentices in Later Medieval London." In *London and the Kingdom: Essays in Honour of Caroline M. Barron*, edited by Matthew Davies and Andrew Prescott, 179–194. Donington: Harlaxton Medieval Studies.

Howard, Alexander Liddon. 1940. *The Worshipful Company of Glass-Sellers of London: From Its Inception to the Present Day*. London: Company of Glass-Sellers.

Hubbard, Eleanor. 2012. *City Women: Money, Sex, and the Social Order in Early Modern London*. Oxford: Oxford University Press.

Hudson, Pat, and Lynette Hunter. 1981. "The Autobiography of William Hart, Cooper, 1776–1857: A Respectable Artisan in the Industrial Revolution." *London Journal* 7 (2): 144–160.

Hudson, William, and John Cottingham Tingey. 1906. *The Records of the City of Norwich*. 2 vols. Norwich: City of Norwich.

Hughes, Thomas Cann, and W. B. Kendall. 1935. *The Rolls of the Freemen of the Borough of Lancaster: 1688 to 1840*. Record Society of Lancashire and Cheshire (Series) 87, 90. Lancaster: Record Society of Lancashire and Cheshire.

Humphries, Jane. 2003. "English Apprenticeship: A Neglected Factor in the First Industrial Revolution." In *The Economic Future in Historical Perspective*, edited by Paul A. David and Mark Thomas, 73–102. Oxford: Oxford University Press.

———. 2010. *Childhood and Child Labour in the British Industrial Revolution*. Cambridge: Cambridge University Press.

Hurley, Beryl, David Mattock, and Tim Morland. 1996. *Salisbury Area Apprenticeships and Wilton Free School*. Devizes: Wiltshire Family History Society.

Hutton, William. 1872. *The Life of William Hutton, and the History of the Hutton Family*. Edited by Llewellynn Jewitt. London: F. Warne.

Ingold, Tim. 2001. "Beyond Art and Technology: The Anthropology of Skill." In *Anthropological Perspectives on Technology*, edited by M. B. Schiffer, 17–31. Albuquerque: University of New Mexico Press.

Innes, Joanna. 2002. "Origins of the Factory Acts: The Health and Morals of Apprentices Act, 1802." In *Law, Crime and English Society, 1660–1830*, edited by J. M. Beattie and Norma Landau. Cambridge: Cambridge University Press.

Innes, Joanna, and Nicholas Rogers. 2000. "Politics and Government 1700–1840." In *The Cambridge Urban History of Britain*. Vol. 2, *1540–1840*, edited by Peter Clark, 529–574. Cambridge: Cambridge University Press.

Iversen, Torben, and David Soskice. 2001. "An Asset Theory of Social Policy Preferences." *American Political Science Review* 95 (4): 875–893.

Jackson, Charles, ed. 1877. *Yorkshire Diaries and Autobiographies in the Seventeenth and Eighteenth Centuries*. Surtees Society 65. Durham: Surtees Society.

Jacob, Margaret C. 2007. "Mechanical Science on the Factory Floor: The Early Industrial Revolution in Leeds." *History of Science* 45 (2): 197–222.

———. 2014. *The First Knowledge Economy: Human Capital and the European Economy, 1750–1850*. Cambridge: Cambridge University Press.

Jacoby, Daniel. 1991a. "Legal Foundations of Human Capital Markets." *Industrial Relations* 30 (2): 229–250.

———. 1991b. "The Transformation of Industrial Apprenticeship in the United States." *Journal of Economic History* 51 (4): 887–910.

Jenkinson, Hilary. 1914. "A Late Surrey Chronicler (Surrey and the Revolution, 1688)." *Surrey Archaeological Collections* 27: 1–20.

J. M. 1750. *The Pocket Remembrancer; or a concise history of the City of London*. London: J. Roberts.

Johnson, Arthur Henry. 1914–22. *The History of the Worshipful Company of the Drapers of London*. 5 vols. Oxford: Oxford University Press.

Jones, D. W. 1988. *War and Economy in the Age of William III and Marlborough*. Oxford: Basil Blackwell.

Jordan, W. K. 1959. *Philanthropy in England, 1480–1660: A Study of the Changing Pattern of English Social Aspirations*. London: George Allen & Unwin.

Jupp, Edward Basil, and William Willmer Pocock. 1887. *An Historical Account of the Worshipful Company of Carpenters of the City of London*. 2nd ed., with a supplement by W. W. Pocock. London: Pickering & Chatto.

Justman, Moshe, and Karine van der Beek. 2015. "Market Forces Shaping Human Capital in Eighteenth-Century London." *Economic History Review* 68 (4): 1177–1202.

Kahan, Marcel, and Michael Klausner. 1997. "Standardization and Innovation in Corporate Contracting (or 'The Economics of Boilerplate')." *Virginia Law Review* 83 (4): 713–770.

Kahl, W. F. 1960. *The Development of the London Livery Companies: An Historical Essay and a Select Bibliography*. Cambridge, MA: Harvard Graduate School of Business Administration.

Kaplan, Steven L. 1981. "The Luxury Guilds in Paris in the Eighteenth Century." *Francia* 9: 257–298.

———. 1993. "L'apprentissage au XVIIIe siècle: Le cas de Paris." *Revue d'histoire moderne et contemporaine* 40 (3): 436–479.

———. 2007. "Reconsidering Apprenticeship: Afterthoughts." In *Learning on the Shop Floor: Historical Perspectives on Apprenticeship*, edited by Bert De Munck, Steven L. Kaplan, and Hugo Soly, 203–219. New York: Berghahn.

———. 2023. *Transmettre, soumettre, socialiser: Essai sur l'apprentissage de Colbert à la Grande Guerre*. Paris: Fayard.

Kaplan, Steven L., C. Crowston, and G. Postel-Vinay. 2009. "Where and Why Apprenticeship in Enlightenment France." Paper presented at Fifteenth World Economic History Congress, Utrecht, 7 August 2009.

Kearsley, George. 1786. *Kearsley's Table of Trades*. London: George Kearsley.

Keene, Derek. 2000. "Metropolitan Values: Migration, Mobility and Cultural Norms, 1300–1700." In *The Development of Standard English, 1300–1800*, edited by L. Wright, 93–114. Cambridge: Cambridge University Press.

Keith-Lucas, Bryan. 1952. *The English Local Government Franchise: A Short History*. Oxford: Basil Blackwell.

———. 1980. *The Unreformed Local Government System*. London: Croom Helm.

Kellett, J. R. 1957–58. "The Breakdown of Gild and Corporation Control over the Handicraft and Retail Trade in London." *Economic History Review* 10 (3): 381–394.

Kelly, Morgan, Joel Mokyr, and Cormac Ó Gráda. 2014. "Precocious Albion: A New Interpretation of the British Industrial Revolution." *Annual Review of Economics* 6:363–389.

———. 2023. "The Mechanics of the Industrial Revolution." *Journal of Political Economy* 131 (1): 59–94.

Kelly, Morgan, and Cormac Ó Gráda. 2016. "Adam Smith, Watch Prices, and the Industrial Revolution." *Quarterly Journal of Economics* 131 (4): 1727–1752.

———. 2022. "Connecting the Scientific and Industrial Revolutions: The Role of Practical Mathematics." *Journal of Economic History* 82 (3): 841–873.

Kent, Joan, and Steve King. 2003. "Changing Patterns of Poor Relief in Some English Rural Parishes circa 1650–1750." *Rural History* 14 (2): 119–156.

Kerry, Charles. 1899. "The Autobiography of Leonard Wheatcroft." *Derbyshire Archaeological Journal* 21: 26–60.

Kha, Henry. 2017. "The Reform of English Divorce Law: 1857–1937." PhD diss., University of Queensland.

King, Gregory. 1936. *Two Tracts*. Edited by G. E. Barnett. Baltimore: Johns Hopkins University Press.

King, Peter. 2004. "The Summary Courts and Social Relations in Eighteenth-Century England." *Past & Present* 183 (1): 125–172.

Kingdon, J. A., ed. 1886. *Facsimile of the Archives of the Worshipful Company of Grocers*. London: Richard Clay for the Grocers' Company.

Kirk, Richard E. G., and Ernest F. Kirk, eds. 1900–1908. *Returns of Aliens Dwelling in the City and Suburbs of London from the Reign of Henry VIII to that of James I*. Proceedings of the Huguenot Society 10. London: Huguenot Society.

Kirke, Henry, ed. 1899. *Extracts from the Diary and Autobiography of the Rev. James Clegg: Nonconformist Minister and Doctor of Medicine, A. D. 1679 to 1755*. Buxton: C. F. Wardley.

Kitch, M. 1986. "Capital and Kingdom: Migration to Later Stuart London." In *The Making of the Metropolis*, edited by A. L. Beier and R. Finlay, 224–251. London: Longman.

Kite, Edward. 1858. "The Guild of Merchants, or Trading Companies Formerly Existing in Devizes." *Magazine of the Wiltshire Archaeological and Natural History Society* 4:160–174.

Klein, Ursula. 2017. "Hybrid Experts." In *The Structures of Practical Knowledge*, edited by M. Valleriani, 287–306. Cham: Springer.

Kleiner, Morris M. 2006. *Licensing Occupations: Ensuring Quality or Restricting Competition?* Kalamazoo, MI: W. E. Upjohn Institute for Employment Research.

Klemp, Marc, Chris Minns, Patrick Wallis, and Jacob Weisdorf. 2013. "Picking Winners? The Effect of Birth Order and Migration on Parental Human Capital Investments in Pre-modern England." *European Review of Economic History* 17 (2): 210–232.

Knights, Mark. 1997. "A City Revolution: The Remodelling of the London Livery Companies in the 1680s." *English Historical Review* 112 (449): 1141–1178.

Knox, William W. 1980. "British Apprenticeship, 1800–1914." PhD diss., Edinburgh University.

Kunnas, Jan. 2016. "Human Capital in Britain, 1760–2009." *Scandinavian Economic History Review* 64 (3): 219–242.

Kussmaul, Ann. 1981. *Servants in Husbandry in Early Modern England.* Cambridge: Cambridge University Press.

Lackington, James. 1793. *Memoirs of the first forty-five years of James Lackington.* London: Author.

Lambert, Bart, and Milan Pajic. 2016. "Immigration and the Common Profit: Native Cloth Workers, Flemish Exiles, and Royal Policy in Fourteenth-Century London." *Journal of British Studies* 55 (4): 633–657.

Lambert, Joseph Malet. 1891. *Two Thousand Years of Gild Life: or, An Outline of the History and Development of the Gild System from Early Times . . . with a Full Account of the Gilds and Trading Companies of Kingston-upon-Hull, from the 14th to the 18th Century.* Hull: Brown and Sons.

Lancy, David F. 2012. "'First You Must Master Pain': The Nature and Purpose of Apprenticeship." *Anthropology of Work Review* 33 (2/3): 113–126.

Landers, John. 1993. *Death and the Metropolis: Studies in the Demographic History of London, 1670–1830.* Cambridge: Cambridge University Press.

Landes, David S. 1983. *Revolution in Time: Clocks and the Making of the Modern World.* Cambridge, MA: Belknap Press.

Lane, Joan. 1996. *Apprenticeship in England, 1600–1914.* London: UCL Press.

Langhamer, Claire. 2006. "Adultery in Post-war England." *History Workshop Journal* 62 (1): 86–115.

Langton, John. 2000. "Urban Growth and Economic Change: From the Late Seventeenth Century to 1841." In *The Cambridge Urban History of Britain*, vol. 2, *1540–1840*, edited by Peter Clark, 451–490. Cambridge: Cambridge University Press.

Lave, Jean, and Etienne Wenger. 1991. *Situated Learning: Legitimate Peripheral Participation.* Cambridge: Cambridge University Press.

Leach, Doreen Sylvia. 2017. "Carpenters in Medieval London c. 1240–c. 1540." PhD diss., University of London.

Leeson, R. A. 1979. *Travelling Brothers: The Six Centuries' Road from Craft Fellowship to Trade Unionism.* London: Granada.

Le Hardy, William, ed. 1905. *Middlesex County Records: Calendar of the Sessions Books 1689–1709.* London: Sir Richard Nicholson.

———, ed. 1930. *Calendar to the Court Minute Books of the Grocers Company, 1556–1692.* London: Guildhall Library.

———, ed. 1931. *Hertfordshire County Records. Calendar to the Sessions Books.* Vol. 7, 1700–1752. Hertford: Elton Longmore.

Le Hardy, William, and Geoffrey Reckitt, eds. 1939. *County of Buckingham Calendar to the Sessions Records.* Vol. 3, 1705–12. Aylesbury: Guy R. Crouch.

Leighton, W. A. 1881. "The Guilds of Shrewsbury." *Transactions of the Shropshire Archaeological and Natural History Society* 4: 193–292.

Levene, Alysa. 2008. "'Honesty, Sobriety and Diligence': Master-Apprentice Relations in Eighteenth- and Nineteenth-Century England." *Social History* 33 (2): 183–200.

———. 2010. "Pauper Apprenticeship and the Old Poor Law in London: Feeding the Industrial Economy?" *Economic History Review* 63 (4): 915–941.

Lever, James. 1891. "A London Citizen's Diary in the 17th and 18th Centuries, c. 1680–1746, ed. A. A. Wallis." *Reliquary* n.s. 5: 90–98.

Lincolnshire Family History Society. n.d. *The Freemen of the City of Lincoln, 1656–1867*. Lincoln: Lincolnshire Family History Society.

London Needlemakers Company. 1876. *The Worshipful Company of Needlemakers of the City of London*. London: Robson and Sons.

Longden, Henry. 1837. *The Life of Mr Henry Longden, Minister of the Gospel*. New York: T. Mason & G. Lane.

López Barahona, Victoria, and José Antolín Nieto Sánchez. 2019. "Artisan Apprenticeship in Early Modern Madrid." In *Apprenticeship in Early Modern Europe*, edited by Maarten Prak and Patrick Wallis, 44–77. Cambridge: Cambridge University Press.

Lovett, A. A., I. D. Whyte, and K. A. Whyte. 1985. "Poisson Regression Analysis and Migration Fields: The Example of the Apprenticeship Records of Edinburgh in the Seventeenth and Eighteenth Centuries." *Transactions of the Institute of British Geographers* 10 (3): 317–332.

Lutkin, Jessica. 2016. "Settled or Fleeting? London's Medieval Immigrant Community Revisited." In *Medieval Merchants and Money: Essays in Honour of James L. Bolton*, edited by Martin Allen and Matthew Davies, 137–156. London: University of London Press.

Luu, Liên. 2005. *Immigrants and the Industries of London, 1500–1700*. Aldershot: Ashgate.

Mackenzie, Eneas. 1827. *Descriptive and Historical Account of the Town and County of Newcastle-upon-Tyne*. Newcastle-upon-Tyne: Mackenzie and Dent.

Manby Smith, Charles. 1853. *The Working Man's Way in the World, Being the Autobiography of a Journeyman Printer*. London: W. & F. G. Cash.

Marchand, Trevor H. J. 2001. *Minaret Building and Apprenticeship in Yemen*. Richmond, Surrey: Curzon Press.

———. 2010. "Making Knowledge: Explorations of the Indissoluble Relation between Minds, Bodies, and Environment." *Journal of the Royal Anthropological Institute* 16 (s1): S1–S21.

Marshall, Alfred. 1890. *Principles of Economics*. London: Macmillan.

Marshall, Tom David Spencer. 2013. "Apprenticeship in Mid-eighteenth-century England: How Did This Ancient Institution Operate during the Commencement of Industrialisation?" DPhil thesis, University of Oxford.

Maruca, Lisa. 2003. "Bodies of Type: The Work of Textual Production in English Printers' Manuals." *Eighteenth-Century Studies* 36 (3): 321–343.

Marx, Karl. 1906. *Capital: A Critique of Political Economy*. Translated by Samuel Moore and Edward B. Aveling. Edited by Friedrich Engels and Ernest Untermann. 3 vols. Chicago: C. H. Kerr.

Mason, Sheila A. 2000. *The History of the Worshipful Company of Framework Knitters: The Art and Mystery of Framework Knitting in England and Wales*. Leicester: Worshipful Company of Framework Knitters.

Matthews, Harold Evan, ed. 1940. *Proceedings, Minutes and Enrolments of the Company of Soapmakers, 1562–1642*. Bristol Record Society 10. Bristol: Bristol Record Society.

Mayer, Edward, and Donald Adamson. 2000. *The Curriers' Company: A Modern History*. London: Worshipful Company of Curriers.

Mayhew, Graham. 1991. "Life-Cycle Service and the Family Unit in Early Modern Rye." *Continuity and Change* 6 (2): 201–226.

McCurrach, M. 1997. *Freemen of the Borough of Ipswich, 1320–1996*. 2 vols. Ipswich: Suffolk Family History Society.

McEwan, Joanne. 2011. "The Lodging Exchange: Space, Authority and Knowledge in Eighteenth-Century London." In *Accommodating Poverty*, edited by Joanne McEwan and Pamela Sharpe, 50–68. London: Palgrave Macmillan.

McGrath, Patrick. 1952. *Records Relating to the Society of Merchant Venturers of the City of Bristol in the 17th Century*. Bristol Record Society 17. Bristol: Bristol Record Society.

McIntosh, Marjorie Keniston. 2014. "Poor Relief in Elizabethan English Communities: An Analysis of Collectors' Accounts." *Economic History Review* 67 (2): 331–357.

McKenzie, D. F., ed. 1961. *Stationers' Company Apprentices 1605–1640*. Charlottesville: Bibliographical Society of the University of Virginia.

Meisenzahl, Ralf, and Joel Mokyr. 2012. "The Rate and Direction of Invention in the British Industrial Revolution: Incentives and Institutions." In *The Rate and Direction of Inventive Activity Revisited*, edited by Josh Lerner and Scott Stern, 443–479. Chicago: University of Chicago Press.

Melhuish, Thomas. 1805. *An Account of the Early Part of the Life and Convincement of Thomas Melhuish, Given by Himself in a Letter*. London: Phillips and Fardon.

Merson, A. L., ed. 1968. *A Calendar of Southampton Apprenticeship Registers, 1609–1740*. Southampton Record Series 12. Southampton: Southampton University Press.

Mill, John Stuart. 1848. *Principles of Political Economy: with some of their applications to social philosophy*. London: John W. Parker.

Millican, Percy. 1934. *The Register of the Freemen of Norwich, 1548–1713*. Norwich: Norwich Corporation.

———. 1952. *The Freeman of Norwich, 1714–1752: A Transcript of the Third Register*. Norfolk Record Society Series 23. Norwich: Norfolk Record Society.

Minns, Chris, and Patrick Wallis. 2012. "Rules and Reality: Quantifying the Practice of Apprenticeship in Early Modern England." *Economic History Review* 65 (2): 556–579.

———. 2013. "The Price of Human Capital in a Pre-industrial Economy: Premiums and Apprenticeship Contracts in 18th-Century England." *Explorations in Economic History* 50 (3): 335–350.

Minoletti, Paul. 2011. "The Transition to Factory Production in the English Wool Textile Industries: Individual and Family Desires for Labour Regulation, 1720–1850." In *Regulating the British Economy, 1660–1850*, edited by Perry Gauci, 217–233. Farnham: Ashgate.

Mitch, David. 1993. "The Role of Human Capital in the First Industrial Revolution." In *The British Industrial Revolution: An Economic Perspective*, edited by Joel Mokyr, 267–307. Boulder, CO: Westview.

Mitchell, David. 2017. *Silversmiths in Elizabethan and Stuart London: Their Lives and Their Marks*. Woodbridge, Suffolk: Boydell.

Moens, W.J.C. 1887. *The Walloons and Their Church at Norwich: Their History and Registers 1565–1832*. Lymington: Printed for the Society.

Mohrenweiser, Jens, and Uschi Backes-Gellner. 2010. "Apprenticeship Training: For Investment or Substitution?" *International Journal of Manpower* 31 (5): 545–562.

Mokyr, Joel. 1990. *The Lever of Riches: Technological Creativity and Economic Progress*. Oxford: Oxford University Press.

———. 2002. *The Gifts of Athena: Historical Origins of the Knowledge Economy*. Princeton, NJ: Princeton University Press.

———. 2009. *The Enlightened Economy: An Economic History of Britain, 1700–1850*. New Haven, CT: Yale University Press.

———. 2020. "The Economics of Apprenticeship." In *Apprenticeship in Early Modern Europe*, edited by Maarten Roy Prak and Patrick Wallis, 20–43. Cambridge: Cambridge University Press.

Moll-Murata, Christine. 2013. "Guilds and Apprenticeship in China and Europe: The Jingdezhen and European Ceramic Industries." In *Technology, Skills and the Pre-modern Economy in the East and West*, edited by Maarten Prak and Jan Luiten van Zanden, 225–258. Leiden: Brill.

Montgomery, James D. 1991. "Social Networks and Labor-Market Outcomes: Toward an Economic Analysis." *American Economic Review* 81 (5): 1408–1418.

More, Charles. 1980. *Skill and the English Working Class, 1870–1914*. London: Croom Helm.

Mortimer, Russell, ed. 1971. *Minute Book of the Men's Meeting of the Society of Friends in Bristol 1667–1686*. Bristol Record Society 26. Bristol: Bristol Record Society.

Muir, Ramsay, and Edith May Platt. 1906. *A History of Municipal Government in Liverpool from the Earliest Times to the Municipal Reform Act of 1835*. Publications of the School of Local History 1. London: Liverpool University Press.

Muldrew, Craig. 1998. *The Economy of Obligation: The Culture of Credit and Social Relations in Early Modern England*. Basingstoke: Macmillan.

Murphy, Kevin M., Andrei Shleifer, and Robert W. Vishny. 1991. "The Allocation of Talent: Implications for Growth." *Quarterly Journal of Economics* 106 (2): 503–530.

Myles, James. 1850. *Chapters in the Life of a Dundee Factory Boy: An Autobiography*. Dundee: J. Myles.

Naidu, Suresh, and Noam Yuchtman. 2013. "Coercive Contract Enforcement: Law and the Labor Market in Nineteenth Century Industrial Britain." *American Economic Review* 103 (1): 107–144.

Neville, Cynthia J. 1996. "Local Sentiment and the 'National' Enemy in Northern England in the Later Middle Ages." *Journal of British Studies* 35 (4): 419–437.

Nicholas, D. 1995. "Child and Adolescent Labour in the Late Medieval City: A Flemish Model in Regional Perspective." *English Historical Review* 110: 1103–1131.

Nicholl, John. 1851. *Some Account of the Worshipful Company of Ironmongers*. London: Nichols.

Nielsen, Klaus. 2008. "Scaffold Instruction at the Workplace from a Situated Perspective." *Studies in Continuing Education* 30 (3): 247–261.

Nieto Sánchez, José Antolín. 2022. "Innovation, Mobility and Knowledge Transfer in Madrid, 1680–1820." In *The Republic of Skill: Artisan Mobility, Innovation, and the Circulation of Knowledge in Premodern Europe*, edited by D. Garrioch, 274–303. Leiden: Brill.

Nieto Sánchez, José Antolín, and Juan Carlos Zofío Llorente. 2016. "The Return of the Guilds: A View from Early Modern Madrid." *Journal of Social History* 50 (2): 247–272.

North, Douglass C., John Joseph Wallis, and Barry R. Weingast. 2009. *Violence and Social Orders: A Conceptual Framework for Interpreting Recorded Human History*. Cambridge: Cambridge University Press.

O'Day, Rosemary. 2000. *The Professions in Early Modern England, 1450–1800: Servants of the Commonweal*. Harlow: Longman.

Ogilvie, Sheilagh C. 1997. *State Corporatism and Proto-industry: The Württemberg Black Forest, 1580–1797*. Cambridge: Cambridge University Press.

———. 2003. *A Bitter Living: Women, Markets, and Social Capital in Early Modern Germany*. Oxford; New York: Oxford University Press.

———. 2004a. "Guilds, Efficiency, and Social Capital: Evidence from German Proto-industry." *Economic History Review* 57 (2): 286–333.

———. 2004b. "How Does Social Capital Affect Women? Guilds and Communities in Early Modern Germany." *American Historical Review* 109 (2): 325–359.

———. 2007. "Can We Rehabilitate the Guilds? A Sceptical Re-appraisal." Cambridge Working Papers in Economics 0745, Faculty of Economics, University of Cambridge. https://doi.org/10.17863/CAM.5174.

———. 2008. "Rehabilitating the Guilds: A Reply." *Economic History Review* 61 (1): 175–182.

———. 2011. *Institutions and European Trade: Merchant Guilds, 1000–1800*. Cambridge: Cambridge University Press.

———. 2019. *The European Guilds: An Economic Analysis*. Princeton, NJ: Princeton University Press.

Oliver, A. M., ed. 1926. *The Register of Freemen of Newcastle upon Tyne from the Corporation Guild and Admission Books*. Newcastle upon Tyne Records Committee 6. Newcastle upon Tyne: Newcastle upon Tyne Records Committee.

Ormrod, W. M., Bart Lambert, and Jonathan Mackman. 2018. *Immigrant England, 1300–1550.* Manchester: Manchester University Press.

Oxley, Joseph. 1837. "Joseph's Offering to His Children. Being Joseph Oxley's Journal of His Life, Travels, and Labours of Love." In *A Select Series, Biographical, Narrative, Epistolary, and Miscellaneous,* edited by John Barclay, 199–389. London: Darton and Harvey.

Palmer, Richard. 1989. "Thomas Corbyn, Quaker Merchant." *Medical History* 33 (3): 371–376.

Palmer, Robert C. 1993. *English Law in the Age of the Black Death.* Chapel Hill: University of North Carolina Press.

Parker, G. 1922. "Early Bristol Medical Institutions, the Medieval Hospitals, and Barber Surgeons." *Transactions of the Bristol and Gloucestershire Archaeological Society* 44: 155–178.

Payne, Dianne Elizabeth. 2008. "Children of the Poor in London, 1700–1780." PhD diss., University of Hertfordshire.

Pearce, Arthur. 1929. *The History of the Butchers' Company.* London: Meat Trades' Journal Company.

Pelling, Margaret. 1988. "Child Health as a Social Value in Early Modern England." *Social History of Medicine* 1 (2): 135–164.

———. 1994. "Apprenticeship, Health and Social Cohesion in Early Modern London." *History Workshop Journal* 37: 33–56.

———. 1995. "Knowledge Common and Acquired: The Education of Unlicensed Medical Practitioners in Early Modern London." In *The History of Medical Education in Britain,* edited by Vivian Nutton and Roy Porter, 250–279. London: Clio Medica.

———. 1998. *The Common Lot: Sickness, Medical Occupations and the Urban Poor in Early Modern England.* London: Longmans.

———. 2019. "Managing Uncertainty and Privatising Apprenticeship: Status and Relationships in English Medicine, 1500–1900." *Social History of Medicine* 32 (1): 34–56.

Pettigree, Andrew. 1986. *Foreign Protestant Communities in Sixteenth-Century London.* Oxford: Oxford University Press.

Petty, William. 1647. *The advice of W.P. to Mr Samuel Hartlib for the advancement of some particular parts of learning.* London.

Pevsner, Nikolaus. 1940. *Academies of Art Past and Present.* Cambridge: Cambridge University Press.

Pfister, Ulrich. 2008. "Craft Guilds and Technological Change: The Engine Loom in the European Silk Ribbon Industry in the Seventeenth and Eighteenth Centuries." In *Guilds, Innovation and the European Economy, 1400–1800,* edited by S. R. Epstein and M. R. Prak, 172–198. Cambridge: Cambridge University Press.

———. 2020. "Urban Population in Germany, 1500–1850." CQE Working Paper 9020, Center for Quantitative Economics, University of Muenster.

Pinches, Sylvia M. 2000. "Charities in Warwickshire in the Eighteenth and Nineteenth Centuries." PhD diss., University of Leicester.

Polanyi, Michael. 1962. *Personal Knowledge: Towards a Post-critical Philosophy.* London: Routledge & Kegan Paul.

———. 1966. *The Tacit Dimension.* London: Routledge & Kegan Paul.

Pomeranz, Kenneth. 2013. "Skills, 'Guilds', and Development: Asking Epstein's Questions to East Asian Institutions." In *Technology, Skills and the Pre-modern Economy in the East and West,* edited by Maarten Prak and Jan Luiten van Zanden, 93–130. Leiden: Brill.

Powell, Thomas. 1631. *Tom of all trades. Or The plaine path-way to preferment.* London: Benjamin Fisher.

Power, Michael, Fiona Lewis, and Di Ascott. 1998. Liverpool Community, 1649–1750. [Data collection.] 10.5255/UKDA-SN-3882-1. Colchester: UK Data Archive. https://beta.ukdataservice.ac.uk/datacatalogue/studies/study?id=3882.

Prak, Maarten. 2008. "Painters, Guilds and the Art Market during the Dutch Golden Age." In *Guilds, Innovation and the European Economy, 1400–1800*, edited by S. R. Epstein and M. R. Prak, 143–171. Cambridge: Cambridge University Press.

———. 2018. *Citizens without Nations: Urban Citizenship in Europe and the World, c. 1000–1789*. Cambridge: Cambridge University Press.

Prak, Maarten, and Jan Luiten van Zanden. 2013. *Technology, Skills and the Pre-modern Economy in the East and the West*. Leiden: Brill.

Prak, Maarten, and Patrick Wallis, eds. 2019. *Apprenticeship in Early Modern Europe*. Cambridge: Cambridge University Press.

Prest, John. 1990. *Liberty and Locality: Parliament, Permissive Legislation and Ratepayers' Democracies in the Nineteenth Century*. Oxford: Clarendon Press.

Price, Roger. 2014a. *Marriages at St James's Church, Bristol: 1559–1753. Chronological Index & Name Index*. Bristol: Bristol & Avon Family History Society.

———. 2014b. *Marriages at Temple Church, Bristol: 1558–1753. Chronological Index & Name Index*. Bristol: Bristol & Avon Family History Society.

———. 2015. *Marriages at Bristol Cathedral: 1615–1754. Chronological Index & Name Index*. Bristol: Bristol & Avon Family History Society.

Prideaux, Walter Sherburne, ed. 1896–97. *Memorials of the Goldsmiths' Company*. 2 vols. London: Eyre and Spottiswoode.

Putnam, Bertha Haven. 1908. *The Enforcement of the Statutes of Labourers during the First Decade after the Black Death, 1349–1359*. New York: Columbia University Press.

Rabuzzi, Daniel A. 1995. "Eighteenth-Century Commercial Mentalities as Reflected and Projected in Business Handbooks." *Eighteenth-Century Studies* 29 (2): 169–189.

Rahikainen, Marjatta. 2004. *Centuries of Child Labour: European Experiences from the Seventeenth to the Twentieth Century*. Aldershot: Ashgate.

Rappaport, Steve Lee. 1983. "Social Structure and Mobility in Sixteenth-Century London." *London Journal* 10 (2): 107–35.

———. 1989. *Worlds within Worlds: Structures of Life in Sixteenth-Century London*. Cambridge: Cambridge University Press.

———. 1991. "Reconsidering Apprenticeship in Sixteenth-Century London." In *Renaissance Society and Culture*, edited by John Monfasani and Ronald G. Musto, 239–261. New York: Italica Press.

Ravenstein, E. G. 1885. "The Laws of Migration." *Journal of the Statistical Society of London* 48 (2): 167–235.

Reddaway, T. F., and Lorna E. M. Walker. 1975. *The Early History of the Goldsmiths Company, 1327–1509*. London: Edward Arnold.

Redford, Arthur. 1926. *Labour Migration in England, 1800–50*. Manchester: Manchester University Press.

Reis, Jaime. 2005. "Economic Growth, Human Capital Formation and Consumption in Western Europe before 1800." In *Living Standards in the Past: New Perspectives on Well-Being in Asia and Europe*, edited by Robert C. Allen, Tommy Bengtsson, and Martin Dribe, 195–225. Oxford: Oxford University Press.

Reith, Reinhold. 2008. "Circulation of Skilled Labour in Late Medieval and Early Modern Central Europe." In *Guilds, Innovation, and the European Economy, 1400–1800*, edited by S. R. Epstein and M. R. Prak, 114–142. Cambridge: Cambridge University Press.

Rice, R. Garraway. 1922. *Sussex Apprentices and Masters, 1710 to 1752: Extracted from the Apprenticeship Books*. Lewes: Sussex Record Society.

Richards, Jake Christopher. 2018. "Anti-slave-trade Law, 'Liberated Africans' and the State in the South Atlantic World, c. 1839–1852." *Past & Present* 241 (1): 179–219.

Richardson, William. 1908. *A Mariner of England: An Account of the Career of William Richardson from Cabin Boy in the Merchant Service to Warrant Officer in the Royal Navy (1780–1819).* London: Murray.

Riello, Giorgio. 2012. "Boundless Competition: Subcontracting and the London Economy in the Late Nineteenth Century." *Enterprise and Society* 13 (3): 504–537.

Ripley, Peter, and A.R.J. Jurica. 1991. *A Calendar of the Registers of the Freemen of the City of Gloucester 1641–1838.* Bristol and Gloucestershire Archaeological Society 4. Stroud: Bristol and Gloucestershire Archaeological Society.

Rising, Winifred M., and Percy Millican. 1959. *An Index of Indentures of Norwich Apprentices Enrolled with the Norwich Assembly: Henry VII–George II.* Vol. 29. Norwich: Norfolk Record Society.

Robson, Leonard Charles Fisher. 1949. *The Farriers of London: Being an Account of the Worshipful Company of Farriers as Described in the Records of the Company.* Leeds: For private circulation.

Rogers, Nicholas. 1989. *Whigs and Cities: Popular Politics in the Age of Walpole and Pitt.* Oxford: Oxford University Press.

Rose, Craig. 1999. *England in the 1690s: Revolution, Religion, and War.* Oxford: Blackwell.

Rosenberger, Lukas. 2022. "Enlightenment, Industrial Revolution, and the Knowledge Economy Essays in (Macro-)Economic History." PhD diss., Ludwig-Maximilians-Universität München.

Roseveare, Henry, ed. 1987. *Markets and Merchants of the Late Seventeenth Century: The Marescoe-David Letters, 1668–1680.* British Academy: Records of Social and Economic History 12. New series. Oxford: Oxford University Press.

Rowe, Margery, and Andrew M. Jackson, eds. 1973. *Exeter Freemen, 1266–1967.* Devon & Cornwall Record Society 1. Extra Series. Exeter: Devon & Cornwall Record Society.

Roy, Tirthankar. 2010. *Company of Kinsmen: Enterprise and Community in South Asian History, 1700–1940.* Oxford: Oxford University Press.

———. 2013. "Apprenticeship and Industrialization in India, 1600–1930." In *Technology, Skills and the Pre-modern Economy in the East and West,* edited by Maarten Prak and Jan Luiten van Zanden, 69–92. Leiden: Brill.

Royal Commission on Municipal Corporations. 1835. *First Report of the Commissioners Appointed to Enquire into the Municipal Corporations in England and Wales: London and Southwark: Provincial England.* Vols. 23–26. London: H.M.S.O.

———. 1837. *Second Report of the Commissioners Appointed to Enquire into the Municipal Corporations in England and Wales: London and Southwark: London Companies.* Vol. 239. London: H.M.S.O.

Rule, John. 1981. *Experience of Labour in Eighteenth-Century Industry.* London: Croom Helm.

———. 1989. "The Property of Skill in the Period of Manufacture." In *The Historical Meanings of Work,* edited by Patrick Joyce, 99–118. Cambridge: Cambridge University Press.

Rushton, Peter. 1991. "The Matter in Variance: Adolescents and Domestic Conflict in the Pre-industrial Economy of Northeast England, 1600–1800." *Journal of Social History* 25 (1): 89–107.

Ryan, Maeve. 2016. "'A moral millstone'? British Humanitarian Governance and the Policy of Liberated African Apprenticeship, 1808–1848." *Slavery & Abolition* 37 (2): 399–422.

Sabel, Charles F., and Jonathan Zeitlin. 2002. *World of Possibilities: Mass Production and Flexibility in Western Industrialization.* Cambridge: Cambridge University Press.

Sacks, David Harris. 1991. *The Widening Gate: Bristol and the Atlantic Economy, 1450–1700.* Berkeley: University of California Press.

Sahle, Esther. 2018. "Quakers, Coercion, and Pre-modern Growth: Why Friends' Formal Institutions for Contract Enforcement Did Not Matter for Early Modern Trade Expansion." *Economic History Review* 71 (2): 418–436.

Salkeld, William. 1773. *Reports of Cases Adjudged in the Court of King's Bench*. New ed. London: W. Strahan.

Schalk, Ruben. 2015. "Splitting the Bill: Matching Schooling to Dutch Labour Markets, 1750–1920." PhD diss., Utrecht University.

———. 2016. "From Orphan to Artisan: Apprenticeship Careers and Contract Enforcement in the Netherlands before and after the Guild Abolition." *Economic History Review* 70 (3): 730–757.

———. 2019. "Apprenticeships with and without Guilds: The Northern Netherlands." In *Apprenticeship in Early Modern Europe*, edited by Maarten Prak and Patrick Wallis, 187–216. Cambridge: Cambridge University Press.

Schalk, Ruben, Patrick Wallis, Clare Crowston, and Claire Lemercier. 2017. "Failure or Flexibility? Exits from Apprenticeship Training in Pre-modern Europe." *Journal of Interdisciplinary History* 48 (2): 131–158.

Schnettler, Sebastian. 2009. "A Structured Overview of 50 Years of Small-World Research." *Social Networks* 31 (3): 165–178.

Schulz, Herbert C. 1943. "The Teaching of Handwriting in Tudor and Stuart Times." *Huntington Library Quarterly* 6 (4): 381–425.

Schwarz, Leonard. 1987. "London Apprentices in the Seventeenth Century: Some Problems." *Local Population Studies* 38: 18–22.

———. 1992. *London in the Age of Industrialisation: Entrepreneurs, Labour Force and Living Conditions, 1700–1850*. Cambridge: Cambridge University Press.

———. 2000. "London 1700–1840." In *The Cambridge Urban History of Britain*, vol. 2, *1540–1840*, edited by Peter Clark, 641–672. Cambridge: Cambridge University Press.

Schwarzberg, Raphaelle. 2016. "The Openness of the London Goldsmiths' Company in the Second Half of the Seventeenth Century: An Empirical Study." *Financial History Review* 23 (2): 245–271.

Scott, Benjamin. 1863. "The Custom of Apprenticeship in the City of London." In *Transactions of the National Association for the Promotion of Social Science: London Meeting 1862*, edited by George W. Hastings, 183–187. London: John W. Parker.

Scott, James B. 1961. *Short Account of the Worshipful Company of Wheelwrights*. Rev. ed. London: Witherby.

Scott, Michael. 2016. *Apprenticeship Disputes in the Lord Mayor's Court of London, 1573–1723*. 2 vols. Apprenticeship Series 1. London: British Record Society.

———, ed. 2019. *The Merchant Taylors' Company of London: Apprentices, 1583–1800*. 3 vols. Apprenticeship Series 2. London: British Record Society.

Seaver, Paul S. 1989. "A Social Contract? Master against Servant in the Court of Requests." *History Today* 39 (9): 50–56.

Sennett, Richard. 2009. *The Craftsman*. London: Penguin.

Sharpe, Pamela. 1991. "Poor Children as Apprentices in Colyton, 1598–1830." *Continuity and Change* 6 (2): 253–270.

Shepard, Alexandra. 2015. *Accounting for Oneself: Worth, Status, and the Social Order in Early Modern England*. Oxford: Oxford University Press.

Shepard, Alexandra, and Judith Spicksley. 2011. "Worth, Age and Social Status in Early Modern England." *Economic History Review* 64 (2): 493–530.

Shephard, Edward J. 1986. "Social and Geographic Mobility of the Eighteenth-Century Guild Artisan: An Analysis of Guild Receptions in Dijon, 1700–90." In *Work in France*, edited by Steven Laurence Kaplan and Cynthia J. Koepp, 97–130. Ithaca, NY: Cornell University Press.

Shoemaker, R. B. 1991. *Prosecution and Punishment: Petty Crime and the Law in London and Rural Middlesex, c. 1660–1725*. Cambridge: Cambridge University Press.

Simonton, Deborah. 1990. "Apprenticeship: Training and Gender in Eighteenth-Century England." In *Markets and Manufactures in Early Industrial Europe*, edited by Maxine Berg, 227–258. London: Routledge.

———. 2000. "Schooling the Poor: Gender and Class in Eighteenth-Century England." *Journal for Eighteenth-Century Studies* 23 (2): 183–202.

———. 2004. "Earning and Learning: Girlhood in Pre-industrial Europe." *Women's History Review* 13 (3): 363–386.

Singleton, John, ed. 1998. *Learning in Likely Places: Varieties of Apprenticeship in Japan*. Cambridge: Cambridge University Press.

Smiles, Samuel. 1866. *Self-Help: With Illustrations of Character Conduct and Perseverance*. New ed. London: John Murray.

Smith, Adam. 1776. *An Inquiry into the Nature and Causes of the Wealth of Nations*. 2 vols. London: W. Strahan and T. Cadell.

Smith, Pamela H. 2022. *From Lived Experience to the Written Word: Reconstructing Practical Knowledge in the Early Modern World*. Chicago: University of Chicago Press.

Smith, S. D. 2005. "Women's Admission to Guilds in Early Modern England: The Case of the York Merchant Tailors', 1693–1776." *Gender and History* 17 (1): 99–126.

Smith, S. R. 1973. "The London Apprentices as Seventeenth-Century Adolescents." *Past & Present* 61: 149–161.

Smits, Wendy, and Thorsten Stromback. 2000. *The Economics of the Apprenticeship System*. Cheltenham: Edward Elgar.

Snell, K.D.M. 1985. *Annals of the Labouring Poor: Social Change and Agrarian England, 1660–1900*. Cambridge: Cambridge University Press.

———. 2006. *Parish and Belonging: Community, Identity, and Welfare in England and Wales, 1700–1950*. Cambridge: Cambridge University Press.

Söderlund, Ernst Frithiof. 1949. *Hantverkarna: D. 2, Stormaktstiden, frihetstiden och gustavianska tiden*. Stockholm: Tiden.

Soskice, David W., and Peter A. Hall. 2001. *Varieties of Capitalism: The Institutional Foundations of Comparative Advantage*. Oxford: Oxford University Press.

Stabel, P. 2004. "Guilds in Late Medieval Flanders: Myths and Realities of Guild Life in an Export-Oriented Environment." *Journal of Medieval History* 30 (2): 187–212.

———. 2007. "Social Mobility and Apprenticeship in Late Medieval Flanders." In *Learning on the Shop Floor: Historical Perspectives on Apprenticeship*, edited by Bert De Munck, Steven L. Kaplan, and Hugo Soly, 158–178. New York: Berghahn.

Steffens, Sven. 2001. "Le métier volé: Transmission des savoir-faire et socialisation dans les métiers qualifiés au XIXe siècle." *Revue du Nord* 15: 121–135.

Steidl, Annemarie. 2007. "Silk Weaver and Purse Maker Apprentices in Eighteenth- and Nineteenth-Century Vienna." In *Learning on the Shop Floor: Historical Perspectives on Apprenticeship*, edited by Bert De Munck, Steven L. Kaplan, and Hugo Soly, 133–157. New York: Berghahn.

Steinberg, Marc W. 2006. "Unfree Labor, Apprenticeship and the Rise of the Victorian Hull Fishing Industry: An Example of the Importance of Law and the Local State in British Economic Change." *International Review of Social History* 51 (2): 243–276.

———. 2016. *England's Great Transformation: Law, Labor, and the Industrial Revolution*. Chicago: University of Chicago Press.

Steinfeld, Robert J. 1991. *The Invention of Free Labor: The Employment Relation in English and American Law and Culture, 1350–1870*. Chapel Hill: University of North Carolina Press.

Stevens, Margaret. 1994. "A Theoretical Model of On-the-Job Training with Imperfect Competition." *Oxford Economic Papers* 46 (4): 537–562.

Stewart, Horace. 1891. *History of the Worshipful Company of Gold and Silver Wyre-drawers*. London: Company of Gold and Silver Wyre-drawers.

Stöger, Georg, and Reinhold Reith. 2019. "Actors and Practices of German Apprenticeship, Fifteenth-Nineteenth Centuries." In *Apprenticeship in Early Modern Europe*, edited by Maarten Prak and Patrick Wallis, 138–162. Cambridge: Cambridge University Press.

Stone, Lawrence. 1966. "Social Mobility in England, 1500–1700." *Past & Present* 33: 16–55.

———. 1975. "The Size and Composition of the Oxford Student Body, 1580–1909." In *The University in Society*, edited by Lawrence Stone, 1: 3–110. Princeton, NJ: Princeton University Press.

Stout, William. 1967. *The Autobiography of William Stout of Lancaster, 1665–1752*. Edited by J. D. Marshall. Remains Historical and Literary Connected with the Palatine Counties of Lancaster and Chester, 3rd series, vol. 14. Manchester: Manchester University Press for the Chetham Society.

Streeck, Wolfgang. 2011. "Skills and Politics: General and Specific." In *The Political Economy of Collective Skill Formation*, edited by Marius R. Busemeyer and Christine Trampusch, 317–352. Oxford: Oxford University Press.

Styles, John. 2007. *The Dress of the People: Everyday Fashion in Eighteenth-Century England*. New Haven, CT: Yale University Press.

Sutton, Anne F. 1998. "The Silent Years of London Guild History before 1300: The Case of the Mercers." *Historical Research* 71 (175): 121–141.

Swanson, Heather. 1988. "The Illusion of Economic Structure: Craft Guilds in Late Medieval English Towns." *Past & Present* (121): 29–48.

———. 1989. *Medieval Artisans: An Urban Class in Late Medieval England*. Oxford: Blackwell.

Tadmor, Naomi. 2001. *Family and Friends in Eighteenth-Century England: Household, Kinship, and Patronage*. Cambridge: Cambridge University Press.

Tawney, R. H. 1909. "The Economics of Boy Labour." *Economic Journal* 19 (76): 517–537.

Tawney, R. H., and Eileen Power, eds. 1924. *Tudor Economic Documents*. 3 vols. London: Longmans.

Taylor, Royston F. 2002. *Calendar of the Court Books of the Borough of New Woodstock 1588–1595*. Vol. 63. Oxford: Oxfordshire Record Society.

Taylor, Royston, Mary Hodges, Pat Crutch, Mollie Moisley, and Mary Haillissey. 2007. *Calendar of the Court Books of the Borough of New Woodstock 1607–1622 (WBM B78/2 & WBM B78/3)*. Oxford: Oxfordshire Record Society.

Teixeira, Pedro Nuno. 2014. "Gary Becker's Early Work on Human Capital—Collaborations and Distinctiveness." *IZA Journal of Labor Economics* 3 (1): 1–20.

Thelen, Kathleen. 2004. *How Institutions Evolve: The Political Economy of Skills in Germany, Britain, the United States and Japan*. Cambridge: Cambridge University Press.

———. 2014. *Varieties of Liberalization and the New Politics of Social Solidarity*. Cambridge: Cambridge University Press.

Thomas, E. G. 1977. "The Old Poor Law and Maritime Apprenticeship." *Mariner's Mirror* 63 (2): 153–161.

Thrift, N. J. 2009. *Shaping the Day: A History of Timekeeping in England and Wales 1300–1800*. Oxford: Oxford University Press.

Tkaczyk, Viktoria. 2017. "'Which Cannot Be Sufficiently Described by My Pen': The Codification of Knowledge in Theater Engineering, 1480–1680." In *The Structures of Practical Knowledge*, edited by Matteo Valleriani, 77–114. Cham: Springer.

Toulmin-Smith, L. 1870. *English Guilds*. Early English Text Society 35. London: Early English Text Society.

Tryon, Thomas. 1705. *Some Memoirs of the Life of Mr. Tho: Tryon, Late of London, merchant*. London: T. Sowle.

Turner, Anthony. 2008. "'Not to hurt of trade': Guilds and Innovation in Horology and Precision Instrument Making." In *Guilds, Innovation and the European Economy, 1400–1800*, edited by S. R. Epstein and M. R. Prak, 264–287. Cambridge: Cambridge University Press.

Turner, Edward. 1883. "Ancient Parochial Account Book of Cowden." *Sussex Archaeological Collections* 20: 91–119.

Twemlow, Jesse Alfred, ed. 1912. *Liverpool Town Books: Proceedings of Assemblies, Common Councils, Portmoot Courts, & c., 1550–1862*. Liverpool: Liverpool University Press.

United Kingdom. House of Commons. 1812–13. *Report from Committee on the Several Petitions, Presented to This House, Respecting the Apprentice Laws of This Kingdom*. H.C. 243.

———. 1815. *Report from the Committee on Parish Apprentices*. H.C. 304.

———. 1816. *Abstract of the Returns of Charitable Donations for the Benefit of Poor Persons, Made by the Ministers and Churchwardens of the Several Parishes and Townships in England and Wales, 1786–88 (Parts I. and II.)*. H.C. 511.

———. 1827. *Commissioners of Inquiry into Charities in England and Wales: Fourteenth Report, Appendix*. H.C. 382.

———. 1861. *Return of Number of Apprentices Bound as Mariners in Merchant Service, 1836–60*. H.C. 170.

University of Oxford. (1681) 2011. *The boys whipt home, or, A rhythme upon The apprentices poem, & c.* Oxford Text Archive, https://hdl.handle.net/20.500.12024/A29065.

Unwin, George. 1963. *The Gilds and Companies of London*. 4th ed. London: Frank Cass.

Unwin, Joan. 1995. "Apprenticeships and Freedoms: The Computer Analysis of the Records of the Cutlers' Company in Sheffield." *Local Historian* 25 (4): 194–208.

Uotila, Merja. 2019. "Rural Artisans' Apprenticeship Practices in Early Modern Finland (1700–1850)." In *Apprenticeship in Early Modern Europe*, edited by Maarten Prak and Patrick Wallis, 163–186. Cambridge: Cambridge University Press.

Van den Wyngaert, Sietske. 2021. "Poor Boys, Poor Chances? Training Underprivileged Youngsters in Early Modern Antwerp (1580–1780)." PhD diss., University of Antwerp.

Van Lottum, Jelle. 2011. "Labour Migration and Economic Performance: London and the Randstad, c. 1600–1800." *Economic History Review* 64 (2): 531–570.

Van Zanden, Jan Luiten. 2009a. *The Long Road to the Industrial Revolution: The European Economy in Global Perspective, 1000–1800*. Leiden: Brill.

———. 2009b. "The Skill Premium and the 'Great Divergence.'" *European Review of Economic History* 13 (1): 121–153.

Venkatesan, Soumhya. 2010. "Learning to Weave, Weaving to Learn . . . What?" *Journal of the Royal Anthropological Institute* 16 (s1): S158–S175.

Waddell, Brodie. 2015. "The Politics of Economic Distress in the Aftermath of the Glorious Revolution, 1689–1702." *English Historical Review* 130 (543): 318–351.

———. 2022. "The Economic Crisis of the 1690s in England." *Historical Journal* 66 (2): 1–22.

Waggett, Ralph W. 2000. *A History of the Worshipful Company of Glovers of London*. Chichester: Phillimore.

Walker, Francis Amasa. 1876. *The Wages Question: A Treatise on Wages and the Wages Class*. London: Macmillan.

Walker, M. J. 1986. "The Extent of the Guild Control of Trades in England c. 1660–1820: A Study Based on a Sample of Provincial Towns and London Companies." PhD diss., Cambridge University.

Walker, Martyn. 2013. "'Encouragement of Sound Education amongst the Industrial Classes': Mechanics' Institutes and Working-Class Membership 1838–1881." *Educational Studies* 39 (2): 142–155.

Wallis, Patrick. 2000. *London Apprentices.* Vol. 32, *Society of Apothecaries, 1617–1669.* London: Society of Genealogists.

———. 2002a. "Controlling Commodities: Search and Reconciliation in the Early Modern Livery Companies." In *Guilds, Society and Economy in London, 1450–1800*, edited by Ian Anders Gadd and Patrick Wallis, 85–100. London: Centre for Metropolitan History.

———. 2002b. "Medicines for London: The Trade, Regulation and Lifecycle of London Apothecaries, c. 1610–c. 1670." DPhil, University of Oxford.

———. 2008. "Apprenticeship and Training in Premodern England." *Journal of Economic History* 68 (3): 832–861.

———. 2012. "Labor, Law, and Training in Early Modern London: Apprenticeship and the City's Institutions." *Journal of British Studies* 51 (4): 791–819.

———. 2019. "Between Apprenticeship and Skill: Acquiring Knowledge outside the Academy in Early Modern England." *Science in Context* 32 (2): 155–170.

Wallis, Patrick, Justin Colson, and David Chilosi. 2018. "Structural Change and Economic Growth in the British Economy before the Industrial Revolution, 1500–1800." *Journal of Economic History* 78 (3): 862–903.

Wallis, Patrick, Clare Crowston, Raoul De Kerf, Bert De Munck, Marcel Hoogenboom, Christopher Kissane, Chris Minns, and Maarten Roy Prak. 2015. "Barriers to Citizenship and Trades in Early Modern Europe." BEUcitizen working paper, Utrecht University.

Wallis, Patrick, and Cliff Webb. 2011. "The Education and Training of Gentry Sons in Early Modern England." *Social History* 36 (1): 36–53.

Wallis, Patrick, Cliff Webb, and Chris Minns. 2010. "Leaving Home and Entering Service: The Age of Apprenticeship in Early Modern London." *Continuity and Change* 25 (3): 377–404.

Walter, John. 2007. "Faces in the Crowd: Gender and Age in the Early Modern English Crowd." In *The Family in Early Modern England*, edited by Helen Berry and Elizabeth A. Foyster, 96–125. Cambridge: Cambridge University Press.

Ward, Joseph P. 1997. *Metropolitan Communities: Trade Guilds, Identity, and Change in Early Modern London.* Stanford, CA: Stanford University Press.

Wareing, John. 1980. "Changes in the Geographical Distribution of the Recruitment of Apprentices to the London Companies, 1486–1750." *Journal of Historical Geography* 6 (3): 241–249.

———. 2017. *Indentured Migration and the Servant Trade from London to America, 1618–1718: 'There is great want of servants'.* Oxford: Oxford University Press.

Watts, Thomas. 1722. *An Essay on the proper method for forming a man of business.* 4th ed. London: Geo. James.

Webb, Cliff. 1994–. *London Livery Company Apprenticeship Registers.* London: Society of Genealogists.

Weber, Max. 1966. *The City.* New York: Free Press.

Webster, Charles. 1975. *The Great Instauration: Science, Medicine and Reform, 1626–1660.* London: Duckworth.

Wegge, Simone A. 1998. "Chain Migration and Information Networks: Evidence from Nineteenth-Century Hesse-Cassel." *Journal of Economic History* 58 (4): 957–986.

Weinstein, Rosemary. 2004. *The History of the Worshipful Company of Feltmakers, 1604–2004.* Chichester: Phillimore.

Welch, Charles. 1902. *History of the Worshipful Company of Pewterers of the City of London.* London: Blades, East, and Blades.

———. 1919–23. *History of the Cutlers' Company of London.* 2 vols. London: The Cutlers' Company.

Whetstone, Charles. 1807. *Truths. No. 1. Or the memoirs of Charles Whetstone, or an exposition of the oppression and cruelty exercised in the Trades and Manufactures of Great Britain.* N.p.

Whittle, Jane. 2017. *Servants in Rural Europe: 1400–1900.* Woodbridge: Boydell.

Wilson, Riley. 2020. "Moving to Jobs: The Role of Information in Migration Decisions." *Journal of Labor Economics* 39 (4): 1083–1128.

Winstanley, Ian G., ed. 1994. *The Diary of Roger Lowe of Ashton-in-Makerfield, Lancashire, 1663–1678: Including a Record of Burials at Winwick Church, 1666–1671.* Wigan: Picks.

Withall, Caroline Louise. 2014. "Shipped Out? Pauper Apprentices of Port Towns during the Industrial Revolution 1750–1870." DPhil diss., University of Oxford.

Withington, Phil. 2005. *The Politics of Commonwealth: Citizens and Freemen in Early Modern England.* Cambridge: Cambridge University Press.

Woodhead, J. R. 1965. *The Rulers of London 1660–1689: A Biographical Record of the Aldermen and Common Councilmen of the City of London.* London: London & Middlesex Archaeological Society.

Woodward, Donald. 1981. "The Background to the Statute of Artificers: The Genesis of Labour Policy, 1558–63." *Economic History Review* 33 (1): 32–44.

Worth, R. N. 1886. "Notes from Two Plymouth Diaries." *Antiquary* 13:242–244.

Wrightson, Keith. 1994. "'Sorts of People' in Tudor and Stuart England." In *The Middling Sort of People: Culture, Society and Politics in England, 1550–1800*, edited by Jonathan Barry and Christopher Brooks, 28–51. London: Macmillan.

Wrigley, E. A. 1967. "A Simple Model of London's Importance in Changing English Society and Economy, 1650–1750." *Past & Present* 37: 44–70.

———. 1985. "Urban Growth and Agricultural Change: England and the Continent in the Early Modern Period." *Journal of Interdisciplinary History* 15 (4): 638–728.

———. 1997. *English Population History from Family Reconstitution, 1580–1837.* Cambridge: Cambridge University Press.

———. 2009. "Rickman Revisited: The Population Growth Rates of English Counties in the Early Modern Period." *Economic History Review* 62 (3): 711–735.

Wrigley, E. A., R. Davies, J. Oeppen, and Roger S. Schofield. 2018. 26 English Parish Family Reconstitutions. [Data collection]. 10.5255/UKDA-SN-853082. Colchester: UK Data Service. https://reshare.ukdataservice.ac.uk/853082/.

Yarbrough, Anne. 1979. "Apprentices as Adolescents in Sixteenth-Century Bristol." *Journal of Social History* 13: 67–81.

———. 1980. "Geographical and Social Origins of Bristol Apprentices, 1542–1565." *Transactions of the Bristol and Gloucestershire Archaeological Society* 98: 113–130.

Zahedieh, Nuala. 2010. *The Capital and the Colonies: London and the Atlantic Economy, 1660–1700.* Cambridge: Cambridge University Press.

Zeev, Nadav Ben, Joel Mokyr, and Karine van der Beek. 2017. "Flexible Supply of Apprenticeship in the British Industrial Revolution." *Journal of Economic History* 77 (1): 208–250.

Zucca Micheletto, Beatrice. 2019. "A Large 'Umbrella': Patterns of Apprenticeship in Eighteenth-Century Turin." In *Apprenticeship in Early Modern Europe*, edited by Maarten Prak and Patrick Wallis, 78–105. Cambridge: Cambridge University Press.

INDEX

Page numbers in italics indicate figures and tables.

The Princeton Economic History of the Western World

Joel Mokyr, Series Editor

Recent titles

The Laissez-Faire Experiment: Why Britain Embraced and Then Abandoned Small Government, 1800–1914, W. Walker Hanlon

The Hidden Victims: Civilian Casualties of the Two World Wars, Cormac Ó Gráda

The Wealth of a Nation: Institutional Foundations of English Capitalism, Geoffrey M. Hodgson

The Corporation and the Twentieth Century: The History of American Business Enterprise, Richard N. Langlois

Pioneers of Capitalism: The Netherlands 1000–1800, Maarten Prak and Jan Luiten van Zanden

Pliny's Roman Economy: Natural History, Innovation, and Growth, Richard P. Saller

Plagues upon the Earth: Disease and the Course of Human History, Kyle Harper

The Israeli Economy: A Story of Success and Costs, Joseph Zeira

Credit Nation: Property Laws and Institutions in Early America, Claire Priest

The Decline and Rise of Democracy: A Global History from Antiquity to Today, David Stasavage

Going the Distance: Eurasian Trade and the Rise of the Business Corporation, 1400–1700, Ron Harris

Escape from Rome: The Failure of Empire and the Road to Prosperity, Walter Scheidel

Trade in the Ancient Mediterranean: Private Order and Public Institutions, Taco Terpstra

Dark Matter Credit: The Development of Peer-to-Peer Lending and Banking in France, Philip T. Hoffman, Gilles Postel-Vinay, and Jean-Laurent Rosenthal

The European Guilds: An Economic Analysis, Sheilagh Ogilvie

The Winding Road to the Welfare State: Economic Insecurity and Social Welfare Policy in Britain, George R. Boyer

The Mystery of the Kibbutz: Egalitarian Principles in a Capitalist World, Ran Abramitzky

Unequal Gains: American Growth and Inequality since 1700, Peter H. Lindert and Jeffrey G. Williamson

Uneven Centuries: Economic Development of Turkey since 1820, Şevket Pamuk

The Great Leveler: Violence and the History of Inequality from the Stone Age to the Twenty-First Century, Walter Scheidel

The Rise and Fall of American Growth: The U.S. Standard of Living since the Civil War, Robert J. Gordon

Brazil in Transition: Beliefs, Leadership, and Institutional Change, Lee J. Alston, Marcus André Melo, Bernardo Mueller, and Carlos Pereira

The Vanishing Irish: Households, Migration, and the Rural Economy in Ireland, 1850–1914, Timothy W. Guinnane

Fragile by Design: The Political Origins of Banking Crises and Scarce Credit, Charles W. Calomiris and Stephen H. Haber

The Son Also Rises: Surnames and the History of Social Mobility, Gregory Clark

Why Did Europe Conquer the World?, Philip T. Hoffman

Lending to the Borrower from Hell: Debt, Taxes, and Default in the Age of Philip II, Mauricio Drelichman and Hans-Joachim Voth

Power to the People: Energy in Europe over the Last Five Centuries, Astrid Kander, Paolo Malanima, and Paul Warde

Cities of Commerce: The Institutional Foundations of International Trade in the Low Countries, 1250–1650, Oscar Gelderblom

Why Australia Prospered: The Shifting Sources of Economic Growth, Ian W. McLean

The Chosen Few: How Education Shaped Jewish History, 70–1492, Maristella Botticini and Zvi Eckstein

Creating Wine: The Emergence of a World Industry, 1840–1914, James Simpson

Distant Tyranny: Markets, Power, and Backwardness in Spain, 1650–1800, Regina Grafe

The Evolution of a Nation: How Geography and Law Shaped the American States, Daniel Berkowitz and Karen B. Clay

The Roman Market Economy, Peter Temin

States of Credit: Size, Power, and the Development of European Polities, David Stasavage

Power over Peoples: Technology, Environments, and Western Imperialism, 1400 to the Present, Daniel R. Headrick

Unsettled Account: The Evolution of Banking in the Industrialized World since 1800, Richard S. Grossman

A Farewell to Alms: A Brief Economic History of the World, Gregory Clark

Power and Plenty: Trade, War, and the World Economy in the Second Millennium, Ronald Findlay and Kevin H. O'Rourke

War, Wine, and Taxes: The Political Economy of Anglo-French Trade, 1689–1900, John V. C. Nye

Cultures Merging: A Historical and Economic Critique of Culture, Eric L. Jones

The European Economy since 1945: Coordinated Capitalism and Beyond, Barry Eichengreen

Feeding the World: An Economic History of Agriculture, 1800–2000, Giovanni Federico

Understanding the Process of Economic Change, Douglass C. North

The Strictures of Inheritance: The Dutch Economy in the Nineteenth Century, Jan Luiten van Zanden and Arthur van Riel

Farm to Factory: A Reinterpretation of the Soviet Industrial Revolution, Robert C. Allen

Quarter Notes and Bank Notes: The Economics of Music Composition in the Eighteenth and Nineteenth Centuries, F. M. Scherer

The Big Problem of Small Change, Thomas J. Sargent and François R. Velde

The Great Divergence: China, Europe, and the Making of the Modern World Economy, Kenneth Pomeranz

Black '47 and Beyond: The Great Irish Famine in History, Economy, and Memory, Cormac Ó Gráda

Growth in a Traditional Society: The French Countryside, 1450–1815, Philip T. Hoffman

A NOTE ON THE TYPE

This book has been composed in Adobe Text and Gotham. Adobe Text, designed by Robert Slimbach for Adobe, bridges the gap between fifteenth- and sixteenth-century calligraphic and eighteenth-century Modern styles. Gotham, inspired by New York street signs, was designed by Tobias Frere-Jones for Hoefler & Co.